The Politi

THE POLITICAL THEORY READER

EDITED BY
PAUL SCHUMAKER

WILEY-BLACKWELL
A John Wiley & Sons, Ltd., Publication

This edition first published 2010

Blackwell Publishing was acquired by John Wiley & Sons in February 2007. Blackwell's publishing program has been merged with Wiley's global Scientific, Technical, and Medical business to form Wiley-Blackwell.

Registered Office
John Wiley & Sons Ltd, The Atrium, Southern Gate, Chichester, West Sussex, PO19 8SQ, United Kingdom

Editorial Offices
350 Main Street, Malden, MA 02148-5020, USA
9600 Garsington Road, Oxford, OX4 2DQ, UK
The Atrium, Southern Gate, Chichester, West Sussex, PO19 8SQ, UK

For details of our global editorial offices, for customer services, and for information about how to apply for permission to reuse the copyright material in this book please see our website at www.wiley.com/wiley-blackwell.

Library of Congress Cataloging-in-Publication Data is available

ISBN Hardback: 9781405189972
ISBN Paperback: 9781405189965

A catalogue record for this book is available from the British Library.

Set in 9.5/11.5pt Minion by SPi Publisher Services, Pondicherry, India

1 2010

Table of Contents

Preface ix
Acknowledgments xiii

1 **Political Theory, Public Philosophy, and Pluralism** 1
Introduction 1
Leo Strauss, "What Is Political Philosophy?" 5
Judith Shklar, "Political Ideology" 9
Theodore J. Lowi, "America's Old and New Public Philosophy" 11
Avigail Eisenberg, "Reconstructing Political Pluralism" 18
William E. Connolly, "Pluralism: A Prelude" 21

PART I IDEOLOGICAL VOICES 27

2 **Nineteenth-Century Ideologies** 29
Introduction 29
John Locke, "The Second Treatise of Government" 31
National Assembly of France, "The Declaration of the Rights of Man and of the Citizen" 37
Edmund Burke, "Reflections on the Revolution in France" 38
Karl Marx and Friedrich Engels, "The Communist Manifesto" 40
Emma Goldman, "Anarchism: What It Really Stands For" 47

3 **Twentieth-Century Ideologies** 51
Introduction 51
Vladimir I. Lenin, "State and Revolution" 53
Giovanni Gentile, "The Philosophic Basis of Fascism" 58
Paul Starr, "Why Liberalism Works" 60
John Kekes, "A Case for Conservatism" 65

4 **Newer Quasi-Ideologies** 73
Introduction 73
Michael J. Sandel, "America's Search for a New Public Philosophy" 75
Richard John Neuhaus, "Public Religion and Public Reason" 79
Susan Moller Okin, "Justice, Gender, and the Family" 82
Arne Naess, "The Environmental Crisis and the Deep Ecological Movement" 87
Michael Hardt and Antonio Negri, "Globalization and Democracy" 92

PART II PHILOSOPHICAL ASSUMPTIONS 99

5 **Ontological Conceptions** 101
Introduction 101
Plato, "The Theory of Forms" 104
Walter Ullman, "Ascending and Descending Theses of Government" 107
Ken Wilber, "The Great Chain of Being" 108
Jean Jacques Rousseau, "On the General Will" 111
Friedrich Engels, "Marx's Materialist Conception of History" 115
Charles Darwin, "Natural Selection" 118
T. H. Huxley, "Evolution and Ethics" 120
Judith Butler, "Contingent Foundations: Feminism and the Question of 'Postmodernism'" 122

6 **Conceptions of Human Nature** 127
Introduction 127
Herbert Deane, "St. Augustine's Conception of Fallen Man" 129
Thomas Hobbes, "The Natural Condition of Mankind" 131
C. B. Macpherson, "The Early Liberal Model of Man" 133
Karl Marx, "Estranged Labor" 137
Peter Kropotkin, "Mutual Aid" 140
John Rawls, "The Rationality and Motivations of Parties in the Original Position" 142
Michael Sandel, "The Procedural Republic and the Unencumbered Self" 144
Bhikhu Parekh, "Conceptualizing Human Beings" 146

7 **Images of Society** 152
Introduction 152
Aristotle, "The Natural Origins of Political Associations" 153
Thomas Hobbes, "The Contractual Origins of Society" 155
Edmund Burke, "The Great Primaeval Contract of Eternal Society" 158
Paul Schumaker, "Social Cleavages and Complex Equality" 160

8 **Epistemological Orientations** 165
Introduction 165
Benjamin Barber, "The Epistemological Frame: Cartesian Politics" 167
Jeremy Bentham, "Of the Principle of Utility" 171
Alasdair MacIntyre, "Narratives of the Good Life Guided by Living Traditions" 173
Richard Rorty, "America's Civic Religion: A Hopeful Pragmatism" 176
Carol Gilligan, "In a Different Voice" 180
John Rawls, "Political Constructivism" 184

PART III POLITICAL PRINCIPLES 189

9 **On Community** 191
Introduction 191
James Madison, "The Federalist No. 10" 193
Rogers M. Smith, "Toward a Theory of Civic Identities" 196
David Held, "Towards a Global Covenant: Global Social Democracy" 200
Kirkpatrick Sale, "Human-Scale Democracy" 204
Robert Dahl, "The Chinese Boxes" 208

10 **On Citizenship** 211
Introduction 211
Michael Walzer, "The Distribution of Membership" 213
Joseph H. Carens, "Aliens and Citizens: The Case For Open Borders" 216
T. H. Marshall, "The Development of Citizen Rights" 222
Iris Marion Young, "Polity and Group Difference: A Critique of the Ideal of Universal Citizenship" 226
Amitai Etzioni et al., "The Responsive Communitarian Platform: Rights and Responsibilities" 231
Niccolo Machiavelli, "The Threat Posed by Corrupt Citizens" 236

11 **On Structure** 238
Introduction 238
John Stuart Mill, "On Liberty" 240
Adam Smith, "The Principles and Virtues of Free Markets" 242
Lawrence E. Harrison, "Progress and Poverty Without Marx" 246
Robert D. Putnam, "The Strange Disappearance of Civic America" 249
Anthony Giddens, "The Third Way and Government" 251
Imam Khomeini, "Islamic Government" 255
John Locke, "A Letter Concerning Toleration" 259

12 **On Rulers** 261
Introduction 261
Robert Dahl, "Guardianship" 263
Edmund Burke, "Speech to the Electors of Bristol" 268
Alexis de Tocqueville, "Unlimited Power of the Majority in the United States and Its Consequences" 268
Joseph Schumpeter, "A Realistic Alternative to the Classical Doctrine of Democracy" 271
Benjamin Barber, "Strong Democracy: Politics in the Participatory Mode" 275
Amy Gutmann and Dennis Thompson, "What Deliberative Democracy Means" 280
William Riker, "Liberalism, Populism, and the Theory of Public Choice" 283

13 **On Authority** 286
Introduction 286
Robert Paul Wolff, "The Conflict Between Authority and Autonomy" 288
Milton Friedman, "The Role of Government in a Free Society" 291
Garrett Hardin, "The Tragedy of the Commons" 295
Benjamin I. Page and James R. Simmons, "What Should Government Do?" 300
William Galston, "Liberalism and Public Morality" 306

14 On Justice 312
Introduction 312
APSA Task Force on Inequality and American Democracy, "American Democracy in an Age of Rising Inequality" 313
John Rawls, "A Kantian Conception of Equality" 320
Irving Kristol, "A Capitalist Conception of Justice" 325
Robert Nozick, "The Entitlement Theory" 330

15 On Change 335
Introduction 335
Michael Oakeshott, "On Being Conservative" 336
Richard Rorty, "Movements and Campaigns" 341
Martin Luther King Jr., "Letter from a Birmingham Jail" 343
Abd Al-Salam Faraj, "The Neglected Duty" 346
Albert Camus, "Rebellion Beyond Nihilism" 349

Preface

Political theory has an honorable past, a vibrant present, and an uncertain future. Studying the history of political ideas – as developed by such great thinkers as Plato, Aristotle, Machiavelli, Hobbes, Locke, Rousseau, Madison, Burke, Hegel, and Marx – has long been central to being an educated person and leading a thoughtful public life. During the past 50 years, the content of political theory has exploded, as the canonical works have been supplemented by important new developments in our thinking about community life and governance. Feminists, environmentalists, and religious fundamentalists are just a few of the "new" voices that have raised and debated issues that had previously received only passing attention. Our basic political identities, opening and closing the borders of our communities, balancing citizen rights and responsibilities, and providing social justice both within and across nation-states are just some of the matters that have spawned intense and stimulating debates – even while older questions, such as those about the desirability and requirements of democracy and the legitimate roles of government, remain hotly contested.

The future of political theory is uncertain, not just because innovative political ideas and paradigmatic changes can occur spontaneously, but also because it remains unclear how a continuation of present trends will be received. As in other fields of inquiry, political theory is experiencing increasing specialization and fragmentation. Contemporary political theorists normally work within particular traditions (such as liberalism and Marxism), emphasize particular concepts (such as justice and citizenship), and focus on more specific topics within such broad conceptual areas (such as global justice and special rights for marginalized groups of citizens). The outburst of books and articles within these traditions and topics makes it difficult, if not impossible, for even professionals to keep abreast of the field as a whole. This development is sometimes viewed with anxiety, as it diminishes the capacity of political theory to play its historical role of integrating political ideas into coherent understandings of the entire range of political activity.

However, there are some ways that this development can be viewed positively. First, persons who do not consider themselves political theorists, but rather specialists in the study of various kinds of political (as well as social and economic) institutions, actions, and events, can more readily access and employ that work in political theory bearing directly on their concerns; in this sense, it is possible to see political theory increasingly informing the work of social scientists generally. Second, it may be that the search for grand and universal theories of politics has been a quixotic and even misguided venture. Perhaps conservatism and communitarianism provide the best answers to questions of community identities, while liberalism provides the best answers to questions of structuring political communities, and socialism and feminism offer important ideas about justice. Moreover, different kinds of political communities (such as cities, nation-states, regional organizations, and global society), other social communities (such as families, voluntary associations, and workplaces), and diverse cultural communities (such as those where secular, Christian, and Islamic values are dominant) may best be guided not by a universal and grand political theory but by political principles that are particular to each of them. Perhaps the future will witness leaders and citizens accessing – with the help of new communication technologies and search engines – relevant specialized work in political theory as resources for generating their own public philosophies to guide the governance of the various particular communities in which they live and work.

This reader introduces students to some of the more significant past and present contributors to political theory and to the central issues that they have raised. It has been developed to complement my introductory text in political theory, *From Ideologies to Public Philosophies*, based on the premise that students require not only the sort of interpretations of the field that texts provide but also they should have direct access to important original sources in it. The readings here are organized so they parallel my account of political theory in *From Ideologies to Public Philosophies*, but instructors could, of course, adopt this reader independently of that text.

Political theory has always been concerned with questions about the good life, the good society, and good government, and political theorists have usually regarded efforts to understand politics without deep concern about such moral and normative matters as incomplete, if not foolish. They generally credit Plato with developing the first major political philosophy, and subsequent works in that tradition have usually been expressed as abstract, complex, and idealized formulations that have eluded widespread intersubjective understandings and clear applications to current political issues. About two centuries ago, ideologies emerged seeking to overcome such difficulties. Various ideologies can be seen as more accessible, applied political philosophies that seek to rally political leaders and citizens behind social and economic goals that could be expressed as general principles having defensible (or at least appealing) philosophical foundations. While ideologies remain important – indeed, many analysts claim that ideological thinking and polarization are more widespread now than ever – political theorists have usually expressed skepticism about ideologies, regarding them as clever intellectual disguises for getting others to support the goals of particular interests at the expense of the public good and the legitimate concerns of others. Ideological thinking seems to resist alternative ideas in ways that make political discussion based on debate among proponents of competing ideologies resemble a winner-take-all sporting event rather than an exercise in political deliberation that seeks the widest possible agreement on how to govern our communities.

As an antidote to ideological thinking, political theorists have increasingly used the term "public philosophy" to capture efforts to develop political principles that have the accessible, applied qualities of ideologies while avoiding their more rigid and closed features. While a great thinker like Locke or Marx could generate a political philosophy and his followers could work out the applied implications and sell this philosophy as an ideology to leaders and citizens of political communities, public philosophies are generated by broader publics – ideally, the most inclusive public possible. Rather than develop their own political principles, political theorists have increasingly sought to become public philosophers who *articulate* what they perceive as the widely accepted public or social understandings of the good life, good society, and good government that prevail in political communities – even while they often criticize these understandings.

I believe that political pluralism is the best term for summarizing such understandings in America and other modern Western societies. In *From Ideologies to Public Philosophies*, I have tried to articulate the broadest consensus that I find among "the friends of pluralism," the most prominent ideological competitors within these societies today. Perhaps the label pluralism is unfortunate because, a half-century ago, political scientists used that term for a much narrower theory of politics than the concept of pluralism had historically conveyed. Along with a growing number of political theorists, I have been involved in expressing pluralism as a more general and basic public philosophy having increasing worldwide appeal. But I doubt that understanding and embracing pluralism exhausts our theoretical needs in politics. While I believe that our first and most basic political commitments should be to pluralism as a set of ideas for tolerating and reconciling our inevitable political differences, I also believe that leaders and citizens need a second and more specific set of *partisan* principles that, compared to the broader public philosophy of pluralism, provide clearer guidance to their immediate political concerns and establish priorities among competing values and ideals. Pluralist societies will always contain people committed to alternative political doctrines containing competing ideas on how our particular political communities should be governed and how emerging issues should be resolved. If people's first commitment is to pluralism, their partisan principles will be more open to alternative viewpoints than is the case when people come to politics with rigid ideological orientations that resist the give-and-take that pluralist politics requires.

This reader provides resources for students seeking to understand both the basic principles of pluralism and many of the partisan principles that might become part of their more specific public philosophies. Such understanding is important for students to become participants in democratic deliberations about public life. Once pluralism as our most basic public philosophy is understood, they can become effective contributors in public conversations that defend, criticize, and transform present social understandings. Once the main issues that all public philosophies address and the leading alternative principles regarding these issues are understood, they can think clearly about the more specific political principles that seem worthy of their allegiance and that they can defend in the company of their fellow citizens. The readings in Chapter 1 address these introductory matters in more depth; they provide overviews of political theory, political philosophy, ideologies, public philosophies, and pluralism.

Part I introduces the ideological traditions whose ideas we can survey, compare and contrast, and critically evaluate as we generate our political commitments. Chapter 2 provides excerpts from canonical texts for the ideological traditions that developed during the nineteenth century: classical liberalism, traditional conservatism, Marxism, and anarchism. In Chapter 3, students are exposed to ideologies that have been most influential in the twentieth century: communism, fascism, contemporary liberalism, and contemporary conservatism. Chapter 4 provides readings from some of the more radical quasi-ideologies that have arisen in recent decades: perspectives like communitarianism, the religious right, feminism, and "green thought" that seek fundamental changes in particular elements of prevailing pluralist public philosophy. Such radicals regard contemporary liberalism as insufficiently committed to various aspects of social equality that have been the concern of the political left,[1] or they regard contemporary conservatism as insufficiently committed to the protection of traditional values that has been the concern of the political right. In subsequent chapters, other radical and more extreme voices will be encountered, as they bear on particular philosophical and political issues.

Part II focuses on philosophical issues. Political theorists have long understood that our most basic political beliefs are often rooted in philosophical assumptions about ontology, human nature, images of society, and epistemology – sometimes only by implication but sometimes clearly specified by those seeking a complete articulation of their political claims. While early modern thought contained great confidence that universal political theory could be built on firm philosophical foundations, this confidence has slowly eroded and many postmodern thinkers wish to expose the limitations of all philosophical foundations and build understandings of politics without such foundations. Contemporary pluralists seem to seek a middle path between these positions, as they acknowledge that philosophical assumptions are never beyond contestation, but also recognize that they cannot be entirely eliminated from deeper political thinking. Pluralists seek as much common ground as possible on basic philosophical assumptions, and believe that this consensus can only be had on "thin" ontologies, minimal assumptions about human nature, unrestrictive images of society, and modest epistemological claims. They believe our commitments to more specific political philosophies than pluralism should be guided by rigorous analysis of thicker philosophical assumptions about the determining role of divine, popular, economic, and other forces on the fate of the world, about more specific ideas about human characteristics and motivations, about the precise composition of societies, and about the best methods for acquiring knowledge about politics.[2]

Alternative ontological bases of political thought are presented in the readings in Chapter 5; they address beliefs in "higher" (often divine) ultimate realities beyond human perceptions about the natural world, assumptions that material forces or human ideas are the ultimate determinants of the course of history, and the postmodern skepticism of any ultimate reality or causal forces. Alternative conceptions of human nature are presented in Chapter 6; some such conceptions focus on human frailties and limitations, while others provide more optimistic accounts of human instincts, capacities, and potential. Alternative images of society are contained in Chapter 7; both cooperative and conflictive conceptions of political societies are presented, as are individualistic and group-centered images of society.

[1] As Sheri Berman argues in *The Primacy of Politics* (New York: Cambridge University Press, 2006), democratic socialism was also highly influential, especially in Western Europe during the twentieth century, and remains an important voice on the radical left. Selections addressing democratic socialist concerns are included throughout this reader.

[2] For a related discussion, see Michael Walzer, *Thick and Thin* (Notre Dame, IN: Notre Dame University Press, 1994).

A variety of attempts to base politics on knowledge other than the pre-modern emphasis on "the word of God," the teachings of some other authority, and traditional understandings are presented in Chapter 8. Readings here propose or discuss various scientific epistemologies that promise some solid political "truth," emphasize more tentative socially constructed political understandings, or criticize all efforts to generate political certainty or even political consensus.

Part III addresses directly the great political issues. Because political theorists focus on different social and economic problems, have different goals that reflect different values (or at least different priorities among values), and bring alternative philosophical assumptions to their thinking, they have expressed and defended a broad array of political principles addressing our most basic concerns as we seek desirable social, economic, and political arrangements. As in *From Ideologies to Public Philosophies*, I organize these concerns into questions of communities, citizenship, structure, rulers, authority, justice, and change. This reader provides extracts from both past and present political theorists containing competing principles on each of these central concerns, as well as readings proposing minimal principles upon which all pluralists can agree.

Chapter 9 deals with the type of political communities (polities) that invoke people's loyalties and support. The attractions of and bases of identity with local, national, and global communities are considered. Chapter 10 provides readings that deal with questions of citizenship. Should polities open or close their borders to new citizens from abroad? What are the rights and responsibilities of citizenship? Are there certain political virtues that all citizens should possess? Chapter 11 deals with how political communities should be structured. Some readings emphasize the need for a large private sphere where individual thoughts and actions are subject to minimal community influences, while others seek more extensive social control over individuals within the community. The roles of economic markets, voluntary associations, cultural norms, religion, and government in structuring community life are addressed in the readings here. Chapter 12 addresses the sorts of people who should govern polities. The desirability and possibility of having rulers who are unaccountable, minimally accountable, and highly accountable to citizens are considered. Whether and how democracy can be strengthened beyond the sorts of representative democracies that presently govern in pluralist societies are questions addressed in other readings in this chapter. In Chapter 13, some readings call for no or very limited government, while others provide arguments for more extensive governmental authority to protect the environment, regulate the economy, and promote certain moral values. The growing economic inequalities and the questions of distributive justice that such inequalities provoke are considered in Chapter 14. John Rawls' egalitarian liberalism and some of the responses his theory has elicited are included in the readings in this chapter. Finally, Chapter 15 addresses the concept of political change – which is useful for summarizing and drawing conclusions arising from issues addressed in earlier chapters. In addition to considering readings that doubt the desirability of significant change, the readings consider various strategies for achieving it.

This reader thus provides a broad survey of the range and scope of political thinking on the most central political issues that thoughtful and informed citizens must confront. To achieve this breadth within the limited space of an anthology, it has, of course, been necessary to extract from larger works those portions that focus on the issues under consideration in various chapters. Some instructors will object to this "reader's digest" approach, but it should be remembered that the purpose of this book is to introduce students to the major contributors to political thought, the central issues they address, and the most important alternative answers they provide. If this reader achieves these goals, students will return for more advanced studies in political theory where they read in their entirety some of the works extracted here, as well as other important books and articles that deserve our attention. But these readings (especially if accompanied by my text) will provide a host of philosophical and political ideas that will engage the interest and deepen the political thinking of most students, and they will provide a basis for stimulating class discussions, as students search for the best answers to the good life, the good society, and good government.

Acknowledgments

The editor and publisher gratefully acknowledge the permission granted to reproduce the copyright material in this book.

Chapter 1, document 1: Leo Strauss, "What is Political Philosophy?" pp. 343–68 from *Journal of Politics*, 19 (August 1957). © Southern Political Science Association, reprinted with permission.

Chapter 1, document 2: Judith Shklar, pp. 1–19 from *Political Theory and Ideology* (New York: Macmillan, 1966).

Chapter 1, document 3: Theodore J. Lowi, pp. 3–6, 42–4, 50–6 from *The End of Liberalism: The Second Republic of the United States*, second edition (New York: W. W. Norton and Co., 1979). © 1979, 1969 by W. W. Norton and Company, Inc. Used by permission of W. W. Norton and Company, Inc.

Chapter 1, document 4: Avigail Eisenberg, pp. 1–7, 168–70 from *Reconstructing Political Pluralism* (SUNY Press, 1995).

Chapter 1, document 5: William E. Connolly, pp. 1–10 from *Pluralism* (Duke University Press, 2005).

Chapter 2, document 1: John Locke, from *The Second Treatise of Government*, in the public domain, this version is at www.ilt.columbia.edu/academic/digitexts/locke/second/locke2nd.txt

Chapter 2, document 2: National Assembly of France, "The Declaration of the Rights of Man and of the Citizen" (1789). In the public domain.

Chapter 2, document 3: Edmund Burke, "Reflections on the Revolution in France" (1790), from the Anchor Books edition, 1973, which is derived from *The Works of the Right Honorable Edmund Burke*, the Riverton edition (London, 1826), Volume 5.

Chapter 2, document 4: Karl Marx and Friedrich Engels, "The Communist Manifesto" (1848), extracted from *The Manifesto of the Communist Party*, authorized English translation (New York: International Publishers, 1948). Available at www.anu.edu.au/polsci/marx/classics/manifesto.html. Reprinted by permission of International Publishers Co., Inc.

Chapter 2, document 5: Emma Goldman, "Anarchism: What It Really Stands For" (1911), from *Anarchism and Other Essays*, available at http://xroads.virginia.edu/~hyper/Goldman/anarchism.html

Chapter 3, document 1: Vladimir I. Lenin "State and Revolution" (1917), pp. 319–35 from *The Lenin Anthology*, edited by Robert C. Tucker (W. W. Norton, 1975), Copyright © 1975, by W. W. Norton & Company, Inc. Used by permission of W. W. Norton & Company, Inc.

Chapter 3, document 2: Giovanni Gentile, "The Philosophic Basis of Fascism" (1929), pp. 49–61 from *Readings on Fascism and National Socialism*, selected by the members of the Department of Philosophy, University of Colorado (Swallow Press, 1952, 1995). Reprinted with permission of Ohio University Press/Swallow Press, Athens, Ohio (www.ohioswallow.com).

Chapter 3, document 3: Paul Starr, "Why Liberalism Works," reprinted with permission from Paul Starr, *The American Prospect*, 18, 4 (April 4, 2007), pp. 34–40. www.prospect.org. *The American Prospect*, 1710 Rhode Island Avenue, NW, 12th Floor, Washington DC 20036.

Chapter 3, document 4: John Kekes, pp. 1–3, 27–47, from *A Case for Conservatism* (Cornell University Press, 1998). Copyright ©1998 by Cornell University. Used by permission of the publisher, Cornell University Press.

Chapter 4, document 1: Michael Sandel, "America's Search for a New Public Philosophy." Copyright © Michael J. Sandel. Originally published in *The Atlantic Monthly* (March 1996), pp. 57–74. Adapted from Michael J. Sandel, *Democracy's Discontent: America in Search of a Public Philosophy* (Harvard University Press, 1996).

Chapter 4, document 2: Richard John Neuhaus, "Public Religion and Public Reason," from Chapter 2 of *The Naked Public Square* (Grand Rapids, MI: William B. Eerdmans Publishing Co., 1984). © 1984, Wm. B. Eerdmans Publishing Company, Grand Rapids, Michigan. Reprinted by permission of the publisher; all rights reserved. ALSO Reprinted by permission of SLL/Sterling Lord Literistic, Inc. Copyright by Richard J. Neuhaus.

Chapter 4, document 3: Susan Moller Okin, pp. 3–23 from *Justice, Gender, and the Family* (Basic Books, Inc., 1989). Reprinted by permission of Basic Books, a member of Perseus Books Group.

Chapter 4, document 4: Arne Naess, "The Environmental Crisis and the Deep Ecological Movement," pp. 23–32 from *Ecology, Community, and Lifestyle* (Cambridge University Press, 1989). © Cambridge University Press 1989, reproduced with permission.

Chapter 4, document 5: Michael Hardt and Antonio Negri, "Globalization and Democracy," from *Implicating Empire: Globalization and Resistance in the 21st-Century World Order*, edited by Stanley Aronowitz and Heather Gautney (New York: Basic Books, Inc., 2003). Reprinted by permission of Basic Books, a member of Perseus Books Group.

Chapter 5, document 1: Plato, "The Theory of Forms" (360 BCE), pp. 164–70 from *The Republic*, translated by G. M. A. Grube (Hackett Publishing Co., 1974). Reprinted by permission of Hackett Publishing Company, Inc. All rights reserved.

Chapter 5, document 2: Walter Ullman, "Ascending and Descending Theses of Government," pp. 12–14 from *A History of Political Thought: The Middle Ages* (Penguin, 1965). Reproduced by permission of Penguin Books Ltd.

Chapter 5, document 3: Ken Wilber, "The Great Chain of Being," pp. 52–65 from the *Journal of Humanistic Psychology*, 33, 3 (Summer 1993). Reprinted by permission of Sage Publications.

Chapter 5, document 4: Jean Jacques Rousseau, "On the General Will" (1762), pp. 98–104 from *Rousseau's Political Writings: A Norton Critical Edition*, edited by Alan Ritter and Julia Conaway Bondanella, translated by Julia Conaway Bondanella. Copyright © 1988 by W. W. Norton & Company, Inc. Used by permission of W. W. Norton & Company, Inc.

Chapter 5, document 5: Friedrich Engels, "Marx's Materialist Conception of History" (1880), from *Socialism: Utopian and Scientific*, translated by Edward Aveling (New York: International Publishers, 1935).

Chapter 5, document 6: Charles Darwin, "Natural Selection" (1859), pp. 53–7 from *Darwin: A Norton Critical Edition*, second edition, edited by Philip Appleman (New York: W. W. Norton, 1979). Copyright © 1979, 1970 by W. W. Norton & Company, Inc. Used by permission of W. W. Norton & Company, Inc.

Chapter 5, document 7: T. H. Huxley, "Evolution and Ethics" (1893), from *The Essays of T. H. Huxley*, edited by Alburey Castell (Crofts Classics, 1948), available at www.gutenberg.org/etext/2940.

Chapter 5, document 8: Judith Butler, "Contingent Foundations: Feminism and the Question of 'Postmodernism,'" pp. 3–17 from Judith Butler and Joan Scott, eds., *Feminists Theorize the Political* (London: Routledge, 1992).

Chapter 6, document 1: Herbert Deane, "St. Augustine's Conception of Fallen Man," pp. 14–48 from *The Political and Social Ideas of St. Augustine* (Columbia University Press, 1963).

Chapter 6, document 2: Thomas Hobbes, "The Natural Condition of Mankind" (1651), from Chapter 13 of *The Leviathan*, edited by Michael Oakeshott (London: Collier-Macmillan Ltd, 1962).

Chapter 6, document 3: C. B. Macpherson, "The Early Liberal Model of Man," pp. 23–43 from *The Life and Times of Liberal Democracy* (Oxford University Press, 1977).

Chapter 6, document 4: Karl Marx, "Estranged Labor" (1844), from *The Marx–Engels Reader*, second edition by Karl Marx and Friedrich Engels, edited by Robert C. Tucker. Copyright © 1978, 1972 by W. W. Norton & Company, Inc. Used by permission of W. W. Norton & Company, Inc.

Chapter 6, document 5: Peter Kropotkin, "Mutual Aid," from *Mutual Aid: A Factor of Evolution* (1902), edited and translated by Paul Avrich (New York: New York University Press, 1972). Reproduced by permission of Penguin Books Ltd.

Chapter 6, document 6: John Rawls, "The Rationality and Motivations of Parties in the Original Position." Reprinted by permission of the publisher from *A Theory of Justice* by John Rawls, pp. 123–7 (Cambridge, MA: The Belknap Press of Harvard University Press). Copyright 1971.

Chapter 6, document 7: Michael Sandel, "The Procedural Republic and the Unencumbered Self," from pp. 81–96 of *Political Theory* (Sage Publications, 1984). Copyright © 1984 by Sage Publications. Reprinted by permission of Sage Publications.

Chapter 6, document 8: Bhikhu Parekh, "Conceptualizing Human Beings," pp. 114–36 from *Rethinking Multiculturalism*, second edition (New York: Palgrave Macmillan, 2006). Reprinted by permission of Palgrave Macmillan.

Chapter 7, document 1: Aristotle, "The Natural Origins of Political Associations" (350 BCE), in *Politics*, translated by Benjamin Jowett, available in the public domain at http://classics.mit.edu/Aristotle/politics.1.one.html.

Chapter 7, document 2: Thomas Hobbes, "The Contractual Origins of Society" (1651), from Chapters 14 and 15 of *The Leviathan*, edited by Michael Oakeshott (London: Collier-Macmillan Ltd, 1962).

Chapter 7, document 3: Edmund Burke, "The Great Primaeval Contract of Eternal Society" (1790), from the Anchor Books edition, 1973, derived from *The Works of the Right Honorable Edmund Burke*, the Riverton edition (London, 1826), Volume 5.

Chapter 7, document 4: Paul Schumaker, "Social Cleavages and Complex Equality," pp. 30–4, 201–2 from *Critical Pluralism, Democratic Performance, and Community Power* (University Press of Kansas, 1991). Reprinted by permission of the University Press of Kansas.

Chapter 8, document 1: Benjamin Barber, "The Epistemological Frame: Cartesian Politics," pp. 46–66 from *Strong Democracy* (University of California Press, 1984). Reprinted by permission of the publisher, The University of California Press.

Chapter 8, document 2: Jeremy Bentham, "Of the Principle of Utility" (1789), pp. 85–9 from "An Introduction to Principles of Morals and Legislation," in *A Bentham Reader*, edited by Mary and Peter Mack (New York: Pegasus, 1969).

Chapter 8, document 3: Alasdair MacIntyre, "Narratives of the Good Life Guided by Living Traditions," pp. 201–7 from *After Virtue* (University Press of Notre Dame, 1981). MacIntyre, Alasdair, *After Virtue*, third edition, © 1981, 1984, 2007 by Alasdair MacIntyre. Published by the University of Notre Dame Press. Reprinted with permission.

Chapter 8, document 4: Richard Rorty, "America's Civic Religion: A Hopeful Pragmatism," reprinted by permission of the publisher from *Achieving Our Country: Leftist Thought In Twentieth-Century America*, by Richard Rorty, pp. 15–16, 18–20, 22–5, 27–9, 37–8, 142–5 (Cambridge, MA: Harvard University Press). Copyright © 1998 by the President and Fellows of Harvard College.

Chapter 8, document 5: Carol Gilligan, "In a Different Voice," reprinted by permission of the publisher from "Woman's Place in Man's Life Cycle" in *In a Different Voice: Psychological Theory and Women's Development* by Carol Gilligan, pp. 1–2, 6, 8, 14, 18–23 (Cambridge, MA: Harvard University Press). Copyright © 1982, 1993 by Carol Gilligan.

Chapter 8, document 6: John Rawls, "Political Constructivism," pp. 89–93 from *Political Liberalism* (Columbia University Press, 1993).

Chapter 9, document 1: James Madison, "The Federalist No. 10," from www.constitution.org/fed/federal10.htm. Originally published in the *Daily Advertiser*, Thursday, November 22, 1787.

Chapter 9, document 2: Rogers M. Smith, "Toward a Theory of Civic Identities," pp. 30–8 from *Civic Ideals: Conflicting Visions of Citizenship in US History* (New Haven, CN: Yale University Press, 1997). Reprinted by permission of the publisher, Yale University Press.

Chapter 9, document 3: David Held, "Towards a Global Covenant: Global Social Democracy," pp. 161–9 from *The Global Covenant* (Cambridge: Polity Press, 2004). Reprinted by permission of Polity Press Ltd.

Chapter 9, document 4: Kirkpatrick Sale, "Human-Scale Democracy," pp. 182–204, 510–15 from *Human Scale* (New York: Coward, McCann & Geoghegan, 1980).

Chapter 9, document 5: Robert Dahl, "The Chinese Boxes," pp. 88–103 from *After the Revolution* (New Haven, CN: Yale University Press, 1970). Reprinted by permission of the publisher, Yale University Press.

Chapter 10, document 1: Michael Walzer, "The Distribution of Membership," pp. 31–63 from *Spheres of Justice* (New York: Basic Books, Inc., 1983). Reprinted by permission of Basic Books, a member of Perseus Books Group.

Chapter 10, document 2: Joseph H. Carens, "Aliens and Citizens: The Case For Open Borders," pp. 251–73 from *Review of Politics*, 47 (Spring 1987). © University of Notre Dame, published by Cambridge University Press, reproduced with permission.

Chapter 10, document 3: T. H. Marshall, "The Development of Citizen Rights," pp. 71–103 from *Class, Citizenship, and Development* (Garden City, NY: Doubleday & Company, Inc., 1964). Reprinted by permission of Pluto Press.

Chapter 10, document 4: Iris Marion Young, "Polity and Group Difference: A Critique of the Ideal of Universal Citizenship," pp. 250–73 from *Ethics*, 99 (January 1989).

Chapter 10, document 5: Amitai Etzioni et al., "The Responsive Communitarian Platform: Rights and Responsibilities," pp. 13–23 from *The Communitarian Reader: Beyond the Essentials*, edited by Amitai Etzioni, Andrew Volmert, and Elanit Rothschild (Lanham, MD: Rowman & Littlefield, 2004). Reprinted by permission of Rowman & Littlefield Publishers, Inc.

Chapter 10, document 6: Niccolo Machiavelli, "The Threat Posed by Corrupt Citizens," pp. 165–70 from *The Discourses* (New York: The Modern Library of Random House, 1950).

Chapter 11, document 1: John Stuart Mill, "On Liberty" (1860), available at www.constitution.org/jsm/liberty.htm.

Chapter 11, document 2: Adam Smith, "The Principles and Virtues of Free Markets" (1776) from *Wealth of Nations*, available at www.adamsmith.org/smith/won-intro.htm.

Chapter 11, document 3: Lawrence E. Harrison, "Progress and Poverty Without Marx," pp. 1, 6–14 from *Who Prospers? How Cultural Values Shape Economic and Political Success* (New York: Basic Books, Inc., 1992). Reprinted by permission of Basic Books, a member of Perseus Books Group.

Chapter 11, document 4: Robert D. Putnam, "The Strange Disappearance of Civic America," pp. 34–48 from *The American Prospect*, 7, 24 (December 1, 1995). Reprinted with permission from Robert Putnam, www.prospect.org. The American Prospect, 1710 Rhode Island Avenue, NW, 12th Floor, Washington DC 20036. All rights reserved.

Chapter 11, document 5: Anthony Giddens, "The Third Way and Government," pp. 55–84 from *The Third Way and Its Critics* (Polity Press, 2000).

Chapter 11, document 6: Imam Khomeini, "Islamic Government," from *Islam and Revolution: Writings and Declarations of Imam Khomeini*, translated by Hamid Algar (Mizan Press, 1981).

Chapter 11, document 7: John Locke, "A Letter Concerning Toleration" (1689) from the translation by William Popple, available at http://18th.eserver.org/toleration.txt.

Chapter 12, document 1: Robert Dahl, "Guardianship," pp. 52–64 from *Democracy and Its Critics* (New Haven, CN: Yale University Press, 1989). Reprinted by permission of the publisher, Yale University Press.

Chapter 12, document 2: Edmund Burke, "Speech to the Electors of Bristol" (November 3, 1774) available at www.ourcivilization.com/smartboard/shop/burkee/extracts/chap4.htm.

Chapter 12, document 3: Alexis de Tocqueville, "Unlimited Power of the Majority in the United States and Its Consequences" (1835), pp. 227–35 from *Democracy in America*, edited by J. P. Mayer and Max Lerner (New York: Harper & Row, 1966). Reprinted by permission of HarperCollins Publishers.

Chapter 12, document 4: Joseph Schumpeter, "A Realistic Alternative to the Classical Doctrine of Democracy," pp. 250–72 from *Capitalism, Socialism, and Democracy* (New York: Harper & Row, 1942, 1950). Reprinted by permission of HarperCollins Publishers.

Chapter 12, document 5: Benjamin Barber, "Strong Democracy: Politics in the Participatory Mode," pp. 145–55 from *Strong Democracy* (Berkeley: University of California Press, 1984). Reprinted by permission of the publisher, The University of California Press.

Chapter 12, document 6: Amy Gutmann and Dennis Thompson, "What Deliberative Democracy Means," pp. 1–21 from *Why Deliberative Democracy?* (Princeton

University Press, 2004) Reprinted by permission of Princeton University Press.

Chapter 12, document 7: William Riker, "Liberalism, Populism, and the Theory of Public Choice," pp. 233–53 from *Liberalism Against Populism* (W. H. Freeman, 1982).

Chapter 13, document 1: Robert Paul Wolff, "The Conflict Between Authority and Autonomy," pp. 3–19 from *In Defense of Anarchism* (Harper & Row, 1970). Reprinted by permission of the publisher, University of California Press.

Chapter 13, document 2: Milton Friedman, "The Role of Government in a Free Society," pp. 22–36 from *Capitalism and Freedom* (University of Chicago Press, 1962).

Chapter 13, document 3: Garrett Hardin, "The Tragedy of the Commons," pp. 1243–8 from *Science*, 162 (1968).

Chapter 13, document 4: Benjamin I. Page and James R. Simmons, "What Should Government Do?" pp. 32–46, 289–93 from *What Government Can Do: Dealing with Poverty and Inequality* (University of Chicago Press, 2000).

Chapter 13, document 5: William Galston, "Liberalism and Public Morality," pp. 129–47 from *Liberals on Liberalism*, edited by Alfonso Damico (Rowman & Littlefield, 1986). Reprinted by permission of Rowman & Littlefield Publishers, Inc.

Chapter 14, document 1: American Political Science Association Task Force on Inequality and American Democracy, "American Democracy in an Age of Rising Inequality," pp. 651–66 from *Perspectives on Politics*, 2, 4 (December 2004) © American Political Science Association, published by Cambridge University Press, reproduced with permission.

Chapter 14, document 2: John Rawls, "A Kantian Conception of Reality," from *Cambridge Review*, 1975. © Cambridge University Press, reproduced with permission.

Chapter 14, document 3: Irving Kristol, "A Capitalist Conception of Justice," pp. 57–69 from *Ethics, Free Enterprise and Public Policy*, edited by Richard DeGeorge and Joseph Pichler (Oxford University Press, 1978). By permission of Oxford University Press, Inc.

Chapter 14, document 4: Robert Nozick, "The Entitlement Theory," pp. 149–63 from *Anarchy, State, and Utopia* (Basic Books, Inc., 1974). Reprinted by permission of Basic Books, a member of Perseus Books Group.

Chapter 15, document 1: Michael Oakeshott, "On Being Conservative," pp. 168–99 from *Rationalism in Politics* (Methuen & Co. Ltd, 1962).

Chapter 15, document 2: Richard Rorty, "Movements and Campaigns," pp. 111–24 from *Achieving Our Country* (Harvard University Press, 1998).

Chapter 15, document 3: Martin Luther King, Jr. "Letter from a Birmingham Jail," April 16, 1963, from http://patriotpost.us/histdocs/Birmjail/html.

Chapter 15, document 4: Abd Al-Salam Faraj, "The Neglected Duty," from *The Neglected Duty: The Creed of Sadat's Assassins and the Emergence of Islamic Militancy in the Middle East*, by Johannes J. G. Jensen (Macmillan Reference, 1986). © 1986 Gale, a part of Cengage Learning, Inc. Reproduced by permission. www.cengage.com/permissions.

Chapter 15, document 5: Albert Camus, "Rebellion Beyond Nihilism," pp. 283–5, 289–92, 302–6 from *The Rebel* (Vintage Books, 1956).

Every effort has been made to trace copyright holders and to obtain their permission for the use of copyright material. The publisher apologizes for any errors or omissions in the above list and would be grateful if notified of any corrections that should be incorporated in future reprints or editions of this book.

Chapter 1

Political Theory, Public Philosophy, and Pluralism

Introduction

- Nation-states are yielding their centrality to the global community, to the betterment (or detriment) of people everywhere.
- National communities should open (or close) their borders to immigrants from other countries who seek citizenship.
- The cultural norms that sustain strong and well-ordered political communities are becoming increasingly debased (or enriched).
- Political life has greatly improved because democratic processes are becoming increasingly adopted globally (or is declining because democracy is eroding in the US or elsewhere).
- To protect and sustain our environment, governments must impose many regulations on economic activity and citizen behaviors (or should allow market forces to function freely and produce those profitable technical innovations that will protect our environment).
- Rising economic inequality creates economic growth for the betterment of everyone (or social polarization that undermines community life).
- We are experiencing increasingly disturbing social, economic, and political problems, so we need to return to our old ways of governing ourselves (or we need revolutionary political changes).

We have all heard such ideas, and most of us have uttered such ideas. To that extent, we are all familiar with political theory, and we all partake in political theory. Politics concerns how we live in community with others, how we cooperate to achieve collective benefits, how we engage in conflict for greater shares of the things we value, and how people are governed. Political theory consists of general or abstract ideas about how politics works and how it should work. Such political ideas flood newspapers, television, radio, and the Internet. Libraries are full of books and journals containing such political ideas, even when they are located in places far removed from collections devoted to elections, legislatures, the law, and other obviously political subjects. Abstract political ideas are discussed not only in governmental forums, but also in classrooms, churches, and taverns. Given the sheer magnitude of political theory, the extent of ignorance and confusion about political life and political ideals is astonishing.[1]

While we are exposed to many theoretical ideas about politics, we seem to comprehend, assimilate, and appreciate few of them. Many such ideas are obviously conflicting, mere opinions of others that have no obvious validity. Many are expressed to serve the interests of others, and seem repugnant to our interests or the public interest. Many seem unrealistic – distortions of the politics we perceive, utopian fantasies containing unattainable goals, and paranoid expressions of others' fears. Many such ideas are simply incoherent – too abstract, too complex, or too removed from our own experiences

[1] Michael X. Delli Carpini and Scott Keeter, *What Americans Know About Politics and Why It Matters* (New Haven: Yale University Press, 1996).

and thinking to make much sense to us. Not surprisingly, people often turn away from political ideas.

But escaping from serious political reflection is dangerous, especially in democracies that proclaim that governance reflects the beliefs and values of their citizens, and even more in democracies where leaders have learned to pander to citizen emotions and mislead the public in order to pursue their own ideological agendas.[2] Democracies that are effective, that are oriented toward the public good, and that seek justice for all require citizens who are competent political thinkers.

Citizen competence no doubt begins with awareness of changing social, cultural, and economic conditions in our communities and with informed judgments about the effectiveness of our leaders and the programs and policies they have established to improve these conditions – or at least prevent their deterioration. Competent citizens must be able to choose effectively among political parties and candidates those that reflect their interests and aspirations and that offer the most promising solutions to social problems, and they must actively pursue their preferred policies between elections. But effective choices and actions presuppose that citizens have some sort of broad cognitive framework to help them choose and act. Citizens need maps that organize various understandings of political life and help them to choose among competing ideas, to judge the directions in which their communities are heading, and to evaluate and hold accountable those who lead them. For competent citizens, political theory is not just a mishmash of conflicting, self-serving, utopian, paranoid, and distant ideas; rather, it provides them comprehensive and coherent maps of political life, helps them sort out valid from dubious ideas, and facilitates their making informed judgments and good political choices.

Four types of maps for organizing and understanding political ideas can be useful. The most general is merely a *conceptual matrix* that organizes ideas along two dimensions. On one axis are arrayed the major political issues (e.g., questions of citizenship, of rulers, of government authority, and of justice) and their philosophical foundations (questions of ontology, human nature, the nature of society, and epistemology). On the other axis are alternative answers to these questions (e.g., as provided by competing ideologies or by different cultural traditions). Sorting political ideas on the basis of the major issues they address and the general perspectives they reflect is the beginning of making sense of political discourse and politics itself. This reader, like my accompanying text (*From Ideologies to Public Philosophies*), is organized on the basis of such a matrix. Chapters 2, 3, and 4 introduce major ideological perspectives. Chapters 5 through 15 provide a sample of readings from these perspectives (and other earlier political theorists not identified with any modern ideology) that provide alternative answers to the major philosophical and political issues developed at the beginning of each chapter. If you encounter a political idea and can place it within a conceptual framework according to the great issue(s) it addresses and the perspective(s) it represents, you will have made a significant step in removing confusion about the bewildering onslaught of political ideas that compete for your attention.

But competent citizens not only can place political ideas in such a matrix, they choose among alternative answers, developing philosophical assumptions and political principles to which they are allegiant. The political principles they adopt and the philosophical assumptions that are the basis of these principles and help provide support and justification for these principles comprise *individual public philosophies* enabling citizens to know where they stand on the concrete political issues that arise in their communities. Most citizens lack comprehensive and coherent political perspectives, while others have simply adopted those of their parents, friends, some charismatic political leader, or the cultures in which they are embedded. But some citizens develop their own political views by thinking long and hard about the alternative ideas on the great issues, adopting those principles that they find most valid and justified. Sometimes these individual public philosophies closely match those of well-established ideologies, but they can also be unique personal constructions. The readings and the way they are organized here are intended to help you develop such a perspective.

Coherent sets of political principles should guide not just individual citizens; they should also guide political communities. A regime or dominant party that has articulated a set of ideas that most citizens have endorsed during elections can govern a polity on the basis of *a specific governing philosophy*. While we often imagine democratic communities as functioning in this way, the failure of candidates and parties to express and remain true to such a philosophy, the failure of citizens to choose among candidates and parties on the basis of their articulated philosophies, and electoral arrangements that make it difficult to ascertain the dominant principles of citizens from electoral outcomes can result in our being governed more by pure power than by any governing philosophy.

[2] Alan Wolfe, *Does American Democracy Still Work?* (New Haven: Yale University Press, 2006).

Since particular regimes and parties have authority for specific time periods, the public philosophies by which they (ideally) govern are many and temporary. In the US, for example, Democrats governed on the basis of a brand of contemporary liberalism during much of the mid-twentieth century, only to give way to a form of contemporary conservatism during the Reagan and Republican years. Bill Clinton brought a somewhat different liberalism to national politics during the 1990s, while George W. Bush governed under another conservatism from 2000 to 2008. Now Barack Obama seeks to govern using a highly pragmatic and nondogmatic form of liberalism. But these variations and changes in governing philosophies should not obscure the existence of a broader public philosophy containing general political principles and (weak) philosophical assumptions to which all these regimes subscribe and to which most Americans (and many leaders and citizens elsewhere) also subscribe. Thus, a fourth map of political theory that people can effectively understand and utilize is composed of these most general ideas that are widely held within political communities and that endure over time, even while different regimes apply their more particular governing philosophies. This most general map of political ideas – which I call *pluralist public philosophy* – helps those with more specific competing principles understand and appreciate their commonalities and thus helps provide a basis of resolving political conflicts in a democratic, civil, and peaceful manner.

While subsequent chapters will provide readings chosen to help you understand and appreciate these various kinds of maps, the readings in this chapter address the "map making" activity of political theorists. It provides some general accounts of what political theorists are trying to achieve and why their work is important. It discusses what political philosophers do, the role of ideologies in political theory, the public philosophies that political theorists have found and seek to promote, and it provides an introduction to pluralism as the most general public philosophy affecting politics today.

Our first selection by Leo Strauss (1899–1973) provides the classical statement about the meaning and importance of political philosophy. It was written in 1957, at a time when political philosophy was "in a state of decay and perhaps putrefaction." Claiming that political philosophers had since Plato been engaged in the search for knowledge of "the nature of political things, and the right, or the good, political order," Strauss discusses the limitations of the "social science positivism" that was ascendant in political science at the beginning of its behavioral revolution and that sought to understand politics in a value-free manner. For Strauss, who taught for many years at the University of Chicago, Claremont College, and St. John's College in Annapolis and who influenced the education of a large group of political philosophers (the Straussians), efforts to understand politics without deep concern about moral and normative matters are incomplete, if not misguided.

Strauss believed that the true activity of a political philosopher was to help relieve the human suffering that occurs from ill-advised attempts to use political power in ways that assume greater understanding and control than humans can actually have; thus, he was not only hostile to the positivist quest for scientific certainty but also to the various ideologies that had arisen since the French Revolution at the end of the eighteenth century. While ideologies are normally regarded as "any visionary and grandiose scheme of social reform," Judith Shklar (1928–92), who had a long and distinguished career as the first woman in Harvard's Department of Government, argues that ideologies are more precisely understood as specific "forms of untruth." She points out that Karl Marx had used the term to reveal that classical liberalism (which was becoming a dominant public philosophy) did not contain universal truths about politics but was instead "a mask" used to obscure the fact that its principles supporting capitalism and representative democracy served the interest of the rising middle class (the bourgeoisie) at the expense of the working class (the proletariat). She also points out that subsequent students of ideology – most notably Karl Mannheim – claim that other public philosophies including democratic socialism, conservatism, communism, and fascism were also mere weapons that particular interests employed in their efforts to gain support and power, and thus succeed in political struggles. In short, Shklar and other students of ideology maintain that none of these outlooks have any claim to providing superior understandings of political life.

Writing in the 1950s and 1960s, Strauss and Shklar lamented the decline of political philosophy. But stimulated by the work of John Rawls (1921–2001) and many others, there was a revival in political philosophy. While Rawls' seminal *A Theory of Justice*, published in 1971, was seen by some as yet another ideology, he subsequently argued in *Political Liberalism* (1993) that his work, like that of other political theorists, actually sought to articulate liberal pluralism as a public philosophy expressing an "overlapping consensus" at least within contemporary Western societies among those holding diverse moral and political doctrines. In Chapters 6, 8, and 14 of this reader, you will encounter some of Rawls' most important ideas in this regard.

If Rawls intended his theory of justice to be a public philosophy, it was a more idealized articulation of political ideas in America than those that actually prevail, at least according to Theodore Lowi, who has been a professor of American Institutions at Cornell University since 1972. In *The End of Liberalism*, first published in 1969 but substantially revised and extended in a subsequent 1979 edition, Lowi argues that America's public philosophy has been transformed since the 1930s. Its old public philosophy was capitalism, understood as a version of classical liberalism that emphasized economic processes and "the sanctity of property and the binding morality of contract." However, its new public philosophy is "interest-group liberalism," in which national government has acquired an expansive role by giving all organized interests access to its authority. According to Lowi, Democrats and Republicans do not really pursue different principles but merely respond to different interests. Lowi can be interpreted as arguing that this new interest-group liberalism is a deformed type of pluralist public philosophy. It must be criticized because its ideas encourage governments to minimize the use of their legitimate powers of coercion and to dispense with philosophically defended standards; instead, such governments merely pursue the sentiments of those who participate and have power.

Our final two selections look more directly at pluralist public philosophy. Avigail Eisenberg – a professor of political science at The University of Victoria (in British Columbia, Canada) – has sought to reconstruct political pluralism. Many political scientists still understand pluralism as either Lowi's interest-group liberalism or as a theory of democratic politics that focuses on the (relatively dispersed) distribution of power among many groups in society and that became the dominant paradigm in the discipline during the 1950s and 1960s. However, most political scientists abandoned pluralism when that formulation encountered many problems and criticisms (such as those suggested by Lowi). Eisenberg regards this understanding of pluralism as limited. Pluralism has a much longer historical legacy that provides a broad array of resources for a more adequate public philosophy – one that focuses on individual moral development as well as the distribution of power and one that not only depicts existing society but also can help transform political life.

William E. Connolly, a professor of political science at Johns Hopkins University, addresses these themes in his recent book entitled *Pluralism*, from which our final extract in this chapter is taken. Connolly takes up the question of whether pluralism – with its uncertainty and relativism, its recognition of the legitimacy of diverse viewpoints and interests, and its commitments to negotiation and compromise among interests – is "a philosophy for wimps." He endorses pluralism because those committed to it "expose and resist such dark resonance machines" that deny and oppress alternative voices. He endorses pluralism, because it permits people to have a "bicameral orientation," a commitment not only to pluralism but also to another "faith, creed, ideology, or philosophy" that enables one to participate as a committed partisan in the public realm. While pluralism has too often been equated with a resignation to politics as it is currently practiced, Connolly proclaims the possibility of being both a pluralist and a person with commitments to radical changes that reduce the deep inequalities that pervade pluralist societies.

In sum, the readings in this chapter invite us to think more clearly about the general modalities of political theory. Political philosophy is not the quest for political certainty, but a search for political understanding in light of human limitations. Political ideologies do not provide clear guidance for political programs and policies, but rather are perspectives that justify the goals of particular interests. Public philosophies are not singular perspectives that demand universal allegiances, but are instead diverse sets of political principles and philosophical assumptions that should be arrived at through careful reflection by both individuals and collectivities. Pluralism is not a well-established paradigm that claims that power is widely and justly distributed in democratic societies, but rather is a general public philosophy that contains the most widely embraced political understandings that people have about the good life, a good society, and good government in a world where most such understandings are highly contested. As such a public philosophy, pluralism remains a work in progress. As such, the voices of all citizens and students can contribute significantly to its articulation and future development.

Leo Strauss, "What Is Political Philosophy?"*

The meaning of political philosophy and its meaningful character are as evident today as they have been since the time when political philosophy first made its appearance in Athens. All political action aims at either preservation or change. When desiring to preserve, we wish to prevent a change to the worse; when desiring to change, we wish to bring about something better. All political action is, then, guided by some thought of better or worse. But thought of better or worse implies thought of the good. The awareness of the good which guides all our actions, has the character of opinion: it is no longer questioned but, on reflection, it proves to be questionable. The very fact that we can question it, directs us towards such a thought of the good as is no longer questionable – towards a thought which is no longer opinion but knowledge. All political action has then in itself a directedness towards knowledge of the good: of the good life, or the good society. For the good society is the complete political good.

If this directedness becomes explicit, if men make it their explicit goal to acquire knowledge of the good life and of the good society, political philosophy emerges. By calling this pursuit political philosophy, we imply that it forms a part of a larger whole: of philosophy. Since political philosophy is a branch of philosophy, even the most provisional explanation of what political philosophy is, cannot dispense with an explanation, however provisional, of what philosophy is. Philosophy, as quest for wisdom, is quest for universal knowledge, for knowledge of the whole. The quest would not be necessary if such knowledge were immediately available. The absence of knowledge of the whole does not mean, however, that men do not have thoughts about the whole: philosophy is necessarily preceded by opinions about the whole. It is, therefore, the attempt to replace opinions about the whole by knowledge of the whole. Instead of "the whole" philosophers also say "all things"; the whole is not a pure ether or an unrelieved darkness in which one cannot distinguish one part from the other, or in which one cannot discern anything. A quest for knowledge of "all things" means quest for knowledge of God, the world, and man – or rather quest for knowledge of the natures of all things: the natures in their totality are "the whole."

Philosophy is essentially not possession of the truth, but quest for the truth. The distinctive trait of the philosopher is that "he knows that he knows nothing," and that his insight into our ignorance concerning the most important things induces him to strive with all his power for knowledge. He would cease to be a philosopher by evading the questions concerning those things or by disregarding them because they cannot be answered. It may be that as regards the possible answers to these questions, the pros and cons will always be in a more or less even balance, and, therefore, the stage of discussion or disputation will never reach the stage of decision. This would not make philosophy futile. [...]

Of philosophy thus understood, political philosophy is a branch. Political philosophy will then be the attempt to replace opinion about the nature of political things by knowledge of the nature of political things. Political things are by their nature subject to approval and disapproval, to choice and rejection, to praise and blame. It is of their essence not to be neutral but to raise a claim to men's obedience, allegiance, decision or judgment. One does not understand them as what they are, as political things, if one does not take seriously their explicit or implicit claim to be judged in terms of goodness or badness, of justice or injustice, i.e., if one does not measure them by some standard of goodness or justice. To judge soundly one must know the true standards. If political philosophy wishes to do justice to its subject matter, it must strive for genuine knowledge of these standards. Political philosophy is the attempt truly to know both the nature of political things and the right, or the good, political order.

All knowledge of political things implies assumptions concerning the nature of political things, i.e., assumptions which concern not merely the given political situation but political life or human life as such. One cannot know anything about a war going on at a given time without having some notion, however dim and hazy, of war as such and its place within human life as such. One cannot see a policeman as a policeman without having made an assumption about law and government as such. The assumptions concerning the nature of political things, which are implied in all knowledge of political things, have the character of opinions. It is only when these assumptions are made the theme of critical and coherent analysis that a philosophic or scientific approach to politics emerges.

The cognitive status of political knowledge is not different from that of the knowledge possessed by the shepherd, the husband, the general, or the cook. Yet the pursuits of these types of man do not give rise to pastoral,

* Leo Strauss, extracted from *Journal of Politics* (August 1957), pp. 343–68.

marital, military, or culinary philosophy because their ultimate goals are sufficiently clear and unambiguous. The ultimate political goal, on the other hand, urgently calls for coherent reflection. The goal of the general is victory, whereas the goal of the statesman is the common good. What victory means is not essentially controversial, but the meaning of the common good is essentially controversial. The ambiguity of the political goal is due to its comprehensive character. Thus the temptation arises to deny, or to evade, the comprehensive character of politics and to treat politics as one compartment among many. This temptation must be resisted if we are to face our situation as human beings, i.e., the whole situation.

Political philosophy as we have tried to circumscribe it, has been cultivated since its beginnings almost without any interruption until a relatively short time ago. Today, political philosophy is in a state of decay and perhaps of putrefaction, if it has not vanished altogether. [...]

If we inquire into the reasons for this great change, we receive these answers: political philosophy is unscientific, or it is unhistorical, or it is both. Science and History, those two great powers of the modern world, have eventually succeeded in destroying the very possibility of political philosophy.

The rejection of political philosophy as unscientific is characteristic of present-day positivism. Positivism is no longer what it desired to be when Auguste Comte originated it. It still agrees with Comte by maintaining that modern science is the highest form of knowledge, precisely because it aims no longer, as theology and metaphysics did, at absolute knowledge of the Why, but only at relative knowledge of the How. But after having been modified by utilitarianism, evolutionism, and neo-Kantianism, it has abandoned completely Comte's hope that a social science modeled on modern natural science would be able to overcome the intellectual anarchy of modern society. In about the last decade of the nineteenth century, social science positivism reached its final form by realizing, or decreeing that there is a fundamental difference between facts and values, and that only factual judgments are within the competence of science: scientific social science is incompetent to pronounce value judgments, and must avoid value judgments altogether.

[...]

It is not necessary to enter here and now into a discussion of the theoretical weaknesses of social science positivism. It suffices to allude to the considerations which speak decisively against this school.

1. It is impossible to study social phenomena, i.e., all important social phenomena, without making value judgments. A man who sees no reason for not despising people whose horizon is limited to their consumption of food and their digestion may be a tolerable econometrist; he cannot say anything relevant about the character of human society. A man who refuses to distinguish between great statesmen, mediocrities, and insane imposters may be a good bibliographer; he cannot say anything relevant about politics and political history. [...]

2. The rejection of value judgments is based on the assumption that the conflicts between different values or value-systems are essentially insoluble for human reason. But this assumption, while generally taken to be sufficiently established, has never been proven. Its proof would require an effort of the magnitude of that which went into the conception and elaboration of the *Critique of Pure Reason;* it would require a comprehensive critique of evaluating reason. What we find in fact are sketchy observations which pretend to prove that this or that specific value conflict is insoluble. It is prudent to grant that there are value conflicts which cannot in fact be settled by human reason. But if we cannot decide which of two mountains whose peaks are hidden by clouds is higher than the other, cannot we decide that a mountain is higher than a molehill? [...]

3. The belief that scientific knowledge, i.e., the kind of knowledge possessed or aspired to by modern science, is the highest form of human knowledge, implies a depreciation of pre-scientific knowledge. If one takes into consideration the contrast between scientific knowledge of the world and pre-scientific knowledge of the world, one realizes that positivism preserves in a scarcely disguised manner Descartes' universal doubt of pre-scientific knowledge and his radical break with it. It certainly distrusts pre-scientific knowledge which it likes to compare to folk-lore. This superstition fosters all sorts of sterile investigations or complicated idiocies. Things which every 10-year-old child of normal intelligence knows are regarded as being in need of scientific proof in order to become acceptable as facts. And this scientific proof which is not only not necessary, is not even possible. To illustrate this by the simplest example: all studies in social science presuppose that its devotees can tell human beings from other beings; this most fundamental knowledge was not

acquired by them in classrooms; and this knowledge is not transformed by social science into scientific knowledge, but retains its initial status without any modification throughout. If this pre-scientific knowledge is not knowledge, all scientific studies which stand or fall with it, lack the character of knowledge. The preoccupation with scientific proof of things which everyone knows well enough, and better, without scientific proof, leads to the neglect of that thinking, or that reflection, which must precede all scientific studies if these studies are to be relevant. [...]

4. Positivism necessarily transforms itself into historicism. By virtue of its orientation by the model of natural science, social science is in danger of mistaking peculiarities of, say, mid-twentieth-century United States, or more generally of modern Western society, for the essential character of human society. To avoid this danger, it is compelled to engage in "cross-cultural research," in the study of other cultures, both present and past. But in making this effort, it misses the meaning of those other cultures, because it interprets them through a conceptual scheme which originates in modern Western society, which reflects that particular society, and which fits at best only that particular society. To avoid this danger, social science must attempt to understand those cultures as they understand or understood themselves: the understanding primarily required of the social scientist is historical understanding. Historical understanding becomes the basis of a truly empirical science of society. But if one considers the infinity of the task of historical understanding, one begins to wonder whether historical understanding does not take the place of the scientific study of society. [...] Not only is social science superseded by historical studies; social science itself proves to be "historical." Reflection on social science as a historical phenomenon leads to the relativization of social science and ultimately of modern science generally. As a consequence, modern science comes to be viewed as one historically relative way of understanding things which is not in principle superior to alternative ways of understanding.

It is only at this point that we come face to face with the serious antagonist of political philosophy: historicism. After having reached its full growth historicism is distinguished from positivism by the following characteristics. (1) It abandons the distinction between facts and values, because every understanding, however theoretical, implies specific evaluations. (2) It denies the authoritative character of modern science, which appears as only one among the many forms of man's intellectual orientation in the world. (3) It refuses to regard the historical process as fundamentally progressive, or, more generally stated, as reasonable. (4) It denies the relevance of the evolutionist thesis by contending that the evolution of man out of non-man cannot make intelligible man's humanity. Historicism rejects the question of the good society, that is to say, of *the* good society because of the essentially historical character of society and of human thought: there is no essential necessity for raising the question of the good society; this question is not in principle coeval with man; its very possibility is the outcome of a mysterious dispensation of fate. The crucial issue concerns the status of those permanent characteristics of humanity, such as the distinction between the noble and the base, which are admitted by the thoughtful historicists: can these permanencies be used as criteria for distinguishing between good and bad dispensations of fate? The historicist answers this question in the negative. He looks down on the permanencies in question because of their objective, common, superficial and rudimentary character: to become relevant, they would have to be completed, and their completion is no longer common but historical. It was the contempt for these permanencies which permitted the most radical historicist in 1933 to submit to, or rather to welcome, as a dispensation of fate, the verdict of the least wise and least moderate part of his nation while it was in its least wise and least moderate mood, and at the same time to speak of wisdom and moderation. The events of 1933 would rather seem to have proved, if such proof was necessary, that man cannot abandon the question of the good society, and that he cannot free himself from the responsibility for answering it by deferring to history or to any other power different from his own reason.

[...]

Regime is the order, the form, which gives society its character. Regime is therefore a specific manner of life. Regime is the form of life as living together, the manner of living of society and in society, since this manner depends decisively on the predominance of human beings of a certain type, on the manifest domination of society by human beings of a certain type. Regime means that whole, which we today are in the habit of viewing primarily in a fragmentized form; regime means simultaneously the form of life of a society, its style of life, its moral taste, form of society, form of state, form of government, spirit of laws. We may try to articulate the simple and unified thought, that expresses itself in the term *politeia*, as follows: life is activity which is directed toward some goal; social life is an activity which is directed toward such a goal as can be pursued only by society; but in order to pursue a specific goal, which is its comprehensive goal, society must be organized, ordered, constructed, constituted in a manner which is in accordance with that goal; this, however, means, that the men in authority must be attuned to that goal.

There is a variety of regimes. Each regime raises a claim, explicitly or implicitly, which extends beyond the boundaries of any given society. These claims conflict, therefore, with each other. There is a variety of conflicting regimes. Thus the regimes themselves, and not our preoccupation as mere bystanders, force us to wonder which of the given conflicting regimes is better, and ultimately, which regime is the best regime. Classical political philosophy is guided by the question of the best regime.

[...]

Whatever the significance of modern natural science may be, it cannot affect our understanding of what is human in man. To understand man in the light of the whole means for modern natural science to understand man in the light of the sub-human. But in that light man as man is wholly unintelligible. Classical political philosophy viewed man in a different light. It was originated by Socrates, and Socrates was so far from being committed to a specific cosmology that his knowledge was knowledge of ignorance. Knowledge of ignorance is not ignorance; it is knowledge of the elusive character of the truth, of the whole. Socrates, then, viewed man in the light of the mysterious character of the whole. He held therefore that we are more familiar with the situation of man as man than with the ultimate causes of that situation. We may also say he viewed man in the light of the unchangeable ideas, i.e., of the fundamental and permanent problems. For to articulate the situation of man means to articulate man's openness to the whole. This understanding of the situation of man which includes then the quest for cosmology rather than a solution to the cosmological problem, was the foundation of classical political philosophy.

To articulate the problem of cosmology means to answer the question of what philosophy is or what a philosopher is. Plato refrained from entrusting the thematic discussion of this question to Socrates. He entrusted it to a stranger from Elea. But even that stranger from Elea did not discuss explicitly what a philosopher is. He discussed explicitly two kinds of men which are easily mistaken for the philosopher, the sophist and the statesman. By understanding both sophistry (in its highest as well as in its lower meanings) and statesmanship, one will understand what philosophy is. Philosophy strives for knowledge of the whole. The whole is the totality of the parts. The whole eludes us, but we know parts: we possess partial knowledge of parts. The knowledge which we possess is characterized by a fundamental dualism which has never been overcome. At one pole we find knowledge of homogeneity: above all in arithmetic, but also in the other branches of mathematics, and derivatively in all productive arts or crafts. At the opposite pole we find knowledge of heterogeneity, and in particular of heterogeneous ends; the highest form of this kind of knowledge is the art of the statesman and of the educator. The latter kind of knowledge is superior to the former for this reason. As knowledge of the ends of human life, it is knowledge of what makes human life complete or whole; it is therefore knowledge of a whole. Knowledge of the ends of man implies knowledge of the human soul; and the human soul is the only part of the whole which is open to the whole and therefore more akin to the whole than anything else is. But this knowledge – the political art in the highest sense – is not knowledge of *the* whole. It seems that knowledge of the whole would have to combine somehow political knowledge in the highest sense with knowledge of homogeneity. And this combination is not at our disposal. Men are therefore constantly tempted to force the issue by imposing unity on the phenomena, by absolutizing either knowledge of homogeneity or knowledge of ends. Men are constantly attracted and deluded by two opposite charms: the charm of competence which is engendered by mathematics and everything akin to mathematics, and the charm of humble awe, which is engendered by meditation on the human soul and its experiences. Philosophy is characterized by the gentle, if firm, refusal to succumb to either charm. It is the highest form of the mating of courage and moderation. In spite of its highness or nobility, it could appear as Sisyphean or ugly, when one contrasts its achievement with its goal. Yet it is necessarily accompanied, sustained and elevated by *eros*. It is graced by nature's grace.

Judith Shklar, "Political Ideology"*

The word "ideology" is so frequently used today that it is easy to forget how very new it is and how uncertain its meaning still remains. Indeed the *Encyclopedia of the Social Sciences*, a very comprehensive work published as late as 1936, has no entry under that heading. It is no exaggeration to say that until the Second World War, and more especially, the Cold War, very few Americans gave any thought to ideology at all. Even in Europe it was not until the interwar period that ideology became a subject of serious scholarly concern. This situation is not really surprising, since the very term only makes its appearance in the last years of the eighteenth century and has always been bedevilled by controversies about its true significance. From the first, ideology has been used colloquially to refer to any visionary and grandiose scheme of social reform. As such it is a word of opprobrium encompassing all political dreams, whatever their nature. However, the main struggle over the significance of ideology does not involve such common usage.[3] The struggle is, rather, a part of the most serious philosophical disagreements about the structure and meaning of human history. It is, above all, concerned with the place of ideas in the shaping of mankind's social development and, more particularly, the role of political ideas. For whatever else ideology may be, historians now agree that it involves those ideas that seem to form an integral part of political–social history, or at least ideas that are seen in a social context.

The range of disputed issues raised by conflicting philosophies of history has, in the modern age, been enormous. Ideology touches upon only some of them, but they are of truly central importance. The first question it raises is whether all ideas – political, religious, scientific, or aesthetic – are the direct products of social situations. What do individual thinkers contribute to the history of ideas? Do they express purely personal experiences and reflections, or do they give voice to group minds? What are the significant groups whose situation finds systematic intellectual expression? Are political philosophers a primary part of social history, or merely pale reflections of some other, more "real", set of historical experiences, even though their authors cannot recognize this? Do ideas shape actions and events, or are they just rationalizations of more basic, subrational drives? What sort of unconscious social impulses are at work here? Above all, does history as a whole follow a determinate pattern which allows the historian to identify some social ideas as "progressive", in contrast to "retrogressive" ones, and to regard the former as historically "right", and the latter as "false"? Is the structure of history, moreover, one of successive group struggles, and so, one of rising and declining, victorious and discarded ideas ... ?

[...] It was certainly the designers of the many new systems of political philosophy in the nineteenth century who earned it the title, "the age of ideology." Curiously, however, the thinker who contributed most to the entire history of ideology, Karl Marx, did not regard philosophers or their works as actors of primary importance on the stage of history. That is why, among other things, he was the founder of the modern theory of ideology.

[...]

Since the mature Marx's main interests were economics and political action, he did not devote more than passing notice to the history of political theory. He never, for example, showed in any detail how the substructure of any given period had determined specific philosophies. In his younger years, however, he had undertaken an intense critique of religion, a subject to which he occasionally returned. It is this part of his writings that is the clearest forerunner of most future theories of ideology. Religion, Marx believed, arose when the division of labor began to alienate man from the work of his hands. In religion men found both a consolation for their actual sufferings, and a vision of an existence which was the exact opposite of their actual situation. As such, religion was both a means of escape from daily suffering and the vehicle for rebellious feelings of the socially helpless and hopelessly weak.[4] When the material conditions creating their misery would disappear, dreams would be replaced by action and religion, the mirror and instrument of oppression, would vanish forever. In the meantime, since it is the duty of philosophers to alter the world, religion must be exposed for the sham it is so that men might be liberated from it. This method of political warfare, by which ideas are "unmasked" to reveal their "real" social roots, was to become the standard technique of ideological warfare in the decades that followed. Marx and Engels employed

* Judith Shklar, extracted from *Political Theory and Ideology* (Macmillan, 1966), pp. 1–19.

[3] Arne Naess et al., *Democracy, Ideology and Objectivity* (Oslo: Oslo University Press, 1956) offers an account of the conflicting definitions of ideology.

[4] Karl Marx, Toward a Critique of Hegel's Philosophy of Right, in Lewis S. Feuer, *Marx and Engels: Basic Writings on Politics and Philosophy* (New York: Doubleday, 1959), pp. 262–263.

this weapon in their attacks upon all rival socialists, whose ideas they tried to destroy, not by showing them to be untrue or illogical, but by "exposing" their hidden class character and tendency to serve the existing state of society.[5] Eventually, to be sure, all political parties came to practice this form of "psychic annihilation" in their mutual struggles, but as Karl Mannheim has said, "socialism in its analysis of ideology worked out a coherent, critical method which was, in effect, an attempt to annihilate the antagonists' utopia by showing that they had their roots in the existing situation."[6] The ferreting out of the social determinants – and so the bias – of the thinking of all his opponents did not for a moment lead Marx to question the roots of his own thinking, which he regarded as scientifically true and in no sense ideological. Marx was no relativist. He clearly believed in the absolute truth of the positive sciences and counted his economics among them. In the classless society, moreover, all the obstacles to the pursuit of truth would necessarily be greatly reduced. Ideology was thus only a specific form of untruth, created by the class system, and one that would disappear as it was unmasked. …

[…]

Although conventional Marxist writings on the history of ideology have been neither very original nor illuminating, Marx, nevertheless, did inspire the most daring and influential of all contemporary theories of ideology, Karl Mannheim's "sociology of knowledge." It is, moreover, a debt that is freely acknowledged.[7] Like Marxism, Mannheim's sociology is a speculative philosophy of history. Although he rejected the Marxian picture of a struggle between three essentially economic classes with a predictable ending, he too saw history as a pattern of struggles between well-defined groups.

[…]

Both [liberalism and Marxism] were, in Mannheim's terms, genuine utopias, since both can be retrospectively recognized as political visions with a significant historical future, both expressing the aspirations of classes that, in very different ways, were to play a central role in their respective epochs. Both eventually became, as they were bound to, mere ideologies. In time they and the groups whose experiences they expressed played out their assigned roles and ceased to have a creative future function. The conservative critique of liberalism, as well as its discovery of history as an organic growth, represented especially the reaction of the remaining feudal and rural elements in Germany. For a brief period in the nineteenth century they and their views inspired and dominated the cultural scene. Presently, however, socialism overcame both the liberal and conservative past. Borrowing a sense of history from conservatism, and a ruthlessly forward-looking activism from liberalism, Marx was the heir of both, to become in his turn the central force of an age. This age, Mannheim thought, was now past and done with, as the classless society was at hand, and Marxism, the last of all possible utopias, was now just an ideology, even though Marx had not been able to foresee that this would be the fate of his doctrine also.

[…]

One way of reconstructing a picture of a group mind is illustrated by Louis Hartz's [work on] the sum of politically articulate Americans at the time of the Revolution.[8] The "objective" state of America, according to Hartz, is a paradoxical one, in that although there were and are economic classes, the one class that had the deepest impact upon the European mind never existed here: the feudal aristocracy. The socio-psychological consequences of the *absence* of this class, and of the struggles against it, have shaped all American political thought and created a uniquely American ideology, just as much as its *presence* has given Europe its own peculiar character. The American bourgeoisie, because it never faced a feudal aristocracy, failed to develop that mixture of resentment of and admiration for aristocratic values and also any sense of identity as a class apart from others. The result is an "irrational Lockeanism," a belief that there is only one set of values because there is only one class, the bourgeoisie, which is not even aware of itself as a class. Taking itself to be a universal order, such a bourgeoisie puts forward libertarian and egalitarian ideology as the only possible one, even when its ideologists are pursuing ends which are in no sense liberal or democratic. It also creates a public mind hostile to and unfamiliar with ideological obstacles and new values which might challenge the self-evidently true ethos. Conflict is regarded as eccentric, agreement as natural, and those remnants of aristocratic society, individuality, differentiation of tastes and manners, and self-assertiveness are discouraged in a social character that seeks security in conformity and unity in alikeness. It gives rise to political

5 Karl Marx, The Class Struggle in France, in Feuer, ibid., pp. 316–317.

6 Karl Mannheim, *Ideology and Utopia* (New York: Harcourt, Brace and Co., n.d.), pp. 38–41, p. 241.

7 Karl Mannheim, *Ideology and Utopia* (London: Routledge and Kegan Paul Ltd., 1936), p. 277.

8 Louis Hartz, *The Liberal Tradition in America* (New York: Harcourt, Brace and World, 1955).

ideas which are alike in that they reflect a middle-class mind whose ascendency has never even been in doubt. ...

[...]

It has indeed been among observers of the governments of Nazi Germany and the Soviet Union that there has been the greatest tendency to stress the role of ideology in shaping political life. This is scarcely surprising, since most Americans only became aware of ideology when they were confronted with these new and hostile political systems. ... While accepting the notion that totalitarian ideologies are "secular religions," Carl J. Friedrich and Zbigniew K. Brzezinski feel that it is impossible to treat the history of the Soviet Union and of Nazi Germany as the simple working out of Marxism and racism respectively.[9] Moreover, the emphasis ought to be put less on the content of these ideologies than on their symbolic and psychological functions within the totalitarian order as a whole. The only really important element in their teachings, the one that sets them apart from all other ideologies, is the glorification of violence. Their mass appeal may well be in just that. In sum, while totalitarian ideologies may draw upon many traditions of political thinking, it is their current use as instruments of mass organization and violent political warfare that is crucial to our understanding of their place in the contemporary world, and not their nonexistent intellectual force. They can be studied only as an integral aspect, but only one among many others, of an operative totalitarian political system, not as an independent historical or spiritual phenomenon.

[...] As the label "the age of ideology" implies, nineteenth-century social thinking was in many ways entirely novel.[10] In its relentless future-directed, prophetic, activist and all-encompassing pretensions, its pseudoscientific aspirations and its dogmatic ways, the typical system of ideas of that century was quite unlike the political theory that preceded it. Whether it is sufficient to say that all the "isms" of the age – the various kinds of liberalism, conservatism, socialism, nationalism, and racism – were surrogate religions, appealing to men dislocated by the Industrial Revolution and the decline of traditional values, cannot be easily determined. Here too there are levels of quality. At their philosophic best, Mill, Hegel, and Marx offered a new and serious interpretation of society and of their age. What made the last century so evidently an "age of ideology" was the way in which political ideas became a part of the new forms of political combat that emerged after the French Revolution. These were but a part of the novel political institutions and forms of government in which the mobilization of public opinion and the organization of political parties and groups played so paramount a part. The unmasking of ideology belonged to that age and its typical political preoccupations – preoccupations that are not a part of the current political life of Europe and the United States. It should not be surprising that the study of the history of political ideas will now be reexamined and interpreted in terms more in keeping with the experiences of the post-ideological age.

[9] Carl J. Friedrich and Zbigniew K. Brzezinski, *Totalitarian Dictatorships and Autocracy* (Cambridge, MA: Harvard University Press, 1956).

[10] E.g., Frederick M. Watkins, *The Age of Ideology: Political Thought, 1750 to the Present* (Englewood Cliffs, NJ: Prentice Hall, 1964).

Theodore J. Lowi, "America's Old and New Public Philosophy"*

The old public philosophy: *capitalist ideology and the automatic society*

The United States is a child of the Industrial Revolution. Its godfather is capitalism and its guardian Providence, otherwise known as the "invisible hand."

Capitalism is an ideology because it is a source of principles and a means of justifying behavior; that is, it is something Americans believe in. It is a liberal ideology because it has always participated in positive attitudes toward progress, individualism, rationality, and nationalism. It is capitalism because its foundation is a capitalistic economic theory and because its standards of legitimacy are capitalistic. It was the public philosophy during the nineteenth century because it dominated all other sources of belief in the formulation of public policy. It is the old public philosophy because it no longer dominates other sources of belief.

In a very important sense, of course, capitalism is not an ideology at all. It is a bundle of economic and technological processes. In this sense capitalism is not something one believes in but rather something one does. One simply amasses wealth and tries to make it produce in the most rational manner by ruthlessly submitting it to the principles of human organization, machines, and

* Theodore J. Lowi, extracted from *The End of Liberalism* (Norton, 1979), pp. 3–6, 42–4, 50–6.

double-entry bookkeeping.[11] Objectively it can be done by private or by public means; capitalistic practices are adopted whenever and wherever rational economic order is sought. But when these objective capitalistic practices are successfully employed privately for many years, as in the United States, institutions develop around them, classes of wealth emerge, power centers organize. Then words are spoken on behalf of these patterns. When repeated often and spread widely these justifying words become the ideology of the thing. When these words end up coloring the Constitution, influencing policies of government, and shaping the very criteria of worth as well as wealth, they constitute a public philosophy.

Capitalism as public philosophy had an immensely strong theoretical core. Karl Marx as economist is an amateur and an imitator in comparison to Adam Smith. Smith's kind of economics appealed to the nineteenth-century American builders for a number of obvious reasons. The most important reason, it seems in retrospect, must have been the reliance of his theory on an automatic, self-regulating society. The second most important reason was, obviously, that it was purely commercial at a time when "being in trade" was still something despicable. In sum, left entirely to their own devices, commercial interests could provide the greatest possible wealth for a nation:

> [When the entrepreneur] intends only his own gain ... he is ... led by an invisible hand to promote an end which was no part of his intention. ... By pursuing his own interest he frequently promotes that of the society more effectually than when he really intends to promote it. ... The statesman, who should attempt to direct private people in what manner they ought to employ their capitals, would not only load himself with a most unnecessary attention, but would assume an authority which could ... nowhere be so dangerous as in the hands of a man who had folly and presumption enough to fancy himself fit to exercise it.[12]

There were other reasons for its appeal. Laissez-faire, as the theory became identified during its elevation to ideological status, made a happy fit with the native American fear of political power. Smith gave systematic reasons for opposition to government, but his reasons merely supplemented and confirmed reasons already widely embraced before and during our Revolution. And why not such confirmation? American grievances were as much against mercantilism as against colonialism. Smith was known and debated during the formative years of the Republic perhaps better in the new country than among the educated classes in England at that time. Hamilton in his *Report on Manufactures* (1791) must have had good reasons to spend the bulk of his first section attempting to refute Smith as regards the application of laissez-faire principles to the new country.[13] Hamilton won his battles but lost his war. If the principles of nineteenth-century economics had not existed the Americans would most certainly have invented them. The Americans accepted the view that there was a natural economic harmony which could only be harmed if touched. The dismal laws of Smith's colleagues Malthus and Ricardo made little difference, for any effort to repeal them could only do still greater injury.

This was the underlying dynamic. Strongly and logically related to it at the level of behavior were the sanctity of property and the binding morality of contract. These notions were justified by the classical economics and were, at one and the same time, additional bulwarks against tyranny. Already imbedded in common law, property and contract were flexible enough to survive the changes in actual property and actual contract as corporations split the property atom into millions of anonymous parts and anonymous corporate giants entered into sacred contracts with tiny suppliers and individual laborers.

Insofar as it also shaped objective constitutional practices and governmental life, capitalist ideology can also be said to have constituted the public philosophy during the same period. Beliefs about popular rule, decentralization of power, and the evils of government were strong; but the case for capitalism as the stronger doctrine can be fairly convincingly documented. Happily for both, the tenets of popular rule and of capitalism generally reinforced each other; but in instances of conflict, American government and public policy were decidedly unresponsive to popular rule ideology. The issue could be *Dred Scott* v. *Sanford*, in which slaves were incorporated into the system by confirmation that they are property under the Fifth Amendment. Or the issue

[11] See Max Weber, *General Economic History* (New York: Collier Books, 1961), pp. 207 ff. Reprinted in Theodore J. Lowi, *Private Life and Public Order* (New York: Norton, 1968). See also Herbert Muller: "Few have heard of Fra Luca Pacioli, the inventor of double-entry bookkeeping; but he has probably had much more influence on human life than has Dante or Michael Angelo." *The Uses of the Past* (New York: Oxford University Press, 1952), p. 257.

[12] Adam Smith, *The Wealth of Nations*, Book IV, reprinted in Lowi, *Private Life*, ibid., p. 12.

[13] Reprinted in part in Lowi, ibid., pp. 111 ff.

could be popularly enacted state regulatory laws, invalidated as unreasonable restraints on contract; many were invalidated as interference with even the process by which contracts are made. Or the issue could be that of the corporation itself, which was given two advantages in nineteenth-century jurisprudence; taken together they strain heavily upon one's sense of logic. On the one hand corporations were merely property, for which the owners, the shareholders, received for themselves total protection and full claim to all profits. On the other hand corporations were defined as persons separate from their owners, so that the death of a corporation affected no owner beyond his shares – because stockholders are not responsible for the debts of the corporation – and yet this "person" was held to enjoy almost all the rights of citizenship under the Bill of Rights and the Fourteenth Amendment.

Following the Civil War, conflicts between capitalism and popular rule increased. But whatever the issue during all of the nineteenth century and part of the twentieth, capitalism won out in a straight fight. In his famous dissent in *Lochner* v. *New York*, Justice Holmes proclaimed, "The Fourteenth Amendment does not enact Mr. Herbert Spencer's Social Statics. ... [A] constitution is not intended to embody a particular economic theory." This doctrine makes Justice Holmes one of the better prophets and one of the worst historians of his day. Spencer was extreme, but his vision of laissez-faire fairly represented an ideology of capitalism that shackled popular-rule ideology, ordaining in effect that popular rule was all right so long as popular institutions chose to do nothing. As soon as state assemblies and Congress became captured by majorities favorable to regular and frequent state intervention, the inconsistencies between the demands of capitalistic ideology and the demands of popular-rule ideology became clear. By the end of the nineteenth century the two were no longer reinforcing at all, and the entire constitutional epoch of 1890–1937 can be characterized as a dialogue between the two.

In the course of that dialogue, capitalism declined as ideology and died as public philosophy. It came to be called conservatism, but that is an incredibly obtuse misnomer that in no way contributes to an understanding of the decline. Capitalism never became conservative. It went into a decline because it became irrevelant and erroneous. The intellectual and theoretical core of the ideology became weakened by generations of belief in itself. Smith and the nineteenth-century liberal economists who followed him were not wrong; in fact, they still hold up for the phenomena with which their theories deal. Capitalist ideology became irrevelant and error-ridden because capitalist ideologues became disloyal to the intellectual spirit of liberal economics. Rather than risk incorporating the new facts of twentieth-century economics and society they closed their minds.

[...]

The new public philosophy: *interest-group liberalism*

Why nineteenth-century liberalism declined

The decline of capitalist ideology as the American public philosophy took the form of a dialogue between a private and a public view of society. This dialogue, between a new liberalism and an old liberalism (redefined as conservatism) comprises the constitutional epoch immediately preceding our own, ending in 1937. During this period there was no prevailing public philosophy but rather two bodies of competing ideology. Liberal and conservative regimes derived their specific uses of government and policy from their general positions, and differences between the two national parties were for the most part clear within these terms. The perennial issue underlying the dialogue was the question of the nature of government itself and whether expansion or contraction of government best produced public good. Expansion of government was demanded by the new liberalism as the means of combating the injustices of a brutal world that would not change as long as we passively submitted ourselves to it. The mark of the new liberalism was its assumption that the instruments of government provided the means for conscious inducement of social change and that outside the capacity for change no experimentation with new institutional forms would be possible. Opposition to such means, but not necessarily to the proposed forms themselves, became the mark of contemporary conservatism.

Across all disagreements there was unanimity on the underlying criteria. These basic criteria were attitude toward government and attitude toward social change. There was also agreement, which persists today, that these two attitudes are consistent and reinforcing, both as guides for leaders in their choices among policies and as criteria for followers in their choices among leaders. For example,

> Conservatism is committed to a discriminating defense of the social order against change and reform (liberalism). ... By the Right, I mean generally those parties and movements that are skeptical of popular governments, oppose the

bright plans of the reformers and dogooders, and draw particular support from men with a sizable stake in the established order. By the Left, I mean generally those parties and movements that demand wider popular participation in government, push actively for reform, and draw particular support from the disinherited, dislocated and disgruntled. As a general rule, to which there are historic exceptions, the Right is conservative or reactionary, the Left is liberal or radical.[14]

These two criteria arose out of a particular constitutional period, were appropriate to that period, and provided a mutually reinforcing basis for doctrine during that period. After 1937, the Constitution did not die from the Roosevelt revolution, as many had predicted, but the basis for the liberal–conservative dialogue did die. Liberalism–conservatism as the source of public philosophy no longer made any sense. Once the principle of positive government in an indeterminable but expanding political sphere was established, criteria arising out of the very issue of expansion became irrelevant.

LIBERALISM–CONSERVATISM: THE EMPTY DEBATE The old dialogue passed into the graveyard of consensus. Yet it persisted. Old habits die hard. Its persistence despite its irrelevance means that the liberal–conservative debate has become almost purely ritualistic. And its persistence even in ritualistic form has produced a number of evil effects among which the most important is the blinding of the nation to the emergence of a new and ersatz public philosophy. The coexistence of a purely ritualistic public dialogue and an ersatz and unrecognized new public philosophy has produced most of the political pathologies of the 1960s and 1970s. The decline of a meaningful dialogue between a liberalism and a conservatism has meant the decline of a meaningful adversary political proceedings in favor of administrative, technical, and logrolling politics. In a nutshell, politics became a question of equity rather than a question of morality. Adjustment comes first, rules of law come last, if at all. The tendency of individuals to accept governmental decisions simply because these decisions are good has probably at no time in American history, save during the Civil War, been less widely distributed and less intensely felt. Cynicism and distrust in everyday political processes have never been more widespread. The emerging public philosophy, interest-group liberalism, has sought to solve the problems of public authority in a large modern state by defining them away. This has simply added the element of demoralization to that of illegitimacy. Interest-group liberalism seeks to justify power by avoiding law and by parceling out to private parties the power to make public policy. A most maladaptive political formula, it was almost inevitably going to produce a crisis of public authority even though its short-run effects seem to be those of consensus and stabilization.

[...]

Interest-group liberalism

The frenzy of governmental activity in the 1960s and 1970s proved that once the constitutional barriers were down the American national government was capable of prompt response to organized political demands. However, that is only the beginning of the story, because the almost total democratization of the Constitution and the contemporary expansion of the public sector has been accompanied by expansion, not contraction, of a sense of distrust toward public objects. Here is a spectacular paradox. It is as though each new program or program expansion had been an admission of prior governmental inadequacy or failure without itself being able to make any significant contribution to order or to well-being. It is as though prosperity had gone up at an arithmetic rate while expectations, and therefore frustrations, had been going up at a geometric rate – in a modern expression of Malthusian Law. Public authority was left to grapple with this alienating gap between expectation and reality.

Why did the expansion of government that helped produce and sustain prosperity also help produce a crisis of public authority? The explanation pursued throughout this volume is that the old justifications for expansion had too little to say beyond the need for the expansion itself. An appropriate public philosophy would have addressed itself to the purposes to which the expanded governmental authority should be dedicated. It would also have addressed itself to the forms and procedures by which that power could be utilized. These questions are so alien to public discourse in the United States that merely to raise them is to be considered reactionary, apolitical, or totally naïve.

[14] Clinton Rossiter, *Conservatism in America* (New York: Knopf, 1955), pp. 12, 15. The term *conservative* came to be attached to nineteenth-century liberals because they favored the government and social order that had become the established fact of the nineteenth-century United States. There is other conservatism in America – racial, aristocratic, ethnic, perhaps even monarchic and feudalistic. But the major part of it is nineteenth-century liberalism grown cold with success. This already suggests the narrow span of the ideological gamut in the United States.

Out of the emerging crisis of public authority developed an ersatz political formula that bears no more relation to those questions than the preceding political formula. The guidance the new formula offers to policy formulation is a set of sentiments that elevated a particular view of the political process above everything else. The ends of government and the justification of one policy or procedure over another are not to be discussed. The *process* of formulation is justified in itself. It takes the pluralist notion that government is an epiphenomenon of politics and makes out of that a new ethics of government.

There are several possible names for the new public philosophy. A strong candidate would be *corporatism*, but its history as a concept gives it several unwanted connotations, such as conservative Catholicism or Italian fascism. Another candidate is *syndicalism*, but among many objections is the connotation of anarchy too far removed from American experience. From time to time other possible labels will be experimented with, but, since the new American public philosophy is something of an amalgam of all of the candidates, some new terminology seems to be called for.

The most clinically accurate term to capture the American variant of all of these tendencies is *interest-group liberalism*. It is liberalism because it is optimistic about government, expects to use government in a positive and expansive role, is motivated by the highest sentiments, and possesses a strong faith that what is good for government is good for the society. It is interest-group liberalism because it sees as both necessary and good a policy agenda that is accessible to all organized interests and makes no independent judgment of their claims. It is interest-group liberalism because it defines the public interest as a result of the amalgamation of various claims. A brief sketch of the working model of interest-group liberalism turns out to be a vulgarized version of the pluralist model of modern political science: (1) Organized interests are homogeneous and easy to define. Any duly elected representative of any interest is taken as an accurate representative of each and every member.[15] (2) Organized interests emerge in every sector of our lives and adequately represent most of those sectors, so that one organized group can be found effectively answering and checking some other organized group as it seeks to prosecute its claims against society.[16] And (3) the role of government is one of insuring access to the most effectively organized, and of ratifying the agreements and adjustments worked out among the competing leaders.

This last assumption is supposed to be a statement of how a democracy works and how it ought to work. Taken together, these assumptions amount to little more than the appropriation of the Adam Smith "hidden hand" model for politics, where the group is the entrepreneur and the equilibrium is not lowest price but the public interest.

These assumptions are the basis of the new public philosophy. The policy behavior of old liberals and old conservatives, of Republicans and Democrats, so inconsistent with the old dialogue, is fully consistent with the critieria drawn from interest-group liberalism: *The most important difference between liberals and conservatives, Republicans and Democrats, is to be found in the interest groups they identify with. Congressmen are guided in their votes, presidents in their programs, and administrators in their discretion by whatever organized interests they have taken for themselves as the most legitimate; and that is the measure of the legitimacy of demands and the only necessary guidelines for the framing of the laws.*

It is one thing to recognize that these assumptions resemble the working methodology of modern political science. But it is quite another to explain how this model was elevated from a hypothesis about political behavior to an ideology about how our democratic polity ought to work.

THE APPEALS OF INTEREST-GROUP LIBERALISM [...] Interest-group liberalism had the approval of political scientists because it could deal with so many of the realities of power. It was further appealing because large interest groups and large memberships could be taken virtually as popular rule in modern dress. And it fit the needs of corporate leaders, union leaders, and government officials desperately searching for support as they were losing communal attachments to their constituencies. Herbert Hoover had spoken out eloquently against

[15] For an excellent inquiry into this assumption and into the realities of the internal life of organized interests, see Grant McConnell, *Private Power and American Democracy* (New York: Knopf, 1966); S. M. Lipset et al., *Union Democracy* (New York: Anchor, 1962); and Raymond Bauer et al., *American Business and Public Policy* (New York: Atherton, 1963).

[16] It is assumed that countervailing power usually crops up somehow, but when it does not, government ought help create it. See John Kenneth Galbraith, *American Capitalism* (Boston: Houghton Mifflin, 1952). Among a number of excellent critiques of the so-called pluralist model, see especially William E. Connolly, ed., *The Bias of Pluralism* (New York: Atherton 1969).

crass individualism and in favor of voluntary collectivism. His belief in this kind of collectivism is what led him to choose, among all his offers, to be Secretary of Commerce in 1921.[17] And the experts on government who were to become the intellectual core of the New Deal and later Democratic administrations were already supporting such views even before the election of Franklin D. Roosevelt. For example,

> [The national associations] represent a healthy democratic development. They rose in answer to certain needs. ... They are part of our representative system.... These groups must be welcomed for what they are, and certain precautionary regulations worked out. The groups must be understood and their proper place in government allotted, if not by actual legislation, then by general public realization of their significance.[18]

After World War II, the academic and popular justifications for interest-group liberalism were still stronger. A prominent American government textbook of the period argued that the "basic concept for understanding the dynamics of government is the multi-group nature of modern society or the modern state."[19] By the time we left the 1960s, with the Democrats back in power, the justifications for interest-group liberalism were more eloquent and authoritative than ever. Take two examples from among the most important intellectuals of the Democratic Party, writing around the time of the return of the Democrats to power in 1960. To John Kenneth Galbraith, "Private economic power is held in check by countervailing power of those who are subjected to it. The first begets the second."[20] Concentrated economic power stimulates power in opposition to it, resulting in a natural tendency toward equilibrium. This is not merely theoretical for Galbraith, although he could not possibly have missed its similarity to Adam Smith; Galbraith was writing a program of positive government action. He admitted that effective countervailing power was limited in the real world and proposed that where it was absent or too weak to do the job, government policy should seek out and support it and, where necessary, create the organizations capable of countervailing. It should be government policy to validate the pluralist theory.

Arthur Schlesinger summarized his views for us in a campaign tract written in 1960. To Schlesinger, the essential difference between the Democratic and Republican Parties is that the Democratic Party is the truly multi-interest party:

> What is the essence of multi-interest administration? It is surely that the leading interests in society are all represented in the interior processes of policy formation – which can be done only if members or advocates of these interests are included in key positions of government.[21]

Schlesinger repeated the same theme in a more sober and reflective book written after John Kennedy's assassination. Following his account of the 1962 confrontation of President Kennedy with the steel industry and the later decision to cut taxes and cast off in favor of expansionary rather than stabilizing fiscal policy, Schlesinger concludes,

> The ideological debates of the past began to give way to a new agreement on the practicalities, of managing a modern economy. There thus developed in the Kennedy years a national accord on economic policy – a new consensus which gave hope of harnessing government, business, and labor in rational partnership for a steadily expanding American economy.[22]

A significant point in the entire argument is that the Republicans would disagree with Schlesinger on the *facts* but not on the *basis* of his distinction. The typical Republican rejoinder would be simply that Democratic administrations are not more multi-interest than Republican. In my opinion this would be almost the whole truth.

The appeal of interest-group liberalism is not simply that it is more realistic than earlier ideologies. There are several strongly positive reasons for its appeal. The first is that it helped flank the constitutional problems of federalism that confronted the expanding national state before the Constitution

[17] For an account of Herbert Hoover's political views and his close relationship to the New Deal, see Grant McConnell, *Private Power*, pp. 62 ff; and Peri Arnold, "Herbert Hoover and the Continuity of American Public Policy," *Public Policy* (Autumn 1972).

[18] E. Pendleton Herring, *Group Representation before Congress* (Baltimore: Johns Hopkins Press, 1929), p. 268. See his reflections of 1936 in Chapter 2 of that book.

[19] Wilfred Binkley and Malcolm Moos, *A Grammar of American Politics* (New York: Knopf, 1950), p. 7. Malcolm Moos became an important idea man in the Eisenhower Administration.

[20] Galbraith, *American Capitalism*, p. 118.

[21] Arthur Schlesinger, Jr., *Kennedy or Nixon – Does It Make Any Difference?* (New York: Macmillan, 1960), p. 43.

[22] Arthur Schlesinger, *A Thousand Days*, as featured in the *Chicago Sun-Times*, January 23, 1966, section 2, p. 3.

was completely democratized. A program like the Extension Service of the Department of Agriculture got around the restrictions of the Interstate Commerce clause by providing for self-administration by a combination of land-grant colleges, local farmer and commerce associations, and organized commodity groups. These appeared to be so decentralized and permissive as to be hardly federal at all. With such programs we begin to see the ethical and conceptual mingling of the notion of organized private groups with the notions of local government and self-government. Ultimately, direct interest-group participation in government became synonymous with self-government; but at first it was probably a strategy to get around the inclination of the Supreme Court to block federal interventions in the economy.

A second positive appeal of interest-group liberalism, strongly related to the first, is that it helped solve a problem for the democratic politician in the modern state where the stakes are so high. This is the problem of enhanced conflict and how to avoid it. The contribution of politicians to society is their skill in resolving conflict. However, direct confrontations are sought only by so-called ideologues and outsiders. Typical American politicians displace and defer and delegate conflict where possible; they face conflict squarely only when they must. Interest-group liberalism offered a justification for keeping major combatants apart and for delegating their conflict as far down the line as possible. It provided a theoretical basis for giving to each according to his claim, the price for which is a reduction of concern for what others are claiming. In other words, *it transformed access and logrolling from necessary evil to greater good.*

A third and increasingly important positive appeal of interest-group liberalism is that it helps create the sense that power need not be power at all, control need not be control, and government need not be coercive. If sovereignty is parceled out among groups, then who is out anything? As a major *Fortune* editor enthusiastically put it, government power, group power, and individual power may go up simultaneously. If the groups to be controlled control the controls, then "to administer does not always mean to rule."[23] The inequality of power and the awesome coerciveness of government are always gnawing problems in a democratic culture. Rousseau's General Will stopped at the boundary of a Swiss canton. The myth of the group and the group will is becoming the answer to Rousseau and the big democracy. Note, for example, the contrast between the traditional and the modern definition of the group: Madison in *Federalist 10* defined the group ("faction") as "a number of citizens, whether amounting to a majority or minority of the whole who are united and actuated by some common impulse of passion, or of interest, *adverse to the right of other citizens, or to the permanent and aggregate interests of the community*" (emphasis added). Modern political science usage took that definition and cut the quotation just before the emphasized part.[24] In such a manner pluralist theory became the handmaiden of interest-group liberalism, and interest-group liberalism became the handmaiden of modern American positive national statehood, and the First Republic became the Second Republic. [...]

Evidence of the fundamental influence of interest-group liberalism can be found in the policies and practices of every Congress and every administration since 1961. The very purpose of this book is to identify, document, and assess the consequences of the preferences that are drawn from the new public philosophy.

[...]

In sum, leaders in modern, consensual democracies are ambivalent about government. Government is obviously the most efficacious way of achieving good purposes, but alas, it is efficacious because it is coercive. To live with that ambivalence, modern policymakers have fallen prey to the belief that public policy involves merely the identification of the problems toward which government ought to be aimed. It pretends that through "pluralism," "countervailing power," "creative federalism," "partnership," and "participatory democracy" the unsentimental business of coercion need not be involved and that unsentimental decisions about how to employ coercion need not really be made at all. Stated in the extreme, the policies of interest-group liberalism are end-oriented but ultimately self-defeating. Few standards of implementation, if any, accompany delegations of power. The requirement of standards has been replaced by the requirement of participation. The requirement of law has been replaced by the requirement of contingency. As a result, the ends of interest-group liberalism are nothing more than sentiments and therefore not really ends at all.

23 Max Ways, "'Creative Federalism' and the Great Society," *Fortune*, January 1966, p. 122.

24 David Truman, *The Governmental Process* (New York: Knopf, 1951), p. 4.

Avigail Eisenberg, "Reconstructing Political Pluralism"*

In the 1990s, political theory has moved beyond the debate between liberalism and communitarianism to explore possibilities which can avoid the putative excesses of both positions. Many of these possibilities are built upon the recognition that contemporary liberal societies contain a plurality of groups, communities, and associations, and that political theory should not aim at overcoming this plurality but rather should strengthen it. In these theories, culture, difference, and identity are crucial. Indeed, the heterogeneity of most societies in these respects is now the central focus of analysis. It is viewed, at the same time, as furnishing a recipe for oppression and as providing a reason for celebration. The aim of this book is to retrieve and reconstruct a legacy of political pluralism that illuminates these developments and clarifies the type of challenges concerning pluralism that are central to contemporary politics.

Striking similarities exist between the new theories of difference and identity and a number of theories dating back to the turn of the century which comprise the tradition of political pluralism in liberal-democratic thought. Political pluralism is usually thought to consist of a set of ideas in postwar political science which held that democracy consists of interest-group competition. This conventional view is mistaken, and this book aims at broadening and deepening our understanding of political pluralism. It does so by examining the resources in the history of political pluralism that are usually given insufficient attention. The main argument is that political pluralism is comprised of two intertwined themes: the distribution of power amongst groups, and the group's power to direct individual development. At the center of the pluralist tradition are the analytical means to understand clearly, within the context of liberal-democratic politics, the political relation between individuals and groups or communities and the relation between a plurality of groups and the state. The tools supplied by political pluralism allow political theory to move beyond the remnants of the liberal–communitarian debate and to approach the new theories of identity and community politics with deeper insight aided by historical hindsight.

* Avigail Eisenberg, extracted from *Reconstructing Political Pluralism* (Albany: State University of New York Press, 1995), pp. 1–7, 168–70.

Generally, what I mean by political pluralism are theories that seek to organize and conceptualize political phenomena on the basis of the plurality of groups to which individuals belong and by which individuals seek to advance and, more importantly, to develop, their interests. This definition emphasizes political, not metaphysical, philosophical, sociological, or psychological pluralism. However, pluralist theories are found at the crossroads of political studies and other disciplines. [...]

Freedom of association is a necessary condition of political pluralism. But pluralist theories go beyond merely accepting the legitimacy of free association and, instead, view association and multiple group affiliations as the central elements of the liberal and democratic aspects of politics. Pluralism is not just tolerated; rather, it is the very life pulse of a healthy polity.

In many political theories, including theories of political pluralism, groups are the key to understanding and reconstructing liberal-democratic politics. There are three reasons for this. First, individuals, when given the freedom, tend to organize themselves into groups. Theories which ignore this fact are criticized for lacking sociological realism. Most significantly, this sociological fact has important implications because it indicates that a politics opposed to the group basis of society must be prepared to coerce individuals to abandon their chosen associative ties. All pluralists recognize that coercion is the only alternative to political pluralism.

Second, groups have a privileged place in liberal-democratic politics because they are the means to vindicating individual interests. If individuals are not driven to form groups in order to appease their instincts, then they do so in order to acquire the resources necessary to address their interests. These resources can be internal or external to the group. Internal resources might include skills or knowledge that group members teach each other and that then can be used to meet the interests of the members as individuals. The "tricks of the trade" are resources often gained in this way. External resources are usually the focus of political pluralism. In pluralism, groups are viewed as the means to acquiring political power. The internal resources which a group possesses are organized in order to capture external resources or power. This power is then used, for instance, to change a governmental policy in a way that advances the interests of the group's members. The idea here is that, whereas the individual is relatively powerless to challenge or change state policy, the aggregation of individuals in a group presents to the state a more formidable contender.

The third reason why groups are the key to liberal-democratic politics is that they help to construct individual identity and are the means to individual development. As communitarians have argued, self-development occurs in a social context. The individual's identity is inexorably tied to the individual's attachments to others or to contexts in which the individual is situated. The role that groups, communities, and associations play in self-development is central to political pluralism as well. [...]

These three reasons – (1) that groups are part of the fabric of sociological reality, (2) that they are the means to political power and thus are instrumental in the pursuit of individual interests, and (3) that they are the means to individual development – partly explain why political pluralism places such importance on groups. But pluralism is not the same as group theory. The political significance of groups in pluralist theory is contained in two additional elements. The first element is that *many* groups coexist in society. The second element is that individuals have *multiple* affiliations and memberships.

For instance, with regards to the first element, pluralism grapples with the need to form groups in order to vindicate interests while insisting that power not be concentrated in one group. The centralized state, the notion of absolute sovereignty, the power elite, are all nemeses of political pluralism. Centralized political power, with its attendant risk of tyranny, is the problem that pluralism seeks to solve without abandoning the group. Historically, part of the pluralist challenge has been to develop the analytic means to distinguish the illegitimate use of power by a group to dominate other groups from the legitimate use of power by a group to vindicate the interests of its members. This challenge is met by adopting a broad view of power that includes both the resources groups can acquire and their influence in shaping the individual's personality. Pluralists insist that in liberal democracy both types of power must be shared by a plurality of groups.

Second, healthy individual development relies on a pluralist context and not simply a group context. Similar to the pluralistic understanding of political power, the critical tools for analyzing the politics of personal development are not found by merely understanding that individuals develop their identities in a social context. Nor is it sufficient to incorporate into one's political theory the mere observation that groups have the power to shape individuals in healthy and unhealthy ways, although in light of contemporary communitarian analysis, a reminder of this fact is entirely apropos. Pluralism holds that the individual requires a multiplicity of developmental contexts in order to enjoy healthy development. Each context develops part of the individual's identity, and together the social contexts provide a critical perspective from which the individual can scrutinize her relation to each context.

It is important to emphasize that, in the pluralist process, the individual is the only agent with legitimacy to negotiate and shape her identity. Pluralists have been unwilling to approach personal development with the disposition of a moral psychologist who is willing to pick and choose among the different facets of the individual's identity those parts which are healthy and those which are diseased. Moreover, to empower the state to make such judgments violates the pluralist program because the power over individual development that this would vest in the state would be so vast as to undermine a pluralistic distribution of power. In order for the individual to have the power to shape her own identity, she must enjoy many affiliations and, crucially, no single group or community may dominate and direct her development. Each group provides for the individual a different vantage from which she can critically assess her attachments to other groups. Reassessing one's attachments requires that a multiplicity of contexts be accessible to the individual. The individual need not be conceptualized as unencumbered by all attachments at once in order to understand how she is the author of her life and identity.

I argue that political pluralism offers the means to resolve the familiar tensions between political power and individual development, between individual autonomy and group membership, and thus between individualism and communitarianism. It focuses on the relation between political power and individual development and seeks to offer the analytic resources to distinguish between the empowerment and domination of groups in society and between the healthy development and social control of individuals. It accomplishes this by (1) insisting that group power not be centralized in society, (2) ensuring that individuals can effectively transform their associational ties, and (3) understanding the relation between group power and individual development.

The historical resources

The historical resources of political pluralism can be categorized into three episodes. The first episode occurs in the United States from the turn of the century until the 1920s and involves the work of John Dewey and William James. The second episode overlaps the first but addresses a distinct set of themes. It includes the work of J. N. Figgis, G. D. H. Cole, Harold J. Laski, and Mary Parker Follett and enjoyed significant attention in Britain and the United States mainly in the 1920s and 1930s. The third episode, again centered in the United States, involves a host of theorists but is chiefly captured here in the postwar pluralism of Robert Dahl.

These three episodes offer different ways in which various thinkers have explored the possibilities that political pluralism offers. They are not meant to represent an exhaustive survey of political pluralist thought. Rather, they have been chosen as vehicles by which to elucidate different ways in which the relation between the two central themes of political pluralism – (1) the distribution of political power to vindicate interests and, (2) the distribution of political power to facilitate individual development – has been conceptualized in political pluralism.

[...]

Dewey found pluralism attractive partly because he saw in it an alternative to the absolutist conception of sovereignty. He also developed a political understanding of personal development in which, again, pluralism was key. But, his theory fails to trace the connection between these two elements and leaves itself open to being misinterpreted as politically absolutist, or, in more contemporary exegesis, communitarian. In light of the seemingly contradictory rhetoric that Dewey used to explain his ideas in the intellectual circles of the 1920s, the key to discovering how to reconcile various aspects of his work is found in the pluralist dimension of his project.

In contrast, Laski's pluralism, while again containing at least a hint of both themes, neglects personal development and comes to reflect an obsessive preoccupation with the consequences of concentrated political power. The thinness of Laski's pluralism and the explanation for why he ultimately abandoned it in favor of a more Marxist approach to state power lay partly in his neglect of the developmental power that groups possess. [...]

The postwar theory of pluralism, which is explored here mostly through the work of Dahl, made prominent both elements of the pluralist equation. But, it was beholden to the standards of political behavioralism and, consequently, attempted to extract the normative dimension from these elements, from the pluralist theory that they comprised, and from democratic theory in general. While this postwar episode contains the pluralism that is most often referred to in contemporary understandings of the doctrine, it offers a distorted purview of the tradition. Nonetheless, the distortions reveal a great deal; the empirical bent of postwar pluralism placed maximal emphasis on the sociological realism and contextualism of pluralism. Existing practices and goods, including existing groups, pathways of socialization, associative ties, and cross-pressures (e.g., multiple affiliations) are legitimized by the functional explanation of democracy offered in postwar pluralism. Conversely, the tradition's radical resources to transform society and improve individual well-being through pluralistic personal development are stifled. In spite of the distortions, the central elements of this episode are those which persist in the other theories as well, namely, the pluralistic distribution of political power and the way in which groups shape individual identity.

[...]

By the late 1970s, Dahl's disposition altered towards pluralism and particularly towards the prospects of the political pluralism which he developed being an adequate basis for upholding democratic values. The problem, Dahl admitted in 1978, was that a system which relied solely on the interplay between associations to decide how resources ought to be distributed will systematically alienate the disadvantaged and disorganized groups in society.

> It is hardly open to doubt that organizational pluralism and the institutional guarantees of polyarchy are not sufficient conditions for a high degree of equality in the distribution of political resources, or, more broadly, status, income, wealth, and other key values.[25]

Moreover, he argued, organizational pluralism may perpetuate group self-interest. Along with Grant McConnell[26] and Theodore Lowi,[27] he noted that the common good gets short shrift as groups vie for self-serving goals. In general, Dahl observed, organizational pluralism may lead to a general "disillusionment

25 Robert A. Dahl, "Pluralism Revisited," *Comparative Politics*, 10, 2 (1978), p. 199.

26 Grant McConnell, *Private Power and American Democracy* (New York: Alfred A. Knopf, 1966).

27 Theodore J. Lowi, *The End of Liberalism: The Second Republic of the United States*, 2nd edn. (New York: W. W. Norton and Co., 1979).

and discontent with the constitutional structure of the polyarchy and more, to polyarchy in general or even to the desirability and feasibility of democracy itself."[28]

The new approach to democracy that Dahl then developed was not one that rejected pluralism as much as it injected normative content into pluralist theory. In *Democracy and Its Critics*, Dahl completely abandons the nonvaluational stance he assumed in the 1950s and frames his analysis with the question, "By what criteria are we to appraise the worth of democracy whether as an ideal or as an actuality?"[29] Part of the answer to this question, Dahl argues, is contained in the idea of intrinsic equality. Polyarchy or political pluralism is the preferred form of democracy because it presents the best way for the interests of all citizens to be given the appropriate consideration.[30] In a manner that echoes Dewey's initial formulation, Dahl states, "... the public good is not necessarily a monolithic goal that can or should be realized by a single, sovereign government. ... 'the public' will consist of many different publics, each of which may have a somewhat different good or set of interests."[31]

So, one explanation for why Dahl abandoned the empirical approach to democracy is because it failed to be the means to vindicate the values, such as equality, that he thought to be important. As he stated in 1978, the problem with polyarchy as a theory of democracy is that it could eventuate in a "stable equilibrium of inequalities."[32] Here, I have argued that a normative commitment to ethical individualism is required to avoid this eventuality. Political pluralism, as well as communitarianism, is bound to tend towards a stable equilibrium of the status quo unless values, which may not be currently adhered to in many communal practices, but which are nonetheless ethically compelling to the community, are entertained as possible standards for that community. [...]

[28] Dahl, "Pluralism Revisited," p. 199.

[29] Robert A. Dahl, *Democracy and Its Critics* (New Haven: Yale University Press, 1989).

[30] See especially Dahl, *Democracy and Its Critics*, chapters 20 and 21.

[31] Dahl, *Democracy and Its Critics*, p. 295.

[32] Dahl, "Pluralism Revisited," p. 200.

William E. Connolly, "Pluralism: A Prelude"*

Charlie Shin posed severe challenges to a 12-year-old. This working-class intellectual participated in the sporadic meetings of local union leaders at our house, intervening in a mild voice from time to time to say, "Maybe it's time for Local 598 to unite against capital" and "From each according to his ability, to each according to his need." The other men – now and then a woman participated – would listen politely and then get on with debates about how to win the next union election, expose the latest scam by management, or get the "rank and file" ready for a "wild-cat" strike. Often they would close the meeting by complaining about Walter Reuther, the president of the UAW whom most of them secretly revered. I did not know quite what to make of Charlie. He was the smartest guy in the room, the least imposing physically, the most militant on some issues, the most sensitive and attentive to others, and sometimes a bit out of touch with tactical questions. Charlie was a Marxist by conviction and a pluralist by disposition. He was also, if I recall correctly, the only man in the bunch who could play the piano. His phrases were the ones that stuck.

One day I saw his picture on the front page of the *Flint Journal*. He had recently been identified as a former member of the Communist Party by the House Un-American Activities Committee. A group of workers had just beaten him up and dumped him on the street in front of the factory gate. Hence the newspaper photo and story. His face had a dazed look, as he was surrounded by toughs whose faces shone with civic virtue. The paper, as I recall, noted the patriotic fervor of the workers. But it also became clear to those close to the scene that many workers in that factory, perhaps a majority, opposed the vigilante action. They were pluralists too. Among them were whites, blacks, Catholics, Protestants, a smattering of Jews, a few atheists. Very few were drawn to Charlie's Marxism. But most respected his disposition, his decency, and his right to work; they wanted to hear his ideas even if they did not endorse them all the way down.

[...]

Charlie is dead now. But if he were to call on the phone today, I would recognize his voice immediately, as you

* William E. Connolly, extracted from *Pluralism* (Durham, NC: Duke University Press, 2005), pp. 1–10.

might register the cadence, emotional tone, and distinctive pronunciation of a friend you have not heard from in years. His voice sticks. Its rhythms and resonance expressed his sensibility. My memory of that voice reminds me that political and ethical commitments are composed by models of inspiration and attraction as well as by sound arguments and intellectual exchanges. The two mix together in ways not registered well enough in most contemporary philosophies of ethics and politics.

I suspect that my commitment to pluralism grows in part out of the memory of Charlie's example, mixed in with the response of those workers who helped him survive during the time of troubles. The anxiety that his fate created could have nudged me in a number of directions, I imagine. Toward Marxism, which attracted but did not capture me. Toward a career far from politics. Or toward the bicameral orientation to citizenship that a culture of pluralism secretes and solicits. I wanted Charlie to have a voice in the world, not to be its Voice. Not much danger of the latter, of course. Above all, McCarthyism became real to me the day Charlie found himself on the street in front of that factory gate. A mélange of legislative committees, judicial decisions, press campaigns, organized rumors, FBI investigations, employee blacklists, film plots, vigilante actions, worker anxieties, corporate proclivities, nervous defense lawyers, overweening judges, and subdued academics generated a dark resonance machine much more ferocious than the sum of its parts. Only a minority embraced it. But it permeated the political atmosphere nonetheless. The union movement never recovered its previous glory. My impression, upon entering graduate school several years later, was that the old resonance machine still cast a pall over left-of-center faculty members, even though a large majority of respondents asserted in well-designed polls that it did not.

Pluralists expose and resist such dark resonance machines. But is pluralism too compromised as a general political stance to do the job? Do pluralists, because of the very bicameral structure of their commitments, lack the fervor to defend the condition they embrace? Perhaps pluralism is a philosophy for wimps, for those whose beliefs are too saturated with uncertainty and ambivalence to take definitive action. I don't think so. Charlie was a Marxist, a pluralist, and a sensitive soul with a strong will. My dad was a radical social democrat, and a tough-guy cultural pluralist. His wife, my mother, was a pluralist above everything else. She helped Charlie's daughters during the difficult time; and she often thought and acted against the tide of the day. A bicameral orientation to citizenship was not self-negating in these cases, nor in innumerable others. Sometimes you hear that the bicameral orientation to citizenship appropriate to pluralism really means relativism. It would be hard to convince innumerable pluralists of that who have put themselves on the line to fight against aggressive, nationalist movements. Bellicose unitarianism is a way of life no pluralist honors, though relativists might be moved to embrace it. Rather, the charge of relativism is the first line of attack advanced by the most aggressive unitarians against pluralism. The accusation does double duty: it drains pluralism of its most attractive qualities, and it vindicates unitarianism as the only alternative to it. At other times you hear that pluralism appeals only to effete elites, academics above all. Ordinary people, it is said, won't tolerate that much ambiguity. Tell that to Charlie, I say, and to workers in Flint who helped restore his job and dignity during a rough time.

The element of truth in this exaggeration, though, is that a bicameral orientation to political life does mean that you keep a foot in two worlds, straddling two or more perspectives to maintain tension between them. A bicameral orientation requires a tolerance of ambiguity in politics, the sort of tolerance that Theodor Adorno in his classic study says is lacking in "the authoritarian personality."[33] There is, first, the faith, doctrine, creed, ideology, or philosophy (I do not distinguish sharply between these) that you adopt as an engaged partisan in the world. Marxism, say. Or a branch of Christianity. Or a particular vision of science. Or Hinduism, Islam, orthodox Judaism, Kantianism, Rawlsianism, neoconservatism, or pragmatism. There is, second, the engrained sense that you should exercise presumptive receptivity toward others when drawing that faith, creed, or philosophy into the public realm. You love your creed; you seldom leave it entirely in the closet when you enter politics. But you appreciate how it appears opaque and profoundly contestable to many who do not participate in it; and you struggle against the tendency to resent this very state of affairs. Pluralists adopt a bicameral orientation to political life. They mix affirmative energies into both sides of that bicameralism. Often, the combination is nourished by a love of the world that overflows the creed embraced in the first instance. It is not necessary to be either an effete intellectual or a hero to adopt a bicameral orientation to politics. A decent respect for the persistent diversity of the human condition suffices.

33 See T. W. Adorno, "Some Aspects of Religious Ideology ..." and "Types and Syndromes," in Else Frenkel-Brunswik, Adorno, Daniel Levinson, and R. Nevitt Sanford, eds., *The Authoritarian Personality* (New York: W. W. Norton, 1950), pp. 727–86.

A lot of things in contemporary life prepare people for the bicameral orientation appropriate to pluralism. Neighborhood life, associational meetings, TV dramas, surprising conversions by friends, relatives, or offspring, new events or movements that bubble into being as if from nowhere, church or temple sermons, interfaith associations, an expansive appreciation of history – the list is almost endless. Indeed, with the impressive acceleration of the fastest zones of culture in contemporary life, it takes massive campaigns stretching from neighborhood crusades through the electronic news media to church indoctrination and police–court actions to turn people against pluralism. McCarthyism was one such campaign in the United States. Some forces in the academy today, fed by right-wing campaigns to cleanse the faculty, would reinstate these pressures. As would the most exclusionary sects in the three religions of the Book and the news reporting on some television channels. The very virulence of these campaigns shows that the bicameral orientation to politics appeals to a significant segment of the populace, distributed across a broad band of gender, class, religious, ethnic, age, and sensual affiliations. While the periodic emergence of a new issue or surprising social movement temporarily throws many for a loop, it takes intensive campaigns by dogmatic constituencies with considerable media, governmental, and corporate power to overturn preliminary dispositions in favor of pluralism. The campaign is often launched by labeling pluralists as relativists, subjectivists, nihilists, or elitists, or merely as self-indulgent. The worry is that such aggressive campaigns are becoming hyperactive again today.

The bicameral orientation to citizenship requires a fair amount of self-cultivation and inter-constituency negotiation to fuel and sustain itself. And the very strength of the cultural predisposition to pluralism in numerous zones of life today mobilizes a series of movements against it.

[...] At each historical juncture distinctive threats to order are identified by unitarians to vindicate sharp constraints on diversity. The idea that each regime must be organized around the same religious faith has had a long run. It continues to find ample expression among the opponents of pluralism. This demand is often linked to other nonnegotiable imperatives, such as the security of the state, the integrity of capitalism, the inviolable demands of sovereignty, and the essential unity of a democratic civilization. The cold war generated McCarthyism as an extreme response to threats that the Soviet Union posed to Christian faith and capitalism together. The terrorism of al Qaeda, in turn, generates new fears, hostilities, and priorities. The McCarthyism of our day, if it arrives, will connect internal state security to an exclusionary version of the Judeo-Christian tradition. So the *expansion* of diversity in faith, within and across states, is good in itself and particularly appropriate to the times.

[...] The idea is to start with the issue of religion, radiating out to pluralism in multiple zones of life. Multidimensional pluralism I call it, arguing that the expansion of diversity in one domain ventilates life in others as well. Consider the radical contention that not only human culture but the nonhuman world contains an unruly element of pluralism within it. William James [contends] that the universe itself is marked by a plurality of forces. The universe includes "litter" as one of its components, as well as a plurality of human and nonhuman actors of different degrees of efficacy, whose agency is not entirely reducible to either the lawlike formulas of classical science or the finalist images historically brought against those models. The Jamesian interpretation of the universe meshes well with the Bergsonian image of time.

On the partisan side of my bicameralism, I embrace much in the thought of James and Bergson. But as a bicameralist, I also realize that a number of creeds, philosophies, and doctrines can be rendered consonant with pluralism. The critical issue is the kind of ethos infused into a doctrine or creed. What counts is how the relational dispositions of people blend into the creeds and philosophies that they embrace and the quality of the institutional ethos of engagement between partisans of different kinds.

A faith, on my reading, is composed of a creed or philosophy plus the sensibility mixed into it. Bergson and James have faith in powers of transcendence that I contest. But that faith is expressed in ways conducive to negotiating a positive ethos of engagement between multiple faiths. James and Bergson enact in their writings the code of bicameralism that they commend to political life writ large.

[...] If there is a paradox of sovereignty, as many theorists contend, the first question to pose is the ethos needed to negotiate that paradox in ways compatible with democratic pluralism. The second is to identify the multiple sites of activism open to citizens who can participate in shaping that ethos. For pluralism is marked not only by a constitutive tension between the already established pattern of diversity and the periodic eruption of new constituencies seeking a place on the register of legitimacy. It is also defined by multiple *sites* of potential citizen action, within and above the state.

[...] While some argue that the achievement of national unity provides the basis from which to reduce economic inequality, I dissent from this view. Under contemporary conditions of rapid mobility within and between states, the drive to national unity itself too readily fosters marginalization of vulnerable minorities. It does so because the rapid pace of late-modern life – the rapid movement of populations, ideas, technologies, identities, and faiths across generations and territorial borders – works against the realization of the national imaginary. So when an effort is made to mobilize public support for the reduction of economic inequality, vocal nationalists on the Right argue against these drives on the grounds, first, that many whom they demean would be included among their beneficiaries and, second, that the programs would undermine fixed capitalist principles undergirding the nation. National health care? That would cover welfare recipients, unwed mothers, and (usually in code language) racial minorities. It would also obstruct the free market. The provision of collective goods to help households make ends meet in the domains of transportation, housing, education, and insurance? These policies would subsidize lazy freeloaders in the cities and undermine the untrammeled free enterprise system around which the nation is built.

In the argument between neoconservative and liberal nationalists over equality, the former hold too many cards.

It seems to me that they will continue to do so until we develop the idea of a thick network pluralism that exceeds both shallow, secular models of pluralism and the thick idea of the highly centered nation. Liberal images of the procedural nation are not only *insufficient* in themselves, they tend to collapse under pressure from rightist orientations to the nation that are more thick and dense.

While there are tensions between deep pluralism and the reduction of economic inequality, at a most basic level each sets a condition of possibility for the other. Part of the connection is definitional: an ethos of pluralism extends the issue of equality from economic culture to other cultural identities. But it is also causal. [...] To make progress in either reducing economic inequality or extending diversity is to improve the prospects for progress on the other front as well.

I have outlined elsewhere programs to reduce inequality that are compatible with deep, multidimensional pluralism. Those programs focus first and foremost on the public infrastructure of consumption in the domains of health care, transportation, public security, education, housing, and retirement. They make it possible for more citizens to make ends meet by rendering the forms of consumption available more inclusive in character. But on what *common basis*, it will be asked, could citizens in such a diverse state unite behind general programs to reduce inequality? Does it not require a unified consensus to promote such an agenda? If so, that carries us right back to the unity of the nation. Right? Not so. In a culture of multidimensional pluralism, support for the reduction of inequality requires the mobilization of a majority assemblage rather than a unified nation. In such an assemblage, some will support the programs in question out of dire need, some out of this or that material interest central to them, some because they seek to meet moral responsibilities or obligations flowing from this creed or that philosophy inspiring them, some because their loyalty to the assemblage encourages them to concede this issue in exchange for others more dear to them, some because they believe that the long-term effects of inequality increase crime, decrease the quality of democracy, and damage the prospects for cultural diversity, some out of considerations that are primarily aesthetic, and most out of a mixture of these considerations, varying in shape and intensity from case to case and constituency to constituency. Further, some who participate in such a majority assemblage will do so because the program resonates deeply with key elements in their identities, interests, or ethical sensibilities, while others are linked to it in more attenuated ways. The difficulties in forging such a majority assemblage are impressive. No question about that. But the strategic promise of reducing inequality improves if you approach the issue through the lens of multidimensional pluralism rather than that of either national unity or the aggregation of material interests.[34]

[34] I first explored ways to reduce economic inequality in a mixed economy with Michael Best in *The Politicized Economy* (Lexington, MA: D. C. Heath, 1976, 1982). There we developed the distinction between exclusive modes of consumption and inclusive modes, supporting the latter in the domains of housing, travel, communication, insurance, and medical care. The unit costs of items in these domains decrease and the quality increases as they are extended more widely. The dominant mode of consumption today is exclusive goods. The difficulties in making ends meet grow as these goods become necessary items of consumption for more and more people. These themes are connected more closely to pluralism in chapter 3 of *The Ethos of Pluralization* (Minneapolis: University of Minnesota Press, 1995) and "Assembling the Left," *Boundary 2*, fall 1999, 47–54. The latter essay appears in a symposium in which Paul Bove, Wendy Brown, Bruce Robbins, and Thomas Dumm speak eloquently to related issues.

A majority assemblage in a culture of multidimensional pluralism is more analogous to a potluck supper than a formal dinner. It is fashioned through a series of resonances between local meetings, internet campaigns, television exposés, church organizations, film portrayals, celebrity testimonials, labor rank-and-file education, and electoral campaigns by charismatic leaders. Multidimensional diversity, inspirational leadership, publicity about the suffering generated by the infrastructure of consumption, micropolitical activity initiated from numerous sites – that is the positive resonance machine to put into motion today.

[...]

It has been suggested to me that my commitment to pluralism exudes an aura of optimism when the time itself calls for pessimism. I agree, certainly, that we live in a dangerous time, and that some of the conditions that place pluralism on the agenda harbor tragic possibilities. The promise is stalked by the dangers of economic collapse, nationalist fervor, cultural war, preemptive state wars, nuclear proliferation, religiostate repression, and more besides. These pressures increase the need for pluralism while throwing up roadblocks. The positive agenda could cascade into a negative spiral. But to me, the first task is to convey neither a mood of optimism nor one of pessimism. Both are spectatorial orientations, anchored in the bureaucrat's desire to assess probabilities. The task, rather, is to probe the shape of positive *possibility* in relation to urgent *needs* of the day. Measured by that standard, pluralism provides the most humane and promising agenda to pursue, even as we encounter strong pressures against it. To bypass pursuit of deep, multidimensional pluralism today would be to fail an elemental test of fidelity to the world.

Part I

Ideological Voices

Chapter 2

Nineteenth-Century Ideologies

Introduction

The readings in this and the next two chapters are intended to introduce some of the ideologies (and less comprehensive quasi-ideologies) that have been developed over the past two centuries. While Shklar argued in the last chapter that most serious political theorists regard ideologies as "untruths" – as ideational weapons used by particular interests – rather than doctrines providing true principles, this recognition does not mean that ideologies contain few if any compelling political ideas. Indeed, if one wants to survey a broad array of alternative answers to the most important and interesting recurring political issues, a very effective approach is to become familiar with competing ideologies. But rather than buy into an ideology because of its emotional appeal (such as its utopian promises to achieve widely sought social and economic goals or its ability to calm our fears about the grave dangers we allegedly face), effective political thinkers question the validity of the ideas contained within various ideologies. They compare and subject to intense critical scrutiny the competing ideas that various ideologies offer and accept only those that survive such reflection.

The nineteenth century is sometimes called the age of ideology, because the concept of ideology first emerged in 1797 when a group of philosophers, the *ideologues*, led by Antoine Louis Claude Destutt de Tracy (1758–1836), founded an institute to mine the ideas developed during the Enlightenment and provide a systemic and rational set of political guidelines to replace the traditions and customs that had previously guided political life. For them, ideology referred to "the science of ideas," and they believed that their science showed the truth of the principles of what is now called classical liberalism.

Classical liberalism was built on ideas that had been circulating for more than a century, dating back at least to Rene Descartes (1596–1650), and certainly included many of those propounded by John Locke (1632–1704), Baron de Montesquieu (1689–1755), Adam Smith (1723–90), Thomas Paine (1739–1809), and others. Such ideas focused on individual freedom and rights (rather than individuals being subordinated to community traditions), free-market economies (rather than older feudal and mercantile arrangements), representative democracies (rather than monarchies and aristocracies), the rule of law (rather than arbitrary decrees), and limited (rather than absolutist) governments.

Our first selection in this chapter provides extracts from Locke's *Second Treatise of Government,* an early and highly influential formulation of many ideas that became absorbed within classical liberalism. Published in 1690, it indirectly defended the Glorious Revolution that transformed England's strong monarchy into a constitutional one and established parliamentary supremacy. Locke, who was a physician and advisor to a leading political opponent of King James II, became a highly influential philosopher whose writings furthered an empirical epistemology, the separation of church and state, and the emerging capitalist economy. Among the liberal ideas you will encounter in this selection are the following: that a natural account of politics requires understanding people in the "state of nature"; that it is rational for such people to form social contracts to establish civil society in order to escape the inconveniences of their natural condition; that such contracts lead to the formation of governments with the legitimate power (or authority) to protect individual rights; that government authority is limited to protecting rights as authorized by citizens; and that citizens are justified in replacing any government that violates their rights.

Locke's ideas were reflected in the American *Declaration of Independence*, but the *Declaration of the Rights of Man and of the Citizen* by the National Assembly of France at the onset of the French Revolution in 1789 provides an even better example of the early liberal emphasis on individual rights. It was these liberal ideas that provoked Edmund Burke (1729–97), the Irish philosopher and leading member of the British parliament, to pen his *Reflections on the Revolution in France* in 1790. The abstract of that work provided here focuses on the value of inherited traditions that liberals too readily swept aside in favor of their idealizations based on speculative reason. More specifically, you will read Burke's famous distinction between "the real rights of men," which we inherit from traditional understandings and institutions, and the natural rights emphasized by liberals, whose "abstract perfection is their practical defect." Much of the political conflict in Europe during the nineteenth century pitted classical liberalism against traditional conservatism. During these struggles, conservatives often looked back to Burke's writings for inspiration and guidance. In contrast, liberals were more open to the reformulation of their ideas. While they continued to emphasize the individual and his rights, they began to justify individual freedoms on utilitarian grounds, as in *On Liberty*, by John Stuart Mill (1806–73), which is featured in Chapter 11.

However, for many radicals the conflict between classical liberalism and traditional conservatism was merely a quarrel among elites. Traditional conservatism represented and defended the interests of the old upper classes: the royalty, the landed aristocracy, the priests, and so forth. Classical liberalism represented and defended the interests of the rising middle classes: the owners of the industrial enterprises that were beginning to dominate economic and social life and other capitalists who owned and controlled productive property and financial institutions. According to radicals, neither of these ideologies provided principles that served the interests of ordinary men and women, the working classes, and the poor.

Today, Marxism is widely regarded as the alternative ideology that represented such interests. Karl Marx (1818–83) was a philosopher, political economist, and revolutionary whose extensive and complex writings provided detailed analyses of capitalism and the limitations of all liberal institutions. His most renowned work remains *The Manifesto of the Communist Party*, which he co-authored in 1848 with his long-time friend, supporter, and collaborator, Friedrich Engels (1820–95). Among the Marxist themes you will encounter in the following abstract are: placing liberalism, its capitalist institutions, and its leading class (the bourgeoisie or owners of industrial enterprises) into historical perspective; the exploitation and domination of workers, and the debased cultures, governments, and laws that capitalism generates; the crises that occur within liberal society and create resistance to it led by its subordinate class (the proletariat or industrial workers); the inevitable revolution against capitalism; the measures that the proletariat will pursue when they emerge victorious after the revolution; and the vague promise of an eventual utopian classless society.

Marxism was not the only left-wing alternative to liberalism and conservatism during the nineteenth century; indeed Marx struggled with anarchists and various "utopian socialists" for control of the First International Workingmen's Association, and anarchists emerged as the strongest force during the 1870s. Anarchism is a much less unified ideology than "orthodox Marxism," as many theorists and revolutionaries provided alternative accounts of its main ideas. But early in the twentieth century, Emma Goldman (1869–1940) – a widely admired free-thinking rebel and activist who was born in Lithuania, moved to New York City when she was 16, and was deported for helping young Americans resist the draft that was enacted during World War I – wrote "Anarchism: What It Really Stands For" in order to define and defend those ideas shared by all anarchists. These include: all governments (including those that Marxists would lead after the revolution) are coercive and unnecessary; the materialist and capitalist institutions that structure social life are evil; "man" – not God, society, or government – is the only object of value, and each human should be a free and active agent creating a mode of living that reflects his ideals; humans have both individual and social instincts, even though the latter have been ignored and repressed by governments and capitalist institutions; and when the energies of humans are no longer "caged into a narrow space [and] whipped daily into submission," humanity's higher and more social nature will enable people to live freely and cooperatively without government. Such sentiments continue to make anarchism an attractive left-wing perspective for those idealists who have become disillusioned with Marxism, due to its connection with communism, which arose in the twentieth century but now appears swept into the dustbins of history.

John Locke, "The Second Treatise of Government"*

Of the state of nature

To understand political power right, and derive it from its original, we must consider, what state all men are naturally in, and that is, a state of perfect freedom to order their actions, and dispose of their possessions and persons, as they think fit, within the bounds of the law of nature, without asking leave, or depending upon the will of any other man.

A state also of equality, wherein all the power and jurisdiction is reciprocal, no one having more than another; there being nothing more evident, than that creatures of the same species and rank, promiscuously born to all the same advantages of nature, and the use of the same faculties, should also be equal one amongst another without subordination or subjection, unless the lord and master of them all should, by any manifest declaration of his will, set one above another, and confer on him, by an evident and clear appointment, an undoubted right to dominion and sovereignty.

[...]

But though this be a state of liberty, yet it is not a state of licence: though man in that state have an uncontrollable liberty to dispose of his person or possessions, yet he has not liberty to destroy himself, or so much as any creature in his possession, but where some nobler use than its bare preservation calls for it. The state of nature has a law of nature to govern it, which obliges every one: and reason, which is that law, teaches all mankind, who will but consult it, that being all equal and independent, no one ought to harm another in his life, health, liberty, or possessions: for men being all the workmanship of one omnipotent, and infinitely wise maker; all the servants of one sovereign master, sent into the world by his order, and about his business; they are his property, whose workmanship they are, made to last during his, not one another's pleasure: and being furnished with like faculties, sharing all in one community of nature, there cannot be supposed any such subordination among us, that may authorize us to destroy one another, as if we were made for one another's uses, as the inferior ranks of creatures are for our's. Every one, as he is bound to preserve himself, and not to quit his station wilfully, so by the like reason, when his own preservation comes not in competition, ought he, as much as he can, to preserve the rest of mankind, and may not, unless it be to do justice on an offender, take away, or impair the life, or what tends to the preservation of the life, the liberty, health, limb, or goods of another.

And that all men may be restrained from invading others' rights, and from doing hurt to one another, and the law of nature be observed, which willeth the peace and preservation of all mankind, the execution of the law of nature is, in that state, put into every man's hands, whereby every one has a right to punish the transgressors of that law to such a degree, as may hinder its violation: for the law of nature would, as all other laws that concern men in this world be in vain, if there were no body that in the state of nature had a power to execute that law, and thereby preserve the innocent and restrain offenders. And if any one in the state of nature may punish another for any evil he has done, every one may do so: for in that state of perfect equality, where naturally there is no superiority or jurisdiction of one over another, what any may do in prosecution of that law, every one must needs have a right to do.

And thus, in the state of nature, one man comes by a power over another; but yet no absolute or arbitrary power, to use a criminal, when he has got him in his hands, according to the passionate heats, or boundless extravagancy of his own will; but only to retribute to him, so far as calm reason and conscience dictate, what is proportionate to his transgression, which is so much as may serve for reparation and restraint: for these two are the only reasons, why one man may lawfully do harm to another, which is that we call punishment. In transgressing the law of nature, the offender declares himself to live by another rule than that of reason and common equity, which is that measure God has set to the actions of men, for their mutual security.

[...]

To this strange doctrine, viz. that in the state of nature every one has the executive power of the law of nature, I doubt not but it will be objected, that it is unreasonable for men to be judges in their own cases, that self-love will make men partial to themselves and their friends: and on the other side, that ill nature, passion and revenge will carry them too far in punishing others; and hence nothing but confusion and disorder will follow, and that therefore God hath certainly appointed government to restrain the partiality and violence of men. I easily grant, that civil government is the proper remedy for the inconveniencies of the state

* John Locke, extracted from *The Second Treatise of Government*: www.ilt.columbia.edu/academic/digitexts/locke/second/locke2nd.txt, accessed April 16, 2008. Originally published 1690.

of nature, which must certainly be great, where men may be judges in their own case. [...]

It is often asked as a mighty objection, where are, or ever were there any men in such a state of nature? To which it may suffice as an answer at present, that since all princes and rulers of independent governments all through the world, are in a state of nature, it is plain the world never was, nor ever will be, without numbers of men in that state.

[...]

And here we have the plain difference between the state of nature and the state of war, which however some men have confounded, are as far distant, as a state of peace, good will, mutual assistance and preservation, and a state of enmity, malice, violence and mutual destruction, are one from another. Men living together according to reason, without a common superior on earth, with authority to judge between them, is properly the state of nature. But force, or a declared design of force, upon the person of another, where there is no common superior on earth to appeal to for relief, is the state of war: and it is the want of such an appeal gives a man the right of war even against an aggressor, tho' he be in society and a fellow subject. [...]

God, who hath given the world to men in common, hath also given them reason to make use of it to the best advantage of life, and convenience. The earth, and all that is therein, is given to men for the support and comfort of their being. And tho' all the fruits it naturally produces, and beasts it feeds, belong to mankind in common, as they are produced by the spontaneous hand of nature; and no body has originally a private dominion, exclusive of the rest of mankind, in any of them, as they are thus in their natural state: yet being given for the use of men, there must of necessity be a means to appropriate them some way or other, before they can be of any use, or at all beneficial to any particular man. The fruit, or venison, which nourishes the wild Indian, who knows no enclosure, and is still a tenant in common, must be his, and so his, i.e., a part of him, that another can no longer have any right to it, before it can do him any good for the support of his life.

Though the earth, and all inferior creatures, be common to all men, yet every man has a property in his own person: this no body has any right to but himself. The labour of his body, and the work of his hands, we may say, are properly his. Whatsoever then he removes out of the state that nature hath provided, and left it in, he hath mixed his labour with, and joined to it something that is his own, and thereby makes it his property. It being by him removed from the common state nature hath placed it in, it hath by this labour something annexed to it, that excludes the common right of other men: for this labour being the unquestionable property of the labourer, no man but he can have a right to what that is once joined to, at least where there is enough, and as good, left in common for others.

[...]

It will perhaps be objected to this, that if gathering the acorns, or other fruits of the earth, etc. makes a right to them, then any one may ingross as much as he will. To which I answer, Not so. The same law of nature, that does by this means give us property, does also bound that property too. God has given us all things richly, 1 Tim. vi. 12. is the voice of reason confirmed by inspiration. But how far has he given it us? To enjoy. As much as any one can make use of to any advantage of life before it spoils, so much he may by his labour fix a property in: whatever is beyond this, is more than his share, and belongs to others. Nothing was made by God for man to spoil or destroy. And thus, considering the plenty of natural provisions there was a long time in the world, and the few spenders; and to how small a part of that provision the industry of one man could extend itself, and ingross it to the prejudice of others; especially keeping within the bounds, set by reason, of what might serve for his use; there could be then little room for quarrels or contentions about property so established.

But the chief matter of property being now not the fruits of the earth, and the beasts that subsist on it, but the earth itself; as that which takes in and carries with it all the rest; I think it is plain, that property in that too is acquired as the former. As much land as a man tills, plants, improves, cultivates, and can use the product of, so much is his property. He by his labour does, as it were, inclose it from the common. Nor will it invalidate his right, to say every body else has an equal title to it; and therefore he cannot appropriate, he cannot inclose, without the consent of all his fellow-commoners, all mankind. God, when he gave the world in common to all mankind, commanded man also to labour, and the penury of his condition required it of him. God and his reason commanded him to subdue the earth, i.e. improve it for the benefit of life, and therein lay out something upon it that was his own, his labour. He that in obedience to this command of God, subdued, tilled and sowed any part of it, thereby annexed to it something that was his property, which another had no title to, nor could without injury take from him.

[...]

Nor is it so strange, as perhaps before consideration it may appear, that the property of labour should be able to over-balance the community of land: for it is labour indeed that puts the difference of value on every thing; and let any one consider what the difference is between an acre of land planted with tobacco or sugar, sown with wheat or barley, and an acre of the same land lying in common, without any husbandry upon it, and he will find, that the improvement of labour makes the far greater part of the value. I think it will be but a very modest computation to say, that of the products of the earth useful to the life of man nine tenths are the effects of labour: nay, if we will rightly estimate things as they come to our use, and cast up the several expences about them, what in them is purely owing to nature, and what to labour, we shall find, that in most of them ninety-nine hundredths are wholly to be put on the account of labour.

[...]

And thus came in the use of money, some lasting thing that men might keep without spoiling, and that by mutual consent men would take in exchange for the truly useful, but perishable supports of life.

And as different degrees of industry were apt to give men possessions in different proportions, so this invention of money gave them the opportunity to continue and enlarge them.

[...]

But since gold and silver, being little useful to the life of man in proportion to food, raiment, and carriage, has its value only from the consent of men, whereof labour yet makes, in great part, the measure, it is plain, that men have agreed to a disproportionate and unequal possession of the earth, they having, by a tacit and voluntary consent, found out, a way how a man may fairly possess more land than he himself can use the product of, by receiving in exchange for the overplus gold and silver, which may be hoarded up without injury to any one; these metals not spoiling or decaying in the hands of the possessor. This partage of things in an inequality of private possessions, men have made practicable out of the bounds of society, and without compact, only by putting a value on gold and silver, and tacitly agreeing in the use of money: for in governments, the laws regulate the right of property, and the possession of land is determined by positive constitutions.

[...]

Of political or civil society

God having made man such a creature, that in his own judgment, it was not good for him to be alone, put him under strong obligations of necessity, convenience, and inclination to drive him into society, as well as fitted him with understanding and language to continue and enjoy it. The first society was between man and wife, which gave beginning to that between parents and children; to which, in time, that between master and servant came to be added: and though all these might, and commonly did meet together, and make up but one family, wherein the master or mistress of it had some sort of rule proper to a family; each of these, or all together, came short of political society, as we shall see, if we consider the different ends, ties, and bounds of each of these.

Conjugal society is made by a voluntary compact between man and woman; and tho' it consist chiefly in such a communion and right in one another's bodies as is necessary to its chief end, procreation; yet it draws with it mutual support and assistance, and a communion of interests too, as necessary not only to unite their care and affection, but also necessary to their common off-spring, who have a right to be nourished, and maintained by them, till they are able to provide for themselves.

[...]

But how a family, or any other society of men, differ from that which is properly political society, we shall best see, by considering wherein political society itself consists.

Man being born, as has been proved, with a title to perfect freedom, and an uncontrolled enjoyment of all the rights and privileges of the law of nature, equally with any other man, or number of men in the world, hath by nature a power, not only to preserve his property, that is, his life, liberty and estate, against the injuries and attempts of other men; but to judge of, and punish the breaches of that law in others, as he is persuaded the offence deserves, even with death itself, in crimes where the heinousness of the fact, in his opinion, requires it. But because no political society can be, nor subsist, without having in itself the power to preserve the property, and in order thereunto, punish the offences of all those of that society; there, and there only is political society, where every one of the members hath quitted this natural power, resigned it up into the hands of the community in all cases that exclude him not from appealing for protection to the law established by it. And thus all private judgment of every particular member being excluded, the community comes to be umpire, by settled standing rules, indifferent, and the same to all parties; and by men having authority from the community, for the execution of those rules, decides all the differences that may happen between any members of that society concerning any matter of right; and punishes those offences which any member hath committed against the society, with such penalties as the law has established: whereby it is easy to discern, who are, and who are not, in political society together. Those who are united into one body, and have a common established law and judicature to appeal to, with authority to decide controversies between them, and punish offenders, are in civil society one with another: but those who have no such common appeal, I mean on earth, are still in the state of nature, each being, where there is no other, judge for himself, and executioner; which is, as I have before shewed it, the perfect state of nature.

[...]

Where-ever therefore any number of men are so united into one society, as to quit every one his executive power of the law of nature, and to resign it to the public, there and there only is a political, or civil society. And this is done, where-ever any number of men, in the state of nature, enter into society to make one people, one body politic, under one supreme government; or else when any one joins himself to, and incorporates with any government already made: for hereby he authorizes the society, or which is all one, the legislative thereof, to make laws for him, as the public good of the society shall require; to the execution whereof, his own assistance (as to his own decrees) is due. And this puts men out of a state of nature into that of a common-wealth, by setting up a judge on earth, with authority to determine all the controversies, and redress the injuries that may happen to any member of the commonwealth; which judge is the legislative, or magistrates appointed by it. And where-ever there are any number of men, however associated, that have no such decisive power to appeal to, there they are still in the state of nature.

[...]

Of the beginning of political societies

Men being, as has been said, by nature, all free, equal, and independent, no one can be put out of this estate, and subjected to the political power of another, without his own consent. The only way whereby any one divests himself of his natural liberty, and puts on the bonds of civil society, is by agreeing with other men to join and unite into a community for their comfortable, safe, and peaceable living one amongst another, in a secure enjoyment of their properties, and a greater security against any, that are not of it. This any number of men may do, because it injures not the freedom of the rest; they are left as they were in the liberty of the state of nature. When any number of men have so consented to make one community or government, they are thereby presently incorporated, and make one body politic, wherein the majority have a right to act and conclude the rest.

For when any number of men have, by the consent of every individual, made a community, they have thereby made that community one body, with a power to act as one body, which is only by the will and determination of the majority: for that which acts any community, being only the consent of the individuals of it, and it being necessary to that which is one body to move one way; it is necessary the body should move that way whither the greater force carries it, which is the consent of the majority: or else it is impossible it should act or continue one body, one community, which the consent of every individual that united into it, agreed that it should; and so every one is bound by that consent to be concluded by the majority. And therefore we see, that in assemblies, impowered to act by positive laws, where no number is set by that positive law which impowers them, the act of the majority passes for the act of the whole, and of course determines, as having, by the law of nature and reason, the power of the whole.

[...]

Of the ends of political society and government

If man in the state of nature be so free, as has been said; if he be absolute lord of his own person and possessions, equal to the greatest, and subject to no body, why will he part with his freedom? why will he give up this empire, and subject himself to the dominion and control of any other power? To which it is obvious to answer, that though in the state of nature he hath such a right, yet the enjoyment of it is very uncertain, and constantly exposed to the invasion of others: for all being kings as much as he, every man his equal, and the greater part no strict observers of equity and justice, the enjoyment of the property he has in this state is very unsafe, very unsecure. This makes him willing to quit a condition, which, however free, is full of fears and continual dangers: and it is not without reason, that he seeks out, and is willing to join in society with others, who are already united, or have a mind to unite, for the mutual preservation of their lives, liberties and estates, which I call by the general name, property.

The great and chief end, therefore, of men's uniting into commonwealths, and putting themselves under government, is the preservation of their property. To which in the state of nature there are many things wanting.

First, There wants an established, settled, known law, received and allowed by common consent to be the standard of right and wrong, and the common measure to decide all controversies between them: for though the law of nature be plain and intelligible to all rational creatures; yet men being biassed by their interest, as well as ignorant for want of study of it, are not apt to allow of it as a law binding to them in the application of it to their particular cases.

Secondly, In the state of nature there wants a known and indifferent judge, with authority to determine all differences according to the established law: for every one in that state being both judge and executioner of the law of nature, men being partial to themselves, passion and revenge is very apt to carry them too far, and with too much heat, in their own cases; as well as negligence, and unconcernedness, to make them too remiss in other men's.

Thirdly, In the state of nature there often wants power to back and support the sentence when right, and to give it due execution, They who by any injustice offended, will seldom fail, where they are able, by force to make good their injustice; such resistance many times makes the punishment dangerous, and frequently destructive, to those who attempt it.

[...]

But though men, when they enter into society, give up the equality, liberty, and executive power they had in the state of nature, into the hands of the society, to be so far disposed of by the legislative, as the good of the society shall require; yet it being only with an intention in every one the better to preserve himself, his liberty and property; (for no rational creature can be supposed to change his condition with an intention to be worse) the power of the society, or legislative constituted by them, can never be supposed to extend farther, than the common good; but is obliged to secure every one's property, by providing against those three defects above mentioned, that made the state of nature so unsafe and uneasy. And so whoever has the legislative or supreme power of any commonwealth, is bound to govern by established standing laws, promulgated and known to the people, and not by extemporary decrees; by indifferent and upright judges, who are to decide controversies by those laws; and to employ the force of the community at home, only in the execution of such laws, or abroad to prevent or redress foreign injuries, and secure the community from inroads and invasion. And all this to be directed to no other end, but the peace, safety, and public good of the people. [...]

Of the dissolution of government

Whenever the legislators endeavour to take away, and destroy the property of the people, or to reduce them to slavery under arbitrary power, they put themselves into a state of war with the people, who are thereupon absolved from any farther obedience, and are left to the common refuge, which God hath provided for all men, against force and violence. Whensoever therefore the legislative shall transgress this fundamental rule of society; and either by ambition, fear, folly or corruption, endeavour to grasp themselves, or put into the hands of any other, an absolute power over the lives, liberties, and estates of the people; by this breach of trust they forfeit the power the people had put into their hands for quite contrary ends, and it devolves to the people, who. have a right to resume their original liberty, and, by the establishment of a new legislative, (such as they shall think fit) provide for their own safety and security, which is the end for which they are in society. What I have said here, concerning the legislative in general, holds true also concerning the supreme executor, who having a double trust put in him, both to have a part in the legislative, and the supreme execution of the law, acts against both, when he goes about to set up his own arbitrary will as the law of the society. He acts also contrary to his trust, when he either employs the force, treasure, and offices of the society, to corrupt the representatives, and gain them to his purposes; or openly preengages the electors, and prescribes to their choice, such, whom he has, by sollicitations, threats, promises, or otherwise, won to his designs; and employs them to bring in such, who have promised before-hand what to vote, and what to enact. Thus to regulate candidates and electors, and new-model the ways of election, what is it but to cut up the government by the roots, and poison the very fountain of public security? for the people having reserved to themselves the choice of their representatives, as the fence to their properties, could do it for no other end, but that they might always be freely chosen, and so chosen, freely act, and advise, as the necessity of the common-wealth, and the public good should, upon examination, and mature debate, be judged to require. [...]

To this perhaps it will be said, that the people being ignorant, and always discontented, to lay the foundation of government in the unsteady opinion and uncertain humour of the people, is to expose it to certain ruin; and no government will be able long to subsist, if the people may set up a new legislative, whenever they take offence at the old one. To this I answer, Quite the contrary. People are not so easily got out of their old forms, as some are apt to suggest. They are hardly to be prevailed with to amend the acknowledged faults in the frame they have been accustomed to. And if there be any original defects, or adventitious ones introduced by time, or corruption; it is not an easy thing to get them changed, even when all the world sees there is an opportunity for it. This slowness and aversion in the people to quit their old constitutions, has, in the many revolutions which have been seen in this kingdom, in this and former ages, still kept us to, or, after some interval of fruitless attempts, still brought us back again to our old legislative of king, lords and commons: and whatever provocations have made the crown be taken from some of our princes heads, they never carried the people so far as to place it in another line.

But it will be said, this hypothesis lays a ferment for frequent rebellion. To which I answer,

First, No more than any other hypothesis: for when the people are made miserable, and find themselves exposed to the ill usage of arbitrary power, cry up their governors, as much as you will, for sons of Jupiter; let them be sacred and divine, descended, or authorized from heaven; give them out for whom or what you please, the same will happen. The people generally ill treated, and contrary to right, will be ready upon any occasion to ease themselves of a burden that sits heavy upon them. They will wish, and seek for the opportunity, which in the change, weakness and accidents of human affairs, seldom delays long to offer itself. He must have lived but a little while in the world, who has not seen examples of this in his time; and he must have read very little, who cannot produce examples of it in all sorts of governments in the world.

Secondly, I answer, such revolutions happen not upon every little mismanagement in public affairs. Great mistakes in the ruling part, many wrong and inconvenient laws, and all the slips of human frailty, will be born by the people without mutiny or murmur. But if a long train of abuses, prevarications and artifices, all tending the same way, make the design visible to the people, and they cannot but feel what they lie under, and see whither they are going; it is not to be wondered, that they should then rouze themselves, and endeavour to put the rule into such hands which may secure to them the ends for which government was at first erected; and without which, ancient names, and specious forms, are so far from being better, that they are much worse, than the state of nature, or pure anarchy; the inconveniencies being all as great and as near, but the remedy farther off and more difficult.

Thirdly, I answer, that this doctrine of a power in the people of providing for their safety a-new, by a new legislative, when their legislators have acted contrary to their trust, by invading their property, is the best fence against rebellion, and the probablest means to hinder it.

[...]

Here, it is like, the common question will be made, Who shall be judge, whether the prince or legislative act contrary to their trust? This, perhaps, ill-affected and factious men may spread amongst the people, when the prince only makes use of his due prerogative. To this I reply, The people shall be judge; for who shall be judge whether his trustee or deputy acts well, and according to the trust reposed in him, but he who deputes him, and must, by having deputed him, have still a power to discard him, when he fails in his trust? If this be reasonable in particular cases of private men, why should it be otherwise in that of the greatest moment, where the welfare of millions is concerned, and also where the evil, if not prevented, is greater, and the redress very difficult, dear, and dangerous?

But farther, this question, (Who shall be judge?) cannot mean, that there is no judge at all: for where there is no judicature on earth, to decide controversies amongst men, God in heaven is judge. He alone, it is true, is judge of the right. But every man is judge for himself, as in all other cases, so in this, whether another hath put himself into a state of war with him, and whether he should appeal to the Supreme Judge, as Ieptha did.

If a controversy arise betwixt a prince and some of the people, in a matter where the law is silent, or doubtful, and the thing be of great consequence, I should think the proper umpire, in such a case, should be the body of the people: for in cases where the prince hath a trust reposed in him, and is dispensed from the common ordinary rules of the law; there, if any men find themselves aggrieved, and think the prince acts contrary to, or beyond that trust, who so proper to judge as the body of the people, (who, at first, lodged that trust in him) how far they meant it should extend?

[...]

To conclude, The power that every individual gave the society, when he entered into it, can never revert to the individuals again, as long as the society lasts, but will always remain in the community; because without this there can be no community, no common-wealth, which is contrary to the original agreement: so also when the society hath placed the legislative in any assembly of men, to continue in them and their successors, with direction and authority for providing such successors, the legislative can never revert to the people whilst that government lasts; because having provided a legislative with power to continue for ever, they have given up their political power to the legislative, and cannot resume it. But if they have set limits to the duration of their legislative, and made this supreme power in any person, or assembly, only temporary; or else, when by the miscarriages of those in authority, it is forfeited; upon the forfeiture, or at the determination of the time set, it reverts to the society, and the people have a right to act as supreme, and continue the legislative in themselves; or erect a new form, or under the old form place it in new hands, as they think good.

National Assembly of France, "The Declaration of the Rights of Man and of the Citizen"*

'The Representatives of the people of France, formed into a NATIONAL ASSEMBLY, considering that ignorance, neglect, or contempt of human rights, are the sole causes of public misfortunes and corruptions of Government, have resolved to set forth, in a solemn declaration, these natural, imprescriptible, and inalienable rights: that this declaration being constantly present to the minds of the members of the body social, they may be ever kept attentive to their rights and their duties: that the acts of the legislative and executive powers of Government, being capable of being every moment compared with the end of political institutions, may be more respected: and also, that the future claims of the citizens, being directed by simple and incontestable principles, may always tend to the maintenance of the Constitution, and the general happiness.

'For these reasons, the NATIONAL ASSEMBLY doth recognize and declare, in the presence of the Supreme Being, and with the hope of his blessing and favour, the following *sacred* rights of men and of citizens:

'I. *Men are born, and always continue, free, and equal in respect of their rights. Civil distinctions, therefore, can be founded only on public utility.*

'II. *The end of all political associations, is, the preservation of the natural and imprescriptible rights of man; and these rights are liberty, property, security, and resistance of oppression.*

'III. *The nation is essentially the source of all sovereignty; nor can any* INDIVIDUAL, *or* ANY BODY OF MEN, *be entitled to any authority which is not expressly derived from it.*

'IV. Political Liberty consists in the power of doing whatever does not injure another. The exercise of the natural rights of every man, has no other limits than those which are necessary to secure to every *other* man the free exercise of the same rights; and these limits are determinable only by the law.

'V. The law ought to prohibit only actions hurtful to society. What is not prohibited by the law, should not be hindered; nor should any one be compelled to that which the law does not require.

'VI. The law is an expression of the will of the community. All citizens have a right to concur, either personally, or by their representatives, in its formation. It should be the same to all, whether it protects or punishes; and *all being equal in its sight, are equally eligible to all honours, places, and employments, according to their different abilities, without any other distinction than that created by their virtues and talents.*

'VII. No man should be accused, arrested, or held in confinement, except in cases determined by the law, and according to the forms which it has prescribed. All who promote, solicit, execute, or cause to be executed, arbitrary orders, ought to be punished; and every citizen called upon, or apprehended by virtue of the law, ought immediately to obey, and renders himself culpable by resistance.

'VIII. The law ought to impose no other penalties but such as are absolutely and evidently necessary: and no one ought to be punished, but in virtue of a law promulgated before the offence, and legally applied.

'IX. Every man being presumed innocent till he has been convicted, whenever his detention becomes indispensable, all rigour to him, more than is necessary to secure his person, ought to be provided against by the law.

'X. No man ought to be molested on account of his opinions, not even on account of his *religious* opinions, provided his avowal of them does not disturb the public order established by the law.

'XI. The unrestrained communication of thoughts and opinions being one of the most precious rights of man, every citizen may speak, write, and publish freely, provided he is responsible for the abuse of this liberty in cases determined by the law.

'XII. A public force being necessary to give security to the rights of men and of citizens, that force is instituted for the benefit of the community, and not for the particular benefit of the persons with whom it is entrusted.

* Originally published 1789.

'XIII. A common contribution being necessary for the support of the public force, and for defraying the other expenses of government, it ought to be divided equally among the members of the community, according to their abilities.

'XIV. Every citizen has a right, either by himself or his representative, to a free voice in determining the necessity of public contributions, the appropriation of them, and their amount, mode of assessment, and duration.

'XV. Every community has a right to demand of all its agents, an account of their conduct.

'XVI. Every community in which a separation of powers and a security of rights is not provided for, wants a constitution.

'XVII. The right to property being inviolable and sacred, no one ought to be deprived of it, except in cases of evident public necessity, legally ascertained, and on condition of a previous just indemnity.'

Edmund Burke, "Reflections on the Revolution in France"*

You will observe, that from Magna Charta to the Declaration of Right, it has been the uniform policy of our constitution to claim and assert our liberties, as an *entailed inheritance* derived to us from our forefathers, and to be transmitted to our posterity; as an estate specially belonging to the people of this kingdom without any reference whatever to any other more general or prior right. By this means our constitution preserves an unity in so great a diversity of its parts. We have an inheritable crown; an inheritable peerage; and an house of commons and a people inheriting privileges, franchises, and liberties, from a long line of ancestors.

This policy appears to me to be the result of profound reflection; or rather the happy effect of following nature, which is wisdom without reflection, and above it. A spirit of innovation is generally the result of a selfish temper and confined views. People will not look forward to posterity, who never look backward to their ancestors. Besides, the people of England well know, that the idea of inheritance furnishes a sure principle of conservation, and a sure principle of transmission; without at all excluding a principle of improvement. It leaves acquisition free; but it secures what it acquires. Whatever advantages are obtained by a state proceeding on these maxims, are locked fast as in a sort of family settlement; grasped as in a kind of mortmain for ever. By a constitutional policy, working after the pattern of nature, we receive, we hold, we transmit our government and our privileges, in the same manner in which we enjoy and transmit our property and our lives. The institutions of policy, the goods of fortune, the gifts of Providence, are handed down, to us and from us, in the same course and order. Our political system is placed in a just correspondence and symmetry with the order of the world, and with the mode of existence decreed to a permanent body composed of transitory parts; wherein, by the disposition of a stupendous wisdom, moulding together the great mysterious incorporation of the human race, the whole, at one time, is never old, or middle-aged, or young, but in a condition of unchangeable constancy, moves on through the varied tenour of perpetual decay, fall, renovation, and progression. Thus, by preserving the method of nature in the conduct of the state, in what we improve we are never wholly new; in what we retain we are never wholly obsolete. By adhering in this manner and on those principles to our forefathers, we are guided not by the superstition of antiquarians, but by the spirit of philosophic analogy. In this choice of inheritance we have given to our frame of polity the image of a relation in blood; binding up the constitution of our country with our dearest domestic ties; adopting our fundamental laws into the bosom of our family affections; keeping inseparable, and cherishing with the warmth of all their combined and mutually reflected charities, our state, our hearths, our sepulchres, and our altars.

[...]

You [French revolutionaries] might, if you pleased, have profited of our example, and have given to your recovered freedom a correspondent dignity. Your privileges, though discontinued, were not lost to memory. Your constitution, it is true, whilst you were out of possession, suffered waste and dilapidation; but you possessed in some parts the walls, and in all the foundations of a noble and venerable castle. You might have repaired those walls; you might have built on those old foundations. Your constitution was suspended before it was perfected; but you had the elements of a constitution very nearly as good as could be wished.

[...]

You had all these advantages in your antient states; but you chose to act as if you had never been moulded into civil society, and had every thing to begin anew. You began ill, because you began by despising every thing that belonged to you. You set up your trade without a capital. If the last generations of your country appeared

* Edmund Burke, extracted from *Reflections on the Revolution in France* (Anchor Books Edition, 1973), which is derived from *The Works of the Right Honorable Edmund Burke*, the Riverton edition (London, 1826), Volume 5. Originally published 1790.

without much lustre in your eyes, you might have passed them by, and derived your claims from a more early race of ancestors. Under a pious predilection for those ancestors, your imaginations would have realized in them a standard of virtue and wisdom, beyond the vulgar practice of the hour: and you would have risen with the example to whose imitation you aspired. Respecting your forefathers, you would have been taught to respect yourselves.

[...]

Far am I from denying in theory; full as far is my heart from withholding in practice (if I were of power to give or to withhold) the *real* rights of men. In denying their false claims of right, I do not mean to injure those which are real, and are such as their pretended rights would totally destroy. If civil society be made for the advantage of man, all the advantages for which it is made become his right. It is an institution of beneficence; and law itself is only beneficence acting by a rule. Men have a right to live by that rule; they have a right to justice; as between their fellows, whether their fellows are in politic function or in ordinary occupation. They have a right to the fruits of their industry; and to the means of making their industry fruitful. They have a right to the acquisitions of their parents; to the nourishment and improvement of their offspring; to instruction in life, and to consolation in death. Whatever each man can separately do, without trespassing upon others, he has a right to do for himself; and he has a right to a fair portion of all which society, with all its combinations of skill and force, can do in his favour. In this partnership all men have equal rights; but not to equal things. He that has but five shillings in the partnership, has as good a right to it, as he that has five hundred pound has to his larger proportion. But he has not a right to an equal dividend in the product of the joint stock; and as to the share of power, authority, and direction which each individual ought to have in the management of the state, that I must deny to be amongst the direct original rights of man in civil society; for I have in my contemplation the civil social man, and no other. It is a thing to be settled by convention.

If civil society be the offspring of convention, that convention must be its law. That convention must limit and modify all the descriptions of constitution which are formed under it. Every sort of legislative, judicial, or executory power are its creatures. They can have no being in any other state of things; and how can any man claim, under the conventions of civil society, rights which do not so much as suppose its existence? Rights which are absolutely repugnant to it? One of the first motives to civil society, and which becomes one of its fundamental rules, is, *that no man should be judge in his own cause*. By this each person has at once divested himself of the first fundamental right of uncovenanted man, that is, to judge for himself, and to assert his own cause. He abdicates all right to be his own governor. He inclusively, in a great measure, abandons the right of self-defence, the first law of nature. Men cannot enjoy the rights of an uncivil and of a civil state together. That he may obtain justice he gives up his right of determining what it is in points the most essential to him. That he may secure some liberty, he makes a surrender in trust of the whole of it.

Government is not made in virtue of natural rights, which may and do exist in total independence of it; and exist in much greater clearness, and in a much greater degree of abstract perfection: but their abstract perfection is their practical defect. By having a right to every thing they want every thing. Government is a contrivance of human wisdom to provide for human *wants*. Men have a right that these wants should be provided for by this wisdom. Among these wants is to be reckoned the want, out of civil society, of a sufficient restraint upon their passions. Society requires not only that the passions of individuals should be subjected, but that even in the mass and body as well as in the individuals, the inclinations of men should frequently be thwarted, their will controlled, and their passions brought into subjection. This can only be done *by a power out of themselves*; and not, in the exercise of its function, subject to that will and to those passions which it is its office to bridle and subdue. In this sense the restraints on men, as well as their liberties, are to be reckoned among their rights. But as the liberties and the restrictions vary with times and circumstances, and admit of infinite modifications, they cannot be settled upon any abstract rule; and nothing is so foolish as to discuss them upon that principle.

The moment you abate any thing from the full rights of men, each to govern himself, and suffer any artificial positive limitation upon those rights, from that moment the whole organization of government becomes a consideration of convenience. This it is which makes the constitution of a state, and the due distribution of its powers, a matter of the most delicate and complicated skill. It requires a deep knowledge of human nature and human necessities, and of the things which facilitate or obstruct the various ends which are to be pursued by the mechanism of civil institutions. The state is to have recruits to its strength, and remedies to its distempers. What is the use of discussing a man's abstract right to food or to medicine? The question is upon the method of procuring and administering them. In that deliberation I shall always advise to call in the aid of the farmer and the physician, rather than the professor of metaphysics.

The science of constructing a commonwealth, or renovating it, or reforming it, is, like every other experimental science, not to be taught *à priori*. Nor is it a short experience that can instruct us in that practical science; because the real effects of moral causes are not always immediate; but that which in the first instance is prejudicial may be excellent in its remoter operation; and its excellence may arise even from the ill effects it produces in the beginning. The reverse also happens; and very plausible schemes, with very pleasing commencements, have often shameful and lamentable conclusions. In states there are often some obscure and almost latent causes, things which appear at first view of little moment, on which a very great part of its prosperity or adversity may most essentially depend. The science of government being therefore so practical in itself, and intended for such practical purposes, a matter which requires experience, and even more experience than any person can gain in his whole life, however sagacious and observing he may be, it is with infinite caution than any man ought to venture upon pulling down an edifice which has answered in any tolerable degree for ages the common purposes of society, or on building it up again, without having models and patterns of approved utility before his eyes.

These metaphysic rights entering into common life, like rays of light which pierce into a dense medium, are, by the laws of nature, refracted from their straight line. Indeed in the gross and complicated mass of human passions and concerns, the primitive rights of men undergo such a variety of refractions and reflections, that it becomes absurd to talk of them as if they continued in the simplicity of their original direction. The nature of man is intricate; the objects of society are of the greatest possible complexity; and therefore no simple disposition or direction of power can be suitable either to man's nature, or to the quality of his affairs. When I hear the simplicity of contrivance aimed at and boasted of in any new political constitutions, I am at no loss to decide that the artificers are grossly ignorant of their trade, or totally negligent of their duty. The simple governments are fundamentally defective, to say no worse of them. If you were to contemplate society in but one point of view, all these simple modes of polity are infinitely captivating. In effect each would answer its single end much more perfectly than the more complex is able to attain all its complex purposes. But it is better that the whole should be imperfectly and anomalously answered, than that, while some parts are provided for with great exactness, others might be totally neglected, or perhaps materially injured, by the over-care of a favourite member.

The pretended rights of these theorists are all extremes; and in proportion as they are metaphysically true, they are morally and politically false. The rights of men are in a sort of *middle*, incapable of definition, but not impossible to be discerned. The rights of men in governments are their advantages; and these are often in balances between differences of good; in compromises sometimes between good and evil, and sometimes, between evil and evil. Political reason is a computing principle; adding, subtracting, multiplying, and dividing, morally and not metaphysically or mathematically, true moral denominations.

By these theorists the right of the people is almost always sophistically confounded with their power. The body of the community, whenever it can come to act, can meet with no effectual resistance; but till power and right are the same, the whole body of them has no right inconsistent with virtue, and the first of all virtues, prudence. Men have no right to what is not reasonable, and to what is not for their benefit; for though a pleasant writer said, *Liceat perire poetis*, when one of them, in cold blood, is said to have leaped into the flames of a volcanic revolution, *Ardentem frigidus Ætnam insiluit*, I consider such a frolic rather as an unjustifiable poetic licence, than as one of the franchises of Parnassus; and whether he were poet or divine, or politician that close to exercise this kind of right, I think that more wise, because more charitable thoughts would urge me rather to save the man, than to preserve his brazen slippers as the monuments of his folly.

Karl Marx and Friedrich Engels, "The Communist Manifesto"*

I. Bourgeois and proletarians[1]

The history of all hitherto existing society is the history of class struggles.

Freeman and slave, patrician and plebeian, lord and serf, guild-master and journeyman, in a word, oppressor

* Karl Marx and Friedrich Engels, extracted from *The Manifesto of the Communist Party*, authorized English translation (New York: International Publishers, 1948), available at www.anu.edu.au/polsci/marx/classics/manifesto.html. Originally published 1848.

1 By bourgeoisie is meant the class of modern Capitalists, owners of the means of social production and employers of wage-labour. By proletariat, the class of modern wage-labourers who, having no means of production of their own, are reduced to selling their labour-power in order to live. [Engels, English edition of 1888]

and oppressed, stood in constant opposition to one another, carried on an uninterrupted, now hidden, now open fight, a fight that each time ended, either in a revolutionary re-constitution of society at large, or in the common ruin of the contending classes.

In the earlier epochs of history, we find almost everywhere a complicated arrangement of society into various orders, a manifold gradation of social rank. In ancient Rome we have patricians, knights, plebeians, slaves; in the Middle Ages, feudal lords, vassals, guild-masters, journeymen, apprentices, serfs; in almost all of these classes, again, subordinate gradations.

The modern bourgeois society that has sprouted from the ruins of feudal society has not done away with class antagonisms. It has but established new classes, new conditions of oppression, new forms of struggle in place of the old ones.

Our epoch, the epoch of the bourgeoisie, possesses, however, this distinctive feature: it has simplified the class antagonisms: Society as a whole is more and more splitting up into two great hostile camps, into two great classes directly facing each other: Bourgeoisie and Proletariat.

From the serfs of the Middle Ages sprang the charted burghers of the earliest towns. From these burgesses the first elements of the bourgeoisie were developed.

[...]

Each step in the development of the bourgeoisie was accompanied by a corresponding political advance of that class. An oppressed class under the sway of the feudal nobility, an armed and self-governing association in the mediaeval commune; here independent urban republic (as in Italy and Germany), there taxable "third estate" of the monarchy (as in France), afterwards, in the period of manufacture proper, serving either the semi-feudal or the absolute monarchy as a counterpoise against the nobility, and, in fact, corner-stone of the great monarchies in general, the bourgeoisie has at last, since the establishment of Modern Industry and of the world-market, conquered for itself, in the modern representative State, exclusive political sway. The executive of the modern State is but a committee for managing the common affairs of the whole bourgeoisie.

The bourgeoisie, historically, has played a most revolutionary part.

The bourgeoisie, wherever it has got the upper hand, has put an end to all feudal, patriarchal, idyllic relations. It has pitilessly torn asunder the motley feudal ties that bound man to his "natural superiors," and has left remaining no other nexus between man and man than naked self-interest, than callous "cash payment." It has drowned the most heavenly ecstasies of religious fervour, of chivalrous enthusiasm, of philistine sentimentalism, in the icy water of egotistical calculation. It has resolved personal worth into exchange value, and in place of the numberless indefeasible chartered freedoms, has set up that single, unconscionable freedom – Free Trade. In one word, for exploitation, veiled by religious and political illusions, it has substituted naked, shameless, direct, brutal exploitation.

The bourgeoisie has stripped of its halo every occupation hitherto honoured and looked up to with reverent awe. It has converted the physician, the lawyer, the priest, the poet, the man of science, into its paid wage-labourers.

The bourgeoisie has torn away from the family its sentimental veil, and has reduced the family relation to a mere money relation.

The bourgeoisie has disclosed how it came to pass that the brutal display of vigour in the Middle Ages, which Reactionists so much admire, found its fitting complement in the most slothful indolence. It has been the first to show what man's activity can bring about. It has accomplished wonders far surpassing Egyptian pyramids, Roman aqueducts, and Gothic cathedrals; it has conducted expeditions that put in the shade all former Exoduses of nations and crusades.

The bourgeoisie cannot exist without constantly revolutionising the instruments of production, and thereby the relations of production, and with them the whole reactions of society. Conservation of the old modes of production in unaltered form, was, on the contrary, the first condition of existence for all earlier industrial classes. Constant revolutionising of production, uninterrupted disturbance of all social conditions, everlasting uncertainty and agitation distinguish the bourgeois epoch from all earlier ones. All fixed, fast-frozen relations, with their train of ancient and venerable prejudices and opinions, are swept away, all new-formed ones become antiquated before they can ossify. All that is solid melts into air, all that is holy is profaned, and man is at last compelled to face with sober senses, his real conditions of life, and his relations with his kind.

[...]

The bourgeoisie, during its rule of scarce one hundred years, has created more massive and more colossal productive forces than have all preceding generations together. Subjection of Nature's forces to man, machinery, application of chemistry to industry and agriculture, steam-navigation, railways, electric telegraphs, clearing of whole continents for cultivation, canalisation of rivers, whole populations conjured out of the ground – what earlier century had even a presentiment that such productive forces slumbered in the lap of social labour?

We see then: the means of production and of exchange, on whose foundation the bourgeoisie built itself up, were generated in feudal society. At a certain stage in the development of these means of production and of exchange, the conditions under which feudal society produced and exchanged, the feudal organization of agriculture and manufacturing industry, in one word, the feudal relations of property became no longer compatible with the already developed productive forces; they became so many fetters. They had to be burst asunder; they were burst asunder.

Into their place stepped free competition, accompanied by a social and political constitution adapted to it, and by the economical and political sway of the bourgeois class.

A similar movement is going on before our own eyes. Modern bourgeois society with its relations of production, of exchange and of property, a society that has conjured up such gigantic means of production and of exchange, is like the sorcerer, who is no longer able to control the powers of the nether world whom he has called up by his spells. For many a decade past the history of industry and commerce is but the history of the revolt of modern productive forces against modern conditions of production, against the property relations that are the conditions for the existence of the bourgeoisie and of its rule. It is enough to mention the commercial crises that by their periodical return put on its trial, each time more threateningly, the existence of the entire bourgeois society. In these crises a great part not only of the existing products, but also of the previously created productive forces, are periodically destroyed. In these crises there breaks out an epidemic that, in all earlier epochs, would have seemed an absurdity – the epidemic of over-production. Society suddenly finds itself put back into a state of momentary barbarism; it appears as if a famine, a universal war of devastation had cut off the supply of every means of subsistence; industry and commerce seem to be destroyed; and why? Because there is too much civilization, too much means of subsistence, too much industry, too much commerce. The productive forces at the disposal of society no longer tend to further the development of the conditions of bourgeois property; on the contrary, they have become too powerful for these conditions, by which they are fettered, and so soon as they overcome these fetters, they bring disorder into the whole of bourgeois society, endanger the existence of bourgeois property. The conditions of bourgeois society are too narrow to comprise the wealth created by them. And how does the bourgeoisie get over these crises? On the one hand by enforced destruction of a mass of productive forces; on the other, by the conquest of new markets, and by the more thorough exploitation of the old ones. That is to say, by paving the way for more extensive and more destructive crises, and by diminishing the means whereby crises are prevented.

The weapons with which the bourgeoisie felled feudalism to the ground are now turned against the bourgeoisie itself.

But not only has the bourgeoisie forged the weapons that bring death to itself; it has also called into existence the men who are to wield those weapons – the modern working class – the proletarians.

In proportion as the bourgeoisie, i.e., capital, is developed, in the same proportion is the proletariat, the modern working class, developed – a class of labourers, who live only so long as they find work, and who find work only so long as their labour increases capital. These labourers, who must sell themselves piece-meal, are a commodity, like every other article of commerce, and are consequently exposed to all the vicissitudes of competition, to all the fluctuations of the market.

Owing to the extreme use of machinery and to division of labour, the work of the proletarians has lost all individual character, and consequently, all charm for the workman. He becomes an appendage of the machine, and it is only the most simple, most monotonous, and most easily acquired knack, that is required of him. Hence, the cost of production of a workman is restricted, almost entirely, to the means of subsistence that he requires for his maintenance, and for the propagation of his race.

[...]

No sooner is the exploitation of the labourer by the manufacturer, so far, at an end, that he receives his wages in cash, than he is set upon by the other portions of the bourgeoisie, the landlord, the shopkeeper, the pawnbroker, etc.

The lower strata of the middle-class – the small tradespeople, shopkeepers, and retired tradesmen generally, the handicraftsmen and peasants – all these sink gradually into the proletariat, partly because their diminutive capital does not suffice for the scale on which Modern Industry is carried on, and is swamped in the competition with the large capitalists, partly because their specialised skill is rendered worthless by new methods of production. Thus the proletariat is recruited from all classes of the population.

The proletariat goes through various stages of development. With its birth begins its struggle with the bourgeoisie. At first the contest is carried on by individual labourers, then by the workpeople of a factory, then by the operatives of one trade, in one locality, against the individual bourgeois who directly exploits them. They direct their attacks not against the bourgeois conditions of production, but against the instruments of production themselves; they destroy imported wares that compete with their labour, they smash to pieces machinery, they set factories ablaze, they seek to restore by force the vanished status of the workman of the Middle Ages.

At this stage the labourers still form an incoherent mass scattered over the whole country, and broken up by their mutual competition. If anywhere they unite to form more compact bodies, this is not yet the consequence of their own active union, but of the union of the bourgeoisie, which class, in order to attain its own political ends, is compelled to set the whole proletariat in motion, and is moreover yet, for a time, able to do so. At this stage, therefore, the proletarians do not fight their enemies, but the enemies of their enemies, the remnants of absolute monarchy, the landowners, the non-industrial bourgeois, the petty bourgeoisie. Thus the whole historical movement is concentrated in the hands of the bourgeoisie; every victory so obtained is a victory for the bourgeoisie.

But with the development of industry the proletariat not only increases in number; it becomes concentrated in greater masses, its strength grows, and it feels that strength more. The various interest and conditions of life within the ranks of the proletariat are more and more equalized, in proportion as machinery obliterates all distinctions of labour, and nearly everywhere reduces wages to the same low level. The growing competition among the bourgeois, and the resulting commercial crises, make the wages of the workers ever more fluctuating. The unceasing improvement of machinery, ever more rapidly developing, makes their livelihood more and more precarious; the collisions between individual workmen and individual bourgeois take more and more the character of collisions between two classes. Thereupon the workers begin to form combinations (Trades Unions) against the bourgeois; they club together in order to keep up the rate of wages; they found permanent associations in order to make provision beforehand for these occasional revolts. Here and there the contest breaks out into riots.

Now and then the workers are victorious, but only for a time. The real fruit of their battles lies, not in the immediate result, but in the ever-expanding union of the workers.

[...]

Finally, in times when the class struggle nears the decisive hour, the process of dissolution going on within the ruling class, in fact within the whole range of society, assumes such a violent, glaring character, that a small section of the ruling class cuts itself adrift, and joins the revolutionary class, the class that holds the future in its hands. Just as, therefore, at an earlier period, a section of the nobility went over to the bourgeoisie, so now a portion of the bourgeoisie goes over to the proletariat, and in particular, a portion of the bourgeois ideologists, who have raised themselves to the level of comprehending theoretically the historical movement as a whole.

Of all the classes that stand face to face with the bourgeoisie today, the proletariat alone is a really revolutionary class. The other classes decay and finally disappear in the face of Modern Industry; the proletariat is its special and essential product.

The lower middle class, the small manufacturer, the shopkeeper, the artisan, the peasant, all these fight against the bourgeoisie, to save from extinction their existence as fractions of the middle class. They are therefore not revolutionary, but conservative. Nay more, they are reactionary, for they try to roll back the wheel of history. If by chance they are revolutionary, they are so only in view of their impending transfer into the proletariat, they thus defend not their present, but their future interests, they desert their own standpoint to place themselves as that of the proletariat.

The "dangerous class," the social scum, that passively rotting mass thrown off the lowest layers of old society, may, here and there, be swept into the movement by a proletarian revolution; its conditions of life, however, prepare it far more for the part of a bribed tool of reactionary intrigue.

[...]

Hitherto, every form of society has been based, as we have already seen, on the antagonism of oppressing and oppressed classes. But in order to oppress a class, certain conditions must be assured to it under which it can, at least, continue its slavish existence. The serf, in the period of serfdom, raised himself to membership in the commune, just as the petty bourgeois, under the yoke of feudal absolutism, managed to develop into the bourgeois. The modern labourer, on the contrary, instead of rising with the progress of industry, sinks deeper and deeper below the conditions of existence of his own class. He becomes a pauper, and pauperism develops more rapidly than population and wealth. And here it becomes evident, that the bourgeoisie is unfit any longer to be the ruling class in society, and to impose its conditions of existence upon society as an over-riding law. It is unfit to rule because it is incompetent to assure an existence to its slave within his slavery, because it cannot help letting him sink into such a state, that it has to feed him instead of being fed by him. Society can no longer live under this bourgeoisie, in other words, its existence is no longer compatible with society.

The essential condition for the existence, and for the sway of the bourgeois class, is the formation and augmentation of capital; the condition for capital is wage-labour. Wage-labour rests exclusively on competition between the labourers. The advance of industry, whose involuntary promoter is the bourgeoisie, replaces the isolation of the labourers, due to competition, by their revolutionary combination, due to association. The development of Modern Industry, therefore, cuts from under its feet the very foundation on which the bourgeoisie produces and appropriates products. What the bourgeoisie, therefore, produces, above all, is its own grave-diggers. Its fall and the victory of the proletariat are equally inevitable.

II. Proletarians and communists

In what relation do the Communists stand to the proletarians as a whole?

The Communists do not form a separate party opposed to other working-class parties.

They have no interests separate and apart from those of the proletariat as a whole.

They do not set up any sectarian principles of their own, by which to shape and mould the proletarian movement.

The Communists are distinguished from the other working-class parties by this only: (1) In the national struggles of the proletarians of the different countries, they point out and bring to the front the common interests of the entire proletariat, independently of all nationality. (2) In the various stages of development which the struggle of the working class against the bourgeoisie has to pass through, they always and everywhere represent the interests of the movement as a whole.

The Communists, therefore, are on the one hand, practically, the most advanced and resolute section of the working-class parties of every country, that section which pushes forward all others; on the other hand, theoretically, they have over the great mass of the proletariat the advantage of clearly understanding the line of march, the conditions, and the ultimate general results of the proletarian movement.

The immediate aim of the Communists is the same as that of all the other proletarian parties: formation of the proletariat into a class, overthrow of the bourgeois supremacy, conquest of political power by the proletariat.

The theoretical conclusions of the Communists are in no way based on ideas or principles that have been invented, or discovered, by this or that would-be universal reformer.

They merely express, in general terms, actual relations springing from an existing class struggle, from a historical movement going on under our very eyes. The abolition of existing property relations is not at all a distinctive feature of Communism.

[...]

Property, in its present form, is based on the antagonism of capital and wage-labour. Let us examine both sides of this antagonism.

To be a capitalist, is to have not only a purely personal, but a social *status* in production. Capital is a collective product and only by the united action of many members, nay, in the last resort, only by the united action of all members of society, can it be set in motion.

Capital is, therefore, not a personal, it is a social power.

When, therefore, capital is converted into common property, into the property of all members of society, personal property is not thereby transformed into social property. It is only the social character of the property that is changed. It loses its class-character.

Let us now take wage-labour.

The average price of wage-labour is the minimum wage. i.e., that quantum of the means of subsistence, which is absolutely requisite to keep the labourer in bare existence as a labourer. What, therefore, the wage-labourer appropriates by means of his labour, merely suffices to prolong and reproduce a bare existence. We by no means intend to abolish this personal appropriation of the products of labour, an appropriation that is made for the maintenance and reproduction of human life, and that leaves no surplus wherewith to command the labour of others. All that we want to do away with, is the miserable character of this appropriation, under which the labourer lives merely to increase capital, and is allowed to live only in so far as the interest of the ruling class requires it.

In bourgeois society, living labour is but a means to increase accumulated labour. In Communist society, accumulated labour is but a means to widen, to enrich, to promote the existence of the labourer.

[...]

Communism deprives no man of the power to appropriate the products of society; all that it does is to deprive him of the power to subjugate the labour of others by means of such appropriation.

It has been objected that upon the abolition of private property all work will cease, and universal laziness will overtake us.

According to this, bourgeois society ought long ago to have gone to the dogs through sheer idleness; for those of its members who work, acquire nothing, and those who acquire anything, do not work. The whole of this objection is but another expression of the tautology: that there can no longer be any wage-labour when there is no longer any capital.

All objections urged against the Communistic mode of producing and appropriating material products, have, in the same way, been urged against the Communistic modes of producing and appropriating intellectual products. Just as, to the bourgeois, the disappearance of class property is the disappearance of production itself, so the disappearance of class culture is to him identical with the disappearance of all culture.

That culture, the loss of which he laments, is, for the enormous majority, a mere training to act as a machine.

But don't wrangle with us so long as you apply, to our intended abolition of bourgeois property, the standard of your bourgeois notions of freedom, culture, law, etc. Your very ideas are but the outgrowth of the conditions of your bourgeois production and bourgeois property, just as your jurisprudence is but the will of your class made into a law for all, a will, whose essential character and direction are determined by the economical conditions of existence of your class.

The selfish misconception that induces you to transform into eternal laws of nature and of reason, the social forms springing from your present mode of production and form of property – historical relations that rise and disappear in the progress of production – this misconception you share with every ruling class that has preceded you. What you see clearly in the case of ancient property, what you admit in the case of feudal property, you are of course forbidden to admit in the case of your own bourgeois form of property.

Abolition of the family! Even the most radical flare up at this infamous proposal of the Communists.

On what foundation is the present family, the bourgeois family, based? On capital, on private gain. In its completely developed form this family exists only among the bourgeoisie. But this state of things finds its complement in the practical absence of the family among the proletarians, and in public prostitution.

The bourgeois family will vanish as a matter of course when its complement vanishes, and both will vanish with the vanishing of capital.

Do you charge us with wanting to stop the exploitation of children by their parents? To this crime we plead guilty.

But, you will say, we destroy the most hallowed of relations, when we replace home education by social.

And your education! Is not that also social, and determined by the social conditions under which you educate, by the intervention, direct or indirect, of society, by means of schools, etc.? The Communists have not invented the intervention of society in education; they do but seek to alter the character of that intervention, and to rescue education from the influence of the ruling class.

The bourgeois clap-trap about the family and education, about the hallowed co-relation of parent and child, becomes all the more disgusting, the more, by the action of Modern Industry, all family ties among the proletarians are torn asunder, and their children transformed into simple articles of commerce and instruments of labour.

But you Communists would introduce community of women, screams the whole bourgeoisie in chorus.

The bourgeois sees in his wife a mere instrument of production. He hears that the instruments of production are to be exploited in common, and, naturally, can come to no other conclusion than that the lot of being common to all will likewise fall to the women.

He has not even a suspicion that the real point aimed at is to do away with the status of women as mere instruments of production. [...]

The Communists are further reproached with desiring to abolish countries and nationality.

The working men have no country. We cannot take from them what they have not got. Since the proletariat must first of all acquire political supremacy, must rise to the leading class of the nation, must constitute itself *the* nation, it is, so far, itself national, though not in the bourgeois sense of the word.

National differences and antagonisms between peoples are daily more and more vanishing, owing to the development of the bourgeoisie, to freedom of commerce, to the world-market, to uniformity in the mode of production and in the conditions of life corresponding thereto.

[...]

The charges against Communism made from a religious, a philosophical, and, generally, from an ideological standpoint, are not deserving of serious examination.

Does it require deep intuition to comprehend that man's ideas, views and conceptions, in one word, man's consciousness, changes with every change in the conditions of his material existence, in his social relations and in his social life?

What else does the history of ideas prove, than that intellectual production changes its character in proportion as material production is changed? The ruling ideas of each age have ever been the ideas of its ruling class.

When people speak of ideas that revolutionise society, they do but express the fact, that within the old society, the elements of a new one have been created, and that the dissolution of the old ideas keeps even pace with the dissolution of the old conditions of existence.

When the ancient world was in its last throes, the ancient relations were overcome by Christianity. When Christian ideas succumbed in the eighteenth century to rationalist ideas, feudal society fought its death battle with the then revolutionary bourgeoisie. The ideas of religious liberty and freedom of conscience merely gave expression to the sway of free competition within the domain of knowledge.

"Undoubtedly," it will be said, "religious, moral, philosophical and juridical ideas have been modified in the course of historical development. But religion, morality, philosophy, political science, and law, constantly survived this change."

"There are, besides, eternal truths, such as Freedom, Justice, etc., that are common to all states of society. But Communism abolishes eternal truths, it abolishes all religion, and all morality, instead of constituting them on a new basis; it therefore acts in contradiction to all past historical experience."

What does this accusation reduce itself to? The history of all past society has consisted in the development of class antagonisms, antagonisms that assumed different forms at different epochs.

But whatever form they may have taken, one fact is common to all past ages, viz., the exploitation of one part of society by the other. No wonder, then, that the social consciousness of past ages, despite all the multiplicity and variety it displays, moves within certain common forms, or general ideas, which cannot completely vanish except with the total disappearance of class antagonisms.

The Communist revolution is the most radical rupture with traditional property relations; no wonder that its development involves the most radical rupture with traditional ideas.

But let us have done with the bourgeois objections to Communism.

We have seen above, that the first step in the revolution by the working class, is to raise the proletariat to the position of ruling class, to win the battle of democracy.

The proletariat will use its political supremacy to wrest, by degrees, all capital from the bourgeoisie, to centralise all instruments of production in the hands of the State, i.e., of the proletariat organised as the ruling class; and to increase the total of productive forces as rapidly as possible.

Of course, in the beginning, this cannot be effected except by means of despotic inroads on the rights of property, and on the conditions of bourgeois production; by means of measures, therefore, which appear economically insufficient and untenable, but which, in the course of the movement, outstrip themselves, necessitate further inroads upon the old social order, and are unavoidable as a means of entirely revolutionising the mode of production.

These measures will of course be different in different countries.

Nevertheless in the most advanced countries, the following will be pretty generally applicable.

1. Abolition of property in land and application of all rents of land to public purposes.
2. A heavy progressive or graduated income tax.
3. Abolition of all right of inheritance.
4. Confiscation of the property of all emigrants and rebels.
5. Centralisation of credit in the hands of the State, by means of a national bank with State capital and an exclusive monopoly.
6. Centralisation of the means of communication and transport in the hands of the State.
7. Extension of factories and instruments of production owned by the State; the bringing into cultivation of waste-lands, and the improvement of the soil generally in accordance with a common plan.
8. Equal liability of all to labour. Establishment of industrial armies, especially for agriculture.
9. Combination of agriculture with manufacturing industries; gradual abolition of the distinction between town and country, by a more equable distribution of the population over the country.
10. Free education for all children in public schools. Abolition of children's factory labour in its present form. Combination of education with industrial production, etc.

When, in the course of development, class distinctions have disappeared, and all production has been concentrated in the hands of a vast association of the whole nation, the public power will lose its political character. Political power, properly so called, is merely the organised power of one class for oppressing another. If the proletariat during its contest with the bourgeoisie is compelled, by the force of circumstances, to organise itself as a class, if, by means of a revolution, it makes itself the ruling class, and, as such, sweeps away by force the old conditions of production, then it will, along with these conditions, have swept away the conditions for the existence of class antagonisms and of classes generally, and will thereby have abolished its own supremacy as a class.

In place of the old bourgeois society, with its classes and class antagonisms, we shall have an association, in which the free development of each is the condition for the free development of all. ...

Emma Goldman, "Anarchism: What It Really Stands For"*

The history of human growth and development is at the same time the history of the terrible struggle of every new idea heralding the approach of a brighter dawn. In its tenacious hold on tradition, the Old has never hesitated to make use of the foulest and cruelest means to stay the advent of the New, in whatever form or period the latter may have asserted itself. Nor need we retrace our steps into the distant past to realize the enormity of opposition, difficulties, and hardships placed in the path of every progressive idea. The rack, the thumbscrew, and the knout are still with us; so are the convict's garb and the social wrath, all conspiring against the spirit that is serenely marching on.

Anarchism could not hope to escape the fate of all other ideas of innovation. Indeed, as the most revolutionary and uncompromising innovator, Anarchism must needs meet with the combined ignorance and venom of the world it aims to reconstruct.

To deal even remotely with all that is being said and done against Anarchism would necessitate the writing of a whole volume. I shall therefore meet only two of the principal objections. [...] First, Anarchism is impractical, though a beautiful ideal. Second, Anarchism stands for violence and destruction, hence it must be repudiated as vile and dangerous. Both the intelligent man and the ignorant mass judge not from a thorough knowledge of the subject, but either from hearsay or false interpretation.

[...]

Someone has said that it requires less mental effort to condemn than to think. The widespread mental indolence, so prevalent in society, proves this to be only too true. Rather than to go to the bottom of any given idea, to examine into its origin and meaning, most people will either condemn it altogether, or rely on some superficial or prejudicial definition of non-essentials.

Anarchism urges man to think, to investigate, to analyze every proposition; but that the brain capacity of the average reader be not taxed too much, I also shall begin with a definition, and then elaborate on the latter.

ANARCHISM: – The philosophy of a new social order based on liberty unrestricted by man-made law; the theory that all forms of government rest on violence, and are therefore wrong and harmful, as well as unnecessary.

The new social order rests, of course, on the materialistic basis of life; but while all Anarchists agree that the main evil today is an economic one, they maintain that the solution of that evil can be brought about only through the consideration of EVERY PHASE of life, – individual, as well as the collective; the internal, as well as the external phases.

A thorough perusal of the history of human development will disclose two elements in bitter conflict with each other; elements that are only now beginning to be understood, not as foreign to each other, but as closely related and truly harmonious, if only placed in proper environment: the individual and social instincts. The individual and society have waged a relentless and bloody battle for ages, each striving for supremacy, because each was blind to the value and importance of the other. The individual and social instincts, – the one a most potent factor for individual endeavor, for growth, aspiration, self-realization; the other an equally potent factor for mutual helpfulness and social well-being.

The explanation of the storm raging within the individual, and between him and his surroundings, is not far to seek. The primitive man, unable to understand his being, much less the unity of all life, felt himself absolutely dependent on blind, hidden forces ever ready to mock and taunt him. Out of that attitude grew the religious concepts of man as a mere speck of dust dependent on superior powers on high, who can only be appeased by complete surrender. All the early sagas rest on that idea, which continues to be the LEITMOTIF of the biblical tales dealing with the relation of man to God, to the State, to society. Again and again the same motif, MAN IS NOTHING, THE POWERS ARE EVERYTHING. Thus Jehovah would only endure man on condition of complete surrender. Man can have all the glories of the earth, but he must not become conscious of himself. The State, society, and moral laws all sing the same refrain: Man can have all the glories of the earth, but he must not become conscious of himself.

Anarchism is the only philosophy which brings to man the consciousness of himself; which maintains that God, the State, and society are non-existent, that their promises are null and void, since they can be fulfilled only through man's subordination. Anarchism is therefore the teacher of the unity of life; not merely in nature, but in man. There is no conflict between the individual

* Emma Goldman, extracted from *Anarchism and Other Essays*, available at: http://xroads.virginia.edu/~hyper/Goldman/anarchism.html, accessed April 14, 2008. Originally published 1911.

and the social instincts, any more than there is between the heart and the lungs: the one the receptacle of a precious life essence, the other the repository of the element that keeps the essence pure and strong. The individual is the heart of society, conserving the essence of social life; society is the lungs which are distributing the element to keep the life essence – that is, the individual – pure and strong.

"The one thing of value in the world," says Emerson, "is the active soul; this every man contains within him. The soul active sees absolute truth and utters truth and creates." In other words, the individual instinct is the thing of value in the world. It is the true soul that sees and creates the truth alive, out of which is to come a still greater truth, the re-born social soul. Anarchism is the great liberator of man from the phantoms that have held him captive; it is the arbiter and pacifier of the two forces for individual and social harmony. To accomplish that unity, Anarchism has declared war on the pernicious influences which have so far prevented the harmonious blending of individual and social instincts, the individual and society.

Religion, the dominion of the human mind; Property, the dominion of human needs; and Government, the dominion of human conduct, represent the stronghold of man's enslavement and all the horrors it entails. Religion! How it dominates man's mind, how it humiliates and degrades his soul. God is everything, man is nothing, says religion. But out of that nothing God has created a kingdom so despotic, so tyrannical, so cruel, so terribly exacting that naught but gloom and tears and blood have ruled the world since gods began.

Anarchism rouses man to rebellion against this black monster. Break your mental fetters, says Anarchism to man, for not until you think and judge for yourself will you get rid of the dominion of darkness, the greatest obstacle to all progress.

Property, the dominion of man's needs, the denial of the right to satisfy his needs. Time was when property claimed a divine right, when it came to man with the same refrain, even as religion, "Sacrifice! Abnegate! Submit!" The spirit of Anarchism has lifted man from his prostrate position. He now stands erect, with his face toward the light. He has learned to see the insatiable, devouring, devastating nature of property, and he is preparing to strike the monster dead.

"Property is robbery," said the great French Anarchist, Proudhon. Yes, but without risk and danger to the robber. Monopolizing the accumulated efforts of man, property has robbed him of his birthright, and has turned him loose a pauper and an outcast. Property has not even the time-worn excuse that man does not create enough to satisfy all needs. The A B C student of economics knows that the productivity of labor within the last few decades far exceeds normal demand a hundredfold. But what are normal demands to an abnormal institution? The only demand that property recognizes is its own gluttonous appetite for greater wealth, because wealth means power; the power to subdue, to crush, to exploit, the power to enslave, to outrage, to degrade. America is particularly boastful of her great power, her enormous national wealth. Poor America, of what avail is all her wealth, if the individuals comprising the nation are wretchedly poor? If they live in squalor, in filth, in crime, with hope and joy gone, a homeless, soilless army of human prey.

[…]

Real wealth consists in things of utility and beauty, in things that help to create strong, beautiful bodies and surroundings inspiring to live in. But if man is doomed to wind cotton around a spool, or dig coal, or build roads for thirty years of his life, there can be no talk of wealth. What he gives to the world is only gray and hideous things, reflecting a dull and hideous existence, – too weak to live, too cowardly to die. Strange to say, there are people who extol this deadening method of centralized production as the proudest achievement of our age. They fail utterly to realize that if we are to continue in machine subserviency, our slavery is more complete than was our bondage to the King. They do not want to know that centralization is not only the death-knell of liberty, but also of health and beauty, of art and science, all these being impossible in a clock-like, mechanical atmosphere.

Anarchism cannot but repudiate such a method of production: its goal is the freest possible expression of all the latent powers of the individual. Oscar Wilde defines a perfect personality as "one who develops under perfect conditions, who is not wounded, maimed, or in danger." A perfect personality, then, is only possible in a state of society where man is free to choose the mode of work, the conditions of work, and the freedom to work. One to whom the making of a table, the building of a house, or the tilling of the soil, is what the painting is to the artist and the discovery to the scientist, – the result of inspiration, of intense longing, and deep interest in work as a creative force. That being the ideal of Anarchism, its economic arrangements must consist of voluntary productive and distributive associations, gradually developing into free communism, as the best means of producing with the least waste of human energy. Anarchism, however, also recognizes the right of the individual, or numbers of individuals, to arrange at all times for other forms of work, in harmony with their tastes and desires.

Such free display of human energy being possible only under complete individual and social freedom, Anarchism directs its forces against the third and greatest foe of all social equality; namely, the State, organized authority, or statutory law, – the dominion of human conduct.

Just as religion has fettered the human mind, and as property, or the monopoly of things, has subdued and stifled man's needs, so has the State enslaved his spirit, dictating every phase of conduct. "All government in essence," says Emerson, "is tyranny." It matters not whether it is government by divine right or majority rule. In every instance its aim is the absolute subordination of the individual. Referring to the American government, the greatest American Anarchist, David Thoreau, said: "Government, what is it but a tradition, though a recent one, endeavoring to transmit itself unimpaired to posterity, but each instance losing its integrity; it has not the vitality and force of a single living man. Law never made man a whit more just; and by means of their respect for it, even the well disposed are daily made agents of injustice." Indeed, the keynote of government is injustice. With the arrogance and self-sufficiency of the King who could do no wrong, governments ordain, judge, condemn, and punish the most insignificant offenses, while maintaining themselves by the greatest of all offenses, the annihilation of individual liberty.

[...]

Unfortunately there are still a number of people who continue in the fatal belief that government rests on natural laws, that it maintains social order and harmony, that it diminishes crime, and that it prevents the lazy man from fleecing his fellows. I shall therefore examine these contentions. A natural law is that factor in man which asserts itself freely and spontaneously without any external force, in harmony with the requirements of nature. For instance, the demand for nutrition, for sex gratification, for light, air, and exercise, is a natural law. But its expression needs not the machinery of government, needs not the club, the gun, the handcuff, or the prison. To obey such laws, if we may call it obedience, requires only spontaneity and free opportunity. That governments do not maintain themselves through such harmonious factors is proven by the terrible array of violence, force, and coercion all governments use in order to live. Thus Blackstone is right when he says, "Human laws are invalid, because they are contrary to the laws of nature."

Unless it be the order of Warsaw after the slaughter of thousands of people, it is difficult to ascribe to governments any capacity for order or social harmony. Order derived through submission and maintained by terror is not much of a safe guaranty; yet that is the only "order" that governments have ever maintained. True social harmony grows naturally out of solidarity of interests. In a society where those who always work never have anything, while those who never work enjoy everything, solidarity of interests is non-existent; hence social harmony is but a myth. The only way organized authority meets this grave situation is by extending still greater privileges to those who have already monopolized the earth, and by still further enslaving the disinherited masses. Thus the entire arsenal of government – laws, police, soldiers, the courts, legislatures, prisons, – is strenuously engaged in "harmonizing" the most antagonistic elements in society.

The most absurd apology for authority and law is that they serve to diminish crime. Aside from the fact that the State is itself the greatest criminal, breaking every written and natural law, stealing in the form of taxes, killing in the form of war and capital punishment, it has come to an absolute standstill in coping with crime. It has failed utterly to destroy or even minimize the horrible scourge of its own creation.

Crime is naught but misdirected energy. So long as every institution of today, economic, political, social, and moral, conspires to misdirect human energy into wrong channels; so long as most people are out of place doing the things they hate to do, living a life they loathe to live, crime will be inevitable, and all the laws on the statutes can only increase, but never do away with, crime. What does society, as it exists today, know of the process of despair, the poverty, the horrors, the fearful struggle the human soul must pass on its way to crime and degradation. Who that knows this terrible process can fail to see the truth in these words of Peter Kropotkin: "Those who will hold the balance between the benefits thus attributed to law and punishment and the degrading effect of the latter on humanity; those who will estimate the torrent of depravity poured abroad in human society by the informer, favored by the Judge even, and paid for in clinking cash by governments, under the pretext of aiding to unmask crime; those who will go within prison walls and there see what human beings become when deprived of liberty, when subjected to the care of brutal keepers, to coarse, cruel words, to a thousand stinging, piercing humiliations, will agree with us that the entire apparatus of prison and punishment is an abomination which ought to be brought to an end."

[...] Anarchism aims to strip labor of its deadening, dulling aspect, of its gloom and compulsion. It aims to make work an instrument of joy, of strength, of color, of real harmony, so that the poorest sort of a man should find in work both recreation and hope.

To achieve such an arrangement of life, government, with its unjust, arbitrary, repressive measures, must be done away with. At best it has but imposed one single mode of life upon all, without regard to individual and social variations and needs. In destroying government and statutory laws, Anarchism proposes to rescue the self-respect and independence of the individual from all restraint and invasion by authority. Only in freedom can man grow to his full stature. Only in freedom will he learn to think and move, and give the very best in him. Only in freedom will he realize the true force of the social bonds which knit men together, and which are the true foundation of a normal social life.

But what about human nature? Can it be changed? And if not, will it endure under Anarchism?

Poor human nature, what horrible crimes have been committed in thy name! Every fool, from king to policeman, from the flatheaded parson to the visionless dabbler in science, presumes to speak authoritatively of human nature. The greater the mental charlatan, the more definite his insistence on the wickedness and weaknesses of human nature. Yet, how can any one speak of it today, with every soul in a prison, with every heart fettered, wounded, and maimed? John Burroughs has stated that experimental study of animals in captivity is absolutely useless. Their character, their habits, their appetites undergo a complete transformation when torn from their soil in field and forest. With human nature caged in a narrow space, whipped daily into submission, how can we speak of its potentialities?

Freedom, expansion, opportunity, and, above all, peace and repose, alone can teach us the real dominant factors of human nature and all its wonderful possibilities.

Anarchism, then, really stands for the liberation of the human mind from the dominion of religion; the liberation of the human body from the dominion of property; liberation from the shackles and restraint of government. Anarchism stands for a social order based on the free grouping of individuals for the purpose of producing real social wealth; an order that will guarantee to every human being free access to the earth and full enjoyment of the necessities of life, according to individual desires, tastes, and inclinations.

[...]

As to methods. Anarchism is not, as some may suppose, a theory of the future to be realized through divine inspiration. It is a living force in the affairs of our life, constantly creating new conditions. The methods of Anarchism therefore do not comprise an iron-clad program to be carried out under all circumstances. Methods must grow out of the economic needs of each place and clime, and of the intellectual and temperamental requirements of the individual. The serene, calm character of a Tolstoy will wish different methods for social reconstruction than the intense, overflowing personality of a Michael Bakunin or a Peter Kropotkin. Equally so it must be apparent that the economic and political needs of Russia will dictate more drastic measures than would England or America. Anarchism does not stand for military drill and uniformity; it does, however, stand for the spirit of revolt, in whatever form, against everything that hinders human growth. All Anarchists agree in that, as they also agree in their opposition to the political machinery as a means of bringing about the great social change.

Chapter 3

Twentieth-Century Ideologies

Introduction

The twentieth century witnessed epic struggles between totalitarian ideologies (communism, fascism, and Nazism) and the various "friends of pluralism" (especially liberals, conservatives, and democratic socialists). After their defeat at the end of World War II, fascism and Nazism lost most of their appeal, and today most thoughtful people regard these ideologies as discredited abominations. When much of Eastern Europe began to escape domination by the Soviet Union at the end of the 1980s, and when the Soviet Union itself collapsed in 1991, communism also lost much appeal. Even countries like China and Cuba that supposedly remain committed to communism seem to depart from its principles in practice.

Pluralist ideologies have not been unscathed by the turbulent events of the past century. Though democratic socialist parties were prominent in post-World War II Western Europe, their governing power has diminished in such countries as France, Germany, and Italy. And those countries still governed by parties nominally committed to democratic socialism (such as Great Britain under the Labour Party) have moved away from such socialist principles as the nationalization of industry and the provision of extensive welfare rights. As socialism has moved to the right and as liberalism has moved to the left, the differences between these two ideologies have become increasingly difficult to detect. Many political theorists now look to such new perspectives as feminism, deep ecologism, radical democracy, civic communitarianism, and egalitarian liberalism for current ideas about how to approach the goals of the radical left (such as more social and economic equality and stronger communal bonds) that had previously been the province of democratic socialists. Some of these perspectives will be introduced in the next chapter.

Contemporary liberalism has certainly moved to the left, at least compared with classical liberal principles. It endorses a much stronger state than its precursor. While it still defends capitalism, it no longer embraces "laissez-faire" principles and is now much more comfortable with regulating the economy on behalf of various social and environmental goals and with redistributing economic resources through various welfare policies. Such shifts in liberal ideas initially strengthened its appeal, at least in the United States during the middle of the twentieth century. However, under conservative assault for its "tax-and-spend policies," its unwillingness to regulate morality, and other such matters, liberal principles lost much appeal, at least until the elections of 2006 enabled the American Democratic Party to control The House of Representatives and the elections of 2008 propelled Barack Obama into the presidency.

Meanwhile, contemporary conservatives have moved away from the outlook of traditional conservatives. Rather than upholding the interests of the upper classes of the past, they now address various contemporary concerns of many ordinary citizens. They seek to stimulate the economic growth that will employ workers and enable both Wall Street corporations and main-street businesses to prosper, to reduce tax burdens by cutting governmental programs, to address the moral concerns of a public dismayed by the lax moral standards resulting from years of liberal neglect, and to ensure that pluralist societies have the military strength to defend themselves from their enemies. But certain seeming contradictions within contemporary conservatism, such as cutting taxes and resources available to government while trying to finance military operations in the Middle East, have recently diminished its appeal.

V. I. Lenin (1870–1924) was a Russian lawyer and revolutionary who was highly influential in transforming Marxism, from a theory about how capitalism would be overthrown and replaced by socialism in such developed Western societies as Great Britain and the United States, into a theoretical foundation for communism as an ideology that justified revolution in nascent capitalist societies like Russia in the early twentieth century and that provided guidance for how victorious Communist Party leaders would govern after their successful revolutions. In his "State and Revolution," written upon his return to Russia from exile in 1917, Lenin stressed the need for a "transition from capitalism to communism" led by "the dictatorship of the proletariat," which Lenin defined as "the organization of the vanguard of the oppressed as a ruling class for the purpose of suppressing the oppressors" in ways that modified Marx's apparent view that the dictatorship over the bourgeoisie would be by the proletariat as a whole and not by a mere vanguard. Here Lenin also stressed that while capitalist exploitation would cease during this transition, there would necessarily continue to be inequalities in the distribution of economic goods corresponding to inequalities in labor. He implied that a strong state would be necessary during the transition in order to collectivize ownership of productive property, to control economic activity, to distribute income according to labor, and to eliminate bourgeois resistance to this regime. He held out the promise that the state would "wither away" after a successful transition, but provided little indication of when that day might arrive.

In Italy, Benito Mussolini (1883–1945) became attracted to many of Lenin's ideas, especially the need for leadership to act on behalf of ordinary citizens, but he eventually supported fascist principles and became leader of the Fascist Party that formed an Italian government in 1922 and ruled until Italy's defeat in World War II appeared imminent. While Mussolini authored many volumes defining and defending fascism, it is now thought that Giovanni Gentile "ghostwrote" some of his most important works. Gentile (1875–1944) was a neo-Hegelian philosopher who held various academic posts and became Mussolini's Minister of Public Education. In "The Philosophic Basis of Fascism," Gentile developed several fascist themes: that an elite few always express the will of a nation and an epoch; that the personality and consciousness of all individuals within a nation must be "reconciled" with the goals of the state; that state law must "embrace the whole life of the people" and thus be "totalitarian" in its control over subjects; that nationalism (in this case Italian spiritualism and greatness) must be emphasized; and that the authority of the state must be absolute. Similar themes were included within Nazi ideology in Germany under Adolf Hitler (1889–1945), but Nazism also incorporated racist themes that make it more discredited today than fascism.

The need to defend pluralist societies from fascism, Nazism, and communism contributed to the need of liberal regimes – especially that of Franklin Delano Roosevelt (1882–1945) in the US – to expand their power. While conservatives stress that FDR's New Deal, initiated in 1933 to lift the country out of its Great Depression, began an unfortunate transformation in liberalism, there is little question that most of the initial growth in the liberal state was on behalf of military purposes – initially to win World War II and then to contain communist expansion. But throughout the twentieth century, liberalism evolved. Especially during the 1960s and 1970s, it endorsed regulating the economy, expanding the welfare state, and satisfying the demands of increasingly assertive portions of the population that had previously been marginalized (such as racial minorities and women). When voters turned toward more conservative leaders and policies, a new generation of liberals (like Bill and Hillary Clinton) began articulating more moderate principles (such as "ending welfare as we know it"). Now Barack Obama appears to have an opportunity to define a liberalism for the twenty-first century. In doing so, he will likely be influenced by such liberal academics as Paul Starr, a Professor of Sociology and Pubic Affairs at Princeton University and a co-editor of the influential liberal monthly, *The American Prospect*. In the article below, Starr discusses key themes for a resurgent liberalism: pragmatism; egalitarianism; extensive individual freedom, initiative, and development; a state with sufficient (although constitutionally limited) power to provide security, enhance opportunity, and promote economic productivity; a commitment to a wide democratic partnership involving cooperation among the many (often marginalized) interests in a pluralist society.

Contemporary conservatism grew as a protest ideology, opposing liberalism's expanding agenda after World War II. Three major criticisms of liberalism have been stressed, enhancing support for the conservative movement. First, conservatives have accused liberals of failed attempts at "social engineering" – of promising to end poverty, racial differences in well-being, environmental deterioration, and so forth even though these problems have no clear or costless solutions. Thus, they claim liberal programs inevitably lead to disappointments and even despair. Second, conservatives have accused liberals of misguided permissiveness, of having a philosophy of value-relativism that refuses to distinguish between moral and sinful lifestyles, and thus has opened the door to abortion on demand, deteriorating family ties and easy divorce, the abuse of drugs and alcohol, a slackening work ethic, and increases in crime. Third, conservatives have accused liberals of putting provision of a wide array of domestic amenities and social spending ahead of a strong military that was initially needed to secure the US and its allies from communism and now is necessary to fight terrorism. But conservatives have had much greater success defining the faults of their ideological opponents than agreeing on a set of principles by which they could govern. (Many liberals accused the administration of George W. Bush of precisely this problem: absent clear principles, it engaged mainly in "pure power politics" with no clear agenda other than its own preservation and enhancement of power.) It is in this light that the final reading of this chapter by John Kekes, professor emeritus in the Department of Philosophy at SUNY–Albany, is compelling, as he attempts to make a positive *Case for Conservatism*. He argues that conservatives have four basic beliefs: skepticism, pluralism, traditionalism, and pessimism. By defining and locating these beliefs as intermediate between extreme alternatives, he articulates a conservatism that is more moderate than the more radical brand of conservatism that others have found in the philosophy of the Bush administration and the current conservative Republicans in Congress who seek to obstruct Obama's liberal agenda.

Vladimir I. Lenin, "State and Revolution"*

The whole theory of Marx is the application of the theory of development – in its most consistent, complete, considered and pithy form – to modern capitalism. Naturally, Marx was faced with the problem of applying this theory both to the *forthcoming* collapse of capitalism and to the *future* development of *future* communism.

On the basis of what *facts*, then, can the question of the future development of future communism be dealt with?

On the basis of the fact that it *has its origin* in capitalism, that it develops historically from capitalism, that it is the result of the action of a social force to which capitalism *gave birth*. There is no trace of an attempt on Marx's part to make up a utopia, to indulge in idle guess-work about what cannot be known. Marx treated the question of communism in the same way as a naturalist would treat the question of the development of, say, a new biological variety, once he knew that it had originated in such and such a way and was changing in such and such a definite direction.

[...]

The first fact that has been established most accurately by the whole theory of development, by science as a whole – a fact that was ignored by the utopians, and is ignored by the present-day opportunists, who are afraid of the socialist revolution – is that, historically, there must undoubtedly be a special stage, or a special phase, of *transition* from capitalism to communism.

2. The transition from capitalism to communism

Marx continued [in *Critique of the Gotha Programme*]: "Between capitalist and communist society lies the period of the revolutionary transformation of the one into the other. Corresponding to this is also a political transition period in which the state can be nothing but *the revolutionary dictatorship of the proletariat.*" Marx bases this conclusion on an analysis of the role played by the proletariat in modern capitalist society, on the data concerning the development of this society, and on the irreconcilability of the antagonistic interests of the proletariat and the bourgeoisie.

Previously the question was put as follows: to achieve its emancipation, the proletariat must overthrow the bourgeoisie, win political power and establish its revolutionary dictatorship.

Now the question is put somewhat differently: the transition from capitalist society – which is developing towards communism – to communist society is impossible without a "political transition period," and the state in this period can only be the revolutionary dictatorship of the proletariat.

* Vladimir I. Lenin, extracted from *The Lenin Anthology*, edited by Robert C. Tucker (New York: W. W. Norton & Co., 1975), pp. 319–35. Originally published 1917.

What, then, is the relation of this dictatorship to democracy?

We have seen that the *Communist Manifesto* simply places side by side the two concepts: "to raise the proletariat to the position of the ruling class" and "to win the battle of democracy." On the basis of all that has been said above, it is possible to determine more precisely how democracy changes in the transition from capitalism to communism.

In capitalist society, providing it develops under the most favourable conditions, we have a more or less complete democracy in the democratic republic. But this democracy is always hemmed in by the narrow limits set by capitalist exploitation, and consequently always remains, in effect, a democracy for the minority, only for the propertied classes, only for the rich. Freedom in capitalist society always remains about the same as it was in the ancient Greek republics: freedom for the slave-owners. Owing to the conditions of capitalist exploitation, the modern wage slaves are so crushed by want and poverty that "they cannot be bothered with democracy," "cannot be bothered with politics"; in the ordinary, peaceful course of events, the majority of the population is debarred from participation in public and political life.

The correctness of this statement is perhaps most clearly confirmed by Germany, because constitutional legality steadily endured there for a remarkably long time – nearly half a century (1871–1914) – and during this period the Social-Democrats were able to achieve far more than in other countries in the way of "utilising legality," and organised a larger proportion of the workers into a political party than anywhere else in the world.

What is this largest proportion of politically conscious and active wage slaves that has so far been recorded in capitalist society? One million members of the Social-Democratic Party – out of fifteen million wage-workers! Three million organised in trade unions – out of fifteen million!

Democracy for an insignificant minority, democracy for the rich – that is the democracy of capitalist society. If we look more closely into the machinery of capitalist democracy, we see everywhere, in the "petty" – supposedly petty – details of the suffrage (residential qualification, exclusion of women, etc.), in the technique of the representative institutions, in the actual obstacles to the right of assembly (public buildings are not for "paupers"!), in the purely capitalist organisation of the daily press, etc., etc. – we see restriction after restriction upon democracy. These restrictions, exceptions, exclusions, obstacles for the poor seem slight, especially in the eyes of one who has never known want himself and has never been in close contact with the oppressed classes in their mass life (and nine out of ten, if not ninety-nine out of a hundred, bourgeois publicists and politicians come under this category); but in their sum total these restrictions exclude and squeeze out the poor from politics, from active participation in democracy.

Marx grasped this *essence* of capitalist democracy splendidly when, in analysing the experience of the Commune, he said that the oppressed are allowed once every few years to decide which particular representatives of the oppressing class shall represent and repress them in parliament!

But from this capitalist democracy – that is inevitably narrow and stealthily pushes aside the poor, and is therefore hypocritical and false through and through – forward development does not proceed simply, directly and smoothly, towards "greater and greater democracy," as the liberal professors and petty-bourgeois opportunists would have us believe. No, forward development, i.e., development towards communism, proceeds through the dictatorship of the proletariat, and cannot do otherwise, for the *resistance* of the capitalist exploiters cannot be *broken* by anyone else or in any other way.

And the dictatorship of the proletariat, i.e., the organisation of the vanguard of the oppressed as the ruling class for the purpose of suppressing the oppressors, cannot result merely in an expansion of democracy. *Simultaneously* with an immense expansion of democracy, which *for the first time* becomes democracy for the poor, democracy for the people, and not democracy for the money-bags, the dictatorship of the proletariat imposes a series of restrictions on the freedom of the oppressors, the exploiters, the capitalists. We must suppress them in order to free humanity from wage slavery, their resistance must be crushed by force; it is clear that there is no freedom and no democracy where there is suppression and where there is violence.

Engels expressed this splendidly in his letter to Bebel when he said, as the reader will remember, that "the proletariat needs the state, not in the interests of freedom but in order to hold down its adversaries, and as soon as it becomes possible to speak of freedom the state as such ceases to exist."

Democracy for the vast majority of the people, and suppression by force, i.e., exclusion from democracy, of the exploiters and oppressors of the people – this is the change democracy undergoes during the *transition* from capitalism to communism.

Only in communist society, when the resistance of the capitalists has been completely crushed, when the capitalists have disappeared, when there are no classes (i.e., when there is no distinction between the members of society as regards their relation to the social means of production), *only* then "the state ... ceases to exist," and *"it becomes possible to speak of freedom."* Only then will a truly complete democracy become possible and be realised, a democracy without any exceptions whatever. And only then will democracy begin to *wither away*, owing to the simple fact that, freed from capitalist slavery, from the untold horrors, savagery, absurdities and infamies of capitalist exploitation, people will gradually *become accustomed* to observing the elementary rules of social intercourse that have been known for centuries and repeated for thousands of years in all copy-book maxims. They will become accustomed to observing them without force, without coercion, without subordination, *without the special apparatus* for coercion called the state.

The expression "the state *withers away*" is very well chosen, for it indicates both the gradual and the spontaneous nature of the process. Only habit can, and undoubtedly will, have such an effect; for we see around us on millions of occasions how readily people become accustomed to observing the necessary rules of social intercourse when there is no exploitation, when there is nothing that arouses indignation, evokes protest and revolts, and creates the need for *suppression*.

And so in capitalist society we have a democracy that is curtailed, wretched, false, a democracy only for the rich, for the minority. The dictatorship of the proletariat, the period of transition to communism, will for the first time create democracy for the people, for the majority, along with the necessary suppression of the exploiters, of the minority. Communism alone is capable of providing really complete democracy, and the more complete it is, the sooner it will become unnecessary and wither away of its own accord.

In other words, under capitalism we have the state in the proper sense of the word, that is, a special machine for the suppression of one class by another, and, what is more, of the majority by the minority. Naturally, to be successful, such an undertaking as the systematic suppression of the exploited majority by the exploiting minority calls for the utmost ferocity and savagery in the matter of suppressing, it calls for seas of blood, through which mankind is actually wading its way in slavery, serfdom and wage labour.

Furthermore, during the *transition* from capitalism to communism suppression is *still* necessary, but it is now the suppression of the exploiting minority by the exploited majority. A special apparatus, a special machine for suppression, the "state," is *still* necessary, but this is now a transitional state. It is no longer a state in the proper sense of the word; for the suppression of the minority of exploiters by the majority of the wage slaves of *yesterday* is comparatively so easy, simple and natural a task that it will entail far less bloodshed than the suppression of the risings of slaves, serfs or wage-labourers, and it will cost mankind far less. And it is compatible with the extension of democracy to such an overwhelming majority of the population that the need for a *special machine* of suppression will begin to disappear. Naturally, the exploiters are unable to suppress the people without a highly complex machine for performing this task, but *the people* can suppress the exploiters even with a very simple "machine," almost without a "machine," without a special apparatus, by the simple *organisation of the armed people* (such as the Soviets of Workers' and Soldiers' Deputies, we would remark, running ahead).

Lastly, only communism makes the state absolutely unnecessary, for there is *nobody* to be suppressed – "nobody" in the sense of a *class*, of a systematic struggle against a definite section of the population. We are not utopians, and do not in the least deny the possibility and inevitability of excesses on the part of *individual persons*, or the need to stop *such* excesses. In the first place, however, no special machine, no special apparatus of suppression, is needed for this; this will be done by the armed people themselves, as simply and as readily as any crowd of civilised people, even in modern society, interferes to put a stop to a scuffle or to prevent a woman from being assaulted. And, secondly, we know that the fundamental social cause of excesses, which consist in the violation of the rules of social intercourse, is the exploitation of the people, their want and their poverty. With the removal of this chief cause, excesses will inevitably begin to *"wither away."* We do not know how quickly and in what succession, but we do know they will wither away. With their withering away the state will also *wither away*.

Without building utopias, Marx defined more fully what can be defined *now* regarding this future, namely, the difference between the lower and higher places (levels, stages) of communist society.

3. The first phase of communist society

In the *Critique of the Gotha Programme*, Marx goes into detail to disprove Lassalle's idea that under socialism the worker will receive the "undiminished" or "full product of his labour." Marx shows that from the whole of the social labour of society there must be deducted a reserve fund, a fund for the expansion of production, a fund for the replacement of the "wear and tear" of machinery, and so on. Then, from the means of consumption must be deducted a fund for administrative expenses, for schools, hospitals, old people's homes, and so on.

Instead of Lassalle's hazy, obscure, general phrase ("the full product of his labour to the worker"), Marx makes a sober estimate of exactly how socialist society will have to manage its affairs. Marx proceeds to make a *concrete* analysis of the conditions of life of a society in which there will be no capitalism, and says: "What we have to deal with here [in analysing the programme of the workers' party] is a communist society, not as it has *developed* on its own foundations, but, on the contrary, just as it *emerges* from capitalist society; which is, therefore, in every respect, economically, morally and intellectually, still stamped with the birthmarks of the old society from whose womb it comes." It is this communist society, which has just emerged into the light of day out of the womb of capitalism and which is in every respect stamped with the birthmarks of the old society, that Marx terms the "first," or lower, phase of communist society.

The means of production are no longer the private property of individuals. The means of production belong to the whole of society. Every member of society, performing a certain part of the socially necessary work, receives a certificate from society to the effect that he has done a certain amount of work. And with this certificate he receives from the public store of consumer goods a corresponding quantity of products. After a deduction is made of the amount of labour which goes to the public fund, every worker, therefore, receives from society as much as he has given to it.

"Equality" apparently reigns supreme.

But when Lassalle, having in view such a social order (usually called socialism, but termed by Marx the first phase of communism), says that this is "equitable distribution," that this is "the equal right of all to an equal product of labour," Lassalle is mistaken and Marx exposes the mistake.

"Equal right," says Marx, we certainly do have here; but it is still a "bourgeois right," which, like every right, *implies inequality*. Every right is an application of an *equal* measure to *different* people who in fact are not alike, are not equal to one another. That is why "equal right" is a violation of equality and an injustice. In fact, everyone, having performed as much social labour as another, receives an equal share of the social product (after the above-mentioned deductions).

But people are not alike: one is strong, another is weak; one is married, another is not; one has more children, another has less, and so on. And the conclusion Marx draws is: "With an equal performance of labour, and hence an equal share in the social consumption fund, one will in fact receive more than another, one will be richer than another, and so on. To avoid all these defects, right would have to be unequal rather than equal."[1]

The first phase of communism, therefore, cannot yet provide justice and equality: differences, and unjust differences, in wealth will still persist, but the *exploitation* of man by man will have become impossible because it will be impossible to seize the *means of production* – the factories, machines, land, etc. – and make them private property.

[...]

Marx not only most scrupulously takes account of the inevitable inequality of men, but he also takes into account the fact that the mere conversion of the means of production into the common property of the whole of society (commonly called "socialism") *does not remove* the defects of distribution and the inequality of "bourgeois right," which *continues to prevail* so long as products are divided "according to the amount of labour performed." Continuing, Marx says: "But these defects are inevitable in the first phase of communist society as it is when it has just emerged, after prolonged birth pangs, from capitalist society. Right can never be higher than the economic structure of society and its cultural development conditioned thereby." And so, in the first phase of communist society (usually called socialism) "bourgeois right" is *not* abolished in its entirety, but only in part, only in proportion to the economic revolution so far attained, i.e., only in respect of the means of production. "Bourgeois right" recognises them as the private property of individuals. Socialism converts them into *common* property. *To that extent* – and to that extent alone – "bourgeois right" disappears.

However, it persists as far as its other part is concerned; it persists in the capacity of regulator (determining factor) in the distribution of products and the allotment of labour among the members of society. The socialist principle, "He who does not work shall not eat," is *already* realised; the other socialist principle, "An equal amount of products for an equal amount of labour," is also *already* realised. But this is not yet communism, and it does not yet abolish "bourgeois right," which gives unequal individuals, in return for unequal (really unequal) amounts of labour, equal amounts of products.

[1] All citations in this section are from Marx's *Critique of the Gotha Program*. [*R. T.*]

This is a "defect," says Marx, but it is unavoidable in the first phase of communism; for if we are not to indulge in utopianism, we must not think that having overthrown capitalism people will at once learn to work for society *without any standard of right*. Besides, the abolition of capitalism *does not immediately create* the economic prerequisites for *such* a change.

Now, there is no other standard than that of "bourgeois right." To this extent, therefore, there still remains the need for a state, which, while safeguarding the common ownership of the means of production, would safeguard equality in labour and in the distribution of products.

The state withers away insofar as there are no longer any capitalists, any classes, and, consequently, no *class* can be *suppressed*.

But the state has not yet completely withered away, since there still remains the safeguarding of "bourgeois right," which sanctifies actual inequality. For the state to wither away completely, complete communism is necessary.

4. The higher phase of communist society

Marx continues:

> In a higher phase of communist society, after the enslaving subordination of the individual to the division of labour and with it also the antithesis between mental and physical labour has vanished, after labour has become not only a livelihood but life's prime want, after the productive forces have increased with the all-round development of the individual, and all the springs of co-operative wealth flow more abundantly – only then can the narrow horizon of bourgeois right be crossed in its entirety and society inscribe on its banners: From each according to his ability, to each according to his needs!

Only now can we fully appreciate the correctness of Engels's remarks mercilessly ridiculing the absurdity of combining the words "freedom" and "state." So long as the state exists there is no freedom. When there is freedom, there will be no state.

The economic basis for the complete withering away of the state is such a high stage of development of communism at which the antithesis between mental and physical labour disappears, at which there consequently disappears one of the principal sources of modern *social* inequality – a source, moreover, which cannot on any account be removed immediately by the mere conversion of the means of production into public property, by the mere expropriation of the capitalists.

This expropriation will make it *possible* for the productive forces to develop to a tremendous extent. And when we see how incredibly capitalism is already *retarding* this development, when we see how much progress could be achieved on the basis of the level of technique already attained, we are entitled to say with the fullest confidence that the expropriation of the capitalists will inevitably result in an enormous development of the productive forces of human society. But how rapidly this development will proceed, how soon it will reach the point of breaking away from the division of labour, of doing away with the antithesis between mental and physical labour, of transforming labour into "life's prime want" – we do not and *cannot* know.

That is why we are entitled to speak only of the inevitable withering away of the state, emphasising the protracted nature of this process and its dependence upon the rapidity of development of the *higher phase* of communism, and leaving the question of the time required for, or the concrete forms of, the withering away quite open, because there is *no* material for answering these questions.

The state will be able to wither away completely when society adopts the rule: "From each according to his ability, to each according to his needs," i.e., when people have become so accustomed to observing the fundamental rules of social intercourse and when their labour has become so productive that they will voluntarily work *according to their ability*. "The narrow horizon of bourgeois right," which compels one to calculate with the heartlessness of a Shylock whether one has not worked half an hour more than somebody else, whether one is not getting less pay than somebody else – this narrow horizon will then be crossed. There will then be no need for society, in distributing products, to regulate the quantity to be received by each; each will take freely "according to his needs."

From the bourgeois point of view, it is easy to declare that such a social order is "sheer utopia" and to sneer at the socialists for promising everyone the right to receive from society, without any control over the labour of the individual citizen, any quantity of truffles, cars, pianos, etc. Even to this day, most bourgeois "savants" confine themselves to sneering in this way, thereby betraying both their ignorance and their selfish defence of capitalism.

Ignorance – for it has never entered the head of any socialist to "promise" that the higher phase of the development of communism will arrive; as for the great socialists' *forecast* that it will arrive, it presupposes not the present productivity of labour and *not the present* ordinary run of people, who, like the seminary students in Pomyalovsky's stories, are capable of damaging the stocks of public wealth "just for fun," and of demanding the impossible.

Until the "higher" phase of communism arrives, the socialists demand the *strictest* control by society *and by the state* over the measure of labour and the measure of consumption; but this control must *start* with the expropriation of the capitalists, with the establishment of workers' control over the capitalists, and must be exercised not by a state of bureaucrats, but by a state of *armed workers.*

Giovanni Gentile, "The Philosophic Basis of Fascism"*

In the definition of Fascism, the first point to grasp is the comprehensive, or as Fascists say, the "totalitarian" scope of its doctrine, which concerns itself not only with political organization and political tendency, but with the whole will and thought and feeling of the nation.

There is a second and equally important point. Fascism is not a philosophy. Much less is it a religion. It is not even a political theory which may be stated in a series of formulae. The significance of Fascism is not to be grasped in the special theses which it from time to time assumes. When on occasion it has announced a program, a goal, a concept to be realized in action, Fascism has not hesitated to abandon them when in practice these were found to be inadequate or inconsistent with the principle of Fascism. Fascism has never been willing to compromise its future. Mussolini has boasted that he is a *tempista*, that his real pride is in "good timing." He makes decisions and acts on them at the precise moment when all the conditions and considerations which make them feasible and opportune are properly matured. This is a way of saying that Fascism returns to the most rigorous meaning of Mazzini's "Thought and Action," whereby the two terms are so perfectly coincident that no thought has value which is not already expressed in action. The real "views" of the *Duce* are those which he formulates and executes at one and the same time.

Is Fascism therefore "anti-intellectual," as has been so often charged? It is eminently anti-intellectual, eminently Mazzinian, that is, if by intellectualism we mean the divorce of thought from action, of knowledge from life, of brain from heart, of theory from practice. Fascism is hostile to all Utopian systems which are destined never to face the test of reality. It is hostile to all science and all philosophy which remain matters of mere fancy or intelligence. It is not that Fascism denies value to culture, to the higher intellectual pursuits by which thought is invigorated as a source of action. Fascist anti-intellectualism holds in scorn a product peculiarly typical of the educated classes in Italy: the *leterato* – the man who plays with knowledge and with thought without any sense of responsibility for the practical world. It is hostile not so much to culture as to bad culture, the culture which does not educate, which does not make men, but rather creates pedants and aesthetes, egotists in a word, men morally and politically indifferent. It has no use, for instance, for the man who is "above the conflict" when his country or its important interests are at stake.

By virtue of its repugnance for "intellectualism," Fascism prefers not to waste time constructing abstract theories about itself. But when we say that it is not a system or a doctrine we must not conclude that it is a blind praxis or a purely instinctive method. If by system or philosophy we mean a living thought, a principle of universal character daily revealing its inner fertility and significance, then Fascism is a perfect system, with a solidly established foundation and with a rigorous logic in its development; and all who feel the truth and the vitality of the principle work day by day for its development, now doing, now undoing, now going forward, now retracing their steps, according as the things they do prove to be in harmony with the principle or to deviate from it.

And we come finally to a third point.

The Fascist system is not a political system, but it has its center of gravity in politics. Fascism came into being to meet serious problems of politics in post-war Italy. And it presents itself as a political method. But in confronting and solving political problems it is carried by its very nature, that is to say by its method, to consider moral, religious, and philosophical questions and to unfold and demonstrate the comprehensive totalitarian character peculiar to it. It is only after we have grasped the political character of the Fascist principle that we are able adequately to appreciate the deeper concept of life which underlies that principle and from which the principle springs. The political doctrine of Fascism is not the whole of Fascism. It is rather its more prominent aspect and in general its most interesting one.

* Giovanni Gentile, extracted from *Readings on Fascism and National Socialism*, selected by the members of the Department of Philosophy, University of Colorado (Swallow Press, 1952), pp. 49–61.

VII

The politic of Fascism revolves wholly about the concept of the national State; and accordingly it has points of contact with nationalist doctrines, along with distinctions from the latter which it is important to bear in mind.

Both Fascism and nationalism regard the State as the foundation of all rights and the source of all values in the individuals composing it. For the one as for the other the State is not a consequence – it is a principle. But in the case of nationalism, the relation which individualistic liberalism, and for that matter socialism also, assumed between individual and State is inverted. Since the State is a principle, the individual becomes a consequence – he is something which finds an antecedent in the State: the State limits him and determines his manner of existence, restricting his freedom, binding him to a piece of ground whereon he was born, whereon he must live and will die. In the case of Fascism, State and individual are one and the same things, or rather, they are inseparable terms of a necessary synthesis.

Nationalism, in fact, founds the State on the concept of nation, the nation being an entity which transcends the will and the life of the individual because it is conceived as objectively existing apart from the consciousness of individuals, existing even if the individual does nothing to bring it into being. For the nationalist, the nation exists not by virtue of the citizen's will, but as datum, a fact, of nature.

For Fascism, on the contrary, the State is a wholly spiritual creation. It is a national State, because, from the Fascist point of view, the nation itself is a creation of the mind and is not a material presupposition, is not a datum of nature. The nation, says the Fascist, is never really made; neither, therefore, can the State attain an absolute form, since it is merely the nation in the latter's concrete, political manifestation. For the Fascist, the State is always *in fieri*. It is in our hands, wholly; whence our very serious responsibility towards it.

But this State of the Fascists which is created by the consciousness and the will of the citizen, and is not a force descending on the citizen from above or from without, cannot have toward the mass of the population the relationship which was presumed by nationalism.

Nationalism identified State with Nation, and made of the nation an entity preexisting, which needed not to be created but merely to be recognized or known. The nationalists, therefore, required a ruling class of an intellectual character, which was conscious of the nation and could understand, appreciate and exalt it. The authority of the State, furthermore, was not a product but a presupposition. It could not depend on the people – rather the people depended on the State and on the State's authority as the source of the life which they lived and apart from which they could not live. The nationalistic State was, therefore, an aristocratic State, enforcing itself upon the masses through the power conferred upon it by its origins.

The Fascist State, on the contrary, is a people's state, and, as such, the democratic State *par excellence*. The relationship between State and citizen (not this or that citizen, but all citizens) is accordingly so intimate that the State exists only as, and in so far as, the citizen causes it to exist. Its formation therefore is the formation of a consciousness of it in individuals, in the masses. Hence the need of the Party, and of all the instruments of propaganda and education which Fascism uses to make the thought and will of the *Duce* the thought and will of the masses. Hence the enormous task which Fascism sets itself in trying to bring the whole mass of the people, beginning with the little children, inside the fold of the Party.

On the popular character of the Fascist State likewise depends its greatest social and constitutional reform – the foundation of the Corporations of Syndicates. In this reform Fascism took over from syndicalism the notion of the moral and educational function of the syndicate. But the Corporations of Syndicates were necessary in order to reduce the syndicates to State discipline and make them an expression of the State's organism from within. The Corporation of Syndicates are a device through which the Fascist State goes looking for the individual in order to create itself through the individual's will. But the individual it seeks is not the abstract political individual whom the old liberalism took for granted. He is the only individual who can ever be found, the individual who exists as a specialized productive force, and who, by the fact of his specialization, is brought to unite with other individuals of his same category and comes to belong with them to the one great economic unit which is none other than the nation.

This great reform is already well under way. Toward it nationalism, syndicalism, and even liberalism itself, were already tending in the past. For even liberalism was beginning to criticize the older forms of political representation, seeking some system of organic representation which would correspond to the structural reality of the State.

The Fascist conception of liberty merits passing notice. The *Duce* of Fascism once chose to discuss the theme of "Force or consent?"; and he concluded that the two terms are inseparable, that the one implies the other and cannot exist apart from the other; that, in other words, the authority of the State and the freedom of the citizen constitute a continuous circle wherein authority presupposes liberty and liberty authority. For freedom can exist only within the State, and the State means authority. But the State is not an entity hovering in the air over the heads of its citizens. It is one with the personality of the citizen. Fascism, indeed, envisages the contrast not as between liberty and authority, but as between a true, a concrete liberty which exists, and an abstract, illusory liberty which cannot exist.

Liberalism broke the circle above referred to, setting the individual against the State and liberty against authority. What the liberal desired was liberty as against the State, a liberty which was a limitation of the State; though the liberal had to resign himself, as the lesser of the evils, to a State which was a limitation on liberty. The absurdities inherent in the liberal concept of freedom were apparent to liberals themselves early in the nineteenth century. It is no merit of Fascism to have again indicated them. Fascism has its own solution of the paradox of liberty and authority. The authority of the State is absolute. It does not compromise, it does not bargain, it does not surrender any portion of its field to other moral or religious principles which may interfere with the individual conscience. But on the other hand, the State becomes a reality only in the consciousness of its individuals. And the Fascist corporative State supplies a representative system more sincere and more in touch with realities than any other previously devised and is therefore freer than the old liberal State.

Paul Starr, "Why Liberalism Works"*

Liberalism is deeply rooted in American soil, so much so that in the years after World War II, many historians and social scientists regarded the liberal project and the American civic creed as more or less the same. The proposition that each of us has a right to "life, liberty, and the pursuit of happiness" remains as good a definition as anyone has ever come up with of liberalism's first principle and America's historic promise.

For some time, however, contemporary liberalism has been under political siege in the United States, and even liberals have at times appeared uncertain about what they stand for. In recent decades, national political leaders who are unquestionably liberal have often been unwilling to say so and unable to articulate a compelling public philosophy, while public-opinion surveys show that many Americans who support liberal positions do not identify themselves as liberals.

Lately, though, the right has been facing its own loss of confidence. No one, not even conservatives, doubts that conservatism is now in deep trouble: divided, uncertain of itself, and with a lot of explaining to do for the fiasco in Iraq. Yet the exhaustion of conservatism is not tantamount to a liberal revival. The Bush administration's manifest failures and the Democrats' triumph in the 2006 elections have created a new opening for liberal argument. The question is now whether liberals can make their case not just for specific policies and candidates but for an alternative public philosophy.

The Bush years have left America with more than just the disaster in Iraq to resolve. Conservative political leadership has failed to confront, and in critical respects has contributed to, some of our most serious long-term problems: growing economic inequality and insecurity, structural deficits in the federal budget, grave threats to the global environment, and increased hostility abroad toward the United States. America needs a different approach rooted in the inclusive, democratic partnerships that are central to the modern liberal tradition – a partnership at home built on the basis of a shared prosperity, and an international partnership in power built on the basis of a cooperative framework of security.

At its heart, the aim of the liberal project is today what it has always been: to build a free, fair, and prosperous society. But liberalism ought never to be confused with mere high-mindedness; it calls for a practical politics, whose ways and means necessarily evolve in response to new conditions and new understandings. A readiness to confront new conditions and absorb the lessons of experience is all the more necessary in a philosophy that asks to be judged by its real effects on human freedom and happiness and the power and peace of nations. Liberalism stands not only for the principle that we all have an equal right to freedom but also for the hypothesis that this is a workable ideal, and that a politics based on liberal principles can produce the power and wealth that make a free society more than a dream.

Liberalism is notoriously difficult to define. The term has been used to describe a sprawling profusion of ideas, practices, movements, and parties in different societies and historical periods. Often emerging as a philosophy of opposition, whether to feudal privilege, absolute monarchy, colonialism, theocracy, communism, or fascism,

* Paul Starr, extracted from *The American Prospect* (April 2007), pp. 34–40.

liberalism has served, as the word suggests, as a force for liberation, or at least liberalization – for the opening up of channels of free initiative.

As a political philosophy in the Anglo-American world, liberalism has two primary senses. In its broader meaning, it refers to the fundamental principles of constitutional government and individual rights shared by modern liberals and conservatives, though often differently interpreted by them. This tradition of *constitutional liberalism* – classical political liberalism – emerged in the seventeenth and eighteenth centuries, culminated in the American and French revolutions, and continues to provide the foundation of the modern liberal state. The classical liberals generally stood for religious liberty, freedom of thought and speech, the division of governmental powers, an independent civil society, and rights of private property and economic freedom that evolved in the nineteenth century into the doctrine of laissez-faire.

Modern democratic liberalism developed out of the more egalitarian aspects of the tradition and serves as the basis of contemporary liberal politics. The relationship between liberalism in these two phases has been predominantly cumulative: While rejecting laissez-faire economic policy, modern liberalism continues to take the broader tradition of constitutional liberalism as its foundation. That is why it is possible to speak not only of the two separately but also of an overarching set of ideas that unites them.

Yet even within the Anglo-American liberal tradition, intellectuals and reformers have started from different premises about human nature, society, and history and have held different views about many matters of deep importance to them, including religion. Historically, liberalism has been defined by a shared, albeit evolving, body of political principles rather than by agreement on the ultimate grounds on which those principles rest.

One of those shared political principles is an equal right to freedom, where freedom has been successively understood during the past three centuries in a more expansive way: first, as a right to civil liberty and freedom from arbitrary power; then, as a right to political liberty and a share in the government; and finally, as a right to basic requirements of human development and security necessary to assure equal opportunity and personal dignity.

Although I have described these ideas as a series of rights, they imply corresponding responsibilities that a liberal society expects of its members, individually and collectively. Inasmuch as individuals enjoy rights to civil liberty and freedom from arbitrary power, they are responsible for their own actions and what they make of their lives.

Inasmuch as citizens enjoy a right to political liberty and a share of their government, they have the responsibilities of citizenship to make democracy work.

And inasmuch as the members of a liberal society have a right to basic requirements of human development, such as education and a minimum standard of security, they have obligations to one another, mutually and through their government, to ensure that conditions exist enabling every person to have the opportunity for success in life.

The liberal project may be defined as the effort to guarantee these freedoms and to create the institutions and forms of character that will lead a people to assume responsibility, not as an external burden imposed upon them but from a force within. This is only a preliminary definition, however, because liberties come into conflict with one another and with other interests, and there must be a way of adjudicating among them that is consistent with the deepest interests in freedom and the public good. Moreover, liberalism consists of principles not only for a just society but also for the design of a state capable of sustaining that society in a world that is far from ideal.

This concern for creating a capable and effective state is critical to understanding how and why liberalism works. Constitutionalism itself, and even more so a liberal constitution with its emphasis on the protection of individual rights, is a system of enabling constraints. The constraints shield individuals from tyranny, but they also strengthen the state's power to act on behalf of its citizens. Checks and balances, requirements for transparency in decision making, and public accountability for performance reduce the odds of capricious, reckless, or self-interested decisions by those in power. Public discussion invites ideas and information that autocrats do not receive or are unlikely to heed. A constitutional state that observes the rule of law is more likely to abide by its promises, pay its debts, and enjoy better credit and lower interest rates. Guarantees of rights, including property rights, enable individuals to make long-term plans and investments and create a more productive economy that redounds to general advantage. Guarantees of religious freedom allow people of different faiths to cooperate under a political order that does not threaten to extinguish any of the various theological doctrines they support.

In short, it is an error to see guarantees of liberty as a source of state weakness. From its beginnings in seventeenth- and eighteenth-century England and America, constitutional liberalism contributed to the development of states that proved not only economically but also militarily successful, even when challenged by regimes more devoted to martial values.

The classical liberal tradition, however, had severe limitations. The liberalism of the eighteenth and early nineteenth centuries was not democratic in a sense we would recognize today: The majority of people – men without property, racial minorities, and women – were denied political rights and full citizenship. In the nineteenth and early twentieth centuries, laissez-faire economics provided a framework of law and policy for industrial capitalism's dynamic growth, but it left most working people in insecurity and poverty. In the same era, while often favoring social reform at home, liberal imperialists supported Western colonialism. The resulting conflicts and disasters nearly brought liberalism to ruin. The old liberal order of limited government, classical economics, and colonialism went up in flames amid total war and the Great Depression, and fascism or communism could easily have emerged from the wreckage to dominate the world.

Modern liberalism, however, transformed its classical inheritance into a genuinely democratic politics that proved stronger and more effective in both war and peace than its critics expected. Liberals now called for true political equality for all, aimed to bring raw capitalism under control in the interests of an expanded circle of opportunity, and supported national self-determination for all peoples and new forms of cooperation among states to promote democracy, human rights, and international peace and security.

Every step of the way, conservatives objected to these movements toward a wider democratic partnership, but as of the mid-twentieth century, liberals had won the argument decisively and had built an electoral majority in support of it. The prevailing view in the liberal democracies held that the extension of political and social rights and economic regulation was not only just but also the basis of a more productive society. And cooperative international organization, far from being a naive delusion, was plainly necessary to meet the twin threats posed by communism, on the one hand, and nuclear extinction, on the other.

Liberals differ from conservatives today not just about government's proper role but more fundamentally about how to produce power and wealth and advance equal rights to freedom in the process. Liberals have insisted that government can take on broader functions without sacrificing individual freedom as long as the law provides strong safeguards against arbitrary power. Modern liberalism, therefore, calls not just for broader social protections but also for stronger guarantees of civil liberties and less government regulation of private moral life. In contrast, modern conservatism has become a combination, in varying degrees, of devotion to the free market and social traditionalism. Each side of conservatism has provided a justification of inequalities that liberalism has attempted to reduce or eliminate.

The two political philosophies offer contrasting ways of resolving conflicts among liberties. Conservatives have generally given higher priority to property rights and, accordingly, to the rights of those with property, whereas liberals have given higher priority and broader scope to other constitutional liberties and civil rights, often those of the historically disadvantaged.

Conservatives and liberals have also responded differently to a phenomenon that did not exist in the eighteenth century when constitutional liberalism took shape: the modern corporation. While conservatives have treated private corporations as analogous to individuals and deserving of the same liberties, liberals have regarded corporations as a phenomenon of power, needing control like government itself. The discipline of power that constitutional liberalism imposes upon the state modern liberalism attempts to impose on the corporation, albeit not in the same way.

As liberal reforms gained ground during the past two centuries, conservatives predicted that they would be morally destructive, economically ruinous, and politically suicidal, while socialist critics maintained that the socioeconomic changes advocated by liberals were merely cosmetic and would make no difference at all. Modern liberalism's historical record turned out to be better than either of these camps anticipated. With increased social expenditures, labor and environmental regulation, and other reforms, the liberal capitalist democracies became more productive, mortality as well as birth rates fell, per capita income rose, and the circle of prosperity expanded. Rather than destroying private wealth, the modern liberal state made it more secure.

In describing these changes, I do not mean to suggest that liberals from the start had a clearly developed theory guiding reforms, much less all the right answers. Rather than formulating policy from speculative axioms, reformers beginning in the mid-nineteenth century increasingly devoted themselves to the gathering and analysis of socioeconomic data. In America, the measures adopted during the Progressive era, New Deal, and Great Society were often ad hoc and experimental, and many failed. But partly through better knowledge, partly by trial and error, liberal governments discovered that certain forms of limited state intervention could help bring the promise of a free and just society closer to fulfillment while reducing the waste of human and physical resources and improving economic performance. Modern liberalism has never been ruled by a theory in the way that free-market conservatism and Marxian socialism have been. A pragmatic emphasis on experience and evidence – on how things work in practice – has been critical in making liberalism work.

Part of the explanation for continued economic expansion during the long rise of public expenditure in the capitalist democracies is that much of the spending has represented investment that otherwise would not have been made. The underlying principle is no different from the one that Adam Smith enunciated in writing of the legitimate role of the state in financing public works and institutions, "which it can never be for the interest of any individual, or small number of individuals, to erect and maintain ... though it may frequently do much more than repay [the expense] to a great society."

What Smith failed to anticipate, however, was how broadly this principle would apply. The development of an urbanized, industrial economy and, more recently, the increased centrality of knowledge and innovation require investments in public goods and services that only government is in a position to make. These are typically complementary to private investment, rather than competitive with it, and involve not just tangible capital assets such as roads, ports, and other aspects of physical infrastructure, but intangible assets as well such as scientific knowledge, education, and public health.

The general point here is that much of what democratic liberalism calls for on grounds of equal rights to opportunity and security also provides a return in economic productivity. In the United States and many other countries, universal primary schooling came on the heels of an expanded franchise. This historical connection between democracy and public education was one of the main reasons that rising taxes and public expenditures did not harm economic growth. The redistributive state turned out also to be, in critical respects, a productive, developmental state, generating wealth as well as power. If we want to know why modern liberalism has worked out economically as well as it has, this is a large part of the answer.

Moreover, social benefits such as unemployment insurance proved not only to stabilize individual incomes but also to function as "automatic stabilizers" for the economy. Because government outlays on benefits rise whenever the economy sags, social spending helps to blunt recessions and prevent a self-reinforcing spiral of decline. Policies softening the hard edges of capitalism have created a margin of security and confidence that enables workers to cope with the uncertainties and risks of technological change and free trade. Protecting workers against sharp declines in their standard of living makes it less likely that they will turn to Luddite and protectionist responses. This, too, is part of the economic logic of liberal social policy.

Not all social spending, however, represents a means of achieving economic stability and growth or a way of ensuring equality of economic opportunity. Some of it simply transfers resources from one group to another. There have been three principled grounds for support of such policies.

The first and most basic of these is properly described as "humanitarian" and involves the relief of immediate suffering – the help we would extend to drowning men without knowing anything about them.

The second is a correlate of the extension of an equal right to political participation. Where wealth is overwhelmingly concentrated in a small oligarchy, political power is sure to follow. Popular self-government requires not that wealth and economic power be equally distributed but that they be widely dispersed.

Third, the liberal state has an obligation to afford its own citizens the equal protection of the law and to treat them with equal respect and concern. To treat people as equals does not necessarily mean recognizing their claims as identical; a disabled child, for example, may require special resources to acquire an education equal to what others receive. The same logic applies to minorities who have suffered persistent social exclusion: more public effort may be required to redress past injustices.

Against all these reasons for redistribution, the liberal project has to weigh other values. Liberalism is egalitarian in the sense that it seeks to achieve a more equal distribution of income and well-being than would otherwise be generated in the marketplace. But it is not committed to achieving a perfect equality in the distribution of goods. Equity requires that those who work harder, take greater risks, or develop their talents to a higher degree be able to recoup a return from their efforts. This incentive is critical to innovation and prosperity, which redound to wider benefit. Liberalism regards the well-being of the least well-off as a central criterion for a just society, and it seeks to provide individuals with some degree of protection against risks beyond their control; but it accepts inequalities insofar as they are to everyone's long-run advantage, and therefore aims for sustainable growth with widely shared gains. The pragmatic disposition of liberalism also implies that policies cannot be derived from moral principles alone, without regard to empirical realities. Experience shows that governments can bring about some results more readily than others.

These considerations tend to lead democratic liberalism in the direction of policies that are dual-purpose: justifiable because they serve both the macroeconomic aims of economic growth and stability and the egalitarian aims of social inclusion – the goal of a shared prosperity. Growth that is widely shared not only raises the standard of living of the middle class and the poor but also strengthens other liberal values. Among the good things that broadly based prosperity buys are tolerance and generosity: Economic growth has historically had strong positive effects on democratization and liberalization. In light of that relationship, the interest in rising living standards ought to be considered, not as crass materialism but rather as a means of achieving a good society in part through secondary effects on public attitudes and politics.

Broadly based prosperity is not what contemporary conservative leadership has given us. Instead, America has seen a growing gap in income and wealth, not just between rich and poor but between those at the very top and everyone else, as the median-income family has failed to receive close to a proportionate share of economic growth. While preaching compassion, conservatives have favored tax cuts and other policies gratifying the appetites of the wealthy on the false premise that a winner-take-all-and-keep-all economy is the only way for the nation to prosper.

Nowhere have the claims of contemporary conservatism proven more hollow and misleading than in foreign policy and defense. Conservatives have cultivated an image of being tough and realistic, ready and willing to use military force to advance America's interests. But rather than augmenting American power, they have recklessly dissipated and degraded it.

The mistakes and malfeasances of recent years have not been the idiosyncratic follies of George W. Bush and Dick Cheney. The conservative movement has long agitated for just what this administration has given them: the unilateral assertion of American power abroad and the unilateral assertion of executive power at home. Externally, the unilateralist impulse has swept aside international alliances, law, and institutions; internally, it has swept aside constitutional checks and balances.

Multilateralism and separation of powers are mechanisms of obligatory consultation, and the same logic underlies them. By enlisting cooperation and reducing the odds of impulsive and narrowly self-interested decisions, consultation with other branches of government and with international allies contributes to a democratic state's power as well as its responsible use. These ideas, particularly about separation of powers, are not entirely alien to conservative philosophy. To the conservative American unilateralist, however, the system of international institutions merely provides the weak with ways to limit the strong, and thereby undercuts America's great and wholesome power. To the liberal internationalist, in contrast, these mechanisms function like internal checks and balances as enabling constraints – they create legitimate and effective power even as they limit it. They foster shared expectations that enable states to cooperate with each other. And the United States, the dominant force in multilateral institutions, has more to gain than to lose from the order they can help establish.

As the world's greatest power, the United States has exceptional leverage in shaping the rules and institutions of the international order. The liberal alternative to assertive nationalism and neoconservatism is not to abandon power for cooperation but to seek additional power and security through a system of partnerships with other countries. That system, moreover, is best founded on the basis of social partnership at home. It is far easier to sustain public support for trade and cooperation with other countries if a nation's own citizens feel that they share in its prosperity and that the good being pursued by the government includes what is good for them.

Shrewd as they were in achieving political power, the Republicans of the Bush era have shown little of that genius in using it. A conservatism that does not want to hear about inequality or the sinking fortunes of the middle class, or about dangers to the global environment, or about unsustainable fiscal policies, or about gaping flaws in plans for war, may prevail in the short run, but the realities will sooner or later make themselves felt, as they did in 2006. A great nation cannot long be governed by wishful and simplistic thinking, denial, obfuscation, and deceit. Costs mount, grievances accumulate, and there comes a reckoning.

The conservative default is liberalism's opportunity – an opportunity to rebuild a political majority by showing how liberal ideas make sense for America and by reopening a conversation with people who believe that liberals have not shown any concern or respect for them. At the heart of any such effort must be a program for shared prosperity to counter the trends toward rising inequality, insecurity, and stress on working families.

But no politics can live on bread alone; the public's concerns are inextricably moral and material. Anyone who worries about the institution of marriage, for example, ought to be receptive to changes in employer policies, the availability of preschool education, and other reforms that would help parents meet their obligations at work and at home. And anyone who favors those reforms ought to make the argument that they are good for stable marriages.

Liberals ought to contest conservatives for the very ground the right claims as its own: morality and patriotism. What is the protection of the global environment if not a moral concern? What are efforts to preserve constitutional liberties if not a patriotic devotion to the true basis of America's greatness? Liberalism should appeal for support on the straightforward basis that conservative economic policies do not serve the interests of the great majority of people. But liberalism ought to do more than that; it ought to remind us of our responsibilities and the power of our traditions and call us to greater interests and purposes than our own.

Nothing has to be reinvented, yet everything has to be reimagined. Constructive ideas for new policies are not wanting, but liberals have to think differently about what those policies are about and how they can be achieved. The era of single-issue progressive causes, each agitating – and litigating – separately, is finished. Liberals have to make the case for progressive policies on the basis of the nation's shared interests and common future. National crisis has in the past often supplied the sense of a common citizenship and the imperative demand to put the greater good ahead of one's own. The task of political leadership now is to evoke that same sentiment: "We are all in this together." This is the work of rebuilding a democratic partnership at home that includes working- and middle-class families, and a partnership with other liberal democracies in defense of our common values and security.

In much of the world, the liberal project is still the creation of constitutional democracy, and liberalism remains an intellectual tradition without deep social and historical roots. But in the United States, the idea that everyone enjoys an equal right to life, liberty, and the pursuit of happiness is part of the national tradition. The story of America is of a nation that has grown greater and stronger by becoming more diverse and inclusive and extending the fruits of liberty more widely among its people. American liberals do not have to invent something new or import a philosophical tradition from abroad. They have only to reclaim the idea of America's greatness as their own.

John Kekes, "A Case for Conservatism"*

It has been said by both defenders and critics of conservatism that it is not a position that lends itself to a systematic statement and defense. Some main reasons adduced in support of this view have been that conservatism is not theoretical but practical, and a practical activity cannot be fully systematized; that conservatism is merely opposition to ill-conceived changes in political arrangements, so it has no substantive content that could be systematized; and that conservatism is a reaction to ideological politics, thus it would be inconsistent to systematize it, since that would make conservatism just another instance of that very ideological approach that it is meant to oppose. There is something to be said for each of these claims. On balance, however, they are all mistaken because conservatism can be systematically stated and defended.

[...]

Good lives may be understood as being both satisfying and beneficial. The pertinent satisfactions are derived from the enjoyment the agents find in the important activities of their lives. The appropriate benefits are those that the agents confer on others. Lives are good if the balance between the satisfactions enjoyed and the benefits conferred, on the one hand, and the dissatisfactions suffered and the harms inflicted, on the other, is strongly in favor of the former. The fundamental aim of the political morality of conservatism is to conserve the political arrangements that have historically shown themselves to be conducive to good lives thus understood.

Conservatism is not alone in being a political morality, aiming at good lives, and judging the goodness of a society by its contribution to the goodness of the lives of the people who live in it. Liberalism and socialism are the most widely favored current alternatives to it. The disagreements among these, and other, political moralities turn on the specific political arrangements that their defenders think a good society ought to have. The case for conservatism is that the political arrangements it favors are more likely than any others to lead to good lives.

The political morality of conservatism rests on four basic beliefs. These beliefs will emerge by considering four distinctions, each of which holds between two extreme beliefs. It will be found that in each case there is a belief intermediate between the extremes, and that is the one

* John Kekes, extracted from *A Case for Conservatism* (Cornell University Press, 1998), pp. 1–3, 27–47.

which is basic to conservatism. The four basic beliefs jointly constitute the strongest version of conservatism and distinguish it both from other versions of conservatism and from other non-conservative political moralities.[2] [...]

Rationalism or fideism

The first distinction poses the question of whether or not conservatives should look beyond their history for the reasons that determine what political arrangements they ought to favor. Some conservatives think so, others do not. To be sure, all conservatives agree that history is the appropriate starting point for their reflection, but some of them believe that it is not a contingent fact that certain political arrangements have historically fostered good lives, while others have been detrimental to them. Conservatives who believe this think that there is a deeper explanation for the historical success or failure of various political arrangements. They believe that there is a rational and moral order in reality. Political arrangements that conform to this order foster good lives, those that conflict with it are bound to make lives worse.

[...]

The belief that rationalism holds the key to dicovering what political arrangements foster good lives is held not only by some conservatives, but also by some left and right-wing radicals who otherwise disagree with these conservatives. These radicals believe that the laws that govern human affairs have been discovered. Some say that the laws are those of history, others that they are of sociology, psychology, sociobiology, or ethology. Their shared view is, however, that a good society is possible only if its political arrangements reflect the relevant laws. Human misery is a consequence of ignorance or wickedness, which leads people to favor arrangements contrary to the laws. History, as they see it, is the painful story of societies banging their collective heads against the wall. They have found the key, however, the door is now open, history has reached its final phase, and from here on all manner of things would be well, if only their prescriptions were followed.

The historical record of societies whose political arrangements were inspired by rationalistic schemes is most alarming. They tended to impose their certainties on unwilling or indoctrinated people, and often made their lives miserable, all the while promising great improvements just after the present crisis, which usually turned out to be permanent. If the present century has a moral achievement, it is the realization that proceeding in this way is morally and politically dangerous.

Opposed to these rationalistically inclined conservatives and nonconservative Utopians are skeptical conservatives. Their skepticism, however, may take either an extreme or a moderate form. The extreme form of skepticism is fideism. It involves reliance on faith and the repudiation of reason. Fideistic conservatives reject reason as a guide to the political arrangements that a good society ought to have. It makes no difference to them whether the reasons are metaphysical, scientific, or merely empirical. They are opposed to relying on reason whatever form it may take. Their opposition is based on their belief that all forms of reasoning are ultimately based on assumptions that must be accepted on faith and that it is possible to juxtapose to any chain of reasoning another chain that is equally plausible and yet incompatible with it.

Their rejection of the guidance of reason, however, leaves fideistic conservatives with the problem of how to decide what political arrangements they ought to favor. The solution they have historically offered is to be guided by faith or to perpetuate the existing arrangements simply because they are familiar. The dangers of either solution have been as evident in the historical

[2] Reliable accounts of some of these disagreements may be found in Noel O'Sullivan, *Conservatism* (New York: St. Martin's Press, 1976) and Anthony Quinton, *The Politics of Imperfection* (London: Faber and Faber, 1978).

For general surveys and bibliographies of conservative ideas, see Kenneth Minogue, "Conservatism," *Encyclopedia of Philosophy*, ed. Paul Edwards (New York: Macmillan, 1967), Anthony O'Hear, "Conservatism," in *The Oxford Companion to Philosophy*, ed. Ted Honderich (Oxford: Oxford University Press, 1995); Anthony Quinton, "Conservatism," *A Companion to Contemporary Political Philosophy*, ed. Robert E. Goodin and Philip Pettit (Oxford: Blackwell, 1993); and Rudolf Vierhaus, "Conservatism," *Dictionary of the History of Ideas*, ed. Philip P. Wiener (New York: Scribner's, 1968).

Three useful anthologies of conservatives writings are Russell Kirk, ed., *Conservative Reader* (Harmondsworth: Penguin, 1982); Jerry Z. Muller, ed., *Conservatism* (Princeton: Princeton University Press, 1997); and Roger Scruton, ed., *Conservative Texts* (New York: St. Martin's Press, 1991).

Some of the classic works that have influenced the development of conservatism are Plato's *Republic*, Aristotle's *Politics, Nicomachean Ethics*, and *Rhetoric*, Machiavelli's *The Prince* and *Discourses*, Montaigne's *Essays*, Hobbes's *Leviathan*, Hume's *Treatise, Enquiries, Essays*, and *History of England*, Burke's *Reflections on the Revolution in France*, Tocqueville's *Democracy in America* and *The Old Regime and the French Revolution*, Hegel's *Philosophy of Right*, Stephen's *Liberty, Equality, Fraternity*, Bradley's *Ethical Studies*, Santayana's *Dominations and Powers*, Wittgenstein's *Philosophical Investigations* and *On Certainty*, and Oakeshott's *Rationalism in Politics* and *On Human Conduct*.

record as the dangers of the preceding approach. Faith breeds dogmatism, the persecution of those who reject it or who hold other faiths, and it provides no ground for regarding the political arrangements it favors as better than contrary ones. Whereas the perpetuation of the status quo on account of its familiarity makes it impossible to improve the existing political arrangements.

A *via media* between the dangerous extremes of rationalistic politics and the fideistic repudiation of reason is skepticism that takes a moderate form. Conservatives who hold this view need not deny that there is a rational and moral order in reality. They are committed only to denying that reliable knowledge of it can be had. Skeptical conservatives are far more impressed by human fallibility than by the success of efforts to overcome it. They think that the claims that some truths are revealed, that some texts are canonical, that some knowledge embodies eternal verities stand in need of persuasive evidence. They regard these claims only as credible as the evidence that is available to support them. But the evidence is as questionable as the claims are that it is adduced to support. According to skeptical conservatives, it is therefore far more reasonable to look to the historical record of various political arrangements than to endeavor to justify or criticize them by appealing to meta-physical or utopian considerations that are bound to be less reliable than the historical record.[3]

Skepticism, however, does not lead conservatives to deny that it is possible to evaluate political arrangements by adducing reasons for or against them. What they deny is that good reasons must be absolute and eternal. The skepticism of these conservatives is, therefore, not a global doubt about it being possible and desirable to be reasonable, to base beliefs on the evidence available in support of them, and to make the strength of beliefs commensurate with the strength of the evidence. Their skepticism is about deducing political conclusions from metaphysical or utopian premises. They want political arrangements to be firmly rooted in the experiences of the people who are subject to them. Since these experiences are unavoidably historical, it is to history that skeptical conservatives look for supporting evidence. They will not try to deduce from metaphysical premises which orifices of the body are suitable for sexual pleasure or evaluate people's desires on the basis of their conformity to some utopian ideal that the people do not share. Skepticism thus avoids the absurdity of basing political arrangements on speculation about what lies beyond experience or of being equally suspicious of all political arrangements because of a global distrust of reason.

Absolutism or relativism

[...] The second distinction that poses questions for conservatives is between two views about the diversity of values. These views have a fundamental influence on the kinds of reasons that their defenders offer for or against particular political arrangements.

Absolutists believe that the diversity of values is apparent, not real. They concede that there are many values, but they think that there is a universal and objective standard that can be appealed to in evaluating the respective importance of all these values.

---

[3] The roots of skeptical conservatism are to be found scattered in Montaigne's *Essays*, Hobbes's *Leviathan*, Hume's *Treatise*, *Enquiries*, *Essays*, and *History of England*, Burke's *Reflections on the Revolution in France*, Tocqueville's *Democracy in America* and *The Old Regime and the French Revolution*, Santayana's *Dominations and Powers*, and Wittgenstein's *Philosophical Investigations* and *On Certainty*.

On Montaigne's conservatism, see John Kekes, *The Examined Life* (University Park: Penn State Press, 1992), chapter 4; on Hobbes's conservatism, see Michael Oakeshott, *Hobbes on Civil Association* (Oxford: Blackwell, 1974); on Hume's conservatism, see Shirley Robin Letwin, *The Pursuit of Certainty* (Cambridge: Cambridge University Press, 1965), part I; Donald W. Livingston, *Hume's Philosophy of Common Life* (Chicago: University of Chicago Press, 1984), chap. 12; and Sheldon S. Wolin, "Hume and Conservatism," *American Political Science Review* 98 (1954), pp. 999–1016; on Tocqueville's conservatism, see Roger Boesche, *The Strange Liberalism of Alexis de Tocqueville* (Ithaca: Cornell University Press, 1987); Frohnen, *Virtue and the Promise of Conservatism;* and Alan S. Kahan, *Aristocratic Liberalism* (New York: Oxford University Press, 1986); on Santayana's conservatism, see John Gray, "George Santayana and the Critique of Liberalism," *The World and I*, February 1989, pp. 593–607; on Wittgenstein's conservatism, see Charles Covell, *The Redefinition of Conservatism*, chap. 1; and J. C. Nyiri, "Wittgenstein's Later Work in Relation to Conservatism" in *Wittgenstein and His Times*, ed. Brian McGuinness (Oxford: Blackwell, 1982).

Some contemporary skeptical conservative works are Lincoln Allison, *Right Principles* (Oxford: Blackwell, 1984); John Gray, *Liberalisms* (London: Routledge, 1989), *Post-liberalism* (New York: Routledge, 1993), and *Beyond the New Right* (London: Routledge, 1993); Shirley Robin Letwin, *The Gentleman in Trollope* (Cambridge: Harvard University Press, 1982); Michael Oakeshott, *Rationalism in Politics, On Human Conduct* (Oxford: Clarendon, 1975) and *The Politics of Faith and the Politics of Scepticism*, ed. Timothy Fuller (New Haven: Yale University Press, 1996).

[...]

It is a considerable embarrassment to absolutists that the candidates for universal and objective standards are also diverse, and thus face the same problems as the values whose diversity is supposed to be diminished by them. Absolutists acknowledge this, and explain it in terms of human shortcomings that prevent people from recognizing the one and true standard. The history of religious wars, revolutions, left and right-wing tyrannies, and persecutions of countless unbelievers, all aiming to rectify human shortcomings, testifies to the dangers inherent in this explanation.

Opposed to absolutism is relativism. Relativists regard the diversity of values as real: there are many values and there are many ways of combining and ranking them. There is no universal and objective standard that could be appealed to in resolving disagreements about the identity and importance of the satisfactions and benefits that form the substance of values. A good society, however, requires some consensus about what is accepted as a possibility and what is placed beyond limits. The political arrangements of a good society reflect this consensus, and the arrangements change as the consensus does. What counts as a value and how seriously it counts depends, then, according to relativists, on the consensus of a society. A value is what is valued in a particular context; all values, therefore, are context-dependent.

[...]

Relativists appear to have the advantage of avoiding the dangers of dogmatism and repression that so often engulf absolutism. This appearance, however, is deceptive. Relativism is no less prone to dogmatism and repression than absolutism. From the fact that the political arrangements of the relativist's society are not thought to be binding outside of it, nothing follows about the manner in which they are held within it. In fact, if the world is full of people and societies whose values are often hostile to the values and political arrangements of the relativist's society, then there is much the more reason to guard jealously those values and political arrangements. If the justification of the political arrangements of a society is the consensus that prevails in it, then any value and any political arrangement becomes justifiable just so long as sufficiently large number of people in the society support the consensus favoring them. Thus slavery, female circumcision, the maltreatment of minorities, child prostitution, the mutilation of criminals, blood feuds, bribery, and a lot of other political arrangements may become sanctioned on the grounds that that is what happens to be valued here.

These pitfalls of the rationalistic aspirations of absolutism and the fideistic orientation of relativism make them unreliable sources of reasons for evaluating political arrangements. It is with some relief then that conservatives may turn to pluralism as an intermediate position between these dangerous extremes. Pluralists are in partial agreement and disagreement with both absolutists and relativists. According to pluralists, there is a universal and objective standard, but it is applicable only to some values. The standard is universal and objective enough to apply to *some* values that must be recognized by all political arrangements that foster good lives, but it is not sufficiently universal and objective to apply to *all* the many diverse values that may contribute to good lives. The standard, in other words, is a minimal one.[4]

It is possible to establish with reference to it some universal and objective values required by all good lives, but the standard does not specify all the values that good lives require. It underdetermines the nature of good lives. It regards some political arrangements as necessary for good lives, and it allows for a generous plurality of possible political arrangements beyond the necessary minimum. The standard operates in the realm of moral necessity, and it leaves open what happens in the realm of moral possibility. The standard thus accommodates part of the universalistic aspiration of absolutism and part of the historicist orientation of relativism. Absolutism prevails in the realm of moral necessity; relativism prevails in the realm of moral possibility.

The source of this standard is human nature.[5] To understand human nature sufficiently for the purposes of this standard does not require plumbing the depths of the soul, unraveling the obscure springs of human motivation, or conducting scientific research. It does not call for any metaphysical commitment and it can be held without subscribing to the existence of a natural law. It is enough for it to concentrate on normal people in a commonsensical way. It will then become obvious that good

[4] Contemporary works of pluralistic conservatism by and large coincide with those of skeptical conservatism, see note 3 above. For an account of pluralism in general, see John Kekes, *The Morality of Pluralism* (Princeton: Princeton University Press, 1993), and Nicholas Rescher, *Pluralism* (Oxford: Clarendon, 1993).

[5] For a general account of the political significance of human nature for politics, see Christopher J. Berry, *Human Nature* (London: Macmillan, 1986). For the specific connection between human nature and conservatism, see Christopher J. Berry, "Conservatism and Human Nature," *Politics and Human Nature*, ed. Ian Forbes and Steve Smith (London: Frances Pinter, 1983).

lives depend on the satisfaction of basic physiological, psychological, and social needs: for nutrition, shelter, and rest; for companionship, self-respect, and the hope for a good or better life; for the division of labor, justice, and predictability in human affairs; and so forth. The satisfaction of these needs is a universal and objective requirement of all good lives, whatever the social context may be in which they are lived. If the political arrangements of a society foster their satisfaction, that is a reason for having and conserving them; if the political arrangements hinder their satisfaction, that is a reason for reforming them.

[...]

Individual or society

The question posed by the third distinction is about the relationship that ought to hold between individuals and the society in which they live.

[...]

Putting individual autonomy before social authority raises two very serious problems. First, it assumes that good lives must be autonomous and cannot involve the systematic domination of their individual constituents by some form of social authority. If this were so, no military or devoutly religious life, no life in static, traditional, hierarchical societies, no life, that is, that involves the subordination of the individual's will and judgment to what is regarded as a higher purpose, could be good. This assumption entails thinking of the vast majority of lives lived outside of prosperous Western societies as bad. The mistake is to slide from the reasonable view that autonomous lives may be good to the unreasonable view that a life cannot be good unless it is autonomous. This way of thinking is not only mistaken in its own right, but it is also incompatible with the pluralism to which liberals who think this way claim themselves to be committed.

Second, if a good society is one that fosters the good lives of the individuals who live in it, then giving precedence to autonomy over authority cannot be right, since autonomous lives may be bad. That the will and judgment of individuals take precedence over the pronouncements of social authority leaves it open whether the resulting lives will be satisfying and beneficial enough to be good. Autonomous lives may be frustrating and harmful. The most casual reflection on history shows that social authority often has to prevail over the individual autonomy of fanatics, criminals, fools, and crazies, if a society is indeed dedicated to fostering good lives.

The problems of letting social authority override individual autonomy are no less serious. What is the reason for thinking that if social authority prevails over individual autonomy, then the resulting lives will be good? Lives cannot be good just because some social authority pronounces them to be such. They must actually be satisfying and beneficial, and whether they are must ultimately be judged by the individuals whose will is unavoidably engaged in causing and enjoying the satisfactions and the benefits. Their will and judgment may of course be influenced by the prescriptions of a social authority. But no matter how strong that influence is, it cannot override the ultimate autonomy of individuals in finding what is satisfying or beneficial for them. As the lamentable historical record shows, however, the importance of autonomy has not prevented countless religious and ideological authorities from stigmatizing individuals who reject their prescriptions as heretics, infidels, class enemies, maladjusted, or living with false consciousness, in bad faith or in a state of sin. The result is a repressive society whose dogmatism is reinforced by specious moralizing.

How then is the question to be answered? Which constituent of good lives should be regarded as the decisive one? The answer, as before, is to eschew the extremes and look for an intermediate assumption that accommodates the salvageable portions of both. There is no need to insist that either individual autonomy or social authority should systematically prevail over the other. Both are necessary for good lives. Instead of engaging in futile arguments about their comparative importance, it is far more illuminating to try to understand the connection between them. In fact, they are parts of two interdependent aspects of the same underlying activity. One aspect is as indispensable as the other. The activity is that of individuals trying to make good lives for themselves. Its two aspects are the individual and the social; autonomy and authority are their respective parts; and the connecting link between them is tradition. The intermediate belief that is reasonably favored by conservatives may therefore be called traditionalism.[6]

A tradition is a set of customary beliefs, practices, and actions that has endured from the past to the present and attracted the allegiance of people so that they wish

6 Traditionalism is an expression that does not appear in any of the works listed below, but the position defended in them is very close to traditionalism so it is perhaps justified to claim affinity with them. See Francis Herbert Bradley, *Ethical Studies*, 2nd edn. (Oxford: Clarendon, 1927), essays 5 and 6; John Kekes, *Moral Tradition and Individuality* (Princeton: Princeton University Press, 1989); Alasdair MacIntyre, *After Virtue* (Notre Dame: University of Notre Dame Press, 1981) and *Whose Justice? Which Rationality?* (Notre Dame: University of Notre Dame Press, 1988); Oakeshott, *On Human Conduct*, and Roger Scruton, *The Meaning of Conservatism* (Harmondsworth: Penguin, 1980).

to perpetuate it. A tradition may be reflective and designed, like the deliberations of the Supreme Court, or unreflective and spontaneous, like sports fans rooting for their teams; it may have a formal institutional framework, like the Catholic Church, or it may be unstructured, like mountain-climbing; it may be competitive, like the Olympics; largely passive, like going to the opera; humanitarian, like the Red Cross; self-centered, like jogging; honorific, like the Nobel Prize; or punitive, like criminal proceedings. Traditions may be religious, horticultural, scientific, athletic, political, stylistic, moral, aesthetic, commercial, medical, legal, military, educational, architectural, and so on and on. They permeate human lives.[7]

When individuals gradually and experimentally form their conceptions of a good life what they are to a very large extent doing is deciding which traditions they should participate in. This decision may be taken from the inside of the traditions into which they were born or in which they were raised, or from the outside of traditions that attract, repel, bore, or interest them. The decisions may be conscious, deliberate, clear-cut yes-or-no choices, they may be ways of unconsciously, unreflectively falling in with familiar patterns, or they may be at various points in between. The bulk of the activities of individuals concerned with living in ways that strike them as good is composed of participation in the various traditions of their society.

As individuals participate in these activities, they of course exercise their autonomy. They make choices and judgments; their wills are engaged; they learn from the past and plan for the future. But they do so in the frameworks of various traditions which authoritatively provide them with the relevant choices, with the matters that are left to their judgments, and with standards that within a tradition determine what choices and judgments are good or bad, reasonable or unreasonable. Their exercise of autonomy is the individual aspect of their conformity to their tradition's authority, which is the social aspect of what they are doing. They act autonomously *by* following the authoritative patterns of the traditions to which they feel allegiance. When a Catholic goes to confession, a violinist gives a concert, a football player scores a touchdown, a student graduates, a judge sentences a criminal, then the individual and the social, the autonomous and the authoritative, the traditional pattern of doing it and a particular agent's doing of it are inextricably mixed. To understand what is going on in terms of individual autonomy is as one-sided as it is to do so in terms of social authority. Each plays an essential role, and understanding what is going on requires understanding both the roles they play and what makes them essential.

Traditionalism rests on this understanding, and is a political response to it. The response is to have and maintain political arrangements that foster the participation of individuals in the various traditions that have historically endured in their society. The reason for fostering them is that good lives depend on participation in a variety of traditions.

[...]

Changes, of course, are often necessary because traditions may be vicious, destructive, stultifying, nay-saying, and thus not conducive to good lives. It is part of the purpose of the prevailing political arrangements to draw distinctions among traditions that are unacceptable, suspect but tolerable, and worthy of encouragement – for example, slavery, pornography, and university education. Traditions that violate the minimum requirements of human nature are prohibited. Traditions that have historically shown themselves to make questionable contributions to good lives may be tolerated but not encouraged. Traditions whose historical record testifies to their importance for good lives are cherished.

The obvious question is *who* should decide which tradition is which and *how* that decision should be made. The answer conservatives give is that the decision should be made by those who are legitimately empowered to do so through the political process of their society and they should make the decisions by reflecting on the historical record of the tradition in question. From this answer three corollaries follow. First, the people who are empowered to make the decisions ought to be those who can reflect well on the historical record. The political process works well if it ends up empowering these people. They are unlikely to be ill-educated, passionate about some single issue, inexperienced, or have qualifications that lie in some other field of endeavor. Conservatives, in a word, will not favor populist politics. Second, a society that proceeds in the manner just indicated will be pluralistic because it fosters a plurality of traditions. It will do so because it sees as the justification of its political arrangements that they foster good lives, and fostering them depends on fostering the traditions

[7] For an account of tradition in general, see Edward Shils, *Tradition* (Chicago: University of Chicago Press, 1981). See also John Casey, "Tradition and Authority," in *Conservative Essays*, ed. Maurice Cowling (London: Cassell, 1978); Thomas Stearns Eliot, "Tradition and the Individual Talent," *The Selected Prose of T.S. Eliot*, ed. Frank Kermode (New York: Farrar, Straus, and Giroux, 1975), and MacIntyre, *After Virtue*, chap. 15.

participation in which may make lives good. Third, the society will be tolerant because it is committed to having as many traditions as possible. This means that its political arrangements will place the burden of proof on those who wish to proscribe a tradition. If a tradition has endured, if it has the allegiance of enough people to perpetuate it, then there is a prima facie case for it. That case may be, and often is, defeated, but the initial presumption is in its favor.

A conservative society that is skeptical, pluralistic, and traditionalist will be in favor of limited government. The purpose of its political arrangements will not be to bring heaven on earth by imposing on people some conception of a good life. No government has a mandate from heaven. The political arrangements of a limited government will interfere as little as possible with the many indigenous traditions that flourish among people subject to it. The purpose of its arrangements will be to enable people to live as they please, rather than to force them to live in a particular way. One of the most important ways of accomplishing this is to have a wide plurality of traditions as a bulwark between individuals and the government that has power over them.

Perfectibility or corruption

[...] Conservatives do not think that the human condition is devoid of hope. They are, however, realistic about the limited control a society has over its future. Their view is *not* that human beings are corrupt and that their evil propensities are uncontrollable. Their view is rather that human beings have both good and evil propensities and neither they nor their societies can exercise sufficient control to make the realization of good propensities reliably prevail over the realization of evil ones. The right sort of political arrangements will help, of course; just as the wrong sort will make matters worse. But even under the best conceivable political arrangements a great deal of contingency will remain, and it will place beyond human control much good and evil. The chief reason for this is that the human efforts to control contingency are themselves subject to the very contingency they aim to control. And that, of course, is the fundamental reason why conservatives are pessimistic and skeptical about the possibility of significant improvement in the human condition. It is thus that the skepticism and pessimism of conservatives reinforce one another.

[...]

If the choice of political arrangements is governed by this conservative attitude, it will result in arrangements that look in two directions: toward fostering what is taken to be good and toward hindering what is regarded as evil. Conservative political arrangements that aim to foster the good are committed to the conditions of good lives: civility, equality, freedom, healthy environment, justice, order, peace, prosperity, rights, security, toleration, and welfare. There need be no significant difference between the items on the conservative list and the ones that liberals, socialists, or others may draw up. There will still be two significant differences, however, between conservative politics and the politics of liberals, socialists, and a great many others.

The first of these differences has already been noted: conservative politics is genuinely pluralistic, whereas the alternative approaches are not. Liberals, socialists, and others are committed to regarding some few conditions of good lives on the list as always having an overriding importance. It is their essential claim, the claim that makes them liberals, socialists, or whatever, that when the conditions they favor conflict with the less favored ones on the list, then the ones they favor should prevail. Conservatives reject this approach. Their commitment is to all the conditions on the list taken jointly and their essential claim is that what is important is the conservation of the whole system of conditions. Its conservation sometimes requires favoring one condition over another, sometimes the reverse. And they hold this to be true for each of the items on the list. Conservatives thus differ from liberals, socialists, and others in refusing to make an a priori commitment to the overriding importance of any particular condition or small number of conditions among all those necessary for good lives.

The second significant difference between conservative politics and most current alternatives to it is the insistence of conservatives on the importance of political arrangements whose purpose is to hinder evil. This difference is a direct result of the pessimism of conservatives and the optimistic belief of others in human perfectibility. Their belief is revealed by the assumption that the prevalence of evil is due to bad political arrangements. If people were not poor, oppressed, exploited, discriminated against, and so forth, they optimistically suppose, then they would be naturally inclined to live good lives. The prevalence of evil, they assume, is due to the political corruption of human nature. If political arrangements were good, there would be no corruption. What is needed, therefore, is to make political arrangements that foster the good. The arrangements that hinder evil are unfortunate and temporary measures needed only until the effects of the good arrangements are generally felt.

Conservatives reject this optimism. They do not think that evil is prevalent merely because of bad political arrangements. They think, to the contrary, that one reason why political arrangements are bad is that those who make them have evil propensities. Political arrangements, after all, are made by people, and they are bound to reflect the propensities of their makers. Since the propensities are subject to contingencies over which human control is insufficient, there is no guarantee whatsoever that political arrangements can be made good. Nor that, if they were made good, they would be sufficient to hinder evil.

Conservatives will insist, therefore, on the necessity and importance of political arrangements that hinder evil. They will stress moral education, the enforcement of morality, the treatment of people according to their moral merit or demerit, the importance of swift and severe punishment for serious crimes, and so on. They will oppose the prevailing attitudes that lead to agonizing over the criminal and forgetting the crime, to perpetuating the absurd fiction of a fundamental moral equality between habitual evil-doers and their victims, to guaranteeing the same freedom and welfare-rights to good and evil people, and so forth.

Political arrangements that are meant to hinder evil are liable to abuse. Conservatives know and care about the historical record that testifies to the dreadful things that have been done to people on the many occasions when such arrangements have gone wrong. The remedy, however, cannot be to refuse to make the arrangements; it must be to make them, learn from history, and try hard to avoid their abuse. Conservatives know that in this respect, as in all others, contingency will cause complete success to elude them. But this is precisely the reason why political arrangements are necessary for hindering evil. Their pessimism will lead conservatives to face the worst and try to deny scope to it, rather than endeavor to erect the City of Man on a far from quiescent volcano.

Note

It is odd but necessary to [have] a note about the [footnotes] to this chapter. In several of the footnotes conservative views will be attributed to various people. This is not meant to imply that the people who hold these views are conservatives. They are conservative in respect to these views, but they also hold other views, and they may or may not be conservative. It is often very difficult to say whether or not a person is conservative, especially since few of the people referred to were concerned with formulating an explicit political morality.

Chapter 4

Newer Quasi-Ideologies

Introduction

During the past four or five decades, many "new voices" have gained prominence, both in popular culture and among academics. Feminism, environmentalism, black (and white) nationalism, Christian (Jewish, and Islamic) fundamentalism, and advocacy for gay and lesbian rights are widely discussed among the public generally. Libertarianism and communitarianism have been extensively explored by academics. Egalitarian liberalism, neoliberalism, social conservatism, and neoconservatism denote some of the many strands of broader ideological perspectives that have distinctive concerns. Such perspectives are called "quasi-ideologies" here to distinguish them from broader and more comprehensive worldviews. They focus on particular problems within pluralist societies and emphasize particular goals that involve more radical changes within pluralism than do more mainstream and comprehensive ideologies – particularly contemporary liberalism and conservatism. Calling these perspectives "new" might be misleading, because the concerns of various forms of feminism, environmentalism, nationalism, fundamentalism, and so forth have been expressed in the past, but broader and politically significant movements on behalf of these concerns are largely recent developments.

In *From Ideologies to Public Philosophies* I distinguish between radical and extreme quasi-ideologies. I argue that radical perspectives seek changes in the underlying structures and norms of pluralist society (rather than more surface changes in who governs and the policies they pursue), even while they work within pluralist politics and accept most of the ideas of pluralist public philosophy. In contrast, extreme perspectives reject pluralist public philosophy and seek to destroy pluralist society. While I continue to believe that this distinction is valuable, I do not explicitly pursue it here. Extracts from proponents of a variety of quasi-ideologies are presented both in this chapter and in subsequent chapters where their particular concerns add important alternatives to conventional understandings of the perennial issues of politics, but I leave it for readers to ponder how radical or extreme are these views.

The first reading in this chapter provides a good introduction to communitarianism. Michael Sandel, professor of government at Harvard where he has taught since 1980, finds that the public philosophies expressed and pursued by both liberal democrats and conservative Republicans do not speak to the discontents of most Americans, and thus we must search for a new public philosophy. He proposes that we consider the ideas of republican theory that emphasize community-regarding participation in politics (and thus must be distinguished from the limited-government themes of the Republican Party). He recognizes that Jean Jacques Rousseau (1712–78) is regarded as a leading proponent of republicanism and that he emphasized a "unitary and uncontestable" conception of the common good, which can be highly coercive. But he finds in Alexis de Tocqueville (1805–59) and other republican theorists a vision of civic involvement that is "more clamorous than consensual," and is more pluralistic than Rousseau's monistic vision that despised differences in political thinking. Thus, Sandel's "search for a public philosophy" reminds us that seeking radical changes to prevailing public philosophies does not necessarily entail a rejection of pluralism.

Richard John Neuhaus – a Catholic priest, author of several books on the role of religion and politics, and influential consultant on such matters during the administration of George W. Bush – takes up Sandel's communitarian concerns, but as a spokesman for the religious right. According to Neuhaus, the context in which moral issues must be debated should include "religiously grounded values." But while religious belief had previously provided a "backstop" to public ethics, secular humanists have largely succeeded in purging "the public square" of religion. According to Neuhaus, the American religious right has muted its dream of living within a nation that is uniformly Christian, but it does seek to weaken those liberal "border patrols" that rigorously enforce the line between the secular and the sacred. He would allow those religious sentiments that are widely held by most citizens to be included in political debate, so long as they are expressed through reasons that are publicly accessible, rather than as religious revelations available only within particular religious traditions.

Our next selection provides a very different radical voice, that of Susan Moller Okin (1946–2004), who was a professor of ethics at Stanford University and a highly respected contributor to feminism. Unlike earlier liberal feminists who sought equal treatment for women under the law, Okin argues that liberal laws treat as equals those that have been made unequal by the conventional division of labor in the family. Despite some changes in family practices, women still bear the lion's share of responsibilities for child-rearing and housekeeping, and the unequal power relationships between husbands and wives in the family leave women vulnerable to social and psychological hurdles when they enter the public sphere. Yet liberal theories of justice had – prior to Okin's ground-breaking work in 1989 – only addressed justice in public life and ignored the injustices that occur in domestic life. Unless there is justice in the family, not only will the oppression of women continue regardless of the "gender neutrality" that is inscribed in our theories of justice and our "equal opportunity" legislation, but our children will fail to learn to be just, because the family is their primary school of justice. Justice cannot be modeled for them in a patriarchal family.

Global warming has brought environmental concerns to public attention during the past decade, but deep green thought precedes this particular concern. Arne Naess (1937–2004), Norway's preeminent philosopher during the twentieth century and an avid mountaineer and political activist on behalf of environmental causes, penned a "platform of the deep ecology movement" in the late 1970s. In our reading by Naess, he articulates many themes of that movement. There is a critical distinction to be made between "shallow environmentalism" (which is primarily concerned with pollution, resource depletion, and sustaining the affluence of people in developed countries) and "deep ecology" that has a much greater veneration of all life forms – humans in underdeveloped areas, animals, and vegetables. According to Naess' "Ecosophy T" philosophy, all life forms have an "equal right to live and blossom." Such flourishing of diversity and richness of life requires that we must ensure that our actions do not have harmful effects on other living beings. Particularly those in rich Western countries must reassess their obsession with economic production and consumption, and this requires changes in our current economic machinery. As others in less-developed countries begin to pursue the material affluence that has been coveted in the West, an "environmental Armageddon" could be hastened.[1]

Global environmental problems are just some of many concerns that the current era of globalization has spawned among the radical left. Michael Hardt (an American literary theorist and political philosopher at Duke University) collaborated with Antonio Negri (an Italian political philosopher who was a professor at Padua University and who was imprisoned on charges of masterminding the assassination of an Italian politician) to write *Empire* (2000) and *Multitude* (2004), which have led some observers to proclaim them the Marx and Engels of the twenty-first century. The selection by them that closes this chapter distills some of the main themes of these works. They claim that a new form of sovereignty now governs the world, narrowing but not eliminating the importance of nation-states. They call this new form of sovereignty "Empire" and see it manifested in a wide range of institutions, actors, and norms. While these institutions have a "democratic logic," they are largely isolated from popular representation and control. Thus, democracy must be reconceptualized; it is no longer a relationship between governments and their populations understood as a "united social body," but rather the actions of a diverse multitude. The people can no longer act as a collectivity, but only as individuals exercising

[1] An updated account of such problems is available in Thomas Friedman's *Hot, Flat, and Crowded* (New York: Farrar, Straus, and Giroux, 2008).

counter-power against the suffocating control that Empire otherwise exerts not only over our actions but our very being. But this does not mean that democracy is no longer possible; rather, it must be reinvented.

Of course, such a brief synopsis of the neo-Marxism or neo-anarchism of Hardt and Negri can hardly pierce the ambiguities in their perspective or convey the breadth of their thinking. When encountering the radical new voices that have come into prominence in recent years, serious political thinkers have few options but to read carefully not just the excerpts of their works, as presented in readers like this, but the larger works from which they are extracted.

Michael J. Sandel, "America's Search for a New Public Philosophy"*

Liberal versus republican freedom

The central idea of the public philosophy by which we live is that freedom consists in our capacity to choose our ends for ourselves. Politics should not try to form the character or cultivate the virtue of its citizens, for to do so would be to "legislate morality." Government should not affirm, through its policies or laws, any particular conception of the good life; instead it should provide a neutral framework of rights within which people can choose their own values and ends.

The aspiration to neutrality finds prominent expression in our politics and law. Although it derives from the liberal tradition of political thought, its province is not limited to those known as liberals, rather than conservatives, in American politics; it can be found across the political spectrum. Liberals invoke the ideal of neutrality when opposing school prayer or restrictions on abortion or attempts by Christian fundamentalists to bring their morality into the public square. Conservatives appeal to neutrality when opposing attempts by government to impose certain moral restraints – for the sake of workers' safety or environmental protection or distributive justice – on the operation of the market economy.

The ideal of free choice also figures on both sides of the debate over the welfare state. Republicans have long complained that taxing the rich to pay for welfare programs for the poor is a form of coerced charity that violates people's freedom to choose what to do with their own money. Democrats have long replied that government must assure all citizens a decent level of income, housing, education, and health care, on the grounds that those who are crushed by economic necessity are not truly free to exercise choice in other domains. Despite their disagreement about how government should act to respect individual choice, both sides assume that freedom consists in the capacity of people to choose their own ends.

So familiar is this vision of freedom that it might seem a permanent feature of the American political tradition. But as a reigning public philosophy, it is a recent arrival, a development of the past half century. Its distinctive character can best be seen by comparison with a rival public philosophy that it gradually displaced: a version of republican political theory.

Central to republican theory is the idea that liberty depends on sharing in self-government. This idea is not by itself inconsistent with liberal freedom. Participating in politics can be one among the ways in which people choose to pursue their individual ends. According to republican political theory, however, sharing in self-rule involves something more. It involves deliberating with fellow citizens about the common good and helping to shape the destiny of the political community. But to deliberate well about the common good requires more than the capacity to choose one's ends and to respect others' rights to do the same. It requires a knowledge of public affairs and also a sense of belonging, a concern for the whole, a moral bond with the community whose fate is at stake. To share in self-rule therefore requires that citizens possess, or come to acquire, certain civic virtues. But this means that republican politics cannot be neutral toward the values and ends its citizens espouse. The republican conception of freedom, unlike the liberal conception, requires a formative politics, a politics that cultivates in citizens the qualities of character that self-government requires.

Both the liberal and the republican understandings of freedom have been present throughout our political experience, but in shifting measure and relative importance. In recent decades the civic, or formative, aspect of our politics has given way to a procedural republic, concerned less with cultivating virtue than with enabling persons to choose their own values. This shift sheds light on our present discontent. For despite its appeal, the liberal vision of freedom lacks the civic resources to

* Michael J. Sandel, extracted from *The Atlantic Monthly* (March 1996), pp. 57–74.

sustain self-government. The public philosophy by which we live cannot secure the liberty it promises, because it cannot inspire the sense of community and civic engagement that liberty requires.

The political economy of citizenship

If American politics is to recover its civic voice, it must find a way to debate questions we have forgotten how to ask. Consider the way we think and argue about economics today, in contrast to the way Americans debated economic policy through much of our history. These days most of our economic arguments revolve around two considerations: prosperity and fairness. Whatever tax policies or budget proposals or regulatory schemes people may favor, they usually defend them on the grounds that they will increase the size of the economic pie or distribute the pieces of the pie more fairly or both.

So familiar are these ways of justifying economic policy that they might seem to exhaust the possibilities. But our debates about economic policy have not always focused solely on the size and the distribution of the national product. Throughout much of American history they have also addressed a different question: what economic arrangements are most hospitable to self-government?

Thomas Jefferson gave classic expression to the civic strand of economic argument. In his *Notes on the State of Virginia* (1787) he argued against developing large-scale domestic manufactures on the grounds that the agrarian way of life made for virtuous citizens, well suited to self-government. [...]

[...] The civic strand of economic argument extended even into the twentieth century, when Progressives grappled with big business and its consequences for self-government.

The curse of bigness

The political predicament of the Progressive Era bears a striking similarity to our own. Then as now, Americans sensed the unraveling of community and feared for the prospects of self-government. Then as now, there was a gap, or a lack of fit, between the scale of economic life and the terms in which people conceived their identities – a gap that many experienced as disorienting and disempowering. The threat to self-government at the turn of the century took two forms: the concentration of power amassed by giant corporations, and the erosion of those traditional forms of authority and community that had governed the lives of most Americans through the first century of the republic. A national economy dominated by vast corporations diminished the autonomy of local communities, traditionally the site of self-government. Meanwhile, the growth of large, impersonal cities, teeming with immigrants, poverty, and disorder, led many to fear that Americans lacked sufficient moral and civic cohesiveness to govern according to a shared vision of the good life.

[...]

In the 1960s, the civic strand of economic argument faded from American political discourse. Confronted with an economy too vast to admit republican hopes of mastery, and tempted by the prospect of prosperity, Americans of the postwar decades found their way to a new understanding of freedom. According to this understanding, our liberty depends not on our capacity as citizens to share in shaping the forces that govern our collective destiny but rather on our capacity as persons to choose our values and ends for ourselves.

From the standpoint of republican political theory, this shift represents a fateful concession; to abandon the formative ambition is to abandon the project of liberty as the republican tradition conceives it. But Americans did not experience the new public philosophy as disempowering – at least not at first. To the contrary, the procedural republic appeared to be a triumph of mastery and self-command. This was owing partly to the historical moment and partly to the promise of the liberal conception of freedom.

The moment of mastery

The procedural republic was born at a rare moment of American mastery. At the end of the Second World War the United States stood astride the world, an unrivaled global power. This power, combined with the buoyant economy of the postwar decades, accustomed a generation of Americans to seeing themselves as masters of their circumstances. John Kennedy's inaugural address gave stirring expression to a generation's conviction that it possessed powers of Promethean proportions. "The world is very different now," Kennedy proclaimed. "For man holds in his mortal hands the power to abolish all forms of human poverty and all forms of human life." We would "pay any price, bear any burden," to assure the success of liberty.

Beyond the bounty of American power, the promise of mastery in the postwar decades had another source in the public philosophy of contemporary liberalism itself. The image of persons as free and independent selves, unbound by moral or communal ties they have not chosen, is a liberating, even exhilarating, ideal. Freed from the dictates of custom or tradition, the liberal self is installed as sovereign, cast as the author of the only obligations that constrain. This image of freedom found expression across the political spectrum. Lyndon Johnson argued the case for the welfare state not in terms of communal obligation but instead in terms of enabling people to choose their own ends: "For more than thirty years, from Social Security to the war against poverty, we have diligently worked to enlarge the freedom of man," he said upon accepting the 1964 Democratic presidential nomination. "And as a result Americans tonight are freer to live as they want to live, to pursue their ambitions, to meet their desires ... than at any time in all of our glorious history." Welfare-rights advocates opposed work requirements, mandatory job training, and family-planning programs for welfare recipients on the grounds that all people, including the poor, "should have the freedom to choose how they may express the meaning of their lives." For their part, conservative critics of Johnson's Great Society also made their arguments in the name of the liberal conception of freedom. The only legitimate functions of government, Barry Goldwater insisted, were those that made it "possible for men to follow their chosen pursuits with maximum freedom." The libertarian economist Milton Friedman opposed Social Security and other mandatory government programs on the grounds that they violated people's rights "to live their lives by their own values."

And so for a time the special circumstances of American life obscured the passing of the civic concept of freedom. But when the moment of mastery expired – when, in 1968, Vietnam, riots in the ghettos, campus unrest, and the assassinations of Martin Luther King Jr. and Robert Kennedy brought a shattering of faith – Americans were left ill-equipped to contend with the dislocation that swirled about them. The liberating promise of the freely choosing self could not compensate for the loss of self-government more broadly conceived. Events spun out of control at home and abroad, and government seemed helpless to respond.

Reagan's civic conservatism

There followed a season of protest that is with us still. As disillusionment with government grew, politicians groped to articulate the frustrations that the reigning political agenda did not address. The most successful, at least in electoral terms, was Ronald Reagan. Although he ultimately failed to allay the discontent he tapped, it is instructive nonetheless to consider the source of his appeal and the way it departed from the prevailing terms of political discourse.

Reagan drew, in different moods and moments, on both the libertarian and the civic strands of American conservatism. The most resonant part of his political appeal derived from the second of these, from his skillful evocation of communal values such as family and neighborhood, religion and patriotism. What set Reagan apart from laissez-faire conservatives also set him apart from the public philosophy of his day: his ability to identify with Americans' yearnings for a common life of larger meanings on a smaller, less impersonal scale than that the procedural republic provides.

Reagan blamed big government for disempowering citizens and proposed a "New Federalism" that would shift power to states and localities, recalling the long-standing republican worry about concentrated power. But Reagan revived this tradition with a difference. Previous advocates of republican political economy had worried about big government and big business alike. For Reagan, the curse of bigness attached to government alone. Even as he evoked the ideal of community, he had little to say about the corrosive effects of capital flight or the disempowering consequences of economic power organized on a vast scale.

Reagan-era Democrats did not challenge Reagan on this score, nor did they otherwise join the debate about community and self-government. Tied to the terms of rights-oriented liberalism, they missed the mood of discontent. The anxieties of the age concerned the erosion of those communities intermediate between the individual and the nation – families and neighborhoods, cities and towns, schools and congregations. But Democrats, once the party of dispersed power, had learned in recent decades to view intermediate communities with suspicion. Too often such communities had been pockets of prejudice, outposts of intolerance, places where the tyranny of the majority held sway. And so, from the New Deal to the civil-rights movement to the Great Society, the liberal project was to use federal power to vindicate individual rights that local communities had failed to protect. This unease with the middle terms of civic life, however honorably acquired, left Democrats ill-equipped to attend to the erosion of self-government.

The civic strand of Reagan's rhetoric enabled him to succeed, where Democrats failed, in tapping the mood of discontent. In the end, however, Reagan's presidency did little to alter the conditions underlying the discontent. He governed more as a market conservative than as a civic conservative. The unfettered capitalism he favored did nothing to repair the moral fabric of families, neighborhoods, and communities and much to undermine them.

The risks of republican politics

Any attempt to revitalize the civic strand of freedom must confront two sobering objections. The first doubts that it is possible to revive republican ideals; the second doubts that it is desirable. The first objection holds that given the scale and complexity of the modern world, it is unrealistic to aspire to self-government as the republican tradition conceives it. From Aristotle's polis to Jefferson's agrarian ideal, the civic conception of freedom found its home in small and bounded places, largely self-sufficient, inhabited by people whose conditions of life afforded the leisure, learning, and commonality to deliberate well about public concerns. But we do not live that way today. To the contrary, we live in a highly mobile continental society, teeming with diversity. Moreover, even this vast society is not self-sufficient but is situated in a global economy whose frenzied flow of money and goods, information and images, pays little heed to nations, much less neighborhoods. How, under conditions such as these, could the civic strand of freedom possibly take hold?

In fact, this objection continues, the republican strand of American politics, for all its persistence, has often spoken in a voice tinged with nostalgia. Even as Jefferson exalted the yeoman farmer, America was becoming a manufacturing nation. And so it was with the artisan republicans of Andrew Jackson's day, the apostles of free labor in Abraham Lincoln's time, and the shopkeepers and pharmacists Brandeis defended against the curse of bigness. In each of these cases – or so it is argued – republican ideals found their expression at the last moment, too late to offer feasible alternatives, just in time to offer an elegy for a lost cause. If the republican tradition is irredeemably nostalgic, then whatever its capacity to illuminate the defects of liberal politics, it offers little that could lead us to a richer civic life.

The second objection holds that even were it possible to recover republican ideals, to do so would not be desirable; given the difficulty of instilling civic virtue, republican politics always runs the risk of coercion. This peril can be glimpsed in Jean-Jacques Rousseau's account of the formative undertaking necessary to a democratic republic. The task of the republic's founder or great legislator, he writes, is no less than "to change human nature, to transform each individual ... into a part of a larger whole from which this individual receives, in a sense, his life and his being." The legislator "must deny man his own forces" in order to make him reliant on the community as a whole. The more nearly each person's individual will is "dead and obliterated," the more likely that person is to embrace the general will. "Thus if each citizen is nothing and can do nothing except in concert with all the others ... one can say that the legislation has achieved the highest possible point of perfection."

The coercive face of soulcraft is by no means unknown among American republicans. For example, Benjamin Rush, a signer of the Declaration of Independence, wanted "to convert men into republican machines" and to teach each citizen "that he does not belong to himself, but that he is public property." But civic education need not take so harsh a form. In practice, successful republican soulcraft involves a gentler kind of tutelage. For example, the political economy of citizenship that informed nineteenth-century American life sought to cultivate not only commonality but also the independence and judgment to deliberate well about the common good. It worked not by coercion but by a complex mixture of persuasion and habituation – what Alexis de Tocqueville called "the slow and quiet action of society upon itself."

The dispersed, differentiated character of American public life in Tocqueville's day and the indirect modes of character formation this differentiation allowed are what separate Rousseau's republican exertions from the civic practices Tocqueville described. Unable to abide disharmony, Rousseau's republican ideal seeks to collapse the distance between persons so that citizens stand in a kind of speechless transparence, or immediate presence to one another. Where the general will prevails, the citizens "consider themselves to be a single body" and there is no need for political argument. "The first to propose [a new law] merely says what everybody has already felt; and there is no question of intrigues or eloquence" to secure its passage.

It is this assumption, that the common good is unitary and uncontestable, not the formative ambition as such, that inclines Rousseau's politics to coercion. It is, moreover, an assumption that republican politics can do without. As America's experience with the political economy of citizenship suggests, the civic conception of freedom does not render disagreement unnecessary. It offers a way of conducting political argument, not transcending it.

Unlike Rousseau's unitary vision, the republican politics Tocqueville described is more clamorous than consensual. It does not despise differentiation. Instead of collapsing the space between persons, it fills this space with public institutions that gather people together in various capacities, that both separate and relate them. These institutions include the townships, schools, religions, and virtue-sustaining occupations that form the "character of mind" and "habits of the heart" a democratic republic requires. Whatever their more particular purposes, these agencies of civic education inculcate the habit of attending to public things. And yet given their multiplicity, they prevent public life from dissolving into an undifferentiated whole.

So the civic strand of freedom is not necessarily coercive. It can sometimes find pluralistic expression. To this extent the liberal objection to republican political theory is misplaced. But the liberal worry does contain an insight that cannot be dismissed: republican politics is risky politics, a politics without guarantees, and the risks it entails inhere in the formative project. To accord the political community a stake in the character of its citizens is to concede the possibility that bad communities may form bad characters. Dispersed power and multiple sites of civic formation may reduce these dangers but cannot remove them.

[...] Since the days of Aristotle's polis, the republican tradition has viewed self-government as an activity rooted in a particular place, carried out by citizens loyal to that place and the way of life it embodies. Self-government today, however, requires a politics that plays itself out in a multiplicity of settings, from neighborhoods to nations to the world as a whole. Such a politics requires citizens who can abide the ambiguity associated with divided sovereignty, who can think and act as multiple situated selves. The civic virtue distinctive to our time is the capacity to negotiate our way among the sometimes overlapping and sometimes conflicting obligations that claim us, and to live with the tension to which multiple loyalties give rise.

The global media and markets that shape our lives beckon us to a world beyond boundaries and belonging. But the civic resources we need to master these forces, or at least to contend with them, are still to be found in the places and stories, memories and meanings, incidents and identities that situate us in the world and give our lives their moral particularity. The task for politics now is to cultivate these resources, to repair the civic life on which democracy depends.

Richard John Neuhaus, "Public Religion and Public Reason"*

The idea of public religion is the subject of great public confusion. The idea is widely accepted that religion is something between an individual and his God. Each person is free to worship the God of her choice. Religion is the business of church and home and has no place in public space. These and other axioms are, it is commonly said, part of the American way. Legally and politically, they are supported by a notion of the "separation of church and state" that is understood to mean the separation of religion and religiously based morality from the public realm.

A competing set of ideas gravitates around the insistent intuition that America is in some significant sense a "Christian nation." Today that is generally thought to be a conservative sentiment. Christians in mainline churches of a liberal political disposition, however, also insist that Christian faith is in some necessary way "relevant" to public policy. Christians, as Christians (and not simply as people of goodwill), have a responsibility to advance a social vision derived from biblical teaching.

[...]

Those who would keep the public square naked of religious symbol and substance are often motivated by a not unreasonable fear. The frequently expressed fear is that politics could degenerate into religious warfare. When one speaks of religion influencing public policy, the immediate question is, *Whose* religion? If one subscribes to the notion that this is in some sense a Christian society, then the question becomes, *Whose* Christianity? Without some basic agreement religiously, the entrance of religion into the public arena would seem to be a formula for open-ended conflict and possible anarchy.

Yet, in the absence of a public ethic, we arrive at that point where, in Alisdair MacIntyre's arresting phrase, "politics becomes civil war carried on by other means."[2] MacIntyre believes that we have already reached that point, and he may be right. A major problem, however, is that a public ethic cannot be reestablished unless it is

* Richard John Neuhaus, extracted from chapter 2 of *The Naked Public Square* (Grand Rapids, MI: William B. Eerdmans Publishing Co., 1984).

2 Alasdair MacIntyre, *After Virtue* (Notre Dame, 1981), p. 236: "... modern politics cannot be a matter of genuine moral consensus. And it is not. Modern politics is civil war carried on by other means."

informed by religiously grounded values. That is, without such an engagement of religion, it cannot be re-established in a way that would be viewed as democratically legitimate. The reason for this is that, in sociological fact, the values of the American people are deeply rooted in religion.

That sociological reality is not necessarily something to be cheered. It simply is. There are other, perhaps more attractive, ways to go about constructing a public ethic. A long and in many respects admirable history of moral philosophy has worked at establishing such an ethic that would be based upon "objective" reason and in no way dependent upon particular religious beliefs. This enterprise, while usually self-consciously secular, is not necessarily hostile to religion. To the contrary, major figures such as Immanuel Kant were at pains to assert that their ethical reasoning was perfectly consonant with Christian faith. In American thought there is ample evidence that the founding fathers – Jefferson, the Adamses, Madison, et al. – had the deepest appreciation of the need for a public ethic and the cultivation of what were called republican virtues. They would also have protested vigorously the suggestion that they shortchanged the importance of particular religions. In their view, a public and universal ethic is to be supported in its observance by the teachings of a variety of faiths. The confidence was frequently expressed that, when it comes to public morality, the sundry sects were, despite their conflicts of doctrine, in essential agreement upon the ethical basics. Still in this century that confidence was reflected in Protestant ecumenical efforts which declared that doctrines divide while ethics and service unite.

Religious belief was seen as a reinforcement, a backstop, if you will, to the public ethic. Religion, especially in its insistence upon ultimate rewards and punishments, was the motivating force for good behavior. But the agreed upon understanding of what constitutes "good" behavior was not to be derived from religious belief. In other words, religion was to motivate and sanction but not to inform or shape the public ethic.

[...]

The idea of a religiously based moral common denominator was soon to come in for hard times, however. The alternative to the common denominator of the American "melting pot" is often described in terms of the rise of pluralism. (Pluralism, as we will have occasion to consider in greater detail, is frequently a synonym for pervasive confusion.) In moments of candor public educators had recognized that the common denominator was somewhat artificial and contrived, too much of what people *really* believed most deeply had to be swept under the carpet in order to maintain the putative consensus. At the same time, there were new and aggressive forces in American cultural and political life that did not go along even with the minimal belief system. The much assailed *Humanist Manifesto* of 1933 was a particularly strident dissent from the consensus. The signers, including John Dewey, the high priest of American public philosophy, must be credited with honesty in their pointing out what might be described as the bootlegging of religion into the public arena, and especially into government schools. That is, the complaint is warranted if one is serious, as the signers of the manifesto were, in believing that America is or should be a secular society.

[...]

Secular humanism has had a pervasive and debilitating effect upon our public life. Without ever having to put them to a vote, without even subjecting them to democratic debate, some of the key arguments of what is properly called secular*ism* have prevailed. There need not be a conspiracy in any coherent or calculated sense for ideas and prejudices to insinuate themselves into our thinking and acting. They are part of the conceptual air we breathe.

One idea that has been insinuated and legally rooted is a peculiar reading of what the First Amendment means for "the separation of church and state." It is not, as some fundamentalists complain, that God has been taken out of our public schools or out of our public life. God, being God, cannot be "taken out" of anything. It is the case that truth claims and normative ethics that have specific reference to God or religion have been, at least in theory, excluded. One says "at least in theory" because, in uncounted classrooms and forums where the business of the *polis* is debated, religiously grounded beliefs continue to play a vigorous part. In everyday fact, people do not and cannot bifurcate themselves so at one moment they are thinking religiously and at another secularly, so to speak. But specific reference to religion, specific claims "tainted" by religious belief, are always subject to challenge. The challengers can usually call in the law on their side.

Thus religion in public space became increasingly surreptitious and suspect. There are remnants in public oaths, prayers in legislatures, and the like. Determined secularists view these as residual inconsistencies that they have not yet got around to extirpating and that may not be worth bothering about. A few belligerent atheists might excite themselves about these matters, but they are not taken seriously and their legal protests are dismissed as nuisance suits.

[...]

In American public life today, abortion law is the single most fevered and volatile question that inescapably joins religion and politics. [...] No other dispute so clearly and painfully illustrates the problematic of the naked public square.

Through specific policy disputes underlying assumptions erupt. It is the underlying assumptions, the cultural postures, if you will, that concern us here. Our own underlying assumption, which needs to be brought to the surface and exposed to examination, is that politics is in large part a function of culture. Beyond that, it is our assumption that at the heart of culture is religion. In this connection "religion" is meant comprehensively. It includes not just those ideas and activities and attitudes that we ordinarily call religious, but all the ways we think and act and interact with respect to what we believe is ultimately true and important. There is nothing frightfully original in this way of connecting politics, culture, and religion. A host of thinkers, including Tillich, Hegel, and Plato, have made the connection in a similar way. With astonishing frequency, however, the connection is neglected in writing about religion and politics today. In American history, of course, the understanding of ultimacies was publicly articulated with specific reference to biblical, Judeo-Christian religion. It is the relatively recent exclusion of that specificity which is now being so vigorously protested by many Americans. They feel that they were not consulted by whoever decided that this is a secular society. And they resent that; they resent it very much.

[...] There is a great deal that is public but not in the ordinary sense of the term political.[3] Family life, work, learning, and entertainment all have public dimensions of interaction, not only interaction with other individuals but also with other communities. For those of us who are not professional politicians or political junkies, what matters to us most does not take place in the political arena as such. The things that matter most happen in the "mediating structures" of our personal and communal existence.[4] These structures – family, neighborhood, church, voluntary association – are the people-sized, face-to-face institutions where we work day by day at our felicities and our fears. The public square is not limited to Government Square. At the same time – and for reasons that may be nearly unavoidable – government impinges upon all public squares.

[...]

In conservative eyes, however, the sins of liberal government are sins of commission: government does many things they think it should not do and forbids them to do things they think they should be free to do. They are notably outraged by governments that, they believe, advance changes in sexual and family mores – areas that could hardly be more value-laden. While accepting the prohibition of mandatory race segregation, they resent deeply programs such as school busing and "affirmative action" aimed at mandatory racial integration. They react vociferously to government actions that get in the way of praying in schools, owning handguns, hiring whom they want, and living where they please. In sum, in very everyday ways they feel assaulted by liberal government as liberals do not feel assaulted by conservative government.

[...]

A fringe of the religious new right would prefer a party that comes right out and says that America is a Christian society. For several decades there has been a proposed constitutional amendment knocking about that says just that. The effective leadership, however, in deference to pluralism, has learned to mute the talk about Christian America. They feel they can work within a party that permits the dream of Christian America to be expressed *sotto voce*. This basis of Republican alliance is strengthened by a Democratic alternative that they perceive as militantly secularist. When they enter the public arena, new right leaders do not insist that everyone there must pass a test of Judeo-Christian moral orthodoxy. They do insist that they will not check their own beliefs in the cloakroom before entering. No longer content to be smugglers, they are in open rebellion against the border patrols that would maintain and even intensify the line between sacred and secular. In the Republican party they find greater sympathy for relaxing the border patrol.

This chapter began by suggesting that the issues joined are more theological than political. A dilemma, both political and theological, facing the religious new right is simply this: *it wants to enter the political arena making public claims on the basis of private truths.* The integrity of politics itself requires that such a proposal be resisted. Public decisions must be made by arguments that are public in character. A public argument is transsubjective. It is not derived from sources of revelation or disposition that are essentially private and

3 For a suggestive discussion of the distinctions between "public" and "political," see Parker Palmer, *The Company of Strangers* (Crossroad, 1981).

4 Peter Berger and Richard John Neuhaus spell out the concept and some policy implications of "mediating structures" in *To Empower People* (American Enterprise Institute, 1977).

arbitrary. The perplexity of fundamentalism in public is that its self-understanding is premised upon a view of religion that is emphatically not public in character. Fundamentalism is the religious variant of what Alisdair MacIntyre calls "modern emotivism." By emotivism is meant that state of affairs in which every moral statement is simply a statement of private preference. It has no inherently normative or public force. Of course it can have great force in public effect if those who agree with it can marshal a majority to their side and thus impose it upon those who do not agree. That is what MacIntyre means when he says that politics becomes civil war carried on by other means.

Fundamentalist leaders rail against secular humanists for creating what I have called the naked public square. In fact, fundamentalism is an indispensable collaborator in that creation. By separating public argument from private belief, by building a wall of strict separationism between faith and reason, fundamentalist religion ratifies and reinforces the conclusions of militant secularism. In order to counter this unwelcome result, the religious new right takes a leaf from the manual of an earlier Christian liberalism: the claim is made that, despite differences in religious belief, there is a core consensus on what is moral. This is the much discussed "moral agenda" on which, presumably, Christians of all stripes and even nonbelievers can come together. That approach will not wash now, however, just as it did not wash for long when employed by earlier religious actors in the public arena. The issues facing our society engage ultimacies. The issues themselves may be penultimate or less, but their resolution requires a publicly discussable sense of more ultimate truths that serve as points of reference in guiding our agreements and disagreements. Such resolution requires a public ethic that we do not now possess.

Groups such as Moral Majority kicked a tripwire alerting us to a pervasive contradiction in our culture and politics. We insist that we are a democratic society, yet we have in recent decades systematically excluded from policy consideration the operatives values of the American people, values that are overwhelmingly grounded in religious belief. We may acknowledge our indebtedness to those who have kicked the tripwire while, at the same time, recognizing that they may be the least helpful in addressing the contradiction they have illuminated. Those who have set off the alarm are at the heart of what is alarming. Fundamentalist morality, which is derived from beliefs that cannot be submitted to examination by public reason, is essentially a private morality. If enough people who share that morality are mobilized, it can score victories in the public arena. But every such victory is a setback in the search for a public ethic.

A serviceable public ethic is not somewhere in our past, just waiting to be found and reinstalled. From the past, however, there may be clues to the reconstruction of such an ethic for our time. In exploring this possibility we should at least entertain the hope that those who kicked, or perhaps merely stumbled over, the tripwire may become partners in that reconstruction.

Susan Moller Okin, "Justice, Gender, and the Family"*

We as a society pride ourselves on our democratic values. We don't believe people should be constrained by innate differences from being able to achieve desired positions of influence or to improve their well-being; equality of opportunity is our professed aim. The Preamble to our Constitution stresses the importance of justice, as well as the general welfare and the blessing of liberty. The Pledge of Allegiance asserts that our republic preserves "liberty and justice for all."

Yet substantial inequalities between the sexes still exist in our society. In economic terms, full-time working women (after some very recent improvement) earn on average 71 percent of the earnings of full-time working men. One-half of poor and three-fifths of chronically poor households with dependent children are maintained by a single female parent. The poverty rate for elderly women is nearly twice that for elderly men.[5] On the political front, [...] one out of nine justices seems to be considered sufficient female representation on the Supreme Court, and the number of men chosen in each congressional election far exceeds the number of women elected in the entire history of the country. Underlying and intertwined with all these inequalities is the unequal distribution of the unpaid labor of the family.

An equal sharing between the sexes of family responsibilities, especially child care, is "the great revolution that has not happened."[6] Women, including mothers of young children, are, of course, working outside the

* Susan Moller Okin, extracted from *Justice, Gender, and the Family* (Basic Books, Inc., 1989), pp. 3–23.

5 US Department of Labor, *Employment and Earnings: July 1987* (Washington, DC: Government Printing Office, 1987).

6 Shirley Williams, in Williams and Elizabeth Holtzman, "Women in the Political World: Observations," *Daedalus*, 116, 4 (Fall, 1987), p. 30.

household far more than their mothers did. And the small proportion of women who reach high-level positions in politics, business, and the professions command a vastly disproportionate amount of space in the media, compared with the millions of women who work at low-paying, dead-end jobs, the millions who do part-time work with its lack of benefits, and the millions of others who stay home performing for no pay what is frequently not even acknowledged as work. Certainly, the fact that women are doing more paid work does not imply that they are more equal. It is often said that we are living in a post-feminist era. This claim, due in part to the distorted emphasis on women who have "made it," is false, no matter which of its meanings is intended. It is certainly not true that feminism has been vanquished, and equally untrue that it is no longer needed because its aims have been fulfilled. Until there is justice within the family, women will not be able to gain equality in politics, at work, or in any other sphere.

The typical current practices of family life, structured to a large extent by gender, are not just. Both the expectation and the experience of the division of labor by sex make women vulnerable. As I shall show, a cycle of power relations and decisions pervades both family and workplace, each reinforcing the inequalities between the sexes that already exist within the other. Not only women, but children of both sexes, too, are often made vulnerable by gender-structured marriage. One-quarter of children in the United States now live in families with only one parent – in almost 90 percent of cases, the mother. [...] The standard of living of divorced women and the children who live with them plummets after divorce, whereas the economic situation of divorced men tends to be better than when they were married.

A central source of injustice for women these days is that the law, most noticeably in the event of divorce, treats more or less as equals those whom custom, workplace discrimination, and the still conventional division of labor within the family have made very unequal. Central to this socially created inequality are two commonly made but inconsistent presumptions: that women are primarily responsible for the rearing of children; and that serious and committed members of the work force (regardless of class) do not have primary responsibility, or even shared responsibility, for the rearing of children. The old assumption of the workplace, still implicit, is that workers have wives at home. It is built not only into the structure and expectations of the workplace but into other crucial social institutions, such as schools, which make no attempt to take account, in their scheduled hours or vacations, of the fact that parents are likely to hold jobs.

Now, of course, many wage workers do not have wives at home. Often, they *are* wives and mothers, or single, separated, or divorced mothers of small children. But neither the family nor the workplace has taken much account of this fact. Employed wives still do by far the greatest proportion of unpaid family work, such as child care and housework. Women are far more likely to take time out of the workplace or to work part-time because of family responsibilities than are their husbands or male partners. And they are much more likely to move because of their husbands' employment needs or opportunities than their own. All these tendencies, which are due to a number of factors, including the sex segregation and discrimination of the workplace itself, tend to be cyclical in their effects: wives advance more slowly than their husbands at work and thus gain less seniority, and the discrepancy between their wages increases over time. Then, because both the power structure of the family and what is regarded as consensual "rational" family decision making reflect the fact that the husband usually earns more, it will become even less likely as time goes on that the unpaid work of the family will be shared between the spouses. Thus the cycle of inequality is perpetuated. Often hidden from view within a marriage, it is in the increasingly likely event of marital breakdown that the socially constructed inequality of married women is at its most visible.

This is what I mean when I say that gender-structured marriage *makes* women vulnerable. These are not matters of natural necessity, as some people would believe. Surely nothing in our natures dictates that men should not be equal participants in the rearing of their children. Nothing in the nature of work makes it impossible to adjust it to the fact that people are parents as well as workers. That these things have not happened is part of the historically, socially constructed differentiation between the sexes that feminists have come to call *gender*. We live in a society that has over the years regarded the innate characteristic of sex as one of the clearest legitimizers of different rights and restrictions, both formal and informal. While the legal sanctions that uphold male dominance have begun to be eroded in the past century, and more rapidly in the last twenty years, the heavy weight of tradition, combined with the effects of socialization, still works powerfully to reinforce sex roles that are commonly regarded as of unequal prestige and worth. The sexual division of labor has not only been a fundamental part of the marriage contract, but so deeply influences us in our formative years that feminists of both sexes who try to reject it can find themselves struggling against it with varying degrees of ambivalence. Based on this linchpin, "gender" – by which I mean *the deeply entrenched institutionalization of sexual difference* – still permeates our society.

The construction of gender

Due to feminism and feminist theory, gender is coming to be recognized as a social factor of major importance. Indeed, the new meaning of the word reflects the fact that so much of what has traditionally been thought of as sexual differences is now considered by many to be largely socially produced.[7] Feminist scholars from many disciplines and with radically different points of view have contributed to the enterprise of making gender fully visible and comprehensible. At one end of the spectrum are those whose explanations of the subordination of women focus primarily on biological difference as causal in the construction of gender,[8] and at the other end are those who argue that biological difference may not even lie at the core of the social construction that is gender[9]; the views of the vast majority of feminists fall between these extremes. The rejection of biological determinism and the corresponding emphasis on gender as a social construction characterize most current feminist scholarship. Of particular relevance is work in psychology, where scholars have investigated the importance of female primary parenting in the formation of our gendered identities,[10] and in history and anthropology,[11] where emphasis has been placed on the historical and cultural variability of gender. Some feminists have been criticized for developing theories of gender that do not take sufficient account of differences *among* women, especially race, class, religion, and ethnicity.[12] While such critiques should always inform our research and improve our arguments, it would be a mistake to allow them to detract our attention from gender itself as a factor of significance. Many injustices are experienced by women *as women*, whatever the differences among them and whatever other injustices they also suffer from.

[...]

Sex discrimination, sexual harassment, abortion, pregnancy in the workplace, parental leave, child care, and surrogate mothering have all become major and well-publicized issues of public policy, engaging both courts and legislatures. Issues of family justice, in particular – from child custody and terms of divorce to physical and sexual abuse of wives and children – have become increasingly visible and pressing, and are commanding increasing attention from the police and court systems. There is clearly a major "justice crisis" in contemporary society arising from issues of gender.

Theories of justice and the neglect of gender

During these same two decades, there has been a great resurgence of theories of social justice. [...] Yet, remarkably, major contemporary theorists of justice have almost without exception ignored the situation I have just described. They have displayed little interest or knowledge of the findings of feminism. [...]

How can theories of justice that are ostensibly about people in general neglect women, gender, and all the inequalities between the sexes? One reason is that most theorists *assume*, though they do not discuss, the traditional, gender-structured family. Another is that they often employ gender-neutral language in a false, hollow way. Let us examine these two points.

The hidden gender-structured family In the past, political theorists often used to distinguish clearly between "private" domestic life and the "public" life of politics and the marketplace, claiming explicitly that the two spheres operated in accordance with different principles. They separated out the family from what they deemed the subject matter of politics, and they made closely related, explicit claims about the nature of women and the appropriateness of excluding from them civil and political life. Men, the subjects of the theories, were able to make the transition back and forth from domestic to public life with ease, largely because of the functions performed by women in the

7 Joan Wallach Scott, *Gender and the Politics of History* (New York: Columbia University Press, 1988), p. 28.

8 Among Anglo-American feminists see, for example, Mary Daly, *Gyn/Ecology: The Metaethics of Radical Feminism* (Boston: Beacon Press, 1978).

9 See, for example, Sylvia Yanagisako and Jane Collier, "The Mode of Reproduction in Anthropology," in Deborah Rhode, ed., *Theoretical Perspectives on Sexual Difference* (New Haven: Yale University Press, 1990).

10 Nancy Chodorow, *The Reproduction of Mothering: Psychoanalysis and the Sociology of Gender* (Berkeley: University of California Press, 1978).

11 Linda Nicholson, *Gender and History* (New York: Columbia University Press, 1986).

12 For such critiques, see bell hooks, *Ain't I a Woman: Black Women and Feminism* (Boston: South End Press, 1981).

family.[13] When we turn to contemporary theories of justice, superficial appearances can easily lead to the impression that they are inclusive of women. In fact, they continue the same "separate spheres" tradition, by ignoring the family, its division of labor, and the related economic dependency and restricted opportunities of most women. The judgment that the family is "nonpolitical" is implicit in the fact that it is simply not discussed in most works of political theory today.

[...]

What is the basis of my claim that the family, while neglected, is *assumed* by theorists of justice? One obvious indication is that they take mature, independent human beings as the subjects of their theories without any mention of how they got to be that way. We know, of course, that human beings develop and mature only as a result of a great deal of attention and hard work, by far the greatest part of it done by women. But when theorists of justice talk about "work," they mean paid work performed in the marketplace. They must be assuming that women, in the gender-structured family, continue to do their unpaid work of nurturing and socializing the young and providing a haven of intimate relations – otherwise there would be no moral subjects for them to theorize about. But these activities apparently take place outside the scope of their theories. Typically, the family itself is not examined in the light of whatever standard of justice the theorist arrives at.[14]

[...]

False gender neutrality Many academics in recent years have become aware of the objectionable nature of using the supposedly generic male forms of nouns and pronouns. As feminist scholars have demonstrated, these words have most often *not* been used, throughout history and the history of philosophy in particular, with the intent to include women. *Man, mankind,* and *he* are going out of style as universal representations, though they have by no means disappeared. But the gender-neutral alternatives that most contemporary theorists employ are often even more misleading than the blatantly sexist use of male terms of reference. For they serve to disguise the real and continuing failure of theorists to confront the fact that the human race consists of persons of two sexes. They are by this means able to ignore the fact that there are *some* socially relevant physical differences between women and men, and the even more important fact that the sexes have had very different histories, very different assigned social roles and "natures," and very different degrees of access to power and opportunity in all human societies up to and including the present.

[...]

False gender neutrality is by no means confined to the realm of theory. Its harmful effects can be seen in public policies that have directly affected large numbers of women adversely. It was used, for example, in the Supreme Court's 1976 decision that the exclusion of pregnancy-related disabilities from employers' disability insurance plans was "not a gender-based discrimination at all." In a now infamous phrase of its majority opinion, the Court explained that such plans did not discriminate against women because the distinction drawn by such plans was between pregnant women and "non-pregnant *persons.*[15]

[...]

The combined effect of the omission of the family and the falsely gender-neutral language in recent political thought is that most theorists are continuing to ignore the highly political issue of gender. The language they use makes little difference to what they actually do, which is to write about men and about only those women who manage, in spite of the gendered structures and practices of the society in which they live, to adopt patterns of life that have been developed to suit the needs of men. The fact that human beings are born as helpless infants – not as the purportedly autonomous actors who populate political theories – is obscured by the implicit assumption of gendered families, operating outside the range of the theories. To a large extent, contemporary theories of justice, like those of the past, are about men with wives at home.

Gender as an issue of justice

For three major reasons, this state of affairs is unacceptable. The first is the obvious point that women must be fully included in any satisfactory theory of justice. The

[13] There is now an abundant literature on the subject of women, their exclusion from nondomestic life, and the reasons given to justify it, in Western political theory. See, for example, Lorenne J. Clark and Lynda Lange, eds., *The Sexism of Social and Political Thought* (Toronto: University of Toronto Press, 1979) and Jeane Bethke Elshtain, *Public Man, Private Woman: Women in Social and Political Thought* (Princeton: Princeton University Press, 1981).

[14] This is commented on and questioned by Francis Schrag, "Justice and the Family," *Inquiry*, 19 (1976), p. 200, and Michael Walzer, *Spheres of Justice* (New York: Basic Books, 1983), chap. 9.

[15] *General Electric v. Gilbert*, 429 U.S. 125 (1976), pp. 135–6; second phrase quoted from *Geduldig v. Aiello*, 417 U.S. 484 (1974), pp. 496–7, emphasis added.

second is that equality of opportunity, not only for women but for children of both sexes, is seriously undermined by the current gender injustices of our society. And the third reason is that, as has already been suggested, the family – currently the linchpin of the gender structure – must be just if we are to have a just society, since it is within the family that we first come to have that sense of ourselves and our relations with others that is at the root of moral development.

Counting women in When we turn to the great tradition of Western political thought with questions about the justice of the treatment of the sexes in mind, it is to little avail. Bold feminists like Mary Astell, Mary Wollstonecraft, William Thompson, Harriet Taylor, and George Bernard Shaw have occasionally challenged the tradition, often using its own premises and arguments to overturn its explicit or implicit justification of the inequality of women. But John Stuart Mill is a rare exception to the rule that those who hold central positions in the tradition almost never question the justice of the subordination of women.

[...]

Unfortunately, much feminist intellectual energy in the 1980s has gone into the claim that "justice" and "right" are masculinist ways of thinking about morality that feminists should eschew or radically revise, advocating a morality of care.[16] The emphasis is misplaced, I think, for several reasons. First, what is by now a vast literature on the subject shows that the evidence for differences in women's and men's ways of thinking about moral issues is not (at least yet) very clear; neither is the evidence about the source of whatever differences there might be.[17] It may well turn out that any differences can be readily explained in terms of roles, including female primary parenting, that are socially determined and therefore alterable. There is certainly no evidence – nor could there be, in such a gender-structured society – for concluding that women are somehow naturally more inclined toward contextuality and away from universalism in their moral thinking, a false concept that unfortunately reinforces the old stereotypes that justify separate spheres. The capacity of reactionary forces to capitalize on the "different moralities" strain in feminism is particularly evident in Pope John Paul II's [...] Apostolic Letter, "On the Dignity of Women," in which he refers to women's special capacity to care for others in arguing for confining them to motherhood or celibacy.

Second, I think the distinction between an ethic of justice and an ethic of care has been overdrawn. The best theorizing about justice, I argue, has integral to it the notions of care and empathy, of thinking of the interests and well-being of others who may be very different from ourselves. It is, therefore, misleading to draw a dichotomy as though they were two contrasting ethics. The best theorizing about justice is not some abstract "view from nowhere," but results from the carefully attentive consideration of *everyone's* point of view. This means, of course, that the best theorizing about justice is not good enough if it does not, or cannot readily be adapted to, include women and their points of view as fully as men and their points of view.

Gender and equality of opportunity The family is a crucial determinant of our opportunities in life, of what we "become." It has frequently been acknowledged by those concerned with real equality of opportunity that the family presents a problem.[18] But though they have discerned a serious problem, these theorists have underestimated it because they have seen only half of it. They have seen that the disparity among families in terms of the physical and emotional environment, motivation, and material advantages they can give their children has a tremendous effect upon children's opportunities in life. [...]

What has not been recognized as an equal opportunity problem, except in feminist literature and circles, is the disparity *within* the family, the fact that its gender structure is itself a major obstacle of equality of opportunity. This is very important in itself, since one of the factors with most influence on our opportunities in life is the social significance attributed to our sex. The opportunities of girls and women are centrally affected by the structure and practices of family life, particularly by the fact that women are almost invariably primary parents. What nonfeminists who see in the family an obstacle to equal opportunity have *not* seen is that the extent to which a family is gender-structured can make the sex we belong to a relatively insignificant aspect of our identity and our life prospects or an all-pervading

16 This claim, originating in the moral development literature, has significantly influenced recent feminist moral and political theory. Two central books are Carol Gilligan, *In a Different Voice* (Cambridge: Harvard University Press, 1982); and Nel Noddings, *Caring: A Feminine Approach to Ethics and Moral Education* (Berkeley: University of California Press, 1984).

17 See, for example, John M. Broughton, "Women's Rationality and Men's Virtues: A Critique of Gender Dualism in Gilligan's Theory of Moral Development," *Social Research*, 50, 3 (1983); Joan Tronto, "'Women's Morality': Beyond Gender Difference to a Theory of Care," *Signs*, 12, 4 (1987).

18 See especially James Fishkin, *Justice, Equal Opportunity and the Family* (New Haven: Yale University Press, 1983).

one. This is because so much of the social construction of gender takes place in the family, and particularly in the institution of female parenting.

Moreover, especially in recent years, with the increased rates of single motherhood, separation, and divorce, the inequalities between the sexes have *compounded* the first part of the problem. The disparity among families has grown largely because of the impoverishment of many women and children after separation or divorce. The division of labor in the typical family leaves most women far less capable than men of supporting themselves, and this disparity is accentuated by the fact that children of separated or divorced parents usually live with their mothers. The inadequacy – and frequent nonpayment – of child support has become recognized as a major social problem. Thus the inequalities of gender are now directly harming many children of both sexes as well as women themselves. Enhancing equal opportunity for women, important as it is in itself, is also a crucial way of improving the opportunities of many of the most disadvantaged children.

As there is a connection among the parts of this problem, so is there a connection among some of the solutions: much of what needs to be done to end the inequalities of gender, and to work in the direction of ending gender itself, will also help to equalize opportunity from one family to another. Subsidized, high-quality day care is obviously one such thing; another is the adaptation of the workplace to the needs of parents.

The family as a school of justice [...]

Almost every person in our society starts life in a family of some sort or other. Fewer of these families now fit the usual, though by no means universal, standard of previous generations, that is, wage-working father, homemaking mother, and children. More families these days are headed by a single parent; lesbian and gay parenting is no longer so rare; many children have two-wage working parents, and receive at least some of their early care outside the home. While its forms are varied, the family in which a child is raised, especially in the earliest years, is clearly a crucial place for early moral development and for the formation of our basic attitudes to others. It is, potentially, a place where we can *learn to be just*. It is especially important for the development of a sense of justice that grows from sharing the experiences of others and becoming aware of the points of view of others who are different in some respects from ourselves, but with whom we clearly have some interests in common.

[...]

In a just society, the structure and practices of families must give women the same opportunities as men to develop their capacities, to participate in political power and influence social choices, and to be economically secure. But in addition to this, families must be just because of the vast influence that they have on the moral development of children. The family is the primary institution of formative moral development. And the structure and practices of the family must parallel those of the larger society if the sense of justice is to be fostered and maintained. While many theorists of justice, both past and present, appear to have denied the importance of at least one of these factors, my own view is that both are absolutely crucial. A society that is committed to equal respect for all of its members, and to justice in social distributions of benefits and responsibilities, can neither neglect the family nor accept family structures and practices that violate these norms, as do current gender-based structures and practices. It is essential that children who are to develop into adults with a strong sense of justice and commitment to just institutions spend their earliest and most formative years in an environment in which they are loved and nurtured, *and* in which principles of justice are abided by and respected. What is a child of either sex to learn about fairness in the average household with two full-time working parents, where the mother does, at the very least, twice as much family work as the father? What is a child to learn about the value of nurturing and domestic work in a home with a traditional division of labor in which the father either subtly or not so subtly uses the fact that he is the wage earner to "pull rank" on or to abuse his wife? What is a child to learn about responsibility for others in a family in which, after many years of arranging her life around the needs of her husband and children, a woman is faced with having to provide for herself and her children but is totally ill-equipped for the task by the life she agreed to lead, has led, and expected to go on leading?

Arne Naess, "The Environmental Crisis and the Deep Ecological Movement"*

The gravity of the situation

Humankind is the first species on earth with the intellectual capacity to limit its numbers consciously and live in an enduring, dynamic equilibrium with other forms

* Arne Naess, extracted from *Ecology, Community, and Lifestyle* (Cambridge University Press, 1989), pp. 23–32.

of life. Human beings can perceive and care for the diversity of their surroundings. Our biological heritage allows us to delight in this intricate, living diversity. This ability to delight can be further perfected, facilitating a creative interaction with the immediate surroundings.

A global culture of a primarily techno-industrial nature is now encroaching upon all the world's milieux, desecrating living conditions for future generations. We – the responsible participants in this culture – have slowly but surely begun to question whether we truly accept this unique, sinister role we have previously chosen. Our reply is almost unanimously negative.

For the first time in the history of humanity, we stand face to face with a choice imposed upon us because our lackadaisical attitude to the production of things and people has caught up with us. Will we apply a touch of self-discipline and reasonable planning to contribute to the maintenance and development of the richness of life on Earth, or will we fritter away our chances, and leave development to blind forces?

A synopsis of what it is which makes the situation so critical could read: *An exponentially increasing, and partially or totally irreversible environmental deterioration or devastation perpetuated through firmly established ways of production and consumption and a lack of adequate policies regarding human population increase.*

The words 'deterioration' and 'devastation' are here understood to mean a change for the worse, a decrease of value. An ethical theory is presupposed, a system which allows one to judge a change as negative. Chemistry, physics, and the science of ecology acknowledge only change, not valued change. But you and I would presumably agree that a change in the bio-conditions of a river or ocean which excluded most forms of life would constitute a deterioration of value. Our evaluative thinking contends that it would constitute a devastation of diversity. The inability of the science of ecology to denounce such processes as the washing away of the soil of rain-forests suggests that we need another approach which involves the inescapable role of announcing values, not only 'facts'.

We need types of societies and communities in which one delights in the value-creative aspects of equilibrium rather than the glorification of value-neutral growth; in which being together with other living beings is more important than exploiting or killing them.

This discussion of the environmental crisis is motivated by the unrealised potential human beings have for varied experience in and of nature: the crisis contributes or could contribute to open our minds to sources of meaningful life which have largely gone unnoticed or have been depreciated in our efforts to adapt to the urbanised, techno-industrial mega-society.

It would be unwise to suppose that improvement can be achieved for the great majority of mankind without severe political contests and profound changes in the economic objectives pursued by the industrial states. Value priorities are socially and economically anchored, and changes in these priorities continuously interplay with other changes in a boundless, dynamic whole.

It would also be dangerous to suppose that any one group has full insight into and power over the techno-economic systems. The profundity of the crisis is due in part to its largely uncontrolled character: developments proceed at an accelerating pace even though no group, class, or nature has necessarily determined, planned, or accepted the next phase. Built-in mechanisms see to it that the tempo does not slacken. The cog-wheels have drawn us into the very machinery we thought was our slave.

Reaching new objectives for progress necessitates greater insight into this machinery, not only within the elites of power, but also within the populace at large. The latter should participate as much as possible both in the formulation of new goals and in suggesting means to reach them.

Production and consumption: ideology and practice

Progress has in all seriousness been measured by the rate of energy consumption and the acquisition and accumulation of material objects. What seems to better the material prerequisites for 'the good life' is given priority without asking if life is experienced as good. But the taste is the proof of the pudding, and more and more people in the so-called affluent societies are finding that its flavour isn't worth the stress. 'I am rich' as an experience is largely, but not entirely, independent of the conventional prerequisites for the good life. High life quality – yes; high standard of living – *tja*.[19]

The politicians and energy experts speak of exponentially increasing energy *needs* as though they were human needs, and not simply demands on the market. The material standard of living and the quality of life are for all intents and purposes thought to be one and the same. This results in demand for exponential material expansion. It is important to realise that percentage growth is exponential and that a yearly growth of 1% or 2% introduces *increasing* social and technical

[19] A Norwegian expression translating roughly as "maybe yes, maybe no."

changes in the course of each year in addition to enormous accumulated changes.

The deep-seated roots of the production and consumption ideology can be traced in all existing industrial states, but perhaps most clearly in the rich Western countries. A great deal of available mental energy within economic life is used to create new so-called needs and entice new customers to increase their material consumption. If it were not, economic crisis and unemployment would soon be upon us, or so it is said.

The dissatisfaction and restlessness due to the artificial tempo and the artificial 'modern' life are conventionally entered on the balance sheet without the batting of an eyelid. A change in the ideology of production and consumption is not possible without considerable change in the economic machinery. At present, the machine seems to require and to produce a distorted attitude to life. Within such a well-oiled system, a revision of value standards in favour of all-round experiential values, life quality rather than standard of living, must sound like a dangerous proposition.

We have 'progressed' to the point where the objectives of the good life must be considered threatening; we are intricately implicated in a system which guarantees short-term well-being in a small part of the world through destructive increases in material affluence. The privileges are regionally reserved because a similar increase of affluence in Africa, Asia or South America is not intended and would hasten the advent of an environmental Armageddon.

[...]

Our ecological knowledge is severely limited; ecopolitical consequences of ignorance

The ecological movement relies upon the results of research in ecology and more recently in conservation biology.[20] But to the great amazement of many, the scientific conclusions are often statements of ignorance: 'We do not know what long-range consequences the proposed interference in the ecosystem will beget, so we cannot make any hard and fast conclusions.' Only rarely can scientists predict with any certainty the effect of a new chemical on even a single small ecosystem.

The so-called ecological doomsday prophecies are statements about catastrophical states of affairs which cannot be precluded *if* certain new policies are *not* put into effect very soon. We know little or nothing about the extent to which such new policies will come into being. The fact that the human population is on a catastrophic course does not lead to the conclusion that catastrophe will occur. The situation is critical because we do not know *whether* the course will be promptly and radically changed.

Politicians and others now attentive to the words of environmental scientists are thunderstruck that science itself is proclaiming so much ignorance! It is a strange feeling to have new, politically brazen policies recommended on the basis of ignorance. But we do not know the consequences! Should we proceed with the project or not? The burden of proof rests with those who are encroaching upon the environment.

Why does the burden of proof rest with the encroachers? The ecosystems in which we intervene are generally in a particular state of balance which there are grounds to assume to be of more service to mankind than states of disturbance and their resultant unpredictable and far-reaching changes. In general, it is not possible to regain the original state after an intervention has wrought serious, undesired consequences. And intervention, ordinarily with a short-sighted gain for some minor part of mankind in view, has a tendency to be detrimental for most or all forms of life.

The study of ecosystems makes us conscious of our ignorance. Faced with experts who, after calling attention to a critical situation, emphasise their lack of knowledge and suggest research programmes which may diminish this lack of knowledge, the most natural response for the politicians is to propose that the matter be put on the table or postponed until more information is available. For example, a proposal which would counter the possible death of forests is postponed in order to gather more information on what makes the trees die. It appears that public and private officials who heed ecological expertise must become accustomed to a new normal procedure: the recommendation and instigation of bold, radical conservation steps justified by the statements of our lack of knowledge.

The deep ecology movement

The term 'deep ecology' was introduced in an article entitled 'The shallow and the deep long-range ecology movement. A summary'[21] Some key paragraphs are reproduced here:

20 See Soulé, Michael E., "What is conservation biology?" *BioScience* 35 (1985), pp. 727–34.

21 Arne Naess, "The shallow and the deep long-range ecological movement. A summary," *Inquiry* 16 (1973), pp. 95–100.

The emergence of ecologists from their former relative obscurity marks a turning point in our scientific communities. But their message is twisted and misused. A shallow, but presently rather powerful, movement, and a deep, but less influential, movement, compete for our attention. I shall make an effort to characterise the two.

1. *The Shallow Ecology movement:*
Fight against pollution and resource depletion. Central objective: the health and affluence of people in the developed countries. [...]

2. *The Deep Ecology movement:*
a. Rejection of the man-in-environment image in favour of *the relational, total-field image*. Organisms as knots in the field of intrinsic relations. An intrinsic relation between two things A and B is such that the relation belongs to the definitions or basic constitutions of A and B, so that without the relation, A and B are no longer the same things. The total field model dissolves not only the man-in-environment concept, but every compact thing-in-milieu concept – except when talking at a superficial or preliminary level of communication.

b. *Biospherical egalitarianism – in principle*. The 'in principle' clause is inserted because any realistic praxis necessitates some killing, exploitation, and suppression. The ecological field worker acquires a deep-seated respect, even veneration, for ways and forms of life. He reaches an understanding from within, a kind of understanding that others reserve for fellow men and for a narrow section of ways and forms of life. To the ecological field worker, *the equal right to live and blossom* is an intuitively clear and obvious value axiom. Its restriction to humans is an anthropocentrism with detrimental effects upon the life quality of humans themselves. This quality depends in part upon the deep pleasure and satisfaction we receive from close partnership with other forms of life. The attempt to ignore our dependence and to establish a master–slave role has contributed to the alienation of man from himself.

In the later 1970s it was difficult to formulate fairly general views which might be agreed upon among people I would characterise as supporters of the deep ecology movement. Finally George Sessions and I formulated eight points [... to propose:]

A platform of the deep ecology movement

(1) The flourishing of human and non-human life on Earth has intrinsic value. The value of non-human life forms is independent of the usefulness these may have for narrow human purposes.

(2) Richness and diversity of life forms are values in themselves and contribute to the flourishing of human and non-human life on Earth.

(3) Humans have no right to reduce this richness and diversity except to satisfy vital needs.

(4) Present human interference with the non-human world is excessive, and the situation is rapidly worsening.

(5) The flourishing of human life and cultures is compatible with a substantial decrease of the human population. The flourishing of non-human life requires such a decrease.

(6) Significant change of life conditions for the better requires change in policies. These affect basic economic, technological, and ideological structures.

(7) The ideological change is mainly that of appreciating *life quality* (dwelling in situations of intrinsic value) rather than adhering to a high standard of living. There will be a profound awareness of the difference between big and great.

(8) Those who subscribe to the foregoing points have an obligation directly or indirectly to participate in the attempt to implement the necessary changes.

The eight formulations are of course in need of clarification and elaboration. A few remarks:

Re (1) Instead of 'biosphere' we might use the term 'ecosphere' in order to stress that we of course do not limit our concern for the life forms in a biologically narrow sense. The term 'life' is used here in a comprehensive non-technical way to refer also to things biologists may classify as non-living: rivers (watersheds), landscapes, cultures, ecosystems, 'the living earth'. Slogans such as 'let the river live' illustrate this broader usage so common in many cultures.

Re (2) So-called simple, lower, or primitive species of plants and animals contribute essentially to the richness and diversity of life. They have value in themselves and are not merely steps toward the so-called higher or rational life forms. The second principle presupposes that life itself, as a process over evolutionary time, implies an increase of diversity and richness.

Why talk about diversity *and* richness? Suppose humans interfere with an ecosystem to such a degree that 1000 vertebrate species are each reduced to a survival minimum. Point (2) is not satisfied. *Richness*, here used for what some others call 'abundance', has been excessively reduced. The maintenance of richness has to do with the maintenance of habitats and the number of individuals (size of populations). No exact count is implied. The main point is that life on Earth may be excessively interfered with even if complete diversity is upheld.

What is said above about species holds also for habitats and ecosystems which show great similarity so that it makes sense to count them.

Re (3) This formulation is perhaps too strong. But, considering the mass of ecologically irresponsible proclamations of human rights, it may be sobering to announce a norm about what they have no right to do.

The term 'vital need' is vague to allow for considerable latitude in judgement. Differences in climate and related factors, together with differences in the structures of societies as they now exist, need to be considered. Also the difference between a means to the satisfaction of the need and the need must be considered. If a whaler in an industrial country quits whaling he may risk unemployment under the present economic conditions. Whaling is for him an important means. But in a rich country with a high standard of living whaling is not a vital need.

Re (4) Status of interference. For a realistic assessment of the global situation, see the unabbreviated version of the IUCN's *World Conservation Strategy* (1980). There are other works to be highly recommended such as Gerald Barney's *Global 2000 Report to the President* of the United States (1980).[22]

People in the materially richest countries cannot be expected to reduce their excessive interference with the non-human world to a moderate level overnight. Less interference does not imply that humans should not modify some ecosystems as do other species. Humans have modified the Earth and will continue to do so. At issue is the nature and extent of such interference.

The fight to preserve and extend areas of wilderness or near-wilderness should continue and should focus on the general ecological functions of these areas (one such function: large wilderness areas are required by the biosphere to allow for continued evolutionary speciation of animals and plants). Present designated wilderness areas and game preserves are not large enough to allow for speciation of large birds and mammals.

Re (5) Limitation of population. The stabilisation and reduction of the human population will take time. Interim strategies need to be developed. But this in no way excuses the present complacency. The extreme seriousness of our current situation must first be more widely recognised. But the longer we wait the more drastic will be the measures needed. Until deep changes are made, substantial decreases in richness and diversity are liable to occur; the rate of extinction of species will be greater than in any other period of Earth history.

A legitimate objection may be that if the present billions of humans deeply change their behaviour in the direction of ecological responsibility, non-human life could flourish. Formulation (5) presupposes that the probability of a deep enough change in economics and technology is too small to take into account.

Re (6) Policy changes required. Economic growth as conceived and implemented today by the industrial states is incompatible with points (1) to (5).

Present ideology tends to value things because they are scarce and because they have a commodity or market value. There is prestige in vast consumption and waste, to mention only two of many relevant factors. Economic growth registers mainly growth in marketable values, not in values generally, including ecological values. Whereas 'self-determination', 'local community', and 'think globally, act locally' will remain key slogans, the implementation of deep changes nevertheless requires increasingly global action in the sense of action across every border, perhaps contrary to the short-range interests of local communities.

Support for global action through non-governmental organisations becomes increasingly important. Many of these organisations are able to act locally from grass roots to grass roots, thus avoiding negative governmental interference.

Cultural diversity today requires advanced technology, that is, techniques that advance the basic goals of each culture. So-called soft, intermediate, and appropriate technologies are steps in this direction.

Re (7) Some economists criticise the term 'quality of life' because it is supposed to be too vague. But, on closer inspection, what they consider to be vague is actually the non-quantifiable nature of the term. One cannot quantify adequately what is important for the quality of life as discussed here, and there is no need to do so.

Re (8) There is ample room for different opinions about priorities. What should be done first, what next? What is most urgent? What is necessary as opposed to what is highly desirable? Different opinions in these matters should not exclude vigorous cooperation.

What is gained from tentatively formulating basic views shared today by most or all supporters of the deep ecology movement? Hopefully it makes it a little easier to localise the movement among the many 'alternative' movements. Hopefully this does not lead to isolation

[22] Editors' note: Much more recent accounts of the global ecological situation are widely available. For example, the Intergovernmental Panel on Climate Change, an organization established by the World Meteorological Organization (WMO) and the United Nations Environmental Program (UNEP), issues annual reports on climatic change. Its report of November 17, 2007, can be found at http://www.ipcc.ch/.

but rather to even better cooperation with many other alternative movements. It might also make some of us more clear about where we stand, and more clear about which disagreements might profitably be reduced and which ones might profitably be sharpened. After all [...] 'diversity' is a high-level norm!

Michael Hardt and Antonio Negri, "Globalization and Democracy"*

The dominant modern notion of democracy has been intimately tied to the nation-state. To investigate the contemporary status of democracy, then, we should look first at the changing powers and role of the nation-state. Many theorists claim, and many others contest, that the diverse phenomena commonly grouped under the term "globalization" have eroded or even negated the powers of nation-states.[23] Too often, however, this is posed as an either/or proposition: either nation-states are still important or there is a new global order. Both, in fact, are true. The era of globalization has not brought the end of the nation-state – nation-states still fulfill extremely important functions in the establishment and regulation of economic, political, and cultural norms – but nation-states have indeed been displaced from the position of sovereign authority. A focus on the concept and practices of sovereignty helps to clarify this discussion.

We propose the concept of Empire to name our contemporary global arrangement. Empire refers above all to a new form of sovereignty that has succeeded the sovereignty of the nation-state, an unlimited form of sovereignty that knows no boundaries or, rather, knows only flexible, mobile boundaries. We borrow the concept of Empire from the ancient Roman figure in which Empire is seen to supersede the alternation of the three classical forms of government – monarchy, aristocracy, and democracy – by combining them in a single sovereign rule. Our contemporary Empire is indeed monarchical, and this is most apparent in times of military conflict when we can see the extent to which the Pentagon, with its atomic weapons and superior military technology, effectively rules the world. The supranational economic institutions, such as the WTO, the World Bank, and the IMF, also at times exercise a monarchical rule over global affairs. Our Empire, however, is also aristocratic, that is, ruled by a limited group of elite actors. The power of nation-states is central here because the few dominant nation-states manage to govern global economic and cultural flows through a kind of aristocratic rule. This aristocracy of nations is revealed clearly, for example, when the G8 nations meet or when the UN security council exercises its authority. The major transnational corporations too in concert and in conflict constitute a form of aristocracy. Finally Empire is also democratic in the sense that it claims to represent the global people, although, as we will argue below, this claim to representation is largely illusory. The entire group of nation-states, the dominant and the subordinated ones together, fulfill the primary role here to the extent that they are assumed in some way to represent their peoples. The UN general assembly is perhaps the most prominent symbol of this democracy of nations. When we recognize that nation-states do not in fact adequately represent their peoples, however, we can have recourse to nongovernmental organizations (NGOs) as the democratic or representative institutions. The functioning of the various different kinds of NGOs as democratic or representative mechanisms is a very complex and important question, which we should not pretend to treat adequately here. In short, Empire is a single sovereign subject that comprehends within its logic all three of these classical forms or levels of rule, the monarchic, the aristocratic, and the democratic. Empire, in other words, is a distinctive form of sovereignty for its ability to include and manage difference within its constitution.

From this perspective we can see that the functions and authority of nation-states have not disappeared. It is probably more accurate to say that the primary functions of nation-states – the regulation of currencies, economic flows, population migrations, legal norms, cultural values, and so forth – have maintained their importance but been transformed through the contemporary processes of globalization. The radical qualitative shift should be recognized rather in terms of sovereignty. Nation-states can no longer claim the role of sovereign or ultimate authority as they could in the modern era. Empire now stands above the nation-states as the final authority and indeed presents a new form of sovereignty.

We should point out that this is a major historical shift only from the perspective of the dominant nation-states. The subordinate nations were never really sovereign. The entry into modernity for many nation-states was the entry into relations of economic and political subordination that undercut any sovereignty to which the

* Michael Hardt and Antonio Negri, extracted from *Implicating Empire: Globalization and Resistance in the 21st-Century World Order*, edited by Stanley Aronowitz and Heather Gautney (New York: Basic Books, Inc., 2003).

[23] The most detailed and influential argument that globalization has not undermined the powers of nation-states and that globalization is in this sense a myth is presented by Paul Hirst and Grahame Thompson, *Globalization in Question: The International Economy and the Possibilities of Governance*, 2nd edn. (Cambridge: Polity, 1999).

nation might pretend. This shift in the form of sovereignty – from the modern sovereignty located in the nation-state to our postmodern imperial sovereignty – nonetheless affects us all. Even where national sovereignty was never a reality, the passage to Empire has transformed our forms of thought and the range of our political possibilities. In the light of Empire we have to reconsider and reconceive all the key concepts of political philosophy.

Democracy unrealized, democracy unrealizable

This brings us back, first and foremost, to the concept of democracy. The dominant modern notion of democracy was, as we claimed at the outset, based on representational institutions and structures within the bounded national space and dependent on national sovereignty.[24] What was represented in the democratic national institutions was the people and hence modern national sovereignty tended to take the form of popular sovereignty. The claim that the nation was sovereign, in other words, tended to become identical to the claim that the people was sovereign. But what or who is the people? The people is not a natural or empirical entity; one cannot arrive at the identity of the people by summing up or even averaging the entire population. The people rather is a *representation* that creates of the population a unity. Three elements are centrally important here. First of all, the people is one, as Hobbes and the entire modern tradition often repeated. The people can be sovereign only as an identity, a unity. Second, the key to the construction of the people is representation. The empirical multiplicity of the population is made an identity through mechanisms of representation – and here we should include both the political and the aesthetic connotations of the term representation. Finally, these mechanisms of representation are based on a notion and a condition of measure – and by measure here we mean not so much a quantifiable condition but rather a bounded one. A bounded or measured multiplicity can be represented as a unity, but the immeasurable, the boundless, cannot be represented. This is one sense in which the notion of the people is intimately tied to the bounded national space. In short, the people is not an immediate nor an eternal identity, but rather the result of a complex process that is proper to a specific social formation and historical period.

We can simplify this complex situation for a moment and consider only the institutional, political mechanisms of representation, of which the electoral process was at least ideologically the most important. The notion of "one person, one vote," for example, was one of the ideals toward which the various modern schema of popular representation and sovereignty tended. There is no need for us to argue here that these schema of popular representation have always been imperfect and in fact largely illusory. There have long been important critiques of the mechanisms of popular representation in modern democratic societies. It is perhaps an exaggeration to characterize elections as an opportunity to choose which member of the ruling class will misrepresent the people for the next two, four, or six years, but there is certainly some truth in it too and low voter turnout is undoubtedly a symptom of the crisis of popular representation through electoral institutions. We think that today, however, popular representation is undermined in a more basic and fundamental way.

In the passage to Empire national space loses its definition, national boundaries (although still important) are relativized, and even national imaginaries are destabilized. As national sovereignty is displaced by the authority of the new supranational power, Empire, political reality loses its measure. In this situation the impossibility of representing the people becomes increasingly clear and thus the concept of the people itself tends to evaporate.

From an institutional, political perspective, imperial sovereignty conflicts with and even negates any conception of popular sovereignty. Consider, for example, the functioning of the supranational economic institutions, such as the World Bank, the IMF, and the WTO. To a large extent the conditionality required by these institutions takes out of the hands of nation-states decisions over economic and social policy. The subordinate nation-states most visibly but also the dominate ones are subject to the rule of these institutions.[25] It is clear that these supranational economic institutions do not and cannot represent the people, except in the most

24 This is the fundamental argument of David Held, *Democracy and the Global Order* (Stanford: Stanford University Press, 1995).

25 Many authors characterize and lament this shift in decision making from national to supranational institutions as the increasing domination of the economic over the political (with the assumption that the nation-state is the only context in which to conduct politics). Several of these authors invoke the work of Karl Polanyi in the argument to re-embed economic markets within social markets. See, for example, James Mittleman, *The Globalization Syndrome* (Princeton: Princeton University Press, 2000), and John Gray, *False Dawn* (New York: The New Press, 1998). In our view it is a mistake to separate the economic and the political in this way and to insist on the autonomy of the political. The supranational economic institutions are also themselves political institutions. The fundamental difference is that these institutions do not allow for (even the pretense of) popular representation.

distant and abstract sense – in the sense, for example, that some nation-states, which in some way represent their peoples, designate representatives to the institutions. If one looks for representation in such institutions, there will always inevitably remain a "democratic deficit." It is no accident, in our view, in other words, that these institutions are so isolated from popular representation. They function precisely to the extent that they are excluded from mechanisms of popular representation.

[...]

Groups call for greater inclusion and representation in the decision-making process of the institutions themselves, demanding, for example, trade union representation or NGO representation or the like. Such demands may have some positive results, but they ultimately face insurmountable obstacles. Our argument casts all this on a much more general plane. If we conceive democracy in terms of a sovereign authority that is representative of the people, then democracy in the imperial age is not only unrealized but actually unrealizable.

Democracy of the multitude

We thus have to explore new forms of democracy, forms that are non-representative or differently representative, to discover a democracy that is adequate to our own times. We have already argued that the modern notion of democracy is intimately tied to national sovereignty and a fixed national space, that the modern notion, in short, is founded on measure. Now we should turn our attention back to explore further the other element in the equation, the people. The people, as we said earlier, is a product of representation. In modern political theory, the people is most strongly configured as the product of the founding contractual act of bourgeois society, as all the modern liberal theorists explain, from Hobbes to Rawls. The contract makes of the population a united social body. This contractual act, however, is nonexistent, mystificatory, and outdated. The contract is nonexistent in the sense that no anthropological or historical fact allows us to assume its reality; rather, the contract negates any memory of its foundation, and this is certainly part of its violence, its fundamental denial of difference. The contract is mystificatory, secondly, in the sense that the people it constructs is presented as equal when the subjects that form it are in fact unequal; the concepts of justice and legitimacy that ground it serve only the strongest who exercise a force of domination and exploitation on the rest of the population. This concept of a people formed through the contract is outdated, finally, because it looks to a society forged by capital: contractualism, people, and capitalism function in fact to make of the plurality a unity, to make of differences an homologous totality, to make of the wealth of all the singular lives of the population the poverty of some and the power of others. But this no longer works: it used to work as long as labor, needs, and desires were so miserable that they received the command of capital as a welcome comfort and a source of security when faced with the risks of the construction of value, the liberation of the imagination, and the organization of society. Today, however, the terms have changed. It is rather our monstrous intelligence and our cooperative power that are put in play: we are a multitude of powerful subjects, a multitude of intelligent monsters.

We thus need to shift our conceptual focus from the people to the multitude. The multitude cannot be grasped in the terms of contractualism – and in general in the terms of transcendental philosophy. In the most general sense, the multitude defies representation because it is a multiplicity, unbounded and immeasurable. The people is represented as a unity but the multitude is not representable because it is monstrous in the face of the teleological and transcendental rationalisms of modernity. In contrast to the concept of the people, the concept of the multitude is a singular multiplicity, a concrete universal. The people constituted a social body but the multitude does not – the multitude is the flesh of life. If on one side we contrast the multitude with the people, on the other side we should contrast it with the masses or the mob. The masses and the mob are most often used to name an irrational and passive social force, dangerous and violent precisely because so easily manipulated. The multitude, in contrast, is an active social agent – a multiplicity that acts. The multitude is not a unity, as is the people, but in contrast to the masses and the mob we can see that it is organized. It is an active, self-organizing agent. One great advantage of the concept of the multitude is that it displaces all the modern arguments based on the fear of the masses and even those about the tyranny of the majority, which have so often served as a kind of blackmail to force us to accept and even call for our own domination.

From the perspective of power, however, what can be done with the multitude? In effect, there is nothing to do with it, because the nexus among the unity of the subject (people), the form of its composition (contract among individuals), and the mode of government (monarchy, aristocracy, and democracy, separate or combined) has been blown apart. The radical modification of the mode of production through the hegemony of immaterial labor-power and cooperative living labor – this ontological, productive, biopolitical revolution – has overturned the parameters of "good government" and destroyed the modern idea of a community that functions for capitalist accumulation, as capitalism imagined it from the beginning.

Allow us a brief parenthesis. Between the fifteenth and sixteenth centuries, when modernity appeared in the form of a revolution, the revolutionaries imagined themselves as monsters. Gargantua and Pantagruel can serve as emblems for all the giants and extreme figures of freedom and invention that have come down to us through the ages and proposed the gigantic task of becoming more free. Today we need new giants and new monsters that bring together nature and history, labor and politics, art and invention to demonstrate the new power that the birth of "general intellect," the hegemony of immaterial labor, the new passions of the abstract activity of the multitude provide to humanity. We need a new Rabelais or, really, several.

Spinoza and Marx spoke of the democracy of the multitude or, rather, a form of democracy that no longer has anything to do with the democracy that along with monarchy and aristocracy comprises the classical forms of government. The democracy that Spinoza advocates is what he calls an *absolute* democracy – absolute in the sense of being unbounded and immeasurable. The conceptions of social contracts and bounded social bodies are thus completely cast aside. When we say that absolute democracy is outside of the theory (and the mystificatory practice) of the classical forms of government we mean also, obviously, that any attempt to realize democracy through the reform of the imperial institutions will be vain and useless. We mean, furthermore, that the only path to realize a democracy of the multitude is the path of revolution. What does it mean, however, to call for a revolutionary democracy adequate to the imperial world? Up to this point we have simply focused on what it is not. It is no longer something that depends on the concept of nation (on the contrary, it is increasingly defined by the struggle against the nation). We have also seen that it is something that does not correspond to the concept of the people and in fact is opposed to any attempt to present as unitary what is different. We need at this point to look to other concepts to help us understand a democracy of the multitude. The concept of counterpower seems fundamental to us when we deal with these new contents of the absolute democracy of the multitude.

Modern counterpower and the paradoxes of modern insurrection

The concept of counterpower consists primarily of three elements: resistance, insurrection, and constituent power. It is important to recognize, however, that like the dominant concept of democracy also the dominant concept of counterpower was defined in modernity by the national space and national sovereignty. The effect was that during the modern era – at least since the French Revolution and throughout the long phase of socialist and communist agitation – the three elements of the concept of counterpower (resistance, insurrection, and constituent power) tended to be viewed as external to one another, and thus functioned as different strategies or at least different historical moments of revolutionary strategy. Once the elements were thus divided the entire concept of counterpower tended to be reduced to one of its elements, the concept of insurrection or, really, civil war.

[...]

The contemporary relevance that emerges from [a] brief history of modern insurrection centers around two facts or, really, one fact with two faces. On one side today, with the decline of national sovereignty and the passage to Empire, gone are the conditions that allowed modern insurrection to be thought and at times to be practiced. Today it thus seems almost impossible even to think insurrection. On the other side, however, what is gone is also exactly the condition that kept modern insurrection imprisoned, in the interminable play between national and international wars. Today, therefore, when considering the question of insurrection we are faced with both a great difficulty and an enormous possibility. Let us move back, however, to the more general consideration of counterpower.

A counterpower of monstrous flesh

With the contemporary decline of the sovereignty of the nation-state, it is possible once again to explore the concept of counterpower in its full form and return to its conceptual foundation. Today the relationship among resistance, insurrection, and constituent power has the possibility to be an absolutely continuous relationship and in each of these moments there is the possibility of the expression of the power of invention. In other words, each of the three moments – resistance, insurrection, and constituent power – can be internal to one another, forming a common means of political expression. The context in which – and against which – this counterpower acts is no longer the limited sovereignty of the nation-state but the unlimited sovereignty of Empire, and thus counterpower too must be reconceived in an unlimited or unbounded way.

Here we are faced with a new imposing and exciting theoretical and political problematic. In our present imperial context we need to rethink the concepts of resistance, insurrection, and constituent power – and rethink too their internal connections, that is, their unity in the concept and practice of counterpower. When we look across the field of contemporary theoretical production we can see that we do already have some tools to work with on this terrain. Certainly, Michel Foucault's development of the concept of resistance along with all the work that has followed on his, the anthropologist James Scott's notion of the weapons of the weak, and all the other work that has emerged on micropolitical resistance should be a foundation for any investigation into this problematic. The great limitation of all this work, however, is that it never manages to discover the internal connection that resistance can have with insurrection and constituent power. Resistance can be a powerful political weapon, in other words, but isolated, individual acts of resistance can never succeed in transforming the structures of power.[26] Today, however, the other two components of counterpower remain completely undeveloped. An insurrection is a collective gesture of revolt, but what are the terms for insurrection today and how can it be put into practice? It should be clear that we can no longer translate insurrection immediately into civil war, as was so common in the modern era, if by "civil" we mean a war within the national space. Insurrection is indeed still a war of the dominated against the rulers within a single society, but that society now tends to be an unlimited global society, imperial society as a whole. How is such an insurrection against Empire put into practice? Who can enact it? Where is the internal connection between the micropolitics of resistance and imperial insurrection? And how can we today conceive of constituent power, that is, the common invention of a new social and political constitution? Finally, we need to think of resistance, insurrection, and constituent power as one indivisible process, the three forged together into a full counterpower and ultimately a new alternative social formation. These are enormous questions and we are only at the very first stages of addressing them.

Rather than confronting them directly it seems better to us to shift registers and take a different view on the entire problematic. We have to find some way to shake off the shackles of reasonableness, to break out of the common forms of thinking about democracy and society, to create more imaginative and inventive perspectives. Let us begin by looking at the most basic foundation of counterpower where its three elements – resistance, insurrection, and constituent power – most intimately correspond. The primary material of counterpower is the flesh, the common living substance in which the corporeal and the intellectual coincide and are indistinguishable. "The flesh is not matter, is not mind, is not substance," Maurice Merleau-Ponty writes. "To designate it, we should need the old term 'element,' in the sense it was used to speak of water, air, earth, and fire, that is, in the sense of a *general thing* ... a sort of incarnate principle that brings a style of being wherever there is a fragment of being. The flesh is in this sense an 'element' of Being."[27] The flesh is pure potentiality, the unformed stuff of life, an element of being. One should be careful, however, not to confuse the flesh with any notion of naked life, which conceives of a living form stripped of all its qualities, a negative limit of life.[28] The flesh is oriented in the other direction, toward the fullness of life. We do not remain flesh, flesh is but an element of being; we continually make of our flesh a form of life.

In the development of forms of life, we discover ourselves as a multitude of bodies and at the same time we recognize that every body is itself a multitude – of molecules, desires, forms of life, inventions. Within each of us resides a legion of demons or, perhaps, of angels – this is the basic foundation, the degree zero of the multitude. What acts on the flesh and gives it form are the powers of invention, those powers that work through singularities to weave together hybridizations of space and metamorphoses of nature – the powers, in short, that modify the modes and forms of existence.

[26] From our perspective Félix Guattari, especially in his work with Deleuze, is the one who has gone furthest to push the notion of resistance toward a conception of molecular revolution.

[27] Maurice Merleau-Ponty, *The Visible and the Invisible*, edited by Claude Lefort, translated by Alphonso Lingus (Evanston, IL: Northwestern University Press, 1968), p. 139. Consider also Antonin Artaud's conception of the flesh: "There are intellectual cries, cries born of the *subtlety* of the marrow. That is what I mean by Flesh. I do not separate my thought from my life. With each vibration of my tongue I retrace all the pathways of my thought in my flesh." Antonin Artaud, "Situation of the Flesh," in *Selected Writings*, translated by Helen Weaver (Berkeley: University of California Press, 1988), p. 110.

[28] See Giorgio Agamben, *Homo Sacer*, translated by Daniel Heller-Roazen (Stanford: Stanford University Press, 1998).

In this context it is clear that the three elements of counterpower (resistance, insurrection, and constituent power) spring forth *together* from every singularity and from every movement of bodies that constitute the multitude. Acts of resistance, collective gestures of revolt, and the common invention of a new social and political constitution pass together through innumerable micropolitical circuits – and thus in the flesh of the multitude is inscribed a new power, a counterpower, a living thing that is against Empire. Here are born the new barbarians, monsters, and beautiful giants that continually emerge from *within* the interstices of imperial power and *against* imperial power itself. The power of invention is monstrous because it is excessive. Every true act of invention, every act, that is, that does not simply reproduce the norm, is monstrous. Counterpower is an excessive, overflowing force, and one day it will be unbounded and immeasurable. This tension between the overflowing and the unbounded is where the monstrous characteristics of the flesh and counterpower take on a heightened importance. As we are waiting for a full epiphany of the (resistant, revolting, and constituent) monsters, there grows a recognition that the imperial system, that is, the contemporary form of repression of the will to power of the multitude, is at this point on the ropes, at the margins, precarious, continually plagued by crisis. (Here is where the weak philosophies of the margin, difference, and nakedness appear as the mystifying figures and the unhappy consciousness of imperial hegemony.)

Against this, the power of invention (or, really, counterpower) makes common bodies out of the flesh. These bodies share nothing with the huge animals that Hobbes and the other theorists of the modern state imagined when they made of the Leviathan the sacred instrument, the pitbull of the appropriative bourgeoisie. The multitude we are dealing with today is instead a multiplicity of bodies, each of which is crisscrossed by intellectual and material powers of reason and affect; they are cyborg bodies that move freely without regard to the old boundaries that separated the human from the machinic. These multiple bodies of the multitude enact a continuous invention of new forms of life, new languages, new intellectual and ethical powers. The bodies of the multitude are monstrous, irrecuperable in the capitalist logic that tries continually to control it in the organization of Empire. The bodies of the multitude, finally, are queer bodies that are insusceptible to the forces of discipline and normalization but sensitive only to their own powers of invention.

When we point to the powers of invention as the key to a formation of counterpower in the age of Empire, we do not mean to refer to some exclusive population of artists or philosophers. In the political economy of Empire the power of invention has become the general and common condition of production. This is what we mean when we claim that immaterial labor and general intellect have come to occupy a dominant position in the capitalist economy.

If, as we have argued, the dominant form of democracy that modernity and European history has bequeathed us – popular, representational democracy – is not only unrealized but actually unrealizable, then one should not view our proposition of an alternative democracy of the multitude as a utopian dream. The unrealizability of the old notion of democracy should rather force us to move forward. This also means that we are entirely within and completely against imperial domination, and there is no dialectical path possible. The only invention that now remains for us is the invention of a new democracy, an absolute democracy, unbounded, immeasurable. A democracy of powerful multitudes, not only of equal individuals but of powers equally open to cooperation, to communication, to creation. Here there are no programmes to propose – and who would dare still today to do such a thing after the twentieth century has ended? All the modern protagonists – the priests, the journalists, the preachers, the politicians – may still be of use to imperial power, but not to us. The philosophical and artistic elements in all of us, the practices of working on the flesh and dealing with its irreducible multiplicities, the powers of unbounded invention – these are the leading characteristics of the multitude. Beyond our unrealized democracy, there is a desire for a common life that needs to be realized. We can perhaps, mingling together the flesh and the intellect of the multitude, generate a new youth of humanity through an enormous enterprise of love.

Part II

Philosophical Assumptions

Chapter 5
Ontological Conceptions

Introduction

Political principles are rooted to a significant degree in underlying philosophical assumptions that will be explored in this and the next three chapters. Political theorists sometimes refer to all such foundational bases for political principles as ontological, but it is useful to distinguish among four types of philosophical assumptions: those dealing with human nature, the nature of society, knowledge or epistemology, and ultimate reality. This chapter focuses on alternative conceptions of ultimate reality, which are ontological issues in the more specific use of that term. When exploring ontological issues, we ask: Is ultimate reality (being) essentially material, ideational, or supernatural? Are our ultimate ends (what becomes of us and of the world) determined by divine or supernatural causes? By material and natural causes? Or are ultimate ends undetermined, subject to human ideals, will, and power?

While the term ontology is unfamiliar to many people and ontological issues may seem overly philosophical and too removed from everyday life to be of much importance to our political thinking, many people have strong though unrecognized ontological beliefs that affect their politics. Some have strong religious convictions that assume that God (or Allah or Yahweh) is ultimate reality, that His will determines our fate, and that if our political behavior and laws depart from His will, He can inflict divine retribution on us. Other people have strong populist convictions that assume that "the people" and "the will of the people" must be the ultimate source of political action and law. Both divine and populist assumptions can be very strong in that those holding them can regard any deviations from the will of God or the people as mistaken and even evil. Strongly held ontological assumptions can thus lead to intolerance of the diversity of political ideas that are central to pluralist public philosophy. Pluralists are comfortable with weaker ontological assumptions that lead to more flexible and open political processes.

The ontological basis of political thinking goes back at least to Plato (427–346 BCE), the ancient Greek philosopher who is often seen as the founder of political theory. In a key section of his *Republic,* he develops "the theory of the forms" as a foundation for his claim that polities should be ruled by philosopher-kings rather than by the uninformed and unruly mob of citizens (that had sentenced his mentor, Socrates, to death for raising unsettling political questions and thus "corrupting the youth"). Plato asks us to consider the possibility that there is a scale of reality or being that begins with images of sensual objects (e.g., photos of political leaders) and ascends to higher levels of reality: next, particular sensual objects themselves (e.g., various political leaders), and then scientific abstractions about classes of such objects (e.g., theories that indicate the qualities of effective political leaders based on reflections and analysis of our accurate perceptions of various leaders). But Plato posits that there is a higher reality than such abstract conceptions: "the forms" are the essences of what is good in the universe that remain invisible to man and inaccessible through scientific or analytical thinking alone. He suggests that there are forms of perfect beauty, wisdom, courage, justice, and other virtues. All visible images and objects and all theoretical abstractions can only be imperfect reflections of such forms, which are the ultimate realities to which we should aspire. There might even be a form of "the Good" itself, which encompasses all other forms. Because "the Good" is not accessible to humans through perception and reasoning, Plato confesses that he cannot describe it but can only provide analogies that give us some intuitive grasp of its existence, as he famously does in his Allegory of the Cave. But Plato suggests that some people have the "inner metal" and can receive extensive training to be far more aware of the forms than ordinary citizens, and that in a good society, such people should rule as "philosopher-kings."

Plato's ontology can be seen as a secular version of subsequent Christian ontology. Christian neo-Platonists developed the idea of "the great chain of being," with God as the ultimate creator and definer of "the good" at the apex of a hierarchy of beings, angels just below God, divinely chosen leaders below them but above ordinary people, who were above other creatures. Walter Ullman (1910–83), a professor of medieval history at Trinity College in Cambridge for many years, points out that during the Middle Ages this "descending" ontology dominated political thinking (and gave rise to theocratic arrangements based on the claim that rulers were divinely selected and guided), but he noticed that even during this era there could be found some conceptions of an "ascending" ontology that located ultimate political reality "in the people or the community itself." While "the overwhelming influence of Christianity" drove ascending ontology underground for many centuries, it resurfaced in the late Middle Ages and became a dominant foundation for liberal and radical politics during the modern era.

According to Ken Wilber, a contemporary contributor to humanistic psychology, many modern philosophers working within various wisdom traditions have reinterpreted the "great chain of being," stressing different levels of reality but abandoning the notion that the concept implies a divine figure at the top of a hierarchy who controls lesser realms. In these renderings, the great chain can be seen as a "holoarchy" rather than a "hierarchy." In Christian terms, reality includes matter, body, mind, soul, and spirit. Humans can assume that they are simply matter, but they can evolve a higher understanding of reality to include spirit itself. Such a reformulation of the great chain of being is essentially ascending rather than descending because humans can develop from holding a narrow and limited understanding of ultimate reality to acquiring a much more complete or holistic understanding of reality that includes lower and higher life forms. In such a great chain of being, a transcendental spirit does not rule over mankind but rather mankind rules itself with a higher consciousness of a unifying "soul of humanity" and a spiritual force that is immanent in all life.

But among many political theorists, the most well-known articulation of the ascending theory was provided by Jean Jacques Rousseau (1712–78), a citizen of Geneva, Switzerland, who lived much of his life in Paris as a struggling musician and literary figure but eventually gained fame as a political philosopher. His writings influenced the French Revolution and many subsequent radical thinkers with populist inclinations. In the following selection from *The Social Contract* (1762), Rousseau presents his famed concept of "the general will." He argues that the state is ultimately founded on the general will, which he defines as an inalienable and indivisible conception of the common good. It is based on the will of the people, but the people can be corrupted and will things other than their common interests or the public good. When the people are informed and seek the common good (which includes their own good but differs from factional, narrow, or selfish conceptions of their own good), their deliberations will normally achieve the inerrant general will. All citizens should be motivated by the general will and submit to it, thus generating a fundamental equality among all citizens. This indivisible and coercive conception of the true will of the people has troubled pluralists – as well as many contemporary "public choice theorists," as we will see in a subsequent selection in Chapter 12 by William Riker.

Because of his emphasis on the idea of a "General Will," Rousseau can be seen as a precursor to the German Idealists, who were highly influential political philosophers during the first part of the nineteenth century. The most widely known idealist, Georg Hegel (1770–1831), declared, "what is rational is actual and what is actual is rational." Hegel's complex and highly abstract ontology is omitted from this reader, but it is difficult to understand our next selection concerning Marx's materialist ontology without a basic introduction to Hegel's idealism. Hegel emphasized that ideas are foundational to actual states and the politics they manifest, that there is an Absolute Idea ("Geist") that is a higher reality than that of the material world, and that history is a process through which this Absolute Idea is revealed. While many competing ideas may be expressed and affect actions in civil society, the state actualizes the ethical Idea as it is understood by those having an elevated consciousness of the universality of the "absolute unmoved end in itself." Such consciousness is historically progressive as it goes through a dialectical process in which certain ideas of the ethical (theses) are opposed by opposite ideas (antitheses); through reason these contradictions are resolved as syntheses that more closely approximate the Absolute; this process repeats itself over time, until the Absolute is completely realized. Some contemporary interpreters claim Hegel believed that the liberal state had realized the Absolute by the early nineteenth century and that subsequent non-liberal states have failed and are no longer tenable precisely because they do not reflect rationality and thus are not "real."[1]

Karl Marx was a student of Hegel, but he could not abide the notion that the actual states of his time – whether they reflected conservative or liberal ideas – could approximate, let alone actualize, rational ethical standards. He regarded "the Hegelian dialectic" as a great inversion of ultimate reality and claimed that the forces that drove history towards its absolute end were material, not ideational. While Hegel suggested that material conditions are determined by ideas, Marx contended the opposite: that material conditions determine the dominant ideas that are expressed about political life and that intellectually justify the politics required by material conditions. As his collaborator, Friedrich Engels, puts it in our next selection from *Socialism: Utopian and Scientific*, the final causes of all social changes are to be sought, "not in men's brains, not in man's better insight into eternal truth and justice, but in changes in the modes of production and exchange." During the present stage of history, capitalist production and exchange are the determining factors, and thus a scientific account of the workings of capitalism will reveal how history will unfold. As we learned by reading the *Communist Manifesto* in Chapter 2, Marx believed that capitalist forces would result in that system's demise and succession by socialism and ultimately communism. Such political ends are economically determined.

This materialist ontology of Marx and Engels was basically within an Anglo-American liberal tradition that dates back to Thomas Hobbes, who also founded his theory on assumptions about natural and material forces. But perhaps Charles Darwin (1809–82), the British naturalist who proposed and provided evidence for his famed theory of evolution, provided the most well-known account of liberalism's materialism. In our brief selection from his *Origin of the Species* (1859), he explains how the forms of life on earth have changed over long periods of time by the workings of natural selection and survival of the fittest: slight biological variations among members of species occur naturally, and those variations that are useful survive while those that are not are eliminated, so that the forms of life naturally evolve in a progressive manner due to natural and material processes.

Darwin did not work out the political implications of these ontological ideas, but "social Darwinists" like Herbert Spencer (1820–88) did. They argued that Darwin's theory implied that politics should not be used to counter the survival of the fittest and the elimination of the weakest members of a species. Such conclusions were rejected by Thomas Henry Huxley (1825–95), another English naturalist who strongly endorsed Darwin's theory but found Spencer's political implications repulsive. He argued that "Men in society are undoubtedly subject to cosmic force," but that social progress involved "checking the cosmic process [of the survival of the fittest] ... by an ethical process." In "Evolution and Ethics," he went on to consider a variety of moral concerns that – if pursued within political communities – can result in human life that is "better than [that] of a brutal savage." In short, Huxley insisted that political life need not be determined by natural and material forces, but rather can be shaped by ethical ideals. Huxley's ethical idealism does not require accepting Platonic perfections or Hegelian absolutes, as his ethical ideas seem to emerge from nothing more than ordinary human intelligence and sentiments. Of course, human intelligence can produce a vast array of moral ideas and there is nothing in Huxley's ontology that enables us to know which ideas will have the greatest influence on political life; moral ideas simply have an independent impact on life, though they leave the ultimate end of life on earth undetermined. Such a thin ontology seems acceptable to various friends of pluralism.

In our final selection in this chapter by Judith Butler, an American feminist and a professor of rhetoric and comparative literature at the University of California–Berkeley, we return to a consideration of ontology in its broadest sense, as all assumptions that are foundational to political thinking. Butler is often associated with postmodernism, a broad term that encompasses the work of scholars in many disciplines who are skeptical of understanding reality by reference to the sort of ontological assumptions discussed in this chapter and to other assumptions about human nature, the nature of society, and knowledge to be encountered in the next three chapters. She points out that postmodernism has been criticized for leading to relativism and nihilism; without foundations on which to build our political theories, everything seems to vanish into thin air, and we are left with only "discourses," "texts,"

[1] Francis Fukuyama, *The End of History and the Last Man* (New York: Free Press, 1992).

and "voices" and without firm principles to guide our thinking and actions. Butler suggests that postmodern skepticism of foundations can better be appreciated by understanding a related intellectual movement, poststructuralism, that has shown that "power pervades the very conceptual apparatus" of foundational thinking. In other words, the philosophical assumptions that are deemed acceptable foundations of political thought are those authorized by those with power – whether the powerful be religious and political authorities, those who own and control economic institutions, or the old guard of male professors who are regarded as leaders of a discipline. Poststructuralists expose such authorized foundations as arbitrary and "contingent," and thus the universal political principles that are built on such foundations are always contestable. She uses the subject of feminism to illustrate her point. If who belongs to the category of "women" is presupposed by reference to certain sexual characteristics, then other possible conceptions of womanhood that might be proposed at "sites of permanent openness" are foreclosed. Butler challenges us to "interrogate the ruse of authority" whenever we encounter a political idea that is based on some ontological assumptions that have no greater claim on our allegiance than that some powerful agents insist upon them.

Plato, "The Theory of Forms"*

d Understand then, I said, that, as we say, there are those two, one reigning over the intelligible kind and realm, the other over the visible (not to say heaven, that I may not appear to play the sophist about the name[2]). So you have two kinds, the visible and the intelligible. – Right.

It is like a line divided[3] into two unequal parts, and then divide each section in the same ratio, that is, the section of the visible and that of the intelligible. You will then have sections related to each other in proportion to their clarity and obscurity. The first section of the visible
e consists of images – and by images I mean shadows in
510 the first instance, then the reflections in water and all those on close-packed, smooth, and bright materials, and all that sort of thing, if you understand me. – I understand.

In the other section of the visible, place the models of the images, the living creatures around us, all plants, and the whole class of manufactured things. – I so place them.

Would you be willing to say that, as regards truth and untruth, the division is made in this proportion: as the opinable is to the knowable so the image is to the model it is made like? – Certainly.

Consider now how the section of the intelligible is to
be divided. – How? b

In such a way that in one section the soul, using as images what before were models, is compelled to investigate from hypotheses, proceeding from these not to a first principle but to a conclusion. The other section which leads to a first principle that is not hypothetical, proceeding from a hypothesis without using the images of the other section, by means of the Forms themselves and proceeding through these. – I do not, he said, quite understand what you mean.

Let us try again, I said, for you will understand more c
easily because of what has been said. I think you know that students of geometry, calculation, and the like

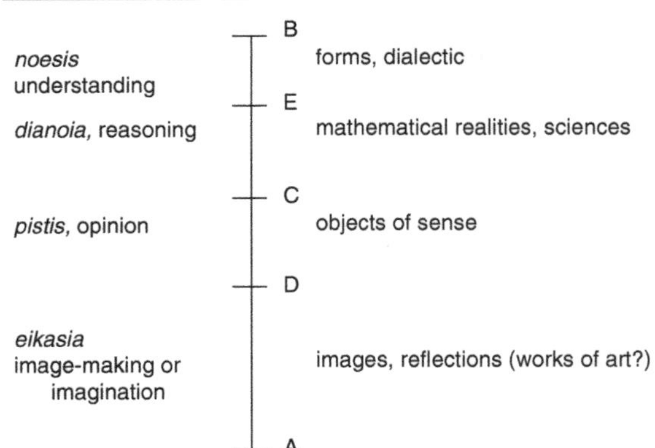

The names of the four mental processes – *noesis*, *dianoia*, *pistis*, and *eikasia* – are more or less arbitrary, and Plato does not use them regularly in these precise senses in the rest of the *Republic*.

* Plato, extracted from *The Republic*, translated by G.M.A. Grube (Hackett Publishing Co., 1974), pp. 164–70. Originally published 360 BCE.

[2] He means play on the similarity of sound between *ouranos*, the sky, and *horaton*, visible.

[3] It is clear that Plato visualizes a vertical line (511d and throughout) with *B* as the highest point in the scale of reality and *A* as the lowest form of existence. The main division is at C. AC is the visible, CB being the intelligible world, AD is the world of images (and perhaps, though Plato does not say so, works of art), mathematical realities are contained in *CE*, the Platonic Forms in *EB*, with the Good presumably at *B*.

assume the existence of the odd and the even, of figures,
of three kinds of angles, and of kindred things in each of
their studies, as if they were known to them. These they
make their hypotheses and do not deem it necessary to
give any account of them either to themselves or to others as if they were clear to all; these are their starting
points, and going through the remaining steps they
d reach an agreed conclusion on what they started out to
investigate. – Quite so, I understand that.

You know also that they use visible figures and talk
about them, but they are not thinking about them but
about the models of which these are likenesses; they are
making their points about the square itself, the diameter
e itself, not about the diameter which they draw, and similarly with the others. These figures which they fashion
and draw, of which shadows and reflections in the water
are images, they now in turn use as images, in seeking to
understand those others in themselves, which one can-
511 not see except in thought. – That is true.

This is what I called the intelligible class, and said that
the soul is forced to use hypotheses in its search for it,
not travelling up to a first principle, since it cannot reach
beyond its hypotheses, but it uses as images those very
things which at a lower level were models and which, in
comparison with their images, were thought to be clear
b and honoured as such. – I understand, he said, that you
mean what happens in geometry and kindred sciences.

Understand also that by the other section of the intelligible I mean that which reason itself grasps by the
power of dialectic. It does not consider its hypotheses as
first principles, but as hypotheses in the true sense of
stepping stones and starting points, in order to reach
that which is beyond hypothesis, the first principle of all
that exists. Having reached this and keeping hold of
what follows from it, it does come down to a conclusion
c without making use of anything visible at all, but proceeding by means of Forms and through Forms to its
conclusions which are Forms.

I understand, he said, but not completely, for you
seem to be speaking of a mighty task – that you wish to
distinguish the intelligible reality contemplated by the
science of dialectic as clearer than that viewed by the so-
called sciences, for which their hypotheses are first principles. The students of these so-called sciences are, it is
true, compelled to study them by thought and not by
sense perception, yet because they do not go back to a
d first principle but proceed from hypotheses, you do
not think that they have any clear understanding of
their subjects, although these can be so understood if
approached from a first principle. You seem to me to call
the attitude of mind of geometers and such reasoning
but not understanding, reasoning being midway
between opinion and understanding.

You have grasped this very satisfactorily, I said. There
are four such processes in the soul, corresponding to the
four sections of our line: understanding for the highest,
reasoning for the second; give the name of opinion to
the third, and imagination to the last. Place these in the
due terms of a proportion and consider that each has as
much clarity as the content of its particular section
shares in truth. – I understand, and I agree and arrange
them as you say. [...]

The allegory of the cave

Next, I said, compare the effect of education and the 514
lack of it upon our human nature to a situation like this:
imagine men to be living in an underground cave-like
dwelling place, which has a way up to the light along its
whole width, but the entrance is a long way up. The men
have been there from childhood, with their neck and
legs in fetters, so that they remain in the same place and b
can only see ahead of them, as their bonds prevent them
turning their heads. Light is provided by a fire burning
some way behind and above them. Between the fire and
the prisoners, some way behind them and on a higher
ground, there is a path across the cave and along this a
low wall has been built, like the screen at a puppet show
in front of the performers who show their puppets
above it. – I see it.

See then also men carrying along that wall, so that
they overtop it, all kinds of artifacts, statues of men,
reproductions of other animals in stone or wood fash- c
ioned in all sorts of ways, and, as is likely, some of the 515
carriers are talking while others are silent. – This is a
strange picture, and strange prisoners.

They are like us, I said. Do you think, in the first place,
that such men could see anything of themselves and
each other[4] except the shadows which the fire casts upon
the wall of the cave in front of them? – How could they,
if they have to keep their heads still throughout life? b

And is not the same true of the objects carried along
the wall? – Quite.

If they could converse with one another, do you not
think that they would consider these shadows to be the
real things? – Necessarily.

4 These shadows of themselves and each other are never mentioned again. A Platonic myth or parable, like a Homeric simile, is often elaborated in considerable detail. These contribute to the vividness of the picture but often have no other function, and it is a mistake to look for any symbolic meaning in them. It is the general picture that matters.

What if their prison had an echo which reached them from in front of them? Whenever one of the carriers passing behind the wall spoke, would they not think that it was the shadow passing in front of them which was talking? Do you agree? – By Zeus I do.

c Altogether then, I said, such men would believe the
truth to be nothing else than the shadows of the artifacts? – They must believe that.

Consider then what deliverance from their bonds and the curing of their ignorance would be if something like this naturally happened to them. Whenever one of them was freed, had to stand up suddenly, turn his head, walk, and look up toward the light, doing all that would give him pain, the flash of the fire would make it impossible
for him to see the objects of which he had earlier seen
d the shadows. What do you think he would say if he was
told that what he saw then was foolishness, that he was now somewhat closer to reality and turned to things that existed more fully, that he saw more correctly? If one then pointed to each of the objects passing by, asked him what each was, and forced him to answer, do you not think he would be at a loss and believe that the things which he saw earlier were truer than the things now pointed out to him? – Much truer.

e If one then compelled him to look at the fire itself, his
eyes would hurt, he would turn round and flee toward those things which he could see, and think that they were in fact clearer than those now shown to him. – Quite so.

And if one were to drag him thence by force up the rough and steep path, and did not let him go before he
516 was dragged into the sunlight, would he not be in phys-
ical pain and angry as he was dragged along? When he came into the light, with the sunlight filling his eyes, he would not be able to see a single one of the things which are now said to be true. – Not at once, certainly.

I think he would need time to get adjusted before he could see things in the world above; at first he would see shadows most easily, then reflections of men and other things in water, then the things themselves. After this he would see objects in the sky and the sky itself more easily at night, the light of the stars and the moon more
b easily than the sun and the light of the sun during the
day. – Of course.

Then, at last, he would be able to see the sun, not images of it in water or in some alien place, but the sun itself in its own place, and be able to contemplate it. – That must be so.

After this he would reflect that it is the sun which provides the seasons and the years, which governs every-
c thing in the visible world, and is also in some way the
cause of those other things which he used to see. – Clearly that would be the next stage.

What then? As he reminds himself of his first dwelling place, of the wisdom there and of his fellow prisoners, would he not reckon himself happy for the change, and pity them? – Surely.

And if the men below had praise and honours from each other, and prizes for the man who saw most clearly the shadows that passed before them, and who could best remember which usually came earlier and which
later, and which came together and thus could most ably d
prophesy the future, do you think our man would desire those rewards and envy those who were honoured and held power among the prisoners, or would he feel, as Homer put it, that he certainly wished to be "serf to another man without possessions upon the earth"[5] and go through any suffering, rather than share their opinions and live as they do? – Quite so, he said, I think he e
would rather suffer anything.

Reflect on this too, I said. If this man went down into the cave again and sat down in the same seat, would his eyes not be filled with darkness, coming suddenly out of the sunlight? – They certainly would.

And if he had to contend again with those who had remained prisoners in recognizing those shadows while
his sight was affected and his eyes had not settled down – 517
and the time for this adjustment would not be short – would he not be ridiculed? Would it not be said that he had returned from his upward journey with his eyesight spoiled, and that it was not worthwhile even to attempt to travel upward? As for the man who tried to free them and lead them upward, if they could somehow lay their hands on him and kill him, they would do so. – They certainly would.

This whole image, my dear Glaucon, I said, must be
related to what we said before. The realm of the visible b
should be compared to the prison dwelling, and the fire inside it to the power of the sun. If you interpret the upward journey and the contemplation of things above as the upward journey of the soul to the intelligible realm, you will grasp what I surmise since you were keen to hear it. Whether it is true or not only the god knows, but this is how I see it, namely that in the intelligible world the Form of the Good is the last to be seen, c
and with difficulty; when seen it must be reckoned to be for all the cause of all that is right and beautiful, to have produced in the visible world both light and the fount

[5] *Odyssey* 11, 489–90, where Achilles says to Odysseus, on the latter's visit to the underworld, that he would rather be a servant to a poor man on earth than king among the dead.

of light, while in the intelligible world it is itself that which produces and controls truth and intelligence, and he who is to act intelligently in public or in private must see it. – I share your thought as far as I am able.

Walter Ullman, "Ascending and Descending Theses of Government"*

[...] Historically speaking, there were two main theses of government and law in the medieval period. Both were operative, though at one time the one, at other times the other, was predominant.

The one conception of government and law, which was also chronologically the earlier one, may be termed the ascending theory. Its main feature is that original power is located in the people, or in the community itself. This was the thesis of government which Tacitus described when he portrayed the manner in which the Germanic tribes were governed. Since original power resided in the people, it was they who in their popular assemblies elected a war leader or a duke or a king, and the like. He had no power other than that which the electing assembly had given him. He was said to represent the community and remained therefore accountable to the popular assembly. Consequently, there existed a *right* of resistance to the ruler's commands as a leader. This right of resistance explains the ease with which a king was deposed and done away with, if in the view of the people he no longer represented their will. Although in course of time the practice developed to elect men into kingship only from certain families, the principle still remained the same. Metaphorically speaking power ascended from the broad base of a pyramid to its apex, the king or duke. The popular assembly controlled the ruler's government, and it was mainly as a court of law that the assembly worked effectively. This ascending theory of government may also be called the populist theory of government, because original power was anchored in the people.

Opposed to this theory was the descending thesis of government. Here original power was located in a supreme being which, because of the prevailing Christian ideas, came to be seen as divinity itself. St. Augustine in the fifth century had said that God distributed the laws to mankind through the medium of kings. And in the thirteenth century St. Thomas Aquinas expressed the same idea when he said that power descended from God. One can here also see a metaphorical pyramid but it was at its apex that the sum-total of power was located. Whatever power was found 'below', was derived from 'above', for, as St. Paul said, 'There is no power but of God.' Here one can speak only of delegated power. It was God who had appointed a vicegerent on earth, and it was, in actual fact, this vicegerent who was held to have embodied original power. Within this thesis the people had no power other than that it had been given 'from above'. Every officer was appointed 'from above' – and not elected by a popular assembly. The supreme officer was responsible to God alone. This theory of government can also be called the theocratic theory, because eventually all power was located in God.

The history of political ideas in the Middle Ages is to a very large extent a history of the conflicts between these two theories of government. As a result of the overpowering influence of Christianity the Germanic peoples adopted the theory inherent in Christian doctrine – which was almost wholly of a Latin–Roman complexion – and the ascending theme was, so to speak, driven underground, not to emerge again as a theoretical proposition until the late thirteenth century. From then onwards the descending thesis of government receded more and more into the background, until only a few remnants are left today.

This adoption of the descending thesis of government makes understandable the very pronounced ecclesiastical and Latin complexion which political thought assumed in the earlier Middle Ages. For its bearers were predominantly, if not exclusively, clerics who were sufficiently educated to express themselves adequately. Until well into the eleventh century there was no such thing as an educated laity; there was no general education for laymen, and whatever education there was, was in the hands of the clergy and almost wholly for the benefit of the clergy. The chanceries and offices of kings and emperors were staffed by clerics, not by laymen. This very strong ecclesiastical character of early political thought marked it off both from ancient – Greek and Roman – as well as modern political thinking.

* Walter Ullman, extracted from *A History of Political Thought: The Middle Ages* (Penguin, 1965), pp. 12–14.

Ken Wilber, "The Great Chain of Being"*

What is the worldview that, as Arthur Lovejoy pointed out, "has been the dominant official philosophy of the larger part of civilized humankind through most of its history"? The worldview that "the greater number of the subtler speculative minds and of the great religious teachers [both East and West] have, in their various fashions, been engaged in"[6]

[...]

Known as the "perennial philosophy" – perennial precisely because it shows up across cultures and across the ages with essentially similar features – this worldview has, indeed, formed the core not only of the world's great wisdom traditions, from Christianity to Buddhism to Taoism, but also of the greatest philosophers, scientists, and psychologists of both East and West, North and South. So overwhelmingly widespread is the perennial philosophy – the details of which I will explain in a moment – that it is either the single greatest intellectual error ever to appear in humankind's history – an error so colossally widespread as to literally stagger the mind – or it is the single most accurate reflection of reality yet to appear.

Central to the perennial philosophy is the notion of "the great chain of being." The idea itself is fairly simple. Reality, according to the perennial philosophy, is not one-dimensional; it is not a flatland of uniform substance stretching endlessly before the eye. Rather, reality is composed of several *different* but *continuous* dimensions. Manifest reality, that is, consists of different grades or levels, reaching from the lowest and most dense and least conscious to the highest and most subtle and most conscious. At one end of this continuum of being or spectrum of consciousness is what we in the West would call "matter" or the insentient and the non-conscious, and at the other end is "spirit" or "godhead" or the "super-conscious" (which is also said to be the all-pervading ground of the entire sequence, as we will see). Arrayed in between are the other dimensions of being arranged according to their individual degrees of reality (Plato), actuality (Aristotle), inclusiveness (Hegel), consciousness (Aurobindo), clarity (Leibniz), value (Whitehead), or knowingness (Garab Dorje).

Sometimes the great chain is presented as having just three major levels: matter, mind, and spirit. Other versions give five levels: matter, body, mind, soul, and spirit. Still others give very exhaustive breakdowns of the great chain; some of the yogic systems give literally dozens of discrete yet continuous dimensions. For the time being, our simple hierarchy of matter to body to mind to soul to spirit will suffice.

The central claim of the perennial philosophy is that *men and women can grow and develop (or evolve) all the way up the hierarchy to Spirit itself*, therein to realize a "supreme identity" with Godhead – the *ens perfectissimum* toward which all growth and evolution yearns.

But before we get to that, the first thing that we can't help but notice is that the great chain is indeed a *hierarchy* – a word that has fallen on very hard times. Originally introduced by the great Christian mystic St. Dionysius, it essentially meant "governing one's life by spiritual principles" ("hiero-" means *sacred* or *holy*, and "-arch" means *governance* or *rule*). But it soon became translated into a political/military power play, where "governance by spirit" came to mean "ruled by the Catholic Church" – a spiritual principle mistranslated into a despotism.

But as used by the perennial philosophy – and indeed, as used in modern psychology, evolutionary theory, and systems theory – hierarchy is simply a ranking of orders of events *according to their holistic capacity*. In any developmental sequence, what is whole at one stage becomes merely a part of a larger whole at the next stage. A letter is part of a whole word, which is part of a whole sentence, which is part of a whole paragraph, and so on. Koestler coined the term *holon* to refer to that which, being a whole at one stage, is a part of a wider whole at the next.[7]

[...]

All developmental and evolutionary sequences that we are aware of proceed by hierarchization, or by orders of increasing holism – molecules to cells to organs to organ systems to organisms to societies of organisms, for example. In cognitive development, we find awareness expanding from simple images that represent only one thing or event to symbols and concepts that represent whole groups or classes of things and events to rules that organize and integrate numerous classes and groups into entire networks. In moral development (male or female), we find a reasoning that moves from the isolated subject to a group or tribe of related subjects, to an entire network of groups beyond any isolated element. And so on.

* Ken Wilber, extracted from the *Journal of Humanistic Psychology*, 33, 3 (Summer 1993), pp. 52–65.

[6] Arthur Lovejoy, *The Great Chain of Being* (Cambridge, MA: Harvard University Press, 1964, 1936).

[7] A. Koestler, *The Ghost in the Machine* (New York: Random House, 1976).

[...]

In any developmental or growth sequence, as a more encompassing stage or holon emerges, it *includes* the capacities and patterns and functions of the previous stage (i.e., of the previous holons) and then adds its own unique (and more encompassing) capacities. In that sense, and that sense only, can the new and more encompassing holon be said to be "higher" or "wider." Whatever the important value of the previous stage, the new stage has *all* of that plus something extra (more integrative capacity, for example), and that "something extra" means "extra value" *relative* to the previous (and less-encompassing) stage. This crucial definition of a "higher stage" was first introduced in the West by Aristotle and in the East by Shankara and Lieh-Tzu; it has been central to the perennial philosophy ever since.

Let me give one example. In cognitive and moral development, in both the boy and the girl, the stage of preoperational or preconventional thought is concerned largely with the individual's own point of view ("narcissistic"). The next stage, the operational or conventional stage, still takes account of the individual's own point of view, but *adds* the capacity to take the view of others into account. Nothing is lost; something is added. And so in this sense it is properly said that this stage is higher or wider, meaning more valuable and useful for a wider range of interactions. Conventional thought is *more valuable* than preconventional thought in establishing a balanced moral response (and postconventional is even more valuable, and so on). As Hegel first put it, and as developmentalists have echoed ever since, each stage is adequate and valuable, but each higher stage is more adequate, and, in that sense only, more valuable (which always means, more holistic).

It is for all these reasons that Koestler, after noting that all hierarchies are composed of holons, or increasing orders of wholeness, pointed out that the correct word for hierarchy is actually *holoarchy*. He is absolutely right, and so from now on I will refer to hierarchy in general, and the great chain in particular, as holoarchy.

So that is normal or natural holoarchy, the sequential or stage-like unfolding of larger networks of increasing wholeness, with the larger or wider wholes being able to exert influence over the lower-order wholes. And as natural, desirable, and unavoidable as that is, you can already start to see how holoarchies *can* go pathological. If the higher levels can exert control over the lower levels, they can also over dominate or even repress and alienate the lower levels. That leads to a whole host of pathological difficulties, in both the individual and society at large.

It is precisely *because* the world is arranged holoarchically, precisely because it contains fields within fields within fields, that things can go so profoundly wrong, that a disruption or pathology in one field can reverberate throughout an entire system. And the "cure" for this pathology, in all systems, is essentially the same: rooting out the pathological holons so the holoarchy itself can return to harmony. The cure does not consist, as the reductionists maintain, in getting rid of holoarchy per se, because, even if that were possible, it would simply result in a uniform, one-dimensional flatland of no value distinctions at all (which is why those critics who toss out holoarchy in general immediately replace it with a new scale of values of their own, i.e., with their own particular holoarchy).

Rather, the "cure" of any diseased system consists in rooting out any holons that have usurped their position in the overall system by abusing their power of upward or downward causation. This is exactly the "cure" we see at work in psychoanalysis (shadow holons refuse integration), critical social theory (opaque ideology usurps open communication), democratic social revolutions (monarchical or fascist holons oppress the body politic), medical science interventions (cancerous holons invade a benign system), radical feminist critiques (patriarchal holons dominate the public sphere), and so on. It is not getting rid of holoarchy per se, but arresting (and integrating) their arrogant holons.

As I said, all of the world's great wisdom traditions are variations of the perennial philosophy, of the great holoarchy of being. In his book *Forgotten Truth*, Huston Smith summarizes the world's major religions in one phrase: "a hierarchy of being and knowing." Chögyam Trungpa, Rinpoche pointed out that *the* essential and background idea pervading all of the philosophies of the East, from India to Tibet to China, lying behind everything from Shintoism to Taoism, is "a hierarchy of earth, human, heaven," which he also pointed out is equivalent to "body, mind, spirit." And Coomaraswamy noted that the world's great religions, bar none, "in their different degrees represent a hierarchy of types or levels of consciousness extending from animal to deity, and according to which one and the same individual may function on different occasions."[8]

Which brings us to the most notorious paradox in the perennial philosophy. We have seen that the wisdom

8 Huston Smith, *Forgotten Truth* (New York: Harper & Row, 1976); Chögyam Trungpa, *Shambhala: Sacred Path of the Warrior* (Boston: Shambhala, 1988); A. Coomaraswamy, *Hinduism and Buddhism* (New York: Philosophical Library, 1943).

traditions subscribe to the notion that reality manifests in levels or dimensions, with each higher dimension being more inclusive and therefore "closer" to the absolute totality of Godhead or Spirit. In this sense, Spirit is the summit of being, the highest rung on the "ladder" of evolution (as long as we don't take that metaphor literally). But it is also true that Spirit is the wood out of which the entire ladder and all its rungs are made; Spirit is the suchness, the isness, the essence of each and every thing that exists.

The first aspect, the highest-rung aspect, is the *transcendental* nature of Spirit – it far surpasses any "worldly" or creaturely or finite things. The entire earth (or even universe) could be destroyed, and Spirit would remain. The second aspect, the wood aspect, is the *immanent* nature of Spirit–Spirit is equally and totally present in all manifest things and events, in nature, in culture, in heaven and on earth, with no partiality. From this angle, no phenomenon is closer to Spirit than another, for all are equally "made of" Spirit. Thus Spirit is *both* the highest *goal* of all development and evolution, and the *ground* of the entire sequence, as present fully at the beginning as at the end. Spirit is prior to this world, but not other to this world.

[...]

We can look now at some of the actual levels of the holoarchy, of the great chain of being, as it appears in the three largest wisdom traditions: Judeo-Christian-Muslim, Buddhism, and Hinduism (although any mature tradition will do). The Christian terms are the easiest, because we already know them and have already been using them: matter, body, mind, soul, and spirit. "Matter" means the physical universe and our physical bodies (e.g., those aspects of existence covered by the laws of physics). "Body" in this case means the emotional body, the "animal" body, sex, hunger, vital life force, and so on (e.g., those aspects of existence studied by biology). "Mind" is the rational, reasoning, linguistic, and imaginative mind (studied by psychology). "Soul" is the higher or subtle mind, the archetypal mind, the intuitive mind, and the essence or the indestructibleness of our own being (studied by theology). And "spirit" is the transcendental summit of our being, our Godhead (studied by contemplative mysticism).

[...]

So soul is both the highest level of individual growth we can achieve, but also the final barrier, the final knot, to complete enlightenment or supreme identity, simply because as transcendental witness it stands back from everything it witnesses. Once we push through the witness position, then the soul or witness itself dissolves and there is only the play of nondual awareness, awareness that does not look at objects but is completely one with all objects (Zen says, "it is like tasting the sky"). The gap between subject and object collapses, the soul is transcended or dissolved, and pure spiritual or nondual awareness – which is very simple, very obvious, very clear – arises. You realize that your being is of all space, vast and open, and everything arising anywhere is arising in you, as spirit, spontaneously.

[...]

And so we can end on a happy note: After being temporarily derailed in the 19th century by a variety of materialistic reductionisms (from scientific materialism to behaviorism to Marxism), the great chain of being, the great holoarchy of being, is back. This temporary derailment – an attempt to reduce the holoarchy of being to its lowest level, matter – was particularly galling in psychology, which first lost its spirit, then its soul, then its mind, and was reduced to studying *only* empirical behavior or bodily drives, a restriction that at any other time or place would be considered a precise definition of insanity.

But now evolutionary holoarchy – the holistic study of the development and self-organization of fields within fields within fields – is once again the dominant theme in virtually all scientific and behavioral disciplines (as we will see), although it goes by many names (Aristotle's "entelechy," to give only one example, is now known as "morphogenetic fields" and "self-organizing systems"). This is not to say that the modern versions of the great holoarchy and its self-organizing principles offer no new insights, for they do, particularly when it comes to the actual evolutionary unfolding of the great chain itself. Each glimpse of the great holoarchy is adequate; each advancing glimpse is more adequate ...

But the essentials are unmistakable. Ludwig von Bertalanffy, the founder of general system theory, summarized it perfectly: "Reality, in the modern conception, appears as a tremendous hierarchical order of organized entities, leading, in a superposition of many levels, from physical and chemical to biological and sociological systems. Such hierarchical structure and combination into systems of ever higher order, *is characteristic of reality as a whole* and of fundamental importance especially in biology, psychology and sociology."[9]

[...]

And the only reason *everybody* doesn't realize this is that it is hiding out under a variety of different names.

9 Ludwig von Bertalanffy, *General System Theory* (New York: Braziller, 1968), pp. 74, 87.

But no matter; realized or not, it is already well under way. And the truly wonderful thing about this homecoming is that modern theory can now, and is now, reconnecting with its rich roots in the perennial philosophy, reconnecting not only with Plato and Aristotle and Plotinus and Maimonides and Spinoza and Hegel and Whitehead in the West but also with Shankara and Padmasambhava and Chih-I and Fa-tsang and Abinavagupta in the East – all made possible by the fact that the perennial philosophy *is* perennial, cutting across times and cultures alike to point to the heart and soul and spirit of humankind.

There is, really, only one major thing left to be done, one fundamental item on the homecoming agenda. Although it is true, as I said, that the unifying paradigm in modern thought, from physics to biology to psychology to sociology, is evolutionary holoarchy [...], nonetheless most orthodox schools of inquiry admit the existence only of matter, body, and mind. The higher dimensions of soul and spirit are not yet accorded quite the same status. We might say that the modern West has still only acknowledged three-fifths of the great holoarchy of being. The agenda, very simply, is to reintroduce the other two-fifths (soul and spirit).

Once we recognize *all* the levels and dimensions of the great chain, we simultaneously acknowledge all the corresponding modes of knowing – not just the eye of flesh, which discloses the physical and sensory world, or just the eye of mind, which discloses the linguistic and logical world, but also the eye of contemplation, which discloses the soul and spirit. When one relies solely on the eye of flesh, the empirical eye, then in psychology one gets behaviorism and in philosophy, positivism (these were the two general movements most responsible for that nasty little nineteenth-century derailment). When we reintroduce the eye of mind we then get, in psychology, the introspective schools including psychoanalysis, gestalt, existential, and humanistic; and in philosophy, we get philosophy proper – phenomenology, hermeneutics, existentialism, critical theory.

And so there is the agenda: Let us take the last step and also reintroduce the eye of contemplation, which, as a scientific and repeatable methodology, discloses soul and spirit. The result is transpersonal psychology and philosophy. And that transpersonal vision is, I submit, the final homecoming, the reweaving of our modern soul with the soul of humanity itself – the true meaning of multiculturalism – so that, standing on the shoulders of giants, we transcend but include, which always means honor, their ever-recurring presence.

Jean Jacques Rousseau, "On the General Will"*

That sovereignty is inalienable

The first and foremost consequence of the principles established above is that the general will alone can direct the forces of the state in accordance with the end for which it was instituted, that is, the common good, for, if the opposition of private interests has made the establishment of societies necessary, the agreement of these same interests has made it possible. It is what these different interests hold in common that forms the social bond, and if there were not some point of agreement among them, no society could exist. Indeed, it is solely on the basis of this common interest that society should be governed.

I say, therefore, that sovereignty, being nothing more than the exercise of the general will, can never be alienated, and that the sovereign, which is merely a collective being, can only be represented by itself; power can indeed be transferred but not will.

In fact, if it is not possible for a particular will to agree on some point with the general will, it is at least impossible for this agreement to be lasting and constant, for the particular will tends by nature towards partiality and the general will towards equality. It is even more impossible to have any guarantee of this agreement, even though it should always exist; this would not be an effect of art but of chance. The sovereign may well say: "I now will what this man wills, or at least what he says he wills," but it cannot say, "What this man wills tomorrow, I too shall will," since it is absurd for the will to give itself fetters for the future, and since no will can consent to anything that is contrary to the good of the being who wills it. If the people, therefore, simply promises to obey, it dissolves itself by that act and loses what makes it a people; at the moment a master exists, there is no longer a sovereign, and from that moment the body politic is destroyed.

This is not to say that the orders of leaders cannot pass for expressions of the general will, as long as the sovereign, free to oppose them, does not do so. In such a case, the consent of the people must be presumed from universal silence. This will be explained at greater length.

* Jean Jacques Rousseau, extracted from The Social Contract, in *Rousseau's Political Writings*, edited by Alan Ritter and Julia Bondanella (W. W. Norton & Co., 1988), pp. 98–104. Originally published 1762.

That sovereignty is indivisible

For the same reason that sovereignty is inalienable, it is indivisible, for the will is general,[10] or it is not; it is the will of the body of the people, or of only a part. In the first case, this declared will is an act of sovereignty and constitutes law; in the second, it is merely a particular will, or an act of magistracy; at the very most it is a decree.

But our political theorists, being unable to divide sovereignty in principle, divide it in its purpose; they divide it into force and will; into legislative power and executive power; into the rights of taxation, justice, and making war; into internal administration and the power of negotiating with foreigners; sometimes they mingle all these parts, and sometimes they separate them. They turn the sovereign into a fantastic being composed as a mosaic of inlaid fragments; it is as if they created man out of several bodies, one of which would provide the eyes, another the arms, another the feet and nothing more. The magicians of Japan, it is said, cut a child into pieces before the eyes of the spectators; then, throwing all the pieces into the air one after another, they make the child fall back to earth alive and completely reassembled. The juggling acts of our political theorists are more or less like this; after having dismembered the social body by a spell worthy of the fair, they reassemble the pieces, we know not how.

This error results from not having formulated an accurate notion of sovereign authority, and from having taken for parts of that authority what were only emanations of it. Thus, for example, the acts of declaring war and making peace have been regarded as acts of sovereignty, but they are not, since each of these acts is not a law, but merely an application of the law, a particular act which determines how the law applies to a particular case, as we shall clearly see when the idea attached to the word *law* has been defined.

By analyzing the other divisions in a similar manner, we would find that whenever we think sovereignty is divided, we are mistaken, and that the rights which are taken to be parts of this sovereignty are always subordinate to it and always presuppose supreme wills which these rights only execute.

It would be impossible to say how much this lack of precision has obscured the determinations of the authors who write on matters of political right, when they have attempted to judge the respective rights of kings and peoples on the basis of the principles they had established. Anyone can see, in Chapters 3 and 4 of the first book of Grotius, how this learned man and his translator Barbeyrac were entangled and hampered by their sophistries, for fear of saying too little or too much in expressing their views, and offending the interests they had to conciliate. Grotius, a refugee in France, discontent with his own country and wishing to pay court to Louis XIII to whom his book is dedicated, spares no pains to deprive the peoples of all their rights and bestow them upon kings in the most artful way possible. This would also have been much to the liking of Barbeyrac, who dedicated his translation to the king of England, George I. But, unfortunately, the expulsion of James II, which he calls abdication, forced him to be on his guard, to equivocate, to be evasive, in order to avoid making William appear to be a usurper.[11] If these two writers had adopted true principles, all these difficulties would have been removed, and they would always have remained consistent, but they would have told the sad truth and paid court only to the people. Indeed, truth does not lead to success, and the people confers neither embassies, professorial chairs, nor pensions.

Whether the general will can err

It follows from what has gone before that the general will is always in the right and always tends toward the public utility, but it does not follow that the decisions of the people are always equally correct. A person always wills his own good, but he does not always see it; the people is never corrupted, but it is often deceived, and it is only then that it appears to will what is bad.[12]

There is often a great difference between the will of all and the general will; the latter looks only to the common interest; the former looks to the private interest and is only a sum of particular wills, but take away from these same wills the pluses and minuses that cancel each

[10] For a will to be general, it is not always necessary for it to be unanimous, but all the votes must be counted; any formal exclusion destroys the generality [Rousseau's note, 1782].

[11] James II was king of England from 1685 to 1688, when he was forced to leave the country during the Glorious Revolution and was replaced by Mary, his Protestant daughter, and her husband, William of Orange, governor of the Netherlands. Parliament imposed conditions in the "Bill of Rights" which limited their authority and that of all their royal successors.

[12] Here Rousseau broaches the main difficulty with his view of a legitimate state as radically democratic: the laws enacted in the sovereign assembly of such a state might be unjust and harmful, since they might not express the general will. *On Social Contract* can be fruitfully read as an attempt to show how a democracy must be organized so that it serves the common good.

other out,[13] and the general will remains as the sum of the differences.

If, when a sufficiently informed people deliberates, the citizens were to have no communication among themselves, the general will would always result from the large number of small differences, and the decision would always be good.[14] But when factions, partial associations, are formed at the expense of the greater one, the will of each of these associations becomes general with respect to its members, and particular with respect to the state; it may then be said that there are no longer as many voters as men, but only as many as there are associations. The differences become less numerous and yield a less general result. Finally, when one of these associations is so large that it prevails over all the others, your result is no longer just a sum of small differences but a single difference; there is, at that point, no longer a general will, and the opinion which prevails is merely a particular one.

It is important, therefore, in order to have a clear enunciation of the general will, that there be no partial association in the state and that each citizen speak only for himself;[15] such was the unique and sublime institution of the great Lycurgus. If there are partial societies, it is necessary to multiply their number and to prevent inequality from existing among them, as Solon, Numa, and Servius did.[16] These precautions are the only good ones for ensuring that the general will is always enlightened, and that the people is not deceived.

13 "Every interest," says the Marquis d'Argenson, "has different principles. The agreement of two particular interests is formed by opposition to that of a third." He might have added that the concurrence of all interests arises in opposition to the interest of each individual. If there were not any different interests, the common interest would hardly exist and would never meet any obstacle; everything would proceed on its own, and politics would cease to be an art [Rousseau's note].

14 The "communication" referred to here is not face to face discussion among citizens in the sovereign assembly, but private caucuses of special interest groups.

15 "It is true," says Machiavelli, "that some divisions harm republics while others benefit them. Those which harm them involve factions and partisans. Since a founder of a republic cannot prevent strife from occurring, he can at least see to it that there are no factions" (*History of Florence*, VII. i) [Rousseau's note].

16 Lycurgus (c. nineth century BC) was a reformer of Spartan and Solon (?638–?559 BC) of Athenian political institutions. The institutions of the Roman Republic, according to tradition, were established by Numa Pompilius (?end of eighth century BC) and reorganized by Servius Tullius (?seventh century BC). Sparta and Republican Rome served Rousseau as inspirations for his vision of democracy.

On the limits of sovereign power

If the state or city is only an artificial body whose life consists in the union of its members, and if the most important of its concerns is its own preservation, it must have a universal and compelling force in order to move and dispose each part in the manner best suited to the whole. Just as nature gives each man absolute power over all his members, the social pact gives the body politic absolute power over all its own; and it is this same power, under the direction of the general will, which bears, as I have said, the name of sovereignty.

But beyond the public person, we have to consider the private persons who compose it, whose life and liberty are naturally independent of it. It is a question, then, of clearly distinguishing the respective rights of the citizens and the sovereign,[17] and the duties the former have to fulfill as subjects from the natural rights they should enjoy as men.

It is agreed that each person alienates through the social pact only the part of his power, possessions, and liberty that will be important to the community, but it must also be agreed that the sovereign alone is the judge of what is important.[18]

A citizen owes to the state all the services he can render, as soon as the sovereign asks for them, but the sovereign, on the other hand, cannot impose on the subjects any restraints that are useless to the community, nor can it even want to do so, for, under the law of reason just as under the law of nature, nothing is done without a cause.

The commitments which bind us to the social body are obligatory only because they are mutual, and their nature is such that in fulfilling them we cannot work for others without also working for ourselves. Why is the general will always in the right, and why do all constantly will the happiness of each person, unless it is because there is no one who does not apply this word *each* to himself and who does not think of himself when voting for all? This proves that equality of right and the notion of justice it produces stem from each man's preference for himself, and, consequently, from the nature of man; that the general will, to be truly so, must be general in its object as well as in its essence; that it must

17 Attentive readers, do not hurry, I beg you, to accuse me here of contradicting myself. I have not been able to avoid it in my terms, given the poverty of language; but wait [Rousseau's note].

18 The fact that the sovereign assembly has unbounded control over each member's fate adds to the urgency of assuring that its decisions are wise and just.

come from all to be applied to all; and that it loses its natural rectitude when it tends toward some individual and determinate object, because, in such a case, we have no real principle of equity to guide us in judging what is foreign to us.[19]

Indeed, as soon as it becomes a question of a particular fact or right on a point which has not been settled by a previous and general agreement, the matter becomes arguable. It is a case in which the interested private individuals are one of the parties and the public the other, but in which I see neither the law that should be followed, nor the judge who should give the decision. It would be ridiculous in such a case to want to refer the matter to an express decision of the general will, which can only be the conclusion of one of the parties, and which is, consequently, for the other party, only a foreign, particular will, inclined on this occasion to injustice, and subject to error. Thus, just as a particular will cannot represent the general will, the general will, in turn, changes in nature when it has a particular object, and, as a general will, it cannot pronounce judgment on either a man or a fact. When the people of Athens, for example, named its leaders or reduced them to the ranks, bestowed honors on one, imposed penalties on another, and, by multitudes of particular decrees, exercised all the functions of government indiscriminately, it no longer had, in such cases, a general will properly speaking; it was no longer acting as sovereign but as magistrate. This will seem contrary to prevailing notions, but I must be given time to set forth my own.

It should be understood from the preceding that what makes the will general is not so much the number of voters as the common interest uniting them, for, in this arrangement, each necessarily submits to the conditions he imposes on others, an admirable concurrence of interest and justice, which gives the common decisions an equitable character which is seen to vanish in the discussion of any particular issue for want of a common interest to unite and identify the ruling of the judge with that of the contending party.

From whatever direction we go back to our principle, we always reach the same conclusion, namely, that the social pact establishes such an equality among the citizens that they all commit themselves under the same conditions and should all enjoy the same rights. Thus, by the very nature of the pact, every act of sovereignty, that is to say, every authentic act of the general will, obligates or favors all citizens equally, so that the sovereign knows only the body of the nation and makes no distinctions between any of those who compose it. What in fact is an act of sovereignty? It is not an agreement between a superior and an inferior, but an agreement between the body and each of its members, a legitimate agreement, because it is based upon the social contract; equitable, because it is common to all; useful, because it can have no other purpose than the general good; and reliable, because it is guaranteed by the public force and the supreme power. As long as the subjects are only bound by agreements of this sort, they obey no one but their own will, and to ask how far the respective rights of the sovereign and citizens extend is to ask to what point the latter can commit themselves to each other, one towards all and all towards one.

We can see from this that the sovereign power, wholly absolute, wholly sacred, and wholly inviolable as it is, does not and cannot exceed the limits of the general agreements, and that every man can fully dispose of whatever has been left to him of his goods and liberty through these agreements, so that the sovereign never has a right to burden one subject more than another, because when the matter becomes a private one, its power is no longer competent.

Once these distinctions have been admitted, it is obviously untrue that under the social contract there is any real renunciation on the part of private individuals, since their situation, as a result of this contract, is actually preferable to what it was previously, and, instead of alienating anything, they have only exchanged, to their advantage, an uncertain and precarious existence for another that is better and more secure, natural independence for liberty, the power to harm others for their own safety, and their force, which others could overcome, for a right that the social union makes invincible. Their very lives, which they have dedicated to the state, are continually protected by it, and when they imperil their lives for the defense of the state, what are they then doing but giving back to the state what they have received from it? What are they doing that they were not doing in greater danger and more frequently in the state of nature, when, engaging in inevitable quarrels, they would, at the risk of their lives, defend their means of

19 One of the means Rousseau counts on most heavily to assure that the sovereign assembly expresses the general will is laid out in this chapter. The enactments passed by the assembly must be general in the sense that they apply equally to all. The assembled citizens would be too tempted to serve private interests, if they could pass enactments for the advantage of particular individuals or groups, rather than the whole community. General rules, on the other hand, have such uncertain benefits and costs for individuals that they cannot readily be crafted so as to advantage particular persons or groups.

preserving them. All have to fight if necessary for the homeland, it is true; but then no one ever has to fight for himself. Do we not still gain something by running part of the risks to insure our safety that we would have to run for ourselves as soon as we are deprived of it?

On the right of life and death

It may be asked how private individuals, having no right to dispose of their own lives, can transfer to the sovereign the very right they do not possess.[20] This question appears difficult to resolve only because it is poorly posed. Every man has the right to risk his own life in order to preserve it. Has it ever been said that anyone who throws himself out a window to escape a fire is guilty of suicide? Has such a crime ever even been imputed to someone who perishes in a storm, even if he was fully aware of the danger when he embarked?

The social treaty has as its end the preservation of the contracting parties. Anyone who desires the end also desires the means, and these means are inseparable from certain risks, even certain losses. Anyone who desires to preserve his life at the expense of others should also give it up for them when it is necessary. Now, the citizen is no longer the judge of the perils to which the law wants him to expose himself, and when the prince[21] has said to him: "It is expedient for the state that you die," he should die, since it is only on this condition that he has lived in safety up to that time, and since his life is no longer merely a blessing of nature, but a conditional gift of the state.

Friedrich Engels, "Marx's Materialist Conception of History"*

The materialist conception of history starts from the proposition that the production of the means to support human life and, next to production, the exchange of things produced, is the basis of all social structure; that in every society that has appeared in history, the manner in which wealth is distributed and society divided into classes or orders is dependent upon what is produced, how it is produced, and how the products are exchanged. From this point of view the final causes of all social changes and political revolutions are to be sought, not in men's brains, not in man's better insight into eternal truth and justice, but in changes in the modes of production and exchange. They are to be sought, not in the *philosophy*, but in the *economics* of each particular epoch. The growing perception that existing social institutions are unreasonable and unjust, that reason has become unreason, and right wrong, is only proof that in the modes of production and exchange changes have silently taken place, with which the social order, adapted to earlier economic conditions, is no longer in keeping. From this it also follows that the means of getting rid of the incongruities that have been brought to light must also be present, in a more or less developed condition, within the changed modes of production themselves. These means are not to be invented by deduction from fundamental principles, but are to be discovered in the stubborn facts of the existing system of production.

What is, then, the position of modern socialism in this connection?

The present structure of society – this is now pretty generally conceded – is the creation of the ruling class of today, of the bourgeoisie. The mode of production peculiar to the bourgeoisie, known, since Marx, as the capitalist mode of production, was incompatible with the feudal system, with the privileges it conferred upon individuals, entire social ranks and local corporations, as well as with the hereditary ties of subordination which constituted the framework of its social organization. The bourgeoisie broke up the feudal system and built upon its ruins the capitalist order of society, the kingdom of free competition, of personal liberty, of the equality, before the law, of all commodity owners, of all the rest of the capitalist blessings. Thenceforward the capitalist mode of production could develop in freedom. Since steam, machinery and the making of machines by machinery transformed the older manufacture into modern industry, the productive forces evolved under the guidance of the bourgeoisie developed with a rapidity and in a degree unheard of before. But just as the older manufacture, in its time, and handicraft, becoming more developed under its influence, had come into collision with the feudal trammels of the guilds, so now modern industry, in its more complete development, comes into collision with the bounds within which the capitalistic mode of production holds it confined. The new productive forces have already outgrown the capitalistic mode of using them. And this

* Friedrich Engels, extracted from *Socialism: Utopian and Scientific*, translated by Edward Aveling (New York: International Publishers, 1935). Originally published 1880.

[20] Locke asks this question in *The Second Treatise of Civil Government*, section 23.

[21] In Rousseau's technical vocabulary, which he does not explain until Book III, chapter 1, the term *prince* refers not to a sovereign, but to the administrative officials charged by the sovereign assembly with the task of executing legislation.

conflict between productive forces and modes of production is not a conflict engendered in the mind of man, like that between original sin and divine justice. It exists, in fact, objectively, outside us, independently of the will and actions even of the men that have brought it on. Modern socialism is nothing but the reflex, in thought, of this conflict in fact; its ideal reflection in the minds, first, of the class directly suffering under it, the working class. …

Active social forces work exactly like natural forces; blindly, forcibly, destructively, so long as we do not understand and reckon with them. But when once we understand them, when once we grasp their action, their direction, their effects, it depends only upon ourselves to subject them more and more to our own will, and by means of them to reach our own ends. And this holds quite especially of the mighty productive forces of today. As long as we obstinately refuse to understand the nature and the character of these social means of action – and this understanding goes against the grain of the capitalist mode of production and its defenders – so long these forces are at work in spite of us, in opposition to us, so long they master us, as we have shown above in detail.

But when once their nature is understood, they can, in the hands of the producers working together, be transformed from master demons into willing servants. The difference is as that between the destructive force of electricity in the lightning of the storm, and electricity under command in the telegraph and the voltaic arc; the difference between a conflagration, and fire working in the service of man. With this recognition at last of the real nature of the productive forces of today, the social anarchy of production gives place to a social regulation of production upon a definite plan, according to the needs of the community and of each individual. Then the capitalist mode of appropriation, in which the product enslaves first the producer and then the appropriator, is replaced by the mode of appropriation of the products that is based upon the nature of the modern means of production; upon the one hand, direct social appropriation, as means to the maintenance and extension of production – on the other, direct individual appropriation, as means of subsistence and of enjoyment.

Whilst the capitalist mode of production more and more completely transforms the great majority of the population into proletarians, it creates the power which, under penalty of its own destruction, is forced to accomplish this revolution. Whilst it forces on more and more the transformation of the vast means of production, already socialised, into state property, it shows itself the way to accomplishing this revolution. *The proletariat seizes political power and turns the means of production into state property.*

But, in doing this, it abolishes itself as proletariat, abolishes all class distinctions and class antagonisms, abolishes also the state as state. Society thus far, based upon class antagonisms, has need of the state. That is, of an organisation of the particular class which was *pro tempore* the exploiting class, an organisation for the purpose of preventing any interference from without with the existing conditions of production, and therefore, especially, for the purpose of forcibly keeping the exploited classes in the condition of oppression corresponding with the given mode of production (slavery, serfdom, wage labour). The state was the official representative of society as a whole; the gathering of it together into a visible embodiment. But it was this only in so far as it was the state of that class which itself represented, for the time being, society as a whole; in ancient times, the state of slave-owning citizens; in the Middle Ages, the feudal lords; in our time, the bourgeoisie. When at last it becomes the real representative of the whole society, it renders itself unnecessary. As soon as there is no longer any social class to be held in subjection; as soon as class rule and the individual struggle for existence based upon our present anarchy in production, with the collisions and excesses arising from these, are removed, nothing more remains to be repressed, and a special repressive force, a state, is no longer necessary. The first act by virtue of which the state really constitutes itself the representative of the whole of society – the taking possession of the means of production in the name of society – this is, at the same time, its last independent act as a state. State interference in social relations becomes, in one domain after another, superfluous, and then dies out of itself; the government of persons is replaced by the administration of things, and by the conduct of processes of production. The state is not "abolished." *It dies out.* This gives the measure of the value of the phrase "a free state," both as to its justifiable use at times by agitators, and as to its ultimate scientific insufficiency; and also of the demands of the so-called anarchists for the abolition of the state out of hand.

Since the historical appearance of the capitalist mode of production, the appropriation by society of all the means of production has often been dreamed of, more or less vaguely, by individuals, as well as by sects, as the ideal of the future. But it could become possible, could become a historical necessity, only when the actual conditions for its realisation were there. Like every other social advance, it becomes practicable, not by mean understanding that the existence of classes is in contradiction to justice, equality, etc., not by the mere willingness to abolish these classes, but by virtue of certain new economic conditions. The separation of society into an exploiting and an exploited class, a ruling and an oppressed class, was the necessary consequence of the deficient and restricted development of production in former times. So long as the total social labour only yields a produce which but slightly exceeds that barely necessary for the existence of all; so long, therefore, as labour engages all or almost all the time of the great majority of the members of society – so long, of necessity, this society is divided into classes. Side by side with the great majority, exclusively bond slaves to labour, arises a class freed from directly productive labour, which looks after the general affairs of society, the direction of labour, state business, law, science, art, etc. It is, therefore, the law of division of labour that lies at the basis of the division into classes. But this does not prevent this division into classes from being carried out by means of violence and robbery, trickery and fraud. It does not prevent the ruling class, once having the upper hand, from consolidating its power at the expense of the working class, from turning their social leadership into an intensified exploitation of the masses.

But if, upon this showing, division into classes has a certain historical justification, it has this only for a given period, only under given social conditions. It was based upon the insufficiency of production. It will be swept away by the complete development of modern productive forces. And, in fact, the abolition of classes in society presupposes a degree of historical evolution, at which the existence, not simply of this or that particular ruling class, but of any ruling class at all, and, therefore, the existence of class distinction itself has become an obsolete anachronism. It presupposes, therefore, the development of production carried out to a degree at which appropriation of the means of production and of the products, and, with this, of political domination, of the monopoly of culture, and of intellectual leadership by a particular class of society, has become not only superfluous, but economically, politically, intellectually a hindrance to development.

This point is now reached. Their political and intellectual bankruptcy is scarcely any longer a secret to the bourgeoisie themselves. Their economic bankruptcy recurs regularly every ten years. In every crisis, society is suffocated beneath the weight of its own productive forces and products, which it cannot use, and stands helpless, face to face with the absurd contradiction that the producers have nothing to consume, because consumers are wanting. The expansive force of the means of production bursts the bonds that the capitalist mode of production had imposed upon them. Their deliverance from these bonds is the one precondition for an unbroken, constantly accelerated development of the productive forces, and therewith for a practically unlimited increase of production itself. Nor is this all. The socialized appropriation of the means of production does away not only with the present artificial restrictions upon production, but also with the positive waste and devastation of productive forces and products that are at the present time the inevitable concomitants of production, and that reach their height in the crises. Further, it sets free for the community at large a mass of means of production and of products, by doing away with the senseless extravagance of the ruling classes of today, and their political representatives. The possibility of securing for every member of society, by means of socialised production, an existence not only fully sufficient materially, and becoming day by day more full, but an existence guaranteeing to all the free development and exercise of their physical and mental faculties – this possibility is now for the first time here, but *it is here*.

With the seizing of the means of production by society, production of commodities is done away with, and simultaneously, the mastery of the product over the producer. Anarchy in social production is replaced by systematic definite organisation. The struggle for individual existence disappears. Then for the first time, man, in a certain sense, is finally marked off from the rest of the animal kingdom, and emerges from mere animal conditions of existence into really human ones. The whole sphere of the conditions of life which environ man, and which have hitherto ruled man, now comes under the dominion and control of man, who for the first time becomes the real, conscious lord of nature, because he has now become master of his own social organisation. The laws of his own social action, hitherto standing face to face with man as laws of nature foreign to and dominating him, will then be used with full understanding, and so mastered by him. Man's own social organisation, hitherto confronting him as a necessity imposed by nature and history, now becomes the result of his own free action. The extraneous objective forces that have hitherto governed history pass under the control of man himself. Only from that time will man himself, more and more consciously, make his own history – only from that time will the social causes set in movement by him have, in the main and in a constantly growing measure, the results intended by him. It is the ascent of man from the kingdom of necessity to the kingdom of freedom.

[...]

To accomplish this act of universal emancipation is the historical mission of the modern proletariat. To thoroughly comprehend the historical conditions and thus the very nature of this act, to impart to the now oppressed proletarian class a full knowledge of the conditions and of the meaning of the momentous act it is called upon to accomplish, this is the task of the theoretical expression of the proletarian movement, scientific socialism.

Charles Darwin, "Natural Selection"*

[...] Can the principle of selection, which we have seen is so potent in the hands of man, apply under nature? I think we shall see that it can act most efficiently. Let the endless number of slight variations and individual differences occurring in our domestic productions, and, in a lesser degree, in those under nature, be borne in mind; as well as the strength of the hereditary tendency. Under domestication, it may be truly said that the whole organisation becomes in some degree plastic. But the variability, which we almost universally meet with in our domestic productions, is not directly produced, as Hooker and Asa Gray have well remarked, by man; he can neither originate varieties, nor prevent their occurrence; he can preserve and accumulate such as do occur. Unintentionally he exposes organic beings to new and changing conditions of life, and variability ensues; but similar changes of conditions might and do occur under nature. Let it also be borne in mind how infinitely complex and close-fitting are the mutual relations of all organic beings to each other and to their physical conditions of life; and consequently what infinitely varied diversities of structure might be of use to each being under changing conditions of life. Can it, then, be thought improbable, seeing that variations useful to man have undoubtedly occurred, that other variations useful in some way to each being in the great and complex battle of life, should occur in the course of many successive generations. If such do occur, can we doubt (remembering that many more individuals are born than can possibly survive) that individuals having any advantage, however slight, over others, would have the best chance of surviving and of procreating their kind? On the other hand, we may feel sure that any variation in the least degree injurious would be rigidly destroyed. This preservation of favourable individual differences and variations, and the destruction of those which are injurious, I have called Natural Selection, or the Survival of the Fittest. Variations neither useful nor injurious would not be affected by natural selection, and would be left either a fluctuating element, as perhaps we see in certain polymorphic species, or would ultimately become fixed, owing to the nature of the organism and the nature of the conditions.

Several writers have misapprehended or objected to the term Natural Selection. Some have even imagined that natural selection induces variability, whereas it implies only the preservation of such variations as arise and are beneficial to the being under its conditions of life. No one objects to agriculturists speaking of the potent effects of man's selection; and in this case the individual differences given by nature, which man for some object selects, must of necessity first occur. Others have objected that the term selection implies conscious choice in the animals which become modified; and it had even been urged that, as plants have no volition, natural selection is not applicable to them! In the literal sense of the word, no doubt, natural selection is a false term; but who ever objected to chemists speaking of the elective affinities of the various elements? – and yet an acid cannot strictly be said to elect the base with which it in preference combines. It has been said that I speak of natural selection as an active power or Deity; but who objects to an author speaking of the attraction of gravity as ruling the movements of the planets? Every one knows what is meant and is implied by such metaphorical expressions; and they are almost necessary for brevity. So again it is difficult to avoid personifying the word Nature; but I mean by Nature, only the aggregate action and product of many natural laws, and by laws the sequence of events as ascertained by us. With a little familiarity such superficial objections will be forgotten.

We shall best understand the probable course of natural selection by taking the case of a country undergoing some slight physical change, for instance, of climate. The proportional numbers of its inhabitants will almost immediately undergo a change, and some species will probably become extinct. We may conclude, from what we have seen of the intimate and complex manner in which the inhabitants of each country are bound together, that any change in the numerical proportions

* Charles Darwin, extracted from *Darwin: A Norton Critical Edition*, 2nd edn., edited by Philip Appleman (New York: W. W. Norton & Co., 1979), pp. 53–7. Originally published 1859.

of the inhabitants, independently of the change of climate itself, would seriously affect the others. If the country were open on its borders, new forms would certainly immigrate, and this would likewise seriously disturb the relations of some of the former inhabitants. Let it be remembered how powerful the influence of a single introduced tree or mammal has been shown to be. But in the case of an island, or of a country partly surrounded by barriers, into which new and better adapted forms could not freely enter, we should then have places in the economy of nature which would assuredly be better filled up, if some of the original inhabitants were in some manner modified; for, had the area been open to immigration, these same places would have been seized on by intruders. In such cases, slight modifications, which in any way favoured the individuals of any species, by better adapting them to their altered conditions, would tend to be preserved; and natural selection would have free scope for the work of improvement.

We have good reason to believe, as shown in the first chapter, that changes in the conditions of life give a tendency to increased variability; and in the foregoing cases the conditions have changed, and this would manifestly be favourable to natural selection, by affording a better chance of the occurrence of profitable variations. Unless such occur, natural selection can do nothing. Under the term of "variations," it must never be forgotten that mere individual differences are included. As man can produce a great result with his domestic animals and plants by adding up in any given direction individual differences, so could natural selection, but far more easily from having incomparably longer time for action. Nor do I believe that any great physical change, as of climate, or any unusual degree of isolation to check immigration, is necessary in order that new and unoccupied places should be left, for natural selection to fill up by improving some of the varying inhabitants. For as all the inhabitants of each country are struggling together with nicely balanced forces, extremely slight modifications in the structure or habits of one species would often give it an advantage over others; and still further modifications of the same kind would often still further increase the advantage, as long as the species continued under the same conditions of life and profited by similar means of subsistence and defence. No country can be named in which all the native inhabitants are now so perfectly adapted to each other and to the physical conditions under which they live, that none of them could be still better adapted or improved; for in all countries, the natives have been so far conquered by naturalised productions, that they have allowed some foreigners to take firm possession of the land. And as foreigners have thus in every country beaten some of the natives, we may safely conclude that the natives might have been modified with advantage, so as to have better resisted the intruders.

As man can produce, and certainly has produced, a great result by his methodical and unconscious means of selection, what may not natural selection effect? Man can act only on external and visible characters: Nature, if I may be allowed to personify the natural preservation or survival of the fittest, cares nothing for appearances, except in so far as they are useful to any being. She can act on every internal organ, on every shade of constitutional difference, on the whole machinery of life. Man selects only for his own good: Nature only for that of the being which she tends. Every selected character is fully exercised by her, as is implied by the fact of their selection. Man keeps the natives of many climates in the same country; he seldom exercises each selected character in some peculiar and fitting manner; he feeds a long and a short beaked pigeon on the same food; he does not exercise a long-backed or long-legged quadruped in any peculiar manner; he exposes sheep with long and short wool to the same climate. He does not allow the most vigorous males to struggle for the females. He does not rigidly destroy all inferior animals, but protects during each varying season, as far as lies in his power, all his productions. He often begins his selection by some half-monstrous form; or at least by some modification prominent enough to catch the eye or to be plainly useful to him. Under Nature, the slightest differences of structure or constitution may well turn the nicely balanced scale in the struggle for life, and so be preserved. How fleeting are the wishes and efforts of man! how short his time! and consequently how poor will be his results, compared with those accumulated by Nature during whole geological periods! Can we wonder, then, that Nature's productions should be far "truer" in character than man's productions that they should be infinitely better adapted to the most complex conditions of life and should plainly bear the stamp of far higher workmanship?

It may metaphorically be said that natural selection is daily and hourly scrutinising, throughout the world, the slightest variations; rejecting those that are bad, preserving and adding up all that are good; silently and insensibly working, *whenever and wherever opportunity offers*, at the improvement of each organic being in relation to its organic and inorganic conditions of life. We see nothing of these slow changes in progress, until the hand of time has marked the lapse of ages, and then so imperfect is our view into long-past geological ages, that we see only that the forms of life are now different from what they formerly were.

T. H. Huxley, "Evolution and Ethics"*

[...]

The majority of us, I apprehend, profess neither pessimism or optimism. We hold that the world is neither so good, nor so bad, as it conceivably might be; and, as most of us have reason, now and again, to discover that it can be. Those who have failed to experience the joys that make life worth living are, probably, in as small a minority as those who have never known the griefs that rob existence of its savor and turn its richest fruits into mere dust and ashes.

Further, I think I do not err in assuming that, however diverse their views on philosophical and religious matters, most men are agreed that the proportion of good and evil in life may be very sensibly affected by human action. I never heard anybody doubt that the evil may be thus increased, or diminished; and it would seem to follow that good must be similarly susceptible of addition or subtraction. Finally, to my knowledge, nobody professes to doubt that, so far forth as we possess a power of bettering things, it is our paramount duty to use it and to train all our intellect and energy to this supreme service of our kind.

Hence the pressing interest of the question, to what extent modern progress in natural knowledge, and, more especially, the general outcome of that progress in the doctrine of evolution, is competent to help us in a great work of helping one another?

The propounders of what are called the "ethics of evolution," when the "evolution of ethics" would usually better express the object of their speculations, adduce a number of more or less interesting facts and more or less sound arguments in favor of the origin of the moral sentiments, in the same way as other natural phenomena, by a process of evolution. I have little doubt, for my own part, that they are on the right track; but as the immoral sentiments have no less been evolved, there is, so far, as much natural sanction for the one as the other. The thief and the murderer follow nature just as much as the philanthropist. Cosmic evolution may teach us how the good and the evil tendencies of man may have come about; but, in itself, it is incompetent to furnish any better reason why what we call good is preferable to what we call evil than we had before. Some day, I doubt not, we shall arrive at an understanding of the evolution of the aesthetic faculty; but all the understanding in the world will neither increase nor diminish the force of the intuition that this is beautiful and that is ugly.

There is another fallacy which appears to me to pervade the so-called "ethics of evolution." It is the notion that because, on the whole, animals and plants have advanced in perfection of organization by means of the struggle for existence and the consequent "survival of the fittest"; therefore men in society, men as ethical beings, must look to the same process to help them towards perfection. I suspect that this fallacy has arisen out of the unfortunate ambiguity of the phrase "survival of the fittest." "Fittest" has a connotation of "best"; and about "best" there hangs a moral flavor. In cosmic nature, however, what is "fittest" depends upon the conditions. Long since, I ventured to point out that if our hemisphere were to cool again, the survival of the fittest might bring about, in the vegetable kingdom, a population of more and more stunted and humbler and humbler organisms, until the "fittest" that survived might be nothing but lichens, diatoms, and such microscopic organisms as those which give red snow its color; while, if it became hotter, the pleasant valleys of the Thames and Isis might be uninhabitable by any animated beings save those that flourish in a tropical jungle. They, as the fittest, the best adapted to the changed conditions, would survive.

Men in society are undoubtedly subject to the cosmic process. As among other animals, multiplication goes on without cessation, and involves severe competition for the means of support. The struggle for existence tends to eliminate those less fitted to adapt themselves to the circumstances of their existence. The strongest, the most self-assertive, tend to tread down the weaker. But the influence of the cosmic process on the evolution of society is the greater the more rudimentary its civilization. Social progress means a checking of the cosmic process at every step and the substitution for it of another, which may be called the ethical process; the end of which is not the survival of those who may happen to be the fittest, in respect of the whole of the conditions which obtain, but of those who are ethically the best.

As I have already urged, the practice of that which is ethically best – what we call goodness or virtue – involves a course of conduct which, in all respects, is opposed to

* Thomas Henry Huxley, extracted from *The Essays of T.H. Huxley*, edited by Alburey Castell (Crofts Classics, 1948). Originally published 1893.

that which leads to success in the cosmic struggle for existence. In place of ruthless self-assertion it demands self-restraint; in place of thrusting aside, or treading down, all competitors, it requires that the individual shall not merely respect, but shall help his fellows; its influence is directed, not so much to the survival of the fittest, as to the fitting of as many as possible to survive. It repudiates the gladiatorial theory of existence. It demands that each man who enters into the enjoyment of the advantages of a polity shall be mindful of his debt to those who have laboriously constructed it; and shall take heed that no act of his weakens the fabric in which he has been permitted to live. Laws and moral precepts are directed to the end of curbing the cosmic process and reminding the individual of his duty to the community, to the protection and influence of which he owes, if not existence itself, at least the life of something better than a brutal savage.

It is from neglect of these plain considerations that the fanatical individualism of our time attempts to apply the analogy of cosmic nature to society. Once more we have a misapplication of the stoical injunction to follow nature; the duties of the individual to the state are forgotten, and his tendencies to self-assertion are dignified by the name of rights. It is seriously debated whether the members of a community are justified in using their combined strength to constrain one of their number to contribute his share to the maintenance of it; or even to prevent him from doing his best to destroy it. The struggle for existence which has done such admirable work in cosmic nature, must, it appears, be equally beneficent in the ethical sphere. Yet if that which I have insisted upon is true; if the cosmic process has no sort of relation to moral ends; if the imitation of it by man is inconsistent with the first principles of ethics; what becomes of this surprising theory?

Let us understand, once for all, that the ethical progress of society depends, not on imitating the cosmic process, still less in running away from it, but in combating it. It may seem an audacious proposal thus to put the microcosm against the macrocosm and to set man to subdue nature to his higher ends; but I venture to think that the great intellectual difference between the ancient times with which we have been occupied and our day, lies in the solid foundation we have acquired for the hope that such an enterprise may meet with a certain measure of success.

The history of civilization details the steps by which men have succeeded in building up an artificial world within the cosmos. Fragile reed as he may be, man, as Pascal says, is a thinking reed: there lies within him a fund of energy operating intelligently and so far akin to that which pervades the universe, that it is competent to influence and modify the cosmic process. In virtue of his intelligence, the dwarf bends the Titan to his will. In every family, in every polity that has been established, the cosmic process in man has been restrained and otherwise modified by law and custom; in surrounding nature, it has been similarly influenced by the art of the shepherd, the agriculturist, the artisan. As civilization has advanced, so has the extent of this interference increased; until the organized and highly developed sciences and arts of the present day have endowed man with a command over the course of non-human nature greater than that once attributed to the magicians. The most impressive, I might say startling, of these changes have been brought about in the course of the last two centuries; while a right comprehension of the process of life and of the means of influencing its manifestations is only just dawning upon us. We do not yet see our way beyond generalities; and we are befogged by the obtrusion of false analogies and crude anticipations. But Astronomy, Physics, Chemistry, have all had to pass through similar phases, before they reached the stage at which their influence became an important factor in human affairs. Physiology, Psychology, Ethics, Political Science, must submit to the same ordeal. Yet it seems to me irrational to doubt that, at no distant period, they will work as great a revolution in the sphere of practice.

The theory of evolution encourages no millennial anticipations. If, for millions of years, our globe has taken the upward road, yet, some time, the summit will be reached and the downward route will be commenced. The most daring imagination will hardly venture upon the suggestion that the power and the intelligence of man can ever arrest the procession of the great year.

Moreover, the cosmic nature born with us and, to a large extent, necessary for our maintenance, is the outcome of millions of years of severe training, and it would be folly to imagine that a few centuries will suffice to subdue its masterfulness to purely ethical ends. Ethical nature may count upon having to reckon with a tenacious and powerful enemy as long as the world lasts. But, on the other hand, I see no limit to the extent to which intelligence and will, guided by sound principles of investigation, and organized in common effort, may modify the conditions of existence, for a period longer than that now covered by history. And much may be done to change the nature of man himself. The intelligence which has converted the brother of the wolf into the faithful guardian of the flock ought to be able to do something towards curbing the instincts of savagery in civilized men.

But if we may permit ourselves a larger hope of abatement of the essential evil of the world than was possible to those who, in the infancy of exact knowledge, faced the problem of existence more than a score of centuries ago, I deem it an essential condition of the realization of that hope that we should cast aside the notion that the escape from pain and sorrow is the proper object of life.

We have long since emerged from the heroic childhood of our race, when good and evil could be met with the same "frolic welcome"; the attempts to escape from evil, whether Indian or Greek, have ended in flight from the battlefield; it remains to us to throw aside the youthful overconfidence and the no less youthful discouragement of nonage. We are grown men, and must play the man

> strong in will
> To strive, to seek, to find, strong in will and not to yield,

cherishing the good that falls in our way, and bearing the evil, in and around us, with stout hearts set on diminishing it. So far, we all may strive in one faith toward one hope:

> It may be that the gulfs will wash us down,
> It may be we shall touch the Happy Isles,
>
> .... but something ere the end,
> Some work of noble note may yet be done.

Judith Butler, "Contingent Foundations: Feminism and the Question of 'Postmodernism'"*

The question of postmodernism is surely a question, for is there, after all, something called postmodernism? Is it an historical characterization, a certain kind of theoretical position, and what does it mean for a term that has described a certain aesthetic practice now to apply to social theory and to feminist social and political theory in particular? Who are these postmodernists? Is this a name that one takes on for oneself, or is it more often a name that one is called if and when one offers a critique of the subject, a discursive analysis, or questions the integrity or coherence of totalizing social descriptions?

* Judith Butler, extracted from Judith Butler and Joan Scott (eds.), *Feminists Theorize the Political* (London: Routledge, 1992), pp. 3–17.

I know the term from the way it is used, and it usually appears on my horizon embedded in the following critical formulations: "if discourse is all there is ...," or "if everything is a text ...," or "if the subject is dead ...," or "if real bodies do not exist ... ." The sentence begins as a warning against an impending nihilism, for if the conjured content of these series of conditional clauses proves to be true, then, and there is always a then, some set of dangerous consequences will surely follow. So 'postmodernism' appears to be articulated in the form of a fearful conditional or sometimes in the form of paternalistic disdain toward that which is youthful and irrational. Against this postmodernism, there is an effort to shore up the primary premises, to establish in advance that any theory of politics requires a subject, needs from the start to presume its subject, the referentiality of language, the integrity of the institutional descriptions it provides. For politics is unthinkable without a foundation, without these premises. But do these claims seek to secure a contingent formation of politics that requires that these notions remain unproblematized features of its own definition? Is it the case that all politics, and feminist politics in particular, is unthinkable without these prized premises? Or is it rather that a specific version of politics is shown in its contingency once those premises are problematically thematized?

To claim that politics requires a stable subject is to claim that there can be no *political* opposition to that claim. Indeed, that claim implies that a critique of the subject cannot be a politically informed critique but, rather, an act which puts into jeopardy politics as such. To require the subject means to foreclose the domain of the political, and that foreclosure, installed analytically as an essential feature of the political, enforces the boundaries of the domain of the political in such a way that that enforcement is protected from political scrutiny. The act which unilaterally establishes the domain of the political functions, then, as an authoritarian ruse by which political contest over the status of the subject is summarily silenced.[22]

[22] Here it is worth noting that in some recent political theory, notably in the writings of Ernesto Laclau and Chantal Mouffe (*Hegemony and Socialist Strategy*, London: Verso, 1986), William Connolly (*Political Theory and Modernity*, Madison: University of Wisconsin Press, 1988), as well as Jean-Luc Nancy and Philippe Lacoue-Labarthe ("Le retrait du politique" in *Le Retrait du politique*, Paris: Editions galilée, 1983), there is an insistence that the political field is of necessity constructed through the production of a determining exterior. In other words, the very domain of politics constitutes itself through the production and naturalization of the "pre-" or "non" political. In Derridean terms, this is the production of a "constitutive

To refuse to assume, that is, to require a notion of the subject from the start is not the same as negating or dispensing with such a notion altogether; on the contrary, it is to ask after the process of its construction and the political meaning and consequentiality of taking the subject as a requirement or presupposition of theory. But have we arrived yet at a notion of postmodernism?

A number of positions are ascribed to postmodernism, as if it were the kind of thing that could be the bearer of a set of positions: discourse is all there is, as if discourse were some kind of monistic stuff out of which all things are composed; the subject is dead, I can never say "I" again; there is no reality, only representations. These characterizations are variously imputed to postmodernism or poststructuralism, which are conflated with each other and sometimes conflated with deconstruction, and sometimes understood as an indiscriminate assemblage of French feminism, deconstruction, Lacanian psychoanalysis, Foucaultian analysis, Rorty's conversationalism and cultural studies. [...]

Do all these theories have the same structure (a comforting notion to the critic who would dispense with them all at once)? Is the effort to colonize and domesticate these theories under the sign of the same, to group them synthetically and masterfully under a single rubric, a simple refusal to grant the specificity of these positions, an excuse not to read, and not to read closely? For if Lyotard uses the term, and if he can be conveniently grouped with a set of writers, and if some problematic quotation can be found in his work, then can that quotation serve as an "example" of postmodernism, symptomatic of the whole?

But if I understand part of the project of postmodernism, it is to call into question the ways in which such "examples" and "paradigms" serve to subordinate and erase that which they seek to explain. For the "whole," the field of postmodernism in its supposed breadth, is effectively "produced" by the example which is made to stand as a symptom and exemplar of the whole; in effect, if in the example of Lyotard we think we have a representation of postmodernism, we have then forced a substitution of the example for the entire field, effecting a violent reduction of the field to the one piece of text the critic is willing to read, a piece which, conveniently, uses the term "postmodern."

[...]

I don't know about the term "postmodern," but if there is a point, and a fine point, to what I perhaps better understand as poststructuralism, it is that power pervades the very conceptual apparatus that seeks to negotiate its terms, including the subject position of the critic; and further, that this implication of the terms of criticism in the field of power is *not* the advent of a nihilistic relativism incapable of furnishing norms, but, rather, the very precondition of a politically engaged critique. To establish a set of norms that are beyond power or force is itself a powerful and forceful conceptual practice that sublimates, disguises and extends its own power play through recourse to tropes of normative universality. And the point is not to do away with foundations, or even to champion a position that goes under the name of antifoundationalism. Both of those positions belong together as different versions of foundationalism and the skeptical problematic it engenders. Rather, the task is to interrogate what the theoretical move that establishes foundations *authorizes*, and what precisely it excludes or forecloses.

It seems that theory posits foundations incessantly, and forms implicit metaphysical commitments as a matter of course, even when it seeks to guard against it; foundations function as the unquestioned and the unquestionable within any theory. And yet, are these "foundations," that is, those premises that function as authorizing grounds, are they themselves not constituted through exclusions which, taken into account, expose the foundational premise as a contingent and contestable presumption. Even when we claim that there is some implied universal basis for a given foundation, that implication and that universality simply constitute a new dimension of unquestionability.

How is it that we might ground a theory or politics in a speech situation or subject position which is "universal," when the very category of the universal has only

---

outside." Here I would like to suggest a distinction between the constitution of a political field that produces *and naturalizes* that constitutive outside and a political field that produces and *renders contingent* the specific parameters of that constitutive outside. Although I do not think that the differential relations through which the political field itself is constituted can ever be fully elaborated (precisely because the status of that elaboration would have to be elaborated as well *ad infinitum*), I do find useful William Connolly's notion of constitutive antagonisms, a notion that finds a parallel expression in Laclau and Mouffe, which suggests a form of political struggle which puts the parameters of the political itself into question. This is especially important for feminist concerns insofar as the grounds of politics ("universality," "equality," "the subject of rights") have been constructed through unmarked racial and gender exclusions and by a conflation of politics with public life that renders the private (reproduction, domains of "femininity") prepolitical.

begun to be exposed for its own highly ethnocentric biases? How many "universalities" are there[23] and to what extent is cultural conflict understandable as the clashing of a set of presumed and intransigent "universalities," a conflict which cannot be negotiated through recourse to a culturally imperialist notion of the "universal" or, rather, which will only be solved through such recourse at the cost of violence? We have, I think, witnessed the conceptual and material violence of this practice in the United States's war against Iraq, in which the Arab "other" is understood to be radically "outside" the universal structures of reason and democracy and, hence, calls to be brought forcibly within. Significantly, the US had to abrogate the democratic principles of political sovereignty and free speech, among others, to effect this forcible return of Iraq to the "democratic" fold, and this violent move reveals, among other things, that such notions of universality are installed through the abrogation of the very universal principles to be implemented. Within the political context of contemporary postcoloniality more generally, it is perhaps especially urgent to underscore the very category of the "universal" as a site of insistent contest and resignification.[24] Given the contested character of the term, to assume from the start a procedural or substantive notion of the universal is of necessity to impose a culturally hegemonic notion on the social field. To herald that notion then as the philosophical instrument that will negotiate between conflicts of power is precisely to safeguard and reproduce a position of hegemonic power by installing it in the metapolitical site of ultimate normativity.

It may at first seem that I am simply calling for a more concrete and internally diverse "universality," a more synthetic and inclusive notion of the universal, and in that way committed to the very foundational notion that I seek to undermine. But my task is, I think, significantly different from that which would articulate a comprehensive universality. In the first place, such a totalizing notion could only be achieved at the cost of producing new and further exclusions. The term "universality" would have to be left permanently open, permanently contested, permanently contingent, in order not to foreclose in advance future claims for inclusion. Indeed, from my position and from any historically constrained perspective, any totalizing concept of the universal will shut down rather than authorize the unanticipated and unanticipatable claims that will be made under the sign of "the universal." In this sense, I am not doing away with the category, but trying to relieve the category of its foundationalist weight in order to render it as a site of permanent political contest.

A social theory committed to democratic contestation within a postcolonial horizon needs to find a way to bring into question the foundations it is compelled to lay down. It is this movement of interrogating that ruse of authority that seeks to close itself off from contest that is, in my view, at the heart of any radical political project. Inasmuch as poststructuralism offers a mode of critique that effects this contestation of the foundationalist move, it can be used as a part of such a radical agenda. Note that I have said, "it can be used": I think there are no necessary political consequences for such a theory, but only a possible political deployment.

If one of the points associated with postmodernism is that the epistemological point of departure in philosophy is inadequate, then it ought not to be a question of subjects who claim to know and theorize under the sign of the postmodern pitted against other subjects who claim to know and theorize under the sign of the modern. Indeed, it is that very way of framing debate that is being contested by the suggestion that the position articulated by the subject is always in some way constituted by what must be displaced for that position to take hold, and that the subject who theorizes is constituted as a "theorizing subject" by a set of exclusionary and selective procedures. For, indeed, who is it that gets constituted as the feminist theorist whose framing of the debate will get publicity? Is it not always the case that power operates in advance, in the very procedures that establish who will be the subject who speaks in the name of feminism, and to whom?

[...]

The critique of the subject is not a negation or repudiation of the subject, but, rather, a way of interrogating its construction as a pregiven or foundationalist premise. At the outset of the war against Iraq, we almost all saw strategists who placed before us maps of the Middle East, objects of analysis and targets of instrumental military action. Retired and active generals were called up by the networks to stand in for the generals on the field whose intentions would be invariably realized in the destruction of various Iraqi military bases. The various affirmations of the early success of these operations

[23] See Ashis Nandy on the notion of alternative universalities in the preface to *The Intimate Enemy: Loss and Recovery of Self under Colonialism* (New Delhi: Oxford University Press, 1983).

[24] Homi Bhabha's notion of "hybridity" is important to consider in this context.

were delivered with great enthusiasm, and it seemed that this hitting of the goal, this apparently seamless realization of intention through an instrumental action without much resistance or hindrance was the occasion, not merely to destroy Iraqi military installations, but also to champion a masculinized Western subject whose will immediately translates into a deed, whose utterance or order materializes in an action which would destroy the very possibility of a reverse strike, and whose obliterating power at once confirms the impenetrable contours of its own subjecthood.

[...]

My suggestion is that agency belongs to a way of thinking about persons as instrumental actors who confront an external political field. But if we agree that politics and power exist already at the level at which the subject and its agency are articulated and made possible, then agency can be *presumed* only at the cost of refusing to inquire into its construction. Consider that "agency" has no formal existence or, if it does, it has no bearing on the question at hand. In a sense, the epistemological model that offers us a pregiven subject or agent is one that refuses to acknowledge that *agency is always and only a political prerogative.* As such, it seems crucial to question the conditions of its possibility, not to take it for granted as an a priori guarantee. We need instead to ask, what possibilities of mobilization are produced on the basis of existing configurations of discourse and power? Where are the possibilities of reworking that very matrix of power by which we are constituted, of reconstituting the legacy of that constitution, and of working against each other those processes of regulation that can destabilize existing power regimes? For if the subject is constituted by power, that power does not cease at the moment the subject is constituted, for that subject is never fully constituted, but is subjected and produced time and again. That subject is neither a ground nor a product, but the permanent possibility of a certain resignifying process, one which gets detoured and stalled through other mechanisms of power, but which is power's own possibility of being reworked. It is not enough to say that the subject is invariably engaged in a political field; that phenomenological phrasing misses the point that the subject is an accomplishment regulated and produced in advance. And is as such fully political; indeed, perhaps *most* political at the point in which it is claimed to be prior to politics itself. To perform this kind of Foucaultian critique of the subject is not to do away with the subject or pronounce its death, but merely to claim that certain versions of the subject are politically insidious.

For the subject to be a pregiven point of departure for politics is to defer the question of the political construction and regulation of the subject itself; for it is important to remember that subjects are constituted through exclusion, that is, through the creation of a domain of deauthorized subjects, presubjects, figures of abjection, populations erased from view. This becomes clear, for instance, within the law when certain qualifications must first be met in order to be, quite literally, a claimant in sex discrimination or rape cases. Here it becomes quite urgent to ask, who qualifies as a "who," what systematic structures of disempowerment make it impossible for certain injured parties to invoke the "I" effectively within a court of law? [...]

There is the refrain that, just now, when women are beginning to assume the place of subjects, postmodern positions come along to announce that the subject is dead (there is a difference between positions of post-structuralism which claim that the subject *never* existed, and postmodern positions which claim that the subject *once* had integrity, but no longer does). Some see this as a conspiracy against women and other disenfranchised groups who are now only beginning to speak on their own behalf. But what precisely is meant by this, and how do we account for the very strong criticisms of the subject as an instrument of Western imperialist hegemony theorized by Gloria Anzaldua,[25] Gayatri Spivak[26] and various theorists of postcoloniality? Surely there is a caution offered here, that in the very struggle toward enfranchisement and democratization, we might adopt the very models of domination by which we were oppressed, not realizing that one way that domination works is through the regulation and production of subjects. Through what exclusions has the feminist subject been constructed, and how do those excluded domains return to haunt the "integrity" and "unity" of the feminist "we"? And how is it that the very category, the subject, the "we," that is supposed to be presumed for the purpose of solidarity, produces the very factionalization it is supposed to quell? Do women want to become subjects on the model which requires and produces an anterior region of abjection, or must feminism become a process which is self-critical about the processes that produce and destabilize identity categories? To take the construction

[25] Gloria Anzaldua, *La Frontera/Borderlands* (San Francisco: Spinsters Ink, 1988).

[26] Gayatri Spivak, "Can the Subaltern Speak?" in *Marxism and the Interpretation of Culture*, eds. Nelson and Grossberg (Chicago: University of Illinois Press, 1988).

of the subject as a political problematic is not the same as doing away with the subject; to deconstruct the subject is not to negate or throw away the concept; on the contrary, deconstruction implies only that we suspend all commitments to that to which the term, "the subject," refers, and that we consider the linguistic functions it serves in the consolidation and concealment of authority. To deconstruct is not to negate or to dismiss, but to call into question and, perhaps most importantly, to open up a term, like the subject, to a reusage or redeployment that previously has not been authorized.

Within feminism, it seems as if there is some political necessity to speak as and for *women*, and I would not contest that necessity. Surely, that is the way in which representational politics operates, and in this country, lobbying efforts are virtually impossible without recourse to identity politics. So we agree that demonstrations and legislative efforts and radical movements need to make claims in the name of women.

But this necessity needs to be reconciled with another. The minute that the category of women is invoked as *describing* the constituency for which feminism speaks, an internal debate invariably begins over what the descriptive content of that term will be. There are those who claim that there is an ontological specificity to women as childbearers that forms the basis of a specific legal and political interest in representation, and then there are others who understand maternity to be a social relation that is, under current social circumstances, the specific and cross-cultural situation of women. And there are those who seek recourse to Gilligan and others to establish a feminine specificity that makes itself clear in women's communities or ways of knowing. But every time that specificity is articulated, there is resistance and factionalization within the very constituency that is supposed to be *unified* by the articulation of its common element. In the early 1980s, the feminist "we" rightly came under attack by women of color who claimed that the "we" was invariably white, and that that "we" that was meant to solidify the movement was the very source of a painful factionalization. The effort to characterize a feminine specificity through recourse to maternity, whether biological or social, produced a similar factionalization and even a disavowal of feminism altogether. For surely all women are not mothers; some cannot be, some are too young or too old to be, some choose not to be, and for some who are mothers, that is not necessarily the rallying point of their politicization in feminism.

I would argue that any effort to give universal or specific content to the category of women, presuming that that guarantee of solidarity is required *in advance*, will necessarily produce factionalization, and that "identity" as a point of departure can never hold as the solidifying ground of a feminist political movement. Identity categories are never merely descriptive, but always normative, and as such, exclusionary. This is not to say that the term "women" ought not to be used, or that we ought to announce the death of the category. On the contrary, if feminism presupposes that "women" designates an undesignatable field of differences, one that cannot be totalized or summarized by a descriptive identity category, then the very term becomes a site of permanent openness and resignifiability. I would argue that the rifts among women over the content of the term ought to be safeguarded and prized, indeed, that this constant rifting ought to be affirmed as the ungrounded ground of feminist theory. To deconstruct the subject of feminism is not, then, to censure its usage, but, on the contrary, to release the term into a future of multiple significations, to emancipate it from the maternal or racialist ontologies to which it has been restricted, and to give it play as a site where unanticipated meanings might come to bear.

[...]

One might well ask: but doesn't there have to be a set of norms that discriminate between those descriptions that ought to adhere to the category of women and those that do not? The only answer to that question is a counter-question: who would set those norms, and what contestations would they produce? To establish a normative foundation for settling the question of what ought properly to be included in the description of women would be only and always to produce a new site of political contest. That foundation would settle nothing, but would of its own necessity founder on its own authoritarian ruse. This is not to say that there is no foundation, but rather, that wherever there is one, there will also be a foundering, a contestation. That such foundations exist only to be put into question is, as it were, the permanent risk of the process of democratization. To refuse that contest is to sacrifice the radical democractic impetus of feminist politics. That the category is unconstrained, even that it comes to serve antifeminist purposes, will be part of the risk of this procedure. But this is a risk that is produced by the very foundationalism that seeks to safeguard feminism against it. In a sense, this risk is the foundation, and hence is not, of any feminist practice.

Chapter 6

Conceptions of Human Nature

Introduction

Simple competing characterizations of human nature are commonplace in our political thinking. Some claim that humans are inherently bad and cannot be trusted; thus extensive government authority is needed to keep people in line. Others claim that humans are inherently good; thus if those institutions and practices that bring out the worst in humans were eliminated, people could coexist without any coercive government.

But more is involved in our conceptions of human nature than such overall judgments. Consider the following questions: Are humans inherently equal and, if so, in what ways, and on what basis? In what ways are humans unequal? What are and what should be basic human motivations and purposes? Are humans rational and autonomous in choosing their own ends, or do others influence their conceptions of the good life and their motivations? Given these several basic questions about human nature and the many plausible answers to them, are there any ideas about human nature that most people can accept as some sort of minimal basis for reaching political agreements?

Some of the complexity of thinking about human nature can be revealed by considering Christian assumptions about "fallen man" as set forth by Saint Augustine (354–430 CE) and as clearly summarized in our first selection by Herbert Deane (1922–91), a professor of political philosophy at Columbia University. Augustine believed that the first humans were created good, but became corrupted when Adam and Eve refused to subordinate themselves to God, and instead chose to exercise the free will that God had granted them to pursue their own desires. Because only goodness had any ontological existence, the fall of man was merely an absence of goodness, and did not make humans evil, but this "original sin" condemned humans to a penal existence in this world. God granted humans various capacities to navigate these difficulties, such as their senses and reason, but all humans are not granted equal capacities in all things, especially their faith in God. Those without such faith have become preoccupied with attaining wealth, fame, and power. Since these are scarce, human desires cannot be satisfied on earth, creating human misery. Such a composite vision of human nature and the human condition led Augustine to believe that no polity (no "City of Man") can ever fundamentally improve the human condition and produce the good life and a good society for humanity. In the early Christian vision, political theory was of little importance because good government was impossible. Political life – like all aspects of the life of fallen man on earth – was simply to be endured.

Deane sees many similarities between Augustinian ideas about human nature and those of Thomas Hobbes (1581–1679), the English philosopher who is usually credited with laying the foundation of much of modern political thought. Both stressed human desires for earthly goods that were scarce and the competition that such desires engendered. But there are important differences in Augustine's and Hobbes' assumptions. Whereas Augustine derived his ideas about human nature by trying to see man from a divine perspective, Hobbes derived his by trying to see man in a natural condition. Understood not as divine creations but as natural material beings, humans are set against each other by their conflicting natural desires. Since men are naturally concerned with themselves, they will want what others have. Natural man does not have equal capacities, as some, for example, are stronger than others, but even the weakest have sufficient strength to kill the strongest, so to that extent they are equal. All men will therefore live in fear of one another as well as in envy for what others have. In their natural condition, men will thus be at war with one another, and life will be miserable. But Hobbes' conception of humans does not condemn mankind to this miserable existence on earth in the way that Augustine assumed. Our passion for peace and our reason provide the possibility that humans can be drawn into some sort of agreement, some articles of peace, which can lead to a better life and a better society on earth than Augustine imagined.

By stressing the self-interested motivations of natural man, Hobbes laid the foundations for a "liberal model of man" that emerged during the next few centuries and is described and analyzed in our next selection by C. B. Macpherson (1911–87), who taught political theory at the University of Toronto. As suggested at the end of his discussion of "the natural condition of mankind," and developed in the next chapter of his masterpiece, *The Leviathan* (1651) – which is provided in the next chapter of this reader – Hobbes believed humans would reason that they should all submit to an earthly power (an absolute government) that could coerce everyone to obey laws that provided social order and that relieved men from the need to constantly defend themselves from encroachments by others, so that they could be industrious and attain a "commodious" life. Other liberals developed a model of "economic man" who was so motivated. According to this model, man was "a maximizer of utilities," seeking his own pleasures without limit, and attaining money became the measure by which such pleasures could be had. According to Macpherson, such a conception of humans led early liberals to support a capitalist society and representative governments that made and enforced laws securing property rights. Such governments would be prevented from abusing their powers and infringing on property rights by giving citizens the right to vote. As economic animals, humans could spend the bulk of their time producing and consuming economic goods, and their involvement in politics could be limited to occasional acts of voting that held government officials accountable.

For Karl Marx, this model of man left humans "estranged" or alienated – having lives as workers within privately owned economic enterprises that were deeply dissatisfying. Because most men did not own productive property (land, factories, machinery, etc.), they had to labor for others who did own such property in exchange for wages. Under capitalism, the worker is exploited because the capitalist does not pay him the full value of his labor. He is estranged from the products he produces, because ownership of them passes to the capitalist (and buyers in the marketplace). He is estranged from nature, because he values it simply for the raw materials that it provides. He is estranged from his co-workers, with whom he must compete for employment and advancement. He is estranged from the process of working, as he engages in tasks that provide little or no intrinsic enjoyment but only a minimal wage that keeps him alive. But mostly he is estranged from his "species-being." While the labor of other animals is limited to taking from nature what they need to satisfy their needs, humans are unique in that they can transform nature; humans can use their creative abilities to make the raw materials of nature much more luxurious. Creative labor is both intrinsically enjoyable and produces genuine affluence. But under capitalism, man is not a creative laborer and is alienated from achieving his human potential as a creative laborer. Only in subsequent socialist and communist societies will humans be able to develop into creative laborers and ultimately live according to their true nature.

Anarchists generally agreed with this conception of man, which Marx developed early in his life before he turned away from such philosophical reflections to focus on developing scientific understandings of capitalism. But anarchists were less preoccupied with "economic man" than liberals and Marxists. They focused on the instincts of humans that caused people to be both egoistic and social. While our egoistic instincts were important, they were overemphasized. In ordinary life, people had long displayed an instinct for *mutual aid*, a term coined and studied by Peter Kropotkin (1842–1921), the Russian noble who gained fame as "the anarchist prince." While this is an instinct that is not unique to humans but is shared with other animals, its positive role in human development and evolution has been ignored. When we are no longer dominated by those institutions and practices that suppress the instinct for mutual aid (such as the competition for political power that arises within democratic governments and for economic gain that is provoked by capitalism), we will be guided by our feelings of "oneness with each human being."

John Rawls doubts that humans will ever have such a sense of oneness. It makes more sense to presume that humans are "mutually disinterested." Like earlier liberals, Rawls thought that political theorists should assume humans do not seek "to confer benefits or to impose injuries on one another" and instead seek to achieve their own life plans, which are furthered by acquiring as many social goods (like income and wealth, power, status, and education) as possible. Yet life goes better for everyone if each has a sense of justice and acts under principles of justice to which all agree. People are rational enough to understand this, and thus they seek agreement on certain principles of justice. To reach such agreement, it is useful if "we try to simulate the original position" – an idealized situation where humans choose their principles of justice while constrained from knowing certain things about their own positions in society and their natural endowments, which of course are different among people and can bias their choices among alternative principles. While the content of their unbiased agreement can await our consideration of alternative theories of justice in Chapter 14, the basic assumptions of human nature that Rawls outlines in the selection here should be grasped now, because they inform many other debates in political theory.

Michael Sandel, for example, takes issue with the account of human nature provided by liberals in general and Rawls in particular. Liberals like Rawls assume that humans seek moral autonomy; they wish to be authors of their own conception of the good life, and have the freedom and resources to pursue that radically personal conception. But from where does *your* conception of the good life come? Have you arrived at it unencumbered by any social influences? Sandel doubts it. We understand ourselves and formulate our life plans under the influence of certain social allegiances. Political theories are inevitably incomplete and misleading if they disregard the fact that humans are socially embedded and have thick social identities that shape their personal and political aspirations.

Is there any way to move beyond these competing assumptions about human nature and achieve a conception of humanity that can produce some political agreements? Bhikhu Parekh, a professor of political theory at the London School of Economics, has recently offered a pluralist and minimalist view of human nature. Only those characteristics that are universal and relatively permanent – that are inherent in the physico-mental structure of all humans – can be regarded as part of human nature. In large part because humans live in different cultural conditions, they differ in their "capacities, emotions, motivations, values, ideals of excellence and so forth." He concludes that a cross-cultural dialogue would be a more satisfactory way to discover universal human values than the efforts of political philosophers over the centuries to discover such values by analyzing human nature.

Herbert Deane, "St. Augustine's Conception of Fallen Man"*

For Augustine, as for all Christians, the world and everything in it were created by God. The world is not eternal; it had a beginning, and the beginning of the world was also the beginning of time. The world will have an end – the Last Judgment – when heaven and earth shall pass away, and a new heaven shall appear, in which the saints will enjoy eternal peace and happiness with God and His angels. Between these two points, the creation of the world and its destruction, is played out the great drama of man's career on earth. The climax of the drama, the moment for which all that went before was simply an anxious prelude, is the Incarnation, the appearance on earth of God in human form with the birth of Jesus Christ; "the Word became flesh and dwelt among us." In order to understand the significance of the Incarnation in the drama of man's salvation, we must return to the first act, to the Garden of Eden and the fall of the first human beings, Adam and Eve.

Like everything else that God created – the heavens, the earth, the seas, plants, and animals – the first man was created good; in *Genesis* we are told that after viewing each of His creatures God saw that it was good. Everything that He created was created out of nothing, *ex nihilo;* there was no eternally existing matter independent of God that He shaped or formed in the process of creation. Obviously, then, there is a clear difference between the Creator and the created. The Creator is unchangeably good, wise, and all-powerful by His very essence; God's goodness, wisdom, and power are not accidents or attributes separable from His being. Like all other created beings, man is good but not incorruptibly, absolutely, or necessarily good. He is mutable and changeable, but as long as he acknowledges his dependence upon and his inferiority to God, his Creator, and obeys His commands, he will be good and happy.[1]

* Herbert Deane, extracted from *The Political and Social Ideas of St. Augustine* (Columbia University Press, 1963), pp. 14–48.

[1] In the text from which this article is extracted, Deane provides extensive endnotes, usually to Latin Biblical quotations and to the Latin versions of St. Augustine's writings. These are omitted here.

Moreover, man has been given the gift of free will, which no other earthly creature possesses; he can, if he wishes to do so, act in a manner contrary to God's command. He can choose to obey or disobey. If he disobeys and turns away from the source of his being, his life will be warped and stunted; the farther he removes himself from God the more wretched, miserable, and imperfect will he become. Augustine adopts the neo-Platonic doctrine that evil has no substantial reality of its own, that it is simply the privation or loss of good. Consequently, evil can inhere only in that which is good but not perfectly good. And since evil is not a substance or a nature, but merely a privation, God is not its author or creator. A created being – a nature or substance – becomes evil insofar as it falls away from its essence or nature and tends toward nonexistence, although by God's Providence nothing in the universe is permitted to decline to the point of nonexistence. Therefore, to the extent that man turns away from God, who is perfect being and goodness, he becomes less good and more evil. The choice is left to man, but, as we shall see, the consequences of the choice are eternally fixed and determined by God.

Man soon misused the free will that God had granted to him. The devil, the chief of the angels who had already fallen from heaven because of their perverse and prideful rebellion against God, tempted Eve to disobey God's command and to eat the fruit of the tree of the knowledge of good and evil, and Eve persuaded Adam to join her in this rebellion against the Creator and Lord of the universe. Thus was committed that "original sin" of disobedience and rebellion against God, which had its root in man's pride and in his presumptuous desire, to which the devil adroitly appealed, to "be like God." "By craving to be more, man becomes less; and by aspiring to be self-sufficing, he fell away from Him who truly suffices him."

It is important to understand clearly what Augustine means by "sin" and "original sin." Sin is to be clearly distinguished from sins, that is, particular acts that are wrong, unjust, or immoral; sin is a pervasive attribute or character of human beings. Sin is disobedience and revolt – man's turning away from God and from His will and His commands, and making himself and his own will and desires the center of his existence. Sin is man's refusal to accept his status as a creature, superior to all other earthly creatures but subordinate to God.

[...]

As a result of the Fall of Adam and Eve, as a consequence of and a punishment for their "original sin" of prideful, arrogant rebellion against God and against their own proper status as creatures, human life in this world became penal. Mortality, death, misery, suffering, crimes, the war of the flesh against the spirit, conflict among men – all these evils, which had no place in human nature as it was created – are the characteristics of fallen man. They are the necessary result and the totally just punishment of that "outrageous wickedness which was perpetrated in Paradise." Moreover, the original sin of egoistic pride and disobedience and its necessary punishment were not confined to our first parents, Adam and Eve. In their sin the whole mass of the human race was condemned, and in all their descendants the originally good nature of man has been and remains radically vitiated and corrupted. [...]

But, even after the Fall, God did not entirely abandon his creature, man. Had He done so, man would have ceased to exist. Even in the misery of sinful existence, God continues to grant to all men the great blessings of His gifts – man's ability to live and to propagate his kind, his senses and his reason, the goods of nature, food and nourishment. But in addition to these gifts, given to both the just and the unjust, God in His infinite mercy has conferred a priceless gift upon a small number of human beings. [...] This minority, the elect, were chosen to receive the gift of faith and, as a consequence, salvation and exemption from the just punishment of sin, without any regard to their future merits or good works. By the operation of unmerited grace those predestined to salvation are released from the just penalty inflicted on the whole mass of fallen mankind and are promised a life of eternal blessedness with God after the Last Judgment, the destruction of the world, and the resurrection of the body.

[...]

By God's free grace a small minority of mankind has been chosen out of the mass of corruption and has been elected to eternal salvation. These men, together with the good angels who never fell away from God, constitute the City of God, and at the end of time, after the resurrection of the body, they will live forever in perfect peace and happiness and in enjoyment of God. The rest of mankind, the vast majority, together with the devil and his angels, are the citizens of the earthly city, which is doomed to eternal punishment. The careers of these two cities from the beginning of time until the end of the world and the relations between their citizens are the theme not only of *The City of God* but of a large number of Augustine's other writings.

The City of God, the true Jerusalem, is the whole assembly of the saints; it is identical with the Church of which Christ is the Head and all the citizens are members, that is, the invisible Church. The human part of the City of God is a single society that extends throughout the whole world and is made up of men of different eras. It is of crucial importance to recognize that Christ explicitly stated that His kingdom, the City of God, is not of this world. By this statement He made it perfectly plain to all men and to their earthly rulers that He had no intention of interfering with their temporal governance, and, more important, He made it clear that no earthly state, city, or association can ever claim to be a part or a representative of the City of God. Precisely because Christ's kingdom is the City of God, it exists eternally in heaven and is not embodied in any human or earthly institution.

[...]

In this heavenly city are found everlasting peace and perfect harmony among the members, since self-love and self-will are completely replaced by "a ministering love that rejoices in the common joy of all, of many hearts makes one, that is to say, secures a perfect concord [*concors*]." In the earthly city, on the contrary, there is constant conflict and strife, not only against the good but among the wicked themselves, since each man and each group seeks a larger share of material goods than the others and each strives for mastery and power over the rest. During this life temporal goods and evils are distributed by God to the men of both cities in accordance with His plans for the world, and there is no correlation between a man's goodness and piety and his earthly happiness and prosperity. In fact, it sometimes seems that the good receive more than their share of misery and suffering. The difference between the two types of man resides not in their fortunes or experiences in this life but in their attitudes toward the good or evil things that befall them. The pilgrims of the City of God are not elated or made proud by earthly prosperity or success, nor are they shattered or broken by calamities or sufferings, which they regard as punishments for their sins or trials of their virtues. To the citizens of the earthly city, however, wealth, fame, and power are the highest goods, and they will do anything that is necessary to obtain them. They regard poverty, sickness, misfortune, and death as absolute disasters, which they will go to any lengths to escape or postpone.

[...]

There is no limit to sinful man's desire for material goods; his life consists in a restless quest for satisfaction by means of one object after another. The moment one desire is satisfied, another rises to demand fulfillment; so there is no rest or surcease for the anguished soul that is seeking happiness in material objects.

[...]

This picture of man's restless striving for material satisfactions reminds us of Hobbes's portrait of natural man, who spends his entire life in the effort to satisfy one desire after another and never attains real repose or enduring satisfaction. And Hobbes's graphic description of the *bellum omnium contra omnes* inevitably comes to mind when Augustine depicts the consequences of the fierce competition for inevitably scarce goods carried on by self-centered men, each one of whom is driven by infinite and insatiable desires. [...]

Thomas Hobbes, "The Natural Condition of Mankind"*

Men by nature equal. Nature hath made men so equal, in the faculties of the body, and mind; as that though there be found one man sometimes manifestly stronger in body, or of quicker mind than another; yet when all is reckoned together, the difference between man, and man, is not so considerable, as that one man can thereupon claim to himself any benefit, to which another may not pretend, as well as he. For as to the strength of body, the weakest has strength enough to kill the strongest, either by secret machination, or by confederacy with others, that are in the same danger with himself.

And as to the faculties of the mind, setting aside the arts grounded upon words, and especially that skill of proceeding upon general, and infallible rules, called science; which very few have, and but in few things; as being not a native faculty, born with us; nor attained, as prudence, while we look after somewhat else, I find yet a greater equality amongst men, than that of strength. For prudence, is but experience; which equal time, equally bestows on all men, in those things they equally apply themselves unto. That which may perhaps make such equality incredible, is but a vain conceit of one's own wisdom, which almost all men think they have in a greater degree, than the vulgar; that is, than all men but themselves, and a few others, whom by fame, or for concurring with themselves, they approve. For such is the nature of men, that howsoever they may acknowledge many others to be more witty, or more eloquent, or

* Thomas Hobbes, extracted from chapter 13 of *The Leviathan*, edited by Michael Oakeshott (London: Collier-Macmillan Ltd, 1962). Originally published 1651.

more learned; yet they will hardly believe there be many so wise as themselves; for they see their own wit at hand, and other men's at a distance. But this proveth rather that men are in that point equal, than unequal. For there is not ordinarily a greater sign of the equal distribution of any thing, than that every man is contented with his share.

From equality proceeds diffidence. From this equality of ability, ariseth equality of hope in the attaining of our ends. And therefore if any two men desire the same thing, which nevertheless they cannot both enjoy, they become enemies; and in the way to their end, which is principally their own conservation, and sometimes their delectation only, endeavour to destroy, or subdue one another. And from hence it comes to pass, that where an invader hath no more to fear, than another man's single power; if one plant, sow, build, or possess a convenient seat, others may probably be expected to come prepared with forces united, to dispossess, and deprive him, not only of the fruit of his labour, but also of his life, or liberty. And the invader again is in the like danger of another.

From diffidence war. And from this diffidence of one another, there is no way for any man to secure himself, so reasonable, as anticipation; that is, by force, or wiles, to master the persons of all men he can, so long, till he see no other power great enough to endanger him: and this is no more than his own conservation requireth, and is generally allowed. Also because there be some, that taking pleasure in contemplating their own power in the acts of conquest, which they pursue farther than their security requires; if others, that otherwise would be glad to be at ease within modest bounds, should not by invasion increase their power, they would not be able, long time, by standing only on their defence, to subsist. And by consequence, such augmentation of dominion over men being necessary to a man's conservation, it ought to be allowed him.

Again, men have no pleasure, but on the contrary a great deal of grief, in keeping company, where there is no power able to over-awe them all. For every man looketh that his companion should value him, at the same rate he sets upon himself: and upon all signs of contempt, or undervaluing, naturally endeavours, as far as he dares, (which amongst them that have no common power to keep them in quiet, is far enough to make them destroy each other), to extort a greater value from his contemners, by damage; and from others, by the example.

So that in the nature of man, we find three principal causes of quarrel. First, competition; secondly, diffidence; thirdly, glory.

The first, maketh men invade for gain; the second, for safety; and the third, for reputation. The first use violence, to make themselves masters of other men's persons, wives, children, and cattle; the second, to defend them; the third, for trifles, as a word, a smile, a different opinion, and any other sign of undervalue, either direct in their persons, or by reflection in their kindred, their friends, their nation, their profession, or their name.

Out of civil states, there is always war of every one against every one. Hereby it is manifest, that during the time men live without a common power to keep them all in awe, they are in that condition which is called war; and such a war, as is of every man, against every man. For WAR, consisteth not in battle only, or the act of fighting; but in a tract of time, wherein the will to contend by battle is sufficiently known: and therefore the notion of *time,* is to be considered in the nature of war; as it is in the nature of weather. For as the nature of foul weather, lieth not in a shower or two of rain; but in an inclination thereto of many days together: so the nature of war, consisteth not in actual fighting; but in the known disposition thereto, during all the time there is no assurance to the contrary. All other time is PEACE.

The incommodities of such a war. Whatsoever therefore is consequent to a time of war, where every man is enemy to every man; the same is consequent to the time, wherein men live without other security, than what their own strength, and their own invention shall furnish them withal. In such condition, there is no place for industry; because the fruit thereof is uncertain: and consequently no culture of the earth; no navigation, nor use of the commodities that may be imported by sea; no commodious building; no instruments of moving, and removing, such things as require much force; no knowledge of the face of the earth; no account of time; no arts; no letters; no society; and which is worst of all, continual fear, and danger of violent death; and the life of man, solitary, poor, nasty, brutish, and short.

It may seem strange to some man, that has not well weighed these things; that nature should thus dissociate, and render men apt to invade, and destroy one another: and he may therefore, not trusting to this inference, made from the passions, desire perhaps to have the same confirmed by experience. Let him therefore consider with himself, when taking a journey, he arms himself, and seeks to go well accompanied; when going to sleep, he locks his doors; when even in his house he locks his chests; and this when he knows there be laws, and public officers, armed, to revenge all injuries shall be done him; what opinion he has of his fellow-subjects, when he rides armed; of his fellow citizens, when he locks his doors; and of his children, and servants, when he locks his chests. Does he not there as much accuse mankind by his actions, as I do by my words? But neither of us accuse man's nature in it. The desires, and other passions of man, are in themselves no sin. No more are the actions, that proceed from those passions, till they know a law that forbids them: which till laws be made they cannot know: nor can any law be made, till they have agreed upon the person that shall make it.

It may peradventure be thought, there was never such a time, nor condition of war as this: and I believe it was never generally so, over all the world: but there are many places, where they live so now. For the savage people in many places of America, except the government of small families, the concord whereof dependeth on natural lust, have no government at all; and live at this day in that brutish manner, as I said before. Howsoever, it may be perceived what manner of life there would be, where there were no common power to fear, by the manner of life, which men that have formerly lived under a peaceful government, use to degenerate into, in a civil war.

But though there had never been any time, wherein particular men were in a condition of war one against another; yet in all times, kings, and persons of sovereign authority, because of their independency, are in continual jealousies, and in the state and posture of gladiators; having their weapons pointing, and their eyes fixed on one another; that is, their forts, garrisons, and guns upon the frontiers of their kingdoms; and continual spies upon their neighbours; which is a posture of war. But because they uphold thereby, the industry of their subjects; there does not follow from it, that misery, which accompanies the liberty of particular men.

In such a war nothing is unjust. To this war of every man, against every man, this also is consequent; that nothing can be unjust. The notions of right and wrong, justice and injustice have there no place. Where there is no common power, there is no law: where no law, no injustice. Force, and fraud, are in war the two cardinal virtues. Justice, and injustice are none of the faculties neither of the body, nor mind. If they were, they might be in a man that were alone in the world, as well as his senses, and passions. They are qualities, that relate to men in society, not in solitude. It is consequent also to the same condition, that there be no propriety, no dominion, no *mine* and *thine* distinct: but only that to be every man's, that he can get: and for so long, as he can keep it. And thus much for the ill condition, which man by mere nature is actually placed in; though with a possibility to come out of it, consisting partly in the passions, partly in his reason.

The passions that incline men to peace. The passions that incline men to peace, are fear of death; desire of such things as are necessary to commodious living; and a hope by their industry to obtain them. And reason suggesteth convenient articles of peace, upon which men may be drawn to agreement. These articles, are they, which otherwise are called the Laws of Nature: whereof I shall speak more particularly [...]

C. B. Macpherson, "The Early Liberal Model of Man"*

[...] There is a sharp break in the path from pre-liberal to liberal democracy. A fresh start was made in the nineteenth century, from a very different base. The earlier concepts of democracy, as we have seen, had rejected class division, believing or hoping that it could be transcended, or even assuming that in some places – Rousseau's Geneva or Jefferson's America – it had been transcended. Liberal democracy, on the contrary, accepted class division, and built on it. (The first formulators of liberal democracy came to its advocacy through a chain of reasoning which started from the assumptions of a capitalist market society and the laws of classical political economy.) These gave them a model of man (as maximizer of utilities) and a model of society (as a collection of individuals with conflicting interests). From those models, and one ethical principle, they deduced the need for government, the desirable functions of government, and hence the desirable system of choosing and authorizing governments. To see how deeply their models of man and society got into their general theory, and hence into their model of liberal democracy as the best form of government, we shall do well to look more closely than is usually done at the theories of the two earliest systematic exponents of liberal democracy, Jeremy Bentham and James Mill.[2]

[...]

* Crawford Brough Macpherson, extracted from *The Life and Times of Liberal Democracy* (Oxford: Oxford University Press, 1977), pp. 23–43.

[2] James Mill's model can be dated precisely at 1820, in his famous article on *Government*. Bentham's may be dated 1820 or 1818, when he produced the twenty-six *Resolutions on Parliamentary Reform*, which would admit to the franchise "all such persons as, being of the male sex, of mature age, and of sound mind, shall ... have been resident either as householders or inmates, within the district or place in which they are called upon to vote".

It must be said that with Bentham and James Mill liberal democracy got off to a poor start. It is not that they were incompetent theorists. On the contrary, Bentham became deservedly famous as a thinker, and the most influential doctrine of the English nineteenth century was named after him. And James Mill, though not of the very first rank, was a clear and forceful writer. And the general theory of Utilitarianism, from which they both deduced the need for a democratic franchise, seemed both fundamentally egalitarian and thoroughly businesslike. (It was both, and that was the trouble. I shall suggest that it was the combination of an ethical principle of equality with a competitive market model of man and society that logically required both thinkers to conclude in favour of a democratic franchise, but made them do so either ambiguously or with reservations.)

The Utilitarian base

The general theory was clear enough. The only rationally defensible criterion of social good was the greatest happiness of the greatest number, happiness being defined as the amount of individual pleasure minus pain. In calculating the aggregate net happiness of a whole society, each individual was to count as one. What could be more egalitarian than that as a fundamental ethical principle?

But to it were added certain factual postulates. Every individual by his very nature seeks to maximize his own pleasure without limit. And although Bentham set out a long list of kinds of pleasure, including many non-material ones, he was clear that the possession of material goods was so basic to the attainment of all other satisfactions that it alone could be taken as the measure of them all. ('Each portion of wealth has a corresponding portion of happiness.'[3] And again: 'Money is the instrument of measuring the quantity of pain or pleasure. Those who are not satisfied with the accuracy of this instrument must find out some other that shall be more accurate, or bid adieu to politics and morals.'[4])

So each seeks to maximize his own wealth without limit. One way of doing this is to get power over others. 'Between wealth and power, the connexion is most close and intimate; so intimate, indeed, that the disentanglement of them, even in the imagination, is a matter of no small difficulty. They are each of them respectively an instrument of production with relation to the other.'[5] And again, 'human beings are the most powerful instruments of production, and therefore everyone becomes anxious to employ the services of his fellows in multiplying his own comforts. Hence the intense and universal thirst for power; the equally prevalent hatred of subjection.'[6]

James Mill was even more forthright. In his 1820 article *Government*, he wrote:

> That one human being will desire to render the person and property of another subservient to his pleasures, notwithstanding the pain or loss of pleasure which it may occasion to that other individual, is the foundation of government. The desire of the object implies the desire of the power necessary to accomplish the object. The desire, therefore, of that power which is necessary to render the persons and properties of human beings subservient to our pleasures is a grand governing law of human nature … The grand instrument for attaining what a man likes is the actions of other men. Power … therefore, means security for the conformity between the will of one man and the acts of other men. This, we presume, is not a proposition which will be disputed.[7]

With this grand governing law of human nature, society is a collection of individuals incessantly seeking power over and at the expense of each other. To keep such a society from flying apart, a structure of law both civil and criminal was seen to be needed. Various structures of law might be capable of providing the necessary order, but, of course, according to the Utilitarian ethical principle, the best set of laws, the best distribution of rights and obligations, was that which would produce the greatest happiness of the greatest number. (This most general end of the laws could, Bentham said, be divided into four subordinate ends: 'to provide subsistence; to produce abundance; to favour equality; to maintain security.'[8]

Bentham's ends of legislation

Bentham's arguments as to how each of these ends could be achieved (and how not) are revealing. Together they amount to a case for a system of unlimited private

[3] *Principles of the Civil Code*, Part I, chapter 6, in Bentham: *The Theory of Legislation*, edited by C. K. Ogden, London, 1931, p. 103. (I have preferred this edition to the version printed in the Bentham *Works* edited by Bowring, vol. i.) On the abstraction from reality required to assert this proposition, see below, at n. 13.

[4] W. Stark (ed.), *Jeremy Bentham's Economic Writings*, i. 117.

[5] *Constitutional Code*, Bk. 1, chapter 9, in *Works*, ed. Bowring, ix. 48.

[6] Stark (ed.): iii. 430.

[7] Section IV (p. 17 of the Barker edition, Cambridge, 1937).

[8] *Principles of the Civil Code*, Part I, chapter 2; Ogden (ed.): op. cit., p. 96.

property and capitalist enterprise, and this apparently deduced from the factual postulates about human nature and a few others. Let us look in turn at his arguments under each head.

First, subsistence. The law need do nothing to ensure that enough will be produced to provide subsistence for everyone.

> What can the law do for subsistence? Nothing directly. All it can do is to create *motives*, that is, punishments or rewards, by the force of which men may be led to provide subsistence for themselves. But nature herself has created these motives, and has given them a sufficient energy. Before the idea of laws existed, *needs* and *enjoyments* had done in that respect all that the best concerted laws could do. Need, armed with pains of all kinds, even death itself, commanded labour, excited courage, inspired foresight, developed all the faculties of man. Enjoyment, the inseparable companion of every need satisfied, formed an inexhaustible fund of rewards for those who surmounted obstacles and fulfilled the end of nature. The force of the physical sanction being sufficient, the employment of the political sanction would be superfluous.[9]

What the laws can do is to 'provide for subsistence indirectly, by protecting men while they labour, and by making them sure of the fruits of their labour. Security for the labourer, security for the fruits of labour; such is the benefit of laws; and it is an inestimable benefit.'[10]

The curious point here is that Bentham, in invoking fear of starvation as a natural incentive to the productive labour which would provide subsistence for everybody, has slipped from thinking of a primitive society ('before the idea of laws existed'), where fear of starvation would have that effect on everybody, to an advanced nineteenth-century industrial society, where that does not apply without an additional proviso. In a primitive society with such a low level of productive technique that the incessant labour of all was needed (and was seen by all to be needed) to avoid general starvation, the fear of starvation would be a sufficient incentive to the productive labour that would produce subsistence for all. But in a society whose productive techniques are sufficient to provide subsistence for everyone without such incessant labour by everyone, like England in Bentham's time, fear of starvation is not in itself a sufficient incentive. In such a society, fear of starvation will be an incentive to incessant labour only where the institutions of property have created a class who have no property in land or working capital, and no claims on society for their support, and hence must sell their labour or starve.

So keen a thinker as Bentham could scarcely have failed to see this, had he not been taking for granted the existence of such a class as inevitable in any economically advanced society. And we know that he did assume this: 'In the highest state of social prosperity, the great mass of citizens will have no resource except their daily industry; and consequently will be always near indigence.'[11] Already we can see the teachings of classical political economy subverting the egalitarian principle.

A similar shift takes place in his argument about 'abundance'. Here he seems to slip from thinking of a society of independent producers to thinking of his own advanced society, applying to the latter a generalization about incentives apparently drawn from the former. No legislation, he says, is needed to encourage individuals to produce abundance of material goods. Natural incentives are enough, because everyone's desire is infinite. Each want satisfied produces a new want. So there is a strong and permanent incentive to produce more. Bentham does not notice that this incentive, which may properly enough be postulated of the capitalist entrepreneur and possibly of the self-employed independent producer, cannot very well apply to the wage-earners, who are 'always near indigence'. He does not see this, because he has created his model of man in the image of the entrepreneur or the independent producer. He could do that because he had no historical sense.

It is only when we come to his argument under the heads of equality and security that we can see the full extent to which his acceptance of capitalism undermined his egalitarian ethical principle. The case for 'equality', that is, for everyone having the same amount of wealth or income, is set out clearly. It rests on what came to be known as the law of diminishing utility, which points out that successive increments of wealth (or of any material goods) bring successively less satisfaction to their holder, or, that a person with ten or a hundred times the wealth of another has much less than ten or a hundred times as much pleasure. Given that all individuals have the same capacity for pleasure, and that 'each portion of wealth has a corresponding portion of happiness', it follows that 'he who has the most wealth has the most happiness', but also that 'the excess in happiness of the richer will not be so great as the excess of his wealth'.[12] From this it follows that aggregate happiness

9 Ibid., Part I, chapter 4; Ogden, p. 100.
10 Ibid.
11 Ibid., Part I, chapter 14; Ogden, p. 127.
12 Ibid., Part I, chapter 6; Ogden, p. 103.

will be greater the more nearly the distribution of wealth approaches equality: maximum aggregate happiness requires that all individuals have equal wealth.

This case for equality requires, as we have noticed, an assumption of equal capacities for pleasure. For if some were assumed to have a greater capacity for pleasure, i.e. a greater sensitivity or sensibility, it could be argued that aggregate happiness would be maximized by their having more wealth than the others. Bentham was not very consistent about this. He prefaced the 'diminishing returns' argument for equality by setting aside 'the particular sensibility of individuals, and … the exterior circumstances in which they may be placed'. These must be set aside, he said, because 'they are never the same for two individuals', so that, without setting those differences aside, 'it will be impossible to announce any general proposition'.[13] Yet elsewhere he pointed out that, besides particular individual differences in sensibility, there were differences between whole categories of individuals. There was a difference in sensibility as between the sexes: 'In point of quantity, the sensibility of the female sex appears in general to be greater than that of the male.'[14] And, of more direct importance in an argument that depends on a relation between pleasure and wealth, Bentham saw a difference in sensibility between those of different 'station, or rank in life': '*Caeteris paribus*, the quantum of sensibility appears to be greater in the higher ranks of men than in the lower.'[15] If Bentham had acknowledged such a property–class differential when making his case for equality of wealth, his case would have been destroyed: he would have been endorsing the position of Edmund Burke. Perhaps he was. Perhaps he saw no need to mention that differential when stating his case for equality because he had already decided that the claims of equality were entirely subordinate to the claims of security.

In any case, having said this much under the head of 'equality', Bentham turned to 'security', that is, security of property and of expectation of return from the use of one's labour and property. Without security of property in the fruits of one's labour, Bentham says, civilization is impossible. No one would form any plan of life or undertake any labour the product of which he could not immediately take and use. Not even simple cultivation of the land would be undertaken if one could not be sure that the harvest would be one's own. The laws, therefore, must secure individual property. And since men differ in ability and energy, some will get more property than others. Any attempt by the law to reduce them to equality would destroy the incentive to productivity. Hence, as between equality and security, the law must have no hesitation: 'Equality must yield.'[16]

[…]

The political requirement

For this kind of society, what kind of state was needed? The political problem was to find a system of choosing and authorizing governments, that is, sets of law-makers and law-enforcers, who would make and enforce the kind of laws needed by such a society. It was a double problem: the political system should both produce governments which would establish and nurture a free market society and protect the citizens from rapacious governments (for by the grand governing principle of human nature every government would be rapacious unless it were made in its own interest not to be so, or impossible for it to be so).

The crucial point in the solution of this double problem turned out to be the extent of the franchise, along with certain devices such as the secret ballot, frequent elections, and freedom of the press, which would make the vote a free and effective expression of the voter's wishes. The extent and genuineness of the franchise became the central question because, by the early nineteenth century in England, theorists were able to take for granted the rest of the framework of representative government: the constitutional provisions whereby legislatures and executives were periodically chosen, and therefore periodically replaceable, by the voters at general elections, and whereby the civil service (and the military) were subordinate to a government thus responsible to the electorate. So the model which the nineteenth-century thinkers started from was a system of representative and responsible government of this kind. The question that was left for them was, what provisions for the extent and genuineness of the franchise would both produce governments which would promote a free market society and protect the citizens from the government.

[…]

Protective democracy for market man

This was the genesis of the first modern model of democracy. It is neither inspiring nor inspired. The democratic franchise provisions were put in the model only belatedly. It is hard to say what had the greater effect in moving the

13 Ibid.

14 *Introduction to the Principles of Morals and Legislation*, chapter 6, in *Collected Works*, London, 1970, p. 64.

15 Ibid., p. 65.

16 *Principles of the Civil Code*, Part I, chapter 11; Ogden, p. 120.

founders of this model to make their franchise democratic in principle: whether it was their realization that nothing less than 'one man, one vote' would placate a working class which was showing signs of becoming seriously politically articulate (as is suggested by Bentham's remark in 1820 that he supposed they wouldn't be satisfied with less), or whether it was the sheer logic of their own case for reform, resting as it did on the assumption of conflicting self-interested maximizing individuals. Either way, it is clear that they allowed themselves a democratic conclusion only because they had convinced themselves that a vast majority of the working-class would be sure to follow the advice and example of 'that intelligent, that virtuous rank', the middle class. It is on that note that James Mill closed his somewhat ambiguous case for a democratic franchise.

In this founding model of democracy for a modern industrial society, then, there is no enthusiasm for democracy, no idea that it could be a morally transformative force; it is nothing but a logical requirement for the governance of inherently self-interested conflicting individuals who are assumed to be infinite desirers of their own private benefits. Its advocacy is based on the assumption that man is an infinite consumer, that his overriding motivation is to maximize the flow of satisfactions, or utilities, to himself from society, and that a national society is simply a collection of such individuals. Responsible government, even to the extent of responsibility to a democratic electorate, was needed for the protection of individuals and the promotion of the Gross National Product, and for nothing more.

I have drawn a harsh, but I think fair, portrait of the founding model of modern Western democracy. It has nothing in common with any of the earlier, pre-industrial visions of a democratic society. The earlier visions had asked for a new kind of man. The founding model of liberal democracy took man as he was, man as he had been shaped by market society, and assumed that he was unalterable. It was on this point chiefly that John Stuart Mill and his humanist liberal followers in the twentieth century attacked the Benthamist model.

Karl Marx, "Estranged Labor"*

We have proceeded from the premises of political economy. We have accepted its language and its laws. We presupposed private property, the separation of labour, capital and land, and of wages, profit of capital and rent of land – likewise division of labour, competition, the concept of exchange-value, etc. On the basis of political economy itself, in its own words, we have shown that the worker sinks to the level of a commodity and becomes indeed the most wretched of commodities; that the wretchedness of the worker is in inverse proportion to the power and magnitude of his production; that the necessary result of competition is the accumulation of capital in a few hands, and thus the restoration of monopoly in a more terrible form; that finally the distinction between capitalist and land-rentier, like that between the tiller of the soil and the factory-worker, disappears and that the whole of society must fall apart into the two classes – the property-*owners* and the property-less *workers.*

[...]

The worker becomes all the poorer the more wealth he produces, the more his production increases in power and range. The worker becomes an ever cheaper commodity the more commodities he creates. With the *increasing value* of the world of things proceeds in direct proportion the *devaluation* of the world of men. Labour produces not only commodities; it produces itself and the worker as a *commodity* – and does so in the proportion in which it produces commodities generally.

This fact expresses merely that the object which labour produces – labour's product – confronts it as *something alien*, as a *power independent* of the producer. The product of labour is labour which has been congealed in an object, which has become material: it is the *objectification* of labour. Labour's realization is its objectification. In the conditions dealt with by political economy this realization of labour appears as *loss of reality* for the workers; objectification as *loss of the object* and *object-bondage*; appropriation as *estrangement*, as *alienation*.

So much does labour's realization appear as loss of reality that the worker loses reality to the point of starving to death. So much does objectification appear as loss of the object that the worker is robbed of the objects most necessary not only for his life but for his work. Indeed, labour itself becomes an object which he can get hold of only with the greatest effort and with the most irregular interruptions. So much does the appropriation of the object appear as estrangement that the more objects the worker produces the fewer can he possess and the more he falls under the dominion of his product, capital.

All these consequences are contained in the definition that the worker is related to the *product of his labour* as to an *alien* object. For on this premise it is clear that the more the worker spends himself, the more powerful

* Karl Marx, *Economic and Philosophical Manuscripts of 1844*, extracted from *The Marx–Engels Reader*, edited by Robert C. Tucker (W. W. Norton & Co., 1972, 1978). Originally published 1844.

the alien objective world becomes which he creates over-against himself, the poorer he himself – his inner world – becomes, the less belongs to him as his own. It is the same in religion. The more man puts into God, the less he retains in himself. The worker puts his life into the object; but now his life no longer belongs to him but to the object. Hence, the greater this activity, the greater is the worker's lack of objects. Whatever the product of his labour is, he is not. Therefore the greater this product, the less is he himself. The *alienation* of the worker in his product means not only that his labour becomes an object, an *external* existence, but that it exists *outside him*, independently, as something alien to him, and that it becomes a power of its own confronting him; it means that the life which he has conferred on the object confronts him as something hostile and alien.

[...]

Till now we have been considering the estrangement, the alienation of the worker only in one of its aspects, i.e., the worker's *relationship to the products of his labour*. But the estrangement is manifested not only in the result but in the *act of production* – within the *producing activity* itself. How would the worker come to face the product of his activity as a stranger, were it not that in the very act of production he was estranging himself from himself? The product is after all but the summary of the activity of production. If then the product of labour is alienation, production itself must be active alienation, the alienation of activity, the activity of alienation. In the estrangement of the object of labour is merely summarized the estrangement, the alienation, in the activity of labour itself.

What, then, constitutes the alienation of labour?

First, the fact that labour is *external* to the worker, i.e., it does not belong to his essential being; that in his work, therefore, he does not affirm himself but denies himself, does not feel content but unhappy, does not develop freely his physical and mental energy but mortifies his body and ruins his mind. The worker therefore only feels himself outside his work, and in his work feels outside himself. He is at home when he is not working, and when he is working he is not at home. His labour is therefore not voluntary, but coerced; it is *forced labour*. It is therefore not the satisfaction of a need; it is merely a *means* to satisfy needs external to it. Its alien character emerges clearly in the fact that as soon as no physical or other compulsion exists, labour is shunned like the plague. External labour, labour in which man alienates himself, is a labour of self-sacrifice, of mortification. Lastly, the external character of labour for the worker appears in the fact that it is not his own, but someone else's, that it does not belong to him, that in it he belongs, not to himself, but to another. Just as in religion the spontaneous activity of the human imagination, of the human brain and the human heart, operates independently of the individual – that is, operates on him as an alien, divine or diabolical activity – in the same way the worker's activity is not his spontaneous activity. It belongs to another; it is the loss of his self.

As a result, therefore, man (the worker) no longer feels himself to be freely active in any but his animal functions – eating, drinking, procreating, or at most in his dwelling and in dressing-up, etc.; and in his human functions he no longer feels himself to be anything but an animal. What is animal becomes human and what is human becomes animal.

Certainly eating, drinking, procreating, etc., are also genuinely human functions. But in the abstraction which separates them from the sphere of all other human activity and turns them into sole and ultimate ends, they are animal.

We have considered the act of estranging practical human activity, labour, in two of its aspects. (1) The relation of the worker to the *product of labour* as an alien object exercising power over him. This relation is at the same time the relation to the sensuous external world, to the objects of nature as an alien world antagonistically opposed to him. (2) The relation of labour to the *act of production* within the *labour* process. This relation is the relation of the worker to his own activity as an alien activity not belonging to him; it is activity as suffering, strength as weakness, begetting as emasculating, the worker's *own* physical and mental energy, his personal life or what is life other than activity – as an activity which is turned against him, neither depends on nor belongs to him. Here we have *self-estrangement*, as we had previously the estrangement of the *thing*.

We have yet a third aspect of *estranged labour* to deduce from the two already considered.

Man is a species being, not only because in practice and in theory he adopts the species as his object (his own as well as those of other things), but – and this is only another way of expressing it – but also because he treats himself as the actual, living species; because he treats himself as a *universal* and therefore a free being.

The life of the species, both in man and in animals, consists physically in the fact that man (like the animal) lives on inorganic nature; and the more universal man is compared with an animal, the more universal is the sphere of inorganic nature on which he lives. Just as plants, animals, stones, the air, light, etc., constitute a part of human consciousness in the realm of theory, partly as objects of natural science, partly as objects of art – his spiritual inorganic nature, spiritual nourishment which he must first prepare to make it palatable and digestible – so too in the realm of practice they constitute a part of human life and human activity. Physically man lives only on these products of nature, whether they appear in the form of food, heating, clothes, a dwelling, or whatever it may be. The universality of man is in practice manifested precisely in the universality which makes all nature his *inorganic* body – both inasmuch as nature is (1) his direct means of life, and (2) the material, the object, and the instrument of his life-activity. Nature is man's *inorganic body* – nature, that is, insofar as it is not itself the human body. Man *lives* on nature – means that nature is his *body*, with which he must remain in continuous intercourse if he is not to die. That man's physical and spiritual life is linked to nature means simply that nature is linked to itself, for man is a part of nature.

In estranging from man (1) nature, and (2) himself, his own active functions, his life-activity, estranged labour estranges the *species* from man. It turns for him the *life of the species* into a means of individual life. First it estranges the life of the species and individual life, and secondly it makes individual life in its abstract form the purpose of the life of the species, likewise in its abstract and estranged form.

For in the first place labour, *life-activity, productive life* itself, appears to man merely as a *means* of satisfying a need – the need to maintain the physical existence. Yet the productive life is the life of the species. It is life-engendering life. The whole character of a species – its species character – is contained in the character of its life-activity; and free, conscious activity is man's species character. Life itself appears only as *a means to life*.

The animal is immediately identical with its life-activity. It does not distinguish itself from it. It is *its life-activity*. Man makes his life-activity itself the object of his will and his consciousness. He has conscious life-activity. It is not a determination with which he directly merges. Conscious life-activity directly distinguishes man from animal life-activity. It is just because of this that he is a species being. Or it is only because he is a species being that he is a Conscious Being, i.e., that his own life is an object for him. Only because of that is his activity free activity. Estranged labour reverses this relationship, so that it is just because man is a conscious being that he makes his life-activity, his *essential* being, a mere means to his *existence*.

In creating an *objective world* by his practical activity, in *working-up* inorganic nature, man proves himself a conscious species being, i.e., as a being that treats the species as its own essential being, or that treats itself as a species being. Admittedly animals also produce. They build themselves nests, dwellings, like the bees, beavers, ants, etc., But an animal only produces what it immediately needs for itself or its young. It produces one-sidedly, whilst man produces universally. It produces only under the dominion of immediate physical need, whilst man produces even when he is free from physical need and only truly produces in freedom therefrom. An animal produces only itself, whilst man reproduces the whole of nature. An animal's product belongs immediately to its physical body, whilst man freely confronts his product. An animal forms things in accordance with the standard and the need of the species to which it belongs, whilst man knows how to produce in accordance with the standard of every species, and knows how to apply everywhere the inherent standard to the object. Man therefore also forms things in accordance with the laws of beauty.

It is just in the working-up of the objective world, therefore, that man first really proves himself to be a *species being*. This production is his active species life. Through and because of this production, nature appears as *his* work and his reality. The object of labour is, therefore, the *objectification of man's species life:* for he duplicates himself not only, as in consciousness, intellectually, but also actively, in reality, and therefore he contemplates himself in a world that he has created. In tearing away from man the object of his production, therefore, estranged labour tears from him his *species life*, his real species objectivity, and transforms his advantage over animals into the disadvantage that his inorganic body, nature, is taken from him.

Similarly, in degrading spontaneous activity, free activity, to a means, estranged labour makes man's species life a means to his physical existence.

The consciousness which man has of his species is thus transformed by estrangement in such a way that the species life becomes for him a means.

Estranged labour turns thus:

(3) *Man's species being*, both nature and his spiritual species property, into a being *alien* to him, into a *means* to his *individual existence*. It estranges man's own body from him, as it does external nature and his spiritual essence, his *human* being.

(4) An immediate consequence of the fact that man is estranged from the product of his labour, from his life-activity, from his species being is the *estrangement of man* from *man*. If a man is confronted by himself, he is confronted by the *other* man. What applies to a man's

relation to his work, to the product of his labour and to himself, also holds of a man's relation to the other man, and to the other man's labour and object of labour.

In fact, the proposition that man's species nature is estranged from him means that one man is estranged from the other, as each of them is from man's essential nature.

[...]

We must bear in mind the above-stated proposition that man's relation to himself only becomes *objective* and *real* for him through his relation to the other man. Thus, if the product of his labour, his labour *objectified*, is for him an *alien*, hostile, powerful object independent of him, then his position toward it is such that someone else is master of this object, someone who is alien, hostile, powerful, and independent of him. If his own activity is to him an unfree activity, then he is treating it as activity performed in the service, under the dominion, the coercion and the yoke of another man.

[...]

Through *estranged, alienated labour*, then, the worker produces the relationship to this labour of a man alien to labour and standing outside it. The relationship of the worker to labour engenders the relation to it of the capitalist, or whatever one chooses to call the master of labour.

Peter Kropotkin, "Mutual Aid"*

If we take now the teachings which can be borrowed from the analysis of modern society, in connection with the body of evidence relative to the importance of mutual aid in the evolution of the animal world and of mankind, we may sum up our inquiry as follows.

In the animal world we have seen that the vast majority of species live in societies, and that they find in association the best arms for the struggle for life: understood, of course, in its wider Darwinian sense – not as a struggle for the sheer means of existence, but as a struggle against all natural conditions unfavourable to the species. The animal species in which individual struggle has been reduced to its narrowest limits, and the practice of mutual aid has attained the greatest development are invariably the most numerous, the most prosperous and the most open to further progress. The mutual protection which is obtained in this case, the possibility of attaining old age and of accumulating experience, the higher intellectual development, and the further growth of sociable habits, secure the maintenance of the species, its extension, and its further progressive evolution. The unsociable species, on the contrary, are doomed to decay.

Going next over to man, we found him living in clans and tribes at the very dawn of the stone age; we saw a wide series of social institutions developed already in the lower savage stage, in the clan and the tribe; and we found that the earliest tribal customs and habits gave to mankind the embryo of all the institutions which made later on the leading aspects of further progress. Out of the savage tribe grew up the barbarian village community; and a new, still wider, circle of social customs, habits and institutions, numbers of which are still alive among ourselves, was developed under the principles of common possession of a given territory and common defence of it, under the jurisdiction of the village folkmote, and in the federation of villages belonging, or supposed to belong, to one stem. And when new requirements induced men to make a new start, they made it in the city, which represented a double network of territorial units (village communities), connected with guilds – these latter arising out of the common prosecution of a given art or craft, or for mutual support and defence.

And finally, in the last two chapters facts were produced to show that, although the growth of the State on the pattern of Imperial Rome had put a violent end to all medieval institutions for mutual support, this new aspect of civilization could not last. The State, based upon loose aggregations of individuals and undertaking to be their only bond of union, did not answer its purpose. The mutual-aid tendency finally broke down its iron rules; it reappeared and reasserted itself in an infinity of associations which now tend to embrace all aspects of life and to take possession of all that is required by man for life and for reproducing the waste occasioned by life.

It will probably be remarked that mutual aid, even though it may represent one of the factors of evolution, covers nevertheless one aspect only of human relations; that by the side of this current, powerful though it may be, there is, and always has been, the other current – the self-assertion of the individual, not only in its efforts to attain personal or caste superiority, economical, political and spiritual, but also in its much more important although less evident function of breaking through the bonds, always prone to become crystallized, which the tribe, the village community, the city, and the State impose upon the individual. In other words, there is the self-assertion of the individual taken as a progressive element.

* Peter Kropotkin, extracted from *Mutual Aid: A Factor of Evolution*, edited and translated by Paul Avrich (New York: New York University Press, 1972). Originally published 1902.

It is evident that no review of evolution can be complete, unless these two dominant currents are analyzed. However, the self-assertion of the individual or of groups of individuals, their struggles for superiority, and the conflicts which resulted therefrom, have already been analysed, described, and glorified from time immemorial. In fact, up to the present time, this current alone has received attention from the epical poet, the annalist, the historian and the sociologist. History, such as it has hitherto been written, is almost entirely a description of the ways and means by which theocracy, military power, autocracy and, later on, the richer classes' rule have been promoted, established and maintained. The struggles between these forces make, in fact, the substance of history. We may thus take the knowledge of the individual factor in human history as granted – even though there is full room for a new study of the subject on the lines just alluded to; while, on the other side, the mutual-aid factor has been hitherto totally lost sight of; it was simply denied, or even scoffed at, by the writers of the present and past generation. It was therefore necessary to show, first of all, the immense part which this factor plays in the evolution of both the animal world and human societies. Only after this has been fully recognized will it be possible to proceed to a comparison between the two factors. …

As to the sudden industrial progress which has been achieved during our own century, and which is usually ascribed to the triumph of individualism and competition, it certainly has a much deeper origin than that. Once the great discoveries of the fifteenth century were made, especially that of the pressure of the atmosphere, supported by a series of advances in natural philosophy – and they were made under the medieval city organization – once these discoveries were made, the invention of the steam-motor, and all the revolution which the conquest of a new power implied, had necessarily to follow. If the medieval cities had lived to bring their discoveries to that point, the ethical consequences of the revolution effected by steam might have been different; but the same revolution in techniques and science would have inevitably taken place. It remains, indeed, an open question whether the general decay of industries which followed the ruin of the free cities, and was especially noticeable in the first part of the eighteenth century, did not considerably retard the appearance of the steam-engine as well as the consequent revolution in arts. When we consider the astounding rapidity of industrial progress from the twelfth to the fifteenth centuries – in weaving, working of metals, architecture and navigation, and ponder over the scientific discoveries which that industrial progress led to at the end of the fifteenth century – we must ask ourselves whether mankind was not delayed in its taking full advantage of these conquests when a general depression of arts and industries took place in Europe after the decay of medieval civilization. Surely it was not the disappearance of the artist-artisan, nor the ruin of large cities and the extinction of intercourse between them, which could favour the industrial revolution; and we know indeed that James Watt spent 20 or more years of his life in order to render his invention serviceable, because he could not find in the last century what he would have readily found in medieval Florence or Brügge, that is, the artisans capable of realizing his devices in metal, and of giving them the artistic finish and precision which the steam-engine requires.

To attribute, therefore, the industrial progress of our century to the war of each against all which it has proclaimed, is to reason like the man who, knowing not the causes of rain, attributes it to the victim he has immolated before his clay idol. For industrial progress, as for each other conquest over nature, mutual aid and close intercourse certainly are, as they have been, much more advantageous than mutual struggle.

However, it is especially in the domain of ethics that the dominating importance of the mutual-aid principle appears in full. That mutual aid is the real foundation of our ethical conceptions seems evident enough. But whatever the opinions as to the first origin of the mutual-aid feeling or instinct may be – whether a biological or a supernatural cause is ascribed to it – we must trace its existence as far back as to the lowest stages of the animal world; and from these stages we can follow its uninterrupted evolution, in opposition to a number of contrary agencies, through all degrees of human development, up to the present times. Even the new religions which were born from time to time – always at epochs when the mutual-aid principle was falling into decay in the theocracies and despotic States of the East, or at the decline of the Roman Empire – even the new religions have only reaffirmed that same principle. They found their first supporters among the humble, in the lowest, downtrodden layers of society, where the mutual-aid principle is the necessary foundation of everyday life; and the new forms of union which were introduced in the earliest Buddhist and Christian communities, in the Moravian brotherhoods and so on, took the character of a return to the best aspects of mutual aid in early tribal life.

Each time, however, that an attempt to return to this old principle was made, its fundamental idea itself was widened. From the clan it was extended to the stem, to the federation of stems, to the nation, and finally – in ideal, at least – to the whole of mankind. It was also refined at the same time. In primitive Buddhism, in primitive Christianity, in the writings of some of the Mussulman teachers, in the early movements of the Reform, and especially in the ethical and philosophical movements of the last century and of our own times, the total abandonment of the idea of revenge, or of 'due reward' – of good for good and evil for evil – is affirmed more and more vigorously. The higher conception of 'no revenge for wrongs,' and of freely giving more than one expects to receive from his neighbours, is proclaimed as being the real principle of morality – a principle superior to mere equivalence, equity, or justice, and more conducive to happiness. And man is appealed to be guided in his acts, not merely by love, which is always personal, or at the best tribal, but by the perception of his oneness with each human being. In the practice of mutual aid, which we can retrace to the earliest beginnings of evolution, we thus find the positive and undoubted origin of our ethical conceptions; and we can affirm that in the ethical progress of man, mutual support – not mutual struggle – has had the leading part. In its wide extension, even at the present time, we also see the best guarantee of a still loftier evolution of our race.

John Rawls, "The Rationality and Motivations of Parties in the Original Position"*

I have assumed throughout that the persons in the original position are rational. But I have also assumed that they do not know their conception of the good. This means that while they know that they have some rational plan of life, they do not know the details of this plan, the particular ends and interests which it is calculated to promote. How, then, can they decide which conceptions of justice are most to their advantage? Or must we suppose that they are reduced to mere guessing? To meet this difficulty, I postulate that they accept the account of the good touched upon in the preceding chapter: they assume that they normally prefer more primary social goods rather than less. Of course, it may turn out, once the veil of ignorance is removed, that some of them for religious or other reasons may not, in fact, want more of these goods. But from the standpoint of the original position, it is rational for the parties to suppose that they do want a larger share, since in any case they are not compelled to accept more if they do not wish to. Thus even though the parties are deprived of information about their particular ends, they have enough knowledge to rank the alternatives. They know that in general they must try to protect their liberties, widen their opportunities, and enlarge their means for promoting their aims whatever these are. Guided by the theory of the good and the general facts of moral psychology, their deliberations are no longer guesswork. They can make a rational decision in the ordinary sense.

The concept of rationality invoked here, with the exception of one essential feature, is the standard one familiar in social theory.[17] Thus in the usual way, a rational person is thought to have a coherent set of preferences between the options open to him. He ranks these options according to how well they further his purposes; he follows the plan which will satisfy more of his desires rather than less, and which has the greater chance of being successfully executed. The special assumption I make is that a rational individual does not suffer from envy. He is not ready to accept a loss for himself if only others have less as well. He is not downcast by the knowledge or perception that others have a larger index of primary social goods. Or at least this is true as long as the differences between himself and others do not exceed certain limits, and he does not believe that the existing inequalities are founded on injustice or are the result of letting chance work itself out for no compensating social purpose.

The assumption that the parties are not moved by envy raises certain questions. Perhaps we should also assume that they are not liable to various other feelings such as shame and humiliation. Now a satisfactory account of justice will eventually have to deal with these matters too, but for the present I shall leave these complications aside. Another objection to our procedure is that it is too unrealistic. Certainly men are afflicted with these feelings. How can a conception of justice ignore this fact? I shall meet this problem by dividing the

* John Rawls, extracted from *A Theory of Justice*, revised edition (Harvard University Press, 1999), pp. 123–7.

17 For this notion of rationality, see A. K. Sen, *Collective Choice and Social Welfare* (San Francisco: Holden-Day, Inc.) chapters 1 and 1* and K. J. Arrow, *Social Choice and Individual Values*, 2nd edition (New York: John Wiley, 1963), chapter II. In *A Theory of Justice*, Rawls also provides citations to other work, especially about rational choice under uncertainty.

argument for the principles of justice into two parts. In the first part, the principles are derived on the supposition that envy does not exist; while in the second, we consider whether the conception arrived at is feasible in view of the circumstances of human life.

One reason for this procedure is that envy tends to make everyone worse off. In this sense it is collectively disadvantageous. Presuming its absence amounts to supposing that in the choice of principles men should think of themselves as having their own plan of life which is sufficient for itself. They have a secure sense of their own worth so that they have no desire to abandon any of their aims provided others have less means to further theirs. I shall work out a conception of justice on this stipulation to see what happens. Later I shall try to show that when the principles adopted are put into practice, they lead to social arrangements in which envy and other destructive feelings are not likely to be strong. The conception of justice eliminates the conditions that give rise to disruptive attitudes. It is, therefore, inherently stable.

The assumption of mutually disinterested rationality, then, comes to this: the persons in the original position try to acknowledge principles which advance their system of ends as far as possible. They do this by attempting to win for themselves the highest index of primary social goods, since this enables them to promote their conception of the good most effectively whatever it turns out to be. The parties do not seek to confer benefits or to impose injuries on one another; they are not moved by affection or rancor. Nor do they try to gain relative to each other; they are not envious or vain. Put in terms of a game, we might say: they strive for as high an absolute score as possible. They do not wish a high or a low score for their opponents, nor do they seek to maximize or minimize the difference between their successes and those of others. The idea of a game does not really apply, since the parties are not concerned to win but to get as many points as possible judged by their own system of ends.

There is one further assumption to guarantee strict compliance. The parties are presumed to be capable of a sense of justice and this fact is public knowledge among them. This condition is to insure the integrity of the agreement made in the original position. It does not mean that in their deliberations the parties apply some particular conception of justice, for this would defeat the point of the motivation assumption. Rather, it means that the parties can rely on each other to understand and to act in accordance with whatever principles are finally agreed to. Once principles are acknowledged the parties can depend on one another to conform to them. In reaching an agreement, then, they know that their undertaking is not in vain: their capacity for a sense of justice insures that the principles chosen will be respected. It is essential to observe, however, that this assumption still permits the consideration of men's capacity to act on the various conceptions of justice. The general facts of human psychology and the principles of moral learning are relevant matters for the parties to examine. If a conception of justice is unlikely to generate its own support, or lacks stability, this fact must not be overlooked. For then a different conception of justice might be preferred. The assumption only says that the parties have a capacity for justice in a purely formal sense: taking everything relevant into account, including the general facts of moral psychology, the parties will adhere to the principles eventually chosen. They are rational in that they will not enter into agreements they know they cannot keep, or can do so only with great difficulty. Along with other considerations, they count the strains of commitment. Thus in assessing conceptions of justice the persons in the original position are to assume that the one they adopt will be strictly complied with. The consequences of their agreement are to be worked out on this basis.

With the preceding remarks about rationality and motivation of the parties the description of the original position is for the most part complete.

[...]

We can turn now to the choice of principles. But first I shall mention a few misunderstandings to be avoided. First of all, we must keep in mind that the parties in the original position are theoretically defined individuals. The grounds for their consent are set out by the description of the contractual situation and their preference for primary goods. Thus to say that the principles of justice would be adopted is to say how these persons would decide being moved in ways our account describes. Of course, when we try to simulate the original position in everyday life, that is, when we try to conduct ourselves in moral argument as its constraints require, we will presumably find that our deliberations and judgments are influenced by our special inclinations and attitudes. Surely it will prove difficult to correct for our various propensities and aversions in striving to adhere to the conditions of this idealized situation. But none of this affects the contention that in the original position rational persons so characterized would make a certain decision. This proposition belongs to the theory of justice. It is another question how well human beings can assume this role in regulating their practical reasoning.

Michael Sandel, "The Procedural Republic and the Unencumbered Self"*

We might begin by considering a certain moral and political vision. It is a liberal vision, and like most liberal visions gives pride of place to justice, fairness, and individual rights. Its core thesis is this: a just society seeks not to promote any particular ends, but enables its citizens to pursue their own ends, consistent with a similar liberty for all; it therefore must govern by principles that do not presuppose any particular conception of the good. What justifies these regulative principles above all is not that they maximize the general welfare, or cultivate virtue, or otherwise promote the good, but rather that they conform to the concept of *right*, a moral category given prior to the good, and independent of it.

This liberalism says, in other words, that what makes the just society just is not the *telos* or purpose or end at which it aims, but precisely its refusal to choose in advance among competing purposes and ends. In its constitution and its laws, the just society seeks to provide a framework within which its citizens can pursue their own values and ends, consistent with a similar liberty for others.

The ideal I've described might be summed up in the claim that the right is prior to the good, and in two senses: the priority of the right means first, that individual rights cannot be sacrificed for the sake of the general good (in this it opposes utilitarianism), and second, that the principles of justice that specify these rights cannot be premised on any particular vision of the good life. (In this it opposes teleological conceptions in general.)

This is the liberalism of much contemporary moral and political philosophy, most fully elaborated by Rawls, and indebted to Kant for its philosophical foundations.[18]

[...]

According to Kant, the right is "derived entirely from the concept of freedom in the external relationships of human beings, and has nothing to do with the end which all men have by nature [i.e., the aim of achieving happiness] or with the recognized means of attaining this end."[19] As such, it must have a basis prior to all empirical ends. Only when I am governed by principles that do not presuppose any particular ends am I free to pursue my own ends consistent with a similar freedom for all.

But this still leaves the question of what the basis of the right could possibly be. If it must be a basis prior to all purposes and ends, unconditioned even by what Kant calls "the special circumstances of human nature,"[20] where could such a basis conceivably be found? Given the stringent demands of the Kantian ethic, the moral law would seem almost to require a foundation in nothing; for any empirical precondition would undermine its priority. "Duty!" asks Kant at his most lyrical, "What origin is there worthy of thee, and where is to be found the root of thy noble descent which proudly rejects all kinship with the inclinations?"[21]

His answer is that the basis of the moral law is to be found in the *subject*, not the object of practical reason, a subject capable of an autonomous will. No empirical end, but rather "a subject of ends, namely a rational being himself, must be made the ground for all maxims of action."[22] Nothing other than what Kant calls "the subject of all possible ends himself" can give rise to the right, for only this subject is also the subject of an autonomous will. [...]

Who or what exactly *is* this subject? It is, in a certain sense, *us*. The moral law, afterall, is a law we give *ourselves;* we don't *find* it, we *will* it. That is how it (and we) escape the reign of nature and circumstance and merely empirical ends. But what is important to see is that the "we" who do the willing are not "we"qua particular persons, you and me, each for ourselves – the moral law is not up to us as individuals – but "we" qua participants in what Kant calls "pure practical reason," "we" qua participants in a transcendental subject.

[...]

* Michael Sandel, extracted from *Political Theory* (Sage Publications, 1984), pp. 81–96.

18 John Rawls, *A Theory of Justice* (Oxford: Oxford University Press, 1971). Immanuel Kant, *Groundwork of the Metaphysics of Morals*, translated by H. J. Paton (1785; New York: Harper and Row, 1956). Kant, *Critique of Pure Reason*, translated by Norman Kemp Smith (1781, 1787; London: Macmillan, 1929). Kant, *Critique of Practical Reason*, translated by L. W. Beck (1788; Indianapolis: Bobbs-Merrill, 1956). Kant, "On the Common Saying: 'This May Be True in Theory, But It Does Not Apply in Practice,'" in Hans Reiss, ed., *Kant's Political Writings* (1793; Cambridge: Cambridge University Press, 1970). Other recent versions of the claim for the priority of the right over good can be found in Robert Nozick, *Anarchy, State and Utopia* (New York: Basic Books, 1974); Ronald Dworkin, *Taking Rights Seriously* (London: Duckworth, 1977); Bruce Ackerman, *Social Justice in the Liberal State* (New Haven: Yale University Press, 1980).

19 Kant (1793), p. 73.

20 Kant (1785), p. 92.

21 Kant (1788), p. 89.

22 Kant (1785), p. 105.

As the subject is prior to its ends, so the right is prior to the good. Society is best arranged when it is governed by principles that do not presuppose any particular conception of the good, for any other arrangement would fail to respect persons as being capable of choice; it would treat them as objects rather than subjects, as means rather than ends in themselves.

We can see in this way how Kant's notion of the subject is bound up with the claim for the priority of right. But for those in the Anglo-American tradition, the transcendental subject will seem a strange foundation for a familiar ethic. Surely, one may think, we can take rights seriously and affirm the primacy of justice without embracing the *Critique of Pure Reason*. This, in any case, is the project of Rawls.

He wants to save the priority of right from the obscurity of the transcendental subject. Kant's idealist metaphysic, for all its moral and political advantage, cedes too much to the transcendent, and wins for justice its primacy only by denying it its human situation. "To develop a viable Kantian conception of justice," Rawls writes, "the force and content of Kant's doctrine must be detached from its background in transcendental idealism" and recast within the "canons of a reasonable empiricism."[23] And so Rawls' project is to preserve Kant's moral and political teaching by replacing Germanic obscurities with a domesticated metaphysic more congenial to the Anglo-American temper. This is the role of the original position.

From transcendental subject to unencumbered self

The original position tries to provide what Kant's transcendental argument cannot – a foundation for the right that is prior to the good, but still situated in the world. Sparing all but essentials, the original position works like this: it invites us to imagine the principles we would choose to govern our society if we were to choose them in advance, before we knew the particular persons we would be – whether rich or poor, strong or weak, lucky or unlucky – before we knew even our interests or aims or conceptions of the good. These principles – the ones we would choose in that imaginary situation – are the principles of justice. What is more, if it works, they are principles that do not presuppose any particular ends.

What they *do* presuppose is a certain picture of the person, of the way we must be if we are beings for whom justice is the first virtue. This is the picture of the unencumbered self, a self understood as prior to and independent of purposes and ends.

Now the unencumbered self describes first of all the way we stand toward the things we have, or want, or seek. It means there is always a distinction between the values I *have* and the person I *am*. To identify any characteristics as *my* aims, ambitions, desires, and so on, is always to imply some subject "me" standing behind them, at a certain distance, and the shape of this "me" must be given prior to any of the aims or attributes I bear. One consequences of this distance is to put the self *itself* beyond the reach of its experience, to secure its identity once and for all. Or to put the point another way, it rules out the possibility of what we might call *constitutive* ends. No role or commitment could define me so completely that I could not understand myself without it. No project could be so essential that turning away from it would call into question the person I am.

For the unencumbered self, what matters above all, what is most essential to our personhood, are not the ends we choose but our capacity to choose them.

[...]

The unencumbered self and the ethic it inspires, taken together, hold out a liberating vision. Freed from the dicates of nature and the sanction of social roles, the human subject is installed as sovereign, cast as the author of the only moral meanings there are. As participants in pure practical reason, or as parties to the original position, we are free to construct principles of justice unconstrained by an order of value antecedently given. And as actual, individual selves, we are free to choose our purposes and ends unbound by such an order, or by custom or tradition or inherited status. So long as they are not unjust, our conceptions of the good carry weight, whatever they are, simply in virtue of our having chosen them. We are, in Rawls' words, "self-originating sources of valid claims."[24]

This is an exhilarating promise, and the liberalism it animates is perhaps the fullest expression of the Enlightenment's quest for the self-defining subject. But is it true? Can we make sense of our moral and political life by the light of the self-image it requires? [...]

Justice and community

[...]

I do not think we can, at least not without cost to those loyalties and convictions whose moral force consists

23 Rawls, "The Basic Structure as Subject," *American Philosophical Quarterly* (1977), p. 165.

24 Rawls, "Kantian Constructivism in Moral Theory," *Journal of Philosophy* 77 (1980), p. 543.

partly in the fact that living by them is inseparable from understanding ourselves as the particular persons we are – as members of this family or community or nation or people, as bearers of that history, as citizens of this republic. Allegiances such as these are more than values I happen to have, and to hold, at a certain distance. They go beyond the obligations I voluntarily incur and the "natural duties" I owe to human beings as such. They allow that to some I owe more than justice requires or even permits, not by reason of agreements I have made but instead in virtue of those more or less enduring attachments and commitments that, taken together, partly define the person I am.

To imagine a person incapable of constitutive attachments such as these is not to conceive an ideally free and rational agent, but to imagine a person wholly without character, without moral depth. For to have character is to know that I move in a history I neither summon nor command, which carries consequences nonetheless for my choices and conduct. It draws me closer to some and more distant from others; it makes some aims more appropriate, others less so. As a self-interpreting being, I am able to reflect on my history and in this sense to distance myself from it, but the distance is always precarious and provisional, the point of reflection never finally secured outside the history itself. But the liberal ethic puts the self beyond the reach of its experience, beyond deliberation and reflection. Denied the expansive self-understandings that could shape a common life, the liberal self is left to lurch between detachment on the one hand, and entanglement on the other. Such is the fate of the unencumbered self, and its liberating promise.

Bhikhu Parekh, "Conceptualizing Human Beings"*

The question whether human beings have a nature cannot be answered unless we are agreed on what we mean by human nature.[25] This is not easy. Some writers take a substantive or thick view, and others a largely formal view of it. Some take a teleological and others a mechanistic view. For some it determines, and for others it only disposes human beings to act in certain ways. Some define it to mean all that characterizes human beings including what they share in common with animals; for others it only refers to what is distinctive to them and marks them off as a distinct species. Given these and other differences, the best way to discuss whether or not human beings have a nature is to concentrate on the minimum on which different views agree or can be expected to agree. [...]

Such a minimalist view of human nature has several advantages. It encompasses a wide variety of views and does not arbitrarily exclude inconvenient ones. It is true that no view, however minimalist, can do equal justice to all of them, for it has to draw a line somewhere and cannot avoid some degree of selectivity. However, as long as the selectivity is based on good reasons and is not too narrow, it provides the only practical basis of discussion. Second, the minimalist view enables us to concentrate on the crucial questions raised by the concept of human nature without getting sidetracked into important but irrelevant questions about its content and mode of operation. Third, if we can show that the concept is problematic even in its minimalist sense, it is bound to be even more so when defined in stronger or more substantive terms.

Minimally, the term human nature refers to those permanent and universal capacities, desires and dispositions – in short, properties – that all human beings share by virtue of belonging to a common species. The properties are permanent in the sense that they continue to belong to human beings as long as they remain what they are, and that, if they were to undergo changes, human nature itself would be deemed to have changed. They are universal in the sense that they are shared by human beings in all ages and societies. This does not mean that there are no exceptions, but rather that those lacking them are to that extent defective or at least not normal. The properties are acquired by virtue of belonging to the human species and not socially or culturally derived. They belong to human beings 'by nature', as

* Bhikhu Parekh, extracted from *Rethinking Multiculturalism*, 2nd edn. (New York: Palgrave Macmillan, 2006), pp. 114–36.

25 The inquiry into human nature presupposes that humans can and should be clearly distinguished from non-humans, that nature and culture can and should be separated, that we can discover human nature fairly accurately, that things of great significance depend on it, and so on. For reasons too complex to discuss here, these and related assumptions became central to Western thought in a way they did not in Hindu, Buddhist, Confucian and Islamic traditions, which have therefore generally taken only limited interest in human nature. In the Western tradition itself Sophists devoted little attention to it. Even Plato is primarily concerned with the structure and hierarchy of the human psyche rather than its constitutive tendencies. Aristotle seems to mark a turning point. The concept of human nature acquires enormous importance in Christianity.

part of their inherited physical and psychological constitution, and constitute their species heritage. Although society might modify them and regulate their expression, it can never altogether eliminate them or alter their inherent tendencies. Finally, the properties are not inert and indeterminate but have a specific character or content and operate in a particular manner. To say that all human beings have a propensity or instinct to preserve themselves is to say that they tend to do all they can to avoid death and life-threatening situations. And to say that they seek to realize themselves, possess an inherent love of God, strive for happiness, have an inclination to do evil, or are naturally curious is to say that they would, as a rule, be inclined to act in a manner intimated by these impulses.

Human beings do seem to have a nature in this sense. They have a common physical and mental structure and all that follows from it. They share a common anatomy and physiological processes, stand erect, possess an identical set of sense organs which operate in an identical manner, have common bodily-derived desires, and so forth. [...]

Thanks to their shared physical and mental structure, human beings also share certain basic needs and common conditions of growth. They require a prolonged period of nurture and all that that implies. They also need to acquire a large body of skills, abilities and dispositions as well as a reasonably coherent conception of the world in order to hold themselves together, build up a stable self, and cope with the inevitable demands of personal and social life. In order to acquire these, they require a stable natural and social environment, close personal relationships, a measure of emotional security, moral norms, and so forth.

Human beings also go through common life-experiences. They mature slowly, reach their peak and begin to suffer losses of or diminutions in their physical and mental powers, grow old, and die. They see their loved ones die, anticipate their own death, experience joys and sorrows and moments of elation and happiness as well as disappointments and frustrations, and undergo changes of mood. They fall in and out of love, are drawn to some and not to others, cannot realize all their dreams and satisfy all their desires, make mistakes, possess limited sympathies, and fall prey to temptations. They carry a large and dimly grasped unconscious all through their lives, and sometimes not only cannot make sense of themselves but are positively puzzled by their thoughts and feelings.

Human beings, then, do seem to have a nature in the sense defined earlier – that is, capacities, emotions and dispositions which are universal, relatively permanent, acquired as part of their species-heritage or by nature, and which tend to generate certain kinds of actions. [...]

While acknowledging that human beings have a shared nature, we may legitimately question its conceptualization, interpretation, the explanatory and normative weight put upon it, and the ways in which it is related to culture in much of traditional philosophy.

[...]

Contrary to what most philosophers have assumed, all attempts to discover human nature beyond what is inherent in their physico-mental structure are open to two great difficulties. Since human beings have always led organized lives, their nature has been so deeply shaped by layers of social influences that we have no direct access to it in its raw or pristine form, and cannot easily detach what is natural from what is manmade or social. Some of those who appreciated the difficulty mistakenly thought they could gain access to human nature by examining the behaviour of our humanoid ancestors, primitive people, children, civilized people in times of social disintegration, or what is universally common. Since our humanoid ancestors have left no records of their thoughts and feelings, we have no knowledge of their nature, and in any case there is no good reason to assume that we must necessarily share a common nature with them. So-called primitive peoples are socially organized and shaped, and do not reveal raw human nature. Children are subject to deep social influences from the moment of their birth and even perhaps conception. When societies disintegrate, their members' behaviour does not reveal raw human nature but their socially shaped character in a climate of chaos and uncertainty. And what is common to all mankind could as well be a result of common processes of socialization rather than an expression of a common nature. In short, human nature is not a brute and empirically verifiable fact, but an inference or a theory which we have no reliable means of corroborating.[26]

Another great difficulty relates to the students of human nature, who are themselves deeply shaped by their society and remain prone to the understandable tendency to mistake the normal and the familiar for the natural. This tendency is further compounded by the fact that an appeal to human nature has unique explanatory and normative advantages. To say that a particular form of behaviour is natural is to forswear the need to look for

[26] C. Geertz, *The Interpretation of Cultures* (New York: Basic Books, 1973), p. 35, n. 49.

further or another explanation. And to say that certain values or ways of life are alone consistent with human nature is to give them a moral finality and to delegitimize alternative values and ways of life. Even the most rigorous and scrupulous philosophers have sometimes availed themselves of the easy advantages offered by appeals to human nature, and argued on the basis of little hard evidence that human beings have an innate tendency to pursue knowledge, love God, maximize pleasure, seek self-realization, and so on and that only such a life gives them 'true' happiness or fulfilment and is worthy of them. This does not mean that we should not appeal to human nature or seek to discover it, but rather that all references to it should be subjected to the strictest scrutiny and viewed with a healthy dose of skepticism.

Fourth and finally, human beings are culturally embedded in the sense that they are born into, raised in and deeply shaped by their cultural communities.[27] Thanks to human creativity, geographical conditions, historical experiences, and so on, different societies develop different systems of meaning, ways of looking at the world, ideals of excellence, traits of temperament and forms of moral and social life, giving different orientation and structure to universally shared human capacities and desires and cultivating wholly new ones of their own. Although skin colour, gender, height and other physical features are universally shared, they are all differently conceptualized and acquire different meaning and significance in different societies. In some societies skin colour is given a deeper metaphysical meaning and made the basis of a differential distribution of power and status, in others it is not even noticed. In some societies male–female distinctions are drawn fairly sharply; in others they are seen as overlapping categories, each sex carrying a bit of the other within itself, so that these societies draw no rigid distinction between masculine and feminine qualities or even between homosexuality and heterosexuality. In some, sexuality is viewed as a natural bodily function like 'scratching an itch', as Bentham once put it, and subjected to the fewest constraints; in others it is invested with cosmic significance, viewed as a quasi-divine activity of generating life, and surrounded with mystique and taboos. Even something as basic and inevitable as death is viewed and experienced differently in different cultures. In some it is a brute fact of life, like the falling of leaves or the diurnal setting of the sun, and arouses no strong emotions; in some others it is a release from the world of sorrow and embraced with joy; in yet others it is a symbol of human weakness, a constant reminder of inadequate human mastery over nature, and accepted with such varied emotions as regret, puzzle, incomprehension and bitterness. Different cultures, again, take different views of human life and the individual's relation to his or her body, leading to very different attitudes to suicide and manners of committing it.

Differences at the level of human capacities, emotions, motivations, values, ideals of excellence and so forth are just as great and in some respects even greater.[28] Although all human beings have the capacity to reason, different cultures cherish and cultivate different forms of it. The Greek *logos*, the Roman *ratio*, the Cartesian *cogito*, the Hobbesian reckoning with consequences, the Benthamite arithmetical reasoning, the Hegelian dialectic and the Indian *buddhi* and *prajnà* represent very different forms of human reason. Some cultures disjoin reason and feeling whereas others find their separation incomprehensible. Some distinguish between theoretical and practical reason or between thinking and willing, whereas others believe that reason has both theoretical and practical impulses built into its very structure. Different cultures also encourage different emotions and feelings. Some develop the concept of conscience and know what guilt and remorse mean; others find these emotions incomprehensible. Some have a poorly developed sense of history and cannot make sense of the desire to gain historical immortality or leave a footnote or a paragraph in history. Some others lack a sense of tradition and cannot make sense of the desire to be worthy of one's ancestors, loyal to their memories, or to cherish their heritage. Although all human beings require a prolonged period of nurture, the mode of upbringing and periodization of life vary greatly. In some cultures children graduate into adulthood without passing through adolescence, in others they never outgrow the latter. Some stress sharp individuation, self-enclosure and a tightly centred

[27] Peter Berger and Thomas Luckman, eds., *The Social Construction of Reality* (Harmondsworth: Penguin, 1966), pp. 67, 69, rightly argue that "human-ness is socio-culturally variable" because "*Homo Sapiens* is always and in the same measure *homo socius*." See also Geertz (1973 op. cit., pp. 43 f, 50–1) where he challenges the widely shared assumption that only what is uniformly shared by humans constitutes their humanity.

[28] For a brief but fascinating analysis of the distinctive style of Indian thought, see A. K. Ramanujan, "Is There an Indian Way of Thinking? An Informal Essay," in M. McKim, ed., *India Through Hindu Categories* (Delhi: Sage, 1990). George Fletcher, "The Case for Linguistic Self-Defense," in R. McKim and J. McMahon, eds., *The Morality of Nationalism* (Princeton: Princeton University Press, 1977) offers a fascinating account of the ties between English language and the common law tradition, and the way in which the former structures legal reasoning.

self; others encourage overlapping selves, openness to others, and a loosely held self.

Different cultures, then, define and constitute human beings and come to terms with the basic problems of human life in their own different ways. Cultures are not superstructures built upon identical and unchanging foundations, or manifestations of a common human essence, but unique human creations that reconstitute and give different meaning and orientation to those properties that all human beings share in common, add new ones of their own, and give rise to different kinds of human beings. Since human beings are culture-creating and capable of creative self-transformation, they cannot passively inherit a shared nature in the same way that animals do.

We might press the point further. As members of a cultural community, human beings *acquire* certain tendencies and dispositions, in some cases as deep and powerful as those they are deemed to possess by nature. Human beings do seek to preserve themselves, but they might develop such a strong religious commitment or patriotic spirit that they think nothing of dying for their religion or their country. They have now acquired a 'second nature' which overrides their 'natural' nature. Since the willingness to die for one's religion or country is not universally shared, it is not a part of universal human nature. However, since it is part of their culturally derived nature, it constitutes their culturally specific or shared human nature. There is no reason why we cannot say with some Chinese philosophers that some components of human nature vary from culture to culture.

The same thing also happens at the individual level. Human beings might so shape themselves that a fierce sense of independence, an uncompromising commitment to integrity, or a passionate love of God or their fellow humans might become woven into their being and become an integral part of their nature. They then not only instinctively and effortlessly act on those inclinations but might even feel helplessly driven by them. These dispositions have the same force as the tendencies deemed to be inherent in their shared human nature, and are just as inseparable and ineradicable from their being. We often call them part of their character to emphasize the fact that they represent their achievements. However, character is not external to who they are, often has the same force as human nature, and constitutes *their* nature.

This means that human beings are articulated at three different but interrelated levels: what they share as members of a common species, what they derive from and share as members of a cultural community, and what they succeed in giving themselves as reflective individuals. All three are parts of their psychological and moral constitution and relate to three different dimensions of their being. What is more, since these are distinctive to them as human beings, they are all part of their human nature. It therefore makes perfect sense to talk of their distinct *individual* natures (as the Hindus and Buddhists do), their nature as members of particular *cultural communities* (as the traditional Chinese do), and their nature as members of the *human species* (as much Western thought has done over the centuries). To equate human nature with only the last is to take too narrow a view of it. Worse, it ontologically and morally privileges the species nature and marginalizes the other two.

[...]

Pluralist universalism

When we understand human beings along the lines I have suggested, the question whether there are universal moral values or norms and how we can judge other cultures appears in a different light. Broadly speaking, the question has received three answers; namely relativism, monism and minimum universalism.[29] Briefly and somewhat crudely, the relativist argues that since moral values are culturally embedded and since each culture is a self-contained whole, they are relative to each society and the search for universal moral values is a logically incoherent enterprise. The monist takes the opposite view that since moral values are derived from human nature, and since the latter is universally common, we can arrive at not only them but also the best way of combining them. The minimum universalist takes the intermediate position, arguing that we can arrive at a body of universal values but that they are few and constitute a kind of floor, or a moral threshold subject to which every society enjoys what Stuart Hampshire calls a 'licence for distinctness'.

[29] For a minimum universalism, see H. L. A. Hart, *The Concept of Law* (Oxford: Clarendon Press, 1961), Michael Walzer, *Thick and Thin: Moral Arguments at Home and Abroad* (Cambridge: Harvard University Press, 1994), and R, Tuck, "Rights and Pluralism," in J. Tully (ed.), *Philosophy in an Age of Pluralism: The Philosophy of Charles Taylor in Question* (Cambridge: Cambridge University Press, 1994). Walzer's "reiterative" universalism cannot easily explain how we can tease out the commonalities between the thick and relatively self-contained moral traditions and translate the categories of one into those of another. For good critiques of Walzer, see R. Bellamy, *Liberalism and Pluralism: Toward a Politics of Compromise* (London: Routledge, 1999, chapter 3) and Joseph Carens, *Culture, Citizenship, and Community* (Oxford: Oxford University Press, 2000, Introduction).

In the light of our discussion, relativism and monism are incoherent doctrines. Relativism ignores the cross-culturally shared human properties and is mistaken in its beliefs that a culture is a tightly integrated and self-contained whole, can be neatly individuated, and determines its members. Monism rests on an untenably substantive view of human nature, ignores the impossibility of deriving moral values from human nature alone, fails to appreciate its cultural mediation and reconstitution, and so on. There is much to be said for minimum universalism. It takes a minimalist view of human nature, appreciates both the cultural embeddedness of human beings and their universally shared properties, recognizes that while values can claim universal validity a way of life cannot, and so on. However, it suffers from several limitations. It naively assumes that the minimum universal values do not come into conflict, and that they are univocal and self-explanatory and mean the same thing in different cultures. Since it sees them as a set of uniform, passive and external constraints and uses them as mechanical yardsticks to judge all cultures, it also ignores the fact that different cultures are bound to balance, prioritize and relate them to their thick moral structures in their own different ways. It would seem that a dialectical and pluralist form of minimum universalism offers the most coherent response to moral and cultural diversity. As we shall see there are universal moral values and there is a creative interplay between them and the thick and complex moral structures of different societies, the latter domesticating and pluralizing the former and being in turn reinterpreted and revised in their light, thus leading to what I might call pluralist universalism.

Unlike Plato's Ideas, moral values are not self-subsistent entities occupying a transcendental realm of their own. They refer to things we consider worth cherishing and realizing in our lives. Since judgments of worth are based on reasons, values are things we have good reasons to cherish, which in our well-considered view deserve our allegiance and ought to form part of the good life. Universal moral values are those we have good reasons to believe to be worthy of the allegiance of all human beings, and are in that sense universally valid or binding. Moral values are meant for beings like us and intended to regulate our lives. Reasons relevant to a discussion of them are therefore of several kinds, such as our assessment of our moral capacities, what we take to be our basic tendencies and limits, the likely consequences of pursuing different values, their compatibility, the ease with which they can be combined into a coherent way of life, and the past and present experiences of societies that lived by them.

Although we might try to arrive at universal values by analysing human nature, universal moral consensus and so on, as philosophers have done over the centuries, the more satisfactory way to arrive at them is through a universal or cross-cultural dialogue.

[...]

In this context, the 1948 United Nations Declaration of Human Rights provides a useful starting point.[30] It was born out of the kind of cross-cultural dialogue referred to earlier and has a genuinely universal feel about it, which is why people all over the world continue to appeal to it, and all subsequent global or continental statements on the subject, while modifying it in some respects, endorse its basic values. These include respect for human life and dignity, equality of rights, respect for personal integrity and inviolability, recognition of basic human worth, and protection of fundamental human interests. These general values in turn entail and are realized by such measures as the prohibition of torture, genocide and slavery, freedom of association, liberty of conscience, equality before the law, fair trial, popular accountability of political power, protection of privacy, and respect for the integrity of familial and other intimate relationships.

[...]

The minimum universal values which we may legitimately insist upon are by their very nature general and need to be interpreted, prioritized, adopted to, and in case of conflict reconciled, in the light of the culture and circumstances of each society. Respect for human life is a universal value, but different societies disagree on when human life begins and ends and what respect for it entails. Again, respect for human life sometimes conflicts with that for human dignity or justice, as when a dying man has lost all control over his bodily functions, or injustices cannot be redressed without recourse to violence. Respect for human dignity requires that we should not humiliate or degrade others or treat them in a cruel and demeaning manner. What constitutes humiliation or cruelty, however, varies with cultures and cannot be universally legislated. In some societies a person would rather be slapped on her face than coldly ignored or subjected to verbal abuse. In some, human dignity is deemed to be violated when parents interfere

[30] For a good discussion of human rights across cultures, see A. An-Na'im, ed., *Human rights in Cross-Cultural Perspectives: A Quest for Consensus* (Philadelphia: University of Pennsylvania Press, 1992), especially the articles by the editor, Richard Falk, William Alford, Virginia Leary, Tom Svensson and Allan McChesney.

with their offsprings' choices of spouses; in others their intervention is taken as a sign that they care enough for their offsprings' dignity and well-being to press their advice on them and save them from making a mess of their lives. Different societies might also articulate, defend and rely on different mechanisms to realize universal values. Some might prefer the language of rights and claims and rely on the state to enforce these. Others might find it too individualist, aggressive, legalistic and state-centred and prefer the language of duty, relying on social conditioning and moral pressure to ensure that their members respect each other's dignity and refrain from harming each other's fundamental interests.

Universal values might also come into conflict with the freely-accepted central values of a cultural community. Women members of some indigenous and traditional communities freely commit themselves to vows of obedience and service to men in their lives and want to have nothing to do with equality. They might be brainwashed and we need to counter that, but should not assume that those who refuse to share our values are all victims of false consciousness. Torture is bad, but members of many religious sects and even some terrorist groups welcome it as a punishment or expiation for grave moral and spiritual or political lapses. Degrading human beings is bad, yet the training for priesthood in many Christian sects involves daily public exposure and humiliation of novices suspected of harbouring 'carnal' thoughts or reading prohibited literature. Human worth is a great value, but many religious groups and even some secular communities see fit to cultivate a feeling of personal and collective worthlessness. Indeed, it is difficult to think of a single universal value which is 'absolute' or inherently inviolable and may never in practice be overridden.[31] Since we rightly consider them as constitutive of the moral minimum due to and from human beings and assign them the greatest moral weight, we must require that the overriding factors be proportionate in their importance and of at least equal moral weight.

Since different societies may legitimately define, trade-off, prioritize, and realize the universal values differently, and even occasionally override some of them, the question arises of how we can prevent them from engaging in specious and self-serving moral reasoning and reinterpreting the values out of existence or emasculating their critical thrust. There is no foolproof way of doing so. All we can do is ask their spokesmen to justify their decisions when they appear unacceptable to us. If they can provide a strong and reasonably compelling defence, we should respect their decisions. If not, we should remain sceptical and press for change.

[31] See John Kekes, *The Morality of Pluralism* (Princeton: Princeton University Press, 1993, pp. 210ff.). We may, of course, make some values absolute by defining them in highly formal and abstract terms, but then they have no normative and critical content. For a balanced discussion of "Asian values," see Daniel Bell, *East Meets West: Human Rights and Democracy in Asia* (Oxford: Clarendon Press, 1999), J. T. H. Tang, ed., *Human rights and International Relations in Asia Pacific* (London: Pinter, 1995), and L. Mehbubani, "An Asian Perspective on Human Rights," in P. van Nees, ed., *Debating Human Rights* (London: Routledge, 1999).

Chapter 7

Images of Society

Introduction

The political communities in which humans live are numerous, varied, and complex. As a foundation for their political principles, political thinkers often reduce this variation and complexity to some basic assumptions that they stress. For example, we saw in the reading by Gentile that fascists believed communities should be homogeneous entities, composed of people united in their devotion to serving the nation. We have also seen in the reading by Macpherson that classical liberals held a model of society as "a collection of individuals with conflicting interests," leading to their endorsement of democratic capitalism.

Many questions can be asked about political communities. For example, which kinds of political communities – ranging from the local to the global – are most important and which kinds should command our greatest allegiance? Answers to these questions are best regarded as political principles and thus will be considered in Chapter 9. But there are questions about political communities that are even more basic, and answers to them can better be described as images of society than as political principles. They deal with what we stress when we observe or think about people who are joined together into on-going associations that influence their collective well-being. How do societies come about? What are their basic features? What should be the features of a good society? Should a society be comprised of people who are similar in specific ways? Insofar as people within societies are different, are there certain categories or groupings that should be acknowledged or emphasized?

Aristotle (384–322 BCE), the student of Plato who became an equally famous Greek philosopher, provided perhaps the first important statement about the origins of society. Various associations arise naturally out of the diverse but complementary needs of people living in proximity to one another. Individual humans cannot provide for all of their own needs, but a political community is "large enough to be nearly or quite self-sufficing," capable of providing its inhabitants access to a good life. Because no true human – but only a god or beast – can survive outside a political community, societies are more important than individuals (and smaller associations like the family).

Aristotle did not assume that political communities were completely united, enabling them to easily reach consensus on their common or complementary needs, but he and other ancients did not regard societies as simply comprised of individuals having opposing interests. As discussed in our selection by Macpherson in the last chapter, the image of society as composed of individuals having adversarial relations rose to prominence in the modern world in general and liberalism in particular. But if individuals living in proximity with one another were thought to have more opposing interests than Aristotle assumed, how are societies formed and maintained? The liberal answer – provided by Hobbes, Locke, Rawls, and many others – is by a social contract. According to Hobbes, men living solitary and adversarial existences in the state of nature would feel very insecure, but they would discover a law of nature: that peace was possible only if everyone joined together to create civil society. In so doing, each would surrender his complete liberty (to seek fulfillment of all their desires, including by seizing others' possessions) and agree to refrain from violating the security of others. But even if everyone took a sacred oath not to violate the rights of others, there must be some coercive power to compel men to uphold their promises. As part of their social contract, they would authorize some common power over them all, to keep them "in awe" because of its ability to punish those who disturb the social order created by their social contract. While liberals have provided various versions of this basic social contract, they generally recognize that the social contract is more hypothetical than actual; inhabitants of a particular territory do not actually live in a state of nature and leave it by explicitly coming to such an agreement. But they tacitly consent to such an agreement by observing its requirements, obeying a sovereign power, and enjoying the resulting peace.

A major difference between Hobbes' and Locke's social contract was that Hobbes thought a perpetual peace required an absolute sovereign, one that must be free to do whatever it deemed necessary to keep the peace, while Locke thought that a sovereign having absolute power could violate the legitimate rights of its subjects; this would engender rebellion (and thus threaten the peace). Revolutionaries in America and France at the end of the eighteenth century drew upon this idea to withdraw allegiance to abusive rulers, which led to Edmund Burke's famous challenge to the idea that a liberal society could be held together by a social contract. Society may be a contract, but it is not held together by the consent of individuals, by members who might withdraw their consent due to particular grievances. Instead, "each contract of each particular state is but a clause in the great primaeval contract of eternal society." For Burke and traditional conservatives, society was eternal and not created by the agreements and destroyed by the disagreement of men at some particular points in history. Societies – with all their particular norms of civility, rules of conduct, governmental authorities, and other traditional devices for maintaining social order – were a great and beneficial gift that each generation had inherited from its ancestors and were obligated to hand down intact to their successors.

While conservative theorists have emphasized the cooperative and unifying aspects of political community and liberals have emphasized the conflicts in societies that arise from competing individual interests, other theorists have images of society that see conflicts and interests as organized into larger aggregations of people. Marx famously envisioned society as divided on the basis of opposing classes. Those attuned to racial differences, of course, see society as divided on the basis of race and ethnicity. Feminists often see society as divided on the basis of gender and sexualities. Pluralists have thought that images of society that emphasize one line of social division, or a single cleavage, are too simple. They have claimed that societies are composed of many groups having a wide variety of complementary and competing interests and interrelationships. They doubt that any cleavage (such as class conflict) is fundamental or that some group (having a particular economic interest) dominates society. Societies can have many cleavages, with specific lines of conflict emerging on a contingent basis – in some social circumstances, at some points in history, and on some particular issues. In the final selection of this chapter, an excerpt from a book I wrote in 1991, *Critical Pluralism,* proposes a "comparative issues method" for analyzing and evaluating various lines of division. This method can detect which cleavages are most common in particular communities, which if any sides on these cleavages is dominant, and whether there might be inequalities in power that lack reasonable explanations. While my application of this method is limited to the community in which I resided during the 1980s, I failed to discover domination by a particular interest, but I did find many persistent lines of cleavage, and inequalities in responsiveness to those on either side of these conflicts. Most of these inequalities had explanations, and perhaps most of these were "reasonable," but there seemed to be an unexplained bias in favor of the middle class. Whether this conception of contingent cleavages constitutes a thin image of society that is agreeable to all pluralists is perhaps doubtful, but I am still offering it!

Aristotle, "The Natural Origins of Political Associations"*

Every state is a community of some kind, and every community is established with a view to some good; for mankind always act in order to obtain that which they think good. But, if all communities aim at some good, the state or political community, which is the highest of all, and which embraces all the rest, aims at good in a greater degree than any other, and at the highest good.

Some people think that the qualifications of a statesman, king, householder, and master are the same, and that they differ, not in kind, but only in the number of their subjects. For example, the ruler over a few is called

* Aristotle, in *Politics*, translated by Benjamin Jowett, available at http://classics.mit.edu/Aristotle/politics.1.one.html, accessed April 28, 2008. Originally published 350 BCE.

a master; over more, the manager of a household; over a still larger number, a statesman or king, as if there were no difference between a great household and a small state. The distinction which is made between the king and the statesman is as follows: when the government is personal, the ruler is a king; when, according to the rules of the political science, the citizens rule and are ruled in turn, then he is called a statesman.

But all this is a mistake; for governments differ in kind, as will be evident to any one who considers the matter according to the method which has hitherto guided us. As in other departments of science, so in politics, the compound should always be resolved into the simple elements or least parts of the whole. We must therefore look at the elements of which the state is composed, in order that we may see in what the different kinds of rule differ from one another, and whether any scientific result can be attained about each one of them.

He who thus considers things in their first growth and origin, whether a state or anything else, will obtain the clearest view of them. In the first place there must be a union of those who cannot exist without each other; namely, of male and female, that the race may continue (and this is a union which is formed, not of deliberate purpose, but because, in common with other animals and with plants, mankind have a natural desire to leave behind them an image of themselves), and of natural ruler and subject, that both may be preserved. For that which can foresee by the exercise of mind is by nature intended to be lord and master, and that which can with its body give effect to such foresight is a subject, and by nature a slave; hence master and slave have the same interest. [...]

The family is the association established by nature for the supply of men's everyday wants, and the members of it are called by Charondas 'companions of the cupboard,' and by Epimenides the Cretan, 'companions of the manger.' But when several families are united, and the association aims at something more than the supply of daily needs, the first society to be formed is the village. And the most natural form of the village appears to be that of a colony from the family, composed of the children and grandchildren, who are said to be suckled 'with the same milk.' And this is the reason why Hellenic states were originally governed by kings; because the Hellenes were under royal rule before they came together, as the barbarians still are. Every family is ruled by the eldest, and therefore in the colonies of the family the kingly form of government prevailed because they were of the same blood. As Homer says:

> "Each one gives law to his children and to his wives."

For they lived dispersedly, as was the manner in ancient times. Wherefore men say that the Gods have a king, because they themselves either are or were in ancient times under the rule of a king. For they imagine, not only the forms of the Gods, but their ways of life to be like their own.

When several villages are united in a single complete community, large enough to be nearly or quite self-sufficing, the state comes into existence, originating in the bare needs of life, and continuing in existence for the sake of a good life. And therefore, if the earlier forms of society are natural, so is the state, for it is the end of them, and the nature of a thing is its end. For what each thing is when fully developed, we call its nature, whether we are speaking of a man, a horse, or a family. Besides, the final cause and end of a thing is the best, and to be self-sufficing is the end and the best.

Hence it is evident that the state is a creation of nature, and that man is by nature a political animal. And he who by nature and not by mere accident is without a state, is either a bad man or above humanity; he is like the

> "Tribeless, lawless, hearthless one,"

whom Homer denounces – the natural outcast is forthwith a lover of war; he may be compared to an isolated piece at draughts.

Now, that man is more of a political animal than bees or any other gregarious animals is evident. Nature, as we often say, makes nothing in vain, and man is the only animal whom she has endowed with the gift of speech. And whereas mere voice is but an indication of pleasure or pain, and is therefore found in other animals (for their nature attains to the perception of pleasure and pain and the intimation of them to one another, and no further), the power of speech is intended to set forth the expedient and inexpedient, and therefore likewise the just and the unjust. And it is a characteristic of man that he alone has any sense of good and evil, of just and unjust, and the like, and the association of living beings who have this sense makes a family and a state.

Further, the state is by nature clearly prior to the family and to the individual, since the whole is of necessity prior to the part; for example, if the whole body be destroyed, there will be no foot or hand, except in an equivocal sense, as we might speak of a stone hand; for when destroyed the hand will be no better than that. But things are defined by their working and power; and we ought not to say that they are the same when they no longer have their proper quality, but only that they have the same name. The proof that the state is a creation of nature and prior to the individual is that the individual, when isolated, is not self-sufficing; and therefore he is like a part in relation to the whole. But he who is unable to live in society, or who has no need because he is sufficient for himself, must be either a beast or a god: he is no part of a state. A social instinct is implanted in all men by nature, and yet he who first founded the state was the greatest of benefactors. For man, when perfected, is the best of animals, but, when separated from law and justice, he is the worst of all; since armed injustice is the more dangerous, and he is equipped at birth with arms, meant to be used by intelligence and virtue, which he may use for the worst ends. Wherefore, if he have not virtue, he is the most unholy and the most savage of animals, and the most full of lust and gluttony. But justice is the bond of men in states, for the administration of justice, which is the determination of what is just, is the principle of order in political society.

Thomas Hobbes, "The Contractual Origins of Society"*

Of the first and second natural laws, and of contracts

Right of nature what. THE RIGHT OF NATURE, which writers commonly call *jus naturale*, is the liberty each man hath, to use his own power, as he will himself, for the preservation of his own nature; that is to say, of his own life; and consequently, of doing any thing, which in his own judgment, and reason, he shall conceive to be the aptest means thereunto.

Liberty what. By LIBERTY, is understood, according to the proper signification of the word, the absence of external impediments: which impediments, may oft take away part of a man's power to do what he would; but cannot hinder him from using the power left him, according as his judgment, and reason shall dictate to him.

A law of nature what. Difference of right and law. A LAW OF NATURE, *lex naturalis*, is a precept or general rule, found out by reason, by which a man is forbidden to do that, which is destructive of his life, or taketh away the means of preserving the same; and to omit that, by which he thinketh it may be best preserved. For though they that speak of this subject, use to confound *jus*, and *lex*, *right* and *law*: yet they ought to be distinguished; because RIGHT, consisteth in liberty to do, or to forbear: whereas LAW, determineth, and bindeth to one of them: so that law, and right, differ as much, as obligation, and liberty; which in one and the same matter are inconsistent.

Naturally every man has right to every thing. The fundamental law of nature. And because the condition of man, as hath been declared in the precedent chapter, is a condition of war of every one against every one; in which case every one is governed by his own reason; and there is nothing he can make use of, that may not be a help unto him, in preserving his life against his enemies; it followeth, that in such a condition, every man has a right to every thing; even to one another's body. And therefore, as long as this natural right of every man to every thing endureth, there can be no security to any man, how strong or wise soever he be, of living out the time, which nature ordinarily alloweth men to live. And consequently it is a precept, or general rule of reason, *that every man, ought to endeavour peace, as far as he has hope of obtaining it; and when he cannot obtain it, that he may seek, and use, all helps, and advantages of war.* The first branch of which rule, containeth the first, and fundamental law of nature; which is, *to seek peace, and follow it.* The second, the sum of the right of nature; which is, *by all means we can, to defend ourselves.*

The second law of nature. From this fundamental law of nature, by which men are commanded to endeavour peace, is derived this second law; *that a man be willing, when others are so too, as far-forth, as for peace, and defence of himself he shall think it necessary, to lay down this right to all things; and be contented with so much liberty against other men, as he would allow other men against himself.* For as long as every man holdeth this right, of doing any thing he liketh; so long are all men in the condition of war. But if other men will not lay down their right, as well as he; then there is no reason for any one, to divest himself of his: for that were to expose himself to prey, which no man is bound to, rather than to dispose himself to peace. This is that law of the Gospel; *whatsoever you require that others should do to you, that do ye to them.* And that law of all men, *quod tibi fieri non vis, alteri ne feceris.* [...]

Renouncing a right, what it is. Transferring right what. Obligation. Duty. Injustice. Right is laid aside, either by simply renouncing it; or by transferring it to another. By *simply* RENOUNCING; when he cares not to whom the benefit thereof redoundeth. By TRANSFERRING; when he intendeth the benefit thereof to some certain person, or persons. And when a man hath in either manner abandoned, or granted away his right; then he is said to be OBLIGED, OR BOUND, not to hinder those, to whom such right is granted, or abandoned, from the benefit of it. [...]

* Thomas Hobbes, extracted from chapters 14 and 15 of *The Leviathan*, edited by Michael Oakeshott (London: Collier-Macmillan Ltd, 1962). Originally published 1651.

Not all rights are alienable. Whensoever a man transferreth his right, or renounceth it; it is either in consideration of some right reciprocally transferred to himself; or for some other good he hopeth for thereby. For it is a voluntary act: and of the voluntary acts of every man, the object is some *good to himself.* And therefore there be some rights, which no man can be understood by any words, or other signs, to have abandoned, or transferred. As first a man cannot lay down the right of resisting them, that assault him by force, to take away his life; because he cannot be understood to aim thereby, at any good to himself. The same may be said of wounds, and chains, and imprisonment; both because there is no benefit consequent to such patience; as there is to the patience of suffering another to be wounded, or imprisoned: as also because a man cannot tell, when he seeth men proceed against him by violence, whether they intend his death or not. And lastly the motive, and end for which this renouncing, and transferring of right is introduced, is nothing else but the security of a man's person, in his life, and in the means of so preserving life, as not to be weary of it. And therefore if a man by words, or other signs, seem to despoil himself of the end, for which those signs were intended; he is not to be understood as if he meant it, or that it was his will; but that he was ignorant of how such words and actions were to be interpreted.

Contract what. The mutual transferring of right, is that which men call CONTRACT.

[...]

Signs of contract express. Promise. Signs of contract, are either *express*, or *by inference.* Express, are words spoken with understanding of what they signify: and such words are either of the time *present*, or *past;* as, *I give, I grant, I have given, I have granted, I will that this be yours:* or of the future; as, *I will give, I will grant:* which words of the future are called PROMISE.

Signs of contract by inference. Signs by inference, are sometimes the consequence of words; sometimes the consequence of silence; sometimes the consequence of actions; sometimes the consequence of forbearing an action: and generally a sign by inference, of any contract, is whatsoever sufficiently argues the will of the contractor.

[...]

Covenants of mutual trust, when invalid. If a covenant be made, wherein neither of the parties perform presently, but trust one another; in the condition of mere nature, which is a condition of war of every man against every man, upon any reasonable suspicion, it is void: but if there be a common power set over them both, with right and force sufficient to compel performance, it is not void. For he that performeth first, has no assurance the other will perform after; because the bonds of words are too weak to bridle men's ambition, avarice, anger, and other passions, without the fear of some coercive power; which in the condition of mere nature, where all men are equal, and judges of the justness of their own fears, cannot possibly be supposed. And therefore he which performeth first, does but betray himself to his enemy; contrary to the right, he can never abandon, of defending his life, and means of living.

But in a civil estate, where there is a power set up to constrain those that would otherwise violate their faith, that fear is no more reasonable; and for that cause, he which by the covenant is to perform first, is obliged so to do.

[...]

Convenants extorted by fear are valid. Covenants entered into by fear, in the condition of mere nature, are obligatory. For example, if I covenant to pay a ransom, or service for my life, to an enemy; I am bound by it: for it is a contract, wherein one receiveth the benefit of life; the other is to receive money, or service for it; and consequently, where no other law, as in the condition of mere nature, forbiddeth the performance, the covenant is valid. Therefore prisoners of war, if trusted with the payment of their ransom, are obliged to pay it: and if a weaker prince, make a disadvantageous peace with a stronger, for fear; he is bound to keep it; unless, as hath been said before, there ariseth some new, and just cause of fear, to renew the war. And even in commonwealths, if I be forced to redeem myself from a thief by promising him money, I am bound to pay it, till the civil law discharge me. For whatsoever I may lawfully do without obligation, the same I may lawfully covenant to do through fear: and what I lawfully covenant, I cannot lawfully break.

[...]

A man's covenant not to defend himself is void. A covenant not to defend myself from force, by force, is always void. For, as I have showed before, no man can transfer, or lay down his right to save himself from death, wounds, and imprisonment, the avoiding whereof is the only end of laying down any right; and therefore the promise of not resisting force, in no covenant transferreth any right; nor is obliging. For though a man may covenant thus, *unless I do so, or so, kill me;* he cannot covenant thus, *unless I do so, or so, I will not resist you, when you come to kill me.* For man by nature chooseth the lesser evil, which is danger of death in resisting; rather than the greater, which is certain and present death in not resisting. And this is granted to be true by all men, in that they lead criminals to execution, and prison, with armed men, notwithstanding that such criminals have consented to the law, by which they are condemned.

[...]

The end of an oath. The form of an oath. The force of words, being, as I have formerly noted, too weak to hold men to the performance of their covenants; there are in man's nature, but two imaginable helps to strengthen it. And those are either a fear of the consequence of breaking their word; or a glory, or pride in appearing not to need to break it. This latter is a generosity too rarely found to be presumed on, especially in the pursuers of wealth, command, or sensual pleasure; which are the greatest part of mankind. The passion to be reckoned upon, is fear; whereof there be two very general objects: one, the power of spirits invisible; the other, the power of those men they shall therein offend. Of these two, though the former be the greater power, yet the fear of the latter is commonly the greater fear. The fear of the former is in every man, his own religion: which hath place in the nature of man before civil society. The latter hath not so; at least not place enough, to keep men to their promises; because in the condition of mere nature, the inequality of power is not discerned, but by the event of battle. So that before the time of civil society, or in the interruption thereof by war, there is nothing can strengthen a covenant of peace agreed on, against the temptations of avarice, ambition, lust, or other strong desire, but the fear of that invisible power, which they every one worship as God; and fear as a revenger of their perfidy. All therefore that can be done between two men not subject to civil power, is to put one another to swear by the God he feareth: which *swearing*, or OATH, is a *form of speech, added to a promise; by which he that promiseth, signifieth, that unless he perform, he renounceth the mercy of his God, or calleth to him for vengeance on himself.* Such was the heathen form, *Let* Jupiter *kill me else, as I kill this beast.* So is our form, *I shall do thus, and thus, so help me God.* And this, with the rites and ceremonies, which every one useth in his own religion, that the fear of breaking faith might be the greater.

[...]

Of other laws of nature

The third law of nature, justice. From that law of nature, by which we are obliged to transfer to another, such rights, as being retained, hinder the peace of mankind, there followeth a third; which is this, *that men perform their covenants made*: without which, covenants are in vain, and but empty words; and the right of all men to all things remaining, we are still in the condition of war.

Justice and injustice what. And in this law of nature, consisteth the fountain and original of JUSTICE. For where no covenant hath preceded, there hath no right been transferred, and every man has right to every thing; and consequently, no action can be unjust. But when a covenant is made, then to break it is *unjust:* and the definition of INJUSTICE, is no other than *the not performance of covenant.* And whatsoever is not unjust, is *just.*

Justice and propriety begin with the constitution of commonwealth. But because covenants of mutual trust, where there is a fear of not performance on either part, as hath been said in the former chapter, are invalid; though the original of justice be the making of covenants; yet injustice actually there can be none, till the cause of such fear be taken away; which while men are in the natural condition of war, cannot be done. Therefore before the names of just, and unjust can have place, there must be some coercive power, to compel men equally to the performance of their covenants, by the terror of some punishment, greater than the benefit they expect by the breach of their covenant: and to make good that propriety, which by mutual contract men acquire, in recompense of the universal right they abandon: and such power there is none before the erection of a commonwealth. And this is also to be gathered out of the ordinary definition of justice in the Schools: for they say, that *justice is the constant will of giving to every man his own.* And therefore where there is no *own*, that is no propriety, there is no injustice; and where there is no coercive power erected, that is, where there is no commonwealth, there is no propriety; all men having right to all things: therefore where there is no commonwealth, there nothing is unjust. So that the nature of justice, consisteth in keeping of valid covenants: but the validity of covenants begins not but with the constitution of a civil power, sufficient to compel men to keep them: and then it is also that propriety begins.

Justice not contrary to reason. The fool hath said in his heart, there is no such thing as justice; and sometimes also with his tongue; seriously alleging, that every man's conservation, and contentment, being committed to his own care, there could be no reason, why every man might not do what he thought conduced thereunto: and therefore also to make, or not make; keep, or not keep covenants, was not against reason, when it conduced to one's benefit. He does not therein deny, that there be covenants; and that they are sometimes broken, sometimes kept; and that such breach of them may be called injustice, and the observance of them justice: but he questioneth, whether injustice, taking away the fear of God, for the same fool hath said in his heart there is no God, may not sometimes stand with that reason, which dictateth to every man his own good; and particularly then, when it conduceth to such a benefit, as shall put a man in a condition, to neglect not only the dispraise, and revilings, but also the power of other men. The kingdom of God is gotten by violence: but what if it could be gotten by unjust violence? were it against reason so to get it, when it is impossible to receive hurt by it? and if it be not against reason, it is not against justice; or else justice is not to be approved for good. From such reasoning as this, successful wickedness hath obtained the name of virtue: and some that in all other things have disallowed the violation of faith; yet have allowed it, when it is for the getting of a kingdom. And the heathen that believed, that Saturn was deposed by his son Jupiter, believed nevertheless the same Jupiter to be the avenger of injustice: somewhat like to a piece of law in Coke's *Commentaries on Littleton;* where he says, if the right heir of the crown be attainted of treason; yet the crown shall descend to him, and *eo instante* the attainder be void: from which instances a man will be very prone to infer; that when the heir apparent of a kingdom, shall kill him that is in possession, though his father; you may call it injustice, or by what other name you will; yet it can never be against reason, seeing all the voluntary actions of men tend to the benefit of themselves; and those actions are most reasonable, that conduce most to their ends. This specious reasoning is nevertheless false.

For the question is not of promises mutual, where there is no security of performance on either side; as when there is no civil power erected over the parties promising; for such promises are no covenants: but either where one of the parties has performed already; or where there is a power to make him perform; there is the question whether it be against reason, that is, against the benefit of the other to perform, or not. And I say it is not against reason. For the manifestation whereof, we are to consider; first, that when a man doth a thing, which notwithstanding any thing can be foreseen, and reckoned on, tendeth to his own destruction, howsoever some accident which he could not expect, arriving may turn it to his benefit; yet such events do not make it reasonably or wisely done. Secondly, that in a condition of war, wherein every man to every man, for want of a common power to keep them all in awe, is an enemy, there is no man who can hope by his own strength, or wit, to defend himself from destruction, without the help of confederates; where every one expects the same defence by the confederation, that any one else does: and therefore he which declares he thinks it reason to deceive those that help him, can in reason expect no other means of safety, than what can be had from his own single power. He therefore that breaketh his covenant, and consequently declareth that he thinks he may with reason do so, cannot be received into any society, that unite themselves for peace and defence, but by the error of them that receive him; nor when he is received, be retained in it, without seeing the danger of their error; which errors a man cannot reasonably reckon upon as the means of his security: and therefore if he be left, or cast out of society, he perisheth; and if he live in society, it is by the errors of other men, which he could not foresee, nor reckon upon; and consequently against the reason of his preservation; and so, as all men that contribute not to his destruction, forbear him only out of ignorance of what is good for themselves.

As for the instance of gaining the secure and perpetual felicity of heaven, by any way; it is frivolous: there being but one way imaginable; and that is not breaking, but keeping of covenant.

And for the other instance of attaining sovereignty by rebellion; it is manifest, that though the event follow, yet because it cannot reasonably be expected, but rather the contrary; and because by gaining it so, others are taught to gain the same in like manner, the attempt thereof is against reason. Justice therefore, that is to say, keeping of covenant, is a rule of reason, by which we are forbidden to do any thing destructive to our life; and consequently a law of nature.

Edmund Burke, "The Great Primaeval Contract of Eternal Society"*

But one of the first and most leading principles on which the commonwealth and the laws are consecrated, is lest the temporary possessors and life-renters in it, unmindful of what they have received from their ancestors, or of what is due to their posterity, should act as if they were the entire masters; that they should not think it amongst their rights to cut off the entail, or commit waste on the inheritance, by destroying at their pleasure the whole original fabric of their society; hazarding to leave to those who come after them, a ruin instead of an habitation – and teaching these successors as little to respect their contrivances, as they had themselves respected the institutions of their forefathers. By this unprincipled facility of changing the state as often, and as much, and in as many ways as there are floating fancies

* Edmund Burke, extracted from *Reflections on the Revolution in France* (Anchor Books Edition, 1973), which is derived from *The Works of the Right Honorable Edmund Burke*, the Riverton edition (London, 1826), Volume 5. Originally published 1790.

or fashions, the whole chain and continuity of the commonwealth would be broken. No one generation could link with the other. Men would become little better than the flies of a summer.

And first of all the science of jurisprudence, the pride of the human intellect, which, with all its defects, redundancies, and errors, is the collected reason of ages, combining the principles of original justice with the infinite variety of human concerns, as a heap of old exploded errors, would be no longer studied. Personal self-sufficiency and arrogance (the certain attendants upon all those who have never experienced a wisdom greater than their own) would usurp the tribunal. Of course, no certain laws, establishing invariable grounds of hope and fear, would keep the actions of men in a certain course, or direct them to a certain end. Nothing stable in the modes of holding property, or exercising function, could form a solid ground on which any parent could speculate in the education of his offspring, or in a choice for their future establishment in the world. No principles would be early worked into the habits. As soon as the most able instructor had completed his laborious course of institution, instead of sending forth his pupil, accomplished in a virtuous discipline, fitted to procure him attention and respect, in his place in society, he would find every thing altered; and that he had turned out a poor creature to the contempt and derision of the world, ignorant of the true grounds of estimation. Who would insure a tender and delicate sense of honour to beat almost with the first pulses of the heart, when no man could know what would be the test of honour in a nation, continually varying the standard of its coin? No part of life would retain its acquisitions. Barbarism with regard to science and literature, unskilfulness with regard to arts and manufactures, would infallibly succeed to the want of a steady education and settled principle; and thus the commonwealth itself would, in a few generations, crumble away, be disconnected into the dust and powder of individuality, and at length dispersed to all the winds of heaven.

To avoid therefore the evils of inconstancy and versatility, ten thousand times worse than those of obstinacy and the blindest prejudice, we have consecrated the state, that no man should approach to look into its defects or corruptions but with due caution; that he should never dream of beginning its reformation by its subversion; that he should approach to the faults of the state as to the wounds of a father, with pious awe and trembling sollicitude. By this wise prejudice we are taught to look with horror on those children of their country who are prompt rashly to hack that aged parent in pieces, and put him into the kettle of magicians, in hopes that by their poisonous weeds, and wild incantations, they may regenerate the paternal constitution, and renovate their father's life.

Society is indeed a contract. Subordinate contracts for objects of mere occasional interest may be dissolved at pleasure – but the state ought not to be considered as nothing better than a partnership agreement in a trade of pepper and coffee, callico or tobacco, or some other such low concern, to be taken up for a little temporary interest, and to be dissolved by the fancy of the parties. It is to be looked on with other reverence; because it is not a partnership in things subservient only to the gross animal existence of a temporary and perishable nature. It is a partnership in all science; a partnership in all art; a partnership in every virtue, and in all perfection. As the ends of such a partnership cannot be obtained in many generations, it becomes a partnership not only between those who are living, but between those who are living, those who are dead, and those who are to be born. Each contract of each particular state is but a clause in the great primaeval contract of eternal society, linking the lower with the higher natures, connecting the visible and invisible world, according to a fixed compact sanctioned by the inviolable oath which holds all physical and all moral natures, each in their appointed place. This law is not subject to the will of those, who by an obligation above them, and infinitely superior, are bound to submit their will to that law. The municipal corporations of that universal kingdom are not morally at liberty at their pleasure, and on their speculations of a contingent improvement, wholly to separate and tear asunder the bands of their subordinate community, and to dissolve it into an unsocial, uncivil, unconnected chaos of elementary principles. It is the first and supreme necessity only, a necessity that is not chosen but chooses, a necessity paramount to deliberation, that admits no discussion, and demands no evidence, which alone can justify a resort to anarchy. This necessity is no exception to the rule; because this necessity itself is a part too of that moral and physical disposition of things to which man must be obedient by consent or force; but if that which is only submission to necessity should be made the object of choice, the law is broken, nature is disobeyed, and the rebellious are outlawed, cast forth, and exiled, from this world of reason, and order, and peace, and virtue, and fruitful penitence, into the antagonist world of madness, discord, vice, confusion, and unavailing sorrow.

Paul Schumaker, "Social Cleavages and Complex Equality"*

Tyrannies permit the strong to dominate the weak. In racist societies, Caucasians normally dominate Africans and Asians. In sexist societies, men normally dominate women. There are many forms of tyranny, but they share a common feature. One segment of society has extensive political power, which it employs to ensure that issues are resolved in ways that uphold its interests and worldview. The counterparts of the dominant interest are the victims because their interests and aspirations are continuously ignored.

Socialists have been concerned about political inequalities, and they often advocate "simple equality."[1] Simple equality would occur if political power were equally distributed between the upper and lower classes, whites and minorities, men and women, and so forth.[2] To achieve simple equality on a specific issue, the policy outcome would have to be equally responsive to the preferences of different segments of the community. To achieve simple equality over a broad range of issues and over time, the victories of the upper class, whites, or men on certain issues would be offset by the victories of the lower class, nonwhites, or women on other issues of comparable importance.

Because simple equality would, by definition, end tyranny, it is an attractive ideal, but pluralists have never fully embraced this ideal. Many issues have outcomes that are inherently dichotomous [...] and they cannot be compromised in ways that are equally responsive to all interests. Equal political power among competing interests will remain an impossibility. If power could be magically distributed equally today, it would become unequally distributed tomorrow, when the next issue is resolved in ways more responsive to one interest than to another. Most importantly, it is not clear that different interests *should* be equally powerful.[3] Perhaps the inequalities that occur can be explained, and perhaps these explanations justify the inequalities.

[...]

Perhaps upper-class domination of the lower class is due to the underrepresentation of the lower class among elected officials. In pluralist policymaking processes, representatives are supposed to be the most powerful participants, and their judgments are likely to be colored by their class backgrounds. The failure of the lower class to elect commissioners who represent their interests can explain the lack of policy responsiveness to the preferences of the lower class.

Perhaps upper-class domination of the lower class is due to the greater participation of the upper class in the resolution of issues. In pluralist processes, representatives are supposed to listen to the arguments of participants, and they are sometimes persuaded by these arguments. The failure of the lower class to participate in these roles can explain their lack of power.

Perhaps upper-class domination is due to support of positions relatively popular with the public. In pluralist processes, representatives should be sensitive to public opinion. If the positions of the lower class are unpopular, they are not likely to be successful in the resolution of community issues.

Finally, perhaps upper-class domination is due to their holding political principles that are more dominant in local political cultures than are the principles held by the lower class. In pluralist processes, policy decisions should reflect dominant community principles. If members of the lower class support policies that undermine dominant community values, their lack of political power is understandable.

Simple inequalities can thus occur because of inequalities in representation, participation, public support for conflicting policy preferences, and cultural acceptance of competing political principles. However, these simple inequalities may not undermine the pluralist goal of complex equality. The ideal of complex equality occurs when there are no significant unexplained inequalities in the political power of competing interests.[4] Conservatives

* Paul Schumaker, extracted from *Critical Pluralism, Democratic Performance, and Community Power* (University Press of Kansas, 1991), pp. 30–4 and 201–2.

1 In *Spheres of Justice: A Defense of Pluralism and Equality* (New York: Basic Books, 1983), pp. 3–30, Michael Walzer uses the concept of "monopoly" to describe simple inequalities of social goods (such as political power), and he uses the term "dominant" to describe those social goods that most often illegitimately invade distributions of other social goods (thus upsetting his conception of complex equality). In the present analysis, the term "dominance" corresponds to Walzer's concept of monopoly but conforms to conventional terminology.

2 In *Equalities* (Cambridge, MA: Harvard University Press, 1981), Douglas Rae et al. have shown that there are many forms of equality. Thus, providing "bloc-regarding" equality among these interests on a group basis may result in "individual-regarding" inequalities.

3 Robert A. Dahl and Charles Lindblom, *Politics, Economics, and Welfare* (Chicago: Chicago University Press, 1976).

4 According to Walzer (*Spheres of Justice*, p. 304), complex equality is achieved in the sphere of political power when inequalities of power are explained by differences in people's persuasiveness. Because the persuasiveness of various interests

and some liberals who hold differentiating (i.e., inegalitarian) principles of justice[5] can thus accept the ideal of complex equality because it permits legitimate inequalities of power.

The criterion of complex equality is thus "reasonable." Pluralists do not label every political inequality tyrannical, but if there are no adequate reasons for significant political inequalities, a prima facie case exists that discrimination has entered into the policymaking process. If the relative powerlessness of the lower class cannot be explained by class differences in representation, participation, popular support, compatibility with the political culture, or other plausible and compelling reasons, it can be concluded that class biases exist. When complex equality is unattained, policymakers discriminate against the lower class – or other subordinant interests – simply because they are lower class. Similarly, when complex equality is unattained, policymakers respond to upper-class people simply because they have more money, more education, and more status. Such discriminations violate pluralist ideals because such matters as wealth, educational background, social status, race, and gender should be irrelevant to the legitimate possession of power.[6]

Though the criterion of complex equality is reasonable, it can also be "radical"; it invites investigation of the causes of inequality. Simply because an inequality can be explained does not mean that it can be justified. If the subordination of the lower class is due to its underrepresentation among elected officials, questions about the legitimacy of such underrepresentation can – and probably will – be raised by those with concerns about inequality. The underlying causes of underrepresentation may be traced to structural features of the electoral system; perhaps lower-class and minority underrepresentation is due to the absence of partisan labels and wards in many local communities.[7] If so, institutional changes can be prescribed and sought. If the subordination of the lower class is due to its holding principles that conflict with dominant cultural values, questions can be raised about the legitimacy of dominant cultural values. Socialists are likely to trace resistance to redistributive principles to the systemic power of capitalism and the ability of capitalists to create cultural values conducive to the needs of capitalism.[8] If so, a transformation of cultural values will be urged as a means of achieving more political equality.[9]

The criterion of complex equality facilitates explanation and evaluation of the inequalities of power between opposite interests defined by various political cleavages. Three phases of analysis must be conducted to determine if communities achieve complex equality.

In the first phase, a sample of issues must be scrutinized to determine the presence or absence of various types of cleavages. Cleavages are defined on the basis of the predominant characteristics – rather than the universal qualities – of the individuals who oppose each other on issues. [...] A cleavage occurs when the majority of people defined by some characteristic (e.g., the upper class) are on one side of the issue, the majority of people with the opposite characteristic (e.g., the lower class) are on the other side of the issue, and the differences are statistically significant.

Although the discussion of complex equality has focused on class cleavages, other kinds of cleavages may be widespread on community issues and may exhibit more extensive and less legitimate inequalities than do those that occur along class lines. Table [1] lists the types of cleavages investigated in the Lawrence study and the interests that may oppose each other when these cleavages occur.

If class, racial, ideological, or other types of cleavages are observed on community issues, the second phase of analysis – the question, Which interests tend to prevail? – must be answered. Just as the standings on the sports pages help fans keep track of the win–loss records of teams in baseball, basketball, and football, so can political standings help keep track of the success of various

defies objective measurement, no attempt is made here to account for simple inequalities in terms of persuasiveness. Nevertheless, Walzer's formulation points to violations of complex equality that can guide empirical research. Complex equality is violated if inequalities are rooted in factors that are not germane to persuasiveness. Arguments should not be more persuasive just because they are made by wealthy or socially prominent people. Other arguments should not be discounted merely because they are made by women, minorities, "radicals" or people having other characteristics irrelevant to an unbiased consideration of the merits of each case.

5 Jennifer Hochschild, *What's Fair: American Beliefs About Distributive Justice* (Cambridge, MA: Harvard University Press, 1981), pp. 60–75.

6 Walzer, *Spheres of Justice*, p. 20.

7 Willis D. Hawley, *Nonpartisan Elections and the Case for Party Politics* (New York: John Wiley, 1973); Susan Welch and Timothy Bledsoe, *Urban Reform and Its Consequences* (Chicago: Chicago University Press, 1988).

8 Steven Lukes, *Power: A Radical View* (London: Macmillan, 1974); John Gaventa, *Power and Powerlessness: Quiescence and Rebellion in an Appalachian Valley* (Urbana: University of Illinois Press, 1980).

9 Manuel Castells, *City and the Grassroots* (Berkeley: University of California Press, 1983).

Table [1] Various community cleavages and the interests that oppose each other when such cleavages arise

- Class
  - The Upper Class: those in the top quartile of a scale of socioeconomic status (SES)
  - The Middle Class: those in the middle quartiles of SES scale
  - The Lower Class: those in the bottom quartile of SES scale
- Neighborhood
  - Country Clubbers: those living in upper-income neighborhoods
  - Split Levellers: those living in middle-income neighborhoods
  - Cellar Dwellers: those living in lower-income neighborhoods
- Racial
  - Whites
  - Minorities
- Gender
  - Men
  - Women
- Age
  - Rookies: those less than 30 years old
  - Veterans: those between 30 and 55 years old
  - Seniors: those over 55 years old
- Length of Residence in the Community
  - Hometowners: those residing in the community more than 20 years
  - Newcomers: community residents for 5 to 20 years
  - Visitors: community residents less than 5 years
- Sector of Employment
  - Public: those who work for governmental agencies
  - Private: those who work in the private sector
- University-Community
  - Gown: students and employees at the university
  - Town: those unaffiliated with the university
- Ideological
  - Liberals: those who define themselves as liberals
  - Conservatives: those who define themselves as conservatives
- Partisan
  - Republicans: those who define themselves as Republicans
  - Democrats: those who define themselves as Democrats
- Ethos
  - Managerialists: those who think government should emphasize businesslike efficiency and other "good government" values
  - Politicos: those who think government should emphasize such political values as openness and fairness
- Other Attitudinal Divisions
  - The Growth Machine: those who prefer rapid economic growth
  - Preservationists: those who prefer no or slow growth
  - Market Providers: those who prefer low taxes and limited public services
  - Public Providers: those who prefer more extensive public services, even if taxes must be raised

interests in community politics. Is the Lower Class in last place in the Class Division? Does the Growth Machine dominate Preservationists on economic development issues? Is there a tight race in the Gender Division suggesting parity between men and women? I describe a procedure that involves relating the preferences of various interests to policy outcomes to determine the win–loss records of the interests listed in Table [1] on the twenty-nine issues examined in this study.[10] These standings indicate that there are extensive simple inequalities among various interests; as in sports,

[10] The larger study from which this excerpt is abstracted examined 29 concrete policy issues, encompassing the more controversial community infrastructure, economic development, land use, social control and social welfare issues that arose in Lawrence, Kansas, during the 1980s. The descriptions of these issues and the data analyses that support the conclusions provided below are detailed in Schumaker, *Critical Pluralism*.

the "have-nots" – those interests that are poor in social and economic resources – are at or near the bottom of the standings in the game of community politics.

The third phase of analysis involves attempts to explain these inequalities. Because inequalities in the success of various interests may be explained by inequalities in representation, participation, popular support, and cultural values, measures of these variables must be attained and incorporated in multivariate models relating the preferences of competing interests to policy outcomes. If the preferences of competing interests are equally potent determinants of policy outcomes when the effects of such variables are controlled, the ideal of complex equality is achieved.

Conclusions

The domination that occurs when responsiveness to the opposing sides of community cleavages is unequal is generally more evident among participants than among citizens in Lawrence. Among citizens, there are few structured cleavages, and the outcomes of issues having class, neighborhood, age, and ideological cleavages among citizens do not persistently favor the upper class, the Country Clubbers, men, or other relatively advantaged people. Nevertheless, there are many structured cleavages among participants, and issues are usually resolved in ways that do favor relatively advantaged participants – especially the middle class, Country Clubbers, Seniors and Veterans, Home-towners, conservatives, Republicans, Market Providers, Managerialists, members of the Growth Machine.

The extensive successes of these advantaged participants on community issues and the extensive failures of their disadvantaged counterparts have a variety of explanations. The number of people who participate in community issues as members of competing teams partially explains, for example, the dominance of Veterans and Seniors over Rookies in the Age Division. The extent to which competing participants engage in various acts of persuasive participation can also help to explain unequal responsiveness, as part of the ineffectiveness of Rookie participants seems to be due to their reluctance to contact officials and make public presentations. Such differences in participation do not explain all forms of domination in Lawrence. Cellar Dwellers in the Neighborhood Division fail despite their extensive participation, and Public Providers are more participatory than Market Providers but are dominated by them. Simply increasing participation does not ensure that subordinate interests will achieve increased levels of power.

Inequalities in representation can help to explain the inequalities in responsiveness that are unexplained by participatory differences. The lower class and Rookies have had almost no representation on policymaking bodies, and Cellar Dwellers have been significantly underrepresented. Not surprisingly, these interests achieved few policy successes. Nevertheless, increased representation may not be the key to equal responsiveness. For example, when Cellar Dweller representation increased on a few issues, there were only marginal increases in responsiveness to the preferences and participation of Cellar Dwellers. This suggests that marginal increases in representation by relatively powerless interests – increases that leave counterparts in control of the commission – are insufficient for promoting equality of political standing.[11]

The public is not equally supportive of the policy positions taken by various interests, and differences in public support can explain inequalities in responsiveness. The positions of the middle class were usually consistent with dominant public opinion, partially explaining the dominance of the middle class. Seniors tended to take more popular positions than Rookies, leading to their more frequent successes, and the dominance of Market Providers over Public Providers is partly explained by their actual and perceived public support.

The different principles of competing interests also help to explain inequalities of success on policy issues. For example, the failures of Cellar Dwellers seem to be partly explained by their seeking public welfare and wanting issues resolved through more politicized and participatory procedures. Because such orientations are at odds with structural economic imperatives, they are resisted. The failures of Rookies seem rooted in their seeking policies involving increased public services and reduced regulation of morality. Because these orientations are resisted by older participants, their dominance in the culture is tenuous, and their potency in the policymaking process is limited. Thus, there seem to be "mobilizations of bias"[12] against certain interests. There is some unresponsiveness to certain interests because the local culture provides only weak support for their principles. There is considerable unresponsiveness to

[11] In *Protest is Not Enough* (Berkeley: University of California Press, 1984) Rufus Browning, Dale Rogers Marshall, and David Tabb develop the argument that relatively powerless interests must be not only represented but "incorporated" (or represented in coalitions that dominate governing bodies) in order to enhance their influence in policymaking.

[12] E. E. Schattschneider, *The Semisovereign People* (Hinsdale, IL: Dryden Press, 1960).

other interests because the city interest in economic growth undermines their principles.

Differences in participation, representation, popular support, and principles do not explain all forms of unequal responsiveness. In Lawrence, for example, these factors do not explain the dominance of the middle class. The bias toward the participation of the middle class – or the absence of complex equality in the Class Division – may not indicate any severe problems in the governance of Lawrence; after all, Lawrence is primarily a middle-class community. However, if the comparative-issues method can demonstrate middle-class biases in Lawrence, it can demonstrate other unexplained inequalities in other communities and thus reveal the presence of racial, gender, and other forms of political discrimination whenever they occur.

Chapter 8
Epistemological Orientations

Introduction

Like ontology, epistemology is a term unfamiliar to many people, and philosophical assumptions about epistemology might seem far removed from our political thinking. But just as people can have strong but unrecognized ontological beliefs, they can also have such epistemological ones. Indeed, it can be argued that epistemological differences are at the root of long-standing conflicts between liberals and conservatives. Liberals have always had a certain optimism about their knowledge of politics that conservatives have found discomforting, if not alarming. Two centuries ago, the Ideologues proclaimed that classical liberal principles constituted "the true science of politics," a claim that more conservative thinkers like John Adams regarded as pure hubris. Traditional conservatives believed political questions could not be resolved by following universally true scientific propositions. They regarded politics as more like an art than a science; just as good artists cannot be guided by rigid scientific rules, accomplished statesmen must apply their own judgments about what works best in the contexts in which they find themselves. Because social and cultural contexts differ, there can be no universal truths about how to govern. Likewise, one of the major criticisms that contemporary conservatives have made of contemporary liberalism is that it engages in misguided "social engineering." Conservatives now charge liberals with holding social scientific theories that claim various problems (like poverty and crime) are ultimately caused by known social conditions and that identify social reforms to be implemented by "big government," which will alter these conditions and thus eliminate the problems. Conservatives claim that the truth of such theories is doubtful – that efforts to engineer a better world by following such theories usually fail or have "unanticipated consequences" (i.e. bad effects that were unknown to liberal reformers when they proposed and implemented their ambitious theoretical schemes).

These examples show that epistemological issues deal with assumptions or claims that people make about knowledge and "truth." The key epistemological issues for politics can be stated simply: What is the role of truth in politics? Can we have certain knowledge or at least tentative knowledge about politics? Or must we accept complete uncertainty about fundamental political questions? How can we achieve truth – or as much knowledge as is humanly possible – about political issues?

Modernity arrived when intellectuals lost confidence in the adequacies of the "knowledge" being bequeathed to them; they thought prevailing (medieval) understandings of the physical universe, social practices, moral conduct, and political life were a mish-mash of conflicting opinions by highly regarded but misleading authorities, a variety of pronouncements by church officials about "divine truth" that rested on arbitrary interpretations of that truth, diverse customs and traditions that were little more than local prejudices, and superstitions born of people's fears about phenomena that they simply did not understand. The scientific revolution, the Enlightenment, and modernity generally sought to replace these dubious understandings with "solid truth."

René Descartes (1596–1650), a French mathematician and philosopher, is widely cited as exemplifying the modern quest for certainty. In our first reading in this chapter, Benjamin Barber, a prominent American democratic theorist who is a professor at the University of Maryland, claims that classical liberal ideas are rooted in a Cartesian method for attaining political truth. This method proposes the existence of "an incorrigible first premise" – such as Descartes' famous "I think, therefore I am," which affirmed the individual as the ground of liberal politics – "from which the concepts, values, standards, and ends of political life can be derived by simple deduction." According to Barber, Descartes' conviction that his method could yield firm political truths "permeates the entire social-contract and state-of-nature tradition" in liberal theory. Barber criticizes this conviction because it seeks to impose and substitute "the orderliness of epistemology" for the "inchoate messiness of the political." Indeed, for Barber and many contemporary political theorists, "politics concerns itself only with those realms where truth is not – or not yet – known."[1]

During the nineteenth century, liberals turned away from Descartes' deductive approach to acquiring political truth, but they did not abandon the quest for firmer political knowledge than provided by ancient and religious authorities or by traditional prejudices and superstitions. Sparked by Jeremy Bentham (1748–1838), an English jurist, philosopher, and reformer, utilitarianism became the epistemological foundation of liberalism. Bentham believed political judgments – and thus the value of all existing and proposed political institutions, policies, and programs – should be based on calculations about their "utility" on those affected. A reform should be adopted if it produced more pleasure than pain for the aggregation of individuals in society than that which it would replace. For Benthamites, utilitarianism promised to base politics on the knowable consequences of political practices and changes in these practices for the happiness of citizens.

Conservatives and contemporary traditional communitarians have always rejected this epistemology. Utilitarians must ultimately base their calculations on assumptions about what is good for individuals, but as Alasdair MacIntyre – a Scottish-born moral philosopher who taught at many American universities – asks in our selection here, "What is the good for me?" And his answer begins with the understanding that "the only criteria for success or failure in a human life as a whole are criteria of success or failure in a narrated or to-be-narrated quest." Ultimately, the good that individuals acknowledge depend on the inspiring stories they are told and on the (living) traditions they bear. This suggests that utilitarian calculations cannot replace traditional understandings as a basis for moral and political knowledge; rather they depend on them. From this perspective, traditions (and our judgments about traditions) are a far more important basis for political life than liberals admit.

Political reformers and revolutionaries have normally claimed that their goals can be understood through scientific formulations that supersede traditional knowledge. Nevertheless, their preferred "scientific method" evolved from the deductive "science of politics" proclaimed by classical liberals. Science became more empirical, as in the work of Karl Marx. His scientific socialism was based on the laws of history and economics as revealed by observing historical and economic facts and, through the process of induction, forming valid generalizations from these facts. Such a science was also, of course, the foundation of Darwin's theory of evolution. During the later part of the nineteenth century, scientific positivism grew in prominence, emphasizing the roles of observation and inductive reasoning to produce natural laws of cause-and-effect.

One problem with positivism, however, is that its strength resides in achieving knowledge based on facts, while politics cannot escape values and value judgments. Marx's scientific socialism could say that a revolution against capitalism was inevitable; but his account of the historical and economic laws that predicted that result could not also claim that such a revolution was good. Darwin's positivism could produce the generalization that the most fit survived the struggle for existence and that this produced more evolved species, but as Huxley maintained in the selection provided in Chapter 5, this process may be at odds with our moral judgments. How to apply an inductive scientific method in the social and political realms where value judgments cannot be escaped has thus been a matter of great concern for twentieth-century political theorists.

One of the most important approaches has been pragmatism, a method historically associated with William James (1842–1910) and Thomas Dewey (1869–1952), but more recently championed by Richard Rorty (1931–2007), a professor of literature, humanities, and philosophy at Princeton, Virginia, and Stanford Universities. For Rorty, pragmatism refuses to believe in the existence of Truth, as some authority that stands over humans. For Rorty, political knowledge

[1] Benjamin Barber, *Strong Democracy* (Berkeley: University of California Press, 1984), p. 139.

cannot rest on any "accurate representation of an antecedently existing reality," rather it rests on the aspirations of a democratic community – on "the preferences we Americans share" such as that for social justice – and with open democratic processes which enable a community to experiment with various ways of approaching such preferences. Pragmatism does not claim that any political end or that any means to an end is "true." It merely endorses democratic experimentation with political means to improve our lives and to discover what works in practice.

But what "preferences" do the members of a democratic community share in common and what meaning do they give to such goals as "social justice"? Many contemporary political theorists recognize the great difficulties that we confront here. Feminist scholars like Carol Gilligan, an American psychologist and professor at New York University, suggest that what we often assume to be universal meanings of terms like justice are really just male conceptions; women bring "a different voice" – one that has too often been ignored – to these matters. She claims that "the presumed neutrality of science, like that of language itself, gives way to the recognition that the categories of knowledge are human constructions" and that the ways that humans construct knowledge depend on many social influences, including, for example, the differences in how boys and girls are raised.

Many political theorists have thus arrived at a "constructivist" approach to achieving political knowledge. This epistemological orientation assumes that knowledge is socially constructed. It matters less how theories or any truth-claims are derived than how they are received, especially in politics. Back in 1962, Thomas Kuhn had noticed that all scientific paradigms are really social constructions in that they depend on acceptance by leading practitioners in a discipline, and that scientific disciplines are less well characterized by small incremental gains in knowledge than by revolutionary shifts in accepted paradigms.[2] This realization has not been lost on *social* constructivists. They recognize that scientific findings, rational models, and other intellectual enterprises can contribute knowledge about social activity, but they focus their attention on whether and how consensus about the validity of such contributions occurs. *Political* constructivists are particularly concerned about how our political communities can reach as much consensus as possible on the principles that govern them, because people who disagree with governing principles will feel excluded and thus disobedient to the coercive governmental powers that rule over them.[3] Our final selection in this chapter provides John Rawls' account of the "procedure of construction" that he endorses. The tentativeness of the knowledge that is produced by such a procedure is something that appeals to contemporary pluralists.

Benjamin Barber, "The Epistemological Frame: Cartesian Politics"*

Liberal democratic theory, like all political theory, depends on particular assumptions about the character of political knowledge. These epistemological assumptions account for many of that theory's strengths and not a few of its weaknesses. The paramount assumption is Cartesian: that there exists a knowable independent ground – an incorrigible first premise or "antecedent immutable reality" – from which the concepts, values, standards, and ends of political life can be derived by simple deduction. It is this sort of inferential certainty that Pufendorf evinces when he claims that it is possible to "reduce moral science to a system as well connected as those of geometry and mechanics and founded upon principles that are equally certain."[4]

John Dewey felt that man's "quest for certainty," rooted in "man's distrust of himself," produced a "desire to get beyond and above himself" through the "transcendence of pure knowledge."[5] Similarly, A. R. Louch speaks of man's "search for ultimate observables" and for a supporting "doctrine of incorrigibility."[6] This futile search seeks a basis for social knowledge secure

* Benjamin Barber, extracted from *Strong Democracy* (University of California Press, 1984), pp. 46–66.

2 Thomas Kuhn, *The Structure of Scientific Revolutions* (Chicago: University of Chicago Press, 1962).

3 From a pluralist perspective, consensus on the everyday issues of politics is less important than that of basic principles, because if people who have lost on an ordinary issue nevertheless believe that the issue has been resolved in accordance with the consensually held principles of the community, they can more easily abide the result.

4 Samuel Pufendorf, *Droit de la nature et de gens*, sect. 2, n. 6.

5 John Dewey, *The Quest for Certainty* (New York: Capricorn, 1960), pp. 6–7.

6 A. R. Louch, *Explanation and Human Action* (Berkeley: University of California Press, 1969), p. 44.

beyond all challenge, one that will endow political practice with the absolute certainty of generic truth.

Louch and Dewey's analyses of the futility of the quest for certain political knowledge reveal their debt to Charles Sanders Peirce. [...]

Peirce sympathized with the need for certainty but regretted the consequences. We should perhaps do the same, for the quest for certainty in political thinking seems more likely to breed orthodoxy than to nurture truth and in practice tends to promote the domination of method over substance. Ironically, this procedure produces a fundamentally unscientific inversion of the "judicious method of the ancients," who, as Dewey remarked, were content to base "their conclusions about knowledge on the nature of the universe in which knowledge occurs."[7] The obsession of recent social-science empiricists with methodology has, by contrast, led them to place epistemology before ontology. In an attempt to mimic the hard sciences, of which they rarely have a true understanding, these social scientists have tried to subordinate every understanding of reality to some orthodox construction of understanding. For a brief period, now happily passed, metatheoretical analysis threatened to become the only legitimate form of political theorizing.

The claim advanced here is that this relentless quest for certainty has been a particular feature of liberal political philosophy from its inception. By rooting the political in a prepolitical realm of the immutable, that quest has worked mischief on both the theory and the practice of politics. Politics, the liberal epistemology insisted, could not be portrayed or understood in political terms but required antiseptic categories untainted by the subject matter that was to be their object. In this insistence, liberals were more Cartesian than Descartes. Descartes wrote, "I was convinced that I must once for all seriously undertake to rid myself of all the opinions which I had formerly accepted, and commence to build anew from the foundation, if I wanted to establish any firm and permanent structure in the sciences."[8] But Descartes fortified himself with conventional beliefs before embarking on his journey of discovery, whereas Hobbes and his successors persuaded themselves that theories of political life had truly to be erected *de novo* on wholly nonpolitical foundations. Political obligation had to rest on the prepolitics of human interaction in a hypothetical state of nature; political freedom had to derive from natural liberty and stand without reference to politics; political rights had to issue from natural rights established without reference to social or political conditions; and the whole subtle complex of social and political relations, which the Greeks thought defined the individual human being from the outset, had to be reduced to a physics-based psychology of individual atoms defined in radical isolation from one another.

This pseudo-Cartesian conviction permeates the entire social-contract and state-of-nature tradition: it is no less evident in recent liberal theorists such as Ackerman, Rawls, and Nozick than in Hobbes. [...]

The point in liberal political theory has been to reconstruct the house of politics, fashioned by the history of human dependency from strange and difficult materials, in a simpler and more familiar medium. If stone presents a smoother facade, then the house of politics must be rebuilt in stone, whatever materials it might have been made of in its original state.

To understand politics is therefore always, necessarily, to deconstruct and depoliticize it: that is to say, to decontaminate it of those exotic and unmanageable elements that resist assimilation by the mind in quest of certainty. This is precisely the program of Hobbes's *Leviathan*: politics is to be refashioned as morals, morals remade as psychology, psychology recast as mechanics, and mechanics recreated as particle physics. From such elemental (and elementary) building blocks as these can be constructed the entire political cosmos: the ends of political action and the norms of political decision as well as the standards of political understanding and the measures of political science. Not even Descartes could have dreamed of so complete a recomposition of the world by minds set on certainty.

Cartesian characteristics of liberal theory

The method of inquiry associated with the bold epistemological presumptions of early liberalism can be characterized as Cartesian in a broad metaphoric sense, but it is also Cartesian in a number of quite specific ways: it tends to be reductionist, genetic, dualistic, speculative, and solipsistic. Liberal political thought – under which heading we have now included theorizing about the social contract, the state of nature, natural rights, and original positions – can be shown to be correspondingly

7 Dewey, *Quest*, p. 41.

8 René Descartes, *Meditations*, edited by E. S. Haldane and G. R. T. Ross (Cambridge: Cambridge University Press, 1970), vol. 2, p. 144.

reductionist, genetic, dualistic, speculative, and solipsistic in specifiably political ways.

To Hobbes, reductionism is self-evidently a desirable method of inquiry. In the "Epistle Dedicatory" to his *Elements of Law*, he insists that to "reduce" the doctrines of justice and of policy in general "to the rules and infallibility of reason, there is no way, but first to put such principles down for a foundation, as passion not mistrusting, may not seek to displace; and afterward to build thereon the truth of cases in the law of nature (which hitherto have been built in the air) by degrees, till the whole be inexpungable."[9] A sturdy house of politics can only arise on an inexpungable and infallible foundation, set deep in prepolitical granite.

John Rawls's "original position" involves a similar reduction. Individual men are decontaminated of the special psychologies and particular interests by which we understand them to be men, so that a political theory of justice can develop from an antiseptic starting place.[10] The theory's success in addressing the political ambiguities and uncertainties of the real world is measured by its remoteness from that world.

Robert Nozick's gloss on Hobbesian method is an even more startling example of reductionist decontamination at play.

[...]

The pitfalls of [such] methodologism are by now so familiar that a single passage from Dewey may serve to recall them. The essence of human affairs, Dewey explains with the patience of a schoolmaster, "is that we cannot indulge in the selective abstractions that are the secret of the success of physical knowing. When we introduce a like simplification into social and moral subjects we eliminate the distinctively human factors: reduction to the physical ensues."[11] Reduction to the physical is a way to circumvent contingency and the uncertainties of accident and fortune that seem indigenous to the world of politics.

[...]

Politics is archetypically experiential and thus experimental in Dewey's sense. It is the art of planning, coordinating, and executing the collective futures of human communities. It is the art of inventing a common destiny for women and men in conflict. To create such a destiny is to be autonomous of necessity and its givens and to be capable of meaningful choice. Reductionism ultimately links the future to a past governed by necessity and leaves freedom without a home in the human scheme of things.

If the Cartesian epistemology of liberal democracy is reductionist in its passion for certainty, it is also genetic in its affection for deductivism. In taking the syllogism as the chief instrument of its logic, the reductive method insists on the priority in political reasoning of the axiom or premise. As in a well-conceived geometry, it excavates starting principles the logical priority of which becomes a warrant for their moral and political priority; the house of politics is then built on foundations laid deep within the excavation.[12]

When reasoning is subsumed to geometry and political understanding is made to depend on syllogistic chains no less apolitical in their conclusions than in their necessarily apolitical premises, then political theory becomes apolitical theory and Burke's charge that geometrical accuracy in moral arguments is the most fallacious of all sophistries seems vindicated.

[...]

This explains why liberal theory often appears to operate in a speculative mode that discomfits Marxists (*The Eleventh Thesis on Feuerbach*), sociologists, conservatives, pragmatists, and other dialectical thinkers with their eyes on history and the concrete social forces that shape it. Genetic reasoning will clearly prefer speculative foundations to concrete realities, and dualism will assure that the two are kept in antiseptic isolation. Theory will be regarded as an autonomous realm that illuminates, guides, and otherwise serves the world of

9 Ibid.

10 John Rawls, *A Theory of Justice* (Cambridge, MA: Harvard University Press, 1971), part 1. Rawls has expressed some striking reservations about this approach in his recent Dewey lectures on Kantian constructivism. He acknowledges that "justifying a conception of justice is not primarily an epistemological problem. The search for reasonable grounds for reaching agreement rooted in our conception of ourselves and in our relation to society replaces the search for moral truth interpreted as fixed by a prior and independent order of objects and relations" ("Kantian Constructivism in Moral Theory," *Journal of Philosophy* 77, 9 [September 1980], p. 519).

This view is obviously more hospitable to the position developed here, but it raises fundamental questions about the notion of rational self-interest on which *A Theory of Justice* seems to be based. For a discussion, see William A. Galston, "Moral Personality and Liberal Theory: Rawls' 'Dewey Lectures'," *Political Theory* 10, 4 (November 1982).

11 Dewey, *Quest*, p. 216.

12 Robert Paul Wolff precisely captures Rawls's preoccupation with axiomatic starting points: "The claim is simply that in our reasoning about moral and social questions, we can choose to perform the same abstractions from particularities that we have learned to perform in our mathematical reasoning" (*Understanding Rawls* [Princeton: Princeton University Press, 1977], p. 121).

action but remains untainted by it. Where the realm of action is dynamic, purposive, and always in process, theory will deliberately attempt to remain static, mechanistic, and causal – precisely in order to capture and subdue the active notions that define politics. The orderliness of epistemology is not merely imposed on but is substituted for the inchoate messiness of the political.

[...]

Underlying the several Cartesian features of liberal political theory is a powerful tradition of philosophical solipsism that can be traced back to Spinoza and Hobbes as well as to Descartes. Bergson remarks that "when man first begins to think, he thinks of himself first." Cartesian liberalism prompts man to think of himself first, second, and last. The tradition understands all knowledge either as a reconstruction of impressions imprinted on the individual subject or as a product of ideas directly apprehended by rational individuals. In both cases – simple empiricism and simple idealism – the mode is radically reflexive. To think is to be conscious of thinking, to reflect on oneself as thinker and on one's mode of thought. Whether it is grounded in a theory of the sense impression or percept as a quasi-physical entity (empiricism) or in a theory of the ideal or the concept as that entity's rational construction (idealism), the process is subjective, individual, and reflexive, and thus thoroughly solipsistic. A premium is placed on the radically isolated consciousness, whether it is perceived as sense perceptor or as rational apprehender.

Yet solipsism would seem to be a rather curious outcome for a method devoted to the pursuit of certainty and objectivity. Reflexivity may seem a self-evident starting point for the Cartesian; but, ironically, it is a point of subjectivity that is immune by definition to common judgment and to communal corroboration. Reflexive thinking quickly becomes a cage separating individual consciousness from the very world that consciousness is intended to mediate and confirm.

[...]

Like empiricism, rationalism seeks to escape the subjectivism of reflexivity. The naturalistic strategy that treats nature as the locus of the principles and laws apprehended by reason presents itself as one rationalist escape. For rationalist naturalism is impervious to the critique that Hume and his successors leveled at naturalism. The apprehending, rational mind asserts that it is not trapped within itself and separated from the real world because it *is* the real world.[13] If minds in collision cannot agree on what is real, it is because one or the other is in error, not because rational knowledge is subjective.

Yet though it associates reason with nature and thus with the real world, this strategy is oblivious to the social character of knowledge and to the ultimate dependence of private reason (however universal its claims) on public corroboration in the setting of human community. Rationalists and empiricists alike lose touch with the reality that is their common object. Thus does the solipsism of Cartesian epistemology serve to reinforce the radical individualism of liberal democratic political theory; thus is created the social analogue of the rational mind or of the sense perceptor – the private, asocial individual defined by absolute liberty, distinguished by utter isolation, and imbued with a sense that he is circumscribed by total solitude.

[...]

Antecedent reality, whether sensed, intuited, or dreamed, is always beyond politics, is always utopian in the sense of being nowhere with respect to its realities. For politics is defined by its *somewhereness*, its concrete historicity in the real world of human beings. Knowledge grounded in nowhere, even where it has a philosophical warranty of truth and certainty, cannot serve politics. Instead, it generates the kinds of confusion we have associated here with American political consciousness.

The alternative, hinted at in Santayana's counsel, is dreams that belong to and are engendered by politics, relative truths that emerge from common life. Politics does not rest on justice and freedom; it is what makes them possible. The object of democracy is not to apply independently grounded abstractions to concrete situations but rather to extrapolate working abstractions from concrete situations. In a word, politics is not the application of Truth to the problem of human relations but the application of human relations to the problem of truth. Justice then appears as an approximation of principle in a world of action where absolute principles are irrelevant.

What we would in any case seem to require in the real political world are not reflexive truths garnered in

[13] I have in mind here not pure philosophical idealism on the model of Kant or Hegel, but rather the Cartesian conviction that subjective consciousness and objective reality cannot effectively be kept separate. A. R. Louch offers this pertinent comment: "The villain of the piece turns out to be the doctrine of incorrigibility. In their search for ultimate observables, classical empiricists were led by the question: have I now got something which would provide the uncontestable basis for any knowledge claim? So they were driven to the equally incompatible extremes of unanalysibility or a mental location of the objects of immediate experience" (*Explanation and Human Action*, p. 44). At his "mental location," idealism and empiricism collide.

reflective equilibrium but enabling norms developed amidst concrete common problems; not absolute certainty but relative conviction; not philosophical incorrigibility but practical agreement; not ultimate knowledge but shared ends, common values, community standards, and public goods in a world where ultimate knowledge may be unattainable. Indeed, democracy may exist entirely without moral foundations; it may be the political answer to the question of moral uncertainty – the form of interaction for people who cannot agree on absolutes. Because democracy generates roots – different roots in different soils – it knows no single environment, no one unchanging soil, no perfect agriculture. Truth in politics seems, as William James said of truth in general, to be something which is "made in the course of experience" rather than something discovered or disclosed and then acted upon.

The Cartesian epistemology of liberal democracy operates from what we may call the fallacy of the independent ground, and its reliance on this fallacy contributes to its thinness as theory. Determined to develop a politics of applied truth (or a politics of passivity reflecting the elusiveness of truth), the liberal must find impossible routes from nowhere (antecedent reality) to somewhere (concrete human relations). He must put down foundations for a ship at sea and try to root moving caravans. He yearns for the stationary in a world that is forever in motion and is all too willing to set a hypothetical sun in motion if only he can make the real earth stand still.

There are epistemological alternatives far more suitable to democracy and to politics in general. An epistemology of process, which could understand truth to be a product of certain modes of common living rather than the foundation of common life, would be free of the metaphysical problems posed by rationalism and empiricism. Men and women would cease to regard themselves as citizens because they once consented to certain abstract truths. Rather, they would see themselves as capable of creating pertinent practical truths because they had become citizens. Citizenship is the root rather than the product of common value; consequently, there must be citizens before there can be common truth.

To the liberal democrat, the citizen is an individual who applies a personal truth to human relations. To another sort of democrat, the citizen is one who contrives common truths in the absence of knowable individual truth. The necessity for common choice and common action in the face of individual uncertainty and collective conflict defines his political world. He knows he must act even while he knows how little he knows. He knows that action can afford neither the agnosticism of skeptical philosophy nor the dogmatism of the quest for reflective certainty.

Jeremy Bentham, "Of the Principle of Utility"*

Nature has placed mankind under the governance of two sovereign masters, *pain* and *pleasure*. It is for them alone to point out what we ought to do, as well as to determine what we shall do. On the one hand the standard of right and wrong, on the other the chain of causes and effects, are fastened to their throne. They govern us in all we do, in all we say, in all we think: every effort we can make to throw off our subjection, will serve but to demonstrate and confirm it. In words a man may pretend to abjure their empire: but in reality he will remain subject to it all the while. The *principle of utility* recognises this subjection, and assumes it for the foundation of that system, the object of which is to rear the fabric of felicity by the hands of reason and of law. Systems which attempt to question it, deal in sounds instead of sense, in caprice instead of reason, in darkness instead of light.

But enough of metaphor and declamation: it is not by such means that moral science is to be improved.

II. The principle of utility is the foundation of the present work: it will be proper therefore at the outset to give an explicit and determinate account of what is meant by it. By the principle[14] of utility is meant that principle which approves or disapproves of every action whatsoever, according to the tendency which it appears

* Jeremy Bentham, extracted from "An Introduction to Principles of Morals and Legislation," in *A Bentham Reader*, edited by Mary and Peter Mack (New York: Pegasus, 1969), pp. 85–9. Originally published 1789.

14 Principle. The word principle is derived from the Latin *principium:* which seems to be compounded of the two words *primus*, first, or chief, and *cipium*, a termination which seems to be derived from *capio*, to take, as in *mancipium*, *municipium*; to which are analogous *auceps*, *forceps*, and others. It is a term of very vague and very extensive signification: it is applied to any thing which is conceived to serve as a foundation or beginning to any series of operations: in some cases, of physical operations: but of mental operations in the present case. The principle here in question may be taken for an act of the mind; a sentiment; a sentiment of approbation; a sentiment which, when applied to an action, approves of its utility, as that quality of it by which the measure of approbation or disapprobation bestowed upon it ought to be governed.

to have to augment or diminish the happiness of the party whose interest is in question: or, what is the same thing in other words, to promote or to oppose that happiness. I say of every action whatsoever; and therefore not only of every action of a private individual, but of every measure of government.

III. By utility is meant that property in any object, whereby it tends to produce benefit, advantage, pleasure, good, or happiness (all this in the present case comes to the same thing), or (what comes again to the same thing) to prevent the happening of mischief, pain, evil, or unhappiness to the party whose interest is considered: if that party be the community in general, then the happiness of the community: if a particular individual, then the happiness of that individual.

IV. The interest of the community is one of the most general expressions that can occur in the phraseology of morals: no wonder that the meaning of it is often lost. When it has a meaning, it is this. The community is a fictitious *body*, composed of the individual persons who are considered as constituting as it were its *members*. The interest of the community then is, what? – the sum of the interests of the several members who compose it.

V. It is in vain to talk of the interest of the community without understanding what is the interest of the individual. [...] A thing is said to promote the interest, or to be *for* the interest, of an individual, when it tends to add to the sum total of his pleasures: or, what comes to the same thing, to diminish the sum total of his pains.

VI. An action then may be said to be conformable to the principle of utility, or, for shortness sake, to utility (meaning with respect to the community at large), when the tendency it has to augment the happiness of the community is greater than any it has to diminish it.

VII. A measure of government (which is but a particular kind of action, performed by a particular person or persons) may be said to be conformable to or dictated by the principle of utility, when in like manner the tendency which it has to augment the happiness of the community is greater than any which it has to diminish it.

VIII. When an action, or in particular a measure of government, is supposed by a man to be conformable to the principle of utility, it may be convenient, for the purposes of discourse, to imagine a kind of law or dictate, called a law or dictate of utility: and to speak of the action in question, as being conformable to such law or dictate.

IX. A man may be said to be a partizan of the principle of utility, when the approbation or disapprobation he annexes to any action, or to any measure, is determined, by and proportioned to the tendency which he conceives it to have to augment or to diminish the happiness of the community: or in other words, to its conformity or unconformity to the laws or dictates of utility.

X. Of an action that is conformable to the principle of utility, one may always say either that it is one that ought to be done, or at least that it is not one that ought not to be done. One may say also, that it is right it should be done: that it is a right action: at least that it is not a wrong action. When thus interpreted, the words *ought*, and *right* and *wrong*, and others of that stamp, have a meaning: when otherwise, they have none.

XI. Has the rectitude of this principle been ever formally contested? It should seem that it had, by those who have not known what they have been meaning. Is it susceptible of any direct proof? It should seem not: for that which is used to prove every thing else, cannot itself be proved: a chain of proofs must have their commencement somewhere. To give such proof is as impossible as it is needless.

XII. Not that there is or ever has been that human creature breathing, however stupid or perverse, who has not on many, perhaps on most occasions of his life, deferred to it. By the natural constitution of the human frame, on most occasions of their lives men in general embrace this principle, without thinking of it: if not for the ordering of their own actions, yet for the trying of their own actions, as well as of those of other men. There have been, at the same time, not many, perhaps, even of the most intelligent, who have been disposed to embrace it purely and without reserve. There are even few who have not taken some occasion or other to quarrel with it, either on account of their not understanding always how to apply it, or on account of some prejudice or other which they were afraid to examine into, or could not bear to part with. For such is the stuff that man is made of: in principle and in practice, in a right track and in a wrong one, the rarest of all human qualities is consistency.

XIII. When a man attempts to combat the principle of utility, it is with reasons drawn, without his being aware of it, from that very principle itself. [...] His arguments, if they prove any thing, prove not that the principle is *wrong*, but that, according to the applications he supposed to be made of it, it is *misapplied*. Is it possible for a man to move the earth? Yes; but he must first find out another earth to stand upon.

XIV. To disprove the propriety of it by arguments is impossible; but, from the causes that have been mentioned, or from some confused or partial view of it, a man may happen to be disposed not to relish it. Where this is the case, if he thinks the settling of his opinions on such a subject worth the trouble, let him take the following steps, and at length, perhaps, he may come to reconcile himself to it.

1. Let him settle with himself, whether he would wish to discard this principle altogether; if so, let him consider what it is that all his reasonings (in matters of politics especially) can amount to?

2. If he would, let him settle with himself, whether he would judge and act without any principle, or whether there is any other he would judge and act by?

3. If there be, let him examine and satisfy himself whether the principle he thinks he has found is really any separate intelligible principle: or whether it be not a mere principle in words, a kind of phrase, which at bottom expresses neither more nor less than the mere averment of his own unfounded sentiments: that is, what in another person he might be apt to call caprice?

4. If he is inclined to think that his own approbation or disapprobation, annexed to the idea of an act, without any regard to its consequences, is a sufficient foundation for him to judge and act upon, let him ask himself whether his sentiment is to be a standard of right and wrong, with respect to every other man, or whether every man's sentiment has the same privilege of being a standard in itself?

5. In the first case, let him ask himself whether his principle is not despotical, and hostile to all the rest of [the] human race?

6. In the second case, whether it is not anarchical, and whether at this rate there are not as many different standards of right and wrong as there are men? and whether even in the same man, the same thing, which is right to-day, may not (without the least change in its nature) be wrong to-morrow? and whether the same thing is not right and wrong in the same place at the same time? and in either case, whether all argument is not at an end? and whether, when two men have said, "I like this," and "I don't like it," they can (upon such a principle) have any thing more to say?

7. If he should have said to himself, No: for that the sentiment which he proposes as a standard must be grounded on reflection, let him say on what particulars the reflection is to turn? If on particulars having relation to the utility of the act, then let him say whether this is not deserting his own principle, and borrowing assistance from that very one in opposition to which he sets it up: or if not on those particulars, on what other particulars?

8. If he should be for compounding the matter, and adopting his own principle in part, and the principle of utility in part, let him say how far he will adopt it?

9. When he has settled with himself where he will stop, then let him ask himself how he justifies to himself the adopting it so far? and why he will not adopt it any farther?

10. Admitting any other principle than the principle of utility to be a right principle, a principle that it is right for a man to pursue: admitting (what is not true) that the word *right* can have a meaning without reference to utility, let him say whether there is any such thing as a *motive* that a man can have to pursue the dictates of it: if there is, let him say what that motive is, and how it is to be distinguished from those which enforce the dictates of utility: if not, then lastly let him say what it is this other principle can be good for?

Alasdair MacIntyre, "Narratives of the Good Life Guided by Living Traditions"*

A central thesis then begins to emerge: man is in his actions and practice, as well as in his fictions, essentially a story-telling animal. He is not essentially, but becomes through his history, a teller of stories that aspire to truth. But the key question for men is not about their own authorship; I can only answer the question "What am I to do?" if I can answer the prior question "Of what story or stories do I find myself a part?" We enter human society, that is, with one or more imputed characters – roles into which we have been drafted – and we have to learn what they are in order to be able to understand how others respond to us and how our responses to them are apt to be construed. It is through hearing stories about wicked stepmothers, lost children, good but misguided kings, wolves that suckle twin boys, youngest sons who receive no inheritance but must make their own way in the world and eldest sons who waste their inheritance on riotous living and go into exile to live with the swine, that children learn or mislearn both what a child and what a parent is, what the cast of characters may be in the drama into which they have been born and what the ways of the world are. Deprive children of stories and you leave them unscripted, anxious stutterers in their actions as in their words. Hence there is no way to give us an understanding of any society, including our own, except through the

* Alasdair MacIntyre, extracted from *After Virtue* (University Press of Notre Dame, 1981), pp. 201–7.

stock of stories which constitute its initial dramatic resources. Mythology, in its original sense, is at the heart of things. Vico was right and so was Joyce. And so too of course is that moral tradition from heroic society to its medieval heirs according to which the telling of stories has a key part in educating us into the virtues. ...

What the narrative concept of selfhood requires is thus twofold. On the one hand, I am what I may justifiably be taken by others to be in the course of living out a story that runs from my birth to my death; I am the *subject* of a history that is my own and no one else's, that has its own peculiar meaning. [...]

To be the subject of a narrative that runs from one's birth to one's death is, I remarked earlier, to be accountable for the actions and experiences which compose a narratable life. It is, that is, to be open to being asked to give a certain kind of account of what one did or what happened to one or what one witnessed at any earlier point in one's life the time at which the question is posed. [...] But to say of someone, under some one description ("The prisoner of the Chateau d'If") that he is the same person as someone characterised quite differently ("The Count of Monte Cristo") is precisely to say that it makes sense to ask him to give an intelligible narrative account enabling us to understand how he could at different times and different places be one and the same person and yet be so differently characterised. Thus personal identity is just that identity presupposed by the unity of the character which the unity of a narrative requires. Without such unity there would not be subjects of whom stories could be told.

The other aspect of narrative selfhood is correlative: I am not only accountable, I am one who can always ask others for an account, who can put others to the question. I am part of their story, as they are part of mine. The narrative of any one life is part of an interlocking set of narratives. Moreover this asking for and giving of accounts itself plays an important part in constituting narratives. Asking you what you did and why, saying what I did and why, pondering the differences between your account of what I did and my account of what I did, and *vice versa*, these are essential constituents of all but the very simplest and barest of narratives. Thus without the accountability of the self those trains of events that constitute all but the simplest and barest of narratives could not occur; and without that same accountability narratives would lack that continuity required to make both them and the actions that constitute them intelligible.

[...]

In what does the unity of an individual life consist? The answer is that its unity is the unity of a narrative embodied in a single life. To ask "What is the good for me?" is to ask how best I might live out that unity and bring it to completion. To ask "What is the good for man?" is to ask what all answers to the former question must have in common. But now it is important to emphasise that it is the systematic asking of these two questions and the attempt to answer them in deed as well as in word which provide the moral life with its unity. The unity of a human life is the unity of a narrative quest. Quests sometimes fail, are frustrated, abandoned or dissipated into distractions; and human lives may in all these ways also fail. But the only criteria for success or failure in a human life as a whole are the criteria of success or failure in a narrated or to-be-narrated quest. A quest for what?

Two key features of the medieval conception of a quest need to be recalled. The first is that without some at least partly determinate conception of the final *telos* there could not be any beginning to a quest. Some conception of the good for man is required. Whence is such a conception to be drawn? Precisely from those questions which led us to attempt to transcend that limited conception of the virtues which is available in and through practices. It is in looking for a conception of *the* good which will enable us to order other goods, for a conception of *the* good which will enable us to extend our understanding of the purpose and content of the virtues, for a conception of *the* good which will enable us to understand the place of integrity and constancy in life, that we initially define the kind of life which is a quest for the good. But secondly it is clear the medieval conception of a quest is not at all that of a search for something already adequately characterised, as miners search for gold or geologists for oil. It is in the course of the quest and only through encountering and coping with the various particular harms, dangers, temptations and distractions which provide any quest with its episodes and incidents that the goal of the quest is finally to be understood. A quest is always an education both as to the character of that which is sought and in self-knowledge.

The virtues therefore are to be understood as those dispositions which will not only sustain practices and enable us to achieve the goods internal to practices, but which will also sustain us in the relevant kind of quest for the good, by enabling us to overcome the harms, dangers, temptations and distractions which we encounter, and which will furnish us with increasing self-knowledge and increasing knowledge of the good. The catalogue of the virtues will therefore include the virtues required to sustain the kind of households and the kind of political communities in which men and women can seek for the good together and the virtues necessary for philosophical enquiry about the character of the good. We have then arrived at a provisional conclusion about the good life for man: the good life for man is the life spent in seeking for the good life for man, and the virtues necessary for the seeking are those which will enable us to understand what more and what else the good life for man is. We have also completed the second stage in our account of the virtues, by situating them in relation to the good life for man and not only in relation to practices. But our enquiry requires a third stage.

For I am never able to seek for the good or exercise the virtues only *qua* individual. This is partly because what it is to live the good life concretely varies from circumstance to circumstance even when it is one and the same conception of the good life and one and the same set of virtues which are being embodied in a human life. What the good life is for a fifth-century Athenian general will not be the same as what it was for a medieval nun or a seventeenth-century farmer. But it is not just that different individuals live in different social circumstances; it is also that we all approach our own circumstances as bearers of a particular social identity. I am someone's son or daughter, someone else's cousin or uncle; I am a citizen of this or that city, a member of this or that guild or profession; I belong to this clan, that tribe, this nation. Hence what is good for me has to be the good for one who inhabits these roles. As such, I inherit from the past of my family, my city, my tribe, my nation, a variety of debts, inheritances, rightful expectations and obligations. These constitute the given of my life, my moral starting point. This is in part what gives my life its own moral particularity.

This thought is likely to appear alien and even surprising from the standpoint of modern individualism. From the standpoint of individualism I am what I myself choose to be. I can always, if I wish to, put in question what are taken to be the merely contingent social features of my existence. I may biologically be my father's son; but I cannot be held responsible for what he did unless I choose implicitly or explicitly to assume such responsibility. I may legally be a citizen of a certain country; but I cannot be held responsible for what my country does or has done unless I choose implicitly or explicitly to assume such responsibility. Such individualism is expressed by those modern Americans who deny any responsibility for the effects of slavery upon black Americans, saying "I never owned any slaves." It is more subtly the standpoint of those other modern Americans who accept a nicely calculated responsibility for such effects measured precisely by the benefits they themselves as individuals have indirectly received from slavery. In both cases "being an American" is not in itself taken to be part of the moral identity of the individual. And of course there is nothing peculiar to modern Americans in this attitude: the Englishman who says, "*I* never did any wrong to Ireland; why bring up that old history as though it had something to do with *me*?" or the young German who believes that being born after 1945 means that what Nazis did to Jews has no moral relevance to his relationship to his Jewish contemporaries, exhibit the same attitude, that according to which the self is detachable from its social and historical roles and statuses. And the self so detached is of course a self very much at home in either Sartre's or Goffman's perspective, a self that can have no history. The contrast with the narrative view of the self is clear. For the story of my life is always embedded in the story of those communities from which I derive my identity. I am born with a past; and to try to cut myself off from that past, in the individualist mode, is to deform my present relationships. The possession of an historical identity and the possession of a social identity coincide. Notice that rebellion against my identity is always one possible mode of expressing it.

Notice also that the fact that the self has to find its moral identity in and through its membership in communities such as those of the family, the neighbourhood, the city and the tribe does not entail that the self has to accept the moral *limitations* of the particularity of those forms of community. Without those moral particularities to begin from there would never be anywhere to begin; but it is in moving forward from such particularity that the search for the good, for the universal, consists. Yet particularity can never be simply left behind or obliterated. The notion of escaping from it into a realm of entirely universal maxims which belong to man as such, whether in its eighteenth-century Kantian form or in the presentation of some modern analytical moral philosophies, is an illusion and an illusion with painful consequences. When men and women identify what are in fact their partial and particular causes too easily and too completely with the cause of some universal principle, they usually behave worse than they would otherwise do.

What I am, therefore, is in key part what I inherit, a specific past that is present to some degree in my present. I find myself part of a history and that is generally to say, whether I like it or not, whether I recognise it or not, one of the bearers of a tradition. [...] What constitutes such traditions?

We are apt to be misled here by the ideological uses to which the concept of a tradition has been put by conservative political theorists. Characteristically such theorists have followed Burke in contrasting tradition with reason and the stability of tradition with conflict. Both contrasts obfuscate. For all reasoning takes place within the context of some traditional mode of thought, transcending through criticism and invention the limitations of what had hitherto been reasoned in that tradition; this is as true of modern physics as of medieval logic. Moreover when a tradition is in good order it is always partially constituted by an argument about the goods the pursuit of which gives to that tradition its particular point and purpose.

So when an institution – a university, say, or a farm, or a hospital – is the bearer of a tradition of practice or practices, its common life will be partly, but in a centrally important way, constituted by a continuous argument as to what a university is and ought to be or what good farming is or what good medicine is. Traditions, when vital, embody continuities of conflict. Indeed when a tradition becomes Burkean, it is always dying or dead.

The individualism of modernity could of course find no use for the notion of tradition within its own conceptual scheme except as an adversary notion; it therefore all too willingly abandoned it to the Burkeans, who, faithful to Burke's own allegiance, tried to combine adherence in politics to a conception of tradition which would vindicate the oligarchical revolution of property of 1688 and adherence in economics to the doctrine and institutions of the free market. The theoretical incoherence of this mismatch did not deprive it of ideological usefulness. But the outcome has been that modern conservatives are for the most part engaged in conserving only older rather than later versions of liberal individualism. Their own core doctrine is as liberal and as individualist as that of self-avowed liberals.

A living tradition then is an historically extended, socially embodied argument, and an argument precisely in part about the goods which constitute that tradition. Within a tradition the pursuit of goods extends through generations, sometimes through many generations. Hence the individual's search for his or her good is generally and characteristically conducted within a context defined by those traditions of which the individual's life is a part, and this is true both of those goods which are internal to practices and of the goods of a single life. Once again the narrative phenomenon of embedding is crucial: the history of a practice in our time is generally and characteristically embedded in and made intelligible in terms of the larger and longer history of the tradition through which the practice in its present form was conveyed to us; the history of each of our own lives is generally and characteristically embedded in and made intelligible in terms of the larger and longer histories of a number of traditions. I have to say "generally and characteristically" rather than "always," for traditions decay, disintegrate and disappear. What then sustains and strengthens traditions? What weakens and destroys them?

The answer in key part is: the exercise or the lack of exercise of the relevant virtues. The virtues find their point and purpose not only in sustaining those relationships necessary if the variety of goods internal to practices are to be achieved and not only in sustaining the form of an individual life in which that individual may seek out his or her good as the good of his or her whole life, but also in sustaining those traditions which provide both practices and individual lives with their necessary historical context. Lack of justice, lack of truthfulness, lack of courage, lack of the relevant intellectual virtues – these corrupt traditions, just as they do those institutions and practices which derive their life from the traditions of which they are the contemporary embodiments. To recognise this is of course also to recognise the existence of an additional virtue, one whose importance is perhaps most obvious when it is least present, the virtue of having an adequate sense of the traditions to which one belongs or which confront one. This virtue is not to be confused with any form of conservative antiquarianism; I am not praising those who choose the conventional conservative role of *laudator temporis acti*. It is rather the case that an adequate sense of tradition manifests itself in a grasp of those future possibilities which the past has made available to the present. Living traditions, just because they continue a not-yet-completed narrative, confront a future whose determinate and determinable character, so far as it possesses any, derives from the past.

Richard Rorty, "America's Civic Religion: A Hopeful Pragmatism"*

Whitman and Dewey were among the prophets of this civic religion. They offered a new account of what America was, in the hope of mobilizing Americans as political agents. The most striking feature of their redescription of our country is its thoroughgoing

* Richard Rorty, extracted from *Achieving Our Country* (Harvard University Press, 1998).

secularism.[15] In the past, most of the stories that have incited nations to projects of self-improvement have been stories about their obligations to one or more gods. For much of European and American history, nations have asked themselves how they appear in the eyes of the Christian God. American exceptionalism has usually been a belief in special divine favor, as in the writings of Joseph Smith and Billy Graham. [...]

Dewey and Whitman wanted Americans to continue to think of themselves as exceptional, but both wanted to drop any reference to divine favor or wrath. They hoped to separate the fraternity and loving kindness urged by the Christian scriptures from the ideas of supernatural parentage, immortality, providence, and – most important – sin. They wanted Americans to take pride in what America might, all by itself and by its own lights, make of itself, rather than in America's obedience to any authority – even the authority of God. Thus Whitman wrote:

> And I call to mankind, Be not curious about God,
> For I who am curious about each am not curious
> about God.[16]

Whitman thought there was no need to be curious about God because there is no standard, not even a divine one, against which the decisions of a free people can be measured. Americans, he hoped, would spend the energy that past human societies had spent on discovering God's desires on discovering one another's desires. Americans will be curious about every other American, but not about anything which claims authority over America.

[...]

"Democracy," Dewey said, "is neither a form of government nor a social expediency, but a metaphysic of the relation of man and his experience in nature."[17] For both Whitman and Dewey, the terms "America" and "democracy" are shorthand for a new conception of what it is to be human – a conception which has no room for obedience to a nonhuman authority, and in which nothing save freely achieved consensus among human beings has any authority at all. Steven Rockefeller is right to say that "[Dewey's] goal was to integrate fully the religious life with the American democratic life."[18] But the sort of integration Dewey hoped for is not a matter of blending the worship of an eternal Being with hope for the temporal realization, in America, of this Being's will. It is a matter of forgetting about eternity. More generally, it is a matter of replacing shared knowledge of what is already real with social hope for what might become real. The word "democracy," Whitman said, "is a great word, whose history ... remains unwritten, because that history has yet to be enacted."[19]

Forgetting about eternity, and replacing knowledge of the antecedently real with hope for the contingent future, is not easy. But both tasks have been a good deal easier since Hegel. Hegel was the first philosopher to take time and finitude as seriously as any Hobbesian

[15] I use "secularism" in the sense of "anticlericalism" rather than of "atheism." Dewey's dislike of "aggressive atheism" is made clear in *A Common Faith*. I have argued elsewhere that Dewey, like James, wanted pragmatism to be compatible with religious belief – but only with a privatized religious belief, not with the sort of religious belief that produces churches, especially churches which take political positions. See Rorty, "Religious Faith, Intellectual Responsibility, and Romance," in Ruth-Anna Putnam, ed., *The Cambridge Companion to William James* (Cambridge: Cambridge University Press, 1997); idem, "Pragmatism as Romantic Polytheism," in Morris Dickstein, ed., *The New Pragmatism* (Durham, NC: Duke University Press, 1998); idem, "Religion as Conversation-Stopper," *Common Knowledge*, 3 (Spring 1994), pp. 1–6. This last is a reply to Stephen Carter's argument that religious voices should be heard in the public square.

[16] *Leaves of Grass*, p. 85. All references to both *Leaves of Grass* and *Democratic Vistas* are to Walt Whitman, *Complete Poetry and Selected Prose* (New York: Library of America, 1982).

[17] John Dewey, "Maeterlinck's Philosophy of Life," in *The Middle Works of John Dewey*, vol. 6 (Carbondale: Southern Illinois University Press, 1978), p. 135. Dewey says that Emerson, Whitman, and Maeterlinck are the only three to have grasped this fact about democracy. Dewey's term "metaphysic" is a bit unfortunate. He might have expressed his meaning better by saying that, Nietzsche to the contrary, democracy is the principal means by which a more evolved form of humanity will come into existence.

Kenneth Burke once wrote (*A Grammar of Motives*, p. 504) that "characters possess *degrees of being* in proportion to the variety of perspectives from which they can with justice be perceived. Thus we could say that plants have 'less being' than animals, because each higher order admits and requires a new dimension of terms not literally relevant to the lower orders." Democratic humanity, Dewey and Burke might have agreed, has "more being" than predemocratic humanity. The citizens of a democratic, Whitmanesque society are able to create new, hitherto unimagined roles and goals for themselves. So a greater variety of perspectives, and of descriptive terms, becomes available to them, and can with justice be used to account for them.

[18] Steven Rockefeller, *John Dewey: Religious Faith and Democratic Humanism* (New York: Columbia University Press, 1991), p. 4.

[19] Whitman, *Democratic Vistas*, p. 960.

materialist, while at the same time taking the religious impulse as seriously as any Hebrew prophet or Christian saint. Spinoza had attempted such a synthesis by identifying God with Nature, but Spinoza still thought it desirable to see things under the aspect of eternity. Hegel rejoined that any view of human history under that aspect would be too thin and abstract to be of any religious use. He suggested that the meaning of human life is a function of how human history turns out, rather than of the relation of that history to something ahistorical. This suggestion made it easier for two of Hegel's readers, Dewey and Whitman, to claim that the way to think about the significance of the human adventure is to look forward rather than upward: to contrast a possible human future with the human past and present.

Marx, unfortunately, has been the most influential of the left-wing Hegelians. But Marx mistakenly thought that Hegel's dialectic could be used for predictive as well as inspirational purposes. That is why Marxists have produced the form of historicism which Karl Popper rightly criticized as impoverished. But there is another form of Hegelian historicism which survives Popper's criticisms intact. In this form, historicism is simply the temporalization of what Plato, and even Kant, try to eternalize. It is the temporalization of ultimate significance, and of awe.

[...]

Whitman, like most American thinkers of the nineteenth century, believed that the Golgotha of the Spirit was in the past, and that the American Declaration of Independence had been an Easter dawn. Because the United States is the first country founded in the hope of a new kind of human fraternity, it would be the place where the promise of the ages would first be realized. Americans would form the vanguard of human history, because, as Whitman says, "the Americans of all nations at any time upon the earth have probably the fullest poetical nature. The United States themselves are essentially the greatest poem."[20] They are also the fulfillment of the human past. "The blossoms we wear in our hats," Whitman wrote, "are the growth of two thousand years."[21]

Whitman thought that we Americans have the most poetical nature because we are the first thoroughgoing experiment in national self-creation: the first nation-state with nobody but itself to please – not even God. We are the greatest poem because we put ourselves in the place of God: our essence is our existence, and our existence is in the future. Other nations thought of themselves as hymns to the glory of God. We redefine God as our future selves.

Neither Dewey nor Whitman, however, was committed to the view that things would *inevitably* go well for America, that the American experiment in self-creation would succeed. The price of temporalization is contingency. Because they rejected any idea of Divine Providence and any idea of immanent teleology, Dewey and Whitman had to grant the possibility that the vanguard of humanity may lose its way, and perhaps lead our species over a cliff. As Whitman put it, "The United States are destined either to surmount the gorgeous history of feudalism, or else prove the most tremendous failure of time."[22] Whereas Marx and Spencer claimed to know what was bound to happen, Whitman and Dewey denied such knowledge in order to make room for pure, joyous hope.

The trouble with Europe, Whitman and Dewey thought, was that it tried too hard for knowledge: it tried to find an answer to the question of what human beings should be like. It hoped to get authoritative guidance for human conduct. One of the first Europeans to suggest abandoning this hope was Wilhelm von Humboldt, a founder of ethnography and a philosopher who greatly influenced Hegel. In a passage which Mill used as the epigraph for his *On Liberty*, von Humboldt wrote that the point of social organization is to make evident "the absolute and essential importance of human development in its richest diversity." Whitman picked up this particular ball from Mill and cited *On Liberty* in the first paragraph of his *Democratic Vistas*. There Whitman says that Mill demands "two main constituents, or sub-strata, for a truly grand nationality – 1st, a large variety of character – and 2nd, full play for human nature to expand itself in numberless and even conflicting directions."[23]

Mill and Humboldt's "richest diversity" and Whitman's "full play" are ways of saying that no past human achievement, not Plato's or even Christ's, can tell us about the ultimate significance of human life. No such achievement can give us a template on which to model our future. The future will widen endlessly. Experiments with new forms of individual and social life will interact and reinforce one another. Individual life will become unthinkably diverse and social life unthinkably free. The moral we should draw from the European past, and in particular from Christianity, is not instruction about the authority under which we should live, but suggestions about how to make ourselves wonderfully different from anything that has been.

20 Whitman, *Leaves of Grass*, p. 5.

21 Ibid., p. 71.

22 Whitman, *Democratic Vistas*, p. 930.

23 Ibid., p. 929.

This romance of endless diversity should not, however, be confused with what nowadays is sometimes called "multiculturalism." The latter term suggests a morality of live-and-let-live, a politics of side-by-side development in which members of distinct cultures preserve and protect their own culture against the incursions of other cultures. Whitman, like Hegel, had no interest in preservation or protection. He wanted competition and argument between alternative forms of human life – a poetic agon, in which jarring dialectical discords would be resolved in previously unheard harmonies. The Hegelian idea of "progressive evolution," which was the nineteenth century's great contribution to political and social thought, is that everybody gets played off against everybody else. This should occur nonviolently if possible, but violently if necessary, as was in fact necessary in America in 1861. The Hegelian hope is that the result of such struggles will be a new culture, better than any of those of which it is the synthesis.[24] This new culture will be better because it will contain more variety in unity – it will be a tapestry in which more strands have been woven together. But this tapestry, too, will eventually have to be torn to shreds in order that a larger one may be woven, in order that the past may not obstruct the future.

[...]

Logic and sermons never convince,
The damp of night drives deeper into my soul.

Only what proves itself to every man and woman is so,
Only what nobody denies is so.[25]

These passages in Whitman can be read as presaging the doctrine that made pragmatism both original and infamous: its refusal to believe in the existence of Truth, in the sense of something not made by human hands, something which has authority over human beings. The closest Hegel got to this pragmatist doctrine was his dictum that philosophy is its own time held in thought.

Despite this historicism, Hegel could never bring himself to assert the primacy of the practical over the theoretical – what Hilary Putnam, defining the essence of pragmatism, has called the primacy of the agent point of view. Dewey, like Marx in the Eleventh Thesis on Feuerbach, took the primacy of the practical all the way. His pragmatism is an answer to the question "What can philosophy do for the United States?" rather than to the question "How can the United States be philosophically justified?" He abandoned the question "Why should one prefer democracy to feudalism, and self-creation to obedience to authority?" in favor of the question "Given the preferences we Americans share, given the adventure on which we are embarked, what should we say about truth, knowledge, reason, virtue, human nature, and all the other traditional philosophical topics?" America will, Dewey hoped, be the first nation-state to have the courage to renounce hope of justification from on high – from a source which is immovable and eternal. Such a country will treat both its philosophy and its poetry as modes of self-expression, rather than ask its philosophers to provide it with reassurance.

The culminating achievement of Dewey's philosophy was to treat evaluative terms such as "true" and "right" not as signifying a relation to some antecedently existing thing – such as God's Will, or Moral Law, or the Intrinsic Nature of Objective Reality – but as expressions of satisfaction at having found a solution to a problem: a problem which may someday seem obsolete, and a satisfaction which may someday seem misplaced. The effect of this treatment is to change our account of progress. Instead of seeing progress as a matter of getting closer to something specifiable in advance, we see it as a matter of solving more problems. Progress is, as Thomas Kuhn suggested, measured by the extent to which we have made ourselves better than we were in the past rather than by our increased proximity to a goal.

Late in his life, Dewey tried to "state briefly the democratic faith in the formal terms of a philosophical proposition." The proposition was that democracy is the only form of moral and social faith which does not "rest upon the idea that experience must be subjected at some point or other to some form of external control: to some 'authority' alleged to exist outside the processes of experience."[26] This formulation echoes Whitman's exclamation, "How long it takes to make this American world see that it is, in itself, the final authority and reliance!"[27] Antiauthoritarianism is the motive behind Dewey's opposition to Platonic and theocentric metaphysics, and behind his more original and far more controversial opposition to the correspondence theory of truth: the idea that truth is a matter of accurate representation of an antecedently existing reality. For Dewey, the idea that there was a reality "out there" with an

24 Whitman hoped that the Era of Reconstruction would be the birth of such a new culture. See David S. Reynolds, *Walt Whitman's America: A Cultural Biography* (New York: Random House, 1995), chapter 14.

25 Whitman, *Leaves of Grass*, p. 56.

26 "Creative Democracy – The Task before Us," in *Later Works of John Dewey*, vol. 14 (Carbondale: Southern Illinois University Press, 1988), p. 229.

27 Whitman, *Democratic Vistas*, p. 956.

intrinsic nature to be respected and corresponded to was not a manifestation of sound common sense. It was a relic of Platonic otherworldliness.

[...]

Hopelessness has become fashionable on the Left – principled, theorized, philosophical hopelessness. The Whitmanesque hope which lifted the hearts of the American Left before the 1960s is now thought to have been a symptom of a naive "humanism."

I see this preference for knowledge over hope as repeating the move made by leftist intellectuals who, earlier in the century, got their Hegelianism from Marx rather than Dewey. Marx thought we should be scientific rather than merely utopian – that we should interpret the historical events of our day within a larger theory. Dewey did not. He thought one had to view these events as the protocols of social experiments whose outcomes are unpredictable.

The Foucauldian Left represents an unfortunate regression to the Marxist obsession with scientific rigor. This Left still wants to put historical events in a theoretical context. It exaggerates the importance of philosophy for politics, and wastes its energy on sophisticated theoretical analyses of the significance of current events. But Foucauldian theoretical sophistication is even more useless to leftist politics than was Engels' dialectical materialism. Engels at least had an eschatology. Foucauldians do not even have that. Because they regard liberal reformist initiatives as symptoms of a discredited liberal "humanism," they have little interest in designing new social experiments.

This distrust of humanism, with its retreat from practice to theory, [...] leads them to look for a frame of reference outside the process of experimentation and decision that is an individual or a national life. Grand theories – eschatologies like Hegel's or Marx's, inverted eschatologies like Heidegger's, and rationalizations of hopelessness like Foucault's and Lacan's – satisfy the urges that theology used to satisfy. These are urges which Dewey hoped Americans might cease to feel. Dewey wanted Americans to share a civic religion that substituted utopian striving for claims to theological knowledge.

Carol Gilligan, "In a Different Voice"*

Over the past ten years, I have been listening to people talking about morality and about themselves. Halfway through that time. I began to hear a distinction in these voices, two ways of speaking about moral problems, two modes of describing the relationship between other and self. Differences represented in the psychological literature as steps in a developmental progression suddenly appeared instead as a contrapuntal theme, woven into the cycle of life and recurring in varying forms in people's judgments, fantasies, and thoughts. The occasion for this observation was the selection of a sample of women for a study of the relation between judgment and action in a situation of moral conflict and choice. Against the background of the psychological descriptions of identity and moral development which I had read and taught for a number of years, the women's voices sounded distinct. It was then that I began to notice the recurrent problems in interpreting women's development and to connect these problems to the repeated exclusion of women from the critical theory-building studies of psychological research.

This book records different modes of thinking about relationships and the association of these modes with male and female voices in psychological and literary texts and in the data of my research. The disparity between women's experience and the representation of human development, noted throughout the psychological literature, has generally been seen to signify a problem in women's development. Instead, the failure of women to fit existing models of human growth may point to a problem in the representation, a limitation in the conception of human condition, an omission of certain truths about life.

The different voice I describe is characterized not by gender but theme. Its association with women is an empirical observation, and it is primarily through women's voices that I trace its development. But this association is not absolute, and the contrasts between male and female voices are presented here to highlight a distinction between two modes of thought and to focus a problem of interpretation rather than to represent a generalization about either sex.

[...]

At a time when efforts are being made to eradicate discrimination between the sexes in the search for social equality and justice, the differences between the sexes are being rediscovered in the social sciences. This discovery occurs when theories formerly considered to be sexually neutral in their scientific objectivity are found instead to reflect a consistent observational and evaluative bias. Then the presumed neutrality of science, like that of language itself, gives way to the recognition that the categories of knowledge are human constructions. The fascination with point of view that has informed the fiction of the twentieth century and the corresponding recognition of the

* Carol Gilligan, extracted from *In a Different Voice* (Harvard University Press, 1982), pp. 1–2, 6–23.

relativity of judgment infuse our scientific understanding as well when we begin to notice how accustomed we have become to seeing life through men's eyes.

[...]

"From very early, then, because they are parented by a person of the same gender ... girls come to experience themselves as less differentiated than boys, as more continuous with and related to the external object-world, and as differently oriented to their inner object-world as well."[28]

Consequently, relationships and particularly issues of dependency, are experienced differently by women and men. For boys and men, separation and individualism are critically tied to gender identity since separation from the mother is essential for the development of masculinity. For girls and women, issues of femininity or feminine identity do not depend on the achievement of separation from the mother or on the progress of individuation. Since masculinity is defined through separation while femininity is defined through attachment, male gender identity is threatened by intimacy while female gender identity is threatened by separation. Thus males tend to have difficulty with relationships, while females tend to have problems with individuation. The quality of embeddedness in social and personal relationships that characterizes women's lives in contrast to men's, however, becomes not only a descriptive difference but also a developmental liability when the milestones of childhood and adolescent development in the psychological literature are markers of increasing separation. Women's failure to separate then becomes by definition a failure to develop.

[...]

These observations about sex difference support the conclusion reached by David McClelland that "sex role turns out to be one of the most important determinants of human behavior; psychologists have found sex differences in their studies from the moment they started doing empirical research." But since it is difficult to say "different" without saying "better" or "worse," since there is a tendency to construct a single scale of measurement, and since that scale has generally been derived from and standardized on the basis of men's interpretations of research data drawn predominantly or exclusively from studies of males, psychologists "have tended to regard male behavior as the 'norm' and female behavior as some kind of deviation from that norm."[29] Thus, when women do not conform to the standards of psychological expectation, the conclusion has generally been that something is wrong with the women.

[...]

Kohlberg's six stages that describe the development of moral judgment from childhood to adulthood are based empirically on a study of eighty-four boys whose development Kohlberg has followed for a period of over twenty years.[30] Although Kohlberg claims universality for his stage sequence, those groups not included in his original sample rarely reach his higher stages.[31] Prominent among those who thus appear to be deficient in moral development when measured by Kohlberg's scale are women, whose judgments seem to exemplify the third stage of his six-stage scale. At this stage morality is conceived in interpersonal terms and goodness is equated with helping and pleasing others. This conception of goodness is considered by Kohlberg and Kramer to be functional in the lives of mature women insofar as their lives take place in the home. Kohlberg and Kramer imply that only if women enter the traditional arena of male activity will they recognize the inadequacy of this moral perspective and progress like men toward higher stages where relationships are subordinated to rules (stage four) and rules to universal principles of justice (stages five and six).[32]

Yet herein lies a paradox, for the very traits that traditionally have defined the "goodness" of women, their care for and sensitivity to the needs of others, are those that mark them as deficient in moral development. In this version of moral development, however, the conception of maturity is derived from the study of men's lives and reflects the importance of individuation in their development. Piaget, challenging the common impression that a developmental theory is built like a pyramid from its base in infancy, points out that a conception of development instead hangs from its vertex of maturity, the point toward which progress is traced. Thus, a change in the definition of maturity does not simply alter the description of the highest stage but recasts the understanding of development, changing the entire account.

28 Nancy Chodorow, *Reproduction of Mothering* (Berkeley: University of California Press, 1978), p. 167.

29 David McClellend, *Power: The Inner Experience* (New York: Irvington, 1975), p. 81.

30 Lawrence Kohlberg, *The Philosophy of Moral Development* (San Francisco: Harper and Row, 1981).

31 See, for example, Carolyn Edwards, "Social Complexity and Moral Development: A Kenyan Study," *Ethos*, 3 (1975), pp. 505–27.

32 Lawrence Kohlberg and R. Kramer, "Continuities and Discontinuities in Child and Adult Moral Development," *Human Development*, vol. 12, 1969, pp. 93–120.

When one begins with the study of women and derives developmental constructs from their lives, the outline of a moral conception different from that described by Freud, Piaget, or Kohlberg begins to emerge and informs a different description of development. In this conception, the moral problem arises from conflicting responsibilities rather than from competing rights and requires for its resolution a mode of thinking that is contextual and narrative rather than formal and abstract. This conception of morality as concerned with the activity of care centers moral development around the understanding of responsibility and relationships, just as the conception of morality as fairness ties moral development to the understanding of rights and rules.

This different construction of the moral problem by women may be seen as the critical reason for their failure to develop within the constraints of Kohlberg's system. Regarding all constructions of responsibility as evidence of a conventional moral understanding, Kohlberg defines the highest stages of moral development as deriving from a reflective understanding of human rights. That the morality of rights differs from the morality of responsibility in its emphasis on separation rather than connection, in its consideration of the individual rather than the relationship as primary, is illustrated by two responses to interview questions about the nature of morality. The first comes from a twenty-five-year-old man, one of the participants in Kohlberg's study:

> [*What does the word morality mean to you?*] Nobody in the world knows the answer. I think it is recognizing the rights of other individuals, not interfering with those rights. Act as fairly as you would have them treat you. I think it is basically to preserve the human being's right to existence. I think that is the most important. Secondly, the human being's right to do as he pleases, again without interfering with somebody else's rights.
>
> [*How have your views on morality changed since the last interview?*] I think I am more aware of an individual's rights now. I used to be looking at it strictly from my point of view, just for me. Now I think I am more aware of what the individual has a right to.

Kohlberg cites this man's response as illustrative of the principled conception of human rights that exemplifies his fifth and sixth stages. Commenting on the response, Kohlberg says: "Moving to a perspective outside of that of his society, he identifies morality with justice (fairness, rights, the Golden Rule), with recognition of the rights of others as these are defined naturally or intrinsically. The human being's right to do as he pleases without interfering with somebody's else's rights is a formula defining rights prior to social legislation."[33]

The second response comes from a woman who participated in the rights and responsibilities study. She also was twenty-five and, at the time, a third-year law student:

> [*Is there really some correct solution to moral problems, or is everybody's opinion equally right?*] No, I don't think everybody's opinion is equally right. I think that in some situations there may be opinions that are equally valid, and one could conscientiously adopt one of several courses of action. But there are other situations in which I think there are right and wrong answers, that sort of inhere in the nature of existence, of all individuals here who need to live with each other to live. We need to depend on each other, and hopefully it is not only a physical need but a need of fulfillment in ourselves, that a person's life is enriched by cooperating with other people and striving to live in harmony with everybody else, and to that end, there are right and wrong, there are things which promote that end and that move away from it, and in that way it is possible to choose in certain cases among different courses of action that obviously promote or harm that goal.
>
> [*Is there a time in the past when you would have thought about these things differently?*] Oh, yeah, I think that I went through a time when I thought that things were pretty relative, that I can't tell you what to do and you can't tell me what to do, because you've got your conscience and I've got mine.
>
> [*When was that?*] When I was in high school. I guess that it just sort of dawned on me that my own ideas changed, and because my own judgment changed, I felt I couldn't judge another person's judgment. But now I think even when it is only the person himself who is going to be affected, I say it is wrong to the extent it doesn't cohere with what I know about human nature and what I know about you, and just from what I think is true about the operation of the universe, I could say I think you are making a mistake.
>
> [*What led you to change, do you think?*] Just seeing more of life, just recognizing that there are an awful lot of things that are common among people. There are certain things that you come to learn promote a better life and better relationships and more personal fulfillment than other things that in general tend to do the opposite, and the things that promote these things, you would call morally right.

[33] Lawrence Kohlberg, "Continuities and Discontinuities in Child and Adult Moral Development Revisited," in *Collected Papers on Moral Development and Education*, Moral Education Research Foundation, Harvard University, 1973.

This response also represents a personal reconstruction of morality following a period of questioning and doubt, but the reconstruction of moral understanding is based not on the primary and universality of individual rights, but rather on what she describes as a "very strong sense of being responsible to the world." Within this construction, the moral dilemma changes from how to exercise one's rights without interfering with the rights of others to how "to lead a moral life which includes obligations to myself and my family and people in general." The problem then becomes one of limiting responsibilities without abandoning moral concern. When asked to describe herself, this woman says that she values "having other people that I am tied to, and also having people that I am responsible to. I have a very strong sense of being responsible to the world, that I can't just live for my enjoyment, but just the fact of being in the world gives me an obligation to do what I can to make the world a better place to live in, no matter how small a scale that may be on." Thus while Kohlberg's subject worries about people interfering with each other's rights, this woman worries about "the possibility of omission, of not helping others when you could help them."

The issue that this woman raises is addressed by Jane Loevinger's fifth "autonomous" stage of ego development, where autonomy, placed in a context of relationships, is defined as modulating an excessive sense of responsibility through the recognition that other people have responsibility for their own destiny. The autonomous stage in Loevinger's account witnesses a relinquishing of moral dichotomies and their replacement with "a feeling for the complexity and multifaceted character of real people and real situations."[34] Whereas the rights conception of morality that informs Kohlberg's principled level (stages five and six) is geared to arriving at an objectively fair or just resolution to moral dilemmas upon which all rational persons could agree, the responsibility conception focuses instead on the limitations of any particular resolution and describes the conflicts that remain.

Thus it becomes clear why a morality of rights and noninterference may appear frightening to women in its potential justification of indifference and unconcern. At the same time, it becomes clear why, from a male perspective, a morality of responsibility appears inconclusive and diffuse, given its insistent contextual relativism. Women's moral judgments thus elucidate the pattern observed in the description of the developmental differences between the sexes, but they also provide an alternative conception of maturity by which these differences can be assessed and their implications traced. The psychology of women that has consistently been described as distinctive in its greater orientation toward relationships and interdependence implies a more contextual mode of judgment and a different moral understanding. Given the differences in women's conceptions of self and morality, women bring to the life cycle a different point of view and order human experience in terms of different priorities.

The myth of Demeter and Persephone, which McClelland cites as exemplifying the feminine attitude toward power, was associated with the Eleusinian Mysteries celebrated in ancient Greece for over two thousand years. As told in the Homeric *Hymn to Demeter*, the story of Persephone indicates the strengths of interdependence, building up resources and giving, that McClelland found in his research on power motivation to characterize the mature feminine style. Although, McClelland says, "it is fashionable to conclude that no one knows what went on in the Mysteries, it is known that they were probably the most important religious ceremonies, even partly on the historical record, which were organized by and for women, especially at the onset before men by means of the cult of Dionysos began to take them over." Thus McClelland regards the myth as "a special presentation of feminine psychology." It is, as well, a life-cycle story par excellence.[35]

Persephone, the daughter of Demeter, while playing in a meadow with her girlfriends, sees a beautiful narcissus which she runs to pick. As she does so, the earth opens and she is snatched away by Hades, who takes her to his underworld kingdom. Demeter, goddess of the earth, so mourns the loss of her daughter that she refuses to allow anything to grow. The crops that sustain life on earth shrivel up, killing men and animals alike, until Zeus takes pity on man's suffering and persuades his brother to return Persephone to her mother. But before she leaves, Persephone eats some pomegranate seeds, which ensures that she will spend part of every year with Hades in the underworld.

The elusive mystery of women's development lies in its recognition of the continuing importance of attachment in the human life cycle. Woman's place in man's life cycle is to protect this recognition while the developmental litany intones the celebration of separation, autonomy, individuation, and natural rights. The myth of Persephone speaks directly to the distortion in this

34 Jane Loevinger and Ruth Wessler, *Measuring Ego Development* (San Francisco: Jossey-Bass, 1970), p. 6.

35 McClelland, *Power: The Inner Experience*, p. 96.

view by reminding us that narcissism leads to death, that the fertility of the earth is in some mysterious way tied to the continuation of the mother–daughter relationship, and that the life cycle itself arises from an alternation between the world of women and that of men. Only when life-cycle theorists divide their attention and begin to live with women as they have lived with men will their vision encompass the experience of both sexes and their theories become correspondingly more fertile.

John Rawls, "Political Constructivism"*

In this lecture [...] we shall see that political constructivism provides political liberalism with an appropriate conception of objectivity.

Political constructivism is a view about the structure and content of a political conception. It says that once, if ever, reflective equilibrium is attained, the principles of political justice (content) may be represented as the outcome of a certain procedure of construction (structure). In this procedure, as modeled by the original position, rational agents, as representatives of citizens and subject to reasonable conditions, select the public principles of justice to regulate the basic structure of society. This procedure, we conjecture, embodies all the relevant requirements of practical reason and shows how the principles of justice follow from the principles of practical reason in union with conceptions of society and person, themselves ideas of practical reason.

The full significance of a constructivist political conception lies in its connection with the fact of reasonable pluralism and the need for a democratic society to secure the possibility of an overlapping consensus on its fundamental political values. The reason such a conception may be the focus of an overlapping consensus of comprehensive doctrines is that it develops the principles of justice from public and shared ideas of society as a fair system of cooperation and of citizens as free and equal by using the principles of their common practical reason. In honoring those principles of justice citizens show themselves autonomous, politically speaking, and thus in a way compatible with their reasonable comprehensive doctrines.

* John Rawls, extracted from *Political Liberalism* (Columbia University Press, 1993), pp. 89–93.

The idea of a constructivist conception

We are here concerned with a constructivist conception of political justice and not with a comprehensive moral doctrine.[36] To fix ideas I first examine moral realism in the form illustrated by rational intuitionism as found in the English tradition in Clarke and Price, and Sidgwick and Ross, among others. [...]

Rational intuitionism may be characterized by four basic features that distinguish it from political constructivism. I state these four features and then describe political constructivism by setting out four corresponding though contrasting features.

The first feature of rational intuitionism says that moral first principles and judgments, when correct, are true statements about an independent order of moral values; moreover, this order does not depend on, nor is it to be explained by, the activity of any actual (human) minds, including the activity of reason.

The second feature says that moral first principles are known by theoretical reason. This feature is suggested by the idea that moral knowledge is gained in part by a kind of perception and intuition, as well as organized by first principles found acceptable on due reflection. It is strengthened by the comparison intuitionists make between moral knowledge and knowledge of mathematics in arithmetic and geometry. The order of moral values is said to lie in God's reason and to direct the divine will.

The third feature concerns the sparse conception of the person. Although not explicitly stated, this feature may be gathered from the fact that rational intuitionism does not require a fuller conception of the person and needs little more than the idea of the self as knower. This is because the content of first principles is given by the order of moral values available to perception and

36 I am indebted to Thomas Nagel and T. M. Scanlon for numerous instructive conversations on the topic of constructivism. The idea of constructivism has not been much discussed outside of the philosophy of mathematics, but I should mention the following: Scanlon's "Contractualism and Utilitarianism"; see, for example, pp. 117f. opposing intuitionism, although the terms "intuitionism" and "constructivism" are not used. To this add: Ronald Dworkin, "Justice and Rights" (1973) in *Taking Rights Seriously* (Cambridge, MA: Harvard University Press, 1977), pp. 159–68, which was the first to suggest that justice as fairness is constructivist, but he understood it differently than I do here; Onora O'Neill, *Constructions of Reason* (Cambridge: Cambridge University Press, 1989), especially chapter 11; and Brian Barry, *Theories of Justice*, vol. I, especially pp. 264–82, 348–53.

intuition as organized and expressed by principles acceptable on due reflection. The main requirement, then, is that we be able to know the first principles expressing those values and to be moved by that knowledge. Here a basic assumption is that recognizing first principles as true gives rise, in a being capable of knowing them, to a desire to act from them for their own sake. Moral motivation is defined by reference to desires that have a special kind of origin: an intuitive knowledge of first principles.

Rational intuitionism is not, to be sure, forced to use this sparse conception of the person. It simply has no need for more complex conceptions of person and society; whereas in constructivism such conceptions are required to provide the form and structure of its constructivist procedure.

Finally, we add a fourth feature: rational intuitionism conceives of truth in a traditional way by viewing moral judgments as true when they are both about and accurate to the independent order of moral values. Otherwise they are false.

The four corresponding though different features of political constructivism are these.

The first feature, as already noted, is that the principles of political justice (content) may be represented as the outcome of a procedure of construction (structure). In this procedure rational agents, as representatives of citizens and subject to reasonable conditions, select the principles to regulate the basic structure of society.

The second feature is that the procedure of construction is based essentially on practical reason and not on theoretical reason. Following Kant's way of making the distinction, we say: practical reason is concerned with the production of objects according to a conception of those objects – for example, the conception of a just constitutional regime taken as the aim of political endeavor – while theoretical reason is concerned with the knowledge of given objects.[37] Note that to say that the procedure of construction is based essentially on practical reason is not to deny that theoretical reason has a role. It shapes the beliefs and knowledge of the rational persons who have a part in the construction; and these persons also use their general capacities of reasoning, inference, and judgment in selecting the principles of justice.

The third feature of political constructivism is that it uses a rather complex conception of person and society to give form and structure to its construction. As we have seen, political constructivism views the person as belonging to political society understood as a fair system of social cooperation from one generation to the next. Persons are said to possess the two moral powers paired with this idea of social cooperation – a capacity for a sense of justice and for a conception of the good. All these stipulations and more are needed to work out the idea that the principles of justice issue from a suitable procedure of construction. Intuitionism's sparse conception of the person would not be adequate to this purpose.

As before, we again add a fourth feature: political constructivism specifies an idea of the reasonable and applies this idea to various subjects: conceptions and principles, judgments and grounds, persons and institutions. In each case, it must, of course, also specify criteria to judge whether the subject in question is reasonable. It does not, however, as rational intuitionism does, use (or deny) the concept of truth; nor does it question that concept, nor could it say that the concept of truth and its idea of the reasonable are the same. Rather, within itself the political conception does without the concept of truth. One thought is that the idea of the reasonable makes an overlapping consensus of reasonable doctrines possible in ways the concept of truth may not. Yet, in any case, it is up to each comprehensive doctrine to say how its idea of the reasonable connects with its concept of truth, should it have one.

If we ask how the reasonable is understood, we say: for our purposes here, the content of the reasonable is specified by the content of a reasonable political conception. The idea of the reasonable itself is given in part, again for our purposes, by the two aspects of persons' being reasonable: their willingness to propose and abide by fair terms of social cooperation among equals and their recognition of and willingness to accept the consequences of the burdens of judgment. Add to this the principles of practical reason and the conceptions of society and person on which the political conception is based. We come to understand this idea by understanding the two aspects of the reasonableness of persons and how these enter into the procedure of construction and why. We decide whether the whole conception is acceptable by seeing whether we can endorse it upon due reflection.

These four corresponding features give a broad contrast between political constructivism and rational intuitionism as a form of moral realism. I add a few remarks to clarify the relations between the two views.

First, it is crucial for political liberalism that its constructivist conception does not contradict rational intuitionism, since constructivism tries to avoid opposing

[37] For Kant's distinction, see *Critique of Practical Reason*, for example Ak:V:15f., 65f., 89f.

any comprehensive doctrine. To explain how this is possible in this case, let us suppose that the argument from the original position is correct: it shows that rational persons under reasonable, or fair, conditions would select certain principles of justice. To be consistent with rational intuitionism, we do not say that the procedure of construction makes, or produces, the order of moral values. For the intuitionist says this order is independent and constitutes itself, as it were. Political constructivism neither denies nor asserts this. Rather, it claims only that its procedure represents an order of political values proceeding from the values expressed by the principles of practical reason, in union with conceptions of society and person, to the values expressed by certain principles of political justice.

Political liberalism adds: this represented order is the most appropriate one for a democratic society marked by the fact of reasonable pluralism. This is because it provides the most reasonable conception of justice as the focus of an overlapping consensus.

Rational intuitionists can also accept the argument from the original position and say that it displays the correct order of values. On these matters, they can agree with political constructivism: from within their own comprehensive view, they can affirm the political conception and join an overlapping consensus. Justice as fairness does not deny what they want to assert: namely, that the order of values displayed by constructivism is backed by an independent order of values that constitutes itself (as stated above as the first feature of intuitionism).

A further point of clarification: both constructivism and rational intuitionism rely on the idea of reflective equilibrium. Otherwise intuitionism could not bring its perceptions and intuitions to bear on each other and check its account of the order of moral values against our considered judgments on due reflection. Similarly, constructivism could not check the formulation of its procedure by seeing whether the conclusions reached match those judgments.

The difference in the views shows up in how they interpret conclusions that are unacceptable and must be revised. The intuitionist regards a procedure as correct because following it correctly usually gives the correct independently given judgment, whereas the political constructivist regards a judgment as correct because it issues from the reasonable and rational procedure of construction when correctly formulated and correctly followed (assuming, as always, that the judgment relies on true information). So if the judgment is not acceptable, intuitionism says that its procedure reflects a mistaken account of the independent order of values. The constructivist says the fault must lie in how the procedure models the principles of practical reason in union with the conceptions of society and person. For the constructivist's conjecture is that the correct model of practical reason as a whole will give the correct principles of justice on due reflection.[38]

Once reflective equilibrium is reached, the intuitionists will say that their considered judgments are now true, or very likely so, of an independent order of moral values. The constructivist will say that the procedure of construction now correctly models the principles of practical reason in union with the appropriate conceptions of society and person. In so doing it represents the order of values most suited to a democratic regime. As to how we find the correct procedure, the constructivist says: by reflection, using our powers of reason. But since we are using our reason to describe itself and reason is not transparent to itself, we can misdescribe our reason as we can anything else. The struggle for reflective equilibrium continues indefinitely, in this case as in all others.

It may already be clear why a political conception that sees the public principles of justice as founded on the principles and conceptions of practical reason is of great significance for a constitutional regime. Still, let us pull the threads together.

Consider again the idea of social cooperation. How are fair terms of cooperation to be determined? Are they to be simply laid down by some outside authority distinct from the persons cooperating, say by God's law? Or are these terms to be accepted by these persons as fair in view of their knowledge of an independent moral order? Or should these terms be established by an undertaking among those persons themselves in view of what they regard as their reciprocal advantage?

Justice as fairness, we said, adopts a form of the last answer. This is because, given the fact of reasonable pluralism, citizens cannot agree on any moral authority, whether a sacred text, or institution. Nor do they agree about the order of moral values, or the dictates of what some regard as natural law. We adopt, then, a constructivist view to specify the fair terms of social cooperation as given by the principles of justice agreed to by the representatives of free and equal citizens when fairly situated. The bases of this view lie in fundamental ideas of

[38] Of course, the repeated failure to formulate the procedure so that it yields acceptable conclusions may lead us to abandon political constructivism. It must eventually add up or be rejected. I am indebted to Anthony Laden for instructive discussion about this and on related points to David Estlund and Gregory Kavka.

the public political culture as well as in citizens' shared principles and conceptions of practical reason. Thus, if the procedure can be correctly formulated, citizens should be able to accept its principles and conceptions along with their reasonable comprehensive doctrine. The political conception of justice can then serve as the focus of an overlapping consensus.

Thus, it is only by affirming a constructivist conception – one which is political and not metaphysical – that citizens generally can expect to find principles that all can accept. This they can do without denying the deeper aspects of their reasonable comprehensive doctrines. Given their differences, citizens cannot fulfill in any other way their conception-dependent desire to have a shared political life on terms acceptable to others as free and equal. This idea of a shared political life does not invoke Kant's idea of autonomy, or Mill's idea of individuality, as moral values belonging to a comprehensive doctrine. The appeal is rather to the political value of a public life conducted on terms that all reasonable citizens can accept as fair. This leads to the ideal of democratic citizens setting their fundamental differences in accordance with an idea of public reason.

To these observations, political liberalism adds that the order represented in the argument from the original position is the most appropriate way to see the political values as ordered. Doing this enables us to state the meaning of an autonomous political doctrine as one that represents, or displays, the political principles of justice – the fair terms of social cooperation – as reached by using the principles of practical reason in union with the appropriate conceptions of persons as free and equal and of society as a fair system of cooperation over time. The argument from the original position exhibits this line of thought. Autonomy is a matter of how the view presents the political values as ordered. Think of this as doctrinal autonomy.

A view is autonomous, then, because in its represented order, the political values of justice and public reason (expressed by their principles) are not simply presented as moral requirements externally imposed. Nor are they required of us by other citizens whose comprehensive doctrines we do not accept. Rather, citizens can understand those values as based on their practical reason in union with the political conceptions of citizens as free and equal and of society as a system of fair cooperation. In affirming the political doctrine as a whole we, as citizens, are ourselves autonomous, politically speaking. An autonomous political conception provides, then, an appropriate basis and ordering of political values for a constitutional regime characterized by reasonable pluralism.

Part III

Political Principles

Chapter 9

On Community

Introduction

All political thinking addresses issues of political community, but the first set of political principles we might contemplate deal with which type of political communities are we thinking about and which we prefer. Perhaps Robinson Crusoe lived outside of any political community, at least for a while, but most of us live in several and will live in different ones during our lifetimes. Though I have always been an American citizen, I've lived in various cities, states, and countries, and I have been a member of various associations within civil society. I am not quite sure which of these communities most determines my social identity and commands my loyalties – or which should. I doubt that each of these communities should be governed by the same political principles. I think I should be principled as a member of various communities, but I find it necessary to decide which principles best apply to each. For example, I am committed to those of participatory democracy in the Political Science Department where I work, but I am comfortable with those of representative democracy for the United States, which is the polity that has issued my passport.

Questions of community that are addressed in this chapter include the following: What are the primary communities, especially political communities (or polities), with which people identify, in which they participate in decision-making regarding their social existence, and in which they incur their primary political obligations? Which sorts of communities – ranging from local to global – are most influential in people's lives? Which should be most influential? What prompts people to identify with and be loyal to particular communities?

The magnitude of these issues might be understood by recalling the US civil war, when the South seceded from the Union and many people, especially in border states, had to wrestle with the question of whether they wanted to remain loyal to the Union or to their home state if it joined the Southern Confederacy. Of course, such questions were of huge importance earlier, when a stronger Federal Union was proposed to replace the weaker original American Confederacy. Our first reading is a classic contribution to political theory addressing that issue: *The Federalist No. 10*. Written by James Madison (1751–1836), a foremost "founding father" of the American Constitution and a future American President, it argues for the creation of a federal union and for citizens transferring much of their state identities and loyalties to the new nation. Madison's argument was that the governance of political communities is always bedeviled by the problem of factions – groups of citizens having special interests contrary to the common interest. Factions cannot be eliminated without suppressing freedom, so the question is how to control the influence of factions. One key way is to "extend the sphere" of government. Smaller communities – for example, the State of Rhode Island – will have fewer factions, but it will be easier for a dominant faction to gain control of its government and impose its special interests on others. Larger communities, like the United States as a whole, will have more factions, but it will be more difficult for any single faction or coalition of factions to gain control of its government; thus the nation is more likely to have a limited government that pursues only those matters that are in the common interest.

Getting people to support a new or reconstructed polity is one thing; maintaining people's allegiances to a polity is another. Rogers M. Smith, a distinguished professor of political science at the University of Pennsylvania, notes that while we often simply accept our membership in polities where we live, neither these polities nor our allegiances to them are natural. All political boundaries are products of protracted political struggles. Larger polities encompass people having diverse ethnicities, religions, languages, and other such traits, and people often identify more with others sharing these traits than with the larger community. Consequently, leaders must forge strong senses of political identity among their followers, and they do so by providing "narratives of peoplehood" that explain why a particular set of people are or should be bound together in a polity and why strong and enduring community bonds are beneficial. Smith insists that these narratives are "virtually always false or at least highly dubious," but they can be "engaging, reassuring, inspiring" and even "intoxicating." In order to pursue their political interests, leaders at different times tell different stories of who a people are, and so narratives of peoplehood contain many tensions and contractions. American leaders, for example, have stressed three themes about Americans: liberal stories stressing individual independence, republican stories stressing self-governance, and ascriptive stories stressing our European and Christian heritages, among others. While the ascriptive stories often conflict with the themes of shared commitments to liberty, equality, and democracy that are stressed by liberalism and republicanism, they reassure many citizens of their self-worth even when they do not live up to liberal and republican values, and they help explain what distinguishes an American from the rest of mankind. In any event, these contradictory stories are the basis for citizenship laws that are themselves inconsistent, sometimes facilitating greater inclusion of blacks, Hispanics, Asians, and other minorities, while sometimes departing from liberal ideals.

National identities everywhere may be undermined by globalization. Increasingly, we may regard ourselves less as Americans, Brits, Mexicans, etc. than as participants in a global economy. But if we increasingly see ourselves as workers, consumers, and investors in a global market, does this mean that we are global *citizens*? Some people, especially "cosmopolitan" global theorists, believe economic globalization must be accompanied by a "global covenant" that produces a global social democracy. David Held, professor of political science and co-director of the study of global governance at the London School of Economics, proposes such a covenant that regulates the international economy through global political institutions that are far more democratic and concerned with social justice and human rights than has been the case thus far. What seems to be required is the development of a global polity. Perhaps such a global polity will not mirror the sort of national polities that Madison endorsed two centuries ago, but some political theorists like Held are trying to specify some of the principles that might apply as we try to invent institutions that are up to the task of governing the emerging global economy.

Despite all the current talk about globalization, many political and social theorists continue to believe that the sort of political communities that work best and deserve our primary allegiances are local ones. Kirkpatrick Sale – a founder and director of the Middlebury Institute, which is dedicated to the study of separatism, secession, and self-determination – believes that we need to reconstruct "human-scale communities." Anthropologists, urban planners, and other scholars have proposed various optimal sizes for communities, but they all seem to endorse living in communities far smaller than the ones where most of us now reside. Sociologists describe mega-cities as places having intractable social problems. Economists argue that larger communities have many disadvantages for business. Ecologists claim that smaller communities are more environmentally sustainable. And smaller communities invite citizen participation in ways that are foreclosed to larger ones.

In our final selection for this chapter, Robert Dahl – professor emeritus at Yale University, probably the leading democratic theorist of his generation, and long recognized as a leading pluralist – asks us to engage in an intellectual experiment in which we try to constitute a democratic government for the world. He argues that we would inevitably demand smaller units that would enable those burdened by majority preferences at the global level to be governed by their own preferences at the local level. Ultimately we would recognize the need for a range of democratic communities, arranged as nested "Chinese boxes." We would endorse a global polity capable of dealing with issues that affect mankind generally, but also want regional, national, state, and local governments to deal with problems best handled on more decentralized levels. He notes that it would be unmanageable to create political communities having jurisdictions that were optimal for every conceivable social problem, and he suggests a variety of pragmatic principles for thinking about the size and forms of political communities. While pluralists might call for further discussion about these principles, they would surely endorse Dahl's conclusion that we need a variety of political communities and that they need to be arranged as "Chinese boxes" from the global to the local.

James Madison, "The Federalist No. 10"*

Among the numerous advantages promised by a well-constructed Union, none deserves to be more accurately developed than its tendency to break and control the violence of faction. The friend of popular governments never finds himself so much alarmed for their character and fate as when he contemplates their propensity to this dangerous vice. He will not fail, therefore, to set a due value on any plan which, without violating the principles to which he is attached, provides a proper cure for it. The instability, injustice, and confusion introduced into the public councils have, in truth, been the mortal diseases under which popular governments have everywhere perished, as they continue to be the favorite and fruitful topics from which the adversaries to liberty derive their most specious declamations. The valuable improvements made by the American constitutions on the popular models, both ancient and modern, cannot certainly be too much admired; but it would be an unwarrantable partiality, to contend that they have as effectually obviated the danger on this side, as was wished and expected. Complaints are everywhere heard from our most considerate and virtuous citizens, equally the friends of public and private faith and of public and personal liberty, that our governments are too unstable, that the public good is disregarded in the conflicts of rival parties, and that measures are too often decided, not according to the rules of justice and the rights of the minor party, but by the superior force of an interested and overbearing majority. However anxiously we may wish that these complaints had no foundation, the evidence of known facts will not permit us to deny that they are in some degree true. It will be found, indeed, on a candid review of our situation, that some of the distresses under which we labor have been erroneously charged on the operation of our governments; but it will be found, at the same time, that other causes will not alone account for many of our heaviest misfortunes; and, particularly, for that prevailing and increasing distrust of public engagements and alarm for private rights, which are echoed from one end of the continent to the other. These must be chiefly, if not wholly, effects of the unsteadiness and injustice with which a factious spirit has tainted our public administration.

By a faction, I understand a number of citizens, whether amounting to a majority or minority of the whole, who are united and actuated by some common impulse of passion, or of interest, adverse to the rights of other citizens, or to the permanent and aggregate interests of the community.

There are two methods of curing the mischiefs of faction: the one, by removing its causes; the other, by controlling its effects.

There are again two methods of removing the causes of faction: the one, by destroying the liberty which is essential to its existence; the other, by giving to every citizen the same opinions, the same passions, and the same interests.

It could never be more truly said than of the first remedy that it was worse than the disease. Liberty is to faction what air is to fire, an aliment without which it instantly expires. But it could not be a less folly to abolish liberty, which is essential to political life, because it nourishes faction, than it would be to wish the annihilation of air, which is essential to animal life, because it imparts to fire its destructive agency.

The second expedient is as impracticable as the first would be unwise. As long as the reason of man continues fallible, and he is at liberty to exercise it, different opinions will be formed. As long as the connection subsists between his reason and his self-love, his opinions and his passions will have a reciprocal influence on each other, and the former will be objects to which the latter will attach themselves. The diversity in the faculties of men, from which the rights of property originate, is not less an insuperable obstacle to a uniformity of interests. The protection of these faculties is the first object of government. From the protection of different and unequal faculties of acquiring property, the possession of different degrees and kinds of property immediately results; and from the influence of these on the sentiments and views

* James Madison, extracted from www.constitution.org/fed/federal10.htm, accessed April 29, 2008. Originally published in the *Daily Advertiser*, Thursday, November 22, 1787.

of the respective proprietors, ensues a division of the society into different interests and parties.

The latent causes of faction are thus sown in the nature of man; and we see them everywhere brought into different degrees of activity, according to the different circumstances of civil society. A zeal for different opinions concerning religion, concerning government, and many other points, as well of speculation as of practice; an attachment to different leaders ambitiously contending for preeminence and power; or to persons of other descriptions whose fortunes have been interesting to the human passions, have, in turn, divided mankind into parties, inflamed them with mutual animosity, and rendered them much more disposed to vex and oppress each other than to cooperate for their common good. So strong is this propensity of mankind to fall into mutual animosities, that where no substantial occasion presents itself, the most frivolous and fanciful distinctions have been sufficient to kindle their unfriendly passions and excite their most violent conflicts. But the most common and durable source of factions has been the various and unequal distribution of property. Those who hold and those who are without property have ever formed distinct interests in society. Those who are creditors, and those who are debtors, fall under a like discrimination. A landed interest, a manufacturing interest, a mercantile interest, a moneyed interest, with many lesser interests, grow up of necessity in civilized nations, and divide them into different classes, actuated by different sentiments and views. The regulation of these various and interfering interests forms the principal task of modern legislation, and involves the spirit of party and faction in the necessary and ordinary operations of the government.

No man is allowed to be a judge in his own cause, because his interest would certainly bias his judgment, and, not improbably, corrupt his integrity. With equal, nay with greater reason, a body of men are unfit to be both judges and parties at the same time; yet what are many of the most important acts of legislation, but so many judicial determinations, not indeed concerning the rights of single persons, but concerning the rights of large bodies of citizens? And what are the different classes of legislators but advocates and parties to the causes which they determine? Is a law proposed concerning private debts? It is a question to which the creditors are parties on one side and the debtors on the other. Justice ought to hold the balance between them. Yet the parties are, and must be, themselves the judges; and the most numerous party, or, in other words, the most powerful faction must be expected to prevail. Shall domestic manufacturers be encouraged, and in what degree, by restrictions on foreign manufacturers? are questions which would be differently decided by the landed and the manufacturing classes, and probably by neither with a sole regard to justice and the public good. The apportionment of taxes on the various descriptions of property is an act which seems to require the most exact impartiality; yet there is, perhaps, no legislative act in which greater opportunity and temptation are given to a predominant party to trample on the rules of justice. Every shilling with which they overburden the inferior number is a shilling saved to their own pockets.

It is in vain to say that enlightened statesmen will be able to adjust these clashing interests and render them all subservient to the public good. Enlightened statesmen will not always be at the helm. Nor, in many cases, can such an adjustment be made at all without taking into view indirect and remote considerations, which will rarely prevail over the immediate interest which one party may find in disregarding the rights of another or the good of the whole.

The inference to which we are brought is, that the *causes* of faction cannot be removed, and that relief is only to be sought in the means of controlling its *effects*.

If a faction consists of less than a majority, relief is supplied by the republican principle, which enables the majority to defeat its sinister views by regular vote. It may clog the administration, it may convulse the society; but it will be unable to execute and mask its violence under the forms of the *Constitution*. When a majority is included in a faction, the form of popular government, on the other hand, enables it to sacrifice to its ruling passion or interest both the public good and the rights of other citizens. To secure the public good and private rights against the danger of such a faction, and at the same time to preserve the spirit and the form of popular government, is then the great object to which our inquiries are directed. Let me add that it is the great desideratum by which alone this form of government can be rescued from the opprobrium under which it has so long labored, and be recommended to the esteem and adoption of mankind.

By what means is this object attainable? Evidently by one of two only. Either the existence of the same passion or interest in a majority at the same time must be prevented, or the majority, having such coexistent passion or interest, must be rendered, by their number and local situation, unable to concert and carry into effect schemes of oppression. If the impulse and the opportunity be suffered to coincide, we well know that neither moral nor religious motives can be relied on as an adequate control. They are not found to be such on the injustice and violence of individuals, and lose their efficacy in proportion to the number combined together, that is, in proportion as their efficacy becomes needful.

From this view of the subject it may be concluded that a pure democracy, by which I mean a society consisting of a small number of citizens, who assemble and administer the government in person, can admit of no cure for the mischiefs of faction. A common passion or interest will, in almost every case, be felt by a majority of the whole; a communication and concert results from the form of government itself; and there is nothing to check the inducements to sacrifice the weaker party or an obnoxious individual. Hence it is that such democracies have ever been spectacles of turbulence and contention; have ever been found incompatible with personal security or the rights of property; and have in general been as short in their lives as they have been violent in their deaths. Theoretic politicians, who have patronized this species of government, have erroneously supposed that by reducing mankind to a perfect equality in their political rights, they would, at the same time be perfectly equalized and assimilated in their possessions, their opinions, and their passions.

A republic, by which I mean a government in which the scheme of representation takes place, opens a different prospect and promises the cure for which we are seeking. Let us examine the points in which it varies from pure democracy, and we shall comprehend both the nature of the cure and the efficacy which it must derive from the Union.

The two great points of difference between a democracy and a republic are: first, the delegation of the government, in the latter, to a small number of citizens elected by the rest; secondly, the greater number of citizens, and greater sphere of country over which the latter may be extended.

The effect of the first difference is, on the one hand, to refine and enlarge the public views, by passing them through the medium of a chosen body of citizens, whose wisdom may best discern the true interest of their country, and whose patriotism and love of justice will be least likely to sacrifice it to temporary or partial considerations. Under such a regulation, it may well happen that the public voice, pronounced by the representatives of the people, will be more consonant to the public good than if pronounced by the people themselves, convened for the purpose. On the other hand, the effect may be inverted. Men of factious tempers, of local prejudices, or of sinister designs, may, by intrigue, by corruption, or by other means, first obtain the suffrages, and then betray the interests of the people. The question resulting is, whether small or extensive republics are more favorable to the election of proper guardians of the public weal; and it is clearly decided in favor of the latter by two obvious considerations:

In the first place, it is to be remarked that however small the republic may be, the representatives must be raised to a certain number, in order to guard against the cabals of a few; and that, however large it may be, they must be limited to a certain number, in order to guard against the confusion of a multitude. Hence, the number of representatives in the two cases not being in proportion to that of the two constituents, and being proportionally greater in the small republic, it follows that, if the proportion of fit characters be not less in the large than in the small republic, the former will present a greater option, and consequently a greater probability of a fit choice.

In the next place, as each representative will be chosen by a greater number of citizens in the large than in the small republic, it will be more difficult for unworthy candidates to practise with success the vicious arts by which elections are too often carried; and the suffrages of the people being more free, will be more likely to center on men who possess the most attractive merit and the most diffusive and established characters.

It must be confessed that in this, as in most other cases, there is a mean, on both sides of which inconveniences will be found to lie. By enlarging too much the number of electors, you render the representative too little acquainted with all their local circumstances and lesser interests; as by reducing it too much, you render him unduly attached to these, and too little fit to comprehend and pursue great and national objects. The federal Constitution forms a happy combination in this respect; the great and aggregate interests being referred to the national, the local and particular to the State legislatures.

The other point of difference is the greater number of citizens and extent of territory which may be brought within the compass of republican than of democratic government; and it is this circumstance principally which renders factious combinations less to be dreaded in the former than in the latter. The smaller the society, the fewer probably will be the distinct parties and interests composing it; the fewer the distinct parties and interests, the more frequently will a majority be found of the same party; and the smaller the number of individuals composing a majority, and the smaller the compass within which they are placed, the more easily will they concert and execute their plans of oppression.

Extend the sphere, and you take in a greater variety of parties and interests; you make it less probable that a majority of the whole will have a common motive to invade the rights of other citizens; or if such a common motive exists, it will be more difficult for all who feel it to discover their own strength and to act in unison with each other. Besides other impediments, it may be remarked that, where there is a consciousness of unjust or dishonorable purposes, communication is always checked by distrust in proportion to the number whose concurrence is necessary.

Hence, it clearly appears, that the same advantage which a republic has over a democracy, in controlling the effects of faction, is enjoyed by a large over a small republic – is enjoyed by the Union over the States composing it. Does this advantage consist in the substitution of representatives whose enlightened views and virtuous sentiments render them superior to local prejudices and to schemes of injustice? It will not be denied that the representation of the Union will be most likely to possess these requisite endowments. Does it consist in the greater security afforded by a greater variety of parties, against the event of any one party being able to outnumber and oppress the rest? In an equal degree does the increased variety of parties comprised within the Union, increase this security. Does it, in fine, consist in the greater obstacles opposed to the concert and accomplishment of the secret wishes of an unjust and interested majority? Here again, the extent of the Union gives it the most palpable advantage.

The influence of factious leaders may kindle a flame within their particular States, but will be unable to spread a general conflagration through the other States. A religious sect may degenerate into a political faction in a part of the Confederacy; but the variety of sects dispersed over the entire face of it must secure the national councils against any danger from that source. A rage for paper money, for an abolition of debts, for an equal division of property, or for any other improper or wicked project, will be less apt to pervade the whole body of the Union than a particular member of it; in the same proportion as such a malady is more likely to taint a particular county or district than an entire State.

In the extent and proper structure of the Union, therefore, we behold a republican remedy for the diseases most incident to republican government. And according to the degree of pleasure and pride we feel in being republicans ought to be our zeal in cherishing the spirit and supporting the character of Federalists.

PUBLIUS

Rogers M. Smith, "Toward a Theory of Civic Identities"*

In this section I sketch a theory of how civic identities are created and sustained. It suggests why the politics of citizenship laws are likely to generate sets of rules filled with anomalies, even contradictions: such laws usually result from compromises among rival views of civic identity that are themselves filled with understandable internal tensions. The account also indicates why, despite their elite origins, citizenship provisions reveal much about whole political cultures, while shaping their politics in basic ways. Most important, it suggests why we should expect American citizenship laws, like the laws of most societies, to express ideologies beyond the liberal and democratic traditions whose power Tocquevillian analysts have well explained.

Citizenship laws – laws designating the criteria for membership in a political community and the key prerogatives that constitute membership – are among the most fundamental of political creations. They distribute power, assign status, and define political purposes. They create the most recognized political identity of the individuals they embrace, one displayed on passports scrutinized at every contested border. They also assign negative identities to the "aliens" they fence out. The attention people give to national citizenship reflects the hard-boiled reality that governments are more likely to use their powers to aid those who are their citizens than those who are not. But citizenship defines political identity even more deeply than this crucial signaling of which guns are likely to be arrayed on a person's behalf. Citizenship laws also literally constitute – they create with legal words – a collective civic identity. They proclaim the existence of a political "people" and designate who those persons are as a people, in ways that often become integral to individuals' senses of personal identity as well.

Citizenship laws are so basic that it is easy to overlook them, just as in sports we usually watch the game and take its rules for granted. And politicians, like athletes, are often happy to let those rules stand so they can get on with trying to win. But like the rules defining who gets to be a player, citizenship laws are first and foremost an institutionalized response to one of the most elemental necessities for organizing and conducting an associated

* Rogers M. Smith, extracted from his *Civic Ideals: Conflicting Visions of Citizenship in US History* (Yale University Press, 1997), pp. 30–8.

enterprise, in this case a political society. Before all else, associations need members. Would-be political leaders need a people to lead, a collection of persons that generally understand themselves and are understood by others as forming one political society. Once a people exists, aspiring leaders then need to convince its membership – by force, logic, or rhetoric – that they will best serve that people's interests and ideals. But this second necessity is greatly shaped by the response to the first: a leader's quest for support is heavily defined by who the members of the leader's people are and what they hope to get out of their political community.

Potential leaders now live in a world with many established peoples and well-defined national boundaries that can at times be taken for granted, as fully as the location of foul territory in a stadium. But here the sports analogy runs out. Games are rarely won by redrawing their constitutive rules while play is under way. Frequently, however, political struggles can be won by altering existing civic boundaries in ways that add or strengthen friends and expel or weaken foes. Hence, contestation over laws defining membership is ongoing in most societies. Sometimes these disputes take place quietly, at the margins of major political conflicts, while most civic rules are left intact because they do not disturb the leading political forces. But at other times, especially when old regimes are being toppled and people are building new ones, battles over membership take center stage, as they have in many parts of the former Soviet bloc. Yet even when they are not venues of great struggles, citizenship laws are essential but potentially incendiary institutions that mirror and shape politics in obvious and subtle ways.

Their importance and volatility stem from the fact that the fundamental task of fostering a "people" is today a difficult challenge in most societies. Almost every state contains many people whose political history, religious or political beliefs, ethnicity, language, or other traits give them reason to decide that their primary political identity and allegiance is to some group other than that defined by the regime governing the territory in which they reside. All modern political boundaries are products of long periods of struggle which have left members of losing sides still living in regimes they can potentially be mobilized to oppose. Even an old nation-state like Great Britain has Irish, Scottish, and Welsh nationalist movements of fluctuating intensity. France has strong traditions of rural localism and conflicts over the "Frenchness" of North African immigrants and their descendants, as well as over the nation's relationship to the European Community. The US has native tribes that have never accepted the national government's claim of sovereignty, black and Chicano nationalists, citizens who believe that their religious memberships outweigh their national allegiance, and many others who at least sometimes do not feel that they are first and foremost Americans. Globally, there may be an indigenous people untouched by the governance of any distant metropol or imperial power, but there are probably none over whom such authority has never been asserted. In a world long shaped by clashing empires and nationalist separatist movements of a sort that are now resurgent, most governments have good reason to fear challenges to their authority over some or all of "their" territories and peoples.

As in all politics, force is one way to meet these challenges, to define who belongs to a people and who does not, especially when a society is first formed but also thereafter. But it is a political truism that few societies can long be kept together, much less effectively governed, by force alone. Most aspirants to power wish to govern people who are genuinely persuaded of these two crucial points: first, that they are one people, and, second, that they are a people well served by following those leaders. Then the tasks of ruling become much simpler.

Thus political leaders need compelling stories to convince their constituents of these things. As the very allegiance of a society's members is at stake, those stories should ideally be so persuasive that the existence of a shared national identity seems to the populace an unshakable truth. Leaders are therefore likely to invoke any and all preexisting senses of common identity they can that will also support their own rule, such as widely shared languages, ancestries, cultural customs, religion, suitable doctrines of "natural" group identity, and histories of oppression (as either conquered or conquerors). Leaders will also point out tangible benefits that people are likely to gain by acting as one society under their governance, such as greater economic resources and growth, heightened military defense against internal and external aggressors, and greater opportunities for members of that society to gain influential political positions.

One crucial further point about the behavior of civic leaders may be harder to accept. As Plato suggested long ago, the stories of civic identity fostered by political elites are virtually always false or at least highly dubious in important respects. To be sure, because these stories are meant to inspire as deep and enduring an allegiance as possible, leaders have an incentive to make them true descriptions of the people's common characteristics and the benefits of embracing a common civic identity. But they have only an incentive, not a categorical imperative; there are powerful countervailing factors. Because no community or leadership is simply natural, and because their members' diverse histories, interests, and perceptions may move many current or desired members of a society to give allegiance to challengers to its incumbent regime, leaders usually foster loyalty by playing as many psychological chords as possible. They worry less about whether their various appeals are true, or whether they fit together logically, than about whether they work politically. They thus simultaneously appeal to lofty rational moralities and thinly veiled greed and lust for power. But most have found irreplaceable the engaging, reassuring, inspiring, often intoxicating charm provided by colorful civic myths.

By *myth* I mean, to cite the *American Heritage Thesaurus*, "a traditional story or tale dealing with ancestors, heroes, supernatural events, etc., that has no proven factual basis but attempts to explain beliefs, practices, or natural phenomena." A *civic myth* is a myth used to explain why persons form a people, usually indicating how a political community originated, who is eligible for membership, who is not and why, and what the community's values and aims are. [...]

Civic myths inspiring faith that memberships are preordained and blessed can especially foster prejudices that may do more than "enlightened reason" to instill "reverence" for the laws constituting their society. That advantage is not easily foregone.

Why might people find partly fictional civic myths so attractive? A reasonable guess is that most people want to believe that a membership as important as that of their political society is an intrinsically right and good one. It takes no high-powered psychology to observe that people also have considerable capacity to believe what they want, including great improbabilities that are intermingled with undeniable truths. And the leaders who propagate civic myths often merge their longings for power into narratives of meaningful civic membership that include elements that they genuinely value, such as a shared religion, ethnicity, language, history, or political ideology. Thus it should be no surprise that the propagators of civic myths are sometimes their truest believers. Their belief then strengthens their power to persuade others.

These points suggest that civic myths have great, perhaps indispensable value. On reflection they may contain much wisdom, enabling people to live together fruitfully and stably, while prompting them to realize the values expressed in their myths in ways that may enrich the lives of all citizens. Civic myths may be "noble lies." But this salutary role is only a possibility, not an inevitability. Civic myths may also cloak the exploitation of citizens by their leaders, demonize innocent outsiders, and foster invidious inequalities among the members of a regime. They may be ugly, ignoble lies.

And they are often likely to be so, just because a populace's acceptance of a civic myth normally aids the power of some leaders against their domestic and foreign opponents, who all offer competing narratives to justify their causes. In the resulting conflicts, political leaders are strongly tempted to exploit harsh implications of their own civic myths to vilify scapegoats outside the society or rivals within it.

[...]

Citizenship laws thus emerge from a variety of often conflicting political imperatives: to maintain arrangements that support a useful sense of civic identity, to include political friends and exclude foes, to add persons who can help promote the regime's prosperity and power, to reinforce narratives of civic identity that foster allegiance to the regime and its current leaders. If, as in most modern pluralist societies, no group or set of leaders has enough power to have its way on every issue, then citizenship laws will also usually be products of compromises among factions and the always partly false civic myths they favor. It would thus be astonishing if the citizenship laws of even a stable, well-established society were an ideologically unified, internally coherent, and intrinsically plausible whole. They are instead likely to be full of anomalies and to satisfy almost no one completely, even though they have enough support to prevail. They are also likely sites of further contests over membership and civic identity that will frequently manifest some of a political society's most vital political cleavages. And most contestants are likely to deploy civic ideologies that contain "naturalizing" ascriptive elements, though some will feature them far more than others.

These considerations suggest, then, why American citizenship laws should also be expected to display deep inconsistencies. They indicate as well why citizenship laws form a more useful map of a society's political culture than may first appear. They are crafted by elites, but elites acting in relation to pressures – sometimes violent, sometimes economic, sometimes political and ideological – exerted by a wide range of constituent and rival groups inside and outside the country. Such groups are, to be sure, often treated as pawns in the struggles of elite power seekers. But pawns often threaten kings, and sometimes take them.

American civic myths

With these general observations in mind, let us turn to the question of the civic ideologies that we are likely to find in America's historical circumstances. Tocquevillian analysts have been right to argue that the absence of a European-style aristocracy, the material circumstances initially limiting gross inequalities among European immigrants, and the usefulness of principles of liberal individual rights and democratic republicanism in America's Revolution all made these traditions central resources for the creation of an American civic community. Many features of liberalism and democratic republicanism have since offered continuing advantages as conceptions of a people's civic identity. Liberal doctrines of individual rights have repeatedly advanced effective claims for personal independence from many repressive structures. They have also supported institutions that provide the rule of law and much domestic tolerance and tranquillity; and they legitimate market systems that generate economic growth. The tremendous appeal of the promise that a liberal society will be a free, peaceful, diverse yet tolerant, and prosperous community should be apparent. Similarly, the conception of society as a democratic republic offers the prospect of political self-governance and of membership in a community of mutually supportive citizens. Again, there are clear attractions in a civic life that is expressive of one's personal dignity, responsive to one's concerns, and shared with sturdy, loyal peers.

Yet whatever their true benefits, even liberalism and republicanism have gained part of their appeal from mythical components. The liberalism of the Declaration of Independence includes the unproved but sanctifying claim that men have individual rights "endowed by their Creator." Both liberal and republican traditions also often invoke stories of social compacts created in a state of nature that represent quasi-religious political creation myths, easily adapted to confer legitimacy on American constitutions. The claim of popular sovereignty – taken to imply that the people as a whole ever do engage or ever have engaged in extensive public deliberation on an egalitarian basis in order to resolve directly any concrete issues of public life – is also a myth or "fiction." [...] Thus even the liberal and republican traditions stressed in standard accounts of American political culture are themselves not simply rationalist political doctrines but also civic myths, much more than those accounts generally acknowledge.

Yet if America was not born equal but instead has had extensive hierarchies justified by illiberal, undemocratic traditions of ascriptive Americanism, we must next ask whether these ideologies and institutions might also have attractions persisting after the founding era. After all, these traditions express what now seem to many to be clear falsehoods, far more than liberalism or republicanism. The answer proposed here is that ideologies of ascriptive Americanism have always done some of the work that civic myths do more effectively than liberalism or democratic republicanism, despite the mythical components that those traditions also possess.

For both liberalism and republicanism, in theory and in practice, place great strains on citizens. Liberal notions of natural rights as expounded in the Declaration of Independence and writings of philosophers like Locke make a prima facie case that all those capable of developing powers of rational self-guidance should be treated as bearers of fairly robust individual rights. Legal systems that automatically subordinate women, blacks, Native Americans, homosexuals, and non-Christians are then presumptively invalid. Even preference for one's countrymen over aliens is suspect if it involves infringements of basic human rights. That is a major reason why the logic of Enlightenment liberalism points away from particular national memberships and toward more inclusive, if not cosmopolitan political arrangements. Democratic republican conceptions of civic identity that stress political participation and community service more easily support devotion to one's country, but they can also have strongly egalitarian implications, suggesting that all ought to possess meaningful civic responsibilities. At a minimum, they militate against the claims of private religious, familial, and cultural groups, as well as personal conscientious choices, to trump duties to contribute to common civic endeavors. But many Americans have instead professed to feel more deeply obliged to such groups than to democratic public life; and they have accordingly wished to maintain white supremacy, to preserve old gender roles, to uphold Protestantism in public life, and in other ways to resist many egalitarian demands in liberal and democratic ideologies. Hence they have been attracted to civic visions that are less threatening than rigorously liberal democratic ones.

Furthermore, the requirements that liberal and democratic republican ideologies set for individuals to gain a secure sense of personal worth are dauntingly high. Liberal morals demand that individuals show themselves to be industrious, rational, and self-reliant, usually via economic productivity. In times of economic distress, especially, many Americans have found it hard to meet those standards; and the workings of markets mean that they will always do so unequally. Democratic republicanism denies the title of "virtuous" to those unwilling or unable to undertake extensive political participation and sacrifices for the public good, despite the pressures of a competitive market economy. Neither doctrine offers much reassurance that even most hard-working individuals will ultimately avoid being eclipsed by their own mortality. Good liberal individuals may be recalled by their families and businesses, a few republican heroes will be celebrated by the republics they helped maintain, but most will soon be lost to human memory.

Frequently, moreover, both philosophical and political proponents of liberal democratic causes have not made much effort to envision and promote alternative arrangements that might cushion the shocks of the quite sweeping changes they have sought. Many reformers called for the end of slavery, equal rights for women, and broader tolerance for all religions largely by decrying the evils of the status quo, not by painting a promising future that could quiet fears. Hence their positions seemed as threatening as advocacy of same-sex marriage appears to many believers in traditional families today.

Finally, and probably most important, in their pure, unalloyed forms, liberal and democratic republican political ideals have offered few reasons why Americans should see themselves as a distinct people, apart from others. [...] If, as Thomas Paine argued, the cause of America was "the cause of all mankind," then there were good reasons for every country to establish republican governments and to protect inalienable rights; but there was no special reason to be a US citizen rather than a citizen of any other similarly free land. [...]

It is thus unsurprising that many Americans have been attracted to ascriptive civic myths assuring them that, regardless of their personal achievements or economic status, their inborn characteristics make them part of a special community, the United States of America, which is, thanks to some combination of nature, history, and God, distinctively and permanently worthy. Those assurances have helped millions of Americans to feel proud and confident about who they are and about their futures, both as individuals and as a national community. [...]

David Held, "Towards a Global Covenant: Global Social Democracy"*

The story of our increasingly global order is not [...] a simple one. Globalization is not, and has never been, a one-dimensional phenomenon. While there has been a massive expansion of global markets which has altered the political terrain, the story of globalization is far from simply economic. Since 1945 there has been a reconnection of international law and morality, as sovereignty is no longer cast merely as effective power but increasingly as legitimate authority defined in terms of the maintenance of human rights and democratic values; a significant entrenchment of universal values concerned with the equal dignity and worth of all human beings in international rules and regulations; the establishment of complex governance systems, regional and global; and the growing recognition that the public good – whether conceived as financial stability, environmental protection or global egalitarianism – requires coordinated multilateral action if it is to be achieved in the long term. Although these developments are currently threatened by the unilateralist stance of the Bush administration, they need to be and can be built upon.

A guiding framework for elaborating on these achievements has been set down in outline in the 'global shift' of the last few decades. The transformation of sovereignty and governance is based, in particular, on values and principles which point beyond statism and nationalism. These are cosmopolitan values and principles which have been deployed to circumscribe and delimit the unacceptable face of state sovereignty. [...] The values and principles at stake – the principles of equal moral worth, equal liberty, the equal political status of all human beings, the common heritage of humankind, among others – lay the ground for a new conception of internationalism. This internationalism is defined by a commitment to cosmopolitan ethical ideals and by the attempt to entrench these in core political, social and economic institutions; it offers a framework for reshaping the nature and form of governance. At its centre is the requirement that legitimate political authority, at all levels, must uphold, and be delimited by, a commitment to the values and principles which underpin political equality, democratic politics, human

* David Held, extracted from "Towards a Global Covenant: Global Social Democracy," in *The Global Covenant* (Cambridge: Polity Press, 2004), pp. 161–9.

rights, political and social justice, and the sound stewardship of the environment. [...]

The contemporary phase of globalization is transforming the foundations of world order, leading away from a world based exclusively on state politics to a new and more complex form of global politics and multilayered governance. At the beginning of the twenty-first century there are good reasons for believing that the traditional international order of states cannot be restored and that the deep drivers of globalization are unlikely to be halted. Accordingly, a fundamental change in political orientation is unavoidable. Changes of outlook are clearly demarcated in the contest between the principal variants in the politics of globalization. Two leading positions – neoliberalism and that of the anti-globalization movement – are both deeply problematic. Whereas neoliberalism simply perpetuates existing economic and political systems and offers no substantial policies to deal with the problems of market failure, the radical anti-globalist position appears deeply naive about the potential for locally based action to resolve, or engage with, the governance agenda generated by the forces of globalization. How can such a politics cope with the challenges posed by overlapping communities of fate?

The same can be said, of course, about the current position of the US administration. If the US acts alone in the world, it cannot deliver core global public goods, such as free trade, financial stability and environmental sustainability, which it depends on for its overall development and prosperity. Moreover, if it acts alone it cannot achieve key domestic objectives, including leading national security goals. The fight against global terrorism requires the global pooling of intelligence, information and resources; the policing of what is left of a secure Afghanistan (Kabul) needs internationally generated resources (financial and personnel); and Iraq itself cannot be legitimately pacified and rebuilt without international cooperation, globally sourced investment and collaboration among many countries helping to supply skilled people of all kinds, from soldiers to engineers.

The alternative position is global social democracy. It seeks to build on the project of social democracy while embracing the achievements of the post-Holocaust multilateral order. Its aim is to adopt some of the values and insights of social democracy while applying them to the new global constellation of economics and politics. National social bargains, as noted in the Introduction, are insufficient to ensure an effective trade-off between the values of social solidarity, the politics of democracy and the efficiencies of the market. The challenge today, as Kofi Annan has written, is to devise a similar bargain or project to underpin the new global economy.[1] The project of global social democracy addresses this call. It is a basis for promoting the rule of international law; greater transparency, accountability and democracy in global governance; a deeper commitment to social justice; the protection and reinvention of community at diverse levels; and the transformation of the global economy into a free and fair rule-based economic order. The politics of global social democracy contains clear possibilities of dialogue between different segments of the 'pro-globalization/anti-globalization' political spectrum, although it will, of course, be contested by opinion at the extreme ends of the spectrum.

Box [1] summarizes the project of global social democracy – the basis of a new global covenant. It does not present an all-or-nothing choice, but rather lays down a direction of change with clear points of orientation. In so doing, it [...] highlights the core recommendations made in the areas of economics, politics and law. [...] Although steps taken to implement the reform programme in each of these areas would constitute a major step forward for progressive politics, it is only by addressing the policy packages in all of them that the programme of global social democracy can ultimately be fulfilled. One of the principal political questions of our time is how such a programme can best be carried out, and how global public goods can best be provided.

A coalition of political groupings could develop to push the agenda of global social democracy further. It could comprise European countries with strong liberal and social democratic traditions; liberal groups in the US which support multilateralism and the rule of law in international affairs; developing countries struggling for freer and fairer trade rules in the world economic system; non-governmental organizations, from Amnesty International to Oxfam, campaigning for a more just, democratic and equitable world order; transnational social movements contesting the nature and form of contemporary globalization; and those economic forces that desire a more stable and managed global economy.

A complex set of parties and commitments would be needed to make a compelling coalition for global social democracy. But while it would be complex, it is not

1 Kofi Annan, "A Compact for a New Century," United Nations Document SG/SM/6881 (January 31, 1999).

Box [1] Towards a new global covenant: global social democracy

Guiding ethical principles
Equal moral worth, equal liberty, equal political status, collective decision-making about public affairs, amelioration of urgent need, development for all, environmental sustainability

Institutional goals
Rule of law, political equality, democratic politics, global social justice, social solidarity and community, economic efficiency, global ecological balance

Priority measures
Economy

- Regulating global markets: salvaging the Doha trade negotiating round; removal of EU and US subsidies of agriculture and textiles; reforming TRIPS; expansion of the terms of reference of the Global Compact
- Promoting development: phasing in trade and financial global market integration (particularly of portfolio capital markets); expanding the negotiating capacity of developing countries at the WTO; enhancing developing country participation in international financial institutions; abolition of debt for highly indebted poor countries (HIPCs); linking debt cancellation to the funding of children's education and basic health; meeting UN aid targets of 0.7 per cent GNP; establishing new international finance facility to aid investment in poorest countries

Governance

- Reform of global governance: establishing a representative Security Council; establishment of Economic and Social Security Council to coordinate poverty reduction and global development policies; creation of environmental IGO; establishment of global issue networks on pressing social and economic problems; strengthening the negotiating capacity of developing countries; developing criteria for fair negotiations among states and non-state actors; improving cooperation among IGOs; enhanced parliamentary scrutiny of regional and international bodies

Law

- Convene an international convention to begin the process of reconnecting the security and human rights agendas through the consolidation of international humanitarian law

Security

- Developing UN Security Council principles and procedures in relation to threats to the peace and the use of armed force to intervene in the affairs of another state; enhancing monitoring capacity of the risks of, and developments concerning, humanitarian crises; implementation of existing global poverty reduction and human development commitments and policies; strengthening of arms control and arms trade regulation

Long-term measures
Economy

- Taming global markets: global antitrust authority; world financial authority; mandatory codes of conduct for MNCs
- Market correcting: mandatory global labour and environmental standards; foreign investment codes and standards
- Market promoting: privileged market access for developing countries where fledgling industries require protection; convention on global labour mobility and economic migration

Governance

- Democratization of national and suprastate governance (multilevel citizenship); global constitutional convention to explore the rules and mandates of new democratic global bodies; establishment of new international tax mechanism; creation of negotiating arenas for new priority issues (e.g. world water court); enhanced global public goods provision

Law

- Establishment of international human rights court with strong supporting regional courts; the expansion of the jurisdictions of the ICC and ICJ; the entrenchment of labour, welfare and environmental standards in the *modus operandi* of corporate practice

Security

- Establishment of permanent peace-making and peacekeeping forces; developing security and human rights threshold tests for membership in key IGOs; security, social exclusion and equity impact reviews of all global development measures impossible to envisage. In fact, some of its core ingredients could be stipulated as follows:

- leading European powers need to commit to the creation of a multilateral order, and not a multipolar one in which they simply pursue their own state interests above all else;
- the EU must address its weak geopolitical and strategic capacity via the development of a rapid reaction force and the creation of a common European defence force;
- the US needs to acknowledge that its long-term strategic, economic and environmental interests can only be achieved collaboratively, and it must, as a matter of principle, accept the opportunities and constraints afforded by multilateral institutions and international regimes;
- developing countries, seeking major aid and overseas investments (public and private), need to accept the establishment of transparent and good governance as part of the requirements to attract investment in the infrastructure of their economies and societies;
- INGOs need to understand that, while their voices in global affairs are important, they represent particular interests which need to be articulated with, and harnessed within, wider frameworks of accountability and justice;
- IGOs utilizing and advocating greater public funding have to recognize that they are part of an international civil service delivering core public goods – and not outposts of particular nation-states or sectional interests. The confusing and conflicting mandates and jurisdictions of IGOs need to be streamlined and clarified;
- regional governance structures, while enhancing and expanding the developmental opportunities of their member states, must commit to keeping regions open for economic and diplomatic engagement with others – in short, they need to nurture open forms of regionalism;
- national governments must recognize that they are stakeholders in global problems and that ownership of these is a crucial first stage in their resolution – national and regional parliaments need to enhance their communication with, understanding of and engagement with supranational governance.

Europe could have a distinctive role in pursuing the cause of global social democracy.[2] As the home of both social democracy and a historic experiment in governance beyond the state, Europe has accumulated a wealth of experience in considering institutional designs for suprastate governance. It offers novel ways of thinking about governance beyond the state which encourage a more accountable and rule-bound – as opposed to more neoliberal or unilateralist – approach to global governance. This is not to suggest that the EU should lead an anti-US coalition of transnational and international forces. On the contrary, it is crucial to recognize the complexity of US domestic politics and the existence of progressive social, political and economic forces seeking to advance a rather different kind of world order from that championed by the current neoconservatives.[3]

While some of those who might coalesce around a movement for global social democracy would inevitably have divergent interests on a wide range of issues, there is potentially an important overlapping sphere of concern among them for the strengthening of multilateralism, building new institutions for providing global public goods, regulating global markets, deepening accountability, protecting the environment and urgently remedying social injustices that kill thousands of men, women and children daily. And there is evidence that the thrust of such a coalition would resonate with people's attitudes to globalization in many parts of the world. A recent poll highlights that while many people have positive views about the broad benefits of globalization, they want a different kind of globalization from the one currently on offer: the integration of economies and societies has to be balanced with the protection of local traditions, with a sustainable pace of life, and with a global social safety net to help ensure equitable life chances.[4]

High stakes

Over the last one hundred years political power has been reshaped and reconfigured. It has been diffused below, above and alongside the nation-state. Globalization has brought large swathes of the world's population 'closer together' in overlapping communities of fate. Yet there are, obviously enough, many reasons for pessimism. There are storm clouds ahead. Globalization has not just integrated peoples and nations, but created new forms of antagonism. The globalization of communications

2 A. McGrew, "Between Two Worlds: Europe in a Globalizing Era," *Government and Opposition*, 27 (Summer, 2002).

3 Joseph Nye, *The Paradox of American Power* (Oxford: Oxford University Press, 2002).

4 B. Stokes, "Global is better," *National Journal* 6 (2003). www.people-press.org.

does not just make it easier to establish mutual understanding, but often highlights what it is that people do not have in common and how and why differences matter. The dominant political game in the 'transnational town' remains geopolitics. Ethnic self-centredness, right-wing nationalism and unilateralist politics are once again on the rise, and not just in the West. However, the circumstances and nature of politics have changed. Like national culture and state traditions, a vibrant internationalism and global social democracy are a cultural and political project, but with one difference: they are better adapted and suited to our regional and global age. Unfortunately, the arguments in support of them have yet to be fully articulated in many parts of the world; and we fail here at our peril.

It is important to return to 9/11 and the war in Iraq and to say what they mean in this context. One cannot accept the burden of putting accountability and justice right in one realm of life – physical security and political cooperation among defence establishments – without at the same time seeking to put it right elsewhere. If the political and the security, the social and the economic dimensions of accountability and justice are separated in the long term – as is the tendency in the global order today – the prospects of a peaceful and civil society will be bleak indeed. Popular support against terrorism, as well as against political violence and exclusionary politics of all kinds, depends on convincing people that there is a legal, responsive and specific way of addressing their grievances. For this reason, globalization without global social democracy could fail.

Against the background of 9/11, the current unilateralist stance of the US and the desperate cycle of violence in the Middle East and elsewhere, the advocacy of global social democracy may appear like an attempt to defy gravity or to walk on water! And, indeed, if it were a case of having to adopt global social democracy all at once or not at all, this would be true. But it is no more the case than was the pursuit of the modern state at the time of its founders. Over the last several decades the growth of multilateralism and the development of international law have created social democratic anchors for the world. These are the basis for the further consolidation of social democratic principles and institutions. Moreover, a coalition of political groupings could emerge to push these achievements further. Of course, how far such forces can unite around these objectives – and can overcome fierce opposition from well-entrenched geopolitical and geoeconomic interests – remains to be seen. The stakes are high, but so too are the potential gains for human security and development if the aspirations for global social democracy can be realized. One thing is clear; existing security and development policies are not working well enough and the case for a new politics and policy mix is overwhelming.

Kirkpatrick Sale, "Human-Scale Democracy"*

But is it not possible to envision the criteria for an optimum community in the modern world? Just as the human measure can guide us in the design of technology and the creation of buildings, can it not provide a guide in the development of communities?

The cardinal task here, it seems to me, is to discover the limits of a human-scale community, the size beyond which – as the Beanstalk Principle would suggest – it ought not to grow. And here, thanks to various anthropological and sociological records, we have a considerable body of interesting evidence.

During most of its prehistorical eons, humankind did not live in settlements much above a thousand people and generally preferred places closer to half of that. John Pfeiffer, the anthropological writer who has perhaps as encyclopedic a vision as anyone in the field, goes so far as to call 500 a "magic number" because it recurs so often in human evolution as the limit of a community:

> The phenomenon becomes clear and meaningful only after taking census figures for a large number of tribes. Such studies reveal a central tendency to cluster at the 500 level, and this tendency is widespread. It holds for the Shoshoni Indians of the Great Plains, the Andaman Islanders in the Bay of Bengal, and other peoples as well as the Australian aborigines.

This number, Pfeiffer suggests, may have been determined by the nature of human communication and culture-sharing mechanisms: "There seems to be a basic limit to the number of persons who can know one another well enough to maintain a tribal identity at the hunter-gatherer level, who communicate by direct confrontation and who live under a diffuse and informal influence, perhaps a council of elders, rather than an active centralized political authority." That number may also have been determined by the optimum number of people for mate-selection.

[...]

* Kirkpatrick Sale, extracted from *Human Scale* (New York: Coward, McCann & Geoghegan, 1980), pp. 182–204, 510–15.

There is another number, or rather range of numbers, similarly "magic" perhaps, that recurs in the examination of community, suggesting another desirable, though somewhat larger, size for human groupings. Again, there is an interesting general agreement on the figures from a wide variety of sources.

Although it was the face-to-face village that was the primary communal unit, many societies, and particularly the more successful, often formed larger bands, or tribes, uniting these villages into a common culture. Anthropological evidence suggests that throughout prehistory the upper limit for such tribes – defined as those who speak the same dialect or language or who unite into an association of villages – was everywhere about 5,000 or 6,000. William Sanders and Paul Baker of Penn State University point out that tribal units sharing common customs, common language, and common territory might have grown as large as this limit but at that point almost always split into new tribes or else imposed a limit on further growth by establishing a central authority capable of governing population. The University of Arizona's William Rathje, after using general systems theory to interpret Mayan culture, has suggested that this 5,000 number may represent a level at which the social system, at least in early societies, had to limit itself to keep from overloading itself with complexities and burning itself out.

This was about the limit of the earliest cities, too, as near as we can reconstruct the sites – not only in the Middle East, an area that has been particularly well surveyed, but in India, China, North Africa, and Central America. A few might have grown to 20,000 and even 50,000 in their latest stages, shortly before collapse, but as a general rule the urban centers of the millennia before Christ seem to have stayed at between 5,000 and 10,000 people.

[...]

Coming down to the present, a range of 5,000 to 10,000 shows up with surprising frequency in the recommendations of architects and city planners for the preferred size of a community. Clarence Perry, the grandfather of contemporary planning and the man who redirected attention back to the idea of small-scale communities in the 1930s when they were first threatened by the onrush of the twentieth-century metropolis, is typical. After years of study he hit upon an ideal "neighborhood unit" of from 3,000 to 9,000 people, with an optimum size at 5,000. His theory was that a neighborhood had to be small enough so that everything important – schools, playgrounds, shops, public buildings – was within easy walking distance, and large enough to support an elementary school and a variety of local stores and services. Both conditions could be satisfied, he determined, with a population of about 1,000 to 1,500 families, or an average of about 5,000 people, distributed at roughly 15–20 people per acre, with the total unit then occupying about a half mile square. Since Perry's formulation, a wide variety of other city planners, of different decades, philosophies, styles, and interests, has also arrived at about the same figure.

Perry's "walking distance" principle in particular has become standard among almost all urban planners who give any thought at all to community. Walter Gropius, the architect, has explained the rationale this way:

> The size of the townships should be limited by the pedestrian range to keep them within a human scale. ... The human being himself, so much neglected during the early machine age, must become the focus of all reconstruction to come. Our stride determines and measures our space- and time-conception and pegs out our local living space. Organic planning has to reckon with the human scale, the "foot," when shaping any physical structure. Violation of the human scale will cause further degeneration of life in cities.

Like Perry, Gropius observed that the maximum distance a person would walk comfortably for ordinary community affairs was about half a mile, and thus he too came up with an optimum "township" size of roughly a half a mile square. Now if we assume that half the space within that area would be given over to public buildings, shops, pathways, and parkland, and if we assume for the remaining 160 acres residential densities somewhere around the models of Gropius and the "garden city" planners, we come up with a range of population – no surprise – around 5,000–8,000 people.

One final piece of evidence on community size comes from Leopold Kohr, who has done more thinking about this from the perspective of the social sciences than anyone to date. Kohr argues that it would take about 80 or 100 adults to provide the *convivial* society, that is to say, the number to "fulfill the companionship function to the fullest" and "to ensure both variety of contacts and constancy of relationships"; but, he says, it would take more than that for an effective *economic* society. In a society with basic specialization – a shoemaker, say, and a baker and a builder and so on – there need to be enough people to consume the goods and services during the course of a year, and 80 or 100 adults is too small a pool; "economic optimum social size," he estimates, requires "a full membership of 4,000 to 5,000 inhabitants." At this level, he argues, "society seems capable of furnishing its members not only with most of the commodities we associate with a high standard of living, but also of surrounding each person with the margin of leisure without which it could not properly perform its original convivial function." And for the optimum *political* society only a few thousand people need be added – "a full population of between 7,000 and 12,000" – to provide a sufficient number who can be spared from basic economic routines to perform legislative, legal, political, and security tasks. This is the size, actually, of various real-world states that survive quite nicely, including the independent state of Nauru in the South Pacific, and such self-administered dependencies as Anguilla, the Cayman Islands, Montserrat, Falkland Islands, Saint Helena, and Tuvalu.

[...]

Thus we seem to have arrived at another set of "magic" numbers, similarly inexact and somewhat elastic but similarly suggestive, which may provide some indication of the nature and the extent of the human-scale city. Obviously we must think of the desirable city as a congeries of neighborhoods and communities, for these have to be the building blocks out of which any larger entity is built; they must continue to supply the rootedness, even as the wider society supplies its diversity. But within that context it is still possible to find enough evidence – sociological, economic, political, and demographic – to permit some reasonable conclusions as to the validity of these magic numbers and the limits of the optimal city.

Sociological

The sociological verdict is generally that the quality of life in the larger American cities is – I can think of no better summary – solitary, poor, nasty, brutish, and short. There are no doubt compensations for it all, in the minds of many, but the studies suggest that, as a rule, as cities get bigger they increase in density, fragmentation, deviance, criminality, social stress, anomie, loneliness, selfishness, alcoholism, mental illness, and racial and ethnic segregation. These ills begin to gather, it seems, somewhere around the 100,000 level, and without doubt the biggest cities are the worst.

[...]

Economic

[...] In big cities today the effects of agglomeration are most likely to be *dis*advantageous for businesses. There are higher transportation and distribution costs because of traffic congestion; higher business costs because of a decrease in the number of hours worked per worker; higher maintenance and cleaning costs because of air pollution; higher energy costs because of the "heat island" effect over cities in the summer and the shading of dense buildings in the winter; higher security costs and higher property-loss rates because of crime and vandalism; higher costs in training new workers because of inferior schools; higher land costs and greater building-construction expenses; and higher insurance rates, higher wages, higher costs of living, and higher taxes.

[...]

Political

[...]

The sheer scale of events and organizations in the smaller city invites participation and creates the feeling that individuals have, or at least can have, some control over the events that affect their lives. Smaller cities also can be more efficient and responsive in meeting citizen needs, since there is likely to be more two-way communication, more and better message-sending to the people in charge, and easier access to their offices. And smaller governing systems are far more adaptable to any crisis, have far better information to rely on, and can depend on greater cooperation from the citizens.

[...]

Could it be that, given human frailty, a modest limit on political effectiveness is inevitable?

Dahl certainly seems to have come to this conclusion. After worrying it over in several books and a number of articles, spending more time on this than any of his academic colleagues have done, he finally decided: "I think that the optimal unit is, or rather could be, the city of intermediate size, bigger than neighborhood, smaller than megalopolis. ... The appropriate size looks to me to be a city between about fifty thousand and several hundred thousand inhabitants."

[...]

[Ecology]

If, further, the community is guided by the tenets of *ecological harmony* and *steady-state* equilibria, it is hardly the type to despoil its environment or readily admit the toxic or polluting industry (which, being in control of its economy, it is free to reject). Conscious of the way it relates to the ecosystem, it would likely establish, and value, its connections to other communities within the bioregion – the city upriver, the town downwind – and keep in check its tendencies to isolation and insularity. Conservative it would certainly be, in the best sense of that word, for that is precisely what recycling and resource recovery, precisely what self-sufficiency, is all about; yet only the most short-sighted would overlook the new biogas invention that came along from elsewhere.

[...]

I am certain that democratically run ecological communities in control of their own destinies will not choose to construct SSTs and DC-10s, MIRV missiles and nuclear bombs, fast-breeder reactors and cyclotrons, CAT scanners and Saturn rockets, Cadillac Sevilles and Astrodomes, TVAs and Alaska pipelines. (They could of course if they wanted to, within their own ecological restrictions, but there might not be much left over for their plows and pitchers.) But I am also certain that the concentrated use of alternative technology (including the cannibalization of elements of existing high technology), coupled with the accelerated energy of individuals in control of their own economies – and absent the absorptive debilitation of the state – will enable communities of quite modest size to achieve all that could be asked for in basic human comfort.

[...]

I have, it will be noted, used the idea of "self-interest" repeatedly. That seems to be precisely the ingredient necessary – paradoxically perhaps – to overcome the deficiencies of a communitarian world. Lucky it is in such abundant supply.

I feel sure that in the long run, the very long run, the experience of an essentially communal society, whether in neighborhoods, communities, or small cities, will diminish the sort of selfishness and egoism familiar to us today. But I see no reason to think that it will happen anytime soon, and since I would rather consider realities than utopias, I assume we should take individual self-interest into account.

Very well. It is in the self-interest of all but a handful of us to stop pollution, overbreeding, overcrowding, crime, anomie, alienation, urban decay ... and the rest of it. It is in the self-interest of all but a demented few of us to find social forms that will permit the greatest amount of personal participation and effective control over institutions, economic forms that allow the greatest amount of real accomplishment with the benefits of comfort and security, political forms that encourage the greatest amount of individual freedom and public happiness. And it is in the self-interest of all to do what is necessary to preserve those forms when once they are achieved or approximated, to maintain the limits at which they can be protected, despite the blandishments of such kings and colonizers and centralizers as may arise.

The difficulties of any human-scale society should not be minimized. But it needs only for each person to confront those difficulties in context – to measure the anguish of face-to-face political negotiation against the frustration of powerlessness, the deprivation of around-the-world vacations against the satisfaction of household artifacts handsome and durable, the nuisance of neighborliness against the cold loneliness of abstract cities – and then to make the rational and, precisely, the self-interested choice.

The truly self-interested individual, in caring about individual needs and satisfactions, would ultimately have to care about the people across the way, the neighborhood around, the community and the city at large, for in the larger contexts the particular needs are satisfied best – especially, as we have seen, those truest and most basic needs, of love and friendship and roots. Self-interest in the long run may be only communal interest, ecological interest, planetary interest. Theodore Roszak, at the first Schumacher Society Lectures in Wales in 1978, explored exactly what this does – what this *can* – mean, and his words stand as a fitting assertion of the resonance of a politics on the human scale:

> As the scale of industrial activity mounts, so also (at least along one important line of contemporary dissent in Western society) do our expectations of personal freedom and fulfillment. This, in turn, becomes an obstacle to the further expansion and integration of the system. So the system begins to *dis*-integrate, a fitful process that gets registered in the news of the day as truancy in the schools, the soaring divorce rate, declining morals and rising turnover in the workforce, the demise of military conscription, a growing reluctance to compete and conform, a general distrust of leaders, experts, official ideals, public institutions ... in brief, the spreading ethos of cynicism and recalcitrance that social theorists refer to as "the twilight of authority," "the crisis of legitimation," etc.
>
> But this disintegration is essentially creative, for, in our rising sense of personhood, we find a peculiarly postindustrial quality of life that is wholly incompatible with the mass processing of superscale systems. So we are moved instinctively to assert the human scale that will give us attention, respect, tender loving care. *In asserting the human scale, we subvert the regime of bigness. In subverting bigness, we save the planet.*

And, not in the least incidentally, ourselves.

Robert Dahl, "The Chinese Boxes"*

I invite you now to engage in a mental experiment which I fear you may resist as preposterous. I want you to imagine that you are trying to constitute a system of rightful government for the world, a system whose laws you would ordinarily feel obliged to obey. I want you to assume further that to be rightful the system must be in some sense "democratic," that it must be designed to facilitate "rule by the people": not just a single people, now, nor *the* people as one parochial ideologue or another might define the people, but rule by the people of the world.

If you resist this exercise, remember that in their Golden Age the Greeks refused to consider seriously a constitution for the whole of Greece, tiny as that entity seems by modern standards. Remember too that as late as the eighteenth century, it was still an article of faith, which the men at the American Constitutional Convention undertook to challenge, that you could not have a republic on a territory as large as the thirteen states. In 1970 a government for the world is, I admit, a fantastic idea; it will not seem so in a century. Nor will it then seem strange to ask whether and to what extent such a government can or should be "democratic," and how it might be.

My reason for asking you to participate in this exercise is, however, not a practical one. I have purely intellectual purposes in mind. Or perhaps spiritual: I am not yet sure of having exorcised a ghost that has been haunting us.

Whenever I try to imagine what such a constitution might be, I am at once drawn to the conclusion that it must contain extensive mutual guarantees limiting the scope of the majority principle. If, as I argued earlier, the majority principle requires such a high degree of trust and consensus that majorities are almost invariably limited even within the nation-state, then surely people of different languages, races, religions, and national origins, far removed from one another in space, speech, and thought, and with no firm habits of political cooperation and mutual trust, will never voluntarily unite or remain under a single constitution unless the matters they value most are protected from invasion by majorities.

[...]

If we assume that the Creation, or the Big Bang, had not totally eradicated all memories of the past, then for many people it would be a natural step to demand some elbow room for smaller units constituted somewhat along the boundaries of the old nation-states. To be sure, some of the nation-states that are now held together more by bayonets and baling wire than by common feeling would like Humpty Dumpty be too fractured for the pieces to be put together again. Yet people sharing a common territory, language, past, and fellow feeling more concrete than abstract humanity would surely demand some decentralization to a unit in which they might reasonably expect to share some aims, feelings, outlooks, and ways of doing things. If you will be patient for the sake of the experiment and let me now make the wildly improbable assumption that these units would be "democratic" (which, because of their size, means polyarchies), our world government now has an intermediate stage of "democracy" in the form of polyarchy-cum-administration.

It is easy to see that only one intermediate stage would be insufficient. For the intermediate units would be either too large or too small. Nations even as small as the Scandinavian democracies are too large to handle satisfactorily all the problems that involve local variation, such as neighborhood planning. As for giant nations, no one has ever devised a sensible scheme by which the people of the United States could govern themselves without several intermediate stages between the people and the federal government. The eleven-tier system of Fridley, Minnesota, may be an absurd proliferation; yet it is a good deal less absurd than trying to govern a world region as large as the United States with no lower levels of authority. If nations are too large for local variations, cities are too small for regional variations of the kind manageable by provinces or the nation-state.

So: you throw in another stage or two of polyarchy-cum-administration, a stage of primary democracy at the neighborhood level, a dash of committee democracy, possibly even an opportunity for referenda.

The system is getting complicated. In practice, any sensible effort to devise a scheme for world democracy would have to be very much more complex than anything we need to envision here. But our mental experiment has, I hope, already made the point I was reaching for. For two thousand years, philosophers who wrote about rule by the people took it for granted that "the people" would be a single, well-defined, and probably small subset of humanity, and that this subset of people would rule through a single, sharply bounded, and completely autonomous state. Just as the consequence of this way of thinking for the Greek democrat was to envision a map of a "democratic" Greece as all fenced off

* Robert Dahl, extracted from *After the Revolution* (Yale University Press, 1970), pp. 88–103.

into autonomous, independent, democratic, and usually warring city-states, each totally legitimate within its own boundaries and totally illegitimate outside them, so the consequence of the ancients' way of thinking about a "democratic" world is to imagine it made up of autonomous, independent, democratic states. Within the walls of their state, the people rule. But they have no authority outside their walls, and therefore no authority for dealing with matters that transcend their boundaries, for example pollution, nuclear testing, and violence.

[...]

Democratic federalist ideas take for granted that there must be several stages of "democratic" governments; that "the people" who are entitled to "rule" at one stage are a subset of "the people" who are entitled to "rule" at a more inclusive stage; and that the rights and obligations of "the people" at various stages are embodied in a system of mutual guarantees.

If you have concurred in my argument up to now, then I think you must agree with me that stages of government fitting together rather like the components of a Chinese box are necessary if "the people" are to "rule" on matters important to them, whether a neighborhood playground, water pollution, or the effective prohibition of nuclear war. From which we must conclude that whatever stages are necessary in order for "the people" to "rule" effectively on matters important to them are also, from a purely democratic point of view, rightful.

Whether you want to say that each stage is equally "democratic" is another question. I do not believe there is any contradiction in saying that in order for the people to make their choices effective on matters of importance to them they will need some stages of government that are less "democratic" than others. Earlier I referred to the need for delegated authority. A representative body, I suggested, may itself be viewed as delegated authority, but in order to be effective representative bodies need to delegate authority still further to administrative bodies. Polyarchy-cum-administration is delegation-cum-delegation. When members of a democratic body delegate some of its authority in order to effectuate their purposes, they will want to insure that the authority is employed for the purposes they have in mind. Delegated authority is subordinate authority. In this sense, delegated authority entails hierarchy. And the more dangerous the authority, or the more open it is to abuse, the stronger we may want the controls within hierarchy to be. If the people who constitute a city's police force were entitled to decide on the purposes for which they would use their power, then the citizens of the city – "the people" – would be unable to rule the city. The fact that this happens too much already is no reason for wanting it to happen more.

In short, if you want to maximize the effectiveness of the people in achieving their purposes, you will need some stages of government that you may consider less "democratic" than others. If you think that polyarchy is less "democratic" than primary democracy, you will nonetheless need to prescribe several stages of polyarchy. What is more, you will need administration, and administration will need hierarchy. Otherwise, "the people" who rule may turn out not to be the people but the bureaucrats. I do not see how we can stretch the meaning of "democratic" authority to include the hierarchy of administration. Consequently we must conclude that rule by the people requires not only democratic forms but also nondemocratic forms of delegated authority.

It would be dishonest and irresponsible of me to draw simple prescriptions from this analysis. The criteria of Personal Choice, Competence, and Economy cannot be applied mechanically. Alas, even the age of computers will not relieve you of hard choices and dangerous decisions.

I cannot therefore exhort you: The only rightful government is primary democracy. Or: Place all your trust in polyarchy. Or: The world must be governed by a federal democracy.

Perhaps the greatest error in thinking about democratic authority is to believe that ideas about democracy and authority are simple and must lead to simple prescriptions. I hope you have seen why this cannot be so. If you do, then we could begin a dialogue on how to develop democracy and rightful authority in our world, our country, our corporations, universities, cities, neighborhoods.

[...]

Must we conclude that an association should be enlarged in every case where it can be shown that by doing so, some matter like pollution can be dealt with more effectively in the larger than in the smaller association? Clearly not. In the first place, we must not relapse into a way of thinking from which I have tried to liberate you: that there must be only a single, all-purpose association, the one sovereign state. Let me remind you again of the now familiar point: we need associations of different dimensions, for different purposes.

In the second place, since you cannot possibly keep a large number of associations at the focus of your attention, energy, and action, it would be foolish to proliferate associations for every problem (as we Americans have a tendency to do). As a practical matter you will have to put some things into your Chinese boxes that do not quite fit, on the ground that the advantages of fewer boxes will outweigh the disadvantages of the inexact fit, at least up to some point that I fear can only be satisfactorily defined in practice.

In the third place, it is crucially important to keep in mind that the extra costs imposed by large organizations are often enormous. That they can bring a matter more fully within their jurisdiction than a smaller organization does not always mean, of course, that they can deal with it effectively. But even if they can, the costs may exceed the gains. Among the costs are the creation of an individual sense of impotence that can be demoralizing and dehumanizing: a feeling that decisions are beyond your control, that your own small voice can never be heard amid the din of a million or a hundred million others, that to the decision makers of the world, engaged today in a lazy game of Indian wrestling and tomorrow, knives drawn, in a struggle to the death, you are as an ant scurrying underfoot, your fate dependent on nothing more than where these giants happen to thrust a foot or crash awkwardly to earth.

It would be comforting to have a crystal-clear rule of action, the kind of rule theorists adore and decision makers disdain. Though I recommend that you deny yourself the dangerous comforts of simplistic thinking, the argument does suggest a few pragmatic principles:

1 If a matter is best dealt with by a democratic association, seek always to have that matter dealt with by the smallest association that can deal with it satisfactorily.
2 In considering whether a larger association would be more satisfactory, do not fail to consider its extra costs, including a possible increase in the sense of individual powerlessness.
3 The Criterion of Economy requires that the number of democratic associations in which you participate are few, even if this means that all are too large or too small for some matters.
4 Remember that the alternatives to a larger association include not only a smaller association but also Autonomous Decisions, for example Consumers' Choice through the market, and so forth.

Chapter 10

On Citizenship

Introduction

Polities are political communities with territorial boundaries and governments having the coercive power to govern the people residing within these boundaries. But are all of these people *citizens*? During the past two centuries, citizenship has been extended to most inhabitants of nations, leaving the most hotly contested issue in this regard one of extending citizenship to immigrants: can national governments and their existing citizens legitimately prevent outsiders from crossing their borders, deny them opportunities to live and work within their societies, and become naturalized citizens themselves? What is involved in citizenship? We usually speak of the rights and responsibilities of citizens, but what are they? We often say that citizens should exhibit certain virtues, but what are the virtues of good citizens? Such are the issues of citizenship.

In his highly influential *Spheres of Justice* (1983), Michael Walzer – now professor emeritus at the Institute for Advanced Study in Princeton – noticed that political theorists had usually assumed that their theories applied to political communities with a given population of citizens, but they were silent about who should be included as citizens within polities. Of course, advocates of the rights of women, minorities, the handicapped, and so forth had made impressive arguments for the inclusion of all such residents of polities into full citizenship, but most contemporary political theorists regarded such claims as self-evident and needed no extensive reflection and defense. They simply assumed that their theories applied to all residents cum citizens, save the immature and the incompetent who might be incapable of exercising adequately the rights and responsibilities that citizenship conferred. What Walzer thought odd was that political theorists had not much considered which outsiders should be admitted as members (first as residents and then as full citizens) into those communities where only limited admission seemed feasible. Perhaps good polities are like elite universities, and "open admissions" would undermine the qualities that make these communities attractive. In any event, Walzer thought that decisions about who to admit into membership of such communities is the *first* issue of justice. Before we can decide how social goods should be distributed among members of a polity, we have to decide who are the members who will be affected by subsequent distributive decisions. In our selection, Walzer concludes that democratic communities have the right to determine their own principles and policies of admission according to their own social understandings of what is necessary to promote their having "communities of character," as long as these determinations were constrained by certain moral requirements.

Joseph Carens, a professor of political science at the University of Toronto, provides an alternative view. He claims "Citizenship in Western liberal democracies is the modern equivalent of feudal privilege. … Restrictive citizenship is hard to justify when one thinks about it closely." In his essay, Carens argues that countries like the United States should have "open admissions," and finds support for his argument in three liberal traditions. Libertarian theory should claim that current restrictive immigration policies are contrary to individual rights. Rawls' egalitarian liberalism suggests that the interests of the least advantaged would be served by open admissions. And utilitarians would calculate that unrestrictive admissions would achieve "the greater good of the greater number." While he finds Walzer's communitarian argument "rich and subtle," he also finds it misleading. Carens argues that the fundamental values of the American tradition call for open borders, not the restrictions on immigration that are currently in place.

So, what rights does citizenship provide? Among serious political theorists, the concept of natural rights has had little currency since it was effectively attacked by such traditional conservatives as Edmund Burke (see Chapter 2). Even classical liberals recognized that citizens abandoned their natural rights when they entered into civil society. Their rights as citizens were those enacted through political processes and set forth in the constitutions that communities adopted, the laws that legislatures enacted, and various judicial determinations. Unlike *human rights* that are more moral than enforceable claims, citizen rights should not be regarded as universal rights that people can claim against any government or people anywhere, but they apply equally to all citizens of a polity. For most theorists, citizen rights were claims to freedoms, opportunities, and goods that people could make by virtue of their equal citizenship. Unlike the unequal distributions that occur in the marketplace, citizen rights were to be distributed by governments equally to all. But beyond such broad understandings, each polity must determine what specific rights citizens should have. T. H. Marshall (1893–1981), a British sociologist who taught at the London School of Economics, believed the best way to understand citizenship rights in Great Britain was to trace three elements of citizenship as they evolved at the national level. Civil rights were those necessary for individual freedom (e.g., freedom of speech, worship, ownership of property, and legal justice) and these could be traced to the seventeenth century when all men were considered free. Political rights were those regarding opportunities to participate in political power, and their formative period was the beginning of the nineteenth century and led to the universal franchise. Social rights involve "the whole range of rights from a modicum of economic welfare and security to [sharing fully] in the social heritage." He argues a broad array of social rights was not enacted until the twentieth century. And the goal of extending social rights has changed from one of "merely" abating poverty to "modifying the whole pattern of social inequality" and thus diminishing the significance of social classes.

But must all citizen rights be provided equally? Iris Marion Young (1949–2006), who was professor of political science at the University of Chicago, argues that equal political rights aim at those needs that citizens hold in common, but that citizens often have different needs. Pluralist societies are composed of a heterogeneous rather than a homogeneous public, including groups of oppressed citizens. Such groups require special rights. They should have the right to those resources necessary to enable the members of the oppressed group to organize and attain a sense of collective empowerment. They should have the right to have their voice represented in public policymaking. And they should have the right to veto specific policies that affect their group directly. Justice requires that such special group rights must supplement the equal citizen rights that pluralist societies provide.

Democratic societies have continuously expanded citizen and group rights, a development supported by civic communitarians such as Amitai Etzioni, a German–Israeli–American professor of sociology at George Washington University. But the platform of The Communitarian Network, an organization founded by Etzioni, declares that all societies need "balances between individuals and groups, rights and responsibilities, and the institutions of state, market, and civil society." While some societies (like China) need to provide more rights to achieve an appropriate balance of citizen rights and responsibilities, others (like the United States) need now to stress citizen responsibilities. The responsibilities of citizens extend beyond those encoded in laws; they must be anchored in the moral consciousness of citizens and in the cultures of communities. If morality is understood as necessary constraints on freedoms, Americans must restore their moral voice. They must seek changes in workplaces to allow parents to better discharge their child-rearing responsibilities and in schools that should more actively provide a moral education. Volunteer work within civil society and the discharge of political duties – such as paying one's fair share of taxes – must be re-emphasized.

Political theorists have always stressed the importance of citizen virtues. The need for virtuous citizens was even recognized by Niccolo Machiavelli (1469–1527) – the diplomat and political philosopher from Florence, Italy, who is renowned for his amoral (some would say immoral) advice to princes that they engage in some unsavory activities to secure power and order. On the basis of his study of ancient republics in his *Discourses on Livy*, he concludes, "a corrupt people ... can never become free." But what virtues should citizens possess, and who should be responsible for insuring the inculcation of the necessary virtues? Pluralists have always been uncomfortable with the ideas that there is any objective list and ranking of virtues and that the state should be less than neutral in resolving differences among conceptions of moral virtue. Yet many friends of pluralism grant the Machiavellian and communitarian point that polities do require a virtuous citizenry. One of the more interesting bodies of political theory to emerge in the past few decades has addressed these issues.[1]

Michael Walzer, "The Distribution of Membership"*

The idea of distributive justice presupposes a bounded world, a community within which distributions take place, a group of people committed to dividing, exchanging, and sharing, first of all among themselves. It is possible to imagine such a group extended to include the entire human race, but no such extension has yet been achieved. For the present, we live in smaller distributive communities. Were the extension ever attempted, its success would depend upon decisions made within these smaller communities and by their members – who distribute decision-making power to one another and avoid, if they possibly can, sharing it with anyone else. When we think today about distributive justice, we think about independent states and commonwealths capable of arranging their own distributions, justly or unjustly. We assume an established group and a fixed population, and so we miss the first and most important distributive question: How is that group constituted?

[...]

Since human beings are highly mobile, large numbers of men and women regularly attempt to change their residence and their membership, moving from unfavored to favored environments. Affluent and free countries are like elite universities; they are besieged by applicants. They have to decide on their own size and character. Whom should they admit? Ought they to have open admissions? Can they choose among applicants? What are the appropriate criteria for distributing membership?

[...]

To how many people do we distribute membership? The larger and philosophically more interesting questions – To what sorts of people? and To what particular people? – are most clearly confronted when we turn to the problems involved in admitting or excluding strangers.

[...]

Admissions policies are shaped partly by arguments about economic and political conditions in the host country, partly by arguments about the character and "destiny" of the host country, and partly by arguments about the character of countries (political communities) in general. The last of these is the most important (in theory, at least), for our understanding of countries in general will determine whether particular countries have the right they commonly claim: to distribute membership for (their own) particular reasons. But few of us have ever had any direct experience of what a country is or of what it means to be a member. We often have strong feelings about our country, but we have only dim perceptions of it. As a political community (rather than a place) it is, after all, invisible; we can actually see only its symbols, its offices, and its representatives. I suspect that we understand it best when we compare it to other, smaller associations whose compass we can more easily grasp, whose entire membership, it may be, we can take in at a glance. For we are all members of formal and informal groups of many different sorts; we know their workings intimately. And all these groups have, and necessarily have, admissions policies. Even if we have never served as state officials, even if we have never emigrated from one country to another, we have all had the experience of accepting or rejecting strangers, and we have all had the experience of being strangers, accepted or rejected. I want to draw upon this experience. My argument will be worked through a series of rough comparisons, in the course of which the special character of the political community will, I hope, become increasingly apparent.

Consider, then, three possible analogues for the political community: we can think of countries as neighborhoods, clubs, or families. [...]

The neighborhood is an enormously complex human association, but it has an ideal form that is at least partially reflected (though also increasingly challenged) in

* Michael Walzer, extracted from *Spheres of Justice* (New York: Basic Books, Inc., 1983), pp. 31–63.

1 For a useful summary, see Will Kymlicka, *Contemporary Political Philosophy*, 2nd edition (New York: Oxford University Press, 2002), Chapter 7.

contemporary American law. It is an association without an organized or legally enforceable admissions policy. Strangers can be welcomed or not welcomed; they cannot be admitted or excluded. Of course, being welcomed or not welcomed is sometimes effectively the same thing as being admitted or excluded, but the distinction is theoretically important. In principle, individuals and families move into a neighborhood for reasons of their own; they choose but are not chosen. Or rather, in the absence of legal controls, the market controls their movements. [...]

It was a common argument in classical political economy that national territory should be as "indifferent" as local space. The same writers who defended free trade in the nineteenth century also defended unrestricted immigration. They argued for perfect freedom of contract, without any sort of political restraint. International society, they thought, should take shape as a world of neighborhoods, with individuals moving freely about, seeking private advancement. In their view, as Henry Sidgwick reports it, the only business of state officials is "to maintain order over [a] particular territory ... but not in any way to determine who is to inhabit this territory, or to restrict the enjoyment of its natural advantages to any particular portion of the human race."[2] Natural advantages (like markets) are open to all comers, within the limits of private-property rights, and if they are used up or devalued by overcrowding, people presumably will move on, into the jurisdiction of new sets of officials.

Sidgwick thinks that this is possibly the "ideal of the future," but he offers three arguments against a world of neighborhoods in the present. First of all, such a world would not allow for patriotic sentiment, and so the "casual aggregates" that would probably result from the free movement of individuals would "lack internal cohesion." Neighbors would be strangers to one another. Second, free movement might interfere with efforts "to raise the standard of living among the poorer classes" of a particular country, since such efforts could not be undertaken with equal energy and equal success everywhere in the world. And third, the promotion of moral and intellectual culture and the efficient working of political institutions might be "defeated" by the continual creation of heterogeneous populations.[3] Sidgwick presents these three arguments as a series of consequentialist considerations that weigh against the benefits of labor mobility and contractual freedom. But they seem to me to have a rather different character. The last two arguments draw their force from the first, but only if the first is conceived in nonutilitarian terms. It is only if patriotic sentiment has some moral basis, only if communal cohesion makes for obligations, only if there are members as well as strangers, that state officials would have any reason to worry especially about the welfare of their own people (and of *all* their own people) and the success of their own culture and politics. For it is at least dubious that the average standard of living of the poorer classes throughout the world would decline under conditions of perfect labor mobility. Nor is there firm evidence that culture cannot thrive in cosmopolitan environments, nor that it is impossible to govern casual aggregations of people. As for the last of these, political theorists long ago discovered that certain sorts of regimes – namely, tyrannical regimes – thrive in the absence of communal cohesion. That perfect mobility leads to tyranny might make for a utilitarian argument against mobility, but such an argument would work only if individual men and women, free to come and go, expressed a desire for some other form of government. And that they might not do.

Perfect labor mobility, however, is probably a mirage, for it is almost certain to be resisted at the local level. Human beings, as I have said, move about a great deal, but this is not because they love to move. They are, most of them, emotionally prone to stay where they are unless their life is very difficult where they are. They experience a tension between love of place and the discomforts of particular places. While some of them leave their homes and become foreigners in new lands, others stay where they are and resent the foreigners in their own land. Hence, if states ever become large neighborhoods, it is likely that neighborhoods will become little states. Their members will organize to defend the local politics and culture against strangers. Historically, neighborhoods have turned into closed communities (leaving aside cases of legal coercion) whenever the state was open: in the cosmopolitan cities of multinational empires, for example, where state officials don't foster any particular identity but permit different groups to build their own institutional structures (as in ancient Alexandria), or in the receiving centers of mass immigration movements (early twentieth-century New York) where the country is an open but also an alien world – or, alternatively, a world full of aliens. The case is similar where the state doesn't exist at all or in areas where it doesn't function. Where welfare monies are raised and spent locally, for example, as in a seventeenth-century English parish, the

2 Henry Sidgwick, *Elements of Politics* (London: Macmillan, 1881), pp. 295–96.

3 Ibid., p. 296.

local people will seek to exclude newcomers who are likely welfare recipients. It is only the nationalization of welfare (or the nationalization of culture and politics) that opens the neighborhood communities to whoever chooses to come in.

[...]

Like clubs, countries have admissions committees. In the United States, Congress functions as such a committee, though it rarely makes individual selections. Instead, it establishes general qualifications, categories for admission and exclusion, and numerical quotas (limits). Then admissible individuals are taken in, with varying degrees of administrative discretion, mostly on a first-come, first-served basis. This sort of thing seems eminently defensible, though that does not mean that any particular set of qualifications and categories ought to be defended. To say that states have a right to act in certain areas is not to say that anything they do in those areas is right. One can argue about particular admissions standards by appealing, for example, to the condition and character of the host country. Such arguments have to be judged morally and politically as well as factually. When defenders of restricted immigration into the United States claimed (in 1920, say) that they were defending a homogeneous white and Protestant country, they were involved in a pretense that can plausibly be called immoral as well as inaccurate – as if nonwhite and non-Protestant citizens were invisible men and women who didn't have to be counted in the national census! Earlier Americans seeing the benefits of economic and geographic expansion had created a pluralist society, and the moral realities of that society ought to have guided the legislators of the 1920s. If we follow the logic of the club analogy, however, we have to say that the earlier decision might have been different, and the United States might have taken shape as a homogeneous community, an Anglo-Saxon nation-state (assuming what happened in any case – the virtual extermination of the Indians, who, understanding correctly the dangers of invasion, struggled as best they could to keep foreigners from their native lands). Decisions of this sort are subject to constraint, but what the constraints are I am not yet ready to say. It is important now to insist that the distribution of membership in American society, and in any ongoing society, is a matter of political decision. The labor market may be given free rein, as it was for many decades in the United States, but that does not happen by an act of nature or of God; it depends upon choices that are ultimately political. What kind of community do the citizens want to create? With what other men and women do they want to share and exchange social goods?

These are exactly the questions that club members answer when they make membership decisions, though usually with reference to a less extensive community and a more limited range of social goods. In clubs, only the founders choose themselves (or one another); all other members have been chosen by those who were members before them. Individuals may be able to give good reasons why they should be selected, but no one on the outside has a right to be inside. The members decide freely on their future associates, and the decisions they make are authoritative and final. Only when clubs split into factions and fight over property can the state intervene and make its own decision as to who the members are. When states split, however, no legal appeal is possible; there is no superior body. Hence, we might imagine states as perfect clubs, with sovereign power over their own selection processes.

But if this description is accurate as to the law, it is not an accurate account of the moral life of political communities. Clearly, citizens often believe themselves morally bound to open the doors of their country – not to anyone who wants to come in, perhaps, but to a particular group of outsiders, recognized as national or ethnic "relatives." In this sense, states are like families rather than clubs, for it is a feature of families that their members are morally connected to people they have not chosen, who live outside the household. In time of trouble, the household is also a refuge. Sometimes, under the auspices of the state, we take in fellow citizens to whom we are not related, as English country families took in London children during the Blitz, but our more spontaneous beneficence is directed at our own kith and kin. The state recognizes what we can call the family principle when it gives priority in immigration to the relatives of citizens. That is current policy in the United States, and it seems especially appropriate in a political community largely formed by the admission of immigrants. It is a way of acknowledging that labor mobility has a social price. Since laborers are men and women with families, one cannot admit them for the sake of their labor without accepting some commitment to their aged parents, say, or their sickly brothers and sisters.

In communities differently formed, where the state represents a nation largely in place, another sort of commitment commonly develops, along lines determined by the principle of nationality. In time of trouble, the state is a refuge for members of the nation, whether or not they are residents and citizens. Perhaps the lines of the political community were drawn years ago so as to exclude their villages and towns; perhaps they are the children or grandchildren of emigrants. They have no legal membership rights, but if they are persecuted in the land where they live, they look to their homeland not only with hope but also with expectation. I am inclined to say that such expectations are legitimate. Greeks driven from Turkey, Turks from Greece, after the wars and revolutions of the early twentieth century, had to be taken in by the states that bore their collective names. What else are such states for? They don't merely preside over a piece of territory and a random collection of inhabitants; they are also the political expression of a common life and (most often) of a national "family" that is never entirely enclosed within their legal boundaries. After World War II, millions of Germans, expelled by Poland and Czechoslovakia, were received and cared for by the two Germanies. Even if these states had been free of all responsibility in the expulsions, they would still have had a special obligation to the refugees. Most states recognize obligations of this sort in practice; some do so in law.

[...]

The distribution of membership is not pervasively subject to the constraints of justice. Across a considerable range of the decisions that are made, states are simply free to take in strangers (or not) – much as they are free, leaving aside the claims of the needy, to share their wealth with foreign friends, to honor the achievements of foreign artists, scholars, and scientists, and to enter into collective security arrangements with foreign states. But the right to choose an admissions policy is more basic than any of these, for it is not merely a matter of acting in the world, exercising sovereignty, and pursuing national interests. What is at stake here is the shape of the community that acts in the world, exercises sovereignty, and so on. Admission and exclusion are at the core of communal independence. They suggest the deepest meaning of self-determination. Without them, there could not be *communities of character*, historically stable, ongoing associations of men and women with some special commitment to one another and some special sense of their common life.[4]

But self-determination in the area of membership is not absolute. It is a right exercised, most often, by national clubs or families, but it is held in principle by territorial states. Hence it is subject both to the claims of affinity and of place and, when territory is considered as a resource, to the claims of necessity too. These are the constraints imposed on immigration. The constraints on naturalization are more severe. Every new immigrant, every refugee taken in, every resident and worker must be offered the opportunities of citizenship. If the community is so radically divided that a single citizenship is impossible, then its territory must be divided too, before the rights of admission and exclusion can be exercised; for these rights are to be exercised only by the political community as a whole (even if in practice some national majority dominates the decision-making) and only with regard to foreigners, not by some members of the community with regard to other members. No community can be half slave, half free, and claim that its admissions policies represent acts of self-determination.

The determination of ethnic minorities by all-powerful majorities, or of slaves by masters, or of aliens and guests by an exclusive band of citizens is not communal freedom but oppression. The men and women of the majority group, the masters, the band of citizens: these people are free, of course, to set up a club, make membership as exclusive as they like, write a constitution, and govern one another. But they can't claim territorial jurisdiction and rule over the people with whom they share the territory. To do that is to act outside their sphere, beyond their rights. It is a form of tyranny. Indeed, the rule of masters and citizens over slaves, aliens, and pariahs is probably the most common form of tyranny in human history. The theory of distributive justice, then, must begin with an account of membership rights. It must vindicate at one time the (limited) right of closure, without which there could be no communities at all, and the internal inclusiveness of the existing communities. For it is only as members somewhere that men and women can hope to share in all the other social goods – security, wealth, honor, culture, and political power – that communal life makes possible.

Joseph H. Carens, "Aliens and Citizens: The Case For Open Borders"*

Borders have guards and the guards have guns. This is an obvious fact of political life but one that is easily hidden from view – at least from the view of those of us who are citizens of affluent Western democracies. To Haitians in small, leaky boats confronted by armed Coast Guard cutters, to Salvadorans dying from heat

[4] I have taken the term "communities of character" from Otto Bauer, in *Austro-Marxism*, edited by Tom Bottomore and Patrick Goode (Oxford: Oxford University Press, 1978), p. 107.

* Joseph H. Carens, extracted from *Review of Politics*, 47 (Spring 1987), pp. 251–73.

and lack of air after being smuggled into the Arizona desert, to Guatemalans crawling through rat-infested sewer pipes from Mexico to California – to these people the borders, guards and guns are all too apparent. What justifies the use of force against such people? Perhaps borders and guards can be justified as a way of keeping out criminals, subversives, or armed invaders. But most of those trying to get in are not like that. They are ordinary, peaceful people, seeking only the opportunity to build decent, secure lives for themselves and their families. On what moral grounds can these sorts of people be kept out? What gives anyone the right to point guns at *them*?

To most people the answer to this question will seem obvious. The power to admit or exclude aliens is inherent in sovereignty and essential for any political community. Every state has the legal and moral right to exercise that power in pursuit of its own national interest, even if that means denying entry to peaceful, needy foreigners. States may choose to be generous in admitting immigrants, but they are under no obligation to do so.[5]

I want to challenge that view. In this essay I will argue that borders should generally be open and that people should normally be free to leave their country of origin and settle in another, subject only to the sorts of constraints that bind current citizens in their new country. The argument is strongest, I believe, when applied to the migration of people from third world countries to those of the first world. Citizenship in Western liberal democracies is the modern equivalent of feudal privilege – an inherited status that greatly enhances one's life chances. Like feudal birthright privileges, restrictive citizenship is hard to justify when one thinks about it closely.

In developing this argument I will draw upon three contemporary approaches to political theory: first that of Robert Nozick; second that of John Rawls; third that of the utilitarians. Of the three, I find Rawls the most illuminating, and I will spend the most time on the arguments that flow from his theory. But I do not want to tie my case too closely to his particular formulations (which I will modify in any event). My strategy is to take advantage of three well-articulated theoretical approaches that many people find persuasive to construct a variety of arguments for (relatively) open borders. I will argue that all three approaches lead to the same basic conclusion: there is little justification for restricting immigration. Each of these theories begins with some kind of assumption about the equal moral worth of individuals. In one way or another, each treats the individual as prior to the community. These foundations provide little basis for drawing fundamental distinctions between citizens and aliens who seek to become citizens. The fact that all three theories converge upon the same basic result with regard to immigration despite their significant differences in other areas strengthens the case for open borders. In the final part of the essay I will consider communitarian objections to my argument, especially those of Michael Walzer, the best contemporary defender of the view I am challenging.

Aliens and property rights

One popular position on immigration goes something like this: "It's our country. We can let in or keep out whomever we want." This could be interpreted as a claim that the right to exclude aliens is based on property rights, perhaps collective or national property rights. Would this sort of claim receive support from theories in which property rights play a central role? I think not, because those theories emphasize *individual* property rights and the concept of collective or national property rights would undermine the individual rights that these theories wish to protect.

Consider Robert Nozick as a contemporary representative of the property rights tradition. Following Locke, Nozick assumes that individuals in the state of nature have rights, including the right to acquire and

[5] The conventional assumption is captured by the Select Commission on Immigration and Refugee Policy: "Our policy – while providing opportunity to a portion of the world's population – must be guided by the basic national interests of the people of the United States." From *U.S. Immigration Policy and the National Interest: The Final Report and Recommendations of the Select Commission on Immigration and Refugee Policy to the Congress and the President of the United States* (1 March 1981). The best theoretical defense of the conventional assumption (with some modifications) is Michael Walzer, *Spheres of Justice* (New York: Basic Books, 1983), pp. 31–63. A few theorists have challenged the conventional assumption. See Bruce Ackerman, *Social Justice in the Liberal State* (New Haven: Yale University Press, 1980), pp. 89–95; Judith Lichtenberg, "National Boundaries and Moral Boundaries: A Cosmopolitan View" in *Boundaries: National Autonomy and Its Limits*, edited by Peter G. Brown and Henry Shue (Totowa, NJ: Rowman and Littlefield, 1981), pp. 79–100, and Roger Nett, "The Civil Right We Are Not Ready For: The Right of Free Movement of People on the Face of the Earth," *Ethics* 81: 212–27. Frederick Whelan has also explored these issues in two interesting unpublished papers.

use property. All individuals have the same natural rights – that is the assumption about moral equality that underlies this tradition – although the exercise of those rights leads to material inequalities. The "inconveniences" of the state of nature justify the creation of a minimal state whose sole task is to protect people within a given territory against violations of their rights.[6]

Would this minimal state be justified in restricting immigration? Nozick never answers this question directly, but his argument at a number of points suggests not. According to Nozick the state has no right to do anything other than enforce the rights which individuals already enjoy in the state of nature. Citizenship gives rise to no distinctive claim. The state is obliged to protect the rights of citizens and noncitizens equally because it enjoys a *de facto* monopoly over the enforcement of rights within its territory. Individuals have the right to enter into voluntary exchanges with other individuals. They possess this right as individuals, not as citizens. The state may not interfere with such exchanges so long as they do not violate someone else's rights.[7]

[...]

Nozick explicitly says that the land of a nation is not the collective property of its citizens. It follows that the control that the state can legitimately exercise over that land is limited to the enforcement of the rights of individual owners. Prohibiting people from entering a territory because they did not happen to be born there or otherwise gain the credentials of citizenship is no part of any state's legitimate mandate. The state has no right to restrict immigration.

Migration and the original position

In contrast to Nozick, John Rawls provides a justification for an activist state with positive responsibilities for social welfare. Even so, the approach to immigration suggested by *A Theory of Justice* leaves little room for restrictions in principle. I say "suggested" because Rawls himself explicitly assumes a closed system in which questions about immigration could not arise. I will argue, however, that Rawls's approach is applicable to a broader context than the one he considers. In what follows I assume a general familiarity with Rawls's theory, briefly recalling the main points and then focusing on those issues that are relevant to my inquiry.

Rawls asks what principles people would choose to govern society if they had to choose from behind a "veil of ignorance," knowing nothing about their own personal situations (class, race, sex, natural talents, religious beliefs, individual goals and values, and so on).

[...]

The original position offers a strategy of moral reasoning that helps to address these concerns. The purpose of the "veil of ignorance" is "to nullify the effects of specific contingencies which put men at odds" because natural and social contingencies are "arbitrary from a moral point of view" and therefore are factors which ought not to influence the choice of principles of justice.[8] Whether one is a citizen of a rich nation or a poor one, whether one is already a citizen of a particular state or an alien who wishes to become a citizen – this is the sort of specific contingency that could set people at odds. A fair procedure for choosing principles of justice must therefore exclude knowledge of these circumstances, just as it excludes knowledge of one's race or sex or social class. We should therefore take a global, not a national, view of the original position.

[...]

Behind the "veil of ignorance," in considering possible restrictions on freedom, one adopts the perspective of the one who would be most disadvantaged by the restrictions, in this case the perspective of the alien who wants to immigrate. In the original position, then, one would insist that the right to migrate be included in the system of basic liberties for the same reasons that one would insist that the right to religious freedom be included: it might prove essential to one's plan of life. Once the "veil of ignorance" is lifted, of course, one might not make use of the right, but that is true of other rights and liberties as well. So, the basic agreement among those in the original position would be to permit no restrictions on migration (whether emigration or immigration).

[...]

Consider the implications of this analysis for some of the conventional arguments for restrictions on immigration. First, one could not justify restrictions on the grounds that those born in a given territory or born of parents who were citizens were more entitled to the benefits of citizenship than those born elsewhere or born of alien parents. Birthplace and parentage are natural

6 Robert Nozick, *Anarchy, State, and Utopia* (New York: Basic Books, 1974), pp. 10–25, 88–119.

7 *Ibid.*, pp. 108–113. Citizens, in Nozick's view, are simply consumers purchasing impartial, efficient protection of preexisting natural rights. Nozick uses the terms "citizen," "client" and "customer" interchangeably.

8 John Rawls, *A Theory of Justice* (Cambridge, MA: Harvard University Press, 1971), p. 136.

contingencies that are "arbitrary from a moral point of view." One of the primary goals of the original position is to minimize the effects of such contingencies upon the distribution of social benefits. To assign citizenship on the basis of birth might be an acceptable procedure, but only if it did not preclude individuals from making different choices later when they reached maturity.

Second, one could not justify restrictions on the grounds that immigration would reduce the economic well-being of current citizens. That line of argument is drastically limited by two considerations: the perspective of the worst-off and the priority of liberty. In order to establish the current citizens' perspective as the relevant worst-off position, it would be necessary to show that immigration would reduce the economic well-being of current citizens below the level the potential immigrants would enjoy if they were not permitted to immigrate. But even if this could be established, it would not justify restrictions on immigration because of the priority of liberty. So, the economic concerns of current citizens are essentially rendered irrelevant.

[...]

Aliens in the calculus

A utilitarian approach to the problem of immigration can take into account some of the concerns that the original position excludes but even utilitarianism does not provide much support for the sorts of restrictions on immigration that are common today. The fundamental principle of utilitarianism is "maximize utility," and the utilitarian commitment to moral equality is reflected in the assumption that everyone is to count for one and no one for more than one when utility is calculated. [...]

If we focus only on economic consequences, the best immigration policy from a utilitarian perspective would be the one that maximized overall economic gains. In this calculation, current citizens would enjoy no privileged position. The gains and losses of aliens would count just as much. Now the dominant view among both classical and neoclassical economists is that the free mobility of capital and labor is essential to the maximization of overall economic gains. But the free mobility of labor requires open borders. So, despite the fact that the economic costs to current citizens are morally relevant in the utilitarian framework, they would probably not be sufficient to justify restrictions.

Economic consequences are not the only ones that utilitarians consider. For example, if immigration would affect the existing culture or way of life in a society in ways that current citizens found undesirable, that would count against open immigration in many versions of utilitarianism. But not in all. Utilitarians disagree about whether all pleasures (or desires or interests) are to count or only some. For example, should a sadist's pleasure be given moral weight and balanced against his victim's pain or should that sort of pleasure be disregarded? What about racial prejudice? That is clearly relevant to the question of immigration. Should a white racist's unhappiness at the prospect of associating with people of color be counted in the calculus of utility as an argument in favor of racial exclusion as reflected, say, in the White Australia policy? What about the desire to preserve a distinctive local culture as a reason for restricting immigration? That is sometimes linked to racial prejudice but by no means always.

[...] Whatever the method of calculation, the concerns of aliens must be counted too. Under current conditions, when so many millions of poor and oppressed people feel they have so much to gain from migration to the advanced industrial states, it seems hard to believe that a utilitarian calculus which took the interests of aliens seriously would justify significantly greater limits on immigration than the ones entailed by the public order restriction implied by the Rawlsian approach.

The communitarian challenge

[...]

My findings about immigration rest primarily on assumptions that I think no defensible moral theory can reject: that our social institutions and public policies must respect all human beings as moral persons and that this respect entails recognition, in some form, of the freedom and equality of every human being. Perhaps some other approach can accept these assumptions while still making room for greater restrictions on immigration. To test that possibility, I will consider the views of the theorist who has done the most to translate the communitarian critique into a positive alternative vision: Michael Walzer.

[...] He thinks that questions of distributive justice should be addressed not from behind a "veil of ignorance" but from the perspective of membership in a political community in which people share a common culture and a common understanding about justice.

I cannot do full justice here to Walzer's rich and subtle discussion of the problem of membership, but I can draw attention to the main points of his argument and to some of the areas of our disagreement. Walzer's central claim is that exclusion is justified by the right of communities to self-determination. The right to exclude is constrained in three important ways, however. First, we have an obligation to provide aid to others who are in dire need, even if we have no established bonds with them, provided that we can do so without excessive cost to ourselves. So, we may be obliged to admit some needy strangers or at least to provide them with some of our resources and perhaps even territory. Second, once people are admitted as residents and participants in the economy, they must be entitled to acquire citizenship, if they wish. Here the constraint flows from principles of justice not mutual aid. The notion of permanent "guest workers" conflicts with the underlying rationale of communal self-determination which justified the right to exclude in the first place. Third, new states or governments may not expel existing inhabitants even if they are regarded as alien by most of the rest of the population.[9]

In developing his argument, Walzer compares the idea of open states with our experience of neighborhoods as a form of open association.[10] But in thinking about what open states would be like, we have a better comparison at hand. We can draw upon our experience of cities, provinces, or states in the American sense. These are familiar political communities whose borders are open. Unlike neighborhoods and like countries, they are formally organized communities with boundaries, distinctions between citizens and noncitizens, and elected officials who are expected to pursue policies that benefit the members of the community that elected them. They often have distinctive cultures and ways of life. Think of the differences between New York City and Waycross, Georgia, or between California and Kansas. These sorts of differences are often much greater than the differences across nation-states. Seattle has more in common with Vancouver than it does with many American communities. But cities and provinces and American states cannot restrict immigration (from other parts of the country). So, these cases call into question Walzer's claim that distinctiveness depends on the possibility of formal closure. What makes for distinctiveness and what erodes it is much more complex than political control of admissions.

This does not mean that control over admissions is unimportant. Often local communities would like to restrict immigration. The people of California wanted to keep out poor Oklahomans during the Depression. Now the people of Oregon would like to keep out the Californians. Internal migrations can be substantial. They can transform the character of communities. (Think of the migrations from the rural South to the urban North.) They can place strains on the local economy and make it difficult to maintain locally funded social programs. Despite all this, we do not think these political communities should be able to control their borders. The right to free migration takes priority.

Why should this be so? Is it just a choice that we make as a larger community (i.e., the nation state) to restrict the self-determination of local communities in this way? Could we legitimately permit them to exclude? Not easily. No liberal state restricts internal mobility. Those states that do restrict internal mobility are criticized for denying basic human freedoms. If freedom of movement within the state is so important that it overrides the claims of local political communities, on what grounds can we restrict freedom of movement across states? This requires a stronger case for the *moral* distinctiveness of the nation-state as a form of community than Walzer's discussion of neighborhoods provides.

Walzer also draws an analogy between states and clubs.[11] Clubs may generally admit or exclude whomever they want, although any particular decision may be criticized through an appeal to the character of the club and the shared understandings of its members. So, too, with states. This analogy ignores the familiar distinction between public and private, a distinction that Walzer makes use of elsewhere.[12] There is a deep tension between the right of freedom of association and the right to equal treatment. One way to address this tension is to say that in the private sphere freedom of association prevails and in the public sphere equal treatment does. You can pick your friends on the basis of whatever criteria you wish, but in selecting people for offices you must treat all candidates fairly. Drawing a line between public and private is often problematic, but it is clear that clubs are normally at one end of the scale and states at the other. So, the fact that private clubs may admit or exclude whomever they choose says nothing about the appropriate admission standards for states. When the state acts it must treat individuals equally.

Against this, one may object that the requirement of equal treatment applies fully only to those who are already *members* of the community. That is accurate as a description of practice but the question is why it should be so. At one time, the requirement of equal treatment

[9] Walzer, *Spheres of Justice*, pp. 33, 45–48, 55–61, 42–44.

[10] *Ibid.*, pp. 36–39.

[11] *Ibid.*, pp. 39–41.

[12] *Ibid.*, pp. 129–64.

did not extend fully to various groups (workers, blacks, women). On the whole, the history of liberalism reflects a tendency to expand both the definition of the public sphere and the requirements of equal treatment. In the United States today, for example, in contrast to earlier times, both public agencies and private corporations may not legally exclude women simply because they are women (although private clubs still may). A white shopkeeper may no longer exclude blacks from his store (although he may exclude them from his home). I think these recent developments, like the earlier extension of the franchise, reflect something fundamental about the inner logic of liberalism.[13] The extension of the right to immigrate reflects the same logic: equal treatment of individuals in the public sphere.

[...]

Any approach like Walzer's that seeks its ground in the tradition and culture of *our* community must confront, as a methodological paradox, the fact that liberalism is a central part of our culture. The enormous intellectual popularity of Rawls and Nozick and the enduring influence of utilitarianism attest to their ability to communicate contemporary understandings and shared meanings in a language that has legitimacy and power in our culture. These theories would not make such sense to a Buddhist monk in medieval Japan. But their individualistic assumptions and their language of universal, ahistorical reason makes sense to us because of *our* tradition, *our* culture, *our* community. For people in a different moral tradition, one that assumed fundamental moral differences between those inside the society and those outside, restrictions on immigration might be easy to justify. Those who are *other* simply might not count, or at least not count as much. But we cannot dismiss the aliens on the ground that they are other, because *we* are the products of a liberal culture.

[...] If my arguments are correct, the general case for open borders is deeply rooted in the fundamental values of our tradition. No moral argument will seem acceptable to *us*, if it directly challenges the assumption of the equal moral worth of all individuals. If restrictions on immigration are to be justified, they have to be based on arguments that respect that principle. Walzer's theory has many virtues that I have not explored here, but it does not supply an adequate argument for the state's right to exclude.

Conclusion

Free migration may not be immediately achievable, but it is a goal toward which we should strive. And we have an obligation to open our borders much more fully than we do now. The current restrictions on immigration in Western democracies – even in the most open ones like Canada and the United States – are not justifiable. Like feudal barriers to mobility, they protect unjust privilege.

Does it follow that there is *no* room for distinctions between aliens and citizens, no theory of citizenship, no boundaries for the community? Not at all. To say that membership is open to all who wish to join is not to say that there is no distinction between members and nonmembers. Those who choose to cooperate together in the state have special rights and obligations not shared by noncitizens. Respecting the particular choices and commitments that individuals make flows naturally from a commitment to the idea of equal moral worth. (Indeed, consent as a justification for political obligation is least problematic in the case of immigrants.) What is *not* readily compatible with the idea of equal moral worth is the exclusion of those who want to join. If people want to sign the social contract, they should be permitted to do so.

Open borders would threaten the distinctive character of different political communities only because we assume that so many people would move if they could. If the migrants were few, it would not matter. A few immigrants could always be absorbed without changing the character of the community. And, as Walzer observes, most human beings do not love to move.[14] They normally feel attached to their native land and to the particular language, culture, and community in which they grew up and in which they feel at home. They seek to move only when life is very difficult where they are. Their concerns are rarely frivolous. So, it is right to weigh the claims of those who want to move against the claims of those who want to preserve the community as it is. And if we don't unfairly tip the scales, the case for exclusion will rarely triumph.

13 I am not arguing that the changes in treatment of women, blacks, and workers were *brought about* by the inner logic of liberalism. These changes resulted from changes in social conditions and from political struggles, including ideological struggles in which arguments about the implications of liberal principles played some role, though not necessarily a decisive one. But from a philosophical perspective, it is important to understand where principles lead, even if one does not assume that people's actions in the world will always be governed by the principles they espouse.

14 Walzer, *Spheres of Justice*, p. 38.

People live in communities with bonds and bounds, but these may be of different kinds. In a liberal society, the bonds and bounds should be compatible with liberal principles. Open immigration would change the character of the community but it would not leave the community without any character. It might destroy old ways of life, highly valued by some, but it would make possible new ways of life, highly valued by others. [...] To commit ourselves to open borders would not be to abandon the idea of communal character but to reaffirm it. It would be an affirmation of the liberal character of the community and of its commitment to principles of justice.

T. H. Marshall, "The Development of Citizen Rights"*

I shall be running true to type as a sociologist if I begin by saying that I propose to divide citizenship into three parts. But the analysis is, in this case, dictated by history even more clearly than by logic. I shall call these three parts, or elements, civil, political and social. The civil element is composed of the rights necessary for individual freedom – liberty of the person, freedom of speech, thought and faith, the right to own property and to conclude valid contracts, and the right to justice. The last is of a different order from the others, because it is the right to defend and assert all one's rights on terms of equality with others and by due process of law. This shows us that the institutions most directly associated with civil rights are the courts of justice. By the political element I mean the right to participate in the exercise of political power, as a member of a body invested with political authority or as an elector of the members of such a body. The corresponding institutions are parliament and councils of local government. By the social element I mean the whole range from the right to a modicum of economic welfare and security to the right to share to the full in the social heritage and to live the life of a civilized being according to the standards prevailing in the society. The institutions most closely connected with it are the educational system and the social services.[15]

[...] In feudal society status was the hall-mark of class and the measure of inequality. There was no uniform collection of rights and duties with which all men – noble and common, free and serf – were endowed by virtue of their membership of the society. There was, in this sense, no principle of the equality of citizens to set against the principle of the inequality of classes. In the medieval towns, on the other hand, examples of genuine and equal citizenship can be found. But its specific rights and duties were strictly local, whereas the citizenship whose history I wish to trace is, by definition, national.

[...]

The story of civil rights in their formative period is one of the gradual addition of new rights to a status that already existed and was held to appertain to all adult members of the community – or perhaps one should say to all male members, since the status of women, or at least of married women, was in some important respects peculiar. This democratic, or universal, character of the status arose naturally from the fact that it was essentially the status of freedom, and in seventeenth-century England all men were free. Servile status, or villeinage by blood, had lingered on as a patent anachronism in the days of Elizabeth, but vanished soon afterwards. This change from servile to free labour has been described by Professor Tawney as 'a high landmark in the development both of economic and political society', and as 'the final triumph of the common law' in regions from which it had been excluded for four centuries. Henceforth the English peasant 'is a member of a society in which there is, nominally at least, one law for all men'.[16] The liberty which his predecessors had won by fleeing into the free towns had become his by right. In the towns the terms 'freedom' and 'citizenship' were interchangeable. When freedom became universal, citizenship grew from a local into a national institution.

The story of political rights is different both in time and in character. The formative period began, as I have said, in the early nineteenth century, when the civil rights attached to the status of freedom had already acquired sufficient substance to justify us in speaking of a general status of citizenship. And, when it began, it consisted, not in the creation of new rights to enrich a status already enjoyed by all, but in the granting of old rights to new sections of the population. In the eighteenth century

* Thomas Humphrey Marshall, extracted from *Class, Citizenship, and Development* (Garden City, NY: Doubleday & Company, Inc., 1964), pp. 71–103.

15 By this terminology, what economists sometimes call 'income from civil rights' would be called 'income from social rights'. Cf. Hugh Dalton, *Some Aspects of the Inequality of Incomes in Modern Communities* (London: G. Routledge and Sons, Ltd, 1929), Part 3, Chapters 3 and 4.

16 R. H. Tawney, *Agrarian Problem in the Sixteenth Century* (1916), pp. 43–4.

political rights were defective, not in content, but in distribution – defective, that is to say, by the standards of democratic citizenship. The Act of 1832 did little, in a purely quantitative sense, to remedy that defect. After it was passed the voters still amounted to less than one-fifth of the adult male population. The franchise was still a group monopoly, but it had taken the first step towards becoming a monopoly of a kind acceptable to the ideas of nineteenth-century capitalism – a monopoly which could, with some degree of plausibility, be described as open and not closed. A closed group monopoly is one into which no man can force his way by his own efforts; admission is at the pleasure of the existing members of the group. The description fits a considerable part of the borough franchise before 1832; and it is not too wide of the mark when applied to the franchise based on freehold ownership of land. Freeholds are not always to be had for the asking, even if one has the money to buy them, especially in an age in which families look on their lands as the social, as well as the economic, foundation of their existence. Therefore the Act of 1832, by abolishing rotten boroughs and by extending the franchise to leaseholders and occupying tenants of sufficient economic substance, opened the monopoly by recognizing the political claims of those who could produce the normal evidence of success in the economic struggle.

It is clear that, if we maintain that in the nineteenth century citizenship in the form of civil rights was universal, the political franchise was not one of the rights of citizenship. It was the privilege of a limited economic class, whose limits were extended by each successive Reform Act. It can nevertheless be argued that citizenship in this period was not politically meaningless. It did not confer a right, but it recognized a capacity. No sane and law-abiding citizen was debarred by personal status from acquiring and recording a vote. He was free to earn, to save, to buy property or to rent a house, and to enjoy whatever political rights were attached to these economic achievements. His civil rights entitled him, and electoral reform increasingly enabled him, to do this.

It was, as we shall see, appropriate that nineteenth-century capitalist society should treat political rights as a secondary product of civil rights. It was equally appropriate that the twentieth century should abandon this position and attach political rights directly and independently to citizenship as such. This vital change of principle was put into effect when the Act of 1918, by adopting manhood suffrage, shifted the basis of political rights from economic substance to personal status. I say 'manhood' deliberately in order to emphasize the great significance of this reform quite apart from the second, and no less important, reform introduced at the same time – namely the enfranchisement of women. But the Act of 1918 did not fully establish the political equality of all in terms of the rights of citizenship. Remnants of an inequality based on differences of economic substance lingered on until, only last year, plural voting (which had already been reduced to dual voting) was finally abolished.

[...]

The original source of social rights was membership of local communities and functional associations. This source was supplemented and progressively replaced by a Poor Law and a system of wage regulation which were nationally conceived and locally administered. The latter – the system of wage regulation – was rapidly decaying in the eighteenth century, not only because industrial change made it administratively impossible, but also because it was incompatible with the new conception of civil rights in the economic sphere, with its emphasis on the right to work where and at what you pleased under a contract of your own making. Wage regulation infringed this individualist principle of the free contract of employment.

[...]

The [Elizabethan] Poor Law treated the claims of the poor, not as an integral part of the rights of the citizen, but as an alternative to them – as claims which could be met only if the claimants ceased to be citizens in any true sense of the word. For paupers forfeited in practice the civil right of personal liberty, by internment in the workhouse, and they forfeited by law any political rights they might possess. This disability of defranchisement remained in being until 1918, and the significance of its final removal has, perhaps, not been fully appreciated.

[...]

The stigma which clung to poor relief expressed the deep feelings of a people who understood that those who accepted relief must cross the road that separated the community of citizens from the outcast company of the destitute.

The Poor Law is not an isolated example of this divorce of social rights from the status of citizenship. The early Factory Acts show the same tendency. Although in fact they led to an improvement of working conditions and a reduction of working hours to the benefit of all employed in the industries to which they applied, they meticulously refrained from giving this protection directly to the adult male – the citizen *par excellence*. And they did so out of respect for his status as a citizen, on the grounds that enforced protective measures curtailed the civil right to conclude a free contract of employment. Protection was confined to women and children, and champions of women's rights were quick to detect the implied insult. Women were protected because they were not citizens. If they wished to enjoy full and responsible citizenship, they must forgo protection. By the end of the nineteenth century such arguments had become obsolete, and the factory code had become one of the pillars in the edifice of social rights.

The history of education shows superficial resemblances to that of factory legislation. In both cases the nineteenth century was, for the most part, a period in which the foundations of social rights were laid, but the principle of social rights as an integral part of the status of citizenship was either expressly denied or not definitely admitted. [...] The education of children has a direct bearing on citizenship, and, when the State guarantees that all children shall be educated, it has the requirements and the nature of citizenship definitely in mind. It is trying to stimulate the growth of citizens in the making. The right to education is a genuine social right of citizenship, because the aim of education during childhood is to shape the future adult. Fundamentally it should be regarded, not as the right of the child to go to school, but as the right of the adult citizen to have been educated. And there is here no conflict with civil rights as interpreted in an age of individualism. For civil rights are designed for use by reasonable and intelligent persons, who have learned to read and write. Education is a necessary prerequisite of civil freedom.

But, by the end of the nineteenth century, elementary education was not only free, it was compulsory. This signal departure from *laissez-faire* could, of course, be justified on the grounds that free choice is a right only for mature minds, that children are naturally subject to discipline, and that parents cannot be trusted to do what is in the best interests of their children. But the principle goes deeper than that. We have here a personal right combined with a public duty to exercise the right. Is the public duty imposed merely for the benefit of the individual – because children cannot fully appreciate their own interests and parents may be unfit to enlighten them? I hardly think that this can be an adequate explanation. It was increasingly recognised, as the nineteenth century wore on, that political democracy needed an educated electorate, and that scientific manufacture needed educated workers and technicians. The duty to improve and civilise oneself is therefore a social duty, and not merely a personal one, because the social health of a society depends upon the civilisation of its members. And a community that enforces this duty has begun to realise that its culture is an organic unity and its civilisation a national heritage. It follows that the growth of public elementary education during the nineteenth century was the first decisive step on the road to the re-establishment of the social rights of citizenship in the twentieth.

[...]

Social rights in the twentieth century

The period of which I have hitherto been speaking was one during which the growth of citizenship, substantial and impressive though it was, had little direct effect on social inequality. Civil rights gave legal powers whose use was drastically curtailed by class prejudice and lack of economic opportunity. Political rights gave potential power whose exercise demanded experience, organization and a change of ideas as to the proper functions of government. All these took time to develop. Social rights were at a minimum and were not woven into the fabric of citizenship. The common purpose of statutory and voluntary effort was to abate the nuisance of poverty without disturbing the pattern of inequality of which poverty was the most obviously unpleasant consequence.

A new period opened at the end of the nineteenth century, conveniently marked by Booth's survey of Life and Labour of the People in London and the Royal Commission on the Aged Poor. It saw the first big advance in social rights, and this involved significant changes in the egalitarian principle as expressed in citizenship. But there were other forces at work as well. A rise of money incomes unevenly distributed over the social classes altered the economic distance which separated these classes from one another, diminishing the gap between skilled and unskilled labour and between skilled labour and non-manual workers, while the steady increase in small savings blurred the class distinction between the capitalist and the propertyless proletarian. Secondly, a system of direct taxation, ever more steeply graduated, compressed the whole scale of disposable incomes. Thirdly, mass production for the home market and a growing interest on the part of industry in the needs and tastes of the common people enabled the less well-to-do to enjoy a material civilization which differed less markedly in quality from that of the rich than it had ever done before. All this profoundly altered the setting in which the progress of citizenship took place. Social integration spread from the sphere of sentiment and patriotism into that of material enjoyment. The components of a civilized and cultured life, formerly the monopoly of the few, were brought progressively within reach of the many, who were encouraged thereby to stretch out their hands towards those that still eluded their grasp. The diminution of inequality strengthened the demand for its abolition, at least with regard to the essentials of social welfare.

These aspirations have in part been met by incorporating social rights in the status of citizenship and thus creating a universal right to real income which is not proportionate to the market value of the claimant. Class-abatement is still the aim of social rights, but it has acquired a new meaning. It is no longer merely an attempt to abate the obvious nuisance of destitution in the lowest ranks of society. It has assumed the guise of action modifying the whole pattern of social inequality. It is no longer content to raise the floor-level in the basement of the social edifice, leaving the superstructure as it was. It has begun to remodel the whole building, and it might even end by converting a skyscraper into a bungalow.

[...]

But I must return to my survey of the social services. The most familiar principle in use is [...] the guaranteed minimum. The State guarantees a minimum supply of certain essential goods and services (such as medical attention and supplies, shelter and education) or a minimum money income available to be spent on essentials – as in the case of Old Age Pensions, insurance benefits and family allowances. Anyone able to exceed the guaranteed minimum out of his own resources is at liberty to do so. Such a system looks, on the face of it, like a more generous version of class-abatement in its original form. It raises the floor-level at the bottom, but does not automatically flatten the superstructure. But its effects need closer examination.

The degree of equalization achieved depends on four things – whether the benefit is offered to all or to a limited class; whether it takes the form of money payment or service rendered; whether the minimum is high or low; and how the money to pay for the benefit is raised. Cash benefits subject to income limit and means test had a simple and obvious equalizing effect. They achieved class-abatement in the early and limited sense of the term. The aim was to ensure that all citizens should attain at least to the prescribed minimum, either by their own resources or with assistance if they could not do it without. The benefit was given only to those who needed it, and thus inequalities at the bottom of the scale were ironed out. The system operated in its simplest and most unadulterated form in the case of the Poor Law and Old Age Pensions. But economic equalization might be accompanied by psychological class discrimination. The stigma which attached to the Poor Law made 'pauper' a derogatory term defining a class. 'Old Age Pensioner' may have had a little of the same flavour, but without the taint of shame.

The general effect of social insurance, when confined to an income group, was similar. It differed in that there was no means test. Contribution gave a right to benefit. But, broadly speaking, the income of the group was raised by the excess of benefits over total expenditure by the group in contributions and additional taxes, and the income gap between this group and those above it was thereby reduced. The exact effect is hard to estimate, because of the wide range of incomes within the group and the varying incidence of the risks covered. When the scheme was extended to all, this gap was reopened, though again we have to take account of the combined effects of the regressive flat-rate levy and the, in part, progressive taxation which contributed to the financing of the scheme. Nothing will induce me to embark on a discussion of this problem. But a total scheme is less specifically class-abating in a purely economic sense than a limited one, and social insurance is less so than a means-test service. Flat-rate benefits do not reduce the gaps between different incomes. Their equalizing effect depends on the fact that they make a bigger percentage addition to small incomes than to large. And, even though the concept of diminishing marginal utility (if one may still refer to it) can strictly be applied only to the rising income of one unchanging individual, that remains a matter of some significance. When a free service, as in the case of health, is extended from a limited income group to the whole population, the direct effect is in part to increase the inequality of disposable incomes, again subject to modification by the incidence of taxes. For members of the middle classes, who used to pay their doctors, find this part of their income released for expenditure on other things.

I have been skating gingerly over this very thin ice in order to make one point. The extension of the social services is not primarily a means of equalizing incomes. In some cases it may, in others it may not. The question is relatively unimportant; it belongs to a different department of social policy. What matters is that there is a general enrichment of the concrete substance of civilized life, a general reduction of risk and insecurity, an equalization between the more and the less fortunate at all levels – between the healthy and the sick, the employed and the unemployed, the old and the active, the bachelor and the father of a large family. Equalization is not so much between classes as between individuals within a population which is now treated for this purpose as though it were one class. Equality of status is more important than equality of income.

Iris Marion Young, "Polity and Group Difference: A Critique of the Ideal of Universal Citizenship"*

An ideal of universal citizenship has driven the emancipatory momentum of modern political life. Ever since the bourgeoisie challenged aristocratic privileges by claiming equal political rights for citizens as such, women, workers, Jews, blacks, and others have pressed for inclusion in that citizenship status. Modern political theory asserted the equal moral worth of all persons, and social movements of the oppressed took this seriously as implying the inclusion of all persons in full citizenship status under the equal protection of the law.

Citizenship for everyone, and everyone the same qua citizen. Modern political thought generally assumed that the universality of citizenship in the sense of citizenship for all implies a universality of citizenship in the sense that citizenship status transcends particularity and difference. Whatever the social or group differences among citizens, whatever their inequalities of wealth, status, and power in the everyday activities of civil society, citizenship gives everyone the same status as peers in the political public. With equality conceived as sameness, the ideal of universal citizenship carries at least two meanings in addition to the extension of citizenship to everyone: (*a*) universality defined as general in opposition to particular; what citizens have in common as opposed to how they differ, and (*b*) universality in the sense of laws and rules that say the same for all and apply to all in the same way; laws and rules that are blind to individual and group differences.

During this angry, sometimes bloody, political struggle in the nineteenth and twentieth centuries, many among the excluded and disadvantaged thought that winning full citizenship status, that is, equal political and civil rights, would lead to their freedom and equality. Now in the late twentieth century, however, when citizenship rights have been formally extended to all groups in liberal capitalist societies, some groups still find themselves treated as second-class citizens. Social movements of oppressed and excluded groups have recently asked why extension of equal citizenship rights has not led to social justice and equality. Part of the answer is straightforwardly Marxist: those social activities that most determine the status of individuals and groups are anarchic and oligarchic; economic life is not sufficiently under the control of citizens to affect the unequal status and treatment of groups. I think this is an important and correct diagnosis of why equal citizenship has not eliminated oppression, but in this article I reflect on another reason more intrinsic to the meaning of politics and citizenship as expressed in much modern thought.

The assumed link between citizenship for everyone, on the one hand, and the two other senses of citizenship – having a common life with and being treated in the same way as the other citizens – on the other, is itself a problem. Contemporary social movements of the oppressed have weakened the link. They assert a positivity and pride in group specificity against ideals of assimilation. They have also questioned whether justice always means that law and policy should enforce equal treatment for all groups. Embryonic in these challenges lies a concept of *differentiated* citizenship as the best way to realize the inclusion and participation of everyone in full citizenship.

In this article I argue that far from implying one another, the universality of citizenship, in the sense of the inclusion and participation of everyone, stands in tension with the other two meanings of universality embedded in modern political ideas: universality as generality, and universality as equal treatment. First, the ideal that the activities of citizenship express or create a general will that transcends the particular differences of group affiliation, situation, and interest has in practice excluded groups judged not capable of adopting that general point of view; the idea of citizenship as expressing a general will has tended to enforce a homogeneity of citizens. To the degree that contemporary proponents of revitalized citizenship retain that idea of a general will and common life, they implicitly support the same exclusions and homogeneity. Thus I argue that the inclusion and participation of everyone in public discussion and decision making requires mechanisms for group representation. Second, where differences in capacities, culture, values, and behavioral styles exist among groups, but some of these groups are privileged, strict adherence to a principle of equal treatment tends to perpetuate oppression or disadvantage. The inclusion and participation of everyone in social and political institutions therefore sometimes requires the articulation of special rights that attend to group differences in order to undermine oppression and disadvantage.

* Iris Marion Young, extracted from *Ethics*, 99 (January 1989), pp. 250–73.

I. Citizenship as generality

Many contemporary political theorists regard capitalist welfare society as depoliticized. Its interest group pluralism privatizes policy-making, consigning it to back-room deals and autonomous regulatory agencies and groups. Interest group pluralism fragments both policy and the interests of the individual, making it difficult to assess issues in relation to one another and set priorities. The fragmented and privatized nature of the political process, moreover, facilitates the dominance of the more powerful interests.[17]

In response to this privatization of the political process, many writers call for a renewed public life and a renewed commitment to the virtues of citizenship. Democracy requires that citizens of welfare corporate society awake from their privatized consumerist slumbers, challenge the experts who claim the sole right to rule, and collectively take control of their lives and institutions through processes of active discussion that aim at reaching collective decisions.[18] In participatory democratic institutions citizens develop and exercise capacities of reasoning, discussion, and socializing that otherwise lie dormant, and they move out of their private existence to address others and face them with respect and concern for justice. Many who invoke the virtues of citizenship in opposition to the privatization of politics in welfare capitalist society assume as models for contemporary public life the civic humanism of thinkers such as Machiavelli or, more often, Rousseau.

With these social critics I agree that interest group pluralism, because it is privatized and fragmented, facilitates the domination of corporate, military, and other powerful interests. With them I think democratic processes require the institutionalization of genuinely public discussion. There are serious problems, however, with uncritically assuming as a model the ideals of the civic public that come to us from the tradition of modern political thought.[19] The ideal of the public realm of citizenship as expressing a general will, a point of view and interest that citizens have in common which transcends their differences, has operated in fact as a demand for homogeneity among citizens. The exclusion of groups defined as different was explicitly acknowledged before this century. In our time, the excluding consequences of the universalist ideal of a public that embodies a common will are more subtle, but they still obtain.

[...]

Several commentators have argued that in extolling the virtues of citizenship as participation in a universal public realm, modern men expressed a flight from sexual difference, from having to recognize another kind of existence that they could not entirely understand, and from the embodiment, dependency on nature, and morality that women represent.[20] Thus the opposition between the universality of the public realm of citizenship and the particularity of private interest became conflated with oppositions between reason and passion, masculine and feminine.

The bourgeois world instituted a moral division of labor between reason and sentiment, identifying masculinity with reason and femininity with sentiment, desire, and the needs of the body. Extolling a public realm of manly virtue and citizenship as independence, generality, and dispassionate reason entailed creating the private sphere of the family as the place to which emotion, sentiment, and bodily needs must be confined.[21] The generality of the public thus depends on excluding women, who are responsible for tending to that private realm, and who lack the dispassionate rationality and independence required of good citizens.

[...]

It is important to recall that universality of citizenship conceived as generality operated to exclude not only women, but other groups as well. European and American republicans found little contradiction in promoting a

17 Theodore Lowi's classic analysis of the privatized operations of interest group liberalism remains descriptive of American politics; see *The End of Liberalism* (New York: Norton, 1969).

18 For an outstanding recent account of the virtues of and conditions for such democracy, see Philip Green, *Retrieving Democracy* (Totowa, NJ: Rowman & Allanheld, 1985).

19 Many who extol the virtues of the civic public, of course, appeal also to a model of the ancient polis. For a recent example, see Murray Bookchin, *The Rise of Urbanization and the Decline of Citizenship* (San Francisco: Sierra Club Books, 1987). In this article, however, I choose to restrict my claims to modern political thought. The idea of the ancient Greek polis often functions in both modern and contemporary discussion as a myth of lost origins, the paradise from which we have fallen and to which we desire to return; in this way, appeals to the ancient Greek polis are often contained within appeals to modern ideas of civic humanism.

20 Hannah Pitkin performs a most detailed and sophisticated analysis of the virtues of the civic public as a flight from sexual difference through a reading of the texts of Machiavelli; see *Fortune Is a Woman* (Berkeley: University of California Press, 1984).

21 See Susan Okin, "Women and the Making of the Sentimental Family," *Philosophy and Public Affairs*, 11 (1982), pp. 65–88; see also Linda Nicholson, *Gender and History: The Limits of Social Theory in the Age of the Family* (New York: Columbia University Press, 1986).

universality of citizenship that excluded some groups, because the idea that citizenship is the same for all translated in practice to the requirement that all citizens be the same. The white male bourgeoisie conceived republican virtue as rational, restrained, and chaste, not yielding to passion or desire for luxury, and thus able to rise above desire and need to a concern for the common good. This implied excluding poor people and wage workers from citizenship on the grounds that they were too motivated by need to adopt a general perspective. The designers of the American constitution were no more egalitarian than their European brethren in this respect; they specifically intended to restrict the access of the laboring class to the public, because they feared disruption of commitment to the general interests.

These early American republicans were also quite explicit about the need for the homogeneity of citizens, fearing that group differences would tend to undermine commitment to the general interest. This meant that the presence of blacks and Indians, and later Mexicans and Chinese, in the territories of the republic posed a threat that only assimilation, extermination, or dehumanization could thwart. Various combinations of these three were used, of course, but recognition of these groups as peers in the public was never an option. Even such republican fathers as Jefferson identified the red and black people in their territories with wild nature and passion, just as they feared that women outside the domestic realm were wanton and avaricious. They defined moral, civilized republican life in opposition to this backward-looking, uncultivated desire that they identified with women and nonwhites.[22] A similar logic of exclusion operated in Europe, where Jews were particular targets.[23]

These republican exclusions were not accidental, nor were they inconsistent with the ideal of universal citizenship as understood by these theorists. They were a direct consequence of a dichotomy between public and private that defined the public as a realm of generality in which all particularities are left behind, and defined the private as the particular, the realm of affectivity, affiliation, need, and the body. As long as that dichotomy is in place, the inclusion of the formerly excluded in the definition of citizenship – women, workers, Jews, blacks, Asians, Indians, Mexicans – imposes a homogeneity that suppresses group differences in the public and in practice forces the formerly excluded groups to be measured according to norms derived from and defined by privileged groups.

[...]

A repoliticization of public life should not require the creation of a unified public realm in which citizens leave behind their particular group affiliations, histories, and needs to discuss a general interest or common good. Such a desire for unity suppresses but does not eliminate differences and tends to exclude some perspectives from the public. Instead of a universal citizenship in the sense of this generality, we need a group differentiated citizenship and a heterogeneous public. In a heterogeneous public, differences are publicly recognized and acknowledged as irreducible, by which I mean that persons from one perspective or history can never completely understand and adopt the point of view of those with other group-based perspectives and histories. Yet commitment to the need and desire to decide together the society's policies fosters communication across those differences.

II. Differentiated citizenship as group representation

[...]

I shall not attempt to define a social group here, but I shall point to several marks which distinguish a social group from other collectivities of people. A social group involves first of all an affinity with other persons by which they identify with one another, and by which other people identify them. A person's particular sense of history, understanding of social relations and personal possibilities, her or his mode of reasoning, values, and expressive styles are constituted at least partly by her or his group identity.

[...]

I think that group differentiation is an inevitable and desirable process in modern societies. We need not settle that question, however. I merely assume that ours is now a group differentiated society, and that it will continue to be so for some time to come. Our political problem is that some of our groups are privileged and others are oppressed.

But what is oppression? In another place I give a fuller account of the concept of oppression.[24] Briefly, a

[22] See Ronald Takaki, *Iron Cages: Race and Culture in 19th Century America* (New York: Knopf, 1979). Don Herzog discusses the exclusionary prejudices of some other early American republicans; see "Some Questions for Republicans," *Political Theory*, 14 (1986), pp. 473–93.

[23] George Mosse, *Nationalism and Sexuality* (New York: Fertig, 1985).

[24] See Iris Marion Young, "Five Faces of Oppression," *Philosophical Forum*, 19, 4 (1988), pp. 270–90.

group is oppressed when one or more of the following conditions occurs to all or a large portion of its members: (1) the benefits of their work or energy go to others without those others reciprocally benefiting them (exploitation); (2) they are excluded from participation in major social activities, which in our society means primarily a workplace (marginalization); (3) they live and work under the authority of others, and have little work autonomy and authority over others themselves (powerlessness); (4) as a group they are stereotyped at the same time that their experience and situation is invisible in the society in general, and they have little opportunity and little audience for the expression of their experience and perspective on social events (cultural imperialism); (5) group members suffer random violence and harassment motivated by group hatred or fear. In the United States today at least the following groups are oppressed in one or more of these ways: women, blacks, Native Americans, Chicanos, Puerto Ricans and other Spanish-speaking Americans, Asian Americans, gay men, lesbians, working-class people, poor people, old people, and mentally and physically disabled people.

Perhaps in some utopian future there will be a society without group oppression and disadvantage. We cannot develop political principles by starting with the assumption of a completely just society, however, but must begin from within the general historical and social conditions in which we exist. This means that we must develop participatory democratic theory not on the assumption of an undifferentiated humanity, but rather on the assumption that there are group differences and that some groups are actually or potentially oppressed or disadvantaged.

I assert, then, the following principle: a democratic public, however that is constituted, should provide mechanisms for the effective representation and recognition of the distinct voices and perspectives of those of its constituent groups that are oppressed or disadvantaged within it. Such group representation implies institutional mechanisms and public resources supporting three activities: (1) self-organization of group members so that they gain a sense of collective empowerment and a reflective understanding of their collective experience and interests in the context of the society; (2) voicing a group's analysis of how social policy proposals affect them, and generating policy proposals themselves, in institutionalized contexts where decision makers are obliged to show that they have taken these perspectives into consideration; (3) having veto power regarding specific policies that affect a group directly, for example, reproductive rights for women, or use of reservation lands for Native Americans.

[...]

Group representation is the best means to promote just outcomes to democratic decision-making processes. The argument for this claim relies on Habermas's conception of communicative ethics. In the absence of a Philosopher King who reads transcendent normative verities, the only ground for a claim that a policy or decision is just is that it has been arrived at by a public which has truly promoted free expression of all needs and points of view. In his formulation of a communicative ethic, Habermas retains inappropriately an appeal to a universal or impartial point of view from which claims in a public should be addressed. A communicative ethic that does not merely articulate a hypothetical public that would justify decisions, but proposes actual conditions tending to promote just outcomes of decision-making processes, should promote conditions for the expression of the concrete needs of all individuals in their particularity.[25] The concreteness of individual lives, their needs and interests, and their perception of the needs and interests of others, I have argued, are structured partly through group-based experience and identity. Thus full and free expression of concrete needs and interests under social circumstances where some groups are silenced or marginalized requires that they have a specific voice in deliberation and decision making.

The introduction of such differentiation and particularity into democratic procedures does not encourage the expression of narrow self-interest; indeed, group representation is the best antidote to self-deceiving self-interest masked as an impartial or general interest. In a democratically structured public where social inequality is mitigated through group representation, individuals or groups cannot simply assert that they want something; they must say that justice requires or allows that they have it. Group representation provides the opportunity for some to express their needs or interests who would not likely be heard without that representation. At the same time, the test of whether a claim on the public is just, or a mere expression of self-interest, is best made when persons making it must confront the opinion of others who have explicitly different, though

25 Jürgen Habermas, *Reason and the Rationalization of Society* (Boston: Beacon, 1983), part. 3. For criticism of Habermas as retaining too universalist a conception of communicative action, see Seyla Benhabib, *Critique, Norm and Utopia* (New York: Columbia University Press, 1986); and Young, "Impartiality and the Civic Public," *Praxis International*, 5, 4 (January 1986).

not necessarily conflicting, experiences, priorities, and needs. As a person of social privilege, I am not likely to go outside of myself and have a regard for social justice unless I am forced to listen to the voice of those my privilege tends to silence.

[...]

III. Universal rights and special rights

A second aspect of the universality of citizenship is today in tension with the goal of full inclusion and participation of all groups in political and social institutions: universality in the formulation of law and policies. Modern and contemporary liberalism hold as basic the principle that the rules and policies of the state, and in contemporary liberalism also the rules of private institutions, ought to be blind to race, gender, and other group differences. The public realm of the state and law properly should express its rules in general terms that abstract from the particularities of individual and group histories, needs, and situations to recognize all persons equally and treat all citizens in the same way.

As long as political ideology and practice persisted in defining some groups as unworthy of equal citizenship status because of supposedly natural differences from white male citizens, it was important for emancipatory movements to insist that all people are the same in respect of their moral worth and deserve equal citizenship. In this context, demands for equal rights that are blind to group differences were the only sensible way to combat exclusion and degradation.

Today, however, the social consensus is that all persons are of equal moral worth and deserve equal citizenship. With the near achievement of equal rights for all groups, with the important exception of gay men and lesbians, group inequalities nevertheless remain. Under these circumstances many feminists, black liberation activists, and others struggling for the full inclusion and participation of all groups in this society's institutions and positions of power, reward, and satisfaction, argue that rights and rules that are universally formulated and thus blind to differences of race, culture, gender, age, or disability, perpetuate rather than undermine oppression.

[...]

To the degree that groups are culturally different equal treatment in many issues of social policy is unjust because it denies these cultural differences or makes them a liability. There are a vast number of issues where fairness involves attention to cultural differences and their effects, but I shall briefly discuss three: affirmative action, comparable worth, and bilingual, bicultural education and service.

Whether they involve quotas or not, affirmative action programs violate a principle of equal treatment because they are race or gender conscious in setting criteria for school admissions, jobs, or promotions. These policies are usually defended in one of two ways. Giving preference to race or gender is understood either as just compensation for groups that have suffered discrimination in the past, or as compensation for the present disadvantage these groups suffer because of that history of discrimination and exclusion.[26] I do not wish to quarrel with either of these justifications for the differential treatment based on race or gender implied by affirmative action policies. I want to suggest that in addition we can understand affirmative action policies as compensating for the cultural biases of standards and evaluators used by the schools or employers. These standards and evaluators reflect at least to some degree the specific life and cultural experience of dominant groups – whites, Anglos, or men. [...]

Although they are not a matter of different treatment as such, comparable worth policies similarly claim to challenge cultural biases in traditional evaluation in the worth of female-dominated occupations, and in doing so require attending to differences. Schemes of equal pay for work of comparable worth require that predominantly male and predominantly female jobs have similar wage structures if they involve similar degrees of skill, difficulty, stress, and so on. [...]

Finally, linguistic and cultural minorities ought to have the right to maintain their language and culture and at the same time be entitled to all the benefits of citizenship, as well as valuable education and career opportunities. This right implies a positive obligation on the part of governments and other public bodies to print documents and to provide services in the native language of recognized linguistic minorities, and to provide bilingual instruction in schools. Cultural assimilation should not be a condition of full social participation, because it requires a person to transform his or her sense of identity, and when it is realized on a group level it means altering or annihilating the group's identity. This principle does not apply to any persons who do not identify with majority language or culture within a society, but only to sizeable linguistic or cultural minorities living in distinct though not necessarily segregated

26 For one among many discussions of such "backward looking" and "forward looking" arguments, see Bernard Boxill, *Blacks and Social Justice* (Totowa, NJ: Rowman & Allanheld, 1984), chapter 7.

communities. In the United States, then, special rights for cultural minorities applies at least to Spanish-speaking Americans and Native Americans.

[...]

Many opponents of oppression and privilege are wary of claims for special rights because they fear a restoration of special classifications that can justify exclusion and stigmatization of the specially marked groups. Such fear has been particularly pronounced among feminists who oppose affirming sexual and gender difference in law and policy. It would be foolish for me to deny that this fear has some significant basis.

Such fear is founded, however, on accession to traditional identification of group difference with deviance, stigma, and inequality. Contemporary movements of oppressed groups, however, assert a positive meaning to group difference, by which a group claims its identity as a group and rejects the stereotypes and labeling by which others mark it as inferior or inhuman. These social movements engage the meaning of difference itself as a terrain of political struggle, rather than leave difference to be used to justify exclusion and subordination. Supporting policies and rules that attend to group difference in order to undermine oppression and disadvantage is, in my opinion, a part of that struggle.

Amitai Etzioni et al., "The Responsive Communitarian Platform: Rights and Responsibilities"*

American men, women, and children are members of many communities – families; neighborhoods; innumerable social, religious, ethnic, workplace, and professional associations; and the body politic itself. Neither human existence nor individual liberty can be sustained for long outside the interdependent and overlapping communities to which all of us belong. Nor can any community long survive unless its members dedicate some of their attention, energy, and resources to shared projects. The exclusive pursuit of private interest erodes the network of social environments on which we all depend, and is destructive to our shared experiment in democratic self-government. For these reasons, we hold that the rights of individuals cannot long be preserved without a communitarian perspective.

A communitarian perspective recognizes both individual human dignity and the social dimension of human existence.

A communitarian perspective recognizes that the preservation of individual liberty depends on the active maintenance of the institutions of civil society where citizens learn respect for others as well as self-respect; where we acquire a lively sense of our personal and civic responsibilities, along with an appreciation of our own rights and the rights of others; where we develop the skills of self-government as well as the habit of governing ourselves, and learn to serve others – not just self.

A communitarian perspective recognizes that communities and polities, too, have obligations – including the duty to be responsive to their members and to foster participation and deliberation in social and political life.

A communitarian perspective does not dictate particular policies; rather, it mandates attention to what is often ignored in contemporary policy debates: the social side of human nature; the responsibilities that must be borne by citizens, individually and collectively, in a regime of rights; the fragile ecology of families and their supporting communities; the ripple effects and long-term consequences of present decisions. The political views of the signers of this statement differ widely. We are united, however, in our conviction that a communitarian perspective must be brought to bear on the great moral, legal, and social issues of our time.

Moral voices

America's diverse communities of memory and mutual aid are rich resources of moral voices – voices that ought to be heeded in a society that increasingly threatens to become normless, self-centered, and driven by greed, special interests, and an unabashed quest for power.

Moral voices achieve their effect mainly through education and persuasion, rather than through coercion. Originating in communities, and sometimes embodied in law, they exhort, admonish, and appeal to what Lincoln called the better angels of our nature. They speak to our capacity for reasoned judgment and virtuous action. It is precisely because this important moral realm, which is neither one of random individual choice nor of government control, has been much neglected

* Amitai Etzioni et al., extracted from *The Communitarian Reader: Beyond the Essentials*, edited by Etzioni, Andrew Volmert, and Elanit Rothschild (Lanham, MD: Rowman & Littlefield, 2004), pp. 13–23.

that we see an urgent need for a communitarian social movement to accord these voices their essential place.

Within history

The basic communitarian quest for balances between individuals and groups, rights and responsibilities, and among the institutions of state, market, and civil society is a constant, ongoing enterprise. Because this quest takes place within history and within varying social contexts, however, the evaluation of what is a proper moral stance will vary according to circumstances of time and place. If we were in China today, we would argue vigorously for more individual rights; in contemporary America, we emphasize individual and social responsibilities.

Not majoritarian but strongly democratic

Communitarians are not majoritarians. The success of the democratic experiment in ordered liberty (rather than unlimited license) depends, not on fiat or force, but on building shared values, habits, and practices that assure respect for one another's rights and regular fulfillment of personal, civic, and collective responsibilities. Successful policies are accepted because they are recognized to be legitimate, rather than imposed. We say to those who would impose civic or moral virtues by suppressing dissent (in the name of religion, patriotism, or any other cause), or censoring books, that their cure is ineffective, harmful, and morally untenable. At the same time divergent moral positions need not lead to cacophony. Out of genuine dialogue clear voices can arise, and shared aspirations can be identified and advanced.

Communitarians favor strong democracy. That is, we seek to make government more representative, more participatory, and more responsive to all members of the community. We seek to find ways to accord citizens more information, and more say, more often. We seek to curb the role of private money, special interests, and corruption in government. Similarly, we ask how "private governments," whether corporations, labor unions, or voluntary associations, can become more responsive to their members and to the needs of the community.

Communitarians do not exalt the group as such, nor do they hold that any set of group values is ipso facto good merely because such values originate in a community. Indeed, some communities (say, neo-Nazis) may foster reprehensible values. Moreover, communities that glorify their own members by vilifying those who do not belong are at best imperfect. Communitarians recognize – indeed, insist – that communal values must be judged by external and overriding criteria, based on shared human experience.

A responsive community is one whose moral standards reflect the basic human needs of all its members. To the extent that these needs compete with one another, the community's standards reflect the relative priority accorded by members to some needs over others. Although individuals differ in their needs, human nature is not totally malleable. Although individuals are deeply influenced by their communities, they have a capacity for independent judgment. The persistence of humane and democratic culture, as well as individual dissent, in Eastern Europe and the Soviet Union demonstrate the limits of social indoctrination.

For a community to be truly responsive – not only to an elite group, a minority or even the majority, but to all its members and all their basic human needs – it will have to develop moral values which meet the following criteria: they must be nondiscriminatory and applied equally to all members; they must be generalizable, justified in terms that are accessible and understandable, for example, instead of claims based upon individual or group desires, citizens would draw on a common definition of justice; and, they must incorporate the full range of legitimate needs and values rather than focusing on any one category, be it individualism, autonomy, interpersonal caring, or social justice.

Restoring the moral voice

History has taught that it is a grave mistake to look to a charismatic leader to define and provide a moral voice for the polity. Nor can political institutions effectively embody moral voices unless they are sustained and criticized by an active citizenry concerned about the moral direction of the community. To rebuild America's moral foundations, to bring our regard for individuals and their rights into a better relationship with our sense of personal and collective responsibility, we must therefore begin with the institutions of civil society.

Start with the family

The best place to start is where each new generation acquires its moral anchoring: at home, in the family. We must insist once again that bringing children into the world entails a moral responsibility to provide, not only material necessities, but also moral education and character formation.

Moral education is not a task that can be delegated to baby sitters, or even professional child-care centers. It requires close bonding of the kind that typically is formed only with parents, if it is formed at all.

Fathers and mothers, consumed by "making it" and consumerism, or preoccupied with personal advancement, who come home too late and too tired to attend to the needs of their children, cannot discharge their most elementary duty to their children and their fellow citizens.

It follows that work places should provide maximum flexible opportunities to parents to preserve an important part of their time and energy, of their life, to attend to their educational moral duties, for the sake of the next generation, its civic and moral character, and its capacity to contribute economically and socially to the commonweal. Experiments such as those with unpaid and paid parental leave, flextime, shared jobs, opportunities to work at home, and for parents to participate as volunteers and managers in childcare centers, should be extended and encouraged.

Above all, what we need is a change in orientation by both parents and workplaces. Child-raising is important, valuable work, work that must be honored rather than denigrated by both parents and the community.

Families headed by single parents experience particular difficulties. Some single parents struggle bravely and succeed in attending to the moral education of their children; while some married couples shamefully neglect their moral duties toward their offspring. However, the weight of the historical, sociological, and psychological evidence suggests that on average two-parent families are better able to discharge their child-raising duties if only because there are more hands – and voices – available for the task. Indeed, couples often do better when they are further backed up by a wider circle of relatives. The issue has been wrongly framed when one asks what portion of parental duties grandparents or other helpers can assume. Their assistance is needed in addition to, not as a substitute for, parental care. Child-raising is by nature labor-intensive. There are no labor-saving technologies, and shortcuts in this area produce woefully deficient human beings, to their detriment and ours.

It follows that widespread divorce, when there are children involved, especially when they are in their formative years, is indicative of a serious social problem. Though divorces are necessary in some situations, many are avoidable and are not in the interest of the children, the community, and probably not of most adults either. Divorce laws should be modified, not to prevent divorce, but to signal society's concern.

Schools: The second line of defense

Unfortunately, millions of American families have weakened to the point where their capacity to provide moral education is gravely impaired. And the fact is that communities have only a limited say over what families do. At best, it will take years before a change in the moral climate restores parenting to its proper status and function for many Americans.

Thus, by default, schools now play a major role, for better or worse, in character formation and moral education. Personal and communal responsibility come together here, for education requires the commitment of all citizens, not merely those who have children in school.

We strongly urge that all educational institutions, from kindergartens to universities, recognize and take seriously the grave responsibility to provide moral education. Suggestions that schools participate actively in moral education are often opposed. The specter of religious indoctrination is quickly evoked, and the question is posed: "Whose morals are you going to teach?"

Our response is straightforward: we ought to teach those values Americans share, for example, that the dignity of all persons ought to be respected, that tolerance is a virtue and discrimination abhorrent, that peaceful resolution of conflict is superior to violence, that generally truth-telling is morally superior to lying, that democratic government is morally superior to totalitarianism and authoritarianism, that one ought to give a day's work for a day's pay, that saving for one's own and one's country's future is better than squandering one's income and relying on others to attend to one's future needs.

The fear that our children will be "brainwashed" by a few educators is far-fetched. On the contrary, to silence the schools in moral matters simply means that the youngsters are left exposed to all other voices and values but those of their educators. For, one way or another, moral education does take place in schools. The only question is whether schools and teachers will passively stand by, or take an active and responsible role. ...

Within communities: A matter of orientation

The ancient Greeks understood this well: A person who is completely private is lost to civic life. The exclusive pursuit of one's self-interest is not even a good prescription for conduct in the marketplace; for no social, political, economic, or moral order can survive that way. Some measure of caring, sharing, and being our brother's and sister's keeper is essential if we are not all to fall back on an ever more expansive government, bureaucratized welfare agencies, and swollen regulations, police, courts, and jails.

Generally, no social task should be assigned to an institution that is larger than necessary to do the job. What can be done by families should not be assigned to an intermediate group – schools, etc. What can be done at the local level should not be passed on to the state or federal level, and so on. There are, of course, plenty of urgent tasks – environmental ones – that do require national and even international action. But to remove tasks to higher levels than is necessary weakens the constituent communities. This principle holds for duties of attending to the sick, troubled, delinquent, homeless, and new immigrants; and for public safety, public health, and protection of the environment – from a neighborhood crime-watch to CPR to sorting the garbage. The government should step in only to the extent that other social subsystems fail, rather than seek to replace them. …

Many social goals … require partnership between public and private groups. Though government should not seek to replace local communities, it may need to empower them by strategies of support, including revenue-sharing and technical assistance. There is a great need for study and experimentation with creative use of the structures of civil society, and public–private cooperation, especially where the delivery of health, educational and social services are concerned.

Last, but not least, we should not hesitate to speak up and express our moral concerns to others when it comes to issues we care about deeply and share with one another. It might be debatable whether or not we should encourage our neighbors to keep their lawns green (which may well be environmentally unsound), but there should be little doubt that we should expect one another to attend to our children, and vulnerable community members. Those who neglect these duties should be explicitly considered poor members of the community.

National and local service, as well as volunteer work, is desirable to build and express a civil commitment. Such activities, bringing together people from different backgrounds and enabling and encouraging them to work together, build community and foster mutual respect and tolerance. …

Duties to the polity

Being informed about public affairs is a prerequisite for keeping the polity from being controlled by demagogues, for taking action when needed in one's own interests and that of others, for achieving justice and the shared future.

Voting is one tool for keeping the polity reflective of its constituent communities. Those who feel that none of the candidates reflect their views ought to seek out other like-minded citizens and seek to field their own candidate rather than retreat from the polity. Still, some persons may discharge their community responsibilities by being involved in nonpolitical activities, say, in volunteer work. Just as the polity is but one facet of interdependent social life, so voting and political activity are not the only ways to be responsible members of society. A good citizen is involved in a community or communities, but not necessarily active in the polity.

Paying one's taxes, encouraging others to pay their fair share, and serving on juries are fully obligatory. One of the most telling ills of our time is the expectation of many Americans that they are entitled to ever more public services without paying for them (as reflected in public opinion polls that show demands to slash government and taxes but also to expand practically every conceivable government function). We all take for granted the right to be tried before a jury of our peers, but, all too often, we are unwilling to serve on juries ourselves.

Cleaning up the polity

We need to revitalize public life so that the two thirds of our citizens who now say they feel alienated or that the polity is not theirs will again be engaged in it.

Campaign contributions to members of Congress and state legislatures, speaking fees, and bribes have become so pervasive that in many areas of public policy and on numerous occasions the public interest is ignored as legislators pay off their debts to special interests. Detailed rationalizations have been spun to justify the system. It is said that giving money to politicians is a form of democratic participation. In fact, the rich can "participate" in this way so much more effectively than the poor that the democratic principle of one-person one-vote is severely compromised. It is said that money buys only access to the politician's ear; but even if money does not buy commitment, access should not be allotted according to the depth of one's pockets. It is said that every group has its pool of money and, hence, as they all grease Congress, all Americans are served. But those who cannot grease at all or not as well lose out and so do long-run public goals that are not underwritten by any particular interest groups.

To establish conditions under which elected officials will be able to respond to the public interest, to the genuine needs of all citizens, and to their own consciences requires that the role of private money in public life be reduced as much as possible. All candidates should receive some public support, as presidential candidates already do, as well as some access to radio and TV.

To achieve this major renewal and revitalization of public life, to reinstitute the prerequisites for attending to the public interest, requires a major social movement, akin to the progressive movement of the beginning of the twentieth century. For even good causes can become special interests if they are not part of such a movement, keeping their strategies and aims in constant dialogue with larger aims and multiple ends. Citizens who care about the integrity of the polity either on the local, state, or national level should band with their fellows to form a neo-progressive communitarian movement. They should persevere until elected officials are beholden – not to special interests – but only to the voters and to their own consciences.

Freedom of speech

The First Amendment is as dear to communitarians as it is to libertarians and many other Americans. Suggestions that it should be curbed to bar verbal expressions of racism, sexism, and other slurs seem to us to endanger the essence of the First Amendment, which is most needed when what some people say is disconcerting to some others. However, one should not ignore the victims of such abuse. Whenever individuals or members of a group are harassed, many nonlegal measures are appropriate to express disapproval of hateful expressions and to promote tolerance among the members of the polity. For example, a college campus faced with a rash of incidents indicating bigotry may conduct a teach-in on intergroup understanding. This, and much more, can be done without compromising the First Amendment. …

Social justice

At the heart of the communitarian understanding of social justice is the idea of reciprocity: each member of the community owes something to all the rest, and the community owes something to each of its members. Justice requires responsible individuals in a responsive community.

Members of the community have a responsibility, to the greatest extent possible, to provide for themselves and their families: honorable work contributes to the commonwealth and to the community's ability to fulfill its essential tasks. Beyond self-support, individuals have a responsibility for the material and moral well-being of others. This does not mean heroic self-sacrifice; it means the constant self-awareness that no one of us is an island unaffected by the fate of others.

For its part, the community is responsible for protecting each of us against catastrophe, natural or man-made; for ensuring the basic needs of all who genuinely cannot provide for themselves; for appropriately recognizing the distinctive contributions of individuals to the community; and for safeguarding a zone within which individuals may define their own lives through free exchange and choice. …

Public safety and public health

The American moral and legal tradition has always acknowledged the need to balance individual rights with the need to protect the safety and health of the public. The Fourth Amendment, for example, guards against unreasonable searches but allows for reasonable ones. …

We differ with the ACLU and other radical libertarians who oppose sobriety checkpoints, screening gates at airports, drug and alcohol testing for people who directly affect public safety (pilots, train engineers, etc.). Given the minimal intrusion involved (an average sobriety checkpoint lasts 90 seconds), the importance of the interests at stake (we have lost more lives, many due to drunken drivers, on the road each year than in the war in Vietnam), and the fact that such measures in the past have not led us down a slippery slope, these and similar reasonable measures should receive full public support.

There is little sense in gun registration. What we need to significantly enhance public safety is domestic disarmament of the kind that exists in practically all democracies. The National Rifle Association suggestion that criminals not guns kill people ignores the fact that thousands are killed each year, many of them children, from accidental discharge of guns, and that people – whether criminal, insane, or temporarily carried away by impulse – kill and are much more likely to do so when armed than when disarmed. The Second Amendment, behind which the NRA hides, is subject to a variety of interpretations, but the Supreme Court has repeatedly ruled, for over a hundred years, that it does not prevent laws that bar guns. We join with those who read the Second Amendment the way it was written, as a communitarian clause, calling for community militias, not individual gun slingers.

When it comes to public health, people who carry sexually transmitted diseases, especially when the illness is nearly always fatal, such as AIDS, should be expected to disclose their illness to previous sexual contacts or help health authorities to inform them, warn all prospective sexual contacts, and inform all health care personnel with whom they come in contact. It is their contribution to help stem the epidemic. At the same time, the carriers' rights against wanton violation of privacy, discrimination in housing, employment, and insurance should be scrupulously protected.

[...]

In conclusion: A question of responsibility

Although some of the responsibilities identified in this manifesto are expressed in legal terms, and the law does play a significant role not only in regulating society but also in indicating which values it holds dear, our first and foremost purpose is to affirm the moral commitments of parents, young persons, neighbors, and citizens to affirm the importance of the communities within which such commitments take shape and are transmitted from one generation to the next. This is not primarily a legal matter. On the contrary, when a community reaches the point at which these responsibilities are largely enforced by the powers of the state, it is in deep moral crisis. If communities are to function well, most members most of the time must discharge their responsibilities because they are committed to do so, not because they fear lawsuits, penalties, or jails. Nevertheless, the state and its agencies must take care not to harm the structures of civil society on which we all depend. Social environments, like natural environments, cannot be taken for granted.

It has been argued by libertarians that responsibilities are a personal matter, that individuals are to judge which responsibilities they accept as theirs. As we see it, responsibilities are anchored in community. Reflecting the diverse moral voices of their citizens, responsive communities define what is expected of people; they educate their members to accept these values; and they praise them when they do and frown upon them when they do not. Although the ultimate foundation of morality may be commitments of individual conscience, it is communities that help introduce and sustain these commitments. Hence the urgent need for communities to articulate the responsibilities they expect their members to discharge, especially in times, such as our own, in which the understanding of these responsibilities has weakened and their reach has grown unclear.

Further work This is only a beginning. This platform is but a point in dialogue, part of an ongoing process of deliberation. It should not be viewed as a series of final conclusions but ideas for additional discussion. We do not claim to have the answers to all that troubles America these days. However, we are heartened by the groundswell of support that our initial efforts have brought to the communitarian perspective. If more and more Americans come forward and join together to form active communities that seek to reinvigorate the moral and social order, we will be able to deal better with many of our communities' problems while reducing our reliance on governmental regulation, controls, and force. We will have a greater opportunity to work out shared public policy based on broad consensus and shared moral and legal traditions. And we will have many more ways to make our society a place in which individual rights are vigilantly maintained, while the seedbeds of civic virtue are patiently nurtured.

Niccolo Machiavelli, "The Threat Posed by Corrupt Citizens"*

[...] And it must be assumed as a well-demonstrated truth, that a corrupt people that lives under the government of a prince can never become free, even though the prince and his whole line should be extinguished; and that it would be better that the one prince should be destroyed by another. For a people in such condition can never become settled unless a new prince be created, who by his good qualities and valor can maintain their liberty; but even then it will last only during the lifetime of the new prince. It was thus that the freedom of Syracuse was preserved at different times by the valor of Dion and Timoleon during their lives, but after their death the city relapsed under the former tyranny. But there is not a more striking example of this than Rome itself, which after the expulsion of the Tarquins was enabled quickly to resume and maintain her liberty; but after the death of Cæsar, Caligula, and Nero, and after the extinction of the entire Cæsarean line, she could not

* Niccolo Machiavelli, extract from *The Discourses* (New York: The Modern Library of Random House, 1950), pp. 165–70. Originally published c.1513–21.

even begin to re-establish her liberty, and much less preserve it. And this great difference in the condition of things in one and the same city resulted entirely from this fact, that at the time of the Tarquins the Roman people was not yet corrupt, whilst under the Cæsars it became corrupt to the lowest degree. [...]

And although the example of Rome is preferable to all others, yet will I cite on this subject some instances amongst peoples known in our times. And therefore I say that no change, however great or violent, could ever restore Milan and Naples to liberty, because the whole people of those states were thoroughly corrupt. This was seen after the death of Philip Visconti, when Milan attempted to recover her liberty, but knew not how, nor was she able to maintain it. It was a great good fortune for Rome, therefore, that no sooner did her kings become corrupt than they were expelled, before the corruption had time to extend to the heart of the people. This corruption caused endless disturbances in Rome; but as the intention of the people was good, these troubles, instead of harming, rather benefited the republic. And from this we may draw the conclusion that, where the mass of the people is sound, disturbances and tumults do no serious harm; but where corruption has penetrated the people, the best laws are of no avail, unless they are administered by a man of such supreme power that he may cause the laws to be observed until the mass has been restored to a healthy condition.

[...]

I will suppose a state to be corrupt to the last degree, so as to present the subject in its most difficult aspect, there being no laws nor institutions that suffice to check a general corruption. For as good habits of the people require good laws to support them, so laws, to be observed, need good habits on the part of the people. Besides, the constitution and laws established in a republic at its very origin, when men were still pure, no longer suit when men have become corrupt and bad. And although the laws may be changed according to circumstances and events, yet it is seldom or never that the constitution itself is changed; and for this reason the new laws do not suffice, for they are not in harmony with the constitution, that has remained intact. To make this matter better understood, I will explain how the government of Rome was constituted and what the nature of the laws was, which together with the magistrates restrained the citizens. The constitution of the state reposed upon the authority of the people, the Senate, the Tribunes, and the Consuls, and upon the manner of choosing and creating the magistrates, and of making the laws. These institutions were rarely or never varied by events; but the laws that restrained the citizens were often altered, such as the law relating to adultery, the sumptuary laws, that in relation to ambition, and many others, which were changed according as the citizens from one day to another became more and more corrupt. Now the constitution remaining unchanged, although no longer suitable to the corrupt people, the laws that had been changed became powerless for restraint; yet they would have answered very well if the constitution had also been modified at the same time with the laws.

And the truth that the original institutions were no longer suitable to a corrupt state is clearly seen in these two main points, – the creation of the magistrates, and the forms used in making the laws. As regards the first, the Roman people bestowed the consulate and the other principal offices only on such as asked for them. This system was very good in the beginning, because only such citizens asked for these places as deemed themselves worthy of them, and a refusal was regarded as ignominious; so that every one strove to make himself esteemed worthy of the honor. But when the city had become corrupt, this system became most pernicious; for it was no longer the most virtuous and deserving, but the most powerful, that asked for the magistratures; and the less powerful, often the most meritorious, abstained from being candidates from fear. [...] Now as to the mode of making the laws. At first a Tribune or any other citizen had the right to propose any law, and every citizen could speak in favor or against it before its final adoption. This system was very good so long as the citizens were uncorrupted, for it is always well in a state that every one may propose what he deems for the public good; and it was equally well that every one should be allowed to express his opinion in relation to it, so that the people, having heard both sides, may decide in favor of the best. But when the citizens had become corrupt, this system became the worst possible, for then only the powerful proposed laws, not for the common good and the liberty of all, but for the increase of their own power, and fear restrained all the others from speaking against such laws; and thus the people were by force and fraud made to resolve upon their own ruin.

Chapter 11

On Structure

Introduction

No perennial political issue received more attention during the twentieth century than that about the respective roles of free markets and governments in structuring political communities. The international conflict between communism and liberal democracy seemed to boil down to a liberal democratic vision that emphasized free-market capitalism with minimal governmental oversight and a communist vision of a strong – even totalitarian – government that denied citizens freedoms to pursue their goals within economic markets. In the US, domestic conflict between liberals and conservatives was less polarized, because both ideologies recognized the need for both capitalism and democratic governments in the organization of society, but liberal voices usually called for less capitalism and more government, while conservatives called for the opposite.

But political theorists have long recognized that questions of structure are more complex than that of the competing and complementary roles of free markets and governments. They have, for example, both stressed and deemphasized the roles of voluntary associations within civil society and of cultural values. They have recognized that other institutions – most notably a strong church – can play a dominant role in structuring society. And still others have wondered whether there is simply too much structure within even liberal and pluralist societies to provide citizens the privacy and freedom that a good life requires.

Our first selection in this chapter addresses the last question. The need for an extensive private sphere of individual freedom is the topic of the classic essay, *On Liberty*, written in 1860 by John Stuart Mill (1806–73) who worked for the British East India Company while developing a body of political thought that earned him the rank as one of the foremost philosophers of the nineteenth century. As a utilitarian, Mill claimed to "forego any advantage which could be derived to my argument from the idea of abstract right." His case for an extensive private sphere rested on utilitarian arguments that pointed out the beneficial consequences of liberty. Freedom of opinion and thus toleration of even the most noxious views are necessary for the emergence of truth and for people having "heart-felt conviction" for the ideas that they affirm. Freedom of action – in even those areas like "traffic in strong drink" and polygamy – is necessary to allow the experiments in living that will enable individuals to learn the effects of their pursuing alternative conceptions of the good life and thus make progressively better choices. Mill issued his famous decree that "the only part of conduct of anyone for which he is amenable to society is that which concerns others," and he asserted that this means that individuals should be free not only from excessive government controls but also from the moral views that dominate cultural life – his "tyranny of the majority."

Even if citizens are granted the liberties that Mill demanded, this does not mean that society would be unstructured. Almost a century earlier, Adam Smith (1723–90), a Scottish moral philosopher and political economist, had produced his famed *Wealth of Nations* (1776) that proclaimed that free markets contained "an invisible hand" that prompted free and self-interested individuals to act as producers and consumers of goods and services in ways that benefited others and contributed to the economic prosperity of their political communities. In our next selection, Smith discusses how the division of labor, economic competition, and market processes (establishing prices and wages on the basis of the laws of supply and demand) can go far in organizing society. He concludes by listing three important functions that markets cannot perform and are thus properly undertaken by governments: protecting individuals from the violence of others, protecting individuals from other injustices, and providing certain public works.

Karl Marx agreed with Smith that economic structures were the key to social progress, but he disagreed, of course, that capitalism would prove to be the best way to organize a political economy. Marx also insisted that economic forces, not the ideas that prevail in the political cultures of communities, were the key causes of progress; for Marx, dominant economic forces simply produced the cultural values necessary to sustain the prevailing economic system; cultural values had no independent effect on the structure of society. This conclusion was famously challenged by Max Weber (1864–1920) who had stressed in the *Protestant Ethic and the Spirit of Capitalism* (1905) how the emergence of Protestant cultural values had played a huge role in promoting capitalism and facilitating economic progress. In our next reading, Lawrence Harrison, director of the Cultural Change Institute at Tufts University, argues "Marx was wrong, Weber was right." After trying to provide some precision to our "fuzzy and elastic" conceptions of culture, he argues that the cultural values that attend democratic capitalism "do a better job of promoting human progress and well-being than other systems." The cultural values found important by Harrison involve a "radius of trust," a rigorous ethical system, a rejection of authoritarianism, and future-regarding economic orientations.

Leading political theorists including Edmund Burke, Georg Hegel, and Alexis de Tocqueville have long recognized the important role of voluntary associations in structuring political communities. The many social organizations that exist in the social sphere ("below the state but beyond the family") provide citizens with social identities and moral purposes and enable them to organize to achieve many collective benefits without depending on governments and to pursue political goals. One of the most influential recent contributions to political theory has been the work of Robert Putnam, a professor of government at Harvard University, on the declining involvement of Americans in voluntary associations. While he detailed his massive research on these trends in *Bowling Alone* (2000), his initial findings and analyses were provided in earlier articles including the one extracted here. He adopts the term "social capital" to summarize his concerns which involve not only our disengagement from voluntary associations (ranging from labor unions to bowling leagues) but also our turning away from cultural values that keep people involved with others (especially their trust of one another). In his larger work, he finds that the decline in social capitalism is unhealthy both for democratic life and individual well-being, and he reaffirms that the major culprit responsible for this problem is television.

In the next selection, Anthony Giddens, a professor emeritus of sociology at the London School of Economics, returns our attention to the role of free markets and government in structuring society. He finds that some older social democrats have an "unreconstructed" emphasis on the role of government while newer free-market globalists (or neoliberals) have overemphasized privatization, the relaxing of economic and trade regulations, and dismantling the welfare state. He thus describes "a third way" that more appropriately balances free markets and government (as well as civil society). According to Giddens, governments must recognize the changes that have occurred in the new global economy and refocus their energies. They must better control the investment of capital in manufacturing, regulate financial markets, and most importantly "build a 'knowledge base' that will release the full potential of the information economy."

But a fourth way of structuring political communities has returned to prominence: theocracies. The primary idea of religious fundamentalists generally and Islamic fundamentalists in particular is that the church must dominate government and structure political communities. A description and defense of Islamic theocracy is provided by Imam Khomeini (1900–89), who was a major instigator of the Iranian Revolution of 1979, became the first Supreme Leader of its Islamic fundamentalist theocracy, and remains a spiritual guide for many Shia Muslims today. He argues that Islamic government is primarily interested in struggling against Western imperialism and pursuing truth and justice. It is "the rule of divine law over men." The sacred texts of Islam (the Qur'an and the Sunna) guide all governance, and all citizens recognize them as worthy of obedience. Thus, no one man (some sort of monarch) rules an Islamic theocracy; only universally recognized divine laws structure such a society.

The classical liberal (and pluralist) response to theocracy was provided more than three centuries ago by John Locke, who sought a solution to the religious wars that occurred during the sixteenth and seventeenth centuries. In "A Letter Concerning Toleration," Locke declared that the coercive power of the state concerns itself only with civil interests; "care of the soul" is not its concern. Since nothing can be more important to humans than their salvation and doing what is "pleasing unto God," each citizen must fear that if his devotion to God were coerced by the state, it would be hypocritical and thus displeasing to Him. Religious society (churches) can offer "exhortation, admonitions, and advices" to community members, but that is the "utmost force of ecclesiastical authority," which should never seek to capture government to further spiritual beliefs.

John Stuart Mill, "On Liberty"*

Like other tyrannies, the tyranny of the majority was at first, and is still vulgarly, held in dread, chiefly as operating through the acts of the public authorities. But reflecting persons perceived that when society is itself the tyrant – society collectively over the separate individuals who compose it – its means of tyrannizing are not restricted to the acts which it may do by the hands of its political functionaries. Society can and does execute its own mandates; and if it issues wrong mandates instead of right, or any mandates at all in things with which it ought not to meddle, it practices a social tyranny more formidable than many kinds of political oppression, since, though not usually upheld by such extreme penalties, it leaves fewer means of escape, penetrating much more deeply into the details of life, and enslaving the soul itself. Protection, therefore, against the tyranny of the magistrate is not enough; there needs protection also against the tyranny of the prevailing opinion and feeling, against the tendency of society to impose, by other means than civil penalties, its own ideas and practices as rules of conduct on those who dissent from them; to fetter the development and, if possible, prevent the formation of any individuality not in harmony with its ways, and compel all characters to fashion themselves upon the model of its own. There is a limit to the legitimate interference of collective opinion with individual independence; and to find that limit, and maintain it against encroachment, is as indispensable to a good condition of human affairs as protection against political despotism.

But though this proposition is not likely to be contested in general terms, the practical question where to place the limit – how to make the fitting adjustment between individual independence and social control – is a subject on which nearly everything remains to be done. ...

* John Stuart Mill, available at www.constitution.org/jsm/liberty.htm, accessed April 30, 2008. Originally published 1860.

The object of this essay is to assert one very simple principle, as entitled to govern absolutely the dealings of society with the individual in the way of compulsion and control, whether the means used by physical force in the form of legal penalties or the moral coercion of public opinion. That principle is that the sole end for which mankind are warranted, individually or collectively, in interfering with the liberty of action of any of their number is self-protection. That the only purpose for which power can be rightfully exercised over any member of a civilized community, against his will, is to prevent harm to others. His own good, either physical or moral, is not a sufficient warrant. He cannot rightfully be compelled to do or forbear because it will be better for him to do so, because it will make him happier, because, in the opinion of others, to do so would be wise or even right. These are good reasons for remonstrating with him, or reasoning with him, or persuading him, or entreating him, but not for compelling him or visiting him with any evil in case he do otherwise. To justify that, the conduct from which it is desired to deter him must be calculated to produce evil to someone else. The only part of the conduct of anyone for which he is amenable to society is that which concerns others. In the part which merely concerns himself, his independence is, of right, absolute. Over himself, over his own body and mind, the individual is sovereign.

It is, perhaps, hardly necessary to say that this doctrine is meant to apply only to human beings in the maturity of their faculties. We are not speaking of children or of young persons below the age which the law may fix as that of manhood or womanhood. Those who are still in a state to require being taken care of by others must be protected against their own actions as well as against external injury. For the same reason we may leave out of consideration those backward states of society in which the race itself may be considered as in its nonage. The early difficulties in the way of spontaneous progress are so great that there is seldom any choice of means for overcoming them; and a ruler full of the spirit of improvement is warranted in the use of any expedients that will attain an end perhaps otherwise unattainable. Despotism is a legitimate mode of government in dealing with barbarians, provided the end be their improvement and the means justified by actually effecting that end. Liberty, as a principle, has no application to any state of things anterior to the time when mankind have become capable of being improved by free and equal discussion. [...]

It is proper to state that I forego any advantage which could be derived to my argument from the idea of abstract right as a thing independent of utility. I regard utility as the ultimate appeal on all ethical questions; but it must be utility in the largest sense, grounded on the permanent interests of man as a progressive being. [...]

Of the liberty of thought and discussion

If all mankind minus one were of one opinion, and only one person were of the contrary opinion, mankind would be no more justified in silencing that one person than he, if he had the power, would be justified in silencing mankind. Were an opinion a personal possession of no value except to the owner, if to be obstructed in the enjoyment of it were simply a private injury, it would make some difference whether the injury was inflicted only on a few persons or on many. But the peculiar evil of silencing the expression of an opinion is that it is robbing the human race posterity as well as the existing generation – those who dissent from the opinion, still more than those who hold it.

[...]

First, if any opinion is compelled to silence, that opinion may, for aught we can certainly know, be true. To deny this is to assume our own infallibility.

Secondly, though the silenced opinion be an error, it may, and very commonly does, contain a portion of truth; and since the general or prevailing opinion on any subject is rarely or never the whole truth, it is only by the collision of adverse opinions that the remainder of the truth has any chance of being supplied.

Thirdly, even if the received opinion be not only true, but the whole truth; unless it is suffered to be, and actually is, vigorously and earnestly contested, it will, by most of those who receive it, be held in the manner of a prejudice, with little comprehension or feeling of its rational grounds. And not only this, but, fourthly, the meaning of the doctrine itself will be in danger of being lost or enfeebled, and deprived of its vital effect on the character and conduct: the dogma becoming a mere formal profession, inefficacious for good, but cumbering the ground and preventing the growth of any real and heart-felt conviction from reason or personal experience.

[...]

Of individuality, as one of the elements of well-being

Such being the reasons which make it imperative that human beings should be free to form opinions and to express their opinions without reserve; and such the baneful consequences to the intellectual, and through that to the moral nature of man, unless this liberty is either conceded or asserted in spite of prohibition; let us next examine whether the same reasons do not require that men should be free to act upon their opinions – to carry these out in their lives without hindrance, either physical or moral, from their fellow men, so long as it is at their own risk and peril. This last proviso is of course indispensable. No one pretends that actions should be as free as opinions. On the contrary, even opinions lose their immunity when the circumstances in which they are expressed are such as to constitute their expression a positive instigation to some mischievous act. An opinion that corn dealers are starvers of the poor, or that private property is robbery, ought to be unmolested when simply circulated through the press, but may justly incur punishment when delivered orally to an excited mob assembled before the house of a corn dealer, or when handed about among the same mob in the form of a placard. Acts, of whatever kind, which without justifiable cause do harm to others may be, and in the more important cases absolutely require to be, controlled by the unfavorable sentiments, and, when needful, by the active interference of mankind. The liberty of the individual must be thus far limited; he must not make himself a nuisance to other people. But if he refrains from molesting others in what concerns them, and merely acts according to his own inclination and judgment in things which concern himself, the same reasons which show that opinion should be free prove also that he should be allowed, without molestation, to carry his opinions into practice at his own cost. That mankind are not infallible; that their truths, for the most part, are only half-truths; that unity of opinion, unless resulting from the fullest and freest comparison of opposite opinions, is not desirable, and diversity not an evil, but a good, until mankind are much more capable than at present of recognizing all sides of the truth, are principles applicable to men's modes of action not less than to their opinions. As it is useful that while mankind are imperfect there should be different opinions, so is it that there should be different experiments of living; that free scope should be given to varieties of character, short of injury to others; and that the worth of different modes of life should be proved practically, when anyone thinks fit to try them. It is desirable, in short, that in things which do not primarily concern others individuality should assert itself. Where not the person's own character but the traditions or customs of other people are the rule of conduct, there is wanting one of the principal ingredients of human happiness, and quite the chief ingredient of individual and social progress. …

Under the name of preventing intemperance, the people of one English colony, and of nearly half the United States, have been interdicted by law from making any use whatever of fermented drinks, except for medical purposes, for prohibition of their sale is in fact, as it is intended to be, prohibition of their use. …

The secretary [of the Alliance for Prohibition] however, says, "I claim, as a citizen, a right to legislate whenever my social rights are invaded by the social act of another." And now for the definition of these "social rights": "If anything invaded my social rights, certainly the traffic in strong drink does. It destroys my primary right of security by constantly creating and stimulating social disorder. It invades my right of equality by deriving a profit from the creation of misery I am taxed to support. It impedes my right to free moral and intellectual development by surrounding my path with dangers and by weakening and demoralizing society, from which I have a right to claim mutual aid and intercourse." A theory of "social rights" the like of which probably never before found its way into distinct language: being nothing short of this – that it is the absolute social right of every individual that every other individual shall act in every respect exactly as he ought; that whosoever fails thereof in the smallest particular violates my social right and entitles me to demand from the legislature the removal of the grievance. So monstrous a principle is far more dangerous than any single interference with liberty; there is no violation of liberty which it would not justify; it acknowledges no right to any freedom whatever, except perhaps to that of holding opinions in secret, without ever disclosing them; for the moment an opinion which I consider noxious passes anyone's lips, it invades all the "social rights" attributed to me by the Alliance. The doctrine ascribes to all mankind a vested interest in each other's moral, intellectual, and even physical perfection, to be defined by each claimant according to his own standard.

[…]

I cannot refrain from adding to these examples of the little account commonly made of human liberty the language of downright persecution which breaks out from the press of this country whenever it feels called on to notice the remarkable phenomenon of Mormonism. … The article of the Mormonite doctrine which is the chief provocative to the antipathy which thus breaks through the ordinary restraints of religious tolerance is its sanction of polygamy; which, though permitted to Mohammedans, and Hindus, and Chinese, seems to excite unquenchable animosity when practiced by persons who speak English and profess to be a kind of Christians. No one has a deeper disapprobation than I have of this Mormon institution; both for other reasons and because, far from being in any way countenanced by the principle of liberty, it is a direct infraction of that principle, being a mere riveting of the chains of one half of the community, and an emancipation of the other from reciprocity of obligation toward them. Still, it must be remembered that this relation is as much voluntary on the part of the women concerned in it, and who may be deemed the sufferers by it, as is the case with any other form of the marriage institution; and however surprising this fact may appear, it has its explanation in the common ideas and customs of the world, which, teaching women to think marriage the one thing needful, make it intelligible that many a woman should prefer being one of several wives to not being a wife at all. Other countries are not asked to recognize such unions, or release any portion of their inhabitants from their own laws on the score of Mormonite opinions. But when the dissentients have conceded to the hostile sentiments of others far more than could justly be demanded; when they have left the countries to which their doctrines were unacceptable and established themselves in a remote corner of the earth, which they have been the first to render habitable to human beings, it is difficult to see on what principles but those of tyranny they can be prevented from living there under what laws they please, provided they commit no aggression on other nations and allow perfect freedom of departure to those who are dissatisfied with their ways.

Adam Smith, "The Principles and Virtues of Free Markets"*

Of the division of labour

The greatest improvement in the productive powers of labour and the greater part of the skill, dexterity, and judgment, with which it is anywhere directed or

* Adam Smith, extracted from *Wealth of Nations*, available at www.adamsmith.org/smith/won-intro.htm. Originally published 1776.

applied seem to have been the effects of the division of labour.

This great increase of the quantity of work which, in consequence of the division of labour, the same number of people are capable of performing is owing to three different circumstances: first, to the increase of dexterity in every particular workman; secondly, to the saving of the time which is commonly lost in passing from one species of work to another; and, lastly, to the invention of a great number of machines which facilitate and abridge labour and enable one man to do the work of many.

It is the great multiplication of the productions of all the different arts, in consequence of the division of labour, which occasions, in a well-governed society, that universal opulence which extends itself to the lowest ranks of the people. Every workman has a great quantity of his own work to dispose of beyond what he himself has occasion for; and every other workman being exactly in the same situation, he is enabled to exchange a great quantity of his own goods for a great quantity, or, what comes to the same thing, for the price of a great quantity of theirs. He supplies them abundantly with what they have occasion for, and they accommodate him as amply with what he has occasion for, and a general plenty diffuses itself through all the different ranks of the society.

... If we examine, I say, all these things and consider what a variety of labour is employed about each of them, we shall be sensible that, without the assistance and cooperation of many thousands, the very meanest person in a civilized country could not be provided, even according to what we very falsely imagine, the easy and simple manner in which he is commonly accommodated. Compared, indeed, with the more extravagant luxury of the great, his accommodation must no doubt appear extremely simple and easy; and yet it may be true, perhaps, that the accommodation of an European prince does not always so much exceed that of an industrious and frugal peasant, as the accommodation of the latter exceeds that of many an African king, the absolute master of the lives and liberties of ten thousand naked savages.

[...]

This division of labour, from which so many advantages are derived, is not originally the effect of any human wisdom, which foresees and intends that general opulence to which it gives occasion. It is the necessary, though very slow and gradual, consequence of a certain propensity in human nature which has in view no such extensive utility – the propensity to truck, barter, and exchange one thing for another.

Whether this propensity be one of those original principles in human nature, of which no further account can be given; or whether, as seems more probable, it be the necessary consequence of the faculties of reason and speech, it belongs not to our present subject to enquire. It is common to all men and to be found in no other race of animals, which seem to know neither this nor any other species of contracts. ...

[...] In almost every other race of animals each individual, when it is grown up to maturity, is entirely independent and, in its natural state, has occasion for the assistance of no other living creature. But man has almost constant occasion for the help of his brethren, and it is in vain for him to expect it from their benevolence only. He will be more likely to prevail if he can interest their self-love in his favour, and show them that it is for their own advantage to do for him what he requires of them. Whoever offers to another a bargain of any kind proposes to do this. "Give me that which I want, and you shall have this which you want," is the meaning of every such offer; and it is in this manner that we obtain from one another the far greater part of those good offices which we stand in need of. It is not from the benevolence of the butcher, the brewer, or the baker that we expect our dinner, but from their regard to their own interest. We address ourselves, not to their humanity, but to their self-love, and never talk to them of our own necessities but of their advantages. Nobody but a beggar chooses to depend chiefly upon the benevolence of his fellow citizens. Even a beggar does not depend upon it entirely. The charity of well-disposed people, indeed, supplies him with the whole fund of his subsistence. But though this principle ultimately provides him with all the necessaries of life which he has occasion for, it neither does nor can provide him with them as he has occasion for them. The greater part of his occasional wants are supplied in the same manner as those of other people – by treaty, by barter, and by purchase. With the money which one man gives him he purchases food. The old clothes which another bestows upon him he exchanges for other old clothes which suit him better, or for lodging, or for food, or for money with which he can buy either food, clothes, or lodging, as he has occasion.

As it is by treaty, by barter, and by purchase, that we obtain from one another the greater part of those mutual good offices which we stand in need of, so it is this same trucking disposition which originally gives occasion to the division of labour. ...

Of the real and nominal price of commodities [...]

Every man is rich or poor according to the degree in which he can afford to enjoy the necessaries, conveniences, and amusements of human life. But after the division of labour has once thoroughly taken place it is but a very small part of these with which a man's own labour can supply him. The far greater part of them he must derive from the labour of other people, and he must be rich or poor according to the quantity of that labour which he can command, or which he can afford to purchase. The value of any commodity, therefore, to the person who possesses it and who means not to use or consume it himself, but to exchange it for other commodities, is equal to the quantity of labour which it enables him to purchase or command. Labour, therefore, is the real measure of the exchangeable value of all commodities.

[...]

But though labour be the real measure of the exchangeable value of all commodities, it is not that by which their value is commonly estimated. It is often difficult to ascertain the proportion between two different quantities of labour. The time spent in two different sorts of work will not always alone determine this proportion. The different degrees of hardship endured and of ingenuity exercised must likewise be taken into account. There may be more labour in an hour's hard work than in two hours' easy business, or in an hour's application to a trade which it cost ten years' labour to learn than in a month's industry at an ordinary and obvious employment. But it is not easy to find any accurate measure either of hardship or ingenuity. In exchanging indeed the different productions of different sorts of labour for one another, some allowance is commonly made for both. It is adjusted, however, not by any accurate measure, but by the higgling and bargaining of the market, according to that sort of rough equality which, though not exact, is sufficient for carrying on the business of common life.

Every commodity, besides, is more frequently exchanged for, and thereby compared with, other commodities than with labour. It is more natural therefore to estimate its exchangeable value by the quantity of some other commodity than by that of the labour which it can purchase. The greater part of people, too, understand better what is meant by a quantity of a particular commodity, than by a quantity of labour. The one is a plain, palpable object; the other an abstract notion which, though it can be made sufficiently intelligible, is not altogether so natural and obvious.

But when barter ceases and money has become the common instrument of commerce, every particular commodity is more frequently exchanged for money than for any other commodity. The butcher seldom carries his beef or his mutton to the baker or the brewer in order to exchange them for bread or for beer; but he carries them to the market, where he exchanges them for money, and afterwards exchanges that money for bread and for beer. The quantity of money which he gets for them regulates, too, the quantity of bread and beer which he can afterwards purchase. It is more natural and obvious to him, therefore, to estimate their value by the quantity of money, the commodity for which he immediately exchanges them, than by that of bread and beer, the commodities for which he can exchange them only by the intervention of another commodity; and rather to say that his butcher's meat is worth threepence or fourpence a pound than that it is worth three or four pounds of bread, or three or four quarts of small beer. Hence it comes to pass that the exchangeable value of every commodity is more frequently estimated by the quantity of money than by the quantity either of labour or of any other commodity which can be had in exchange for it.

[...]

Of the natural and market price of commodities

There is in every society or neighbourhood an ordinary or average rate both of wages and profit in every different employment of labour and stock. This rate is naturally regulated, ... partly by the general circumstances of the society, their riches or poverty, their advancing, stationary, or declining condition, and partly by the particular nature of each employment.

There is likewise in every society or neighbourhood an ordinary or average rate of rent which is regulated, too, ... partly by the general circumstances of the society or neighbourhood in which the land is situated, and partly by the natural or improved fertility of the land.

These ordinary or average rates may be called the natural rates of wages, profit, and rent at the time and place in which they commonly prevail.

When the price of any commodity is neither more nor less than what is sufficient to pay the rent of the land, the wages of the labour, and the profits of the stock employed in raising, preparing, and bringing it to market, according to their natural rates, the commodity is then sold for what may be called its natural price.

The commodity is then sold precisely for what it is worth, or for what it really costs the person who brings it to market. …

The actual price at which any commodity is commonly sold is called its market price. It may either be above, or below, or exactly the same with its natural price.

… Though the market price of every particular commodity is … continually gravitating, if one may say so, towards the natural price, yet sometimes particular accidents, sometimes natural causes, and sometimes particular regulations of police, may, in many commodities, keep up the market price, for a long time together, a good deal above the natural price.

When, by an increase in the effectual demand, the market price of some particular commodity happens to rise a good deal above the natural price, those who employ their stocks in supplying that market are generally careful to conceal this change. If it was commonly known, their great profit would tempt so many new rivals to employ their stocks in the same way that, the effectual demand being fully supplied, the market price would soon be reduced to the natural price, and perhaps for some time even below it. If the market is at a great distance from the residence of those who supply it, they may sometimes be able to keep the secret for several years together, and may so long enjoy their extraordinary profits without any new rivals. Secrets of this kind, however, it must be acknowledged, can seldom be long kept; and the extraordinary profit can last very little longer than they are kept.

Secrets in manufactures are capable of being longer kept than secrets in trade. A dyer who has found the means of producing a particular colour with materials which cost only half the price of those commonly made use of, may, with good management, enjoy the advantage of his discovery as long as he lives, and even leave it as a legacy to his posterity. …

Such enhancements of the market price are evidently the effects of particular accidents, of which, however, the operation may sometimes last for many years together.

Some natural productions require such a singularity of soil and situation that all the land in a great country which is fit for producing them may not be sufficient to supply the effectual demand. The whole quantity brought to market, therefore, may be disposed of to those who are willing to give more than what is sufficient to pay the rent of the land which produced them, together with the wages of the labour and the profits of the stock which were employed in preparing and bringing them to market, according to their natural rates. Such commodities may continue for whole centuries together to be sold at this high price. …

A monopoly granted either to an individual or to a trading company has the same effect as a secret in trade or manufactures. The monopolists, by keeping the market constantly under-stocked, by never fully supplying the effectual demand, sell their commodities much above the natural price and raise their emoluments, whether they consist in wages or profit, greatly above their natural rate.

The price of monopoly is upon every occasion the highest which can be got. The natural price, or the price of free competition, on the contrary, is the lowest which can be taken, not upon every occasion indeed, but for any considerable time together. The one is upon every occasion the highest which can be squeezed out of the buyers, or which, it is supposed, they will consent to give. The other is the lowest which the sellers can commonly afford to take, and at the same time continue their business.

The exclusive privileges of corporations, statutes of apprenticeship, and all those laws which restrain, in particular employments, the competition to a smaller number than might otherwise go into them, have the same tendency, though in a less degree. They are a sort of enlarged monopolies, and may frequently, for ages together, and in whole classes of employments, keep up the market price of particular commodities above the natural price, and maintain both the wages of the labour and the profits of the stock employed about them somewhat above their natural rate.

[…]

Of the revenue of the sovereign or commonwealth

[…]

All systems either of preference or of restraint, therefore, being thus completely taken away, the obvious and simple system of natural liberty establishes itself of its own accord. Every man, as long as he does not violate the laws of justice, is left perfectly free to pursue his own interest his own way, and to bring both his industry and capital into competition with those of any other man or order of men. The sovereign is completely discharged from a duty in the attempting to perform which he must always be exposed to innumerable delusions, and for the proper performance of which no human wisdom or knowledge could ever be sufficient – the duty of superintending the industry of private people and of directing it towards the employments most suitable to the interest of the society. According to the system of natural liberty, the sovereign has only three duties to attend to – three duties of great importance, indeed, but plain and intelligible to common understandings: first, the duty of protecting the society from the violence and invasion of other independent societies; secondly, the duty of protecting, as far as possible, every member of the society from the injustice or oppression of every other member of it or the duty of establishing an exact administration of justice; and, thirdly, the duty of erecting and maintaining certain public works and certain public institutions which it can never be for the interest of any individual or small number of individuals to erect and maintain, because the profit could never repay the expense to any individual or small number of individuals, though it may frequently do much more than repay it to a great society.

Lawrence E. Harrison, "Progress and Poverty Without Marx"*

> *The central conservative truth is that it is culture, not politics, that determines the success of a society. The central liberal truth is that politics can change a culture and save it from itself.*
> —Daniel Patrick Moynihan, *The New Republic* (July 7, 1986)

Why do some nations and ethnic groups do better than others? Climate, resource endowment, geographic location and size, policy choices, and sheer luck are among the relevant factors. But it is values and attitudes – culture – that differentiate ethnic groups and are mainly responsible for such phenomena as Latin America's persistent instability and inequity, Taiwan's and Korea's economic "miracles," and the achievements of the Japanese – in Japan, in Brazil, and in America.

Culture changes, for good and for bad. In the span of three decades, Spain has turned away from its traditional, authoritarian, hierarchical value system, which was at the root of both Spain's and Hispanic America's backwardness, and has immersed itself in the progressive Western European mainstream. During the same period, a racial revolution has occurred in America that has brought two-thirds of America's blacks into the mainstream – and the middle class. Yet, in the same three decades, the United States as a nation has experienced economic and political decline, principally, I believe, because of the erosion of the traditional American values – work, frugality, education, excellence, community – that had contributed so much to our earlier success.

[...]

Marx was wrong, Weber was right

History has proven that Karl Marx was wrong; it may well be proving that Max Weber was right. Analyzing family income levels of Protestants, Catholics, and Jews in the German city of Baden in 1904–5, Weber found that Protestants did substantially better than Catholics and that Jews did better than either. The analysis led to Weber's masterwork, *The Protestant Ethic and the Spirit of Capitalism*, which explained why the values and attitudes inculcated by ascetic Calvinism were a more effective motivator of entrepreneurship, capital accumulation, and community responsibility than the values and attitudes inculcated by confessional Roman Catholicism.

Weber's emphasis on religion has prompted his critics to highlight two apparent anomalies: (1) the Catholic countries France, Italy, and Spain have grown more rapidly than most Protestant countries in Western Europe in recent decades; and (2) if "religion" (culture) is decisive, why are the Chinese so much more successful overseas than in China?

It is obvious that religion is but one of several roots of culture; after all, atheists and agnostics have values and attitudes. Moreover, Western Europe and North America have experienced a process of secularization, particularly in this century, that has reduced religion's impact on culture while expanding the impact of the education system and the media, above all, television.

[...]

How culture influences progress

Admittedly, the word *culture* is fuzzy and elastic. It can define group or national value systems, attitudes, religious and other institutions, intellectual achievement, artistic expression, daily behavior, customs, lifestyle, and many other characteristics. When we focus on the relationship between culture and progress, however, its definition becomes more manageable. In this book, I am addressing those aspects of culture that influence group or national political, economic, and social performance.

* Lawrence E. Harrison, extracted from *Who Prospers? How Cultural Values Shape Economic and Political Success* (New York: Basic Books, 1992), pp. 1, 6–14.

Culture is a coherent system of values, attitudes, and institutions that influences individual and social behavior in all dimensions of human experience.

[...]

Progressive societies encourage experimentation and criticism and help people both discover their talents and interests and mesh them with the right jobs. The idea of merit permeates such societies, and people are judged more by their performance than by their family background or class. Political pluralism and broad citizen participation are likely to evolve in such an environment. The freedom that nourishes the expression of human creative capacity also nourishes democratic political systems, stability, and continuity.

What has been demonstrated in this century, particularly in the last decade, is that democratic capitalism does a better job of promoting human progress and well-being than other systems. But, as the experience of most Third World countries in recent decades shows, the building of durable democratic capitalist institutions can be dauntingly difficult, particularly since cultural traditions that nurture progress are not likely to be in place.

What, then, are the cultural forces that facilitate or suppress the expression of human creative capacity and that influence movement toward or away from this increasingly universal aspirational model? There are, in my view, four fundamental factors: (1) the degree of identification with others in a society – the radius of trust, or the sense of community; (2) the rigor of the ethical system; (3) the way authority is exercised within the society; and (4) attitudes about work, innovation, saving, and profit. These factors flow from the overarching world view of a society, what social scientists refer to as "cognitive orientation" or "cognitive view." It is shaped by geographic and historical factors and, in the case of traditional societies, also by the idea, inculcated by stagnation that has persisted over centuries, that progress is possible only at the expense of others. In such societies, the time focus is the present or the past. In progressive cultures, the time focus is the future. An examination of these four factors will help clarify the link between values and progress.

The radius of trust Identification with others in the society – the sense of community – is synonymous with social empathy and is a foundation of trust. Trust is of transcendental importance to the viability of pluralistic political systems. It comes crucially into play, for example, when power is transferred from the ins to the outs. It affects attitudes about cooperation and compromise, both indispensable to the smooth functioning of democratic politics. Where trust and identification are scant, political polarization, confrontation, and autocratic government are likely to emerge.

Trust is also important to the pluralistic, decentralized economic systems that have proved to be the most efficient and productive. Successful enterprise usually depends on effective organization and cooperation, which, in turn, depend on trust.

Commercial and industrial enterprises – and public administration – in low-trust countries are usually weighted down by centralization, including a variety of checking mechanisms and procedures designed, ostensibly, to assure conformity and to control dishonesty. Particularly in public administration, such controls not only stifle governmental creativity and private entrepreneurship but lend themselves to corruption and perpetuate privilege, as Hernando De Soto has documented so tellingly in the case of Peru.[1]

The radius of identification, or social empathy, is a key determinant of social equity and progress. If there is a relatively high degree of identification, as in Japan, the politically and economically powerful are more likely to concern themselves with the well-being of the masses. That concern is reflected, through budget allocations, in high levels of literacy and public health. Similarly, philanthropy, notably absent in most Latin American countries, is a likely consequence of an extended radius of identification. Countries like Costa Rica and Israel, which also show a high level of identification and empathy, are prone to democratic political systems that reinforce the claim of the masses to attention to their needs and aspirations.

In most poor countries, the radius of identification and trust is substantially confined to the family. What is outside the family is an object of indifference, even hostility. Familistic societies are usually characterized by nepotism and other forms of corruption, as well as antisocial behavior such as tax evasion, littering, and aversion to organization and cooperation for common purposes and causes.

The rigor of the ethical system The ethical system often derives from religion, although that is not the case with the East Asian countries. In *The Protestant Ethic and the Spirit of Capitalism*, Weber focused on the link between religion and economic performance, particularly the impetus given to entrepreneurship, saving, and

1 Hernando De Soto, *El Otro Sendero* (Lima: Editorial El Barranco, 1986).

investing by a combination of Protestant asceticism and the Calvinist doctrines of calling and election. *Calling* requires an individual to discharge the personal and social responsibilities of his or her station in life; *election* is the doctrine that God has blessed a chosen few whose state of grace is apparent from their prosperity. But Weber also recognized the important link between ethics and economic performance, and he believed that the Roman Catholic emphasis on the afterlife and what he perceived as a more flexible ethical system put Catholics at a disadvantage to Protestants and Jews in this life: "The God of Calvinism demanded of his believers not single good works, but a life of good works combined into a unified system. There was no place for the very human Catholic cycle of sin, repentance, atonement, release, followed by renewed sin."[2]

[...]

The exercising of authority Traditionally, authority has been seen in Hispanic America as a license. There is truth, albeit sometimes exaggerated and overgeneralized, in the stereotype of the Hispanic American male who sees life as a struggle to achieve the power that comes with authority, which, once achieved, is to be used in his own interest, unrestrained by concerns with the rights of others, constitutional checks and balances, or even prudence. Those who find the stereotype offensive and without foundation should ponder why the typical Latin American chief of state leaves office vastly enriched. I hasten to acknowledge that there are exceptions.

But beyond the costs in terms of the frustration of democracy and justice, diverted resources, bad policies, and quixotic adventures (for example, the decision of Argentina's military to attack the Falkland Islands), authoritarianism in Latin America – in the home, the church, school, government, business – probably also contributes to the suppression of risk taking, innovation, and entrepreneurship by constantly penalizing initiative.[3] The authoritarianism of the mandarins, including Mao, has, I believe, similarly suppressed economic growth in China.

Authoritarianism implies a hierarchical view of the world, one that nurtures paternalism, patron–client relationships, and social rigidity, conditions commonly found in the Third World. But authoritarianism is not peculiar to the Third World, as German history attests. It has traditionally flourished in Taiwan, Korea, and Japan, all of whose economic performance in recent decades has astonished the world. [...]

Work, innovation, saving, and profit Positive attitudes about work may reflect religious influence, as Weber points out with respect to Protestantism. As we shall see in the two chapters on East Asian countries, religion is not the only source of such attitudes, which usually incorporate (1) the belief that rationality presents a tool with which the world can be manipulated and wealth increased, (2) a consequent high emphasis on education, and (3) an orientation toward the future that encourages planning and saving.[4] The implications of such attitudes for economic development are obvious. But the same attitudes also have important effects on political and social progress by influencing the way public officials go about their work: the extent of their vision, the significance they attach to planning, the effort and sense of responsibility they exert in shaping and executing policies.

Closely related to the value attached to work is the extent to which a society promotes creativity and entrepreneurship. David McClelland has argued that child-rearing practices are the principal reason some countries and ethnic groups produce proportionally more entrepreneurs than others. He believes that the years between five and twelve are crucial to a child's achievement motivation. He cites evidence that during this key growth period, moderate parental pressures are optimal and children's achievement tendencies are reinforced by: reasonably high parental standards at a time when a child can handle them; limited parental interference; and expressed parental pleasure in their children's achievements. McClelland believes that an authoritarian style of child rearing undermines a child's creativity, and he consequently believes that in most societies it is advantageous for mothers, rather than fathers, to take the leading role in child rearing.[5]

[...]

2 Max Weber, *The Protestant Ethic and the Spirit of Capitalism* (New York: Scribner, 1950), p. 117.

3 This is a point made forcefully about Argentina by Tomás Roberto Fillol in *Social Factors in Economic Development* (Cambridge: MIT Press, 1961).

4 In *The Unheavenly City Revisited* (Boston and Toronto: Little, Brown, 1974), Edward Banfield emphasizes future orientation as a principal motivator of upward mobility in America.

5 David McClelland, *The Achieving Society* (Princeton: D. Van Nostrand, 1961).

To recapitulate, I believe that significant differences in political, economic, and social development among countries can usually be explained by differences in trust and identification, ethical codes, the way authority is exercised, and the value attached to work, innovation, and planning.

Robert D. Putnam, "The Strange Disappearance of Civic America"*

For the last year or so, I have been wrestling with a difficult mystery: [...] the strange disappearance of social capital and civic engagement in America. By "social capital," I mean features of social life – networks, norms, and trust – that enable participants to act together more effectively to pursue shared objectives. (Whether or not their shared goals are praiseworthy is, of course, entirely another matter.) I use the term "civic engagement" to refer to people's connections with the life of their communities, not only with politics.

[...]

Evidence for the decline of social capital and civic engagement comes from a number of independent sources. Surveys of average Americans in 1965, 1975, and 1985, in which they recorded every single activity during a day – so-called "time-budget" studies – indicate that since 1965 time spent on informal socializing and visiting is down (perhaps by one-quarter) and time devoted to clubs and organizations is down even more sharply (by roughly half). Membership records of such diverse organizations as the PTA, the Elks club, the League of Women Voters, the Red Cross, labor unions, and even bowling leagues show that participation in many conventional voluntary associations has declined by roughly 25 percent to 50 percent over the last two to three decades. Surveys show sharp declines in many measures of collective political participation, including attending a rally or speech (off 36 percent between 1973 and 1993), attending a meeting on town or school affairs (off 39 percent), or working for a political party (off 56 percent).

Some of the most reliable evidence about trends comes from the General Social Survey (GSS), conducted nearly every year for more than two decades. The GSS demonstrates, at all levels of education and among both men and women, a drop of roughly one-quarter in group membership since 1974 and a drop of roughly one-third in social trust since 1972. (Trust in political authorities, indeed in many social institutions, has also declined sharply over the last three decades, but that is conceptually a distinct trend.) Slumping membership has afflicted all sorts of groups, from sports clubs and professional associations to literary discussion groups and labor unions. Only nationality groups, hobby and garden clubs, and the catch-all category of "other" seem to have resisted the ebbing tide. Gallup polls report that church attendance fell by roughly 15 percent during the 1960s and has remained at that lower level ever since, while data from the National Opinion Research Center suggest that the decline continued during the 1970s and 1980s and by now amounts to roughly 30 percent. [...]

Of course, American civil society is not moribund. Many good people across the land work hard every day to keep their communities vital. Indeed, evidence suggests that America still outranks many other countries in the degree of our community involvement and social trust. But if we examine our lives, not our aspirations, and if we compare ourselves not with other countries but with our parents, the best available evidence suggests that we are less connected with one another. [...] Why, beginning in the 1960s and accelerating in the 1970s and 1980s, did the fabric of American community life begin to fray? Why are more Americans bowling alone?

The usual suspects

Many possible answers have been suggested for this puzzle: busy-ness and time pressure; economic hard times (or, according to alternative theories, material affluence); residential mobility; suburbanization; the movement of women into the paid labor force and the stresses of two-career families; disruption of marriage and family ties; changes in the structure of the American economy, such as the rise of chain stores, branch firms, and the service sector; the 1960s, most of which actually happened in the 1970s, including Vietnam, Watergate, and disillusion with public life, and the cultural revolt against authority (sex, drugs, and so on); growth of the welfare state; the civil rights revolution; and television, the electronic revolution, and other technological changes.

[...]

Our efforts thus far to identify the major sources of civic disengagement have been singularly unfruitful. In all our statistical analyses, however, one factor, second

* Robert D. Putnam, extracted from *The American Prospect*, 7, 24 (December 1, 1995), pp. 34–48.

only to education, stands out as a predictor of all forms of civic engagement and trust.[6]

[...]

Our prime suspect

[...]

I have discovered only one prominent suspect against whom circumstantial evidence can be mounted, and in this case, it turns out, some directly incriminating evidence has also turned up. This is not the occasion to lay out the full case for the prosecution, nor to review rebuttal evidence for the defense, but I want to present evidence that justifies indictment.

The culprit is television.

First, the timing fits. The long civic generation was the last cohort of Americans to grow up without television, for television flashed into American society like lightning in the 1950s. In 1950 barely 10 percent of American homes had television sets, but by 1959, 90 percent did, probably the fastest diffusion of a major technological innovation ever recorded. The reverberations from this lightning bolt continued for decades, as viewing hours grew by 17–20 percent during the 1960s and by an additional 7–8 percent during the 1970s.

[...]

Evidence of a link between the arrival of television and the erosion of social connections is, however, not merely circumstantial. The links between civic engagement and television viewing can be instructively compared with the links between civic engagement and newspaper reading. The basic contrast is straightforward: newspaper reading is associated with high social capital, TV viewing with low social capital.

[...]

In other words, each hour spent viewing television is associated with less social trust and less group membership, while each hour reading a newspaper is associated with more. An increase in television viewing of the magnitude that the US has experienced in the last four decades might directly account for as much as one-quarter to one-half of the total drop in social capital, even without taking into account, for example, the indirect effects of television viewing on newspaper readership or the cumulative effects of lifetime viewing hours. [...]

[6] Much of *The American Prospect* the article from which this reading is extracted, and several chapters of Putnam's subsequent *Bowling Alone*, discusses the evidence that largely or partly exonerates "the usual suspects." He finds that more education increases social capital, but because we have become more educated while simultaneously losing social capital, this finding only adds to the puzzle. Only partially exonerated because the evidence is inclusive or because they have only minor effects on the loss of social capital are: the changing role of women, increases in divorce and the loosening of family bonds, and the gains resulting from the civil rights movements.

How might TV destroy social capital?

Time displacement Even though there are only 24 hours in everyone's day, most forms of social and media participation are positively correlated. People who listen to lots of classical music are more likely, not less likely, than others to attend Cubs games. Television is the principal exception to this generalization – the only leisure activity that seems to inhibit participation outside the home. TV watching comes at the expense of nearly every social activity outside the home, especially social gatherings and informal conversations. TV viewers are homebodies.

[...]

In short, television privatizes our leisure time.

Effects on the outlooks of viewers An impressive body of literature suggests that heavy watchers of TV are unusually skeptical about the benevolence of other people – overestimating crime rates, for example. This body of literature has generated much debate about the underlying causal patterns, with skeptics suggesting that misanthropy may foster couch-potato behavior rather than the reverse. While awaiting better experimental evidence, however, a reasonable interim judgment is that heavy television watching may well increase pessimism about human nature. Perhaps too, as social critics have long argued, both the medium and the message have more basic effects on our ways of interacting with the world and with one another. Television may induce passivity, as Neil Postman has claimed.

Effects on children TV consumes an extraordinary part of children's lives, about 40 hours per week on average. Viewing is especially high among pre-adolescents, but it remains high among younger adolescents: time-budget studies suggest that among youngsters aged 9 to 14 television consumes as much time as all other discretionary activities combined, including playing, hobbies, clubs, outdoor activities, informal visiting, and just hanging out. The effects of television on childhood socialization have, of course, been hotly debated for more than three decades. The most reasonable conclusion from a welter of sometimes conflicting results appears to be that heavy television watching probably increases aggressiveness (although perhaps not actual violence), that it probably reduces school achievement, and that it is statistically associated with "psychosocial malfunctioning," although how much of this effect is self-selection and how much causal remains much debated. The evidence is, as I have said, not yet enough to convict, but the defense has a lot of explaining to do.

[...]

In an astonishingly prescient book, *Technologies without Borders*, published in 1991 after his death, Ithiel de Sola Pool concluded that the electronic revolution in communications technology was the first major technological advance in centuries that would have a profoundly decentralizing and fragmenting effect on society and culture. [...] This perspective invites us not merely to consider how technology is privatizing our lives – if, as it seems to me, it is – but to ask whether we like the result, and if not, what we might do about it. Those are questions we should, of course, be asking together, not alone.

Anthony Giddens, "The Third Way and Government"*

The traditional left, and many other social democrats too, tend to operate with an unreconstructed notion of the state. Their aim is to replace the market, as far as possible, with state power in order to realize social goals. Modernizing social democrats should argue for a different standpoint. In the wake of the receding influence of free-market philosophies, it is a fundamental task to revive public institutions. However, it won't do to identify public institutions solely with government and the state. Following the decline or collapse of the other 'ways', third way politics has to look for a different basis of social order.

Its point of view could be described as *structural pluralism*. The 'design options' offered by the two rival political positions were monistic – they looked either to government or to the market as the means of coordinating the social realm. Others have turned to the community or civil society as the ultimate sources of social cohesion. However, social order, democracy and social justice cannot be developed where one of these sets of institutions is dominant. A balance between them is required for a pluralistic society to be sustained. Moreover, each has to be looked at afresh in the light of contemporary social changes.

* Anthony Giddens, extracted from *The Third Way and Its Critics* (Polity Press, 2000), pp. 55–84.

One of the lessons to be learned from the fall of communism, and from the statist zeal of old-style social democracy, is that – even when applied to desirable social ends – state power can become stifling and bureaucratic. The neoliberal opponents of big government, as Offe says, 'must be granted the point that excessive statism often inculcates dispositions of dependency, inactivity, rent-seeking, red tape, clientelism, authoritarianism, cynicism, fiscal irresponsibility, avoidance of accountability, lack of initiative, and hostility to innovation, if not outright corruption – and so often on either side of the administration–client divide'.[7]

These considerations explain the emphasis the third way places on personal responsibility, as well as upon the transparency and reform of state mechanisms. As against the traditional left, it is emphasized that it isn't only the market that creates perverse or disruptive consequences for those exposed to it. Government and the state do so as well and – just like the market – call forth active responses. Welfare clients, for instance, do not simply 'accept' benefits given to them. They react actively and with discrimination to what is on offer, while state action changes their social environments in unpredictable ways. [...]

Obviously social democrats should not join with the free-marketeers in denigrating the state and all its works. Government and the state perform many tasks essential to any civilized society. The democratic left believed in the mixed economy, and therefore saw the state and markets in some sort of balance. Yet there is no doubt that in many countries the state, national and local, became too large and cumbersome. The inefficiency and wastefulness that state institutions frequently display provided fertile ground for the growth of neoliberalism and diminished the standing of the public sphere as a whole. As private companies downsized, adopted flatter hierarchies and sought to become more responsive to customer needs, the limitations of bureaucratic state institutions stood out in relief.

Acknowledging these developments does not imply arguing that governments have to adopt a diminished role in the world. Reform of the state can give government more influence than before rather than less. There is a difference between a *big state*, as measured by the number of its functionaries or the size of its budget, and a *strong state*. In any given circumstance, we can ask: will a marginal increase in the scope of the state improve

[7] Clause Offe, "The present historical transformation and some basic design options for social institutions." Paper presented at the seminar on "Society and Reform of the State," San Paulo, March 26–9, 1998, p. 7.

access of citizens to basic social and economic goods, or would a decrease actually serve these ends better?

The idea that the state should be reduced to a 'caretaker' capacity is plainly inadequate. The minimal state ideology ignores the limitations of markets just as thoroughly as the traditional left does the pathologies of the state. Government must play a basic role in sustaining the social and civic frameworks upon which markets actually depend. It is a fantasy, for example, to suppose that taxation can be reduced to a bare minimum and social order still be maintained, or economic prosperity created.

The reconstruction of public institutions, and confidence in their performance, is a first priority in contemporary societies. States have become inadequate in the provision of public goods, social protection, and civic order. The issue is not, as the critics seem to think, that the size of the state has fallen too far – on the contrary, in most societies it has stayed the same, or continued to grow. States can be simultaneously oversized *and* underperforming, and face legitimacy deficits as a result. But we need also to adjust government and state power to the exigencies of a globalizing era, with the changes in sovereignty this brings in its train. In addition, we have to address the requirements of governance that new risk situations bring about. These are mostly not 'traditional' demands, that can be met merely by providing further resources for existing state institutions.

Third way politics looks to transform government and the state – to make them as effective and quick on their feet as many sectors of business have now become. These aims have to be achieved through structural reform, not through turning state institutions into markets or quasi-markets. Many business firms have reformed themselves in recent years, but not by making themselves like markets. The most effective firms have debureaucratized, looked for the benchmarking of standards, and have accorded greater autonomy in decision-making to lower levels of the organization. Government should seek to achieve similar results within its own agencies.

It is quite untrue to say that the only way to breathe new life into public institutions is to privatize them, necessary though this sometimes may be. As an example, we can look at one such institution, the postal service in the country normally thought to be the home of privatized industry, the US. The US Post Service (USPS) had long been losing money – some $9 billion over two decades up to the mid-1990s. [...]

Yet in 1995 the service made one of the most remarkable turnarounds ever seen in any enterprise, moving from a loss of $800 million the previous year to a profit of $1.8 billion. Since then it has made substantial profits each year – the first time an increased profit had ever been made without postal price rises. The change was made by a thoroughgoing shake-up of the organization, designed to make every employee responsive to the needs of customers, with incentives for meeting stated aims. [...] Bureaucratic rules of procedure were dissolved in favour of devolved decision-making, responsive to client needs. Next-day delivery targets are now nearly always met, or exceeded.

The self-reform of government and the state needs not only to meet efficiency goals, but to respond to the voter apathy from which even the most established democratic states are suffering. In many countries, levels of trust in political leaders and other authority figures have declined, while the proportions voting in elections and expressing an interest in parliamentary politics have also dropped. [...]

Many people feel that government has become remote from their everyday lives and concerns. They believe that politics has become a corrupt affair, distant from the democratic ideals that supposedly inspire it. Neither worry is easily remedied, since in an era of globalization national politicians have less control over some of the influences affecting their citizens than they did.

However, reform of government and the mechanisms of the state can contribute to redressing the balance. In what has become an open information society, the established democracies are *not democratic enough*. What is needed is a second wave of democratization – or what I call the democratizing of democracy. The democratizing of democracy will require differing policies depending upon a country's history and its level of prior democratization. For many, it involves constitutional reform, the stripping away of archaic symbols and privileges, plus measures to introduce greater transparency and accountability. It is also likely to include 'experiments with democratization' such as the use of electronic referenda, revived forms of direct democracy and citizens' juries.

[...]

Communitarianism and government

Disenchantment with neoliberal policies, plus the problems of governability just referred to, were factors leading to the rise of communitarian thinking over recent years. According to communitarians, the consolidating of communities, and of civil society as a whole, are to overcome the social disintegration brought about by the dominance of the marketplace. The communitarians have had a direct and visible influence upon the New Democrats and New Labour, as well as upon social democratic parties elsewhere. Communitarianism represents a 'call to restore civic virtues' and 'to shore up the moral foundations of society'.[8]

In the communitarian view, a stable sense of self has to be anchored in a community – such as one's family of origin, or ethnic, religious or national communities. Communities are the source of the ethical values that make a wholesome civic life possible. In a general way, such a view is surely correct. Moreover, contrary to what is sometimes assumed, globalization creates favourable conditions for the renewal of communities. This is because globalization has a 'push-down' effect, promoting the local devolution of power and bottom-up community activism.

Communitarianism, however, has its problems, well established in the now extensive literature to which it has given rise. The term 'community' does too much work in communitarian theory: a society or a nation, for example, is only a community in an elliptical sense. Moreover, if they become too strong, communities breed identity politics, and with it the potential for social division, or even disintegration. Even in its milder forms, identity politics tends to be exclusivist, and difficult to reconcile with the principles of tolerance and diversity upon which an effective civil society depends. Hence it is to civil society more generally, rather than to 'the community', that we should turn as an essential element of third way politics.

Civil society is fundamental to constraining the power of both markets and government. Neither a market economy nor a democratic state can function effectively without the civilizing influence of civic association. [...]

The state and government do not represent the public domain when they become detached from their roots in civic association. The rule of law, the basic prerequisite of democratic government, can't exist without unwritten codes of civic trust. Civil society, rather than the state, supplies the grounding of citizenship, and is hence crucial to sustaining an open public sphere.

Third way politics and economic globalization

In the reform of state and government, as well as in economic policy, third way politics looks to respond to the great social transformations of the end of the twentieth century: globalization, the rise of the new knowledge-based economy, changes in everyday life, and the emergence of an active, reflexive citizenry. [...]

That economic globalization is real, and different from analogous processes in the past, has become increasingly difficult to dispute – whatever some of the critics might say.[9] This is most obviously true in the case of world currency markets. Average daily turnover on the global foreign exchange market has increased from $180 million twenty years ago to $1.5 trillion today. The total portfolio of cross-border holdings of bank deposits and loans grew from $1 billion in 1981 to $5.5 billion in 1996. These statistics represent more than just a very large increase in the volume of economic transactions. The basic character of the world economy has changed, partly because of the dominance of financial markets over trade in goods and commodities, and partly because of the ever-growing role of knowledge as a force of production.

[...]

The knowledge economy

The knowledge economy is not as yet all-conquering, but it is well on the way to being so. [...]

The dynamic sectors of the economy today are in finance, computers and software, telecommunications, biotechnology and the communications industries. The telecommunications industry in the US employs more people than the car and car-parts industries combined. Measured in terms of annual turnover, the health and medical industry in the US is bigger than oil refining, aircraft and car production, logging, steel and shipping put together.

[...]

Government will not be able to play an effective role in the new economy if it goes on the defensive. As the transformations noted above occur, citizens will need the help of government just as much as they used to; but state intervention has to be redirected, and cooperation with other agencies will be essential.

We could think of the influences involved as a triangle:

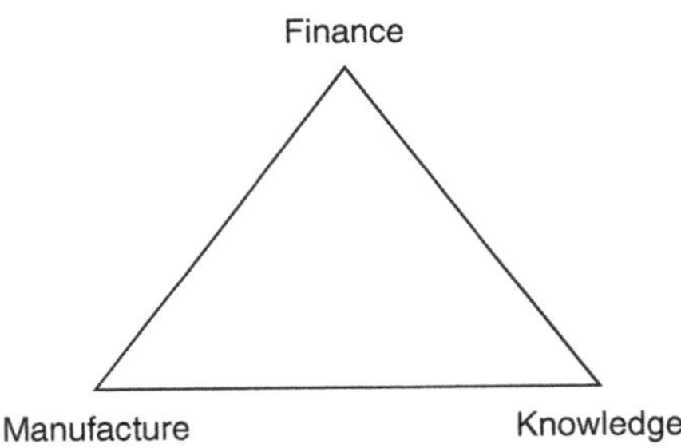

[8] Amitai Etzioni, *The Spirit of Community* (London: Fontana, 1995), p. 31.

[9] For the best account of this debate see David Held, Anthony McGrew, David Goldblatt and Jonathan Perraton, *Global Transformations: Politics, Economics and Culture* (Cambridge: Polity Press, 1999).

In the old economy, industrial manufacture was the dominant point of the triangle. Financial markets were geared to the needs of industrial production, although of course they always had a life of their own. In the globalizing economy, financial markets have much more autonomy – in effect, they scrutinize the efforts of producers. Knowledge is much less subservient to manufacture, since it becomes more and more the key to productivity. Financial markets grow increasingly diverse, driven as they are by the increasing complexity of available market knowledge. Control of manufacturing capital, the regulation of financial markets – these remain major tasks for left-of-centre governments. But the other point of the triangle becomes even more important. Government needs to build a 'knowledge base' that will release the full potential of the information economy.

Old-style social democracy concentrated on industrial policy and Keynesian demand measures, while the neoliberals focused on deregulation and market liberalization. Third way economic policy needs to concern itself with different priorities – with education, incentives, entrepreneurial culture, flexibility, devolution and the cultivation of social capital. Third way thinking emphasizes that a strong economy presumes a strong society, but doesn't see this connection as coming from old-style interventionism. The aim of macroeconomic policy is to keep inflation low, limit government borrowing, and use active supply-side measures to foster growth and high levels of employment.

The key force in human capital development obviously has to be education. It is the main public investment that can foster both economic efficiency and civic cohesion. Education isn't a static input into the knowledge economy, but is itself becoming transformed by it. It has traditionally been seen as a preparation for life – an attitude that persisted as it became more and more widely available. Primary school education became mandatory for everyone, then an extended period of secondary school education. Higher education expanded, taking on increasing numbers of students. But the underlying idea remained that of acquiring the qualifications needed to get a start in adulthood.

Education needs to be redefined to focus on capabilities that individuals will be able to develop through life. Orthodox schools and other educational institutions are likely to be surrounded, and to some extent subverted, by a diversity of other learning frameworks. Internet technology, for instance, might bring educational opportunities to mass audiences.

[...]

The question of flexibility

Product, capital and labour markets must all be flexible for an economy today to be competitive. 'Flexibility' for many is a red rag to a bull. Especially as applied to labour markets, flexibility implies deregulation, making workers more vulnerable to economic insecurity and expanding the numbers of in-work poor. Flexibility does indeed entail deregulation – getting rid of, or reshaping, rules and regulations that hamper innovation and technological change. Increasing flexibility can't be costless – trade-offs are involved. Yet it can't be stressed too strongly how high the social and personal costs are where there is large-scale unemployment, and especially where there are many long-term unemployed.

The statistics on job creation are instructive. In almost all industrial countries there are more jobs now than a quarter of a century ago. The sole exceptions are Sweden, Finland, and Spain. In the US 45% more net jobs were created over that period and in Canada almost as many. For Japan, the figure is 24%. In the EU countries, on the other hand, there was on average only a 4% growth in jobs. A high proportion – about half – of the new net jobs created in the US were in skilled or professional occupations. Contrary to some interpretations, those who have profited most, in relative terms, are women and ethnic minority groups, including Afro-Americans.

[...]

A statutory thirty-five-hour working week would seem to be the opposite of flexibility, but there are some signs that it is in fact helping to promote it. French employers are seeking to introduce shift working and weekend working, coupled with more part-time working, as means of adapting fruitfully to the directive. If these changes occur, the initiative could bear fruit. On the other hand, if it is applied rigidly, it is likely to block needed reforms rather than obviate the need for them.

Some leftist critics say that active labour market policies are essentially irrelevant, because the jobs have to be there in the first place. The most important mechanism of job creation is economic growth. But economic growth does not solve labour market problems on its own. Thus between 1984 and 1994 the EU countries had average growth rates of 2.3%, in spite of the negligible increase in the net number of new jobs.

[...]

Social capital

The cultivation of social capital is integral to the knowledge economy. The 'new individualism' that goes along with globalization is not refractory to cooperation and collaboration – cooperation (rather than hierarchy) is positively stimulated by it. Social capital refers to trust networks that individuals can draw upon for social support, just as financial capital can be drawn upon to be used for investment. Like financial capital, social capital can be expanded – invested and reinvested.

[...]

Innovation in the old economy was often the result of separate processes of research, development and production. In the knowledge-based economy, innovation stems more from networks and collaborative ventures. Firms are increasingly turning to networks of suppliers and customers to develop novel ideas and technologies. There were only 750 inter-firm alliances registered in the US during the 1970s. Between 1987 and 1992 there were 20,000. The range of industry ties with universities has also grown rapidly.

[...]

In the past, some on the left have viewed the 'third sector' (the voluntary sector) with suspicion. Government and other professional agencies should as far as possible take over from third-sector groups, which are often amateurish and dependent upon erratic charitable impulses. Developed in an effective manner, however, third-sector groups can offer choice and responsiveness in the delivery of public services. They can also help promote local civic culture and forms of community development.

[...]

Third-sector groups can also combine effectively with business to foster social programmes. Rosabeth Moss Kanter's work, based on comparative research carried out in different cities and regions of the US, is instructive in this respect. She found a number of companies, and groups of companies, becoming involved in social development in ways quite different from the past. Businesses have usually supported the social sector either by giving money to community activities or by contributing their employees' time for volunteer work. They have treated the third sector as a 'dumping ground' for 'spare cash, obsolete equipment and tired executives on their way out'.[10] Such philanthropy at arm's length has made little dent upon America's enduring social problems. The 'new paradigm', as Moss Kanter calls it, is quite different. It involves using social needs as a basis for the development of ideas, technologies and long-term investments. The firms concerned are using their best people and cutting-edge technologies.

An example is the programme begun by Bell Atlantic in the early 1990s, installing computer networks in schools. The company gave state-of-the-art computers to students to use at home, allowing them access to the network for interactive learning activities. Most of the students were from poor backgrounds, while the schools concerned were close to failing. The schools have since become national role models, while the company gained from the experience by discovering new ways of handling data transmission in the service of education.

Sceptical observers, Moss Kanter points out, are liable to see such endeavours simply as 'public relations ploys'. But, in the cases she studied, 'this would be an extremely costly and risky way to get a favourable press'. The primary justification 'is the new knowledge and capabilities that will stem from innovation'.

Conclusion

Reform of government and the state, a core theme of third way politics, is closely related to the economic changes signalled by the knowledge economy. In the contemporary world, contrary to what the neoliberals say, we need more government than before, not less. However, such government has to track the impact of globalization, and must stretch both below and above the level of the nation state. In an increasingly fast-moving world, government and the state also need to be quick on their feet, as well as democratic and transparent.

The economic interventions of government have to be different from those of the past. Those on the old left always say 'regulate, regulate', and greater regulation of economic life, in some respects and some contexts, is necessary. But deregulation can also be just as important, in areas where restrictions inhibit innovation, job creation or other basic economic goals. Government is not there only to constrain markets and technological change – it has just as significant a role in helping them work for the social good. To do so, it will often have to draw upon the resources of civil society; these resources are needed for effective governance too. [...]

Imam Khomeini, "Islamic Government"*

The subject of the governance of the faqih (*vilayat-faqih*[11]) provides us with the opportunity to discuss

[10] Rosabeth Moss Kanter, "From spare change to real change: the social sector as a site for business innovation." *Harvard Business Review*, 77, 3 (May–June 1999), pp. 122–32, 128.

* Imam Khomeini, extracted from *Islam and Revolution: Writings and Declarations of Imam Khomeini*, translated by Hamid Algar (Mizan Press, 1981).

[11] *Faqih*: one learned in the principles and ordinances of Islamic law, or more generally, in all aspects of the faith.

certain related matters and questions. The governance of the *faqih* is a subject that in itself elicits immediate assent and has little need of demonstration, for anyone who has some general awareness of the beliefs and ordinances of Islam will unhesitatingly give his assent to the principle of the governance of the *faqih* as soon as he encounters it; he will recognize it as necessary and self-evident. If little attention is paid to this principle today, so that it has come to require demonstration, it is because of the social circumstances prevailing among the Muslims in general, and in the teaching institution in particular. These circumstances, in turn, have certain historical roots to which I will now briefly refer.

From the very beginning, the historical movement of Islam has been to contend with the Jews, for it was they who first established anti-Islamic propaganda and engaged in various stratagems, and as you can see, this activity continues down to the present. Later they were joined by other groups, who were in certain respects more satanic than they. These new groups began their imperialist penetration of the Muslim countries about three hundred years ago, and they regarded it as necessary to work for the extirpation of Islam in order to attain their ultimate goals. It was not their aim to alienate the people from Islam in order to promote Christianity among them, for the imperialists really have no religious belief, Christian or Islamic. Rather, throughout this long historical period, and going back to the Crusades, they felt that the major obstacle in the path of their materialistic ambitions and the chief threat to their political power was nothing but Islam and its ordinances, and the belief of the people in Islam. They therefore plotted and campaigned against Islam by various means.

The preachers they planted in the religious teaching institution, the agents they employed in the universities, government educational institutions, and publishing houses, and the orientalists who work in the service of the imperialist states – all these people have pooled their energies in an effort to distort the principles of Islam. As a result, many persons, particularly the educated, have formed misguided and incorrect notions of Islam.

Islam is the religion of militant individuals who are committed to truth and justice. It is the religion of those who desire freedom and independence. It is the school of those who struggle against imperialism. But the servants of imperialism have presented Islam in a totally different light.

[...]

In order to demonstrate to some degree how great the difference is between Islam and what is presented as Islam, I would like to draw your attention to the difference between the Qur'an and the books of *hadith*,[12] on the one hand, and the practical treatises of jurisprudence, on the other. The Qur'an and the books of *hadith*, which represent the sources for the commands and ordinances of Islam, are completely different from the treatises written by the *mujtahids*[13] of the present age both in breadth of scope and in the effect they are capable of exerting on the life of society. The ratio of Qur'anic verses concerned with the affairs of society to those concerned with ritual worship is greater than a hundred to one. Of the approximately fifty sections of the corpus of *hadith* containing all the ordinances of Islam, not more than three or four sections relate to matters of ritual worship and the duties of man toward his Creator and Sustainer. A few more are concerned with questions of ethics, and all the rest are concerned with social, economic, legal, and political questions – in short, the gestation of society.

[...]

In just the same way that there are laws setting forth the duties of worship for man, so too there are laws, practices, and norms for the affairs of society and government. Islamic law is a progressive, evolving, and comprehensive system of law. All the voluminous books that have been compiled from the earliest times on different areas of law, such as judicial procedure, social transactions, penal law, retribution, international relations, regulations pertaining to peace and war, private and public law – taken together, these contain a mere sample of the laws and injunctions of Islam. There is not a single topic in human life for which Islam has not provided instruction and established a norm. ...

[...]

Islamic government does not correspond to any of the existing forms of government. For example, it is not a tyranny, where the head of state can deal arbitrarily with the property and lives of the people, making use of them as he wills, putting to death anyone he wishes, and enriching anyone he wishes by granting landed estates and distributing the property and holdings of the people. The Most Noble Messenger (peace be upon him), the Commander of the Faithful (peace be upon him), and the other caliphs did not have such powers. Islamic government is neither tyrannical nor absolute, but

12 *Hadith:* a tradition setting forth a saying or deed of the Prophet, or in Shi'i usage, of one of the Twelve Imams.

13 *Mujtahid:* an authority on divine law who practices *itihad*, that is, "the search for a correct opinion ... in the deducing of the specific provisions of the law from its principles and ordinances."

constitutional. It is not constitutional in the current sense of the word, i.e., based on the approval of laws in accordance with the opinion of the majority. It is constitutional in the sense that the rulers are subject to a certain set of conditions in governing and administering the country, conditions that are set forth in the Noble Qur'an and the Sunna of the Most Noble Messenger. It is the laws and ordinances of Islam comprising this set of conditions that must be observed and practiced. Islamic government may therefore be defined as the rule of divine law over men.

The fundamental difference between Islamic government, on the one hand, and constitutional monarchies and republics, on the other, is this: whereas the representatives of the people or the monarch in such regimes engage in legislation, in Islam the legislative power and competence to establish laws belongs exclusively to God Almighty. The Sacred Legislator of Islam is the sole legislative power. No one has the right to legislate and no law may be executed except the law of the Divine Legislator. It is for this reason that in an Islamic government, a simple planning body takes the place of the legislative assembly that is one of the three branches of government. This body draws up programs for the different ministries in the light of the ordinances of Islam and thereby determines how public services are to be provided across the country.

The body of Islamic laws that exist in the Qur'an and the Sunna has been accepted by the Muslims and recognized by them as worthy of obedience. This consent and acceptance facilitates the task of government and makes it truly belong to the people. In contrast, in a republic or a constitutional monarchy, most of those claiming to be representatives of the majority of the people will approve anything they wish as law and then impose it on the entire population.

Islamic government is a government of law. In this form of government, sovereignty belongs to God alone and law is His decree and command. The law of Islam, divine command, has absolute authority over all individuals and the Islamic government. Everyone, including the Most Noble Messenger (peace be upon him) and his successors, is subject to law and will remain so for all eternity – the law that has been revealed by God, Almighty and Exalted, and expounded by the tongue of the Qur'an and the Most Noble Messenger. If the Prophet assumed the task of divine viceregency upon earth, it was in accordance with the divine command. God, Almighty and Exalted, appointed him as His viceregent, "the viceregent of God upon earth"; he did not establish a government on his own initiative in order to be leader of the Muslims. Similarly, when it became apparent that disagreements would probably arise among the Muslims because their acquaintance with the faith was recent and limited, God Almighty charged the Prophet, by way of revelation, to clarify the question of succession immediately, there in the middle of the desert. Then the Most Noble Messenger (upon whom be peace) as his successor, in conformity and obedience to the law, not because he was his own son-in-law or had performed certain services, but because he was acting in obedience to God's law, as its executor.[14]

In Islam, then, government has the sense of adherence to law; it is law alone that rules over society. Even the limited powers given to the Most Noble Messenger (upon whom be peace) and those exercising rule after him have been conferred upon them by God. Whenever the Prophet expounded a certain matter or promulgated a certain injunction, he did so in obedience to divine law, a law that everyone without exception must obey and adhere to. Divine law obtains both for the leader and the led; the sole law that is valid and imperative to apply is the law of God. Obedience to the Prophet also takes place in accordance with divine decree, for God says: "And obey the Messengers" (Qur'an, 4:50). Obedience to those entrusted with authority is also on the basis of divine decree: "And obey the holders of authority from among you" (Qur'an, 4:50). Individual opinion, even if it be that of the Prophet himself, cannot intervene in matters of government or divine law; here, all are subject to the will of God.

Islamic government is not a form of monarchy, especially not an imperial system. In that type of government, the rulers are empowered over the property and persons of those they rule and may dispose of them entirely as they wish. Islam has not the slightest connection with this form and method of government. For this reason we find that in Islamic government, unlike monarchical and imperial regimes, there is not the slightest trace of vast palaces, opulent buildings, servants and retainers, private equerries, adjutants to their heir apparent, and all the other appurtenances of monarchy that consume as much as half of the national budget. You will know how the Prophet lived, the Prophet who was the head of the Islamic state and its ruler. The same mode of life was preserved by his successors until the beginning of the Umayyad period. [...] According to

[14] It is the belief of Shi'i Muslims that the Prophet appointed Imam 'Ali as his successor at a gathering near the pool of Khumm during his return to Medine from Mecca, after having performed the last pilgrimage in his life.

tradition, he once bought two tunics, and finding one of them better than the other, he gave the better one to his servant Qanbar. The other he kept for himself, and since its sleeves were too long for him, he tore off the extra portion. In this torn garment the ruler of a great, populous and prosperous realm clothed himself.

If this mode of conduct had been preserved, and government has retained its Islamic form, there would have been no monarchy and no empire, no usurpation of the lives and property of the people, no oppression and plunder, no encroachment on the public treasury, no vice and abomination. Most forms of corruption originate with the ruling class, the tyrannical ruling family and the libertines that associate with them. It is these rulers who establish centers of vice and corruption, who build centers of vice and wine-drinking, and spend the income of the religious endowments constructing cinemas.[15]

If it were not for these profligate royal ceremonies,[16] this reckless spending, this constant embezzlement, there would never be any deficit in the national budget forcing us to bow in submission before America and Britain and request aid or a loan from them. Our country has become needy on account of this reckless spending, this endless embezzlement, for are we lacking in oil? Do we have no minerals, no natural resources? We have everything, but this parasitism, this embezzlement, this profligacy – all at the expense of the people and the public treasury – have reduced us to a wretched state. Otherwise he [the Shah] would not need to go all the way to America and bow down before that ruffian's desk, begging for help.

[...]

The qualifications essential for the ruler derive directly from the nature and form of Islamic government. In addition to general qualifications like intelligence and administrative ability, there are two other essential qualifications: knowledge of the law and justice.

After the death of the Prophet (upon whom be peace), differences arose concerning the identity of the person who was to succeed him, but all the Muslims were in agreement that his successor should be someone knowledgeable and accomplished; there was disagreement only as to his identity.

Since Islamic government is a government of law, knowledge of the law is necessary for the ruler, as has been laid down in tradition. Indeed such knowledge is necessary not only for the ruler, but also for anyone holding a post or exercising some government function. The ruler, however, must surpass all others in knowledge. In laying claim to the Imamate, our Imams also argued that the ruler must be more learned than everyone else. The objections raised by the Shi'i *ulama* are also to the same effect. A certain person asked the caliph a point of law and he was unable to answer; he was therefore unfit for the position of leader and successor to the Prophet. Or again, a certain act he performed was contrary to the laws of Islam; hence he was unworthy of his high post.

Knowledge of the law and justice, then, constitute fundamental qualifications in the view of the Muslims. Other matters have no importance or relevance in this connection. Knowledge of the nature of the angels, for example, or of the attributes of the Creator, Exalted and Almighty, is of no relevance to the question of leadership. In the same vein, one who knows all the natural sciences, uncovers all the secrets of nature, or has a good knowledge of music does not thereby qualify for leadership or acquire any priority in the matter of exercising government over those who know the laws of Islam and are just. The sole matters relevant to rule, those that were mentioned and discussed in the time of the Most Noble Messenger (upon whom be peace) and our Imams (upon whom be peace) and were, in addition, unanimously accepted by the Muslims, are: (1) the knowledgeability of the ruler or caliph, i.e., his knowledge of the provisions and ordinances of Islam; and (2) his justice, i.e., his excellence in belief and morals.

[...]

Huge amounts of capital are being swallowed up; our public funds are being embezzled; our oil is being plundered; and our country is being turned into a market for expensive, unnecessary goods by the representatives of foreign companies, which makes it possible for foreign capitalists and their local agents to pocket the people's money. A number of foreign states carry off our oil after drawing it out of the ground, and the negligible sum they pay to the regime they have installed returns to their pockets by other routes. As for the small amount that goes into the treasury, God only knows what it is spent on. All of this is a form of "consumption of what is forbidden" that takes place on an enormous scale, in fact on an international scale. It is not merely an evil, but a hideous and most dangerous evil. Examine carefully the conditions of society and the actions of the government and its component

15 After the Revolution, extensive evidence came to light of misappropriation of the religious endowments. Land was being given to cabaret singers and members of the royal family by the state-controlled administration of the endowments. See the article on this subject in the Tehran daily *Kayhan*, Isfand 27, 1357/March 18, 1979.

16 A reference to the coronation ceremonies of 1967.

organs, and then you will understand what hideous "consumption of what is forbidden" is taking place now. If an earthquake occurs in some corner of the country, it too becomes a means for the ruling profiteers to increase their illegal income; they fill their pockets with the money that is supposed to go to the victims of the earthquake. Whenever our oppressive, anti-national rulers enter into agreements with foreign states or companies, they pocket huge amounts of our people's money and lavish additional huge sums on their foreign masters. It is a veritable flood of forbidden consumption that sweeps past up, right before our eyes. All this misappropriation of wealth goes on and on: in our foreign trade and in the contracts made for the exploitation of our mineral wealth, the utilization of our forests and other natural resources, construction work, road building, and the purchase of arms from the imperialists, both Western and communist.

We must end all this plundering and usurpation of wealth. The people as a whole have a responsibility in this respect, but the responsibility of the religious scholars is graver and more critical. We must take the lead over other Muslims in embarking on this sacred *jihad*, this heavy undertaking; because of our rank and position, we must be in the forefront. If we do not have the power today to prevent these misdeeds from happening and to punish these embezzlers and traitors, these powerful thieves that rule over us, then we must work to gain that power. At the same time, to fulfill our minimum obligation, we must not fail to expound the truth and expose the thievery and mendacity of our rulers. When we come to power, we will not only put the country's political life, economy, and administration back in order, we will also whip and chastise the thieves and the liars.

John Locke, "A Letter Concerning Toleration"*

The commonwealth seems to me to be a society of men constituted only for the procuring, preserving, and advancing their own civil interests.

Civil interests I call life, liberty, health, and indolency of body; and the possession of outward things, such as money, lands, houses, furniture, and the like.

It is the duty of the civil magistrate, by the impartial execution of equal laws, to secure unto all the people in general and to every one of his subjects in particular the just possession of these things belonging to this life. If anyone presume to violate the laws of public justice and equity, established for the preservation of those things, his presumption is to be checked by the fear of punishment, consisting of the deprivation or diminution of those civil interests, or goods, which otherwise he might and ought to enjoy. But seeing no man does willingly suffer himself to be punished by the deprivation of any part of his goods, and much less of his liberty or life, therefore, is the magistrate armed with the force and strength of all his subjects, in order to the punishment of those that violate any other man's rights.

Now that the whole jurisdiction of the magistrate reaches only to these civil concernments, and that all civil power, right and dominion, is bounded and confined to the only care of promoting these things; and that it neither can nor ought in any manner to be extended to the salvation of souls, these following considerations seem unto me abundantly to demonstrate.

First, because the care of souls is not committed to the civil magistrate, any more than to other men. It is not committed unto him, I say, by God; because it appears not that God has ever given any such authority to one man over another as to compel anyone to his religion. Nor can any such power be vested in the magistrate by the consent of the people, because no man can so far abandon the care of his own salvation as blindly to leave to the choice of any other, whether prince or subject, to prescribe to him what faith or worship he shall embrace. For no man can, if he would, conform his faith to the dictates of another. All the life and power of true religion consist in the inward and full persuasion of the mind; and faith is not faith without believing. Whatever profession we make, to whatever outward worship we conform, if we are not fully satisfied in our own mind that the one is true and the other well pleasing unto God, such profession and such practice, far from being any furtherance, are indeed great obstacles to our salvation. For in this manner, instead of expiating other sins by the exercise of religion, I say, in offering thus unto God Almighty such a worship as we esteem to be displeasing unto Him, we add unto the number of our other sins those also of hypocrisy and contempt of His Divine Majesty.

In the second place, the care of souls cannot belong to the civil magistrate, because his power consists only in outward force; but true and saving religion consists in the inward persuasion of the mind, without which nothing can be acceptable to God. And such is the nature of the

* John Locke, from the translation by William Popple, available at http://18th.eserver.org/toleration.txt, accessed April 27, 2008. "A Letter Concerning Toleration" was first published 1689.

understanding, that it cannot be compelled to the belief of anything by outward force. Confiscation of estate, imprisonment, torments, nothing of that nature can have any such efficacy as to make men change the inward judgement that they have framed of things.

It may indeed be alleged that the magistrate may make use of arguments, and, thereby; draw the heterodox into the way of truth, and procure their salvation. I grant it; but this is common to him with other men. In teaching, instructing, and redressing the erroneous by reason, he may certainly do what becomes any good man to do. Magistracy does not oblige him to put off either humanity or Christianity; but it is one thing to persuade, another to command; one thing to press with arguments, another with penalties. This civil power alone has a right to do; to the other, goodwill is authority enough. Every man has commission to admonish, exhort, convince another of error, and, by reasoning, to draw him into truth; but to give laws, receive obedience, and compel with the sword, belongs to none but the magistrate. And, upon this ground, I affirm that the magistrate's power extends not to the establishing of any articles of faith, or forms of worship, by the force of his laws. For laws are of no force at all without penalties, and penalties in this case are absolutely impertinent, because they are not proper to convince the mind. Neither the profession of any articles of faith, nor the conformity to any outward form of worship (as has been already said), can be available to the salvation of souls, unless the truth of the one and the acceptableness of the other unto God be thoroughly believed by those that so profess and practise. But penalties are no way capable to produce such belief. It is only light and evidence that can work a change in men's opinions; which light can in no manner proceed from corporal sufferings, or any other outward penalties.

In the third place, the care of the salvation of men's souls cannot belong to the magistrate; because, though the rigour of laws and the force of penalties were capable to convince and change men's minds, yet would not that help at all to the salvation of their souls. For there being but one truth, one way to heaven, what hope is there that more men would be led into it if they had no rule but the religion of the court and were put under the necessity to quit the light of their own reason, and oppose the dictates of their own consciences, and blindly to resign themselves up to the will of their governors and to the religion which either ignorance, ambition, or superstition had chanced to establish in the countries where they were born? In the variety and contradiction of opinions in religion, wherein the princes of the world are as much divided as in their secular interests, the narrow way would be much straitened; one country alone would be in the right, and all the rest of the world put under an obligation of following their princes in the ways that lead to destruction; and that which heightens the absurdity, and very ill suits the notion of a Deity, men would owe their eternal happiness or misery to the places of their nativity.

These considerations, to omit many others that might have been urged to the same purpose, seem unto me sufficient to conclude that all the power of civil government relates only to men's civil interests, is confined to the care of the things of this world, and hath nothing to do with the world to come.

Let us now consider what a church is. A church, then, I take to be a voluntary society of men, joining themselves together of their own accord in order to the public worshipping of God in such manner as they judge acceptable to Him, and effectual to the salvation of their souls.

[...]

The end of a religious society (as has already been said) is the public worship of God and, by means thereof, the acquisition of eternal life. All discipline ought, therefore, to tend to that end, and all ecclesiastical laws to be thereunto confined. Nothing ought nor can be transacted in this society relating to the possession of civil and worldly goods. No force is here to be made use of upon any occasion whatsoever. For force belongs wholly to the civil magistrate, and the possession of all outward goods is subject to his jurisdiction.

But, it may be asked, by what means then shall ecclesiastical laws be established, if they must be thus destitute of all compulsive power? I answer: they must be established by means suitable to the nature of such things, whereof the external profession and observation – if not proceeding from a thorough conviction and approbation of the mind – is altogether useless and unprofitable. The arms by which the members of this society are to be kept within their duty are exhortations, admonitions, and advices. If by these means the offenders will not be reclaimed, and the erroneous convinced, there remains nothing further to be done but that such stubborn and obstinate persons, who give no ground to hope for their reformation, should be cast out and separated from the society. This is the last and utmost force of ecclesiastical authority. No other punishment can thereby be inflicted than that, the relation ceasing between the body and the member which is cut off. The person so condemned ceases to be a part of that church.

Chapter 12

On Rulers

Introduction

Citizens of democratic communities typically believe that the most important political issues that they must decide involve which of the competing candidates and parties deserves their vote when elections are held. Such issues are no doubt important, but political theorists think questions about rulers run deeper. They involve questions about what type of people should govern and how rulers should be related to their subjects. Most political communities now stress their commitment to democratic norms and practices, but this commitment hardly settles these abstract questions about rulers. Do voters, their elected representatives, or perhaps certain unelected elites have the most power? Within nominal democracies, should citizens or representatives be more empowered? And what are the appropriate behaviors of both citizens and representatives in a democratic society?

But democracy is not the only reasonable answer to the question of who should govern. Throughout the ages, political philosophers have considered various alternatives to democracy – including monarchies, aristocracies, and other forms of elite rule. Most historians and political scientists have found very few democracies prior to the nineteenth century, and it is only the second and third waves of democratic transformations that have occurred since World War II that has produced a world where most countries are democracies (of some sort) and where allegiance to democracy is widespread. Robert Dahl, whose work we first encountered in Chapter 9, claims that the attractive alternatives to democracy can be reduced to a single vision: guardianship.

Guardianship is based on the premise that there are great inequalities in the capacity of various people to rule. At the top of a hierarchy of capabilities, one can envision a guardian class, just as Plato proposed in *The Republic*. Perhaps there exists a small group of people who have more wisdom than others (because in Platonic terms they have acquired an understanding of "the Good," or because in Leninist terms they form a "vanguard" that better understands the true interests of the proletariat than do the workers themselves). Perhaps this group also has superior technical competence, in that they – unlike most people – know best the means to attain good ends. Perhaps this group also has superior moral virtue in that they – again, unlike most people – do not seek political power to pursue their own interests but always aim for the common good and justice. Being ruled by guardians would seem very attractive, if people having such wisdom, technical competence, and moral virtue could be identified and trained, and if others lacked these qualities. There in fact have been impressive examples of guardian regimes – such as in Confucian China. Despite the case that can be made for guardianship, Dahl rejects this alternative to democracy (in chapters of his *Democracy and Its Critics* not included here).

One reason that guardianship seems unattractive is that – both in theory and practice – one of its defining features is that such rulers are not accountable to their subjects; after all, how could ordinary citizens – lacking wisdom, competence, and virtue – possibly stand in judgment of those possessing these qualities? Nevertheless, most people do not quite trust anyone to have and display at all times the qualities attributed to ideal guardians, and so they at least want to have opportunities to hold their leaders accountable. Requiring rulers to stand for reelection and giving citizens certain minimal political rights that enable their making reasonable collective judgments about the performance of their rulers are the minimal requirements of a (weak) democracy.

Perhaps the classic defense of this minimal conception of democracy was provided by Edmund Burke, the Irish statesman we encountered as a spokesman for traditional conservatism in Chapter 2. When seeking election to Parliament as a representative of Bristol, he told electors (that small group of citizens who had voting rights at that time) that, if elected, he would not pander to their views. He claimed that what a representative owed his constituents was limited to his exercising his best judgment about what served the interests of the nation as a whole in the long run; he rejected completely the notion that constituents could deliver mandates or instruct their representatives on how to vote in Parliament to secure their local interests. In short, Burke stressed that while he might be democratically accountable, he would act to the best of his ability as a guardian. The debate about whether representatives should act as "Burkean trustees" or as "instructed delegates" of the districts that elect them still rages.

During the 1830s, the French historian Alexis de Tocqueville (1805–59) observed a more populist version of democracy that was emerging in America. Democracy's most significant problem, according to Tocqueville, was its tendency towards becoming a "tyranny of the majority." Whether enacted in law or simply the dominant opinion in the country, the views of the majority "know no obstacle which can retard, much less halt, its progress and give it time to hear the wails of those it crushes as it passes." In short, in a populist democracy, the majority can abuse its power.

Respect for some of the virtues of guardianship and concern for some of the problems of popular rule led Joseph Schumpeter (1883–1950), who was educated as an economist in Austria and who taught for 20 years at Harvard University, to propose a reconceptualization of democracy. What he called "the classical conception" of democracy stressed that citizens themselves have certain capacities (principally the ability to know the common good and the virtue to pursue it) and that democratic processes enabled citizens either directly (by referendum) or indirectly (by selecting representatives) to enact and implement laws reflecting their collective judgments about the contents of the common good. After subjecting this classical conception to critical scrutiny, Schumpeter proposed another conception of democracy: it is a political system in which the role of the people is limited to producing a government. The democratic method involves citizens choosing in competitive elections among individuals or parties who seek political power. Democracy is nothing more – and nothing less – than this. In our selection from his most acclaimed book, *Capitalism, Socialism, and Democracy* (1942), he provides seven defenses for his "realistic" conception of democracy.

Many political scientists and citizens accept Schumpeter's model, but "strong" and "deliberative" democrats do not. Perhaps the most well-known advocate of strong democracy is Benjamin Barber, whose work we first encountered in Chapter 8. In the selection below, he criticizes representative democracy on several grounds, but the most important is epistemological; for Barber, there simply is no "independent ground" for political judgment other than strong democracy itself: a highly participatory process in which private individuals transform themselves into "free citizens" and their "private interests into public goods." Strong democracy does not emphasize consensus, as do such conceptions of democracy as those associated with Rousseau (whose unitary conception of the "general will" we encountered in Chapter 5). Instead, strong democracy is highly contentious. It seeks the widest possible expression of different views and transforms conflict into a tool for public thinking. Strong democracy is not so much a process by which communities reach political decisions as it is a process that enables citizens to be their own politicians and that creates "mutualism" within political communities, making them worthy of our allegiance.

Deliberative democracy is closely related to strong democracy – as Barber stresses the centrality of deliberation by citizens – but defenders of deliberative democracy seem more amenable to representation than Barber. Amy Gutmann (President of the University of Pennsylvania) and Dennis Thompson (Professor of Political Philosophy at Harvard University) summarize "what deliberative democracy means" in our next selection. Most generally, deliberative democracy requires of representatives that they justify their decisions in terms that are accessible to all citizens. The objective of deliberative democracy is not to reach some sort of academic consensus on the principles of government but to arrive at binding policy decisions; while consensus on such decisions is unlikely and indeed is not sought, the goal of deliberation is expressed by "the principle of economy of moral disagreement." Deliberation aims to minimize our differences with our opponents and offer them our mutual respect. One might conclude that deliberative democrats seek a "talk-centric" version of democratic engagement rather than a "vote-centric" version of democracy that simply tabulates people's pre-existing opinions and determines political outcomes on the basis of prevalent opinions.

This is a much more demanding conception of democracy than those that prevail. In everyday politics, people who think of themselves as strong democrats often refer to themselves as populists. They think democracy is a system that is responsive to "the will of the people," no matter the content or the basis of people's views. In a popular democracy, each citizen has a preference on issues, each citizen counts equally, and democracy is about counting votes to see which view is more popular; that view must prevail, else the system is not democratic. William Riker (1920–93), an American political scientist who was central in founding the influential "Rochester School" of positive political theory, maintains in our final selection in this chapter that this school has shown the inadequacies – indeed the impossibilities – of such a model of democracy. Even if we thought that pre-existing individual preferences were legitimate data for reaching democratic decisions – an idea which strong and deliberative democrats reject – there simply is no single fair and adequate procedure for aggregating individual preferences into a stable collective judgment. While the proof of this conclusion depends on fairly complex mathematical reasoning, the implications of social choice theory are fairly straightforward. Just as one problem with theocratic government is that – even though everyone might want to live in accordance with the Will of God – we have no satisfactory way of knowing precisely what is the Divine Will, so the problem of popular government is that – even though everyone might want to live in accordance with the popular will – we have no satisfactory way of determining what that is. Riker concludes that this problem with a populist conception of democracy means that the only surviving conception of democracy is the liberal one, which constrains rulers by the twin devices of constitutional limits on their powers and holding them accountable through elections. Perhaps. But does this mean that strong and deliberative democratic theorists have contributed little or nothing to the perennial question of who should rule?

Robert Dahl, "Guardianship"*

A perennial alternative to democracy is government by guardians. In this view, the notion that ordinary people can be counted on to understand and defend their own interests – much less the interests of the larger society – is preposterous. Ordinary people, these critics insist, are clearly not qualified to govern themselves. The assumption by democrats that ordinary people are qualified, they say, ought to be replaced by the opposing proposition that rulership should be entrusted to a minority of persons who are specially qualified to govern by reason of their superior knowledge and virtue.

Most beautifully and enduringly presented by Plato in *The Republic*,[1] the idea of guardianship has exerted a powerful pull throughout human history. Although a rudimentary democracy may well have existed for millennia among our ancestral hunter-gatherers, in recorded history hierarchy[2] is older than democracy. Both as an idea and as a practice, throughout recorded history hierarchy has been the rule, democracy the exception. Even in the later twentieth century, when lip service is all but universally given to the legitimacy of "rule by the people," only a minority of the countries of the world, and only a minority of the people of the world, are governed by regimes that might qualify as "democracies" in a modern sense. In practice, then, hierarchy is democracy's most formidable rival; and because the claim of guardianship is a standard justification

* Robert Dahl, extracted from *Democracy and Its Critics* (New Haven, CN: Yale University Press, 1989), pp. 52–64.

1 A minority of scholars argue that Plato really intended to show the impossibility of a regime like that described in *The Republic*. It is true that on close textual analysis Plato's argument is more ambiguous and complex than it appears to be on the surface. Here I assume one plausible interpretation and make no claim that it is the only reasonable interpretation.

2 I use the term here to include all forms of rule in which leaders exercise a very high degree of unilateral control over nonleaders: "Two pragmatic but not precise tests can be used to distinguish a hierarchical organization. Non-leaders cannot peacefully displace leaders after explicit or implicit voting; and leaders substantially decide when, in what conditions, and with whom consultation takes place" (Robert A. Dahl and Charles E. Lindblom, *Politics, Economics, and Welfare*, 2nd edition (Chicago: University of Chicago Press, 1976), p. 227.

for hierarchical rule, as an idea guardianship is democracy's most formidable rival.

One further point. Although the idea of guardianship is often used in its most vulgar form as a rationalization for corrupt, brutal, and inept authoritarian regimes of all kinds, the argument for it does not collapse simply because it has been badly abused. When we apply the same harsh test to democratic ideas, they too are often found wanting in practice. For both democracy and hierarchy, their worst failures are relevant to a judgment about these two alternatives. But so too are the more successful instances of each, as well as the relative feasibility and desirability of the ideal standards of democracy and guardianship.

Visions of guardianship

The idea of guardianship has appealed to a great variety of political thinkers and leaders in many different guises and in many different parts of the world over most of recorded history. If Plato provides the most familiar example, the practical ideal of Confucius, who was born more than a century before Plato, has had far more profound influence over many more people and persists to the present day, deeply embedded in the cultures of several countries, including China, where it offers a vigorous though not always overt competition to Marxism and Leninism for political consciousness. To mention Karl Marx and Nikolai Lenin is to remind us of another, perhaps more surprising version of guardianship: Lenin's doctrine of the vanguard party with its special knowledge of the laws of history and, as a consequence, its special, indeed its unique, claim to rule. […]

To Plato, political knowledge constituted the royal science, the supreme art: "No other art or science will have a prior or better right than in the royal science to care for human society and to rule over men in general" (*Statesman*, in *Dialogues* II, Jowett, trans., para. 276, p. 303). The essence of the art and science of politics is, of course, knowledge of the good of the community, the polis. Just as all men are not of equal excellence as physicians or pilots, so some are superior in their knowledge of the political art. And just as excellence as a physician or a pilot requires training, so too men and women must be carefully selected and rigorously trained in order to achieve excellence in the art and science of politics. The guardians must not only, like true philosophers, be completely devoted to the search for truth and, like true philosophers, discern more clearly than all others what is best for the community, but they must also be wholly dedicated to achieving that end and therefore must possess no interests of their own inconsistent with the good of the polis. Thus they would unite the truth seeking and knowledge of the true philosopher with the dedication of a true king or a true aristocracy – if such could exist – to the good of the community over which they rule.

Obviously rule by philosopher-kings would be unlikely to come about by chance. To create such a republic and the class of guardians to rule over it would require exceptional care, including, certainly, much attention to the selection and education of the guardians. Yet if such a republic were to come into existence, its citizens, recognizing the excellence of the rulers and their unswerving commitment to the good of the community, would give to it their support and loyalty. In this sense, in the language not of Plato but of modern democratic ideas, we could say that the government of the guardians would enjoy the consent of the governed.

[…]

While no single interpretation can do justice to the variations among the many different visions of guardianship, it is possible to construct an account that I think fully captures the essentials of the argument. In a discussion with a modern democrat, a contemporary advocate of guardianship might make a case along the following lines.

Three shared assumptions

ARISTOS: You're badly mistaken if you think that you and I begin from diametrically opposed assumptions. […] I'm quite willing to accept an assumption that I presume democrats like you believe is important to your case for democracy: that the interests of all human beings ought to be given equal consideration. […] In fact, what I want to argue is that only a body of highly qualified people – guardians, if you like – can reasonably be counted on to possess both the knowledge and virtue needed to serve the good of everyone subject to the laws.

DEMO: I'm beginning to see where your path will veer away from mine.

ARISTO: Before I show you why you really ought to join me on that path, I want to call your attention to still another assumption we both share. Though this may surprise you, you really *do* agree with me that the process of governing the state ought to be restricted to those who are qualified to govern. I know most democrats recoil from such an idea. You fear that by openly admitting to this assumption you'll give the game away at the start to those of us who support guardianship. Certainly in your democratic theory, philosophy, and argument this dangerous premise is rarely made explicit, precisely because it is so dangerous to your case. Yet I don't believe that any important political philosopher in the democratic tradition – Locke, Rousseau, Jeremy Bentham, James Mill, for example – has ever rejected it, though perhaps only John Stuart Mill made it fully explicit.[3] You know as well as I that your great advocates of democracy have always considered that a substantial proportion of persons are just unqualified to participate in governing. [...]

In all democratic countries, children are still excluded from full citizenship, as they always have been. Why? Because every grown-up knows that children are not qualified to govern. Surely you agree. Children are denied the rights of full citizenship simply and solely because they are unqualified. Their exclusion demonstrates conclusively that democratic theory and practice share with the theory and practice of guardianship the assumption that governing must be restricted to those who are qualified to govern.[4]

So the issue between us, my good friend, is the answer to the question posed by Plato: who *are* the best qualified to govern? Will the interests of ordinary folk best be protected by themselves, acting so far as they may be able through the democratic process, or by a body of meritorious leaders who possess exceptional knowledge and virtue?

[...]

Perhaps it would help to avoid confusion if you will let me make a distinction between what I mean by guardianship and what you just called meritocracy. Meritocracy, which is a pretty recent term, usually refers, as you suggested, to a body of officials selected exclusively by merit and competition but who are at least nominally subordinate to others – a cabinet, prime minister, president, legislature, and the like. Meritocracy in this sense might in principle be perfectly consistent with your idea of the democratic process, provided only that the authorities who control the bureaucracies are themselves subject to the democratic process. The experts in the bureaucracies, then, might be conceived of as indirect agents of the demos, just as the elected representatives might be seen as direct agents. I think this interpretation is a rather farfetched account of the real world, but once again let's assume it as a sort of theoretical model. "Meritocracy" then could refer to a bureaucracy based on merit that operates within a democratic regime, under the full control of elected leaders. But a meritocracy in this sense isn't at all what I mean by guardianship. Guardianship isn't a mere modification of a democratic regime; it's an alternative to democracy, a fundamentally different *kind* of regime. By guardianship I mean a regime in which the state is governed by meritorious rulers who consist of a minority of adults, quite likely a very small minority, *and who are not subject to the democratic process*. That's why I prefer to call the rulers by Plato's more evocative term "guardians."

The qualifications of the qualified

DEMO: I suppose the difference between us will now turn on what you mean by "qualified."

ARISTOS: No, I think we may agree on what we *mean* by "qualified." Where we're going to disagree is on *who* is qualified. You'll probably agree with me that in order to be qualified to govern – to be politically competent – people should possess three qualities. People who govern should have an adequate understanding of the proper ends, goals, or objectives that the government should strive to reach. Let me call this the quality of *moral understanding* or *moral capacity*. You exclude children from the demos because they lack the moral capacity to govern: they don't know what the government should do even to protect their own interests as children. In the same way, if ordinary people don't understand their own interests, you would have to concede that like children they are morally unqualified to govern themselves.

DEMO: But in my judgment most people understand their own interests better than your guardians are likely to!

ARISTO: A base and baseless dogma. But if you'll allow me, I'd like to proceed. Even if ordinary people adequately understood their own interests, they would

[3] On John Stuart Mill, see particularly Dennis Thompson, *John Stuart Mill and Representative Government* (Princeton: Princeton University Press, 1976).

[4] Conceivably, democrats might not entirely agree among themselves on a somewhat different issue: should persons who may not *now* be qualified nonetheless be admitted to full citizenship if it can be foreseen that participation may be necessary or sufficient for them to become qualified within some reasonable time? Depending on how democrats answer this question, they might also disagree on another. Suppose that members of some well-defined group are not now qualified, but *no other persons* can be safely counted on to protect their interests. What is the best solution? In his *Considerations on Representative Government* (1861), J. S. Mill implicitly acknowledged this dilemma but never quite confronted it. He chose instead to contend that qualifications must take precedence over the benefits of participation. Many contemporary democrats would find his solution unacceptable.

still not be fully qualified to govern. Since it would be utterly useless if people knew the right ends – whether their own interests or some other good – but failed to act to achieve them, those who govern should also possess a strong disposition actually to seek good ends. It's not enough to know what is best, or, like most modern philosophers and other academics, merely to talk about it. To be qualified to govern, rulers – whether guardians or the demos – must actively attempt to bring it about. This quality or disposition I like to call by an old name *virtue*. When moral understanding and virtue are combined in the same person, they make for *morally competent* rulers. But even moral competence is not sufficient: we all know what the road to Hell is paved with. Rulers should also know the best, most efficient, and most appropriate means to achieve desirable ends. In short, they ought to possess adequate *technical* or *instrumental knowledge*.[5]

No single one of these qualities, or even any pair, would be enough. All three are necessary. To be properly qualified to govern, I say, one should be both morally competent and instrumentally competent. In combination, then, the three qualities define *political competence*. I can't help thinking that you really agree with me about the need for political competence as a requirement for ruling, no matter whether the rulers are my guardians or your demos.

Demo: Not so fast! If I accept the assumptions so far, haven't I already conceded your case for guardianship?

Aristos: That may be so. But on what grounds can you reasonably reject the premises? Would you or anyone else argue that people who definitely lack political competence – children, for example – are nevertheless entitled to participate fully in governing this country? You democrats simply must confront the elementary implications of the undeniable fact that you choose deliberately to exclude children from the demos. If we agree that children aren't qualified to govern, even though they may someday become qualified, then no matter how uncomfortable it may be to acknowledge it, you have already accepted the premise that people who are definitely unqualified should not be permitted to participate fully in governing.

[...]

Demo: [...] I believe just the opposite is true: an adequate level of moral competence is widely distributed among human beings, and in any case no distinctively superior moral elite can be identified or safely entrusted with the power to rule over the rest. I think Jefferson and the philosophers of the Scottish Enlightenment were correct in holding that most human beings possess a fundamental sense of right and wrong that is not significantly stronger in some groups than in others. If anything, ordinary folk may often have a clearer judgment on elementary moral issues than their supposed superiors. Jefferson once wrote: "State a moral case to a ploughman and a professor. The former will decide it as well and often better than the latter because he has not been led astray by artificial rules" (quoted in Wills 1978, 203). [...]

Aristos: Aren't you greatly exaggerating the moral capacity of the average person? To begin with, many people seem to lack much understanding of their *own* basic needs, interests, or good, whichever you prefer. Isn't it a fact that very few people bother to reflect very deeply, if at all, as to what would constitute a good life? [...]

[...] Can you deny that a great many people – not children, mind you, but adults – are unable or unwilling to do whatever may be necessary to acquire an elementary understanding of their own needs, their own interests, their own good? If they don't even understand their own interests, aren't they, like children, incompetent to govern themselves?

And if they are incompetent to govern themselves, surely they are even less competent to govern others. Don't most people find it difficult, perhaps even impossible, to take the good of others – very many others, anyway – into account in making decisions? Their deficiency is partly in knowledge, partly in virtue. It is, heaven knows, often difficult in a world as complex as ours to know enough to judge accurately where your own interests lie. But it's infinitely more daunting to acquire an adequate understanding of the good of other people in your society.

[...]

In political life most of us lack the quality I've called virtue: we just aren't very strongly predisposed to act in behalf of the general good. That's why individual and group interests usually prevail over general interests in democratic countries.

So the question is this: if both knowledge and virtue are required for moral competence, and moral competence is required for political competence, are we really justified in believing that very many people are politically competent? And if they aren't, can they be qualified to govern? The clear answer seems to be no.

[5] These are essentially J. S. Mill's criteria. See the excellent discussion in Thompson's *John Stuart Mill and Representative Government* (1976), pp. 54ff.

DEMO: Even if I were prepared to grant all that you say (and I'm not) I still wouldn't conclude that guardianship would be better than democracy unless you could show me that your proposed guardians, whoever they may be, would definitely possess both the knowledge and the virtue that you contend most people lack. As to that, I am profoundly skeptical.

[...]

ARISTOS: Anyone who professes to believe that people are about equally well qualified to govern can't be much of a skeptic. But maybe I can overcome your doubts with some further observations. Consider technical knowledge for a moment. If it's problematic, to say the least, whether very many people possess the moral qualifications for ruling, their lack of technical competence seems to me undeniable. Today, most questions of public policy involve highly technical issues. I'm thinking partly about questions of obvious technicality like nuclear weapons and strategies, nuclear waste disposal, the regulation of recombinant DNA research, the desirability of a manned space program; I could go on and on with examples. But I also mean matters much closer to everyday life: health care and delivery, social security, unemployment, inflation, tax reform, crime, welfare programs ...

We who aren't experts on these matters could deal with them more intelligently if the experts agreed on technical solutions, or, failing that, if we could judge the comparative expertise of the experts. But experts don't agree, and we don't know how to evaluate the qualifications of the experts.

DEMO: But isn't that a fatal flaw in your argument? If the best-qualified experts disagree, why should we make them guardians? Incidentally, how would your guardians settle their disagreements – by majority rule?

ARISTOS: A nice debating point. But you mustn't assume that expert technicians are qualified to be guardians. Most of them probably aren't. The guardians would have to be carefully trained and carefully selected for their special qualities of knowledge and virtue. Plato devotes an extraordinary amount of attention in *The Republic* to the education of the guardians, and every serious advocate of guardianship since then has done likewise. Unlike the haphazard process of selecting leaders in your democratic system, recruiting and educating the future guardians is a central element in the idea of guardianship.

DEMO: But how would you go about that? Your solution gets more and more demanding. It's not for nothing that Plato's *Republic* is generally dismissed as a utopia.

[...]

ARISTOS: I don't think it's useful to draw up detailed blueprints, as utopian writers like to do. Your democratic systems weren't built from utopian blueprints. They were built by applying general principles and ideas to concrete historical situations. The guardians would of course be experts of a certain kind. They would be experts in the art of governing. They would be specialists whose specialization would give them superiority as rulers in comparison not only with ordinary people but also with other kinds of experts: economists, physicists, engineers, and so on.

[...]

In a well ordered society, just as some persons would receive the rigorous training and meritocratic selection essential to the art and science of the physician, so also others would be rigorously trained and selected to function well as rulers. Because rulership is so crucial – it has never been more so than today – nothing could be of greater importance than the education of our rulers, whether they are to be ordinary citizens in your democracy or specialized leaders in my system of guardianship.

[...]

DEMO: I must say, despite your disavowal of any intention to portray a utopia, like Plato you do begin to sound more and more utopian. Imperfect as they are, democracies really do exist. The idea of guardianship might be fine as a utopian fancy, but applying it to the real world is something else again. [...] Are there any good examples of guardianship?

ARISTOS: I was hoping you'd ask. A most impressive case is the Republic of Venice. It endured, though of course not unchanged, for about eight centuries. For sheer endurance that's worthy of the *Guinness Book of World Records*. It not only endured. As regimes go in the history of mankind, it has to be counted as exceptionally successful. [...] I could cite other examples, too, such as the Republic of Florence under the Medici in the fifteenth century, or even China during the periods of stability and prosperity under the rule of an emperor and a bureaucracy greatly influenced by Confucian ideas of meritocratic rule.

So you would be mistaken if you were to say that the ideal of guardianship is impossible of fulfillment in at least a reasonably satisfactory approximation, which is the most we can ask of political ideals.

Edmund Burke, "Speech to the Electors of Bristol"*

I am sorry I cannot conclude without saying a word on a topic touched upon by my worthy colleague. I wish that topic had been passed by at a time when I have so little leisure to discuss it. But since he has thought proper to throw it out, I owe you a clear explanation of my poor sentiments on that subject.

He tells you that 'the topic of instructions has occasioned much altercation and uneasiness in this city'; and he expresses himself (if I understand him rightly) in favour of the coercive authority of such instructions.

Certainly, Gentlemen, it ought to be the happiness and glory of a representative to live in the strictest union, the closest correspondence, and the most unreserved communication with his constituents. Their wishes ought to have great weight with him; their opinions high respect; their business unremitted attention. It is his duty to sacrifice his repose, his pleasure, his satisfactions, to theirs – and above all, ever, and in all cases, to prefer their interest to his own.

But his unbiased opinion, his mature judgment, his enlightened conscience, he ought not to sacrifice to you, to any man, or to any set of men living. These he does not derive from your pleasure – no, nor from the law and the Constitution. They are a trust from Providence, for the abuse of which he is deeply answerable. Your representative owes you, not his industry only, but his judgment; and he betrays, instead of serving you, if he sacrifices it to your opinion.

My worthy colleague says, his will ought to be subservient to yours. If that be all, the thing is innocent. If government were a matter of will upon any side, yours, without question, ought to be superior. But government and legislation are matters of reason and judgment, and not of inclination; and what sort of reason is that in which the determination precedes the discussion, in which one set of men deliberate and another decide, and where those who form the conclusion are perhaps three hundred miles distant from those who hear the arguments?

To deliver an opinion is the right of all men; that of constituents is a weighty and respectable opinion, which a representative ought always to rejoice to consider. But *authoritative* instructions, *mandates* issued, which the member is bound blindly and implicitly to obey, to vote, and to argue for, though contrary to the clearest convictions of his judgment and conscience – these are things utterly unknown to the laws of this land, and which arise from a fundamental mistake of the whole order and tenor of our Constitution.

Parliament is not a *congress* of ambassadors from different and hostile interests, which interests each must maintain, as an agent and advocate, against other agents and advocates; Parliament is a *deliberative* assembly of *one* nation, with *one* interest – that of the whole – where not local purposes, not local prejudices, ought to guide, but the general good, resulting from the general reason of the whole. You choose a member, indeed; but when you have chosen him, he is not member of Bristol, but he is a member of *Parliament*. If the local constituent should have an interest, or should form an hasty opinion evidently opposite to the real good of the rest of the community, the member for that place ought to be as far as any other from any endeavour to give it effect. I beg pardon for saying so much on this subject; I have been unwillingly drawn into it; but I shall ever use a respectable frankness of communication with you. Your faithful friend, your devoted servant, I shall be to the end of my life: a flatterer you do not wish for. On this point of instructions, however, I think it scarcely possible we ever can have any sort of difference. Perhaps I may give you too much, rather than too little trouble.

* Edmund Burke's "Speech to the Electors of Bristol" is available at www.ourcivilization.com/smartboard/shop/burkee/extracts/chap4.htm, accessed April 30, 2008. The speech was made on November 3, 1774.

Alexis de Tocqueville, "Unlimited Power of the Majority in the United States and Its Consequences"*

The very essence of democratic government consists in the absolute sovereignty of the majority; for there is nothing in democratic states which is capable of resisting it. Most of the American constitutions have sought to increase this natural strength of the majority by artificial means.

The legislature is, of all political institutions, the one which is most easily swayed by the will of the majority. The Americans determined that the members of the legislature should be elected by the people *directly*, and for a *very brief term*, in order to subject them, not only to

* Alexis de Tocqueville, extracted from *Democracy in America*, edited by J. P. Mayer and Max Lerner (New York: Harper & Row, 1966), pp. 227–35. Originally published 1835.

the general convictions, but even to the daily passions, of their constituents. The members of both houses are taken from the same classes in society, and nominated in the same manner; so that the movements of the legislative bodies are almost as rapid, and quite as irresistible, as those of a single assembly. It is to a legislature thus constituted, that almost all the authority of the government has been intrusted.

At the same time that the law increased the strength of those authorities which of themselves were strong, it enfeebled more and more those which were naturally weak. It deprived the representatives of the executive power of all stability and independence; and, by subjecting them completely to the caprices of the legislature, it robbed them of the slender influence which the nature of a democratic government might have allowed them to exercise. In several States, the judicial power was also submitted to the election of the majority; and in all of them, its existence was made to depend on the pleasure of the legislative authority, since the representatives were empowered annually to regulate the stipend of the judges.

Custom has done even more than law. A proceeding is becoming more and more general in the United States, which will, in the end, do away with the guaranties of representative government: it frequently happens that the voters, in electing a delegate, point out a certain line of conduct to him, and impose upon him certain positive obligations which he is pledged to fulfil. With the exception of the tumult, this comes to the same thing as if the majority itself held its deliberations in the market-place.

Several other circumstances concur to render the power of the majority in America not only preponderant, but irresistible. The moral authority of the majority is partly based upon the notion, that there is more intelligence and wisdom in a number of men united than in a single individual, and that the number of the legislators is more important than their quality. The theory of equality is thus applied to the intellects of men; and human pride is thus assailed in its last retreat by a doctrine which the minority hesitate to admit, and to which they will but slowly assent. Like all other powers, and perhaps more than any other, the authority of the many requires the sanction of time in order to appear legitimate. At first, it enforces obedience by constraint; and its laws are not *respected* until they have been long maintained.

The right of governing society, which the majority supposes itself to derive from its superior intelligence, was introduced into the United States by the first settlers; and this idea, which of itself would be sufficient to create a free nation, has now been amalgamated with the manners of the people and the minor incidents of social life.

The French, under the old monarchy, held it for a maxim that the king could do no wrong; and if he did do wrong, the blame was imputed to his advisers. This notion made obedience very easy; it enabled the subject to complain of the law, without ceasing to love and honor the lawgiver. The Americans entertain the same opinion with respect to the majority.

The moral power of the majority is founded upon yet another principle, which is, that the interests of the many are to be preferred to those of the few. It will readily be perceived that the respect here professed for the rights of the greater number must naturally increase or diminish according to the state of parties. When a nation is divided into several great irreconcilable interests, the privilege of the majority is often overlooked, because it is intolerable to comply with its demands.

If there existed in America a class of citizens whom the legislating majority sought to deprive of exclusive privileges which they had possessed for ages, and to bring down from an elevated station to the level of the multitude, it is probable that the minority would be less ready to submit to its laws. But as the United States were colonized by men holding equal rank, there is as yet no natural or permanent disagreement between the interests of its different inhabitants.

There are communities in which the members of the minority can never hope to draw over the majority to their side, because they must then give up the very point which is at issue between them. Thus, an aristocracy can never become a majority whilst it retains its exclusive privileges, and it cannot cede its privileges without ceasing to be an aristocracy.

In the United States, political questions cannot be taken up in so general and absolute a manner; and all parties are willing to recognize the rights of the majority, because they all hope at some time to be able to exercise them to their own advantage. The majority, therefore, in that country, exercise a prodigious actual authority, and a power of opinion which is nearly as great; no obstacles exist which can impede or even retard its progress, so as to make it heed the complaints of those whom it crushes upon its path. This state of things is harmful in itself, and dangerous for the future. …

[…]

A majority taken collectively is only an individual, whose opinions, and frequently whose interests, are opposed to those of another individual, who is styled a minority. If it be admitted that a man possessing absolute power may misuse that power by wronging his adversaries, why should not a majority be liable to the same reproach? Men do not change their characters by uniting with each other; nor does their patience in the presence of obstacles increase with their strength. For my own part, I cannot believe it; the power to do everything, which I should refuse to one of my equals, I will never grant to any number of them.

I do not think, for the sake of preserving liberty, it is possible to combine several principles in the same government so as really to oppose them to one another. The form of government which is usually termed *mixed* has always appeared to me a mere chimera. Accurately speaking, there is no such thing as a *mixed government*, in the sense usually given to that word, because, in all communities, some one principle of action may be discovered which preponderates over the others. England, in the last century, – which has been especially cited as an example of this sort of government, – was essentially an aristocratic state, although it comprised some great elements of democracy; for the laws and customs of the country were such that the aristocracy could not but preponderate in the long run, and direct public affairs according to its own will. The error arose from seeing the interests of the nobles perpetually contending with those of the people, without considering the issue of the contest, which was really the important point. When a community actually has a mixed government, – that is to say, when it is equally divided between adverse principles, – it must either experience a revolution, or fall into anarchy.

I am therefore of opinion, that social power superior to all others must always be placed somewhere; but I think that liberty is endangered when this power finds no obstacle which can retard its course, and give it time to moderate its own vehemence.

Unlimited power is in itself a bad and dangerous thing. Human beings are not competent to exercise it with discretion. God alone can be omnipotent, because his wisdom and his justice are always equal to his power. There is no power on earth so worthy of honor in itself, or clothed with rights so sacred, that I would admit its uncontrolled and all-predominant authority. When I see that the right and the means of absolute command are conferred on any power whatever, be it called a people or a king, an aristocracy or a democracy, a monarchy or a republic, I say there is the germ of tyranny, and I seek to live elsewhere, under other laws.

In my opinion, the main evil of the present democratic institutions of the United States does not arise, as is often asserted in Europe, from their weakness, but from their irresistible strength. I am not so much alarmed at the excessive liberty which reigns in that country, as at the inadequate securities which one finds there against tyranny.

When an individual or a party is wronged in the United States, to whom can he apply for redress? If to public opinion, public opinion constitutes the majority; if to the legislature, it represents the majority, and implicitly obeys it; if to the executive power, it is appointed by the majority, and serves as a passive tool in its hands. The public force consists of the majority under arms; the jury is the majority invested with the right of hearing judicial cases; and in certain States, even the judges are elected by the majority. However iniquitous or absurd the measure of which you complain, you must submit to it as well as you can.

If, on the other hand, a legislative power could be so constituted as to represent the majority without necessarily being the slave of its passions, an executive so as to retain a proper share of authority, and a judiciary so as to remain independent of the other two powers, a government would be formed which would still be democratic, without incurring hardly any risk of tyranny.

I do not say that there is a frequent use of tyranny in America, at the present day; but I maintain that there is no sure barrier against it, and that the causes which mitigate the government there are to be found in the circumstances and the manners of the country, more than in its laws.

[...]

Power exercised by the majority in America upon opinion

It is in the examination of the exercise of thought in the United States, that we clearly perceive how far the power of the majority surpasses all the powers with which we are acquainted in Europe. Thought is an invisible and subtile power, that mocks all the efforts of tyranny. At the present time, the most absolute monarchs in Europe cannot prevent certain opinions hostile to their authority from circulating in secret through their dominions, and even in their courts. It is not so in America; as long as the majority is still undecided, discussion is carried on; but as soon as its decision is irrevocably pronounced, every one is silent, and the friends as well as the opponents of the measure unite in assenting to its propriety. The reason of this is perfectly clear: no monarch is so absolute as to combine all the powers of society in his own hands, and to conquer all opposition, as a majority is able to do, which has the right both of making and of executing the laws.

The authority of a king is physical, and controls the actions of men without subduing their will. But the majority possesses a power which is physical and moral at the same time, which acts upon the will as much as upon the actions, and represses not only all contest, but all controversy.

I know of no country in which there is so little independence of mind and real freedom of discussion as in America. In any constitutional state in Europe, every sort of religious and political theory may be freely preached and disseminated; for there is no country in Europe so subdued by any single authority, as not to protect the man who raises his voice in the cause of truth from the consequences of his hardihood. If he is unfortunate enough to live under an absolute government, the people are often upon his side; if he inhabits a free country, he can, if necessary, find a shelter behind the throne. The aristocratic part of society supports him in some countries, and the democracy in others. But in a nation where democratic institutions exist, organized like those of the United States, there is but one authority, one element of strength and success, with nothing beyond it.

Joseph Schumpeter, "A Realistic Alternative to the Classical Doctrine of Democracy"*

I. The common good and the will of the people

The eighteenth-century philosophy of democracy may be couched in the following definition: the democratic method is that institutional arrangement for arriving at political decisions which realizes the common good by making the people itself decide issues through the election of individuals who are to assemble in order to carry out its will. Let us develop the implications of this.

It is held, then, that there exists a Common Good, the obvious beacon light of policy, which is always simple to define and which every normal person can be made to see by means of rational argument. There is hence no excuse for not seeing it and in fact no explanation for the presence of people who do not see it except ignorance – which can be removed – stupidity and anti-social interest. [...] Thus every member of the community, conscious of that goal, knowing his or her mind, discerning what is good and what is bad, takes part, actively and responsibly, in furthering the former and fighting the latter and all the members taken together control their public affairs.

It is true that the management of some of these affairs requires special aptitudes and techniques and will therefore have to be entrusted to specialists who have them. This does not affect the principle, however, because these specialists simply act in order to carry out the will of the people exactly as a doctor acts in order to carry out the will of the patient to get well. It is also true that in a community of any size, especially if it displays the phenomenon of division of labor, it would be highly inconvenient for every individual citizen to have to get into contact with all the other citizens on every issue in order to do his part in ruling or governing. It will be more convenient to reserve only the most important decisions for the individual citizens to pronounce upon – say by referendum – and to deal with the rest through a committee appointed by them – an assembly or parliament whose members will be elected by popular vote. This committee or body of delegates, as we have seen, will not represent the people in a legal sense but it will do so in a less technical one – it will voice, reflect or represent the will of the electorate. Again as a matter of convenience, this committee, being large, may resolve itself into smaller ones for the various departments of public affairs. Finally, among these smaller committees there will be a general-purpose committee, mainly for dealing with current administration, called cabinet or government, possibly with a general secretary or scapegoat at its head, a so-called prime minister.

As soon as we accept all the assumptions that are being made by this theory of the polity – or implied by it – democracy indeed acquires a perfectly unambiguous meaning and there is no problem in connection with it except how to bring it about. Moreover we need only forget a few logical qualms in order to be able to add that in this case the democratic arrangement would not only be the best of all conceivable ones, but that few people would care to consider any other. It is no less obvious however that these assumptions are so many statements of fact every one of which would have to be proved if we are to arrive at that conclusion. And it is much easier to disprove them.

There is, first, no such thing as a uniquely determined common good that all people could agree on or be made to agree on by the force of rational argument. This is due not primarily to the fact that some people may want

* Joseph Schumpeter, extracted from *Capitalism, Socialism, and Democracy* (New York: Harper & Row, 1942, 1950), pp. 250–72.

things other than the common good but to the much more fundamental fact that to different individuals and groups the common good is bound to mean different things. [...]

Secondly, even if a sufficiently definite common good – such as for instance the utilitarian's maximum of economic satisfaction – proved acceptable to all, this would not imply equally definite answers to individual issues. Opinions on these might differ to an extent important enough to produce most of the effects of "fundamental" dissension about ends themselves. [...]

But, third, as a consequence of both preceding propositions, the particular concept of the will of the people or the *volonté générale* that the utilitarians made their own vanishes into thin air. For that concept presupposes the existence of a uniquely determined common good discernible to all. Unlike the romanticists the utilitarians had no notion of that semi-mystic entity endowed with a will of its own – that "soul of the people" which the historical school of jurisprudence made so much of. They frankly derived their will of the people from the wills of individuals. And unless there is a center, the common good, toward which, in the long run at least, *all* individual wills gravitate, we shall not get that particular type of "natural" *volonté générale*. The utilitarian center of gravity, on the one hand, unifies individual wills, tends to weld them by means of rational discussion into the will of the people and, on the other hand, confers upon the latter the exclusive ethical dignity claimed by the classic democratic creed. *This creed does not consist simply in worshiping the will of the people as such* but rests on certain assumptions about the "natural" object of that will which object is sanctioned by utilitarian reason. Both the existence and the dignity of this kind of *volonté générale* are gone as soon as the idea of the common good fails us. And both the pillars of the classical doctrine inevitably crumble into dust.

[...]

In the realm of public affairs there are sectors that are more within the reach of the citizen's mind than others. This is true, first, of local affairs. Even there we find a reduced power of discerning facts, a reduced preparedness to act upon them, a reduced sense of responsibility. We all know the man – and a very good specimen he frequently is – who says that the local administration is not his business and callously shrugs his shoulders at practices which he would rather die than suffer in his own office. High-minded citizens in a hortatory mood who preach the responsibility of the individual voter or taxpayer invariably discover the fact that this voter does not feel responsible for what the local politicians do. Still, especially in communities not too big for personal contacts, local patriotism may be a very important factor in "making democracy work." Also, the problems of a town are in many respects akin to the problems of a manufacturing concern. The man who understands the latter also understands, to some extent, the former. The manufacturer, grocer or workman need not step out of his world to have a rationally defensible view (that may of course be right or wrong) on street cleaning or town halls.

Second, there are many national issues that concern individuals and groups so directly and unmistakably as to evoke volitions that are genuine and definite enough. The most important instance is afforded by issues involving immediate and personal pecuniary profit to individual voters and groups of voters, such as direct payments, protective duties, silver policies and so on. Experience that goes back to antiquity shows that by and large voters react promptly and rationally to any such chance. But the classical doctrine of democracy evidently stands to gain little from displays of rationality of this kind. Voters thereby prove themselves bad and indeed corrupt judges of such issues, and often they even prove themselves bad judges of their own long-run interests, for it is only the short-run promise that tells politically and only short-run rationality that asserts itself effectively.

However, when we move still farther away from the private concerns of the family and the business office into those regions of national and international affairs that lack a direct and unmistakable link with those private concerns, individual volition, command of facts and method of inference soon cease to fulfill the requirements of the classical doctrine. What strikes me most of all and seems to me to be the core of the trouble is the fact that the sense of reality is so completely lost. Normally, the great political questions take their place in the psychic economy of the typical citizen with those leisure-hour interests that have not attained the rank of hobbies, and with the subjects of irresponsible conversation. These things seem so far off; they are not at all like a business proposition; dangers may not materialize at all and if they should they may not prove so very serious; one feels oneself to be moving in a fictitious world.

This reduced sense of reality accounts not only for a reduced sense of responsibility but also for the absence of effective volition. One has one's phrases, of course, and one's wishes and daydreams and grumbles: especially, one has one's likes and dislikes. But ordinarily they do not amount to what we call a will – the psychic counterpart of purposeful responsible action. In fact, for the private citizen musing over national affairs there is no scope for such a will and no task at which it could develop. He is a member of an unworkable committee, the committee of the whole nation, and this is why he expends less disciplined effort on mastering a political problem than he expends on a game of bridge.

The reduced sense of responsibility and the absence of effective volition in turn explain the ordinary citizen's ignorance and lack of judgment in matters of domestic and foreign policy which are if anything more shocking in the case of educated people and of people who are successfully active in non-political walks of life than it is with uneducated people in humble stations. Information is plentiful and readily available. But this does not seem to make any difference. Nor should we wonder at it. We need only compare a lawyer's attitude to his brief and the same lawyer's attitude to the statements of political fact presented in his newspaper in order to see what is the matter. In the one case the lawyer has qualified for appreciating the relevance of his facts by years of purposeful labor done under the definite stimulus of interest in his professional competence; and under a stimulus that is no less powerful he then bends his acquirements, his intellect, his will to the contents of the brief. In the other case, he has not taken the trouble to qualify; he does not care to absorb the information or to apply to it the canons of criticism he knows so well how to handle; and he is impatient of long or complicated argument. All of this goes to show that without the initiative that comes from immediate responsibility, ignorance will persist in the face of masses of information however complete and correct. It persists even in the face of the meritorious efforts that are being made to go beyond presenting information and to teach the use of it by means of lectures, classes, discussion groups. Results are not zero. But they are small. People cannot be carried up the ladder.

Thus the typical citizen drops down to a lower level of mental performance as soon as he enters the political field. He argues and analyzes in a way which he would readily recognize as infantile within the sphere of his real interests. He becomes a primitive again. His thinking becomes associative and affective. And this entails two further consequences of ominous significance.

First, even if there were no political groups trying to influence him, the typical citizen would in political matters tend to yield to extra-rational or irrational prejudice and impulse. [...]

Second, however, the weaker the logical element in the processes of the public mind and the more complete the absence of rational criticism and of the rationalizing influence of personal experience and responsibility, the greater are the opportunities for groups with an ax to grind. [...] The only point that matters here is that, Human Nature in Politics being what it is, they are able to fashion and, within very wide limits, even to create the will of the people. What we are confronted with in the analysis of political processes is largely not a genuine but a manufactured will. And often this artefact is all that in reality corresponds to the *volonté générale* of the classical doctrine. So far as this is so, the will of the people is the product and not the motive power of the political process.

The ways in which issues and the popular will on any issue are being manufactured is exactly analogous to the ways of commercial advertising. We find the same attempts to contact the subconscious. We find the same technique of creating favorable and unfavorable associations which are the more effective the less rational they are. We find the same evasions and reticences and the same trick of producing opinion by reiterated assertion that is successful precisely to the extent to which it avoids rational argument and the danger of awakening the critical faculties of the people. And so on. Only, all these arts have infinitely more scope in the sphere of public affairs than they have in the sphere of private and professional life. The picture of the prettiest girl that ever lived will in the long run prove powerless to maintain the sales of a bad cigarette. There is no equally effective safeguard in the case of political decisions. Many decisions of fateful importance are of a nature that makes it impossible for the public to experiment with them at its leisure and at moderate cost. Even if that is possible, however, judgment is as a rule not so easy to arrive at as it is in the case of the cigarette, because effects are less easy to interpret.

[...]

Thus information and arguments that are really driven home are likely to be the servants of political intent. Since the first thing man will do for his ideal or interest is to lie, we shall expect, and as a matter of fact we find, that effective information is almost always adulterated or selective and that effective reasoning in politics consists mainly in trying to exalt certain propositions into axioms and to put others out of court; it thus reduces to the psycho-technics mentioned before. The reader who thinks me unduly pessimistic need only ask himself whether he has never heard – or said himself – that this or that awkward fact must not be told publicly, or that a certain line of reasoning, though valid, is undesirable. If men who according to any current standard are perfectly honorable or even high-minded reconcile themselves to the implications of this, do they not thereby show what they think about the merits or even the existence of the will of the people?

There are of course limits to all this. And there is truth in Jefferson's dictum that in the end the people are wiser than any single individual can be, or in Lincoln's about the impossibility of "fooling all the people all the time." But both dicta stress the long-run aspect in a highly significant way. It is no doubt possible to argue that given time the collective psyche will evolve opinions that not infrequently strike us as highly reasonable and even shrewd. History however consists of a succession of short-run situations that may alter the course of events for good. If all the people can in the short run be "fooled" step by step into something they do not really want, and if this is not an exceptional case which we could afford to neglect, then no amount of retrospective common sense will alter the fact that in reality they neither raise nor decide issues but that the issues that shape their fate are normally raised and decided for them. More than anyone else the lover of democracy has every reason to accept this fact and to clear his creed from the aspersion that it rests upon make-believe.

[...]

Another theory of democracy

Competition for political leadership [...] It will be remembered that our chief troubles about the classical theory centered in the proposition that "the people" hold a definite and rational opinion about every individual question and that they give effect to this opinion – in a democracy – by choosing "representatives" who will see to it that that opinion is carried out. Thus the selection of the representatives is made secondary to the primary purpose of the democratic arrangement which is to vest the power of deciding political issues in the electorate. Suppose we reverse the roles of these two elements and make the deciding of issues by the electorate secondary to the election of the men who are to do the deciding. To put it differently, we now take the view that the role of the people is to produce a government, or else an intermediate body which in turn will produce a national executive or government. And we define: the democratic method is that institutional arrangement for arriving at political decisions in which individuals acquire the power to decide by means of a competitive struggle for the people's vote.

Defense and explanation of this idea will speedily show that, as to both plausibility of assumptions and tenability of propositions, it greatly improves the theory of the democratic process.

First of all, we are provided with a reasonably efficient criterion by which to distinguish democratic governments from others. We have seen that the classical theory meets with difficulties on that score because both the will and the good of the people may be, and in many historical instances have been, served just as well or better by governments that cannot be described as democratic according to any accepted usage of the term. Now we are in a somewhat better position partly because we are resolved to stress a *modus procedendi* the presence or absence of which it is in most cases easy to verify.

For instance, a parliamentary monarchy like the English one fulfills the requirements of the democratic method because the monarch is practically constrained to appoint to cabinet office the same people as parliament would elect. A "constitutional" monarchy does not qualify to be called democratic because electorates and parliaments, while having all the other rights that electorates and parliaments have in parliamentary monarchies, lack the power to impose their choice as to the governing committee: the cabinet ministers are in this case servants of the monarch, in substance as well as in name, and can in principle be dismissed as well as appointed by him. Such an arrangement may satisfy the people. The electorate may reaffirm this fact by voting against any proposal for change. The monarch may be so popular as to be able to defeat any competition for the supreme office. But since no machinery is provided for making this competition effective the case does not come within our definition.

Second, the theory embodied in this definition leaves all the room we may wish to have for a proper recognition of the vital fact of leadership. The classical theory did not do this but, as we have seen, attributed to the electorate an altogether unrealistic degree of initiative which practically amounted to ignoring leadership. But collectives act almost exclusively by accepting leadership – this is the dominant mechanism of practically any collective action which is more than a reflex. Propositions about the working and the results of the democratic method that take account of this are bound to be infinitely more realistic than propositions which do not. They will not stop at the execution of a *volonté générale* but will go some way toward showing how it emerges or how it is substituted or faked. What we have termed Manufactured Will is no longer outside the theory, an aberration for the absence of which we piously pray; it enters on the ground floor as it should.

Third, however, so far as there are genuine group-wise volitions at all – for instance the will of the unemployed to receive unemployment benefit or the will of other groups to help – our theory does not neglect them. On the contrary we are now able to insert them in exactly the role they actually play. Such volitions do not as a rule assert themselves directly. Even if strong and definite they remain latent, often for decades, until they are called to life by some political leader who turns them into political factors. This he does, or else his agents do it for him, by organizing these volitions, by working them up and by including eventually appropriate items in his competitive offering. The interaction between sectional interests and public opinion and the way in which they produce the pattern we call the political situation appear from this angle in a new and much clearer light.

Fourth, our theory is of course no more definite than is the concept of competition for leadership. This concept presents similar difficulties as the concept of competition in the economic sphere, with which it may be usefully compared. In economic life competition is never completely lacking, but hardly ever is it perfect. Similarly, in political life there is always some competition, though perhaps only a potential one, for the allegiance of the people. To simplify matters we have restricted the kind of competition for leadership which is to define democracy, to free competition for a free vote. The justification for this is that democracy seems to imply a recognized method by which to conduct the competitive struggle, and that the electoral method is practically the only one available for communities of any size. But though this excludes many ways of securing leadership which should be excluded, such as competition by military insurrection, it does not exclude the cases that are strikingly analogous to the economic phenomena we label "unfair" or "fraudulent" competition or restraint of competition. And we cannot exclude them because if we did we should be left with a completely unrealistic ideal. Between this ideal case which does not exist and the cases in which all competition with the established leader is prevented by force, there is a continuous range of variation within which the democratic method of government shades off into the autocratic one by imperceptible steps. But if we wish to understand and not to philosophize, this is as it should be. The value of our criterion is not seriously impaired thereby.

Fifth, our theory seems to clarify the relation that subsists between democracy and individual freedom. If by the latter we mean the existence of a sphere of individual self-government the boundaries of which are historically variable – *no* society tolerates absolute freedom even of conscience and of speech, *no* society reduces that sphere to zero – the question clearly becomes a matter of degree. We have seen that the democratic method does not necessarily guarantee a greater amount of individual freedom than another political method would permit in similar circumstances. It may well be the other way round. But there is still a relation between the two. If, on principle at least, everyone is free to compete for political leadership by presenting himself to the electorate, this will in most cases though not in all mean a considerable amount of freedom of discussion *for all*. [...]

Sixth, it should be observed that in making it the primary function of the electorate to produce a government (directly or through an intermediate body) I intended to include in this phrase also the function of evicting it. The one means simply the acceptance of a leader or a group of leaders, the other means simply the withdrawal of this acceptance. This takes care of an element the reader may have missed. He may have thought that the electorate controls as well as installs. But since electorates normally do not control their political leaders in any way except by refusing to reelect them or the parliamentary majorities that support them, it seems well to reduce our ideas about this control in the way indicated by our definition. [...]

Seventh, our theory sheds much-needed light on an old controversy. Whoever accepts the classical doctrine of democracy and in consequence believes that the democratic method is to guarantee that issues be decided and policies framed according to the will of the people must be struck by the fact that, even if that will were undeniably real and definite, decision by simple majorities would in many cases distort it rather than give effect to it. Evidently the will of the majority is the will of the majority and not the will of "the people." The latter is a mosaic that the former completely fails to "represent."

Benjamin Barber, "Strong Democracy: Politics in the Participatory Mode"*

A well-known adage has it that under a representative government the voter is free only on the day he casts his ballot. Yet even this act may be of dubious consequence in a system where citizens use the franchise only to select an executive or judicial or legislative elite that in turn exercises every other duty of civic importance.

* Benjamin Barber, extracted from *Strong Democracy* (Berkeley: University of California Press, 1984), pp. 145–55.

To exercise the franchise is unhappily also to renounce it. The representative principle steals from individuals the ultimate responsibility for their values, beliefs, and actions. And it is far less hospitable to such primary Western values as freedom, equality, and social justice than weak democrats might wish.

Representation is incompatible with freedom because it delegates and thus alienates political will at the cost of genuine self-government and autonomy. As Rousseau warned, "The instant a people allows itself to be represented it loses its freedom."[6] Freedom and citizenship are correlates; each sustains and gives life to the other. Men and women who are not directly responsible through common deliberation, common decision, and common action for the policies that determine their common lives are not really free at all, however much they enjoy security, private rights, and freedom from interference.

Representation is incompatible with equality because, in the astute words of the nineteenth-century French Catholic writer Louis Veuillot, "when I vote my equality falls into the box with my ballot – they disappear together."[7] Equality, construed exclusively in terms of abstract personhood or of legal and electoral equity, omits the crucial economic and social determinants that shape its real-life incarnation. In the absence of community, equality is a fiction that not merely divides as easily as it unites but that raises the specter of a mass society made up of indistinguishable consumer clones.

Representation, finally, is incompatible with social justice because it encroaches on the personal autonomy and self-sufficiency that every political order demands, because it impairs the community's ability to function as a regulating instrument of justice, and because it precludes the evolution of a participating public in which the idea of justice might take root.[8]

Freedom, equality, and justice are in fact all *political* values that depend for their theoretical coherence and their practical efficacy on self-government and citizenship. They cannot be apprehended or practiced except in the setting of citizenship. They are not coterminous with the condition of politics, they are aspects of a satisfactory response to the condition of politics. They cannot be externally defined and then appropriated for political use; rather, they must be generated and conditioned by politics.

This point relates directly to the problem of the independent ground. In each of the three versions of weak democracy, the banished independent ground (in whose place a mode of politics is supposed to operate) is covertly reintroduced in the guise of such notions as noblesse oblige (the wisdom of an authoritative elite), or the free market (the absolute autonomy of the individual as an irrefutable premise of pluralist market and contract relations). Yet the definition of the political condition developed above would suggest that it is precisely such notions as "wisdom," "rights," and "freedom" that need to be given meaning and significance within the setting of democratic politics. These terms and others like them are essentially contestable: their meaning is subject to controversy at a fundamental level and cannot be discovered by abstract reasoning or by an appeal to external authority.[9] This is why they become the focus of discourse in democratic politics: they do not define but are defined by politics.

Representative democracy suffers, then, both from its reliance on the representative principle and from its vulnerability to seduction by an illicit rationalism – from the illusion that metaphysics can establish the meaning of debatable political terms. By permitting, even encouraging, the reintroduction of independent grounds, representative modes of democracy subvert the very political process that was supposed to meet and overcome the absence of such grounds. By subordinating the will and judgment of citizens to abstract norms about which there can be no real consensus, these modes demean citizenship itself and diminish correspondingly the capacities of a people to govern itself. And by allowing heteronomous notions of right to creep into the

6 Jean Jacques Rousseau, *The Social Contract*, book 3, chapter 15. A later philosopher writing in the same vein insists upon "the logical impossibility of the 'representative' system." Since "the will of the people is not transferable, nor even the will of the single individual, the first appearance of professional leadership marks the beginning of the end" (Robert Michels, *Political Parties: A Sociological Study of the Oligarchical Tendencies of Modern Democracy* [Glencoe, IL: Free Press, 1915; reprinted, 1949], pp. 33–4).

7 Cited by Michels, *Political Parties*, p. 39; my translation.

8 Court-ordered busing programs, which are "right" by every legal standard, nonetheless manage to remedy the effects of public prejudice only by destroying public responsibility and activity in a realm (schooling) that is traditionally associated with vigorous neighborhood civic activity. Here the principle of right collides with the principle of participation, and the damage done to the latter imperils, in the long run, the possibility of sustaining the former by democratic means.

9 The idea of "essential contestability," first developed in a philosophical setting by W. B. Gallie, has been given an illuminating political context by William Connolly in *The Terms of Political Discourse* (Lexington, MA: Heath, 1974).

politics of self-legislation, they fatally undermine the autonomy on which all real political freedom depends. Citizens become subject to laws they did not truly participate in making; they become the passive constituents of representatives who, far from reconstituting the citizens' aims and interests, usurp their civic functions and deflect their civic energies.

To the extent that these criticisms apply, thin democracy is not very democratic, nor even convincingly political. For all the talk about politics in Western democratic regimes, it is hard to find in all the daily activities of bureaucratic administration, judicial legislation, executive leadership, and party policy-making anything that resembles citizen engagement in the creation of civic communities and in the forging of public ends. Politics has become what politicians do; what citizens do (when they do anything) is vote for the politicians.

Two alternative forms of democracy seem to hold out some hope that these difficulties can be alleviated through the activation of citizenship and community. The first, which I call *unitary democracy*, is motivated by the need for consensus but ultimately betrays the democratic impulse – particularly when it is separated from the small-scale institutions out of which it arose. The second, *strong democracy*, seems able to remedy a number of the shortcomings of weak democracy without falling prey to the excesses of unitary democracy. It is the argument of this book that the strong form of democracy is the only form that is genuinely and completely democratic. It may also be the only one capable of preserving and advancing the political form of human freedom in a modern world that grows ever more hostile to traditional liberal democracy.

Unitary democracy The unitary form of democracy is defined by politics in the consensual mode and seems at first glance to eschew representation (if not politics itself) in pursuit of its central norm, unity. It calls for all divisive issues to be settled unanimously through the organic will of a homogeneous or even monolithic community – often identified symbolically as a race or nation or people or communal will.

[...]

In larger settings, however, where the community becomes an impersonal abstraction and individuals relate anonymously and anomically with masses of strangers, unitary democracy can turn malevolent, can be perilous to freedom and citizenship and ruinous to democracy.

[...]

As I have suggested, whether the consensual community is large and abstract (as in the case of fascism in its pure, national form) or small and face-to-face (as in the case of the homogeneous eighteenth-century New England town or the rural Swiss commune) will determine whether unitary democracy becomes vicious or merely irrelevant.[10] But in neither case is it consistently participatory (since it undermines self-legislation) or genuinely political (since it "wills" away conflict). For the identification of individual with collectivity – which permits a government in the unitary mode to speak not only for but *as* "The People" – conceals and obscures the representative relationship that actually obtains between citizens and governing organs. Moreover, the symbolic collectivity denoted by such abstract terms as *the nation* or *the Aryan Race* or *the communal will* – since it is no longer circumscribed by the actual wills (or choices) of individual citizens acting in concert – usually turns out to be a cipher for some surreptitious set of substantive norms. It turns out, in other words, to be camouflage for the reintroduction of independent grounds, a stalking horse for Truth in the midst of politics, a Trojan Horse carrying Philosophers, Legislators, and other seekers of Absolute Certainty into the very inner sanctum of democracy's citadel. And so, in the place where we expect finally to hear the voices of active citizens determining their own common destiny through discourse and deliberation, we hear instead the banished voice of hubris, of would-be-truth and of could-be-right, which were unable to get a hearing on their own merits. Had they done so, the occasion for politics, democratic or otherwise, would never have arisen.

Thus does the promise of unitary democracy fade: unable to escape weak democracy's dependency on representation and the covert independent ground, it adds to them all the grave risks of monism, conformism, and coercive consensualism. No wonder that liberal democrats cringe at the prospect of "benevolent" direct democratic alternatives. With the perils of unitary democracy in mind, they justifiably fear the remedy for representation more than its ills.

The central question for the future of democracy thus becomes: is there an alternative to liberal democracy that does not resort to the subterfuges of unitary democracy? In the absence of a safe alternative, it is the better part of prudence to stick by the representative forms of democracy, deficiencies and all.

10 Even in such benign settings as the Vermont town meeting or an urban crisis cooperative, direct democracy can be problematic. See for example Jane J. Mansbridge's sociologically astute study *Beyond Adversary Democracy* (New York: Basic Books, 1980).

Strong democracy: politics in the participatory mode

The future of democracy lies with strong democracy – with the revitalization of a form of community that is not collectivistic, a form of public reasoning that is not conformist, and a set of civic institutions that is compatible with modern society. Strong democracy is defined by politics in the participatory mode: literally, it is self-government by citizens rather than representative government in the name of citizens. Active citizens govern themselves directly here, not necessarily at every level and in every instance, but frequently enough and in particular when basic policies are being decided and when significant power is being deployed. Self-government is carried on through institutions designed to facilitate ongoing civic participation in agenda-setting, deliberation, legislation, and policy implementation (in the form of "common work"). Strong democracy does not place endless faith in the capacity of individuals to govern themselves, but it affirms with Machiavelli that the multitude will on the whole be as wise as or even wiser than princes and with Theodore Roosevelt that "the majority of the plain people will day in and day out make fewer mistakes in governing themselves than any smaller body of men will make in trying to govern them."[11]

Considered as a response to the dilemmas of the political condition, strong democracy can be given the following formal definition: *strong democracy in the participatory mode resolves conflict in the absence of an independent ground through a participatory process of ongoing, proximate self-legislation and the creation of a political community capable of transforming dependent private individuals into free citizens and partial and private interests into public goods.*

The crucial terms in this strong formulation of democracy are *activity, process, self-legislation, creation,* and *transformation.* Where weak democracy eliminates conflict (the anarchist disposition), represses it (the realist disposition), or tolerates it (the minimalist disposition), strong democracy *transforms conflict.* It turns dissensus into an occasion for mutualism and private interest into an epistemological tool of public thinking.

Participatory politics deals with public disputes and conflicts of interest by subjecting them to a never-ending process of deliberation, decision, and action. Each step in the process is a flexible part of ongoing procedures that are embedded in concrete historical conditions and in social and economic actualities. In place of the search for a prepolitical independent ground or for an immutable rational plan, strong democracy relies on participation in an evolving problem-solving community that creates public ends where there were none before by means of its own activity and of its own existence as a focal point of the quest for mutual solutions. In such communities, public ends are neither extrapolated from absolutes nor "discovered" in a preexisting "hidden consensus." They are literally forged through the act of public participation, created through common deliberation and common action and the effect that deliberation and action have on interests, which change shape and direction when subjected to these participatory processes.

Strong democracy, then, seems potentially capable of transcending the limitations of representation and the reliance on surreptitious independent grounds without giving up such defining democratic values as liberty, equality, and social justice. Indeed, these values take on richer and fuller meanings than they can ever have in the instrumentalist setting of liberal democracy. For the strong democratic solution to the political condition issues out of a self-sustaining dialectic of participatory civic activity and continuous community-building in which freedom and equality are nourished and given political being. Community grows out of participation and at the same time makes participation possible; civic activity educates individuals how to think publicly as citizens even as citizenship informs civic activity with the required sense of publicness and justice. Politics becomes its own university, citizenship its own training ground, and participation its own tutor. Freedom is what comes out of this process, not what goes into it. Liberal and representative modes of democracy make politics an activity of specialists and experts whose only distinctive qualification, however, turns out to be simply that they engage in politics – that they encounter others in a setting that requires action and where they have to find a way to act in concert. Strong democracy is the politics of amateurs, where every man is compelled to encounter every other man without the intermediary of expertise.

This universality of participation – every citizen his own politician – is essential, because the "Other" is a construct that becomes real to an individual only when

[11] "The People are wiser and more constant than Princes," writes Machiavelli in his *Discourses on Livy*, book 1, chapter 58. Roosevelt is cited in R. A. Allen, "The National Initiative Proposal: A Preliminary Analysis," *Nebraska Law Review*, 58, 4 (1979), p. 1011.

he encounters it directly in the political arena. He may confront it as an obstacle or approach it as an ally, but it is an inescapable reality in the way of and on the way to common decision and common action. *We* also remains an abstraction when individuals are represented either by politicians or as symbolic wholes. The term acquires a sense of concreteness and simple reality only when individuals redefine themselves as citizens and come together directly to resolve a conflict or achieve a purpose or implement a decision. Strong democracy creates the very citizens it depends upon *because* it depends upon them, because it permits the representation neither of *me* nor of *we*, because it mandates a permanent confrontation between the *me* as citizen and the "Other" as citizen, forcing *us* to think in common and act in common. The citizen is by definition a *we*-thinker, and to think of the *we* is always to transform how interests are perceived and goods defined.

This progression suggests how intimate the ties are that bind participation to community. Citizenship is not a mask to be assumed or shed at will. It lacks the self-conscious mutability of a modern social "role" as Goffman might construe it. In strong democratic politics, participation is a way of defining the self, just as citizenship is a way of living. The old liberal notion, shared even by radical democrats such as Tom Paine, was that a society is "composed of distinct, unconnected individuals [who are] continually meeting, crossing, uniting, opposing, and separating from each other, as accident, interest, and circumstances shall direct."[12] Such a conception repeats the Hobbesian error of setting participation and civic activity apart from community. Yet participation without community, participation in the face of deracination, participation by victims or bondsmen or clients or subjects, participation that is uninformed by an evolving idea of a "public" and unconcerned with the nurturing of self-responsibility, participation that is fragmentary, part-time, half-hearted, or impetuous – these are all finally sham, and their failure proves nothing.

It has in fact become a habit of the shrewder defenders of representative democracy to chide participationists and communitarians with the argument that enlarged public participation in politics produces no great results. Once empowered, the masses do little more than push private interests, pursue selfish ambitions, and bargain for personal gain, the liberal critics assert. Such participation is the work of prudent beasts and is often less efficient than the ministrations of representatives who have a better sense of the public's appetites than does the public itself. But such a course in truth merely gives the people all the insignia and none of the tools of citizenship and then convicts them of incompetence. Social scientists and political elites have all too often indulged themselves in this form of hypocrisy. They throw referenda at the people without providing adequate information, full debate, or prudent insulation from money and media pressures and then pillory them for their lack of judgment. They overwhelm the people with the least tractable problems of mass society – busing, inflation, tax structures, nuclear safety, right-to-work legislation, industrial waste disposal, environmental protection (all of which the representative elites themselves have utterly failed to deal with) – and then carp at their uncertainty or indecisiveness or the simple-mindedness with which they muddle through to a decision. But what general would shove rifles into the hands of civilians, hurry them off to battle, and then call them cowards when they are overrun by the enemy?

Strong democracy is not government by "the people" or government by "the masses," because a people are not yet a citizenry and masses are only nominal freemen who do not in fact govern themselves. Nor is participation to be understood as random activity by maverick cattle caught up in the same stampede or as minnow-school movement by clones who wiggle in unison. As with so many central political terms, the idea of participation has an intrinsically normative dimension – a dimension that is circumscribed by citizenship. Masses make noise, citizens deliberate; masses behave, citizens act; masses collide and intersect, citizens engage, share, and contribute. At the moment when "masses" start deliberating, acting, sharing, and contributing, they cease to be masses and become citizens. Only then do they "participate."

Or, to come at it from the other direction, to be a citizen *is* to participate in a certain conscious fashion that presumes awareness of and engagement in activity with others. This consciousness alters attitudes and lends to participation that sense of the *we* I have associated with community. To participate *is* to create a community that governs itself, and to create a self-governing community *is* to participate. Indeed, from the perspective of strong democracy, the two terms *participation* and *community* are aspects of one single mode of social being: citizenship. Community without participation first breeds unreflected consensus and uniformity, then

12 Tom Paine, "Dissertation on First Principles of Government," in *Writings*, edited by N. D. Conway (New York: G. P. Putnam's Sons, 1894–1896, 8 vols.), vol. 3, p. 268.

nourishes coercive conformity, and finally engenders unitary collectivism of a kind that stifles citizenship and the autonomy on which political activity depends. Participation without community breeds mindless enterprise and undirected, competitive interest-mongering. Community without participation merely rationalizes collectivism, giving it an aura of legitimacy. Participation without community merely rationalizes individualism, giving it the aura of democracy.

This is not to say that the dialectic between participation and community is easily institutionalized. Individual civic activity (participation) and the public association formed through civic activity (the community) call up two strikingly different worlds. The former is the world of autonomy, individualism, and agency; the latter is the world of sociability, community, and interaction. The world views of individualism and communalism remain at odds; and institutions that can facilitate the search for common ends without sabotaging the individuality of the searchers, and that can acknowledge pluralism and conflict as starting points of the political process without abdicating the quest for a world of common ends, may be much more difficult to come by than a pretty paragraph about the dialectical interplay between individual participation and community. Yet it is just this dialectical balance that strong democracy claims to strike.

Amy Gutmann and Dennis Thompson, "What Deliberative Democracy Means"*

To go to war is the most consequential decision a nation can make. Yet most nations, even most democracies, have ceded much of the power to make that decision to their chief executives – to their presidents and prime ministers. Legislators are rarely asked or permitted to issue declarations of war. The decision to go to war, it would seem, is unfriendly territory for pursuing the kind of reasoned argument that characterizes political deliberation.

Yet when President George W. Bush announced that the United States would soon take military action against Saddam Hussein, he and his advisors recognized the need to justify the decision not only to the American people but also to the world community. Beginning in October 2002, the administration found itself engaged in argument with the US Congress and, later, with the United Nations. During the months of preparation for the war, Bush and his colleagues, in many different forums and at many different times, sought to make the case for a preventive war against Iraq. Saddam Hussein, they said, was a threat to the United States because he had or could soon have weapons of mass destruction, and had supported terrorists who might have struck again against the United States. Further, he had tyrannized his own people and destabilized the Middle East.

In Congress and in the United Nations, critics responded, concurring with the judgment that Hussein was a terrible tyrant but challenging the administration on all its arguments in favor of going to war before exhausting the nonmilitary actions that might have controlled the threat. As the debate proceeded, it became clear that almost no one disagreed with the view that the world would be better off if Saddam Hussein no longer ruled in Iraq, but many doubted that he posed an imminent threat, and many questioned whether he actually supported the terrorists who had attacked or were likely to attack the United States.

This debate did not represent the kind of discussion that deliberative democrats hope for, and the deliberation was cut short once US troops began their invasion in March 2003. [...]

The imperfect deliberation that preceded the war prepared the ground for the less imperfect deliberation that followed.

Thus even in a less than friendly environment, deliberative democracy makes an appearance, and with some effect. Both the advocates and the foes of the war acted as if they recognized an obligation to justify their views to their fellow citizens. (That their motives were political or partisan is less important than that their actions were responsive to this obligation.) This problematic episode can help us discern the defining characteristics of deliberative democracy if we attend to both the presence and the absence of those characteristics in the debate about the war.

What is deliberative democracy?

Most fundamentally, deliberative democracy affirms the need to justify decisions made by citizens and their representatives. Both are expected to justify the laws they would impose on one another. In a democracy, leaders should therefore give reasons for their decisions, and respond to the reasons that citizens give in return.

* Amy Gutmann and Dennis Thompson, extracted from *Why Deliberative Democracy?* (Princeton University Press, 2004), pp. 1–21.

But not all issues, all the time, require deliberation. Deliberative democracy makes room for many other forms of decision-making (including bargaining among groups, and secret operations ordered by executives), as long as the use of these forms themselves is justified at some point in a deliberative process. Its first and most important characteristic, then, is its *reason-giving* requirement.

The reasons that deliberative democracy asks citizens and their representatives to give should appeal to principles that individuals who are trying to find fair terms of cooperation cannot reasonably reject. The reasons are neither merely procedural ("because the majority favors the war") nor purely substantive ("because the war promotes the national interest or world peace"). They are reasons that should be accepted by free and equal persons seeking fair terms of cooperation.

[...]

A second characteristic of deliberative democracy is that the reasons given in this process should be *accessible* to all the citizens to whom they are addressed. To justify imposing their will on you, your fellow citizens must give reasons that are comprehensible to you. If you seek to impose your will on them, you owe them no less. This form of reciprocity means that the reasons must be public in two senses. First, the deliberation itself must take place in public, not merely in the privacy of one's mind. In this respect deliberative democracy stands in contrast to Rousseau's conception of democracy, in which individuals reflect on their own on what is right for the society as a whole, and then come to the assembly and vote in accordance with the general will.[13]

The other sense in which the reasons must be public concerns their content. A deliberative justification does not even get started if those to whom it is addressed cannot understand its essential content. It would not be acceptable, for example, to appeal only to the authority of revelation, whether divine or secular in nature. Most of the arguments for going to war against Iraq appealed to evidence and beliefs that almost anyone could assess. Although President Bush implied that he thought God was on his side, he did not rest his argument on any special instructions from his heavenly ally (who may or may not have joined the coalition of the willing).

[...]

The third characteristic of deliberative democracy is that its process aims at producing a decision that is *binding* for some period of time. In this respect the deliberative process is not like a talk show or an academic seminar. The participants do not argue for argument's sake; they do not argue even for truth's own sake (although the truthfulness of their arguments is a deliberative virtue because it is a necessary aim in justifying their decision). They intend their discussion to influence a decision the government will make, or a process that will affect how future decisions are made. At some point, the deliberation temporarily ceases, and the leaders make a decision. The president orders troops into battle, the legislature passes the law, or citizens vote for their representatives. Deliberation about the decision to go to war in Iraq went on for a long period of time, longer than most preparations for war. Some believed that it should have gone on longer (to give the UN inspectors time to complete their task). But at some point the president had to decide whether to proceed or not. Once he decided, deliberation about the question of whether to go to war ceased.

Yet deliberation about a seemingly similar but significantly different question continued: was the original decision justified? Those who challenged the justification for the war of course did not think they could undo the original decision. They were trying to cast doubt on the competence or judgment of the current administration. They were also trying to influence future decisions – to press for involving the United Nations and other nations in the reconstruction effort, or simply to weaken Bush's prospects for reelection.

This continuation of debate illustrates the fourth characteristic of deliberative democracy – its process is *dynamic*. Although deliberation aims at a justifiable decision, it does not presuppose that the decision at hand will in fact be justified, let alone that a justification today will suffice for the indefinite future. It keeps open the possibility of a continuing dialogue, one in which citizens can criticize previous decisions and move ahead on the basis of that criticism. Although a decision must stand for some period of time, it is provisional in the sense that it must be open to challenge at some point in the future. [...]

13 Jean Jacques Rousseau, *Du contrat social*, in *Political Writings*, vol. II, edited by C. E. Vaughan (Cambridge: Cambridge University Press, 1915), Bk. II, ch. 3; Bk. IV, ch. 1. Rousseau worried that if citizens were to come together in the assembly to discuss what the general will should be, they would be tempted to make compromises, and perhaps even form factions which by their nature do not express the general will. A modern, less extreme version of this view (which does not rule out public deliberation) is developed by Robert Goodin, who argues for what he calls "deliberation within," not because he fears factional politics but because he thinks any other kind of deliberation is impractical in large-scale democracies [*Reflective Democracy* (Oxford: Oxford University Press, 2003)].

Deliberative democrats care as much about what happens after a decision is made as about what happens before. Keeping the decision-making process open in this way – recognizing that its results are provisional – is important for two reasons. First, in politics as in much of practical life, decision-making processes and the human understanding upon which they depend are imperfect. We therefore cannot be sure that the decisions we make today will be correct tomorrow, and even the decisions that appear most sound at the time may appear less justifiable in light of later evidence. Even in the case of those that are irreversible, like the decision to attack Iraq, reappraisals can lead to different choices later than were planned initially. Second, in politics most decisions are not consensual. Those citizens and representatives who disagreed with the original decision are more likely to accept it if they believe they have a chance to reverse or modify it in the future. And they are more likely to be able to do so if they have a chance to keep making arguments.

One important implication of this dynamic feature of deliberative democracy is that the continuing debate it requires should observe what we call the principle of the economy of moral disagreement. In giving reasons for their decisions, citizens and their representatives should try to find justifications that minimize their differences with their opponents. Deliberative democrats do not expect deliberation always or even usually to yield agreement. How citizens deal with the disagreement that is endemic in political life should therefore be a central question in any democracy. Practicing the economy of moral disagreement promotes the value of mutual respect (which is at the core of deliberative democracy). By economizing on their disagreements, citizens and their representatives can continue to work together to find common ground, if not on the policies that produced the disagreement, then on related policies about which they stand a greater chance of finding agreement. Cooperation on the reconstruction of Iraq does not require that the parties at home and abroad agree about the correctness of the original decision to go to war. Questioning the patriotism of critics of the war, or opposing the defense expenditures that are necessary to support the troops, does not promote an economy of moral disagreement.

Combining these four characteristics, we can define deliberative democracy as a form of government in which free and equal citizens (and their representatives), justify decisions in a process in which they give one another reasons that are mutually acceptable and generally accessible, with the aim of reaching conclusions that are binding in the present on all citizens but open to challenge in the future.[14] This definition obviously leaves open a number of questions. [...]

How democratic is deliberation?

[...]

In the early modern period, deliberation was more explicitly contrasted with democracy. When the term "deliberative" was first used to refer to political discussion (evidently as early as 1489), it referred to discussion within a small and exclusive group of political leaders. By the eighteenth century, deliberation was part of a defense of political representation that pointedly resisted appeals to popular opinion. Edmund Burke's "Speech to the electors of Bristol," which declared that "Parliament is a deliberative assembly," is famously a defense of a trustee conception of representation that today seems more aristocratic than democratic.[15]

[...]

More than any other theorist, Jürgen Habermas is responsible for reviving the idea of deliberation in our time, and giving it a more thoroughly democratic foundation. His deliberative politics is firmly grounded in the idea of popular sovereignty.[16] The fundamental source of legitimacy is the collective judgment of the people. This is to be found not in the expression of an unmediated popular will, but in a disciplined set of practices defined by the deliberative ideal. [...]

But here the point to keep in mind is that the democratic element in deliberative democracy should turn

14 Although this definition is intended to capture what we believe to be the essential characteristics of deliberative democracy, deliberative democrats disagree among themselves about many of its features. For a recent sample of the disputes and other conceptions, see James Bohman and William Rehg, eds., *Deliberative Democracy* (Cambridge, MA: MIT Press, 1997); Jon Elster, *Deliberative Democracy* (Cambridge: Cambridge University Press, 1998); Stephen Macedo, ed., *Deliberative Politics* (Oxford: Oxford University Press, 1999); John Dryzek, *Deliberative Democracy and Beyond* (Oxford: Oxford University Press, 2000); David Estlund, ed., *Democracy* (Oxford: Blackwell, 2002); and Frank Cunningham, *Theories of Democracy* (London and New York: Routledge, 2002), pp. 163–83.

15 Edmund Burke, *Burke's Politics*, in R. Hoffman and P. Levack, eds. (New York: Knopf, 1959), p. 115.

16 Jürgen Habermas, *Between Facts and Norms: Contributions to a Discourse Theory of Law and Democracy* (Cambridge, MA: MIT Press, 1996). Also see his "Discourse Ethics," in *Moral Consciousness and Communicative Action*, translated by Christian Lenhardt and Shierry Weber Nicholsen (Cambridge, MA: MIT Press, 1993), p. 94.

not on how purely procedural the conception is but on how fully inclusive the process is. While deliberation is now happily married to democracy – and Habermas deserves much of the credit for making the match – the bond that holds the partners together is not pure proceduralism. What makes deliberative democracy democratic is an expansive definition of who is included in the process of deliberation – an inclusive answer to the questions of who has the right (and effective opportunity) to deliberate or choose the deliberators, and to whom do the deliberators owe their justifications. In this respect, the traditional tests of democratic inclusion, applied to deliberation itself, constitute the primary criterion of the extent to which deliberation is democratic. [...]

William Riker, "Liberalism, Populism, and the Theory of Public Choice"*

The process of compounding individual choices into a social choice does not inspire confidence in the quality of majorities or similar amalgamations for decision. I will now summarize the conclusions of the previous chapters, setting forth the difficulties with amalgamation.

Conclusion 1. If there are more than two alternatives on any issue – as is almost always the case for any reasonably free, open, and fair political system – then there exist a wide variety of methods by which the values of members may be incorporated into the social decision. [...]

The difference in methods would not occasion much difficulty for democratic theory if one method were clearly technically or morally superior to others. Yet this is not the case. A good argument can be made for the fairness or efficiency or both of most of the majoritarian or positional methods and even of the utilitarian methods – which is indeed why methods in each category have been invented and recommended. The difference among the methods is simply that they are fair or efficient in different ways because they embody different ethical principles. Unfortunately, there seems to be no way to show that one such ethical principle is morally superior to another. Consequently, there is no fundamental reason of prudence or morality for preferring the amalgamation produced by one method to the amalgamation produced by another.

[...]

Conclusion 2. Suppose, however, that the people in a society have decided to use a particular method of voting and to define as fair the outcomes produced by that method. Because of the revelations from Arrow's theorem, from Gibbard's and Satterthwaite's theorems, and from Black and Newing's and Plott's and McKelvey's and Schofield's notions of equilibrium and related developments, there is no reason to suppose that one profile of individual values will always produce the same outcome with that method. Consequently, the alternative outcomes by a particular method on a particular profile cannot be said to be a fair or true amalgamation, even though the method itself is assumed to be fair. In that sense, we never know what an outcome means, whether it is a true expression of public opinion or not. Every reasonably fair method of voting can be manipulated in several ways. Since we cannot know whether manipulation has occurred, the truth and meaning of *all* outcomes is thereby rendered dubious.

One method of manipulation is strategic voting, wherein voters vote contrary to their true tastes in order to bring about an outcome more desirable than the outcome from voting truthfully. [...] It is possible, even probable, that strategic voting is commonplace in the real world, as evidenced by the frequency of allegations of, for example, vote-trading. If so, then *all* voting is rendered uninterpretable and meaningless. Manipulated outcomes are meaningless because they are manipulated, and unmanipulated outcomes are meaningless because they cannot be distinguished from manipulated ones.

[...]

This, then, is the second conclusion: outcomes of any particular method of voting lack meaning because often they are manipulated amalgamations rather than fair and true amalgamations of voters' judgments and because we can never know for certain whether an amalgamation has in fact been manipulated.

[...]

What does this conclusion imply for the two views of voting in democracy? Can either populism or liberalism stand up?

Clearly populism cannot survive. The essence of populism is this pair of propositions:

1 What the people, as a corporate entity, want ought to be social policy.
2 The people are free when their wishes are law.

* William Riker, extracted from *Liberalism Against Populism* (W. H. Freeman, 1982), pp. 233–53.

[...]

Populism as a moral imperative depends on the existence of a popular will discovered by voting. But if voting does not discover or reveal a will, then the moral imperative evaporates because there is nothing to be commanded. If the people speak in meaningless tongues, they cannot utter the law that makes them free. Populism fails, therefore, not because it is morally wrong, but merely because it is empty.

In the history of political ideas, a similar rejection of a moral imperative on the ground that it was uninterpretable occurred in the sixteenth and seventeenth centuries when religious directives on politics lost their presumed clarity. So long as the spiritual authority of the pope was unquestioned, he could state the political content of moral and divine law. With the success of the Reformation, however, there were many conflicting voices speaking for God, no one of which was more clearly vested with divine quality than another. Thus, even though no one seriously questioned the existence of the Divinity or the authority of divine direction of human politics, the direction nevertheless failed simply because no one could be sure what the Divinity said. Modern secular political thought begins with that uncertainty. Similarly I believe that in the next generation populist claims will be rejected simply because it will be realized that, however desirable they might be, they are based on a flawed technique that renders populism unworkable.

[...]

Given that social choice theory reveals populism to be inconsistent and absurd, how does the liberal interpretation of voting fare? For democracy, this is a crucial question. Since populism and liberalism, as I have defined them, exhaust the possibilities and since populism must be rejected, then, if liberalism cannot survive, democracy is indefensible. Fortunately, liberalism survives, although in a curious and convoluted way. Liberalism does not demand much from voting, and hence the restrictions placed on the justification of voting by social choice theory do not quite render the liberal ideal unattainable.

The essence of the liberal interpretation of voting is the notion that voting permits the rejection of candidates or officials who have offended so many voters that they cannot win an election. This is, of course, a negative ideal. It does *not* require that voting produce a clear, consistent, meaningful statement of the popular will. It requires only that voting produce a decisive result: that this official or this party is retained in office or rejected. This very restricted expectation about voting can, I believe, easily coexist with all the defects we have observed in the voting mechanism. If so, then liberalism survives.

[...]

Madison was correct, I believe, in his assertion that constitutional limits preserve liberal democracy. Fortunately the limits he helped provide retain most of their original force. Yet in the American political tradition there has always been a strong strand of populism, usually expressed as the notion that the winners of an election ought to be able immediately to embody their platform in law and policy. This was, for example, the basis for the attack by Jacksonians on bureaucratic tenure, for the attack by populist political philosophers (such as Charles Beard and J. Allen Smith) on constitutional limitations of all sorts, for the persistent advocacy of a rigid system of two disciplined political parties (thus allowing a "majority" immediately to enact its program), and finally in recent decades for the idealization of "presidential leadership" – a euphemism for transcending constitutional limitations by the domination of a populistically endorsed, quasi-monarchical president.

Along with the populist notion of an unfettered agent (whether party or president) of the popular will, there is also the notion that the popular will can express itself directly, as in legislation by referenda and even by public opinion polls. The device of referendum was developed in the progressive era – an epoch of the populist spirit – to provide a "truer" expression of the popular will than statutes produced by legislatures, which were, it was argued, merely distorting intermediaries of the popular will. Since that time there has been considerable disillusionment with referenda because they have produced both inconsistent and bizarre legislation. Still, the populist belief in direct democracy dies hard, even though it can in no wise escape the defects of manipulation. So now there is considerable enthusiasm for using cable television to conduct elections on the content of statutes and even of administrative policy. Presumably citizens will listen to debate and then vote by push button, supplanting thereby the need for any kind of legislature.

[...]

The present situation in the United States is, therefore, that, although the fundamental constitutional limitations remain, populists persistently seek to undermine them. Since the twentieth century is a populist era worldwide, our homegrown populists may well succeed.

Populism puts democracy at risk. Democracy requires control of rulers by electoral santions; the spirit of populism and populist institutions allows rulers to tamper with this sanction, thereby rendering it a weak defense against the tyranny of officials. The maintenance of democracy requires therefore the minimization of the risk in populism.

How can we minimize the risk? This is the great question of political prudence forced on us by the revelations of social choice theory. I will conclude this survey with some remarks on this practical problem.

The main defense against populist excesses is the maintenance of the constitutional limitations inherited from eighteenth-century Whiggery. It would probably help also to have a citizenry aware of the emptiness of the populist interpretation of voting. And surely a wide dissemination of the discoveries of social choice theory is a desirable additional defense. But the dissemination of a rather arcane theory is a task for generations. (It took me a score of years of reflection on Black's and Arrow's discoveries to reject the populism I had initially espoused.) Consequently, the fundamental method to preserve liberty is to preserve ardently our traditional constitutional restraints – decentralized parties and multicameral government.

Chapter 13
On Authority

Introduction

Issues of political authority deal with the legitimate powers of government and their rulers. The most important such functions are normally specified in constitutions, as those who write and adopt such documents act as political theorists trying to develop principles about the roles of good government. But constitutions seldom provide the last word on these important matters. While the American Constitution enumerates various governmental powers and various limitations on these powers, it is not clear why American society should be bound by the judgments of a small group of "founders" whose knowledge of government was primitive by contemporary standards and who could hardly anticipate more than two centuries ago what would today be required of good government.[1]

Contemporary liberals and conservatives debate the role of constitutions in defining governmental authority. Many conservatives claim to be "strict constructionists." They maintain that contemporary governmental authority must be understood in terms of the literal and narrow definitions that the founders initially employed when writing the Constitution. They believe that ratification of the Constitution constituted a permanent agreement among citizens about what they authorize their government to do. In contrast, many liberals claim "judicial activism" is required. They say that judicial bodies (especially the US Supreme Court) must constantly reinterpret the wording in the Constitution in light of social changes and modern conditions. For example, they question whether the founders' language about the role of government in regulating the limited interstate commerce that existed at the end of the eighteenth century can be the final word on what governments should do to regulate those businesses that are active in the global economy.

Thus, the debate on political authority goes deeper than discerning what constitutions permit and forbid governments to do. What should governments do? In what realms of community life should governments exercise authority? What constraints on individual freedom in such areas as economic behavior, social interaction, religious worship, and personal lifestyles can governmental authorities legitimately impose? What extensions and restrictions on governmental authority are needed?

Our first selection here addresses the question of whether *any* governmental authority is morally legitimate? Robert Paul Wolff, currently a professor of Afro-American Studies at the University of Massachusetts–Amherst who has described himself as a philosophical anarchist, doubts that governments have any legitimate power or authority. He writes that by definition there is a conflict between governmental authority and individual autonomy. While government authority can be understood in a descriptive sense – as what citizens *acknowledge* to be the powers of their governments – it can also be understood in a prescriptive

[1] See Robert Dahl, *How Democratic is the American Constitution?* second edition (New Haven: Yale University Press, 2004).

sense – as those powers that citizens *ought* to concede to their governments. Individual autonomy can be understood in a metaphysical sense – as the human capacity to exercise free will – but it can also be understood in a moral sense – as addressing whether individuals ought to be morally responsible for their own actions. Wolff claims that there can be no doubt about our moral autonomy. Because individuals are endowed with the ability to choose, the capacity to make judgments about right and wrong, reason, etc., it is simply inhuman for individuals to fail to accept and assert their moral autonomy. But acceptance of our autonomy means we cannot concede that government has any authority to determine our moral responsibilities. Thus whatever powers we grant to government on prudential grounds, we can never regard these powers as legitimate. We should never cease to ask whether we think that the way governments employ their powers is consistent with our moral judgments, and we should only obey those governmental commands that are consistent with our own moral judgments.

Wolff's provocative argument can be attacked on many grounds, but it can surely be questioned by those who find some governmental authority necessary. Almost everyone would concede the necessity of maintaining the peace – that Hobbes, Locke, Smith, and other classical liberals were right to claim that rational individuals grant to government the power to protect their lives, liberties, and property. In our next selection, Milton Friedman (1912–2006), a Nobel laureate in economics who taught for many years at the University of Chicago and Stanford, expands this classical liberal model, drawing on his understanding of economic theory to list more precisely what governments should and should not be able to do. His conclusions are generally regarded as libertarian or contemporary conservative, because he thinks social conflict can be avoided by leaving as many issues as possible to resolution in the free market. But he recognizes that markets can only function after governments have made various provisions for the maintenance of law and order, the enforcement of contracts, the definition of property rights, the prevention of monopoly, the regulation of "neighborhood effects," and so forth. Perhaps most provocative is the list of activities currently undertaken by governments that Friedman finds unjustified by any economic principles.

Garrett Hardin (1915–2003), an ecologist at the University of California–Santa Barbara, provides a quite different perspective on political authority. Contrary to classical liberals like Adam Smith and free-market economic theory, there are important occasions when "the invisible hand" does not convert individual freedom into the public good. The classical example occurs when herdsmen are free to have their beasts graze on common pastures. It is in the interest of each herdsman to increase the size of his herd, but if all herdsmen would do so under conditions of complete freedom, the total demand on the pasture would bring the commons to ruin. So it is in almost every area of ecology. It might be desirable for every couple to have additional children, but when all do so, the carrying capacity of the planet is threatened. It might be in the interest of each individual to dispose of his wastes in a manner that contributes a minuscule amount to the earth's pollution, but if we all do so, we spoil our environment. Simply appealing to the moral consciousness of individuals is "self-defeating," according to Hardin. Only "mutual coercion mutually agreed upon" – the regulations that a democratic government would impose on each of us regarding everything from procreation limits to disposing of our garbage – can enable us to escape "the tragedy of the commons."

When people exercise their freedoms in economic markets, some people are highly successful and some fail, resulting in extensive poverty and economic inequality – topics that are so important that they dominate current discussions of justice, as indicated in our next chapter. But before turning to what governments *should* do to eliminate poverty, it is important to consider what governments *can* do in this regard. It is commonly believed that there is little government can do without undermining economic efficiency and growth. Most simply, when governments redistribute income and wealth from the successful to the unsuccessful, it creates disincentives for people to invest their energies and capital in things that will allow them to escape poverty or even become very rich – to work hard to improve their own condition and contribute to a larger gross national product. However, Benjamin Page, a professor of political science at the University of Chicago, and James Simmons, a professor of political science at the University of Wisconsin–Oshkosh, challenge this understanding in our next selection. When governments decide which fiscal and monetary policies to pursue when seeking to stimulate economic growth, they can make those choices – like attacking unemployment – that better the conditions of the least well off. Many social insurance programs – like social security – have track records that show that they have reduced poverty. Many educational and training policies have proven to be good investments economically while also increasing opportunities for the poor. According to Page and Simmons, there is "no reason at all to despair about the capacity of governments to deal with the problems of poverty and inequality."

Another area of great debate regarding the authority of government is whether or not it should remain neutral on the moral issues – often centering on sexuality and abortion – that inevitably creep into (and sometimes seem to dominate) political life. Many previous readings here – such as those by Michael Sandel, Richard Neuhaus, and John Locke's *Letter on Toleration* – have already focused on this issue, but what do pluralists think about such matters? Our final reading in this section by William Galston – a political theorist who teaches at the University of Maryland, is a fellow at the Brookings Institution, and served as a domestic policy advisor to Bill Clinton – provides such a perspective. Galston claims that despite liberal theorists' insistence on the neutrality of the state on moral questions, liberals have always upheld certain moral and even religious values in practice. He claims that American political culture long maintained a delicate balance between liberal secular values, Christian moral maxims, and the mores of Protestants. But the civil rights movement, by giving recognition to the legitimacy of social differences, unleashed the recognition of moral differences that extend far beyond any that might exist between black and white Americans. Traditional morality was assaulted by a revitalized "expressive individualism" and by Supreme Court rulings that seemed overly permissive to many. The result has been a country that is increasingly divided on the principle and meaning of government neutrality. Conservatives simply cannot accept that government is being neutral when it leaves issues of abortion up to the free choice of individuals. They claim that "permitting abortion cannot be construed as neutrality." And liberals cannot deny that their philosophy "contains a specific account of the virtues and the good life." When such things are better understood, it should be possible to maintain a proper balance between extensive intrusion on the moral autonomy of individuals and abdication of any publicly proclaimed moral positions and standards.

Robert Paul Wolff, "The Conflict Between Authority and Autonomy"*

The concept of authority

Politics is the exercise of the power of the state, or the attempt to influence that exercise. Political philosophy is therefore, strictly speaking, the philosophy of the state. If we are to determine the content of political philosophy, and whether indeed it exists, we must begin with the concept of the state.

The state is a group of persons who have and exercise supreme authority within a given territory. Strictly, we should say that a *state* is a group of persons who have supreme authority within a given territory *or over a certain population*. [...]

Authority is the right to command, and correlatively, the right to be obeyed. It must be distinguished from power, which is the ability to compel compliance, either through the use or the threat of force. When I turn over my wallet to a thief who is holding me at gunpoint, I do so because the fate with which he threatens me is worse than the loss of money which I am made to suffer. I grant that he has power over me, but I would hardly suppose that he has *authority*, that is, that he has a right to demand my money and that I have an obligation to give it to him. When the government presents me with a bill for taxes, on the other hand, I pay it (normally) even though I do not wish to, and even if I think I can get away with not paying. It is, after all, the duly constituted government, and hence it has a *right* to tax me. It has *authority* over me. Sometimes, of course, I cheat the government, but even so, I acknowledge its authority, for who would speak of "cheating" a thief?

To *claim* authority is to claim the right to be obeyed. To *have* authority is then – what? It may mean to have that right, or it may mean to have one's claim acknowledged and accepted by those at whom it is directed. The term "authority" is ambiguous, having both a descriptive and a normative sense. Even the descriptive sense refers to norms or obligations, of course, but it does so by *describing* what men believe they ought to do rather than by *asserting* that they ought to do it.

Corresponding to the two senses of authority, there are two concepts of the state. Descriptively, the state may be defined as a group of persons who are *acknowledged* to have supreme authority within a territory – acknowledged, that is, by those over whom the authority is asserted. The study of the forms, characteristics, institutions, and functioning of *de facto* states, as we may call them, is the providence of political science. If we take the term in its prescriptive signification, the state is a group of persons who have the *right* to exercise supreme authority within a territory. The discovery, analysis, and demonstration of the forms and principles of legitimate authority – of the right to rule – is called political philosophy.

* Robert Paul Wolff, extracted from *In Defense of Anarchism* (Harper & Row, 1970), pp. 3–19.

[...]

There are, of course, many reasons why men actually acknowledge claims of authority. The most common, taking the whole of human history, is simply the prescriptive force of tradition. The fact that something has always been done in a certain way strikes most men as a perfectly adequate reason for doing it that way again. Why should we submit to a king? Because we have always submitted to kings. But why should the oldest son of the king become king in turn? Because oldest sons have always been heirs to the throne. The force of the traditional is engraved so deeply on men's minds that even a study of the violent and haphazard origins of a ruling family will not weaken its authority in the eyes of its subjects.

Some men acquire the aura of authority by virtue of their own extraordinary characteristics, either as great military leaders, as men of saintly character, or as forceful personalities. Such men gather followers and disciples around them who willingly obey without consideration of personal interest or even against its dictates. The followers believe that the leader has a *right to command,* which is to say, *authority.*

Most commonly today, in a world of bureaucratic armies and institutionalized religions, when kings are few in number and the line of prophets has run out, authority is granted to those who occupy official positions. As Weber has pointed out, these positions appear authoritative in the minds of most men because they are defined by certain sorts of bureaucratic regulations having the virtues of publicity, generality, predictability, and so forth. We become conditioned to respond to the visible signs of officiality, such as printed forms and badges. Sometimes we may have clearly in mind the justification for a legalistic claim to authority, as when we comply with a command because its author is an *elected* official. More often the mere sight of a uniform is enough to make us feel that the man inside it has a right to be obeyed.

That men accede to claims of supreme authority is plain. That men *ought* to accede to claims of supreme authority is not so obvious. Our first question must therefore be, Under what conditions and for what reasons does one man have supreme authority over another? The same question can be restated, Under what conditions can a state (understood normatively) exist?

[...]

What can be inferred from the existence of *de facto* states is that men *believe* in the existence of legitimate authority, for of course a *de facto* state is simply a state whose subjects believe it to be legitimate (i.e., really to have the authority which it claims for itself). They may be wrong. Indeed, *all* beliefs in authority may be wrong – there may be not a single state in the history of mankind which has now or ever has had a right to be obeyed. It might even be impossible for such a state to exist; that is the question we must try to settle. But so long as men believe in the authority of states, we can conclude that they possess the concept of *de jure* authority.

The normative concept of the state as the human community which possesses rightful authority within a territory thus defines the subject matter of political philosophy proper. However, even if it should prove impossible to present a deduction of the concept – if, that is, there can be no *de jure* state – still a large number of moral questions can be raised concerning the individual's relationship with *de facto* states. We may ask, for example, whether there are any moral principles which ought to guide the state in its lawmaking, such as the principle of utilitarianism, and under what conditions it is right for the individual to obey the laws. We may explore the social ideals of equality and achievement, or the principles of punishment, or the justifications for war. All such investigations are essentially applications of general moral principles to the particular phenomena of (*de facto*) politics. Hence, it would be appropriate to reclaim a word which has fallen on bad days, and call that branch of the study of politics *casuistical politics.* Since there are men who acknowledge claims to authority, there are *de facto* states. Assuming that moral discourse in general is legitimate, there must be moral questions which arise in regard to such states. Hence, casuistical politics as a branch of ethics does exist. It remains to be decided whether political philosophy proper exists.

The concept of autonomy

The fundamental assumption of moral philosophy is that men are responsible for their actions. From this assumption it follows necessarily, as Kant pointed out, that men are metaphysically free, which is to say that in some sense they are capable of choosing how they shall act. Being able to choose how he acts makes a man responsible, but merely choosing is not in itself enough to constitute *taking* responsibility for one's actions. Taking responsibility involves attempting to determine what one ought to do, and that, as philosophers since Aristotle have recognized, lays upon one the additional burdens of gaining knowledge, reflecting on motives, predicting outcomes, criticizing principles, and so forth.

[...]

Every man who possesses both free will and reason has an obligation to take responsibility for his actions, even though he may not be actively engaged in a continuing process of reflection, investigation, and deliberation about how he ought to act. A man will sometimes announce his willingness to take responsibility for the consequences of his actions, even though he has not deliberated about them, or does not intend to do so in the future. Such a declaration is, of course, an advance over the refusal to take responsibility; it at least acknowledges the existence of the obligation. But it does not relieve the man of the duty to engage in the reflective process which he has thus far shunned. It goes without saying that a man may take responsibility for his actions and yet act wrongly. When we describe someone as a responsible individual, we do not imply that he always does what is right, but only that he does not neglect the duty of attempting to ascertain what is right.

The responsible man is not capricious or anarchic, for he does acknowledge himself bound by moral constraints. But he insists that he alone is the judge of those constraints. He may listen to the advice of others, but he makes it his own by determining for himself whether it is good advice. He may learn from others about his moral obligations, but only in the sense that a mathematician learns from other mathematicians – namely by hearing from them arguments whose validity he recognizes even though he did not think of them himself. He does not learn in the sense that one learns from an explorer, by accepting as true his accounts of things one cannot see for oneself.

Since the responsible man arrives at moral decisions which he expresses to himself in the form of imperatives, we may say that he gives laws to himself, or is self-legislating. In short, he is *autonomous*. As Kant argued, moral autonomy is a combination of freedom and responsibility; it is a submission to laws which one has made for oneself. The autonomous man, insofar as he is autonomous, is not subject to the will of another. He may do what another tells him, but not *because* he has been told to do it. He is therefore, in the political sense of the word, *free*.

Since man's responsibility for his actions is a consequence of his capacity for choice, he cannot give it up or put it aside. He can refuse to acknowledge it, however, either deliberately or by simply failing to recognize his moral condition. [...]

Even after he has subjected himself to the will of another, an individual remains responsible for what he does. [...]

There are many forms and degrees of forfeiture of autonomy. A man can give up his independence of judgment with regard to a single question, or in respect of a single type of question. For example, when I place myself in the hands of my doctor, I commit myself to whatever course of treatment he prescribes, but only in regard to my health. I do not make him my legal counselor as well. A man may forfeit autonomy on some or all questions for a specific period of time, or during his entire life. He may submit himself to all commands, whatever they may be, save for some specified acts (such as killing) which he refuses to perform. From the example of the doctor, it is obvious that there are at least some situations in which it is reasonable to give up one's autonomy. Indeed, we may wonder whether, in a complex world of technical expertise, it is ever reasonable *not* to do so!

[...] I may decide that I ought to do what that person is commanding me to do, and it may even be that his issuing the command is the factor in the situation which makes it desirable for me to do so. For example, if I am on a sinking ship and the captain is giving orders for manning the lifeboats, and if everyone else is obeying the captain *because he is the captain*, I may decide that under the circumstances I had better do what he says, since the confusion caused by disobeying him would be generally harmful. But insofar as I make such a decision, I am not *obeying his command*; that is, I am not acknowledging him as having authority over me. I would make the same decision, for exactly the same reasons, if one of the passengers had started to issue "orders" and had, in the confusion, come to be obeyed.

[...]

The moral condition demands that we acknowledge responsibility and achieve autonomy wherever and whenever possible. Sometimes this involves moral deliberation and reflection; at other times, the gathering of special, even technical, information. The contemporary American citizen, for example, has an obligation to master enough modern science to enable him to follow debates about nuclear policy and come to an independent conclusion. There are great, perhaps insurmountable, obstacles to the achievement of a complete and rational autonomy in the modern world. Nevertheless, so long as we recognize our responsibility for our actions, and acknowledge the power of reason within us, we must acknowledge as well the continuing obligation to make ourselves the authors of such commands as we may obey. [...]

The conflict between authority and autonomy

The defining mark of the state is authority, the right to rule. The primary obligation of man is autonomy, the refusal to be ruled. It would seem, then, that there can be no resolution of the conflict between the autonomy of the individual and the putative authority of the state. Insofar as a man fulfills his obligation to make himself the author of his decisions, he will resist the state's claim to have authority over him. That is to say, he will deny that he has a duty to obey the laws of the state *simply because they are the laws*. In that sense, it would seem that anarchism is the only political doctrine consistent with the virtue of autonomy.

Now, of course, an anarchist may grant the necessity of *complying* with the law under certain circumstances or for the time being. He may even doubt that there is any real prospect of eliminating the state as a human institution. But he will never view the commands of the state as *legitimate*, as having a binding moral force. [...]

The dilemma which we have posed can be succinctly expressed in terms of the concept of a *de jure* state. If all men have a continuing obligation to achieve the highest degree of autonomy possible, then there would appear to be no state whose subjects have a moral obligation to obey its commands. Hence, the concept of a *de jure* legitimate state would appear to be vacuous, and philosophical anarchism would seem to be the only reasonable political belief for an enlightened man.

Milton Friedman, "The Role of Government in a Free Society"*

The use of political channels, while inevitable, tends to strain the social cohesion essential for a stable society. The strain is least if agreement for joint action need be reached only on a limited range of issues on which people in any event have common views. Every extension of the range of issues for which explicit agreement is sought strains further the delicate threads that hold society together. If it goes so far as to touch an issue on which men feel deeply yet differently, it may well disrupt the society. Fundamental differences in basic values can seldom if ever be resolved at the ballot box; ultimately they can only be decided, though not resolved, by conflict. The religious and civil wars of history are a bloody testament to this judgment.

The widespread use of the market reduces the strain on the social fabric by rendering conformity unnecessary with respect to any activities it encompasses. The wider the range of activities covered by the market, the fewer are the issues on which explicitly political decisions are required and hence on which it is necessary to achieve agreement. In turn, the fewer the issues on which agreement is necessary, the greater is the likelihood of getting agreement while maintaining a free society. [...]

I turn now to consider more specifically, though still in very broad terms, what the areas are that cannot be handled through the market at all, or can be handled only at so great a cost that the use of political channels may be preferable.

Government as rule-maker and umpire

It is important to distinguish the day-to-day activities of people from the general customary and legal framework within which these take place. The day-to-day activities are like the actions of the participants in a game when they are playing it; the framework, like the rules of the game they play. And just as a good game requires acceptance by the players both of the rules and of the umpire to interpret and enforce them, so a good society requires that its members agree on the general conditions that will govern relations among them, on some means of arbitrating different interpretations of these conditions, and on some device for enforcing compliance with the generally accepted rules. As in games, so also in society, most of the general conditions are the unintended outcome of custom, accepted unthinkingly. At most, we consider explicitly only minor modifications in them, though the cumulative effect of a series of minor modifications may be a drastic alteration in the character of the game or of the society. In both games and society also, no set of rules can prevail unless most participants most of the time conform to them without external sanctions; unless that is, there is a broad underlying social consensus. But we cannot rely on custom or on this consensus alone to interpret and to enforce the rules; we need an umpire. These then are the basic roles of government in a free society: to provide a means whereby we can modify the rules, to mediate differences among us on the meaning of the rules, and to enforce compliance with the rules on the part of those few who would otherwise not play the game.

The need for government in these respects arises because absolute freedom is impossible. However attractive anarchy may be as a philosophy, it is not feasible in a world of imperfect men. Men's freedoms can conflict, and when they do, one man's freedom must be limited to preserve another's – as a Supreme Court Justice once put it, "My freedom to move my fist must be limited by the proximity of your chin."

* Milton Friedman, extracted from *Capitalism and Freedom* (University of Chicago Press, 1962), pp. 22–36.

The major problem in deciding the appropriate activities of government is how to resolve such conflicts among the freedoms of different individuals. In some cases, the answer is easy. There is little difficulty in attaining near unanimity to the proposition that one man's freedom to murder his neighbor must be sacrificed to preserve the freedom of the other man to live. In other cases, the answer is difficult. In the economic area, a major problem arises in respect of the conflict between freedom to combine and freedom to compete. What meaning is to be attributed to "free" as modifying "enterprise"? In the United States, "free" has been understood to mean that anyone is free to set up an enterprise, which means that existing enterprises are not free to keep out competitors except by selling a better product at the same price or the same product at a lower price. In the continental tradition, on the other hand, the meaning has generally been that enterprises are free to do what they want, including the fixing of prices, division of markets, and the adoption of other techniques to keep out potential competitors. Perhaps the most difficult specific problem in this area arises with respect to combinations among laborers, where the problem of freedom to combine and freedom to compete is particularly acute.

A still more basic economic area in which the answer is both difficult and important is the definition of property rights. The notion of property, as it has developed over centuries and as it is embodied in our legal codes, has become so much a part of us that we tend to take it for granted, and fail to recognize the extent to which just what constitutes property and what rights the ownership of property confers are complex social creations rather than self-evident propositions. Does my having title to land, for example, and my freedom to use my property as I wish, permit me to deny to someone else the right to fly over my land in his airplane? Or does his right to use his airplane take precedence? Or does this depend on how high he flies? Or how much noise he makes? Does voluntary exchange require that he pay me for the privilege of flying over my land? Or that I must pay him to refrain from flying over it? The mere mention of royalties, copyrights, patents; shares of stock in corporations; riparian rights, and the like, may perhaps emphasize the role of generally accepted social rules in the very definition of property. It may suggest also that, in many cases, the existence of a well specified and generally accepted definition of property is far more important than just what the definition is.

Another economic area that raises particularly difficult problems is the monetary system. Government responsibility for the monetary system has long been recognized. It is explicitly provided for in the constitutional provision which gives Congress the power "to coin money, regulate the value thereof, and of foreign coin." There is probably no other area of economic activity with respect to which government action has been so uniformly accepted. [...]

In summary, the organization of economic activity through voluntary exchange presumes that we have provided, through government, for the maintenance of law and order to prevent coercion of one individual by another, the enforcement of contracts voluntarily entered into, the definition of the meaning of property rights, the interpretation and enforcement of such rights, and the provision of a monetary framework.

Action through government on grounds of technical monopoly and neighborhood effects

The role of government just considered is to do something that the market cannot do for itself, namely, to determine, arbitrate, and enforce the rules of the game. We may also want to do through government some things that might conceivably be done through the market but that technical or similar conditions render it difficult to do in that way. These all reduce to cases in which strictly voluntary exchange is either exceedingly costly or practically impossible. There are two general classes of such cases: monopoly and similar market imperfections, and neighborhood effects.

Exchange is truly voluntary only when nearly equivalent alternatives exist. Monopoly implies the absence of alternatives and thereby inhibits effective freedom of exchange. [...] Monopoly may also arise because it is technically efficient to have a single producer or enterprise. I venture to suggest that such cases are more limited than is supposed but they unquestionably do arise. A simple example is perhaps the provision of telephone services within a community. I shall refer to such cases as "technical" monopoly.

[...]

Technical monopoly may on occasion justify a *de facto* public monopoly. It cannot by itself justify a public monopoly achieved by making it illegal for anyone else to compete. For example, there is no way to justify our present public monopoly of the post office. It may be argued that the carrying of mail is a technical monopoly and that a government monopoly is the least of evils. Along these lines, one could perhaps justify a government post office but not the present law, which makes it illegal for anybody else to carry mail. If the delivery of mail is a technical monopoly, no one will be able to succeed in competition with the government. If it is not, there is no reason why the government should be engaged in it. The only way to find out is to leave other people free to enter.

[...]

A second general class of cases in which strictly voluntary exchange is impossible arises when actions of individuals have effects on other individuals for which it is not feasible to charge or recompense them. This is the problem of "neighborhood effects". An obvious example is the pollution of a stream. The man who pollutes a stream is in effect forcing others to exchange good water for bad. These others might be willing to make the exchange at a price. But it is not feasible for them, acting individually, to avoid the exchange or to enforce appropriate compensation.

A less obvious example is the provision of highways. In this case, it is technically possible to identify and hence charge individuals for their use of the roads and so to have private operation. However, for general access roads, involving many points of entry and exit, the costs of collection would be extremely high if a charge were to be made for the specific services received by each individual, because of the necessity of establishing toll booths or the equivalent at all entrances.

[...]

Parks are an interesting example because they illustrate the difference between cases that can and cases that cannot be justified by neighborhood effects, and because almost everyone at first sight regards the conduct of National Parks as obviously a valid function of government. In fact, however, neighborhood effects may justify a city park; they do not justify a national park, like Yellowstone National Park or the Grand Canyon. What is the fundamental difference between the two? For the city park, it is extremely difficult to identify the people who benefit from it and to charge them for the benefits which they receive. If there is a park in the middle of the city, the houses on all sides get the benefit of the open space, and people who walk through it or by it also benefit. To maintain toll collectors at the gates or to impose annual charges per window overlooking the park would be very expensive and difficult. The entrances to a national park like Yellowstone, on the other hand, are few; most of the people who come stay for a considerable period of time and it is perfectly feasible to set up toll gates and collect admission charges. This is indeed now done, though the charges do not cover the whole costs. If the public wants this kind of an activity enough to pay for it, private enterprises will have every incentive to provide such parks. And, of course, there are many private enterprises of this nature now in existence. I cannot myself conjure up any neighborhood effects or important monopoly effects that would justify governmental activity in this area.

Considerations like those I have treated under the heading of neighborhood effects have been used to rationalize almost every conceivable intervention. In many instances, however, this rationalization is special pleading rather than a legitimate application of the concept of neighborhood effects. Neighborhood effects cut both ways. They can be a reason for limiting the activities of government as well as for expanding them.

[...]

Action through government on paternalistic grounds

Freedom is a tenable objective only for responsible individuals. We do not believe in freedom for madmen or children. The necessity of drawing a line between responsible individuals and others is inescapable, yet it means that there is an essential ambiguity in our ultimate objective of freedom. Paternalism is inescapable for those whom we designate as not responsible.

The clearest case, perhaps, is that of madmen. We are willing neither to permit them freedom nor to shoot them. It would be nice if we could rely on voluntary activities of individuals to house and care for the madmen. But I think we cannot rule out the possibility that such charitable activities will be inadequate, if only because of the neighborhood effect involved in the fact that I benefit if another man contributes to the care of the insane. For this reason, we may be willing to arrange for their care through government.

Children offer a more difficult case. The ultimate operative unit in our society is the family, not the individual. Yet the acceptance of the family as the unit rests in considerable part on expediency rather than principle. We believe that parents are generally best able to protect their children and to provide for their development into responsible individuals for whom freedom is appropriate. But we do not believe in the freedom of parents to do what they will with other people. The children are responsible individuals in embryo, and a believer in freedom believes in protecting their ultimate rights.

To put this in a different and what may seem a more callous way, children are at one and the same time consumer goods and potentially responsible members of society. The freedom of individuals to use their economic resources as they want includes the freedom to use them to have children – to buy, as it were, the services of children as a particular form of consumption. But once this choice is exercised, the children have a value in and of themselves and have a freedom of their own that is not simply an extension of the freedom of the parents.

The paternalistic ground for governmental activity is in many ways the most troublesome to a liberal; for it involves the acceptance of a principle – that some shall decide for others – which he finds objectionable in most applications and which he rightly regards as a hallmark of his chief intellectual opponents, the proponents of collectivism in one or another of its guises, whether it be communism, socialism, or a welfare state. Yet there is no use pretending that problems are simpler than in fact they are. There is no avoiding the need for some measure of paternalism. As Dicey wrote in 1914 about an act for the protection of mental defectives, "The Mental Deficiency Act is the first step along a path on which no sane man can decline to enter, but which, if too far pursued, will bring statesmen across difficulties hard to meet without considerable interference with individual liberty."[2] There is no formula that can tell us where to stop. We must rely on our fallible judgment and, having reached a judgment, on our ability to persuade our fellow men that it is a correct judgment, or their ability to persuade us to modify our views. We must put our faith, here as elsewhere, in a consensus reached by imperfect and biased men through free discussion and trial and error.

Conclusion

A government which maintained law and order, defined property rights, served as a means whereby we could modify property rights and other rules of the economic game, adjudicated disputes about the interpretation of the rules, enforced contracts, promoted competition, provided a monetary framework, engaged in activities to counter technical monopolies and to overcome neighborhood effects widely regarded as sufficiently important to justify government intervention, and which supplemented private charity and the private family in protecting the irresponsible, whether madman or child – such a government would clearly have important functions to perform. The consistent liberal is not an anarchist.

Yet it is also true that such a government would have clearly limited functions and would refrain from a host of activities that are now undertaken by federal and state governments in the United States, and their counterparts in other Western countries. Succeeding chapters will deal in some detail with some of these activities, and a few have been discussed above, but it may help to give a sense of proportion about the role that a liberal would assign government simply to list, in closing this chapter, some activities currently undertaken by government in the US, that cannot, so far as I can see, validly be justified in terms of the principles outlined above:

1. Parity price support programs for agriculture.
2. Tariffs on imports or restrictions on exports, such as current oil import quotas, sugar quotas, etc.
3. Governmental control of output, such as through the farm program, or through prorationing of oil as is done by the Texas Railroad Commission.
4. Rent control, such as is still practiced in New York, or more general price and wage controls such as were imposed during and just after World War II.
5. Legal minimum wage rates, or legal maximum prices, such as the legal maximum of zero on the rate of interest that can be paid on demand deposits by commercial banks, or the legally fixed maximum rates that can be paid on savings and time deposits.
6. Detailed regulation of industries, such as the regulation of transportation by the Interstate Commerce Commission. This had some justification on technical monopoly grounds when initially introduced for railroads; it has none now for any means of transport. Another example is detailed regulation of banking.
7. A similar example, but one which deserves special mention because of its implicit censorship and violation of free speech, is the control of radio and television by the Federal Communications Commission.
8. Present social security programs, especially the old-age and retirement programs compelling people in effect (*a*) to spend a specified fraction of their income on the purchase of retirement annuity, (*b*) to buy the annuity from a publicly operated enterprise.
9. Licensure provisions in various cities and states which restrict particular enterprises or occupations or professions to people who have a license, where the license is more than a receipt for a tax which anyone who wishes to enter the activity may pay.
10. So-called "public-housing" and the host of other subsidy programs directed at fostering residential construction such as FHA and VA guarantee of mortgage, and the like.

[2] A. V. Dicey, *Lectures on the Relation between Law and Public Opinion in England during the Nineteenth Century*, third edition (London: Macmillan & Co., 1914), p. 11.

11. Conscription to man the military services in peacetime. The appropriate free market arrangement is volunteer military forces; which is to say, hiring men to serve. There is no justification for not paying whatever price is necessary to attract the required number of men. Present arrangements are inequitable and arbitrary, seriously interfere with the freedom of young men to shape their lives, and probably are even more costly than the market alternative. (Universal military training to provide a reserve for war time is a different problem and may be justified on liberal grounds.)

12. National parks, as noted above.

13. The legal prohibition on the carrying of mail for profit.

14. Publicly owned and operated toll roads, as noted above.

This list is far from comprehensive.

Garrett Hardin, "The Tragedy of the Commons"*

[...] An implicit and almost universal assumption of discussions published in professional and semipopular scientific journals is that the problem under discussion has a technical solution. A technical solution may be defined as one that requires a change only in the techniques of the natural sciences, demanding little or nothing in the way of change in human values or ideas of morality.

In our day (though not in earlier times) technical solutions are always welcome. [But] the class of "no technical solution problems" has members. My thesis is that the "population problem," as conventionally conceived, is a member of this class. How it is conventionally conceived needs some comment. It is fair to say that most people who anguish over the population problem are trying to find a way to avoid the evils of overpopulation without relinquishing any of the privileges they now enjoy. They think that farming the seas or developing new strains of wheat will solve the problem – technologically. I try to show here that the solution they seek cannot be found. The population problem cannot be solved in a technical way. [...]

* Garrett Hardin, extracted from *Science*, 162 (1968), pp. 1243–8.

What shall we maximize?

Population, as Malthus said, naturally tends to grow "geometrically," or, as we would now say, exponentially. In a finite world this means that the per-capita share of the world's goods must decrease. Is ours a finite world?

A fair defense can be put forward for the view that the world is infinite; or that we do not know that it is not. But, in terms of the practical problems that we must face in the next few generations with the foreseeable technology, it is clear that we will greatly increase human misery if we do not, during the immediate future, assume that the world available to the terrestrial human population is finite. "Space" is no escape.[3]

A finite world can support only a finite population; therefore, population growth must eventually equal zero. (The case of perpetual wide fluctuations above and below zero is a trivial variant that need not be discussed.) When this condition is met, what will be the situation of mankind? Specifically, can Bentham's goal of "the greatest good for the greatest number" be realized?

No – for two reasons, each sufficient by itself. The first is a theoretical one. It is not mathematically possible to maximize for two (or more) variables at the same time. This was clearly stated by von Neumann and Morgenstern,[4] but the principle is implicit in the theory of partial differential equations, dating back at least to D'Alembert (1717–83).

The second reason springs directly from biological facts. To live, any organism must have a source of energy (for example, food). This energy is utilized for two purposes: mere maintenance and work. For man, maintenance of life requires about 1,600 kilocalories a day ("maintenance calories"). Anything that he does over and above merely staying alive will be defined as work, and is supported by "work calories" which he takes in. Work calories are used not only for what we call work in common speech; they are also required for all forms of enjoyment, from swimming and automobile racing to playing music and writing poetry. If our goal is to maximize population it is obvious what we must do: we must make the work calories per person approach as close to zero as possible. No gourmet meals, no vacations, no sports, no music, no literature, no art. ... I think that everyone will grant, without argument or proof, that

[3] G. Hardin, *Journal of Heredity*, 50, 68 (1959); S. von Hoernor, *Science*, 137, 18 (1962).

[4] J. von Neumann and O. Morgenstern, *Theory of Games and Economic Behavior* (Princeton University Press, 1947), p. 11.

maximizing population does not maximize goods. Bentham's goal is impossible.

In reaching this conclusion I have made the usual assumption that it is the acquisition of energy that is the problem. The appearance of atomic energy has led some to question this assumption. However, given an infinite source of energy, population growth still produces an inescapable problem. The problem of the acquisition of energy is replaced by the problem of its dissipation, as J. H. Fremlin has so wittily shown.[5] The arithmetic signs in the analysis are, as it were, reversed; but Bentham's goal is unobtainable. The optimum population is, then, less than the maximum.

[...]

We can make little progress in working toward optimum population size until we explicitly exorcise the spirit of Adam Smith in the field of practical demography. In economic affairs, *The Wealth of Nations* (1776) popularized the "invisible hand," the idea that an individual who "intends only his own gain," is, as it were, "led by an invisible hand to promote ... the public interest."[6] Adam Smith did not assert that this was invariably true, and perhaps neither did any of his followers. But he contributed to a dominant tendency of thought that has ever since interfered with positive action based on rational analysis, namely, the tendency to assume that decisions reached individually will, in fact, be the best decisions for an entire society. If this assumption is correct it justifies the continuance of our present policy of *laissez faire* in reproduction. If it is correct we can assume that men will control their individual fecundity so as to produce the optimum population. If the assumption is not correct, we need to reexamine our individual freedoms to see which ones are defensible.

Tragedy of freedom in a commons

The rebuttal to the invisible hand in population control is to be found in a scenario first sketched in a little-known pamphlet in 1833 by a mathematical amateur named William Forster Lloyd (1794–1852)[7] We may well call it "the tragedy of the commons," using the word "tragedy" as the philosopher Whitehead used it[8]: "The essence of dramatic tragedy is not unhappiness. It resides in the solemnity of the remorseless working of things." He then goes on to say, "This inevitableness of destiny can only be illustrated in terms of human life by incidents which in fact involve unhappiness. For it is only by them that the futility of escape can be made evident in the drama."

The tragedy of the commons develops in this way. Picture a pasture open to all. It is to be expected that each herdsman will try to keep as many cattle as possible on the commons. Such an arrangement may work reasonably satisfactorily for centuries because tribal wars, poaching, and disease keep the numbers of both man and beast well below the carrying capacity of the land. Finally, however, comes the day of reckoning, that is, the day when the long-desired goal of social stability becomes a reality. At this point, the inherent logic of the commons remorselessly generates tragedy.

As a rational being, each herdsman seeks to maximize his gain. Explicitly or implicitly, more or less consciously, he asks, "What is the utility *to me* of adding one more animal to my herd?" This utility has one negative and one positive component.

1. The positive component is a function of the increment of one animal. Since the herdsman receives all the proceeds from the sale of the additional animal, the positive utility is nearly +1.
2. The negative component is a function of the additional overgrazing created by one more animal. Since, however, the effects of overgrazing are shared by all the herdsmen, the negative utility for any particular decision-making herdsman is only a fraction of −1.

Adding together the component partial utilities, the rational herdsman concludes that the only sensible course for him to pursue is to add another animal to his herd. And another. ... But this is the conclusion reached by each and every rational herdsman sharing a commons. Therein is the tragedy. Each man is locked into a system that compels him to increase his herd without limit – in a world that is limited. Ruin is the destination toward which all men rush, each pursuing his own best interest in a society that believes in the freedom of the commons. Freedom in a commons brings ruin to all.

Some would say that this is a platitude. Would that it were! In a sense, it was learned thousands of years ago, but natural selection favors the forces of psychological denial.[9] The individual benefits as an individual from his

[5] J. H. Fremlin, *New Scientist*, 415 (1964), p. 285.

[6] A. Smith, *The Wealth of Nations* (New York: Modern Library, 1937), p. 423.

[7] W. F. Lloyd, *Two Lectures on the Checks to Population* (Oxford: Oxford University Press, 1833).

[8] A. N. Whitehead, *Science and the Modern World* (New York: Mentor, 1948), p. 17.

[9] G. Hardin, ed., *Population, Evolution, and Birth Control* (San Francisco: Freeman, 1964), p. 56.

ability to deny the truth even though society as a whole, of which he is a part, suffers. Education can counteract the natural tendency to do the wrong thing, but the inexorable succession of generations requires that the basis for this knowledge be constantly refreshed.

[...]

In an approximate way, the logic of the commons has been understood for a long time, perhaps since the discovery of agriculture or the invention of private property in real estate. But it is understood mostly only in special cases which are not sufficiently generalized. Even at this late date, cattlemen leasing national land on the Western ranges demonstrate no more than an ambivalent understanding, in constantly pressuring federal authorities to increase the head count to the point where overgrazing produces erosion and weed-dominance. Likewise, the oceans of the world continue to suffer from the survival of the philosophy of the commons. Maritime nations still respond automatically to the shibboleth of the "freedom of the seas." Professing to believe in the "inexhaustible resources of the oceans," they bring species after species of fish and whales closer to extinction.[10]

The National Parks present another instance of the working out of the tragedy of the commons. At present, they are open to all, without limit. The parks themselves are limited in extent – there is only one Yosemite Valley – whereas population seems to grow without limit. The values that visitors seek in the parks are steadily eroded. Plainly, we must soon cease to treat the parks as commons or they will be of no value to anyone.

What shall we do? We have several options. We might sell them off as private property. We might keep them as public property, but allocate the right to enter them. The allocation might be on the basis of wealth, by the use of an auction system. It might be on the basis of merit, as defined by some agreed-upon standards. It might be by lottery. Or it might be on a first-come, first-served basis, administered to long queues. These, I think, are all objectionable. But we must choose – or acquiesce in the destruction of the commons that we call our National Parks.

Pollution

In a reverse way, the tragedy of the commons reappears in problems of pollution. Here it is not a question of taking something out of the commons, but of putting something in – sewage, or chemical, radioactive, and heat wastes into water; noxious and dangerous fumes into the air; and distracting and unpleasant advertising signs into the line of sight. The calculations of utility are much the same as before. The rational man finds that his share of the cost of the wastes he discharges into the commons is less than the cost of purifying his wastes before releasing them. Since this is true for everyone, we are locked into a system of "fouling our own nest," so long as we behave only as independent, rational, free-enterprisers.

The tragedy of the commons as a food basket is averted by private property, or something formally like it. But the air and waters surrounding us cannot readily be fenced, and so the tragedy of the commons as a cesspool must be prevented by different means, by coercive laws or taxing devices that make it cheaper for the polluter to treat his pollutants than to discharge them untreated. [...]

The pollution problem is a consequence of population. It did not much matter how a lonely American frontiersman disposed of his waste. "Flowing water purifies itself every ten miles," my grandfather used to say, and the myth was near enough to the truth when he was a boy, for there were not too many people. But as population became denser, the natural chemical and biological recycling processes became overloaded, calling for a redefinition of property rights.

How to legislate temperance?

Analysis of the pollution problem as a function of population density uncovers a not generally recognized principle of morality, namely: *the morality of an act is a function of the state of the system at the time it is performed.*[11] Using the commons as a cesspool does not harm the general public under frontier conditions, because there is no public; the same behavior in a metropolis is unbearable. A hundred and fifty years ago a plainsman could kill an American bison, cut out only the tongue for his dinner, and discard the rest of the animal. He was not in any important sense being wasteful. Today, with only a few thousand bison left, we would be appalled at such behavior.

In passing, it is worth noting that the morality of an act cannot be determined from a photograph. One does not know whether a man killing an elephant or setting fire to the grassland is harming others until one knows the total system in which his act appears. "One picture is worth a thousand words," said an ancient Chinese; but it may take ten thousand words to validate it. It is as tempting to ecologists as it is to reformers in general to

10 S. McVay, *Scientific American* 216, 8 (1966), p. 13.

11 J. Fletcher, *Situation Ethics* (Philadelphia: Westminster, 1966).

try to persuade others by way of the photographic shortcut. But the essence of an argument cannot be photographed: it must be presented rationally – in words.

That morality is system-sensitive escaped the attention of most codifiers of ethics in the past. "Thou shalt not ..." is the form of traditional ethical directives which make no allowance for particular circumstances. The laws of our society follow the pattern of ancient ethics, and therefore are poorly suited to governing a complex, crowded, changeable world. Our epicyclic solution is to augment statutory law with administrative law. Since it is practically impossible to spell out all the conditions under which it is safe to burn trash in the back yard or to run an automobile without smog-control, by law we delegate the details to bureaus. The result is administrative law, which is rightly feared for an ancient reason – *Quis custodiet ipsos custodes?* – Who shall watch the watchers themselves? John Adams said that we must have a "government of laws and not men." Bureau administrators, trying to evaluate the morality of acts in the total system, are singularly liable to corruption, producing a government by men, not laws.

Prohibition is easy to legislate (though not necessarily to enforce); but how do we legislate temperance? Experience indicates that it can be accomplished best through the mediation of administrative law. We limit possibilities unnecessarily if we suppose that the sentiment of *Quis custodiet* denies us the use of administrative law. We should rather retain the phrase as a perpetual reminder of fearful dangers we cannot avoid. The great challenge facing us now is to invent the corrective feedbacks that are needed to keep custodians honest. We must find ways to legitimate the needed authority of both the custodians and the corrective feedbacks.

Freedom to breed is intolerable

The tragedy of the commons is involved in population problems in another way. In a world governed solely by the principle of "dog eat dog" – if indeed there ever was such a world – how many children a family had would not be a matter of public concern. Parents who bred too exuberantly would leave fewer descendants, not more, because they would be unable to care adequately for their children. David Lack and others have found that such a negative feedback demonstrably controls the fecundity of birds.[12] But men are not birds, and have not acted like them for millenniums, at least.

If each human family were dependent only on its own resources; *if* the children of improvident parents starved to death; *if*, thus, over-breeding brought its own "punishment" to the germ line – *then* there would be no public interest in controlling the breeding of families. But our society is deeply committed to the welfare state[13] and hence is confronted with another aspect of the tragedy of the commons.

In a welfare state, how shall we deal with the family, the religion the race, or the class (or indeed any distinguishable and cohesive group) that adopts overbreeding as a policy to secure its own aggrandizement?[14] To couple the concept of freedom to breed with the belief that everyone born has an equal right to the commons is to lock the world into a tragic course of action.

Unfortunately this is just the course of action that is being pursued by the United Nations. In late 1967, some thirty nations agreed to the following: "The Universal Declaration of Human Rights describes the family as the natural and fundamental unit of society. It follows that any choice and decision with regard to the size of the family must irrevocably rest with the family itself, and cannot be made by anyone else."[15]

It is painful to have to deny categorically the validity of this right. [...] If we love the truth we must openly deny the validity of the Universal Declaration of Human Rights, even though it is promoted by the United Nations. [...]

Conscience is self-eliminating

It is a mistake to think that we can control the breeding of mankind in the long run by an appeal to conscience. Charles Galton Darwin made this point when he spoke on the centennial of the publication of his grandfather's great book. The argument is straightforward and Darwinian.

People vary. Confronted with appeals to limit breeding, some people will undoubtedly respond to the plea more than others. Those who have more children will produce a larger fraction of the next generation than those with more susceptible consciences. The differences will be accentuated, generation by generation.

In C. G. Darwin's words: "It may well be that it would take hundreds of generations for the progenitive instinct

12 D. Lack, *The Natural Regulation of Animal Numbers* (Oxford: Clarendon Press, 1954).

13 H. Girvetz, *From Wealth to Welfare* (Stanford University Press, 1950).

14 G. Hardin, *Perspectives in Biology and Medicine*, 6, 366 (1963).

15 U Thant, *International, Planned Parenthood News*, 168 (February 1968), p. 3.

to develop in this way, but if it should do so, nature would have taken her revenge, and the variety *Homo contracipiens* would become extinct and would be replaced by the variety *Homo progenitivus*."[16]

[...] The argument has here been stated in the context of the population problem, but it applies equally well to any instance in which society appeals to an individual exploiting a commons to restrain himself for the general good – by means of his conscience. To make such an appeal is to set up a selective system that works toward the elimination of conscience from the race.

Pathogenic effects of conscience

The long-term disadvantage of an appeal to conscience should be enough to condemn it; but it has serious short-term disadvantages as well. If we ask a man who is exploiting a commons to desist "in the name of conscience," what are we saying to him? What does he hear? – not only at the moment but also in the wee small hours of the night when, half asleep, he remembers not merely the words we used but also the nonverbal communication cues we gave him unawares? Sooner or later, consciously or subconsciously, he senses that he has received two communications, and that they are contradictory: 1. (intended communication) "If you don't do as we ask, we will openly condemn you for not acting like a responsible citizen"; 2. (the unintended communication) "If you *do* behave as we ask, we will secretly condemn you for a simpleton who can be shamed into standing aside while the rest of us exploit the commons."

Everyman then is caught in what Bateson has called a "double bind." Bateson and his co-workers have made a plausible case for viewing the double bind as an important causative factor in the genesis of schizophrenia.[17] The double bind may not always be so damaging, but it always endangers the mental health of anyone to whom it is applied. "A bad conscience," said Nietzsche, "is a kind of illness."

To conjure up a conscience in others is tempting to anyone who wishes to extend his control beyond the legal limits. Leaders at the highest level succumb to this temptation. Has any president during the past generation failed to call on labor unions to moderate voluntarily their demands for higher wages, or to steel companies to honor voluntary guidelines on prices? I can recall none. The rhetoric used on such occasions is designed to produce feelings of guilt in noncooperators.

For centuries it was assumed without proof that guilt was a valuable, perhaps even an indispensable, ingredient of the civilized life. Now, in this post-Freudian world, we doubt it.

Paul Goodman speaks from the modern point of view when he says: "No good has ever come from feeling guilty, neither intelligence, policy, nor compassion. The guilty do not pay attention to the object but only to themselves, and not even to their own interests, which might make sense, but to their anxieties."[18]

[...]

Since proof is difficult, we may even concede that the results of anxiety may sometimes, from certain points of view, be desirable. The larger question we should ask is whether, as a matter of policy, we should ever encourage the use of a technique the tendency (if not the intention) of which is psychologically pathogenic. We hear much talk these days of responsible parenthood; the coupled words are incorporated into the titles of some organizations devoted to birth control. Some people have proposed massive propaganda campaigns to instill responsibility into the nation's (or the world's) breeders. But what is the meaning of the word conscience? When we use the word responsibility in the absence of substantial sanctions are we not trying to browbeat a free man in a commons into acting against his own interest? Responsibility is a verbal counterfeit for a substantial quid pro quo. It is an attempt to get something for nothing.

[...]

Mutual coercion mutually agreed upon

The social arrangements that produce responsibility are arrangements that create coercion, of some sort.

[...]

Coercion is a dirty word to most liberals now, but it need not forever be so. As with the four-letter words, its dirtiness can be cleansed away by exposure to the light, by saying it over and over without apology or embarrassment. To many, the word coercion implies arbitrary decisions of distant and irresponsible bureaucrats; but this is not a necessary part of its meaning. The only kind of coercion I recommend is mutual coercion, mutually agreed upon by the majority of the people affected.

16 S. Tax, ed., *Evolution After Darwin* (University of Chicago Press, 1960), vol. 2, p. 469.

17 G. Bateson, D. D. Jackson, J. Haley, J. Weakland, *Behavioral Science*, 1, 251 (1956).

18 P. Goodman, *New York Review of Books* 10, 8 (May 23, 1968), p. 22.

To say that we mutually agree to coerecion is not to say that we are required to enjoy it, or even to pretend we enjoy it. Who enjoys taxes? We all grumble about them. But we accept compulsory taxes because we recognize that voluntary taxes would favor the conscienceless. We institute and (grumblingly) support taxes and other coercive devices to escape the horror of the commons.

[...]

Recognition of necessity

Perhaps the simplest summary of this analysis of man's population problems is this: the commons, if justifiable at all, is justifiable only under conditions of low-population density. As the human population has increased, the commons has had to be abandoned in one aspect after another.

First we abandoned the commons in food gathering, enclosing farm land and restricting pastures and hunting and fishing areas. These restrictions are still not complete throughout the world.

Somewhat later we saw that the commons as a place for waste disposal would also have to be abandoned. Restrictions on the disposal of domestic sewage are widely accepted in the Western world; we are still struggling to close the commons to pollution by automobiles, factories, insecticide sprayers, fertilizing operations, and atomic energy installations.

In a still more embryonic state is our recognition of the evils of the commons in matters of pleasure. There is almost no restriction on the propagation of sound waves in the public medium. The shopping public is assaulted with mindless music, without its consent. Our government has paid out billions of dollars to create a supersonic transport which would disturb 50,000 people for every one person whisked from coast to coast 3 hours faster. Advertisers muddy the airwaves of radio and television and pollute the view of travelers. We are a long way from outlawing the commons in matters of pleasure. Is this because our Puritan inheritance makes us view pleasure as something of a sin, and pain (that is, the pollution of advertising) as the sign of virtue?

Every new enclosure of the commons involves the infringement of somebody's personal liberty. Infringements made in the distant past are accepted because no contemporary complains of a loss. It is the newly proposed infringements that we vigorously oppose; cries of "rights" and "freedom" fill the air. But what does "freedom" mean? When men mutually agreed to pass laws against robbing, mankind became more free, not less so. Individuals locked into the logic of the commons are free only to bring on universal ruin; once they see the necessity of mutual coercion, they become free to pursue other goals. I believe it was Hegel who said, "Freedom is the recognition of necessity."

The most important aspect of necessity that we must now recognize, is the necessity of abandoning the commons in breeding. No technical solution can rescue us from the misery of overpopulation. Freedom to breed will bring ruin to all. At the moment, to avoid hard decisions many of us are tempted to propagandize for conscience and responsible parenthood. The temptation must be resisted, because an appeal to independently acting consciences selects for the disappearance of all conscience in the long run, and an increase in anxiety in the short.

The only way we can preserve and nurture other and more precious freedoms is by relinquishing the freedom to breed, and that very soon. "Freedom is the recognition of necessity" – and it is the role of education to reveal to all the necessity of abandoning the freedom to breed. Only so, can we put an end to this aspect of the tragedy of the commons.

Benjamin I. Page and James R. Simmons, "What Should Government Do?"*

What should government do about the extensive poverty and the extreme and growing inequality of income and wealth in the United States?

One possible answer to this question is "nothing." Perhaps we can trust market forces to fairly reward merit and punish sloth; let the chips fall where they may. [...] Don't government programs inevitably violate individual freedoms, waste resources, and get bogged down in bureaucratic inefficiency? Are we sure that anything *can* be done about poverty and inequality without causing dependency and making the problems worse? Perhaps everyone should just concentrate on getting ahead and forget about those who fall behind.

[...]

Practically everyone in the industrialized West – and, increasingly, people around the world – believes that government should keep public order, define and protect property rights, enforce contracts, and create and manage the money supply.

* Benjamin I. Page and James R. Simmons, extracted from *What Government Can Do: Dealing with Poverty and Inequality* (University of Chicago Press, 2000), pp. 32–46, 289–93.

In order for markets to work well, it is clearly essential to *define and protect property rights.* Legal provisions are needed to determine exactly how ownership of various kinds of property is established, what rights owners have, how those rights are enforced, and how ownership can be altered. Only when property rights are clear and enforceable is it possible for people to buy and sell goods, hire employees, accumulate capital, and build up businesses. Only with well-defined and transferable property rights can goods be produced, traded, and consumed in an efficient fashion. And only government has the authority and legitimacy to create and enforce property rights.

The basic idea is simple enough. One of the most ancient functions of governments has been to establish who owns which land and personal property and to protect them against theft or destruction. Police forces and courts are needed to punish or deter violations of property rights. The law must make clear just what people can and cannot do with their property and how they can sell or lease it to others or pass it on to heirs by inheritance. Constitutional or other provisions may also be needed to limit the ways in which government itself can interfere with private property.

In a complex modern economy, however, the definition and protection of property become very complicated. New forms of ownership must be invented and implemented. Limited-liability corporations, for example, which are so crucial to the high-volume production and distribution of goods and services, exist only because governments recognize them as legal "persons" – entitled to own, to contract, to sue and be sued – while shielding their owners (stockholders) and managers from most forms of personal liability. The corporation is a creature of government. For a modern economy to work properly, government laws and regulations must deal with many abstract forms of property, including corporate stocks and bonds and rights to ideas ("intellectual property"). They must define the nature and powers of partnerships, trusts, and a host of other institutions. They must spell out the meaning of, and enforce, a welter of different provisions in commercial contracts. And they must make clear when and how private property rights have to give way to other public and private purposes, through liability laws, zoning, taxes, condemnation, and the like.[19]

Governments permit corporations to be organized and to act as legal persons, for example, not because there is some sort of natural "right" to do so, but because corporations are thought capable of bringing benefits to society as a whole. In return for the valuable legal privileges given to them, therefore, it might not be unreasonable for government to require that corporations meet specific social obligations. Such obligations could be enforced through such measures as revising state-granted corporate charters, imposing serious criminal penalties for illegal behavior, depriving them of tax breaks or subsidies in cases of serious infractions of civil law, and perhaps even withdrawing political rights (to lobby and the like) upon criminal conviction, just as people convicted of felonies lose the right to vote.[20]

In addition to defining and protecting private property, governments need to *create and manage a supply of money,* that is, of a medium of exchange that people can use conveniently to buy and sell things with. Only governments have the power and the legitimacy to declare what is and what is not "legal tender," to print paper money or moneylike obligations including Treasury bonds and notes, to guarantee that money will maintain its value, and to regulate the size of the money supply so that it is neither too small nor too large.

One reason we need to mention these obvious functions of government is to make clear that it is artificial to distinguish sharply between "public" and "private" in a modern economy. The idea of a free market without government – an idea that some libertarians seem to embrace – is an illusion. Governments create and enforce the property rights and other legal arrangements that make modern markets possible. And governments not only create markets, but also inevitably alter and modify markets by making choices among a host of alternative legal arrangements, many of which may have important implications for poverty and inequality. It would be rather peculiar to attack the legitimacy of any and all government "interference" with the private economy when government action makes such an economy possible. The real question is what sorts of government action are *desirable* and what sorts are not.

[...]

Economists have developed theories of *public goods,* or *social* or *collective goods,* invoking such examples

19 See Morton J. Horowitz, *The Transformation of American Law, 1780–1860* (Cambridge, MA: Harvard University Press, 1977) and Alan Trachtenberg, *The Incorporation of America: Culture and Society in the Gilded Age* (New York: Hill and Wang, 1982).

20 See Richard L. Grossman and Frank T. Adams, "Exercising Power over Corporations Through State Charters," in *The Case Against the Global Economy: and for a turn toward the local,* edited by Jerry Mander and Edward Goldsmith (San Francisco: Sierra Club Books, 1996), pp. 374–89.

(imperfect examples) as clean water, clean air, national defense, and public order. Markets alone generally fail to provide public goods in an optimal fashion. Sometimes they fail to provide them at all. In order to promote economic efficiency, therefore, governments may have to act.[21]

This is most obvious in the case of an ideal, theoretically "pure" public good. A pure public good is one with completely *nonrival* and *nonexcludible consumption.* Nonrivalness means that there is no rivalry among consumers: no matter how many people consume such a good (perhaps the view of a beautiful mountain, for example), the cost of producing it does not increase. Nonexcludibility means that once the good (say, clean air) is produced, no one can be excluded from consuming it or be forced to pay for doing so. If a good has the characteristic of nonexcludibility, private markets will fail to produce it no matter how many people want it. When consumption is nonrival, the price (which is economically most efficient if it is set equal to marginal cost) should ideally be zero because it costs nothing for an additional person to consume the good. But what sort of businessperson would produce a good and then sell it for nothing? With nonexcludibility, there is no way to require consumers to pay any price at all, so, again, who would produce it? Economic theorists have shown that the result is highly inefficient.[22]

Take the traditional (though rather archaic) example of a lighthouse, which has some of the features of a public good. Consumption is more or less nonrival: it costs no more to let 50 ships – or 500 ships – use a light than it costs to let a single vessel use it. Also, once the light is shining, it is hard to exclude any ship from seeing it or to force a ship to pay for doing so. Left to themselves, therefore, private entrepreneurs have little or no incentive to build lighthouses. If we want to prevent ships from breaking up on the rocks, governments may have to act.[23]

[…]

A third function of government advocated by many economists and others is that of promoting economic growth and stability – ensuring that the entire economy grows at a desirable rate, does not suffer from excessively high levels of unemployment or inflation, and does not fall into damaging recessions or depressions.[24]

Economic theory does not offer very firm prescriptions about these matters. There is no agreed formula stating how much current consumption should be foregone for the sake of economic growth. Indeed, the relative importance of various causes of economic growth – aggregate demand, investment in plant and equipment, technological innovation, workforce education, public works infrastructure – is subject to debate, so it is difficult to assess exactly what should be done about them. There is even sharper disagreement about inflation and unemployment. In the short run, at least, there may exist a trade-off between the two: when unemployment declines, inflation tends to increase. Macroeconomic theorists disagree about which is the greater evil, what level of unemployment – if any – is "natural" (below which inflation is likely to accelerate), and what, if anything, government can and should do. Similar arguments concern whether and how government should try to smooth out economic fluctuations, counteracting the business cycle.[25]

In the 1980s, a chorus of conservative economists and policy advocates argued that government cannot and should not do much about any of these things except to fight inflation; efforts at short-run stimulation of the economy are futile because people see through their temporary nature and adapt in ways that defeat the policy efforts. Government, they said, should simply keep the money supply steady, stand aside, and let the great engine of free enterprise chug down the tracks, producing whatever growth and employment it can.[26] The appeal of this sort of laissez-faire doctrine tends to fade,

[21] Richard A. Musgrave and Peggy B. Musgrave, *Public Finance in Theory and Practice*, third edition (New York: McGraw-Hill, 1980) discuss public goods in the context of the "allocation" function of government.

[22] Paul A. Samuelson, "Diagrammatic Exposition of a Theory of Public Expenditure," *Review of Economics and Statistics*, 37 (1955), pp. 350–6. See also Musgrave and Musgrave, *Public Finance in Theory and Practice*, chapters 3 and 4.

[23] Ronald Coase and others have asserted that unaided private entrepreneurs have in fact built lighthouses, but the historical evidence appears to refute this proposition. British entrepreneurs were assisted by funds from government-enforced collection of port tolls, government-granted-monopolies and the like. See David van Zandt, "The Lessons of the Lighthouse: 'Government' or 'Private' Provision of Goods," *Journal of Legal Studies*, 22 (1993), pp. 47–72.

[24] Musgrave and Musgrave, *Public Finance in Theory and Practice*, call this the "stabilization" function of government.

[25] Macroeconomics textbooks differ from one to another and tend to change their tunes over time in response to economic events. Contrast, for example, the enthusiastic Keynesianism and pro-full employment attitude of Baumol and Blinder with the scepticism and strongly anti-inflation stand of Gordon. See William J. Baumol and Alan S. Blinder, *Macroeconomics: Principles and Policy*, seventh edition (Fort Worth, TX: Dryden Press, 1993); Robert J. Gordon, *Macroeconomics*, fifth edition (New York: HarperCollins, 1990).

[26] See David K. H. Begg, *The Rational Expectations Revolution in Macroeconomics: Theories and Evidence* (Baltimore: Johns Hopkins University Press, 1982); Preston J. Miller, *The Rational Expectations Revolution in Macroeconomics: Readings from the Front Line* (Cambridge, MA: MIT Press, 1994).

however, when things go badly wrong – as they did in the 1990–1 recession, one of the most severe economic contractions since World War II. High rates of inflation or unemployment, deep recessions, and slow economic growth invariably lead to calls for government action. Most Americans believe that the government has some degree of responsibility to make the overall economy work properly. For that matter, government probably has no choice but to try: it is so deeply involved in the economy that it is bound to have profound effects, and it may as well try to make those effects positive rather than negative.

One set of tools for macroeconomic policy making involves *fiscal* policy: the overall levels of taxes and spending, and the balance or imbalance between them. Budget deficits, representing an excess of spending over tax revenues, tend to stimulate aggregate demand, which in turn (under certain conditions, at least) produces higher levels of employment, counteracts recessions, and promotes higher levels of economic growth. The thought of John Maynard Keynes, though much contested, retains considerable vigor: many economists and others still argue that the government ought deliberately to run substantial deficits in times of recession in order to stimulate economic recovery. Other economists, especially in the period after the Reagan-era surge in annual US budget deficits, have maintained that reducing the deficit and then paying off part of the accumulated national debt should be the highest priority in American politics.

[...]

A second tool of macroeconomic policy involves management of the money supply and interest rates. By printing paper money or by issuing bonds, notes, and other moneylike obligations, the government can have major effects on interest rates, inflation, unemployment, and economic growth. "Tight money," when money is made hard to borrow by means of slow growth in the money supply and/or direct raising of interest rates by the Federal Reserve Board, tends to reduce inflation, but also to slow growth and to increase unemployment. An expanding money supply and low interest rates have the opposite effects. [...]

Historically, economic growth has eventually trickled down to help the poor; a rising tide has tended to lift all boats – though, as we saw in the last chapter, it did not do so in the 1970s and 1980s. Choices between unemployment and inflation can affect the rich and the poor quite differently. Wealthy creditors who loan their money out at fixed interest rates – the holders of bonds, for example – hate unanticipated inflation, which erodes the value of their assets, whereas ordinary working people are much more devastated by unemployment.

Dealing with poverty and inequality

A fourth possible function of government, the one of most interest to us in this book, derives from the fact that market outcomes may produce a highly unequal distribution of income and wealth. We may want government to do something to help the poor or to reduce inequality. Even Milton Friedman has taken this point. *Capitalism and Freedom* at one point hedged on the issue, maintaining that it is "difficult to justify" either accepting or rejecting an ethic of market-driven incomes equal to people's marginal product. But it also expressed openness to an extensive income-redistribution program in the form of a "negative income tax," which, Friedman argued, would minimally upset market allocations.[27] Others have taken it to be a major function of government, if not *the* major function, to provide a safety net for the neediest and to reduce excessive inequalities in wealth and income.[28]

[...]

If we love individual freedom and want all people to enjoy it, for example, we must recognize that there is not much freedom for the destitute. Disability, illness, hunger, and exposure to the elements are not conducive to a wide range of choices or to full self-development. Nor is bondage to a dead-end, low-paying job. Similarly, if we cherish the value of equal opportunity, the idea that everyone should have an equal chance at the "starting line" of life's competition, we must realize – at least when pressed – that accidents of birth and environment greatly advantage some and severely handicap others. Without compensatory action by government or some other agency, formally equal opportunity is likely to be an illusion. If we believe in fair treatment for all human beings, we are bound to see that much deprivation results from factors beyond people's control and requires collective help.

None of these values – not social order, sense of community, individual freedom, self-development, equal opportunity, or fair treatment – points toward total and complete equality. Each of them calls up a somewhat different vision of exactly what government should do. Nor, as we noted, does the utilitarian criterion of maximizing

27 Milton Friedman, *Capitalism and Freedom* (Chicago: University of Chicago Press, 1962), pp. 164–5, 191–2.

28 Musgrave and Musgrave, *Public Finance in Theory and Practice*, call this the "distribution" function of government. Most non-economists refer to "redistribution."

aggregate happiness prescribe perfect equality. The danger of losing some productive investment and work indicates that we should stop short of complete leveling. Just how far we should go depends both on how strong our egalitarian values are and on empirical questions about the precise terms of what Arthur Okun called the "big tradeoff" between efficiency and equity. As Okun put it, a bucket that carries (redistributes) income from one person to another may be leaky.[29]

[We] will be much concerned with the question of just how leaky – or how watertight – the "Okun bucket" actually is in the case of various specific policies. As we will see, the empirical evidence does not in fact establish the existence of such rigid barriers against redistribution as are often assumed in popular rhetoric. In a number of cases, equity and efficiency can go harmoniously together. The efficiency and practicality of measures to deal with poverty and inequality depend partly on just what our aims are and how well we design policy tools to accomplish them.

[...]

Conclusion

There are many reasons therefore to think that governments *should* act to reduce poverty and inequality, if they can do so in ways that do not entail too many costs: without too much inefficiency, for example, and without seriously infringing on individual liberties. Our review of the evidence indicates that government *can* in fact do so. The old canard that governments cannot do anything right is simply not correct. Nor is the newer claim that globalization renders national governments completely impotent. Yes, globalization does exert pressure against certain types of egalitarian programs, but those pressures are much less overpowering than is often supposed. Some important kinds of egalitarian programs (investment in education, for example; childhood health and nutrition; income supplements for low-wage work) actually can confer global competitive advantages, rather than disadvantages. Yes, it requires creativity and care to design programs to maximize their effectiveness, while minimizing red tape and bureaucratic interference. But such creativity and care are well within the reach of our experts, political leaders, and citizenry.

Right now, in fact, the US federal, state, and local governments *do,* in many efficient and effective ways, contribute to the reduction of poverty and inequality. At the same time, there remains much more that can and should be done. To make further progress requires recognizing and surmounting certain political and economic obstacles.

Programs that work [...] US social insurance programs, which offer certain kinds of protection that private insurance markets cannot provide, make very significant contributions to reducing poverty and inequality. Social Security in particular – the very foundation of American social policy – does more than any other government program to keep people's incomes above the poverty line. Without Social Security old age benefits, many more millions of elderly Americans would be poor, as many millions were before the enactment and expansion of the program.

That great reduction in poverty has been accomplished with a high degree of efficiency. Social Security's administrative costs amount to only about 1 percent of total payments. The poverty reduction has been achieved through a near-universal system of forced savings linked to work, in which people contribute while they are working and then quite properly feel entitled to benefits when they retire. The antipoverty effects are real; payroll contributions to Social Security have not merely replaced private savings that would have occurred without the program.

To be sure, Social Security is largely a middle-class program designed to smooth out individuals' earnings over their life cycles and to prevent disastrous losses of income upon retirement. It only modestly reduces inequality between the lifetime earnings of high- and low-income people. True also, the long-term financial health of the program will probably require some new resources, but those can be obtained relatively easily through such methods as extending the payroll tax to higher incomes, drawing on general tax revenues, and/or investing some tax revenues in higher-yield securities. The chief challenge for Social Security right now is simply to keep the program intact against forces working for benefit cuts or destructive privatization schemes.

Similarly, US social insurance programs do a reasonably good job of helping Americans who have severe disabilities that prevent them from working. Together with the Americans with Disabilities Act's legal provisions for nondiscrimination and mainstreaming, the benefits of Social Security's Disability Insurance (DI) and Supplemental

[29] See Arthur M. Okun, *Equality and Efficiency: The Big Tradeoff* (Washington, DC: Brookings, 1975). Any tradeoff between equality and efficiency would also affect the extent of equalization under Rawls' maximum criterion.

Security Income (SSI) have helped most gravely disabled Americans to avoid impoverishment.

Again, the Medicare program for the aged, despite its gaps in coverage, has greatly helped the elderly with medical expenses and (together with Medicaid) has prevented millions of people from sinking into poverty under the weight of bills for hospitals, doctors, and nursing homes. Although Medicare's scope and efficiency could be bettered by a universal health insurance system, the first task for the twenty-first century is simply to augment its financial resources and protect the program from benefit cutting or privatizing.

[...] It is possible to operate a fair tax system that sets tax rates according to ability to pay and reduces the inequality of after-tax incomes. A progressive personal income tax – at one time reviled as a form of "communism" – can accomplish those aims, as is clear from several periods of our history. It can do so at rather low administrative expense (vigorous enforcement efforts more than pay for themselves, though anti-government legislators have cut back enforcement in recent years) and without serious negative effects on work efforts or savings.

The income tax is also a useful vehicle for what may be the most effective of all work-encouraging antipoverty programs, the Earned Income Tax Credit (EITC). The refundable EITC has brought the total earnings of millions of low-wage workers close to or just above the poverty threshold. The EITC puts some reality behind the all-too-facile American promise that everyone who works hard can get a decent income. It does so in a way that is cheap to administer, reduces income maintenance expenses, and encourages increased work effort, thus increasing economic output and helping rather than hurting the United States in global competition.

In education and training, too, [...] various US government policies have enjoyed a great deal of success: considerably more success than they are usually given credit for. It is fashionable to disparage the US system of public elementary and secondary education as ineffective, internationally inferior, and perhaps hopeless. But this trashing – sometimes inflicted by armchair critics who are less than fully committed to a multicultural, egalitarian society – ignores the awesome magnitude of the tasks we want our schools to perform. It slights the schools' real achievements in accomplishing those tasks. We ask our public schools to teach everyone the basics, to socialize children of diverse cultural and linguistic backgrounds, to cope with economic and racial segregation, and to make up for absent or neglectful parents, all while working with limited amounts of unequally distributed money. The federal Elementary and Secondary Education Act has provided important resources for poor students and poor school districts. With federal government help, the system of higher education, too, has done a great deal of excellent teaching and research and has provided pathways to upward mobility for many Americans of modest background. Educational opportunities are certainly not equal for all Americans, and much needs to be done to improve this situation, but our educational system has the potential – to some extent already realized – to build up nearly everyone's skills and talents.

Several programs specifically designed to help educate and train the disadvantaged have demonstrated the capacity to do so. Head Start, despite surprisingly pinched funding, has helped prepare millions of poor children for school. Childhood health and nutrition programs provide some of the food and medical care that is essential for the development of sound minds in sound bodies. Special education helps many disabled children to acquire cognitive and social skills and the ability to function in mainstream society. Vocational education, apprenticeships, retraining, and welfare-to-work programs (particularly those that offer help with day care and transportation, as well as job training) have all demonstrated the capacity to prepare even severely disadvantaged Americans for useful work. Some of these programs require a substantial investment of resources in each trainee, but the trainees and society as a whole generally get good returns on the investment in terms of lifelong reductions in income maintenance payments, increased productive work, and more fulfilling lives.

[...] US public policies have fallen considerably short of the ideal of providing jobs for everyone at good wages. Yet here, too, effective policy tools are available and have been successful when used. The trick is to use them. When the US Congress, the president, and the Federal Reserve Board encourage economic growth through moderately expansive fiscal policies and low interest rates, for instance, the economy does tend to grow, unemployment falls, and the lowest-wage workers do better. (On the other hand, obsession with deficits and inflation has sometimes led to excessively tight money and unnecessarily steep recessions, in which low-income workers have suffered most.) Job creation through public service employment, when tried, has worked fairly well, and it could easily be made to work better. The minimum wage (when set at a reasonable level and not allowed to fall behind increases in the cost of living), together with the EITC, does a great deal to make sure that all work is rewarded by a living wage.

Antidiscrimination laws and regulations have helped reduce employment discrimination based on arbitrary factors like race and gender.

United States government policies have even successfully provided at least one important part of a minimal standard of living. [...] The Food Stamps program, our only near-comprehensive effort to provide an essential good to everyone in need, has sharply reduced the extent of hunger and malnutrition in America from the outrageously high levels that existed in the 1960s. Weathering years of ideological attacks and misleading rhetoric, Food Stamps have accomplished this very important task with limited and declining levels of fraud and with administrative costs that are reasonable, given the difficulty of determining eligibility and enforcing complex rules (some administrative costs could be saved by simplifying the rules and making Food Stamps universal). The much smaller and more grudging program of rental vouchers, and the experience of other countries like Canada with universal health insurance, makes clear that governments also have the capacity – not yet realized in the United States – to provide everyone with the basic necessities of shelter and medical care.

Amid the antigovernment rhetoric of the 1980s, John Schwarz wrote *America's Hidden Success,* documenting a number of important accomplishments of US social programs.[30] Yet the false images and outrageous assertions of government failure that Schwarz chronicled have proved surprisingly persistent – even as both the need for government action and the accomplishments of government have grown. We see no reason at all to despair about the capacity of governments to deal with the problems of poverty and inequality. The challenge is to make better use of that capacity.

William Galston, "Liberalism and Public Morality"*

During the past generation, the view has arisen that a liberal polity must remain systematically neutral on the widest possible range of moral and religious questions. During this same period, religious fundamentalism has attained an influence not seen in the United States for more than half a century. It is my thesis that these two developments are intimately related and that, considered together, they have much to teach us about the nature of liberalism.

Early liberal theorists worked to disentangle civil society from destructive religious quarrels. But they nevertheless assumed that civil society needed morality and that publicly effective morality rested on religion. Juridical liberalism, which focused on the exercise of liberty and the limits of government, presumed a foundation of individual moral restraint. In a liberal society, however, the civil authority would not directly enforce this moral code. Rather, the private sphere – primarily the family and voluntary religious associations – would sustain the moral foundations of a decent and orderly public sphere.

This understanding of the proper relation among politics, morality, and religion dominated the American Founding. It suffuses Tocqueville's analysis. In clearly recognizable form, it survived well into the twentieth century. In the past generation, however, this understanding came under attack, and the delicate balance between juridical liberalism and its social preconditions was disrupted. Influential forces equated liberty with the absence of all restraints. The Supreme Court encouraged this tendency, and it reinterpreted the Constitution to require impartiality, not just among religious faiths, but also between religion and irreligion. Many influential philosophers argued that the essence of liberalism was public neutrality on the widest possible range of moral issues. Thus, in John Rawls's view, "the liberal state rests on a conception of equality between human beings as moral persons, as creatures having a conception of the good and capable of a sense of justice. ... *Systems of ends are not ranked in value.*[31] And for Ronald Dworkin, the liberal state "must be neutral on ... the question of the good life. ... political decisions must be, so far as is possible, independent of any particular conception of the good life."[32] Early liberals maintained that, while the public sphere should eschew direct involvement in moral and religious issues, it must nonetheless draw moral sustenance from the private sphere. Contemporary liberals reply that the public institutions of liberalism do not and cannot rest on any particular conception of the good or of religion.

* William Galston, extracted from *Liberals on Liberalism*, edited by Alfonso Damico (Rowman & Littlefield, 1986), pp. 129–47.

[30] John E. Schwarz, *America's Hidden Success: A Reassessment of Public Policy from Kennedy to Reagan*, revised edition (New York: Norton, 1988).

[31] John Rawls, *A Theory of Justice* (Cambridge: Harvard University Press, 1971), p. 19; emphasis added.

[32] Ronald Dworkin, "Liberalism," in *Public and Private Morality*, edited by Stuart Hampshire (Cambridge: Cambridge University Press, 1978), p. 127.

This new dispensation soon encountered difficulties. To begin with, it was not firmly rooted in a popular consensus. The purely juridical understanding of liberalism was accepted by some elites, but by only a relatively small fraction of ordinary citizens. Worse, actualizing the juridical understanding meant dismantling long-established practices such as school prayer and restraints on pornography, a process that understandably evoked strong passions. The counterreaction was not slow to take shape. But although it depicts itself as purely defensive, this wave of fundamentalism in fact wishes to go well beyond the status quo ante, to a commingling of religion and the civil order that threatens the centuries-old doctrine of toleration itself.

Neither juridicalism nor fundamentalism can serve as an adequate basis for a liberal society. An urgent task of liberal theory, then, is to reflect anew on the moral preconditions of liberalism and to establish, more precisely than heretofore, how these preconditions can coexist with liberalism's powerful juridical tendencies. The following remarks, a somewhat untidy amalgam of historical and theoretical analyses, are offered as a point of departure for this task.

[...]

Early liberal theory is sometimes described as discarding concern for moral virtue altogether in favor of an orientation toward the non-moral goods of self-preservation, liberty, and property. This depiction is a half-truth. Early liberals do indeed reject the Aristotelian account of virtue as an intrinsic good. But they do not wholly extrude virtue from liberal theory. Rather, they redefine it as an instrumental good, essential for the attainment of the nonmoral goods that constitute the ends of liberal politics.

In this spirit, Hobbes constructs nineteen "laws of nature," the knowledge of which, he insists, is the "true moral philosophy."

> All men agree on this, that peace is good, and therefore also the way, or means of peace, which ... are justice, gratitude, modesty, equity, mercy, and the rest of the laws of nature, are good. ... But the writers of moral philosophy, though they acknowledge the same virtues and vices [do not see] wherein consisted their goodness; nor that they come to be praised as the means of peaceable, sociable, and comfortable living.[33]

Similarly, Locke supplements the juridical account of liberal government in the *Second Treatise* with his *Thoughts Concerning Education*, which spells out the virtues that support a liberal polity and society – self-denial, civility, justice, courage, humanity, industry, and truthfulness, among others. As Nathan Tarcov has argued, these virtues "are based on the same insights as his politics and serve the same goals, the preservation of oneself and others and avoidance of the injustice and contention that so disturb human life."[34] Lockean liberty is not just a fact, but rather an achievement: "Locke saw that we have to be willing to deny our desires, face our fears, endure our pains, and take pains in labor in order to preserve our equal liberty and avoid being either tyrants or slaves."[35]

While Locke defends a version of individual morality supportive of liberal politics, he also lays the foundation for what in our time has become an assault on the very concept of a public morality, carried out in the name of liberalism itself. I refer, of course, to the argument of the *Letter Concerning Toleration*.

Locke's challenge in the *Letter* was to define the appropriate relation between religion and the civil order. This was not merely a theoretical matter. In the wake of the Reformation, Europe had been wracked by a century of religious warfare. All the combatants sought to restore the unity of Christendom by imposing their version of religious truth through the coercive power of the state. In circumstances of deep diversity, these efforts ensured endless strife. Locke's doctrine of toleration (or, in our terms, state neutrality) was an attempt to reestablish the possibility of decent politics in the context of abiding disagreements about fundamental religious questions.

Setting to one side theses proceeding from Christianity itself, Locke may be said to make five arguments in favor of religious toleration or state neutrality, divided into three categories: arguments based on the nature of religious truth, on the nature of coercion, and on the nature of politics.

The first of these arguments may be called *epistemological neutrality*. For a wide range of religious disputes, Locke insists, no rational adjudication is possible among competing claims. This does not (necessarily) mean that there is no religious truth. But it does mean that no judge "on earth" is competent to determine it.[36] Locke's religious epistemology thus denies the basic premise through which public religious coercion is customarily justified.

33 Thomas Hobbes, *Leviathan*, chapter 15.

34 *Locke's Education for Liberty* (Chicago: University of Chicago Press, 1984), p. 183.

35 Ibid., pp. 210–11.

36 James H. Tully, ed., *A Letter Concerning Toleration* (Indianapolis: Hackett, 1983), p. 32.

Locke does not, however, rest his case on the elusiveness of religious truth. Even if religious truth could be intersubjectively established, he argues, the coercive weapons at the disposal of civil society could not possibly achieve their purported end – the inculcation of true belief or faith. "True and saving religion," Locke observes, "consists in the inward persuasion of the Mind, without which nothing is acceptable to God. And such is the nature of the understanding, that it cannot be compelled to the belief of any thing by outward force."[37] This argument I will call *ontological neutrality*.

Locke's third argument, *character-based neutrality*, also revolves around the nature of coercion, but from a moral rather than ontological standpoint. Those who use the power of the state to suppress religious dissent regularly invoke as their motive their love of truth and the desire to save souls. In fact, Locke contends, these self-appointed guardians of orthodoxy are moved by cruelty and lust for power.[38]

The remaining two arguments focus on the nature of politics. *Rights-based neutrality* rests on Locke's concept of limited government. Human beings enter into civil society to attain and protect nonmoral goods: goods of the body and external possessions. To secure these goods, the civil magistrate is created and invested with coercive power. It follows, Locke insists, that the sovereign's legitimate sway extends no further than this initial grant: "the whole jurisdiction of the Magistrate reaches only to these Civil Concernments [and] neither can nor ought in any manner to be extended to the salvation of souls."[39]

Even if it were proper for the magistrate to intervene in the religious practices of the citizenry, it would not be wise to do so. Locke's final argument, *prudential neutrality*, draws important conclusions from the fact of religious differences. In circumstances of deep diversity, Locke contends, the consequences of trying to impose uniformity are worse than the consequences of accepting the existence of controversial opinions – even deeply implausible opinions. History shows that religious coercion yields not agreement and civil concord, but rather discord, destruction, and war. The sovereign once invested with the power to enforce truth can turn that power against the truth. And finally, the suppression of diversity is in no way necessary to the peace and good order of civil society. Diversity is a threat to peace only if the magistrate is repressive.[40]

Locke's thesis may be summarized in three propositions. Because religious truth cannot be known with certainty, efforts to impose truth through coercion lack rational warrant. Even if religious truth could be established, faith cannot be imposed through coercion. And even if coercion could succeed, it would be wrong to employ it.

Locke's argument is less sweeping than the contemporary doctrine of state neutrality in two respects. To begin with, Locke distinguishes between coercion and persuasion. The fact that the sovereign cannot legitimately command a specific religious belief does not mean that civil authority cannot make arguments on behalf of that belief.[41] Second, Locke insists that in cases of conflict, civil authority takes precedence over religious faith. The key criterion is the maintenance of civil order. Opinions that threaten the peace of society need not be tolerated. So, for example, Locke declares that "No Opinion contrary to human society, or to those moral Rules which are necessary to the preservation of Civil Society, are to be tolerated by the Magistrate."[42] (Locke has no doubt that such a core morality *is* politically essential.) Nor should magistrates tolerate religions that diminish their legitimate sovereignty, such as those faiths that preach or imply allegiance to a foreign sovereign. Finally, the magistrate cannot tolerate those "who deny the Being of a God" because "Promises, Covenants, and Oaths, which are the bond of Humane Society, can have no hold upon an Atheist. The taking away of God, tho but even in thought, dissolves all."[43]

The flip-side of Locke's strictures against atheism is the remarkable convergence he discerns among all forms of religious faith, not just Christianity or even monotheism: "Neither Pagan, nor Mahumetan, nor Jew, ought to be excluded from the Civil Rights of the Commonwealth, because of his religion. ... the Commonwealth, which embraces indifferently all Men that are honest, peaceable, and industrious, requires it not."[44] In short, Locke suggests, civil society rests on certain opinions and moral rules, and religion *as such* tends to be consistent with, and supportive of, these prerequisites for a decent society. (The one exception is those religions whose teaching dilutes or divides civil sovereignty.) It follows that the sovereign should encourage all faiths without regard

37 Ibid., p. 27.

38 Ibid., pp. 23–24, 34–35.

39 Ibid., pp. 26, 43–44, 46–48.

40 Ibid., pp. 33, 42, 52–53.

41 Ibid., p. 27.

42 Ibid., p. 49.

43 Ibid., p. 51.

44 Ibid., p. 54.

to doctrinal distinctions. To be sure, civil authority may legitimately indicate a preference for certain doctrines over others, but not in a manner that impedes the free exercise of competing doctrines.

For Locke, then, the fact that religious doctrinal conflicts cannot be rationally resolved does not suggest that moral virtues and rules are equally unknowable. On the contrary: our rational knowledge of morality undergirds both the critique of religious intolerance and the principles governing the relations between religion and public order.

[...]

This Lockean understanding was the orthodox view among the American Founders.

[...]

By Tocqueville's time, then, a distinctively American political culture had been forged. Its major elements were three: the essentially secular principles of democratic liberalism, the moral maxims derived from Christianity, and the mores of Protestant Americans – in particular, white Anglo-Saxon males.

This amalgam proved remarkably enduring. At the turn of the century, Lord Bryce nicely captured its delicate balance between liberal and religious tendencies.

> It is accepted as an axiom by all Americans that the civil power ought to be not only neutral and impartial as between different forms of faith, but ought to leave these matters entirely on one side. [Nevertheless,] the national government, and the state governments do give Christianity [and by that he meant Protestant Christianity] a species of recognition inconsistent with the view that civil government should be absolutely neutral in religious matters.[45]

[...]

This unstable combination was still intact and clearly recognizable as late as the early 1950s. [...] Today, this cultural consensus is gone, replaced by pitched battles on numerous fronts. The critical event in this transformation was, I believe, the civil rights movement.

[...]

The civil rights movement was more than an appeal to the moral equality of human beings and the political equality of citizens. It was also the legitimation of social differences. Black Americans, after all, had a distinctive group identity, forged in the crucible of slavery and discrimination. This identity was in no way incompatible with American principles. But it was very far from the dominant white culture. Black Americans argued that they could not rightly be asked to surrender their distinctiveness as the price of full admission into our society. What makes us a nation, they argued, was voluntary adherence to shared political and moral principles – not forced assimilation to the mores of any social group. This argument, too, carried the day, and many long-suppressed elements of the black experience began to enter the mainstream of American culture.

The civil rights movement was pivotal, I suggest, not just because it so altered the condition of black Americans, but also because it became an inspirational metaphor for other aggrieved groups. In ensuing years, the subordination of women to men, of youth to age, of deviant sexuality to traditional families, of nonbelief to religion – all these hierarchies and more were challenged in the name of freedom, equality, and the recognition of legitimate differences.

This assault on traditional morality was pushed forward by two other forces.

It is a commonplace to stress the individualism of American culture. But, as Robert Bellah and his coauthors have recently reminded us, from the outset there has been a tension between Benjamin Franklin's utilitarian individualism (a lineal descendent of Lockean morality) and the expressive individualism of Emerson and Whitman. Each places the individual at the center of the moral universe. But while utilitarian individualism teaches that personal goals can be achieved in society only through adherence to moral and prudential maxims of self-restraint, expressive individualism argues that the fullness of being, craved by each individual, stands in opposition to the constraints of morality and society.[46] During the 1960s, this ancestral tension within the individualist tradition resurfaced in the form of generational warfare. Unlimited self-expression was held to be not only good in itself, but fully compatible with – indeed, mandated by – the classic liberal distinction between the public and private spheres.

The assault on traditional morality was also spurred on by the Supreme Court. Key decisions on school prayer, pornography, criminal justice, and abortion sharpened the line between public and private, widened individual freedom, and emphasized the requirement of state neutrality in areas previously seen as the legitimate arena for collective moral judgment.

45 *The American Commonwealth*, quoted in Philip B. Kurland, *Religion and the Law: Of Church and State and the Supreme Court* (Chicago: University of Chicago Press, 1978), pp. 18, 26.

46 Robert N. Bellah, Richard Madsen, William M. Sullivan, Ann Swidler, and Steven M. Tipton, *Habits of the Heart: Individualism and Commitment in American Life* (Berkeley: University of California Press, 1985), pp. 32–35.

In short, during the past generation, the longstanding balance between juridical liberal principles and a complex of traditional moral beliefs, many of which rested on religious foundations, was disrupted, with liberalism in the ascendency and tradition in retreat. From the unquestionable fact that many traditional practices, chief among them racial discrimination, violated liberal principles was inferred the dubious conclusion that traditionalism *as a whole* was opposed to the actualization of those principles.

Not surprisingly, these developments were received variously in different sectors of society. Among groups constrained or aggrieved by traditional practices, the rise of the secular, putatively neutral state was interpreted as the civil rights movement writ large – that is, as the long-overdue decision to live up to our founding principles. Among the partisans of what I am calling the tradition, the response was quite different. They wondered how school prayer could be unconstitutional if it had been part of our national life under the constitution for more than a century and a half. They wondered how legislation that assisted all schools could possibly be seen as an unconstitutional establishment of religion. They wondered how abortion could be transformed from a state issue to a national question, let alone a constitutional right. From their standpoint, the new assertion of strict state neutrality on matters of morals and religion was anything but neutral. Indeed, the defenders of the tradition saw it as an assault on the very foundations of public order.

[...]

To some extent, this disagreement revolves around differing interpretations of "neutrality." Juridical liberals typically argue as follows: toward every action, the public authority may take one of three stances. It may command the performance of the action; it may prohibit the action; or it may promulgate neither commands nor prohibitions, in which case individuals may choose for themselves. In this last case, the state is said to be neutral because it offers no authoritative judgment. Thus the state commands draft registration, prohibits murder, and permits – but takes no stand on – abortion.

Traditionalists do not accept this as an adequate account of neutrality. To permit a certain class of actions, they argue, is to make the public judgment that those actions are not wrong. No one denies that the state should prohibit murder. To permit abortion is therefore to determine (at least implicitly) that abortion is not murder. But this is precisely the issue between proponents and opponents of abortion. Permitting abortion cannot be construed as neutrality, because it rests on a substantive moral judgment that is anything but neutral.

[...]

Every contemporary liberal theory that begins by promising to do without a substantive theory of the good ends by betraying that promise. Indeed, all of them covertly rely on the same triadic theory of the good, which assumes, first, the worth of human existence; second, the worth of human purposiveness and of the fulfillment of human purposes; and finally, the worth of rationality as the chief constraint on social principles and actions. If we may call the belief in the worth of human existence and purposiveness the root assumption of humanism, then the liberal theory of the good is the theory of rationalist humanism.[47]

From this liberal theory of the good, moreover, there follows a canon of liberal virtues. The worth of human existence implies restraints on actions that terminate human life or diminish its quality – prohibitions, that is, against bloodthirstiness and cruelty. The worth of human purposiveness implies, first, the inappropriateness of denigrating worldly existence in light of the world to come; and second, the imperative of honoring a wide range of diverse human ends, a virtue we have come to call tolerance. The worth of rationality implies the virtues of civility and self-restraint in the conduct of both private and public life.

If this account is correct, then liberalism, far from embracing a thoroughgoing neutrality concerning human ends and human conduct, in fact requires a commitment to a specific account of the virtues and of the good.

[...]

These conflicting theses – that traditionalism and liberalism are opposed, and that they are mutually supportive – can be reconciled. My suggestion is that there is a substantial area of overlap between these two forces, as well as significant areas of conflict.

The relationship of mutual support obtains as long as both focus on what they share. It is supplanted by antagonism when one – or both – choose to emphasize what divides them. Pushed to the limit, the principles and practices of a liberal society tend inevitably to corrode moralities that rest either on traditional forms of social organization or on the stern requirements of revealed religion. Pushed to the limit, tradition and religion can end by denying the diversity – and the freedoms – at the heart of liberal society.

47 William A. Galston, "Defending Liberalism," *American Political Science Review*, 76, 3, pp. 621–9.

So, for example, the Moral Majority pushes its concern for the moral foundations of our institutions too far. As Harvey Mansfield, Jr. has written,

> The Moral Majority ... is concerned above all with the souls of Americans, but it has difficulty in finding a universal definition of the healthy individual suitable for a free, secular society. ... The Moral Majority seems to want to abolish the distinction between state and society.[48]

[48] Harvey C. Mansfield, Jr., "The American Election: Entitlements Versus Opportunity," *Government and Opposition*, 20, 1, p. 17.

But equally, liberal theorists (and activists) who deny the existence of legitimate public involvement in matters such as family stability, sexual conduct, moral education, and religion are unwittingly undermining the values and institutions they seek to support.

Liberal politics is in part the maintenance of proper balance between these tendencies – avoiding the extremes of moral intrusion that unduly restricts diversity and of moral abdication that gives illiberal tendencies full scope for development. Somewhere between the Moral Majority and the American Civil Liberties Union lies the art of liberal statemanship.

Chapter 14

On Justice

Introduction

Political theorists as diverse as Plato and John Rawls have suggested and proclaimed that justice is the first virtue of any political community. While we form and join political communities in order to cooperate and increase the available stock of social goods, each of us wants and expects our fair share when wealth, income, political power, social recognition, education, and other resources and opportunities are distributed. But what is a fair distribution? How fairly are money and other social goods distributed? What principles and procedures should be used to achieve more fair distributions?

How social goods are distributed is of great importance because it affects our individual destinies. Who is willing to cooperate in social production but receive such a small reward that they feel exploited and without the resources to live a decent – let alone a full – life? But how social goods are distributed is an issue that runs deeper than their effects on individuals. Social distributions influence the goodness and stability of political communities understood as collective entities, and they affect the character of their political processes.

It has been widely observed that, during the past three or four decades, social distributions, particularly of income and wealth, have become increasingly unequal in most political communities but especially in the United States. This prompted the American Political Science Association to do something it has seldom done: form a task force to make recommendations addressing a pressing political problem. That task force, chaired by Lawrence Jacobs – a political science professor at the University of Minnesota – and comprised of a virtual who's who in the discipline, issued its report at the end of 2004; our first selection provides key extracts from it. The report provides not only data on the extent and increase of inequality in the United States (and to a lesser extent in other countries like Great Britain and France), but it also reports the discipline's understandings of some of the causes and effects of rising economic inequality. It points out that such inequality is undermining American democracy, because it affects participation and policy responsiveness. Simply put, the affluent are far more likely to participate than the poor and to receive what they want from government; the rise in economic inequalities thus reduces the political equalities that democracies claim to provide. The report also points out that while rising economic inequalities have many causes, governmental policies themselves constitute one important set of such causes. Other Western democracies seem to have found policies that have dampened the increase in economic inequalities in their societies in ways that the US has not.

But are these increases in inequality unjust? The data reported by the APSA Task Force (unlike those reported by more radical authors and organizations) show that while the rich have become a lot richer in recent years, the poor have also achieved some modest gains. If everyone – or at least the average citizen within various economic classes – has gotten better off, who is to complain?

The most ambitious attempt to answer this question was provided by John Rawls in his 1971 magnum opus, *A Theory of Justice*. Our second selection is an effort by Rawls to explain his complex theory in ways that might be readily understood by the informed public. Rawls argues that "a well-ordered society is effectively regulated by a public conception of justice," which means that all citizens would use their reason to choose the same principles of justice, and everyone – governmental authorities as well as all citizens – would be guided in politics by these universally acknowledged principles. But what principles would we all acknowledge and why? To put Rawls' conclusions succinctly, we would all insist on being treated equally while permitting only those inequalities that benefit everyone, especially the least prosperous among us. In large part we would choose principles that protect the life chances of the disadvantaged members of the community, because if we adopt "the veil of ignorance" to conceal our own natural talents and our social circumstances that might bias our thinking, we would fear that we might be among the least well-heeled.

Our final two selections in this chapter reject such equalitarian concerns. Irving Kristol, a founder of "neo-conservatism" and its influential journal (*The Public Interest*) and a long-time associate of the American Enterprise Institute, provides and defends a capitalist conception of justice. Capitalist ideology does not regard unequal distributions as unfair. What it does promise is that following its principles improves the conditions of most people (if not literally everyone). It also provides a reasonable explanation for inequalities: if some get more than others, "the reason is to be found in their different contributions to the economy." But the major reason for upholding a capitalist conception of justice, according to Kristol, is that it avoids the authoritarianism implied by egalitarian theories. If we think that market justice is inadequate and pursue "social justice," someone will have to determine continuously what a socially just distribution requires and then use governmental power to deliver the desired result, but people will continuously disagree on what social justice requires and would resent continuous infringements on their freedom to provide it.

Robert Nozick (1938–2002), who like Rawls was a long-time professor of philosophy at Harvard University, responded to Rawls' theory when he published *Anarchy, State, and Utopia* in 1974. According to Nozick, principles of justice are not properly concerned with "the end results" of distributions, which preoccupy egalitarians like Rawls. Instead, they are concerned only with the process by which distributions occur. If unequal distributions result because of acts of production and exchange undertaken by free men and women – if they occur without any force or fraud – then each person is entitled to what (s)he has acquired. Nozick's libertarian theory of justice has many things in common with Kristol's capitalist theory, but notice that Kristol suggests that there should be a pattern to our economic distributions such that the more one contributes to the supply of demanded goods, the more one should receive in economic rewards. Nozick denies that this is a requirement of justice, as some people can be recipients of favorable exchanges even if they have not engaged in much production of economic goods.

Perhaps we see some merit in both capitalist and libertarian conceptions of justice, but we also have the sort of moral sympathies that Rawls' theory invokes and that Page and Simmons described in their selection in the last chapter. While pluralists are busy attempting to find principles that give adequate attention to these different concerns, there remains plenty of room for individual reflection and class discussion on this issue.

APSA Task Force on Inequality and American Democracy, "American Democracy in an Age of Rising Inequality"*

Equal political voice and democratically responsive government are cherished American ideals. Indeed, the United States is vigorously promoting democracy abroad. Yet, what is happening to democracy at home? Our country's ideals of equal citizenship and responsive government may be under growing threat in an era of persistent and rising inequalities. Disparities of income, wealth, and access to opportunity are growing more sharply in the United States than in many other nations, and gaps between races and ethnic groups persist. Progress toward realizing American ideals of democracy may have stalled, and in some arenas reversed.

We have reached this conclusion as members of the Task Force on Inequality and American Democracy formed under the auspices of the 14,000-member American Political Science Association (APSA). As one

* American Political Science Association Task Force on Inequality and American Democracy, extracted from *Perspectives on Politics*, 2, 4 (December 2004), pp. 651–66.

of several task forces formed to enhance the public relevance of political science, ours was charged to review and assess the best current scholarship about the health and functioning of US democracy in a time of rising inequality. We have surveyed the evidence about three interlinked areas of concern and their consequences: citizen participation, government responsiveness, and patterns of public-policy making. We have done our work as experts, paying close attention to data and evidence in all of their ambiguity.[1] Yet we also speak as concerned citizens of American democracy.

Generations of Americans have worked to equalize citizen voice across lines of income, race, and gender. Today, however, the voices of American citizens are raised and heard unequally. The privileged participate more than others and are increasingly well organized to press their demands on government. Public officials, in turn, are much more responsive to the privileged than to average citizens and the least affluent. Citizens with low or moderate incomes speak with a whisper that is lost on the ears of inattentive government, while the advantaged roar with a clarity and consistency that policy makers readily heed. The scourge of overt discrimination against African Americans and women has been replaced by a more subtle but still potent threat – the growing concentration of the country's wealth and income in the hands of the few.

Equal rights, rising economic inequality, and American democracy

American society has become both more and less egalitarian in recent decades. Following the civil rights revolution of the 1950s and 1960s, racial segregation and exclusion were no longer legally or socially acceptable. Whites and African Americans began to participate together in schools and colleges, the job market, and political and civic organizations. Gender barriers have also been breached since the 1960s, with women now able to pursue most of the same economic and political opportunities as men. Many other previously marginalized groups have also gained rights to full participation in American institutions and have begun to demand – and to varying degrees enjoy – the dignity of equal citizenship.[2]

But as US society has become more integrated across barriers of race, ethnicity, gender, and other longstanding forms of social exclusion, it has simultaneously suffered growing gaps of income and wealth. Gaps have grown not just between the poor and the rest of society, but also between privileged professionals, managers, and business owners on the one hand, and the middle strata of regular white- and blue-collar employees on the other hand. Many middle-class families are just barely staying afloat with two parents working.[3] And many African Americans, Latinos, and women who head families find themselves losing ground. There are signs of increased segregation by, for example, income and race in public schools.[4] Meanwhile, the rich and the super-rich have become much more so – especially since the mid-1970s. Indeed, the richest 1 percent of Americans has pulled away from not only the poor but also the middle class.

Rising economic inequality has been documented by extensive research, using diverse methodologies, which has analyzed authoritative government and nongovernment data.[5] Perfect income equality would mean that each fifth or quintile of the population (arrayed by income) would receive 20 percent of the country's income.[6] However, in 2001 the most affluent fifth received 47.7 percent of family income; the middle class

1 In addition to the sources specifically cited in this report, we rely upon evidence and citations in three broad reviews of the social science research prepared by our task force, focusing respectively on "Inequalities of Political Voice," "Inequality and American Governance," and "Inequality and Public Policy." See http://www.apsanet.org/inequality.

2 John D. Skrentny, *The Minority Rights Revolution* (Cambridge, MA: Belknap Press of Harvard University Press, 2002).

3 Timothy M. Smeeding, "Globalization, Inequality, and the Rich Countries of the G-20: Evidence from the Luxembourg Income Study Working Group," Luxembourg Income Study Working Paper 320 (July 2002).

4 Erica Frankenberg, Chumgmei Lee, and Gary Orfield, *A Multiracial Society with Segregated Schools: Are We Losing the Dream?* (Cambridge, MA: Harvard Civil Rights Project, 2002).

5 Data on economic inequality has been collected from authoritative sources including the US government (e.g., US Bureau of the Census, US Bureau of Labor Statistics, US Bureau of Economic Analysis, and US Internal Revenue Service) and the Luxembourg Income Study. Information on the distribution of income and other economic rewards in the United States can be found in Lawrence Mishel, Jared Bernstein, and Heather Boushey, *The State of Working America 2002/2003* (Ithaca: Cornell University Press, 2003). Evidence that compares income and wealth distributions in the United States and other advanced industrial democracies can be found in the Luxembourg Income Study (http://www.lisproject.org).

6 The next few paragraphs are based on Mishel, Bernstein, and Boushey, *The State of Working America 2002/2003*, 52–57, 86–94, 277–307, and table 1.8.

(the third and fourth fifths) earned 15.5 percent and 22.9 percent, respectively while the bottom two quintiles each received less than 10 percent. (Twenty-one percent of family income went to the top 5 percent.) Put simply, the richest 20 percent obtained nearly half of the country's income.

The highest earners, of course, have always enjoyed a disproportionate hold over income. The top quintile has enjoyed more than 40 percent of income in the United States since 1947. What stands out over the [last quarter-century] is the sharp and unmistakable *increase* in the concentration of income at the top. [...]

During this period members of the top fifth saw their income increase by 61.6 percent, much faster than any other part of the income distribution. Indeed, the top 5 percent grew even faster – 87.5 percent. The bottom fifth experienced the lowest rate of income growth in the same period (10.3 percent). Even the middle income groups grew at half or less the rate of the most affluent. [...]

Even as the distribution of income has moved rapidly to the top, the most affluent have attained a larger slice of the country's wealth (as defined by stock holdings, mutual funds, retirement savings, ownership of property, and other assets). [...] The top 1 percent of households drew 16.6 percent of all income but commanded more than double this proportion of the country's wealth (38.1 percent). By contrast, the supermajority of the country – the bottom 90 percent of households – earned the majority of household income (58.8 percent) but controlled only 29 percent of the country's wealth.[7] The tilted distribution of wealth in 1998 reflects a change. From 1979 to 2000, the share of income paid out in wages and benefits declined, while the portion tied to capital income rose – a unique development in post-World War II America.

Disparities in wealth and income have increased faster in the United States than in Canada, France, Germany, Italy, and nearly all other advanced industrial democracies. [Comparing] income trends for American families with those of British and French families [...] all three countries reduced inequality from the end of World War I until the 1960s. But the United States, from the mid-1970s on, rapidly diverged from its two allies in this respect. By 1998 the share of income accruing to the very rich was two or three times higher in the United States than in Britain and France.

Disparities are particularly striking when it comes to race. Since the civil rights era, the absolute levels of income and wealth enjoyed by African Americans and Hispanics have risen, but income and especially wealth remain far behind levels for white America. Living conditions, too, remain tenuous for the black middle class and continue to lag far behind. And, of course, the quality of life for African Americans below the middle class is even more precarious.

[...]

Economic inequalities in the United States result from a variety of causes – including developments in technology, transformations in family life, and market forces that promote global integration.[8] We leave it to others to pinpoint the precise economic and social changes that explain the rise in economic inequality. Many nations have faced the same changes as the United States; comparative research, however, indicates that the policies pursued by various governments matter. Regulations, tax policy, and social programs, for example, have been successfully used elsewhere to buffer market-generated increases in socioeconomic inequalities.[9] Policies pursued – or not pursued – help to explain sharper socioeconomic disparities in the United States compared to nearly all other advanced industrialized countries.

How concerned should we be about persistent and rising socioeconomic inequalities? According to opinion surveys, Americans accept considerable disparities of

7 Although the Federal Reserve's Survey was conducted near the stock market's peak (1999), the value of the stock market remained at or near record levels even after its sharp decline (1999 to 2001), with the wealthiest households enjoying much of the gain.

8 Gary Burtless, "Growing American Inequality: Sources and Remedies," in *Setting the National Priorities: The 2000 Election and Beyond*, edited by Henry Aaron and Robert Reischauer (Washington, DC: Brookings Institution, 1999), pp. 137–65; Richard Freeman, ed., *Working Under Different Rules* (New York: Russell Sage Foundation, 1994); Richard Freeman and Lawrence Katz, "Rising Wage Inequality: The United States vs. Other Advanced Nations," in Freeman, ed., *Working Under Different Rules*, pp. 29–62; Smeeding, "Globalization, Inequality, and the Rich Countries of the G-20"; Peter Gottschalk and Timothy Smeeding, "Cross-national Comparisons of Earnings and Income Inequality," *Journal of Economic Literature*, 35, 2 (1997), pp. 633–97; Sheldon Danziger and Daniel Weinberg, "The Historical Record," in *Confronting Poverty: Prescriptions for Change*, edited by Sheldon Danziger, Gary Sandefur, and Daniel Weinberg (Cambridge, MA: Harvard University Press, 1994), pp. 18–50.

9 Rigorous cross-national studies are available at http://www.lisproject.org. Our research review, "Inequality and Policy," discusses evidence regarding the distributional consequences of overall government policy and individual policies.

income and wealth – much more than their European counterparts do.[10] Unequal economic outcomes are seen as largely reflecting differences among individuals rather than flaws in the economic system. Americans support private property and free enterprise, and see much of the skewed distribution of wealth and income as a legitimate result of differences in individual talent and effort.

Americans accept economic inequalities only when they are sure that everyone has an equal chance to get ahead. Research shows that upward mobility remains an avenue of advancement for some Americans. But the number of Americans who are able to enjoy the fruits of upward mobility does not come close to offsetting the rise in economic disparities among the many.[11] The evidence demonstrates that economic opportunity and upward mobility are declining, challenging a core precept of the American dream.

Even more clearly, Americans celebrate and expect equal democratic rights. Americans fervently believe that everyone should have an equal say in our democratic politics and what government does. They embrace the ideal enunciated by the Declaration of Independence that "all men are created equal," which in our time is taken to mean that every citizen – regardless of income, gender, race, and ethnicity – should have an equal voice in representative government.

According to the National Elections Studies (NES) and other evidence, Americans are increasingly worried about disparities of participation, voice, and government responsiveness.[12] [...]

The evidence our task force has compiled suggests that our fellow citizens are right to be concerned about the health of our democracy. We find disturbing inequalities in the political voice expressed through elections and other avenues of participation. We find that our governing institutions are much more responsive to the privileged than to other Americans. And we find that the policies fashioned by our government today may be doing less than celebrated programs of the past to promote equal opportunity and security, and to enhance citizen dignity and participation. Indeed, trends in all three areas – citizen voice, government decision making, and public policy – may together be amplifying the influence of the few and promoting government unresponsiveness to the values and needs of the many. Such a negative spiral can, in turn, prompt Americans to become increasingly discouraged about the effectiveness of democratic governance, spreading cynicism and withdrawal from elections and other arenas of public life.

Unequal voices

Only some Americans fully exercise their rights as citizens, and they usually come from the more advantaged segments of society. Those who enjoy higher incomes, more occupational success, and the highest levels of formal education are the ones most likely to participate in politics and make their needs and values known to government officials.

Our review of research on inequality and political participation as well as other components of American political life demonstrates an extraordinary association between economic and political inequality. [...]

Voting is the most obvious means for Americans to exercise their rights of citizenship, yet only a third of eligible voters participate in midterm congressional elections and only about half turn out for today's presidential elections. Even voters in presidential elections tend to be from the ranks of the most advantaged Americans. Figure [1], based on a national survey of Americans in 1990, compares the political activity of two income groups (each of which constituted roughly one-fifth of the sample) – those having family incomes below $15,000 and those at the top of the income ladder, with family incomes over $75,000. Nearly 9 out of 10 individuals in families with incomes over $75,000 reported voting in presidential elections while only half of those in families with incomes under $15,000 reported voting.

[...]

[10] David L. Weakliem, Robert Andersen, and Anthony F. Heath, "The Directing Power? A Comparative Study of Public Opinion and Income Distribution" (Storrs, CT: Department of Sociology, University of Connecticut, 2003); Benjamin I. Page and Robert Y. Schapiro, *The National Public: Fifty Years of Trends in American Policy Preferences* (Chicago: University of Chicago Press, 1992).

[11] Peter Gottschalk, "Inequality, Income Growth, and Mobility: The Basic Facts," *Journal of Economic Perspectives*, 11, 2 (1997), pp. 21–40; Timothy Smeeding, "Public Policy and Economic Inequality: The United States in Comparative Perspective," paper prepared for Campbell Institute Seminar, Inequality and American Democracy (February 20, 2004): www.maxwell.syr.edu/campbell/Events/smeeding.pdf; Walter Benn Michaels, "Diversity's False Solace," *New York Times Magazine* (April 11, 2004).

[12] Unless otherwise noted, the data cited in this paragraph are from NES; see especially the chapters by Gary Orren, "Fall from Grace: The Public's Loss of Faith in Government," and Robert J. Blendon, John M. Benson, Richard Morin, Drew E. Altman, Mollyann Brodie, Marios Brossard, and Matt James, "Changing Attitudes in America," in Joseph S. Nye, Jr., Philip D. Zelikow, and David C. King, eds., *Why People Don't Trust Government* (Cambridge, MA: Harvard University Press, 1997).

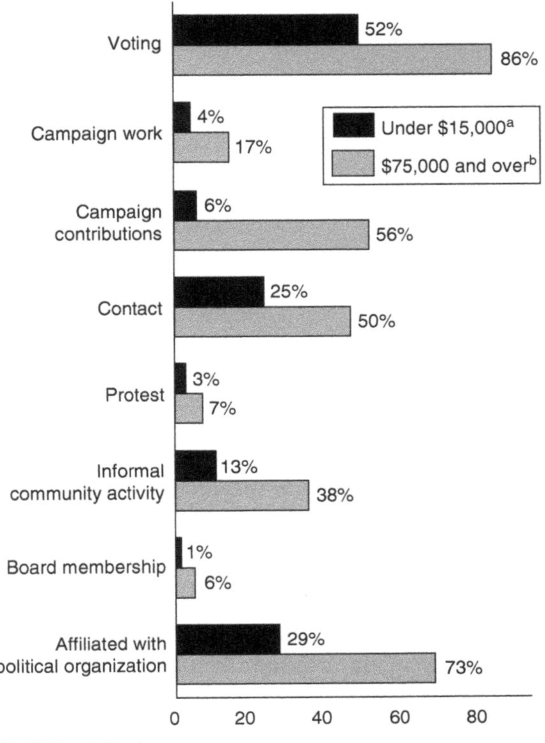

Figure [1] Percentage active in various political activities: high- and low-income groups

Low and unequal voting is sobering in part because casting a ballot is America's most widespread form of political participation. Many fewer than half of the Americans who vote in presidential elections take part in more time-consuming and costly political activities, such as making financial contributions to candidates, working in electoral campaigns, contacting public officials, getting involved in organizations that take political stands, and demonstrating for or against political causes.

[...]

Disparities in participation mean that the concerns of lower- or moderate-income Americans, racial and ethnic minorities, and legal immigrants are systematically less likely to be heard by government officials. In contrast, the interests and preferences of the better-off are conveyed with clarity, consistency, and forcefulness.

Unequal political voice matters because the advantaged convey very different messages to government officials than do the rest of the citizenry. For example, Americans who participate in politics are much less likely than many of their fellow citizens to have known the necessity of having to work extra hours to get by. The privileged are unlikely to have delayed medical treatment for economic reasons or cut back on their spending for food or their children's education. Those Americans who would be most likely to raise issues about basic opportunities and needs – from escaping poverty to securing jobs, education, health care, and housing – tend to be the least likely to participate in politics. The less advantaged are so absent from discussions in Washington that government officials are likely to hear about their concerns, if at all, from privileged advocates who try to speak for them.[13]

Political voice is also unequal because Americans who are very active in politics often have more intense or extreme views than average citizens. They tend, for instance, to identify themselves as far more conservative or liberal. The most loyal partisans and fringe activists have become more prominent in US politics in recent times with the erosion of such mass mobilizing organizations as voluntary associations and unions, a development that may have significant consequences for American governance. The intense and unrelenting expressions of "extremists" (combined with the proliferation of interest groups speaking for specialized constituencies) make it harder for government to work out compromises or to respond to average citizens, who may have more middle-of-the-road opinions about a range of important matters, from abortion to tax cuts.[14]

How government responds

Generations of reformers have understood a simple truth: what government officials hear influences what they do. What citizens do or don't do in politics affects what happens in the halls of government. Because government officials today hear more clearly and more often from privileged and highly active citizens, policy

[13] Sidney Verba, Kay Lehman Schlozman, and Henry E. Brady, *Voice and Equality: Civic Voluntarism in American Politics* (Cambridge, MA: Harvard University Press, 1995).

[14] Morris P. Fiorina, "Extreme voices: A dark side of civic engagement," in *Civic Engagement in American Democracy*, edited by Theda Skocpol and Morris P. Fiorina (Washington, DC, and New York: Brookings Institution Press and Russell Sage Foundation, 1999), pp. 396–425; Theda Skocpol, "Diminished democracy: From membership to management in American civic life" (Norman: University of Oklahoma Press, 2003).

makers are less likely to respond readily to the concerns of the majority. The skew in political participation toward the advantaged increases the probability of policies that tilt toward maintaining the status quo and continue to reward the organized and already well-off.

[...]

Today politicians are *not* usually directly bribed by political contributors or moneyed interests. Research does not support the idea that specific votes in Congress are directly determined by campaign contributions.[15] What wealthy citizens and moneyed interests do gain from their big contributions is influence over who runs for office and a *hearing* from politicians and government officials.

Money is the oxygen of today's elections, given the reliance of candidates on high-priced consultants and expensive media advertisements.[16] Big contributors have the power to discourage or perhaps suffocate unfriendly candidates by denying them early or consistent funding. After the election, moreover, government officials need information to do their jobs, and research shows that big contributors earn the privilege of meeting regularly with policy makers in their offices. Money buys the opportunity to present self-serving information or raise some problems for attention rather than others.

Generous contributors also attend countless rounds of fund-raisers. They build relationships with government officials who can undertake helpful, low-profile actions – inserting a rider into an omnibus bill, expediting the scheduling of a bill that has been languishing in committee, or making sure that threatening regulatory legislation receives minimal funding for implementation. Equally important, legislators can decide to pay more attention to the kinds of concerns that big contributors press forward, such as requests for a narrowly targeted subsidy, tax cut, or regulatory exemption, than to problems of broader democratic import.

[...]

Recent changes in how Congress designs legislation reinforce and expand the advantages of the organized. Government money to fund projects – from building highways and waterways to constructing buildings – has long been allocated to well-organized and vocal groups with connections inside Washington. A century ago, the reforms of the Progressive Era aimed to end machine politics that doled out government funds, or "pork," in exchange for votes and campaign contributions. Civil service exams, government oversight, and a more watchful press put a stop to the crudest forms of corruption. But the best-organized still feast on discretionary government spending because members of Congress remain convinced that pork produces votes and campaign contributors.

New developments within Congress have more finely targeted government largess to narrow factions. As the two parties have polarized into increasingly warring tribes, the majority party in Congress has funneled greater proportions of defense contracts, transportation funding, appropriation earmarks for higher-education institutions, and other programs to the districts of fellow partisans. Members of Congress have further directed government funds coming into their districts to specific geographic areas that vote at higher rates and provide their greatest support.[17]

[...]

15 Stephen Ansolabehere, John M. de Figueiredo, and James M. Snyder, "Why is there so little money in US politics?" Working Paper 9409 (Cambridge, MA: National Bureau of Economic Research, 2003a), *Journal of Economic Perspectives*, 17, 1 (2003b), pp. 105–30; John R. Wright, "PACs, contributions and roll calls: An organizational perspective," *American Political Science Review*, 79, 2 (1985), pp. 400–14; John R. Wright, "Contributions, lobbying, and committee voting in the U.S. House of Representatives," *American Political Science Review*, 84, 2 (1990), pp. 417–38.

16 J. David Gopoian, "What makes PACs tick? An analysis of the allocation patterns of economic interest groups," *American Journal of Political Science*, 28, 2 (1984), pp. 259–81; Richard L. Hall and Frank W. Wayman, "Buying time: Moneyed interests and the mobilization of bias in congressional committees," *American Political Science Review*, 84, 3 (1990), pp. 797–820; Randall S. Kroszner and Thomas Stratmann, "Interest group competition and the organization of Congress: Theory and evidence from financial services political action committees," *American Economic Review*, 88, 5 (1998), pp. 1163–87; Laura Langbein, "Money and access: Some empirical evidence," *Journal of Politics*, 48, 4 (1986), pp. 1052–62.

17 Steven Balla, Eric Lawrence, Forrest Maltzman, and Lee Sigelman, "Partisanship, blame avoidance, and the distribution of legislative pork," *American Journal of Political Science*, 46, 3 (2002), pp. 515–25; Thomas Carsey and Barry Rundquist, "Party and committee in distributive politics: Evidence from defense spending," *Journal of Politics*, 61, 4 (1999), pp. 1156–69; Frances Lee, "Senate representation and coalition building in distributive politics," *American Political Science Review*, 94, 1 (2000), pp. 59–72; Steven Levitt and James Snyder, "Political parties and the distribution of federal outlays," *American Journal of Political Science*, 39, 4 (1995), pp. 958–80; Steven Levitt and James Snyder, "The impact of federal spending on House election outcomes," *Journal of Political Economy*, 105, 1 (1997), pp. 30–53.

Skewed participation among citizens and the targeting of government resources to partisans and the well-organized ensure that government officials disproportionately respond to business, the wealthy, and the organized when they design America's domestic and foreign policies.[18]

Recent research strikingly documents that the votes of US senators are far more influenced by the policy preferences of each senator's rich constituents than by the preferences of the senator's less privileged constituents.[19] In particular, income-weighted preferences were much more influential than simple averages of state opinion, especially for Republican senators. Constituents at the 75th percentile of the income distribution had almost three times as much influence as those at the 25th percentile on their senators' general voting patterns, and even more disproportional influence on specific salient roll call votes on the minimum wage, civil rights, government spending, and abortion. The preferences of constituents in the bottom fifth of the income distribution had little or no effect on their senators' votes.

The bias in government responsiveness toward the affluent is evident not only in Congress but also in national government policy more generally. Government officials who design policy changes are more than twice as responsive to the preferences of the rich as to the preferences of the least affluent.[20] The rich have even greater leverage, moreover, when their preferences diverge substantially from the preferences of the poor. The rich generally win "class warfare" in government offices.

[...]

Missed opportunities for democratic government

What government does not do is just as important as what it does.[21] It is difficult, however, to pin down the effect of disparities of influence on what government fails to do. Through much of US history, our government has responded to the life circumstances of ordinary citizens by enacting major policies to spread opportunities and provide security to millions of individuals and families. Numerous studies by scholars and independent researchers document that public education, Social Security and Medicare, the GI Bill, home-mortgage programs, and many other efforts have enhanced the quality of life for millions of regular Americans.

These broadly inclusive government programs have also encouraged ordinary citizens to become more active participants in our democracy. The United States pioneered schooling for all and has spent as much as or more than many advanced industrialized countries on it since the 1800s. Promotion of education has helped to open the door to opportunity for students who work hard, to propel the country's economy, and to lower economic disparities. It has also boosted participation in volunteer organizations and democratic life. The GI Bill extended generous assistance to attend universities, community colleges, and vocational schools for millions of veterans of World War II and the Korean War.[22] Since the 1970s, federal programs like Pell Grants and state initiatives have allowed millions of lower- and middle-income students to pursue post-secondary schooling.

Similarly, Social Security, which provides protection against low income in retirement to employees who

18 Lawrence R. Jacobs and Robert Y. Shapiro, "Issues, candidate image and priming: The use of private polls in Kennedy's 1960 presidential campaign," *American Political Science Review*, 88, 3 (1994), pp. 527–40. Robert S. Erikson, Michael B. MacKuen, and James A. Stimson, in *The Macro Polity* (New York: Cambridge University Press, 2002) offer an alternative interpretation. Our research review, "Inequality and American Governance," discusses this alternative account, noting, in part, that the empirical analysis of the full political system in Erikson, MacKuen, and Stimson is not inconsistent with the account offered here.

19 Larry M. Bartels, "Economic inequality and political representation," paper presented at the 2002 Annual Meeting of the American Political Science Association, Boston. http://www.princeton.edu/~bartels/papers.

20 A 10 percentage point increase in support for policy change among the best-off (i.e., those in the 90th percentile of the income distribution) was associated with a 4.8 percentage point increase in the likelihood of a corresponding policy change; the preferences of the poorest (i.e., individuals in the 10th percentile of the income distribution) produced only a 2 percentage point increase in the likelihood of a corresponding policy shift. See Martin Gilens, "Public opinion and Democratic responsiveness: Who gets what they want from government?" Paper presented at the Inequality and American Democracy Conference, Princeton, NJ, November 7–8, 2003. http://www.princeton.edu/~csdp/events/pdfs/Gilens.pdf.

21 This point is developed in Jacob S. Hacker, "Privatizing risk without privatizing the welfare state: The hidden politics of social policy retrenchment in the United States," *American Political Science Review*, 98, 2 (2004), pp. 243–60.

22 Suzanne Merrler, "Bringing the state back in to civic engagement: Policy feedback effects of the G.I. Bill for World War II veterans," *American Political Science Review*, 96, 2 (2002), pp. 351–65.

contribute to the system, has helped to foster an extraordinary level of participation by the elderly in the electoral process and civic life. Social Security has encouraged participation by low- and moderate-income seniors, which means that the elderly are less subject to the skew in favor of the affluent and better-educated that generally characterizes political participation in the United States.[23]

America can boast, then, of a distinguished track record of government programs that have not only enhanced opportunity and security for the many, but also promoted democracy by expanding political voice.

But what are the equivalents of such broadly responsive programs today? The educational and training benefits for America's all-volunteer military are modest compared with those in the original GI Bill and, consequently, they have been less effective in boosting the schooling of veterans to the level of nonveterans.[24] Moreover, rising tuition, the declining value of individual Pell Grants, and state budget cuts have made higher education less affordable to nonveterans at a time when its economic value has risen and its contribution to counteracting the bias in political participation is invaluable.[25]

While Social Security protects and engages seniors, few government programs ensure opportunity and security and encourage political engagement for Americans who are not elderly. This situation reinforces the preoccupation of political leaders with improving the programs of the aged rather than assisting young and old alike. The fact that nonelderly Americans are less engaged in politics than the elderly makes it less likely that our government will adequately address the many challenges faced by working-age adults and their children – access to affordable health care, paying for higher education, and finding ways to care for family members when parents must work full-time. Judging from public opinion surveys, large majorities of Americans would like our government to find ways to support citizens of all ages as they face old and new challenges. Our government, however, is too often failing to respond.

[...]

The Declaration of Independence promised that all American citizens would enjoy equal political rights. Nearly every generation has returned to this promise and struggled to elevate the performance of American democracy to its high ideals. The promise of American democracy is threatened again. The threat is less overt than the barriers of law or social custom conquered by earlier generations. Today, the risk is that rising economic inequality will solidify longstanding disparities in political voice and influence, and perhaps exacerbate such disparities. Our government is becoming less democratic, responsive mainly to the privileged and not a powerful instrument to correct disadvantages and look out for the majority. If disparities of participation and influence become further entrenched – and if average citizens give up on democratic government – unequal citizenship could take on a life of its own, weakening American democracy for a long time to come.

[23] Andrea Louise Campbell, *How Policies Make Citizens; Senior Political Activism and the American Welfare State* (Princeton: Princeton University Press, 2003).

[24] Jere Cohen, Rebecca Warner, and David Segal, "Military Service and educational attainment in the all-Volunteer Force," *Social Science Quarterly*, 76, 1 (1995), pp. 88–104.

[25] National Center for Public Policy and Higher Education, *Losing Ground: A National Status Report on the Affordability of American Higher Education* (San Jose, CA, 2002) http://www.highereducation.org/reports/losing_ground/ar.shtml.

John Rawls, "A Kantian Conception of Equality"*

My aim in these remarks is to give a brief account of the conception of equality that underlies the view expressed in *A Theory of Justice* and the principles considered there. I hope to state the fundamental intuitive idea simply and informally; and so I make no attempt to sketch the argument from the original position. In fact, this construction is not mentioned until the end and then only to indicate its role in giving a Kantian interpretation to the conception of equality already presented.

I

When fully articulated, any conception of justice expresses a conception of the person, of the relations between persons, and of the general structure and ends of social co-operation. To accept the principles that represent a conception of justice is at the same time to accept an ideal of the person; and in acting from these principles we realize such an ideal. Let us begin, then, by trying to describe the kind of person we might want to be and the form of society we might wish to live in and to shape our interests and character. In this way we arrive at the notion of a well-ordered society. I shall first describe this notion and then use it to explain a Kantian conception of equality.

* John Rawls, extracted from *Cambridge Review*, 1975.

First of all, a well-ordered society is effectively regulated by a public conception of justice. That is, it is a society all of whose members accept, and know that the others accept, the same principles (the same conception) of justice. It is also the case that basic social institutions and their arrangement into one scheme (the basic structure) actually satisfy, and are on good grounds believed by everyone to satisfy, these principles. Finally, publicity also implies that the public conception is founded on reasonable beliefs that have been established by generally accepted methods of inquiry; and the same is true of the application of its principles to basic social arrangements. This last aspect of publicity does not mean that everyone holds the same religious, moral, and theoretical beliefs: on the contrary, there are assumed to be sharp and indeed irreconcilable differences on such questions. But at the same time there is a shared understanding that the principles of justice, and their application to the basic structure of society, should be determined by considerations and evidence that are supported by rational procedures commonly recognized.

Secondly, I suppose that the members of a well-ordered society are, and view themselves as, free and equal moral persons. They are moral persons in that, once they have reached the age of reason, each has, and views the others as having, a realized sense of justice; and this sentiment informs their conduct for the most part. That they are equal is expressed by the supposition that they each have, and view themselves as having, a right to equal respect and consideration in determining the principles by which the basic arrangements of their society are to be regulated. Finally, we express their being free by stipulating that they each have, and view themselves as having, fundamental aims and higher-order interests (a conception of their good) in the name of which it is legitimate to make claims on one another in the design of their institutions. At the same time, as free persons they do not think of themselves as inevitably bound to, or as identical with, the pursuit of any particular array of fundamental interests that they may have at any given time; instead, they conceive of themselves as capable of revising and altering these final ends and they give priority to preserving their liberty in this regard.

In addition, I assume that a well-ordered society is stable relative to its conception of justice. This means that social institutions generate an effective supporting sense of justice. Regarding society as a going concern, its members acquire as they grow up an allegiance to the public conception and this allegiance usually overcomes the temptations and strains of social life.

Now we are here concerned with a conception of justice and the idea of equality that belongs to it. Thus, let us suppose that a well-ordered society exists under circumstances of justice. These necessitate some conception of justice and give point to its special role. First, moderate scarcity obtains. This means that although social co-operation is productive and mutually advantageous (one person's or group's gain need not be another's loss), natural resources and the state of technology are such that the fruits of joint efforts fall short of the claims that people make. And second, persons and associations have contrary conceptions of the good that lead them to make conflicting claims on one another; and they also hold opposing religious, philosophical, and moral convictions (on matters the public conception leaves open) as well as different ways of evaluating arguments and evidence in many important cases. Given these circumstances, the members of a well-ordered society are not indifferent as to how the benefits produced by their co-operation are distributed. A set of principles is required to judge between social arrangements that shape this division of advantages. Thus the role of the principles of justice is to assign rights and duties in the basic structure of society and to specify the manner in which institutions are to influence the overall distribution of the returns from social cooperation. The basic structure is the primary subject of justice and that to which the principles of justice in the first instance apply.

It is perhaps useful to observe that the notion of a well-ordered society is an extension of the idea of religious toleration. Consider a pluralistic society, divided along religious, ethnic, or cultural lines in which the various groups have reached a firm understanding on the scheme of principles to regulate their fundamental institutions. While they have deep differences about other things, there is public agreement on this framework of principles and citizens are attached to it. A well-ordered society has not attained social harmony in all things, if indeed that would be desirable; but it has achieved a large measure of justice and established a basis for civic friendship, which makes people's secure association together possible.

II

The notion of a well-ordered society assumes that the basic structure, the fundamental social institutions and their arrangement into one scheme, is the primary subject of justice. What is the reason for this assumption? First of all, any discussion of social justice must take the nature of the basic structure into account. Suppose we begin with the initially attractive idea that the social process should be allowed to develop over time as free agreements fairly arrived at and fully honoured require. Straightaway we need an account of when agreements are free and the conditions under which they are reached are fair. In addition, while these conditions may be satisfied at an earlier time, the accumulated results of agreements in conjunction with social and historical contingencies are likely to change institutions and opportunities so that the conditions for free and fair agreements no longer hold. The basic structure specifies the background conditions against which the actions of individuals, groups, and associations take place. Unless this structure is regulated and corrected so as to be just over time, the social process with its procedures and outcomes is no longer just, however free and fair particular transactions may look to us when viewed by themselves.

[...]

The justice of the basic structure is, then, of predominant importance. The first problem of justice is to determine the principles to regulate inequalities and to adjust the profound and long-lasting effects of social, natural, and historical contingencies, particularly since these contingencies combined with inequalities generate tendencies that, when left to themselves, are sharply at odds with the freedom and equality appropriate for a well-ordered society. In view of the special role of the basic structure, we cannot assume that the principles suitable to it are natural applications, or even extensions, of the familiar principles governing the actions of individuals and associations in everyday life which take place within its framework. Most likely we shall have to loosen ourselves from our ordinary perspective and take a more comprehensive viewpoint.

III

I shall now state and explain two principles of justice, and then discuss the appropriateness of these principles for a well-ordered society. They read as follows:

1 Each person has an equal right to the most extensive scheme of equal basic liberties compatible with a similar scheme of liberties for all.
2 Social and economic inequalities are to meet two conditions: they must be (a) to the greatest expected benefit of the least advantaged, and (b) attached to offices and positions open to all under conditions of fair opportunity.

The first of these principles is to take priority over the second; and the measure of benefit to the least advantaged is specified in terms of an index of social primary goods. These goods I define roughly as rights, liberties, and opportunities, income and wealth, and the social bases of self-respect. Individuals are assumed to want these goods whatever else they want, or whatever their final ends. The least advantaged are defined very roughly, as the overlap between those who are least favoured by each of the three main kinds of contingencies. Thus this group includes persons whose family and class origins are more disadvantaged than others, whose natural endowments have permitted them to fare less well, and whose fortune and luck have been relatively less favourable, all within the normal range (as noted below) and with the relevant measures based on social primary goods. Various refinements are no doubt necessary, but this definition of the least advantaged suitably expresses the link with the problem of contingency and should suffice for our purposes here.

[...]

Now the members of a well-ordered society are free and equal; so let us first consider the fittingness of the two principles to their freedom, and then to their equality. These principles reflect two aspects of their freedom, namely, liberty and responsibility, which I take up in turn. In regard to liberty, recall that people in a well-ordered society view themselves as having fundamental aims and interests which they must protect, if this is possible. It is partly in the name of these interests that they have a right to equal consideration and respect in the design of their society. A familiar historical example is the religious interest; the interest in the integrity of the person, freedom from psychological oppression and from physical assault and dismemberment is another. The notion of a well-ordered society leaves open what particular expression these interests take; only their general form is specified. But individuals do have interests of the requisite kind and the basic liberties necessary for their protection are guaranteed by the first principle.

It is essential to observe that these liberties are given by a list of liberties; important among these are freedom of thought and liberty of conscience, freedom of the person and political liberty. These liberties have a central range of application within which they can be limited and compromised only when they conflict with other basic liberties. Since they may be limited when they clash with one another, none of these liberties is absolute; but however they are adjusted to form one system, this system is to be the same for all. It is difficult, perhaps impossible, to give a complete definition of these liberties independently from the particular circumstances, social, economic, and technological, of a given well-ordered society. Yet the hypothesis is that the general form of such a list could be devised with sufficient exactness to sustain this conception of justice. Of course, liberties not on the list, for example, the right to own certain kinds of property (e.g., means of production), and freedom of contract as understood by the doctrine of laissez-faire, are not basic, and so they are not protected by the priority of the first principle.[26]

One reason, then, for holding the two principles suitable for a well-ordered society is that they assure the protection of the fundamental interests that members of such a society are presumed to have. [...] As I noted earlier, they do not think of themselves as unavoidably tied to any particular array of fundamental interests; instead they view themselves as capable of revising and changing these final ends. They wish, therefore, to give priority to their liberty to do this, and so their original allegiance and continued devotion to their ends are to be formed and affirmed under conditions that are free. Or, expressed another way, members of a well-ordered society are viewed as responsible for their fundamental interests and ends. While as members of particular associations some may decide in practice to yield much of this responsibility to others, the basic structure cannot be arranged so as to prevent people from developing their capacity to be responsible, or to obstruct their exercise of it once they attain it. Social arrangements must respect their autonomy and this points to the appropriateness of the two principles.

IV

These last remarks about responsibility may be elaborated further in connection with the role of social primary goods. As already stated, these are things that people in a well-ordered society may be presumed to want, whatever their final ends. And the two principles assess the basic structure in terms of certain of these goods: rights, liberties, and opportunities, income and wealth, and the social bases of self-respect. The latter are features of the basic structure that may reasonably be expected to affect people's self-respect and self-esteem (these are not the same) in important ways.[27] Part (a) of the second principle (the difference principle, or as economists prefer to say, the maximum criterion) uses an index of these goods to determine the least advantaged. [...]

It is not suggested that people must modify their desires and ends whatever their circumstances. The doctrine of primary goods does not demand the stoic virtues. Society for its part bears the responsibility for upholding the principles of justice and secures for everyone a fair share of primary goods (as determined by the difference principle) within a framework of equal liberty and fair equality of opportunity. It is within the limits of this division of responsibility that individuals and associations are expected to form and moderate their aims and wants. Thus among the members of a well-ordered society there is an understanding that as citizens they will press claims for only certain kinds of things, as allowed for by the principles of justice. Passionate convictions and zealous aspirations do not, as such, give anyone a claim upon social resources or the design of social institutions. For the purposes of justice, the appropriate basis of interpersonal comparisons is the index of primary goods and not strength of feeling or intensity of desire. The theory of primary goods is an extension of the notion of needs, which are distinct from aspirations and desires. One might say, then, that as citizens the members of a well-ordered society collectively take responsibility for dealing justly with one another founded on a public and objective measure of (extended) needs, while as individuals and members of associations they take responsibility for their preferences and devotions.

V

I now take up the appropriateness of the two principles in view of the equality of the members of a well-ordered society. The principles of equal liberty and fair opportunity (part (b) of the second principle) are a natural expression of this equality; and I assume, therefore, that such a society is one in which some form of democracy exists. Thus our question is: by what principle can members of a democratic society permit the tendencies of the basic structure to be deeply affected by social chance, and natural and historical contingencies?

Now since we are regarding citizens as free and equal moral persons (the priority of the first principle of equal liberty gives institutional expression to this), the obvious starting point is to suppose that all other social primary goods, and in particular income and wealth, should be equal: everyone should have an equal share. But society must take organizational requirements and economic efficiency into account. So it is unreasonable to stop at equal division. The basic structure should allow inequalities so long as these improve everyone's

[26] This paragraph confirms H. L. A. Hart's interpretation. See his discussion of liberty and its priority, *Chicago Law Review*, April 1973, pp. 536–40.

[27] I discuss certain problems in interpreting the account of primary goods in "Fairness to Goodness," *Philosophical Review*, October 1976, pp. 536–54.

situation, including that of the least advantaged, provided these inequalities are consistent with equal liberty and fair opportunity. Because we start from equal shares, those who benefit least have, so to speak, a veto; and thus we arrive at the difference principle. Taking equality as the basis of comparison those who have gained more must do so on terms that are justifiable to those who have gained the least.

In explaining this principle, several matters should be kept in mind. First of all, it applies in the first instance to the main public principles and policies that regulate social and economic inequalities. It is used to adjust the system of entitlements and rewards, and the standards and precepts that this system employs. Thus the difference principle holds, for example, for income and property taxation, for fiscal and economic policy; it does not apply to particular transactions or distributions, nor, in general, to small scale and local decisions, but rather to the background against which these take place. No observable pattern is required of actual distributions, nor even any measure of the degree of equality (such as the Gini coefficient) that might be computed from these.[28] What is enjoined is that the inequalities make a functional contribution to those least favoured. [...]

At first sight, it may appear that the difference principle is arbitrarily biased toward the least favoured. But suppose, for simplicity, that there are only two groups, one significantly more fortunate than the other. Society could maximize the expectations of either group but not both, since we can maximize with respect to only one aim at a time. It seems plain that society should not do the best it can for those initially more advantaged; so if we reject the difference principle, we must prefer maximizing some weighted mean of the two expectations. But how should this weighted mean be specified? Should society proceed as if we had an equal chance of being in either group (in proportion to their size) and determine the mean that maximizes this purely hypothetical expectation? Now it is true that we sometimes agree to draw lots but normally only to things that cannot be appropriately divided or else cannot be enjoyed or suffered in common.[29] And we are willing to use the lottery principle even in matters of lasting importance if there is no other way out. (Consider the example of conscription.) But to appeal to it in regulating the basic structure itself would be extraordinary. There is no necessity for society as an enduring system to invoke the lottery principle in this case; nor is there any reason for free and equal persons to allow their relations over the whole course of their life to be significantly affected by contingencies to the greater advantage of those already favoured by these accidents. No one had an antecedent claim to be benefited in this way; and so to maximize a weighted mean is, so to speak, to favour the more fortunate twice over. Society can, however, adopt the difference principle to arrange inequalities so that social and natural contingencies are efficiently used to the benefit of all, taking equal division as a benchmark. So while natural assets cannot be divided evenly, or directly enjoyed or suffered in common, the results of their productive efforts can be allocated in ways consistent with an initial equality. Those favoured by social and natural contingencies regard themselves as already compensated, as it were, by advantages to which no one (including themselves) had a prior claim. Thus they think the difference principle appropriate for regulating the system of entitlements and inequalities.

VI

The conception of equality contained in the principles of justice I have described as Kantian, I shall conclude by mentioning very briefly the reasons for this description. [...]

To suggest the main idea, think of the notion of a well-ordered society as an interpretation of the idea of a kingdom of ends thought of as a human society under circumstances of justice. Now the members of such a society are free and equal and so our problem is to find a rendering of freedom and equality that it is natural to describe as Kantian; and since Kant distinguished between positive and negative freedom, we must make room for this contrast. At this point I resorted to the idea of the original position: I supposed that the conception of justice suitable for a well-ordered society is the one that would be agreed to in a hypothetical situation that is fair between individuals conceived as free and equal moral persons, that is, as members of such a society. Fairness of the circumstances under which agreement is reached transfers to the fairness of the principles agreed to. The original position was designed so that the conception of justice that resulted would be appropriate.

Particularly important among the features of the original position for the interpretation of negative freedom are the limits on information, which I called the veil of ignorance. Now there is a stronger and a weaker form of

[28] For a discussion of such measures, see A. K. Sen, *On Economic Inequality* (Oxford, 1973), chapter 2.

[29] At this point I adapt some remarks of Thomas Hobbes. See *Leviathan*, chapter 15, under the thirteenth and fourteenth laws of nature.

these limits. The weaker supposes that we begin with full information, or else that which we possess in everyday life, and then proceed to eliminate only the information that would lead to partiality and bias. The stronger form has a Kantian explanation: we start from no information at all; for by negative freedom Kant means being able to act independently from the determination of alien causes; to act from natural necessity is to subject oneself to the heteronomy of nature. We interpret this as requiring that the conception of justice that regulates the basic structure, with its deep and long-lasting effects on our common life, should not be adopted on grounds that rest on a knowledge of the various contingencies. Thus when this conception is agreed to, knowledge of our social position, our peculiar desires and interests, or of the various outcomes and configurations of natural and historical accident is excluded. One allows only that information required for a rational agreement. This means that, so far as possible, only the general laws of nature are known together with such particular facts as are implied by the circumstances of justice.

Of course, we must endow the parties with some motivation, otherwise no acknowledgement would be forthcoming. Kant's discussion in the *Groundwork* of the second pair of examples indicates, I believe, that in applying the procedure of the categorical imperative he tacitly relied upon some account of primary goods. In any case, if the two principles would be adopted in the original position with its limits on information, the conception of equality they contain would be Kantian in the sense that by acting from this conception the members of a well-ordered society would express their negative freedom. They would have succeeded in regulating the basic structure and its profound consequences on their persons and mutual relationships by principles the grounds for which are suitably independent from chance and contingency.

In order to provide an interpretation of positive freedom, two things are necessary: first, that the parties are conceived as free and equal moral persons must play a decisive part in their adoption of the conception of justice; and second, the principles of this conception must have a content appropriate to express this determining view of persons and must apply to the controlling institutional subject. Now if correct, the argument from the original position seems to meet these conditions. The assumption that the parties are free and equal moral persons does have an essential role in this argument; and as regards content and application, these principles express, on their public face as it were, the conception of the person that is realized in a well-ordered society. They give priority to the basic liberties, regard individuals as free and responsible masters of their aims and desires, and all are to share equally in the means for the attainment of ends unless the situation of everyone can be improved, taking equal division as the starting point. A society that realized these principles would attain positive freedom, for these principles reflect the features of persons that determined their selection and so express a conception they give to themselves.

Irving Kristol, "A Capitalist Conception of Justice"*

It is fashionable these days for social commentators to ask, "Is capitalism compatible with social justice?" I submit that the only appropriate answer is "No." Indeed, this is the only possible answer. The term "social justice" was invented in order *not* to be compatible with capitalism.

What is the difference between "social justice" and plain, unqualified "justice?" Why can't we ask, "Is capitalism compatible with justice?" We can, and were we to do so, we would then have to explore the idea of justice that is peculiar to the capitalist system, because capitalism certainly does have an idea of justice.

"Social justice," however, was invented and propagated by people who were not much interested in understanding capitalism. These were nineteenth-century critics of capitalism – liberals, radicals, socialists – who invented the term in order to insinuate into the argument a quite different conception of the good society from the one proposed by liberal capitalism. As it is used today, the term has an irredeemably egalitarian and authoritarian thrust. Since capitalism as a socioeconomic or political system is neither egalitarian nor authoritarian, it is in truth incompatible with "social justice."

Let us first address the issue of egalitarianism. In a liberal or democratic capitalist society there is, indeed, a connection between justice and equality. Equality before the law and equality of political rights are fundamental to a liberal capitalist system and, in historical fact, the ideological Founding Fathers of liberal capitalism all did believe in equality before the law and in some form of equality of political rights. The introduction of the term "social justice" represents an effort to stretch the idea of justice that is compatible with capitalism to cover *economic* equality as well. Proponents of something

* Irving Kristol, extracted from *Ethics, Free Enterprise and Public Policy*, edited by Richard DeGeorge and Joseph Pichler (Oxford University Press, 1978), pp. 57–69.

called "social justice" would persuade us that economic equality is as much a right as are equality before the law and equality of political rights. As a matter of fact, these proponents move in an egalitarian direction so formidably that inevitably *all* differences are seen sooner or later to be unjust. Differences between men and women, differences between parents and children, differences between human beings and animals – all of these, as we have seen in the last 10 or 15 years, become questionable and controversial.

A person who believes in "social justice" is an egalitarian. I do not say that he or she necessarily believes in perfect equality; I do not think anyone believes in perfect equality. But "social justice" advocates are terribly interested in far more equality than a capitalist system is likely to deliver. Capitalism delivers many good things but, on the whole, economic equality is not one of them. It has never pretended to deliver economic equality. Rather, capitalism has always stood for equality of economic opportunity, reasonably understood to mean the absence of official barriers to economic opportunity.

We are now in an egalitarian age when Harvard professors write books wondering whether there is a problem of "social justice" if some people are born of handsome parents and are therefore more attractive than others. This is seriously discussed in Cambridge and in other learned circles. Capitalism is not interested in that. Capitalism says there ought to be no *official* barriers to economic opportunity. If one is born of handsome or talented parents, if one inherits a musical skill, or mathematical skill, or whatever, that is simply good luck. No one can question the person's right to the fruits of such skills. Capitalism believes that, through equal opportunity, each individual will pursue his happiness as he defines it, and as far as his natural assets (plus luck, good or bad) will permit. In pursuit of that happiness everyone will, to use that familiar phrase of Adam Smith, "better his condition."

Thus, capitalism says that equal opportunity will result in everyone's bettering his or her condition. And it does. The history of the world over the past 200 years shows that capitalism did indeed permit and encourage ordinary men and women in the pursuit of their happiness to improve their condition. Even Marx did not deny this. We are not as poor as our grandparents. We are all better off because individuals in pursuit of happiness, and without barriers being put in their way, are very creative, innovative, and adept at finding ways for societies to be more productive, thereby creating more wealth in which everyone shares.

Now, although individuals do better their condition under capitalism, they do not better their condition equally. In the pursuit of happiness, some will be more successful than others. Some will end up with more than others. Everyone will end up with *somewhat* more than he had – everyone. But some people will end up with a lot more than they had and some with a little more than they had. Capitalism does not perceive this as a problem. It is assumed that since everyone gets more, everyone ought to be content. If some people get more than others, the reason is to be found in their differential contributions to the economy. In a capitalist system, where the market predominates in economic decision making, people who – in whatever way – make different productive inputs into the economy receive different rewards. If one's input into the economy is great, one receives a large reward; if one's input is small, one receives a modest reward. The determination of these rewards is by public preferences and public tastes as expressed in the market. [...]

Capitalism does recognize, incidentally, that luck is a very important factor affecting the distribution of rewards in a market system. (As a matter of fact, all systems recognize this point except modern utopian systems, such as socialism.) Obviously, in order for a person to collect rewards of whatever kind, he has to be alive. The fact that he is alive is a matter of luck. He could have been hit by a truck. He could have developed cancer at the age of twelve. It happens to people all the time. All sorts of terrible things could have happened to reduce his income potential. The fact that they did not is luck.

Some of us who move about in the business world have met people who turn out to be millionaires. We wonder why. They don't seem very bright; they don't seem to have any special skills. Why are they millionaires? The answer is that they were in the right place at the right time and had just enough wit, in the old-fashioned sense of the term, to take advantage of their situation. Economic input under capitalism is a very peculiar and mysterious thing, which is one of the reasons that critics of capitalism get so upset about it. One never knows who is going to become enormously successful because one never knows what the market is going to reward. Who would have guessed that a Mr. Ray Kroc, who just resigned at age 75 as chairman of the board of McDonald's, would be worth $200 million or more? From what? Making hamburgers? The answer is that he saw something that others did not see. He saw that the American public would be happy buying hamburgers of high, standardized quality, served in a clean, attractive place. It sounds absurd to put it that way, because it is so obvious and banal. That is all he saw, and he invented McDonald's. There are in this country hundreds and thousands of people who are millionaires simply because they saw something that others did not see. They are not very brilliant. They just happened to be lucky and have the initiative to capitalize on it, as Mr. Kroc just happened to walk into a hamburger stand and get the idea for McDonald's.

This is the way the system works. It rewards people in terms of their contribution to the economy as measured and defined by the marketplace – namely, in terms of the free preferences of individual men and women who have money in their pockets and are free to spend it or not on this, that, or the other as they please. Economic justice under capitalism means the differential reward to individuals is based on their productive input *to the economy*. I emphasize "to the economy" because input is measured by the marketplace.

Is it "just" that Mr. Ray Kroc should have made so much money by merely figuring out a new way of selling hamburgers? They are the same old hamburgers, just better made, better marketed. Is it fair? Capitalism says it is fair. He is selling a good product; people want it; it is fair. It is "just" that he has made so much money.

However, capitalism doesn't say only that. It also understands that it is an exaggeration to say that literally *everyone* betters his condition when rewards are based on productive input. There are some people who are really not capable of taking part in the race at all because of mental illness, physical illness, bad luck, and so on. Such persons are simply not able to take advantage of the opportunity that does exist.

Capitalism as originally conceived by Adam Smith was not nearly so heartless a system as it presented itself during the nineteenth century. Adam Smith didn't say that people who could make no productive input into the economy through no fault of their own should be permitted to starve to death. Though not a believer, he was enough of a Christian to know that such a conclusion was not consistent with the virtue of charity. He understood that such people had to be provided for. There has never been any question of that. Adam Smith wrote two books. The book that first made him famous was not *The Wealth of Nations* but *The Theory of Moral Sentiments*, in which he said that the highest human sentiment is sympathy – the sympathy that men and women have for one another as human beings. Although *The Wealth of Nations* is an analysis of an economic system based on self-interest, Adam Smith never believed for a moment that human beings were strictly economic men or women. It took some later generations of economists to come up with that idea. Adam Smith understood that people live in a society, not just in an economy, and that they feel a sense of social obligation to one another, as well as a sense of engaging in mutually satisfactory economic transactions.

In both these books, but especially in *The Theory of Moral Sentiments*, Adam Smith addressed himself to the question, "What do the rich do with their money once they get it?" His answer was that they reinvest some of it so that society as a whole will become wealthier and everyone will continue to be able to improve his or her condition to some degree. Also, however, the rich will engage in one of the great pleasures that wealth affords: the expression of sympathy for one's fellow human beings. [...] Although capitalism has long been accused of being an inhumane system, we forget that capitalism and humanitarianism entered the modern world together. Name a modern, humane movement – criminal reform, decent treatment of women, kindness to animals, etc. Where does it originate? They all came from the rising bourgeoisie at the end of the eighteenth century. They were all middle-class movements. The movements didn't begin with peasants or aristocrats. Peasants were always cruel to animals and aristocrats could not care less about animals, or about wives, for that matter. It was the bourgeoisie, the capitalist middle class, that said animals should be treated with consideration, that criminals should not be tortured, that prisons should be places of punishment, yes, but humane places of punishment. It was the generation that helped establish the capitalist idea and the capitalist way of thinking in the world that brought these movements to life. Incidentally, the anti-slavery movement was also founded by middle-class men and women who had a sense of social responsibility toward their fellow citizens.

So it is simply and wholly untrue that capitalism is a harsh, vindictive, soulless system. A man like Adam Smith would never have dreamed of recommending such a system. No, he recommended the economic relations which constitute the market system, the capitalist system, on the assumption that human beings would continue to recognize their social obligations to one another and act upon this recognition with some degree of consistency. Incidentally, he even seems to have believed in a progressive income tax.

However, something very peculiar happened after Adam Smith. Something very odd and very bad happened to the idea of capitalism and its reputation after the first generation of capitalism's intellectual Founding Fathers. The economics of capitalism became a "dismal science." One cannot read *The Wealth of Nations* and have any sense that economics is a dismal science. It is an inquiry into the causes of the wealth of nations that tells people how to get rich. It says, "If you organize your economic activities this way, everyone will get richer." There is nothing pessimistic about that, nothing dismal about that. It was an exhilarating message to the world.

Unfortunately, what gave capitalism a bad name in the early part of the nineteenth century was not the socialist's criticism of capitalism but, I fear, the work of the later capitalist economists. We do not even have a really good intellectual history of this episode because people who write histories of economic thought tend not to be interested in intellectual history, but in economics. For some reason, Malthus and then Ricardo decided that capitalist economics should not deal with the production of wealth but rather with its distribution. Adam Smith had said everyone could improve his condition. Malthus said the situation was hopeless, at least for the lower classes.

[...]

It is nineteenth-century capitalist economic thought, with its incredible emphasis on the impossibility of improving the condition of the working class – even as the improvement was obviously taking place – that gave great popularity and plausibility to the socialist critique of capitalism and to the redistributionist impulse that began to emerge. This impulse, which is still so appealing, makes no sense. A nation can redistribute to its heart's content and it will not affect the average person one bit. There just isn't ever enough to redistribute. Nevertheless, once it became "clear" in the nineteenth century that there was no other way, redistribution became a very popular subject.

This absolutely insane folly on the part of capitalist economists, which gave capitalism a bad name, was followed by an even worse event. I do not like the term "free enterprise." I prefer the simple word, "capitalism." Here is why. The words "free enterprise" to describe capitalism, so far as I have been able to determine, enter our vocabulary in the latter part of the nineteenth century. "Capitalism" is a term invented by socialists, but it can be a neutral term, almost a technical term. There happened to be no other term around to describe that economic system, but various conservatively inclined, procapitalist people – procapitalist ideologues, I would say – decided they did not like the word "capitalism." They substituted "free enterprise" as part of a neo-Darwinian theory of the economy. "Free enterprise" emerged out of a conception of the economy and the society which said: "We'll all engage in competition, a war of all against all, and some of us will do better and some of us will survive; others will do worse and won't survive. That's tough and that's all there is to it. Of course, the majority will not survive." The majority did not greet this intelligence with glad tidings. The majority, on the whole, thought that this was not a very good way to live, that human society should not be constituted under the law of the jungle. So "free enterprise" and its connotations only continued to give capitalism a bad name.

I am convinced that capitalism has been slandered more by its defenders than by its critics. During the nineteenth century, as the socialists said that capitalism could not improve the condition of the working class, and capitalist economists agreed, the condition of the working class continued to improve. In the twentieth century, economists finally caught up with reality and decided that there really was such a thing as economic growth and that it was indeed possible, Malthus and Ricardo to the contrary notwithstanding. By then it was almost too late. For one century we had capitalism given a bad name by its friends and by its enemies, and it will take a long time to wash that reputation away, if it ever can be done.

[...]

However, I think the more important thrust of the term "social justice" has to do with its authoritarian meaning rather than its egalitarian meaning. The term "social" prefixed before the word "justice" has a purpose and an effect which is to abolish the distinction between the public and the private sectors, a distinction which is absolutely crucial for a liberal society. It is the very definition of a liberal society that there be a public sector and a large, private sector where people can do what they want without government bothering them. What is a "social problem?" Is a social problem something that government can ignore? Would anyone say we have a social problem but it is not the business of government? Of course not.

The term "social justice" exists in order to identify those issues about which government should get active. A social problem is a problem that gives rise to a governmental policy, which is why people who believe in the expansion of the public sector are always inventing, discovering, or defining more and more social problems in our world. The world has not become any more problematic than it ever was. The proliferation of things called "social problems" arises out of an effort to get government more and more deeply involved in the lives of private citizens in an attempt to "cope with" or "solve" these "problems." Sometimes real problems are posed. Rarely are they followed by real solutions.

The idea of "social justice," however, assumes not only that government will intervene but that government will have, should have, and can have an authoritative knowledge as to what everyone merits or deserves in terms of the distribution of income and wealth. After all, if we do not like the inequality that results from the operation of the market, then who is going to make the decision as to the distribution of services and wealth? Some authority must be found to say so-and-so deserves more than so-and-so. Of course, the only possible such authority in the modern world is not the Church but the State. To the degree that one defines "social justice" as a kind of protest against the capitalist distribution of income, one proposes some other mechanism for the distribution of income. Government is the only other mechanism that can make the decisions as to who gets what, as to what he or she "deserves," for whatever reason.

The assumption that the government is able to make such decisions wisely, and therefore that government should make such decisions, violates the very premises of a liberal community. A liberal community exists on the premise that there is no such authority. If there were an authority which knew what everyone merited and could allocate it fairly, why would we need freedom? There would be no point in freedom. Let the authority do its work. Now, we have seen the experience of non-liberal societies, and not all of it is bad. I would not pretend that a liberal society is the only possible good society. If one likes the values of a particular non-liberal society, it may not be bad at all. There are many non-liberal societies I admire: monasteries are non-liberal societies, and I do not say they are bad societies. They are pretty good societies – but they are not liberal societies. The monk has no need for liberty if he believes there is someone else, his superior, who knows what is good for him and what reward he merits.

Once we assume that there is a superior authority who has authoritative knowledge of the common good and of the merits and demerits of every individual, the ground of a liberal society is swept away, because the very freedoms that subsist and thrive in a liberal society all assume that there is no such authoritative knowledge. Now, this assumption is not *necessarily* true. Maybe there is someone who really does have an authoritative knowledge of what is good for all of us and how much we all merit. We who choose a liberal society are skeptical as to the possibility. In any case, we think it is more likely that there will be ten people all claiming to have different versions of what is good for all of us and what we should all get, and therefore we choose to let the market settle it. It is an amicable way of not getting involved in endless philosophical or religious arguments about the nature of the true, the good, and the beautiful.

I emphasize that if we want a society that aims at social justice, then we must have a society with a powerful consensus on values, with no significant disagreements as to what is good, what is bad, what is desirable, what is undesirable, what the good life is, what the not-so-good life is. [...]

Those who have an idea of "social justice" need an authority to enforce that idea of "social justice." What is the point of knowing "social justice" and not doing anything about it? Now, such enforcement is really self-enforcement in a monastery because this is a consensual community and everyone assents to its values. There are no big arguments taking place over values. But in our kind of society there are disagreements, and "social justice" can be achieved only if the government *imposes* consensus on people. In fact, this is what is happening to a greater degree every day. To impose "social justice," there must be an authority. That is, there must be someone who says he knows what it is. Those who make this claim can, further, claim power in the name of their knowledge of justice. Given power, they might possibly create a society that is better than a liberal society in some ways. However, I don't think this is likely in our complicated and diverse civilization. More likely, they will produce the kind of system found in the Communist nations or in other authoritarian nations where government insists that it knows what "social justice" is and imposes it on a dissenting people simply by force.

We cannot have a liberal society, with all the freedoms that prevail in a liberal society, if we glibly assume that "social justice" has a precise meaning which we can define and upon which we can agree, and which it then becomes the function of government to impose. In our world today, [...] there is a class of people who do believe that they can define "social justice," that they have an authoritative conception of the common good that should be imposed on the society by using the force of government. These people, products of our graduate and professional schools, for the most part, can be called "the new class."

[...]

This group does not want people to be recompensed on the basis of contributions to the *economy*, which is the capitalist definition of justice, but on the basis of their contributions to the *society* – as the group determines the worth of that contributions. In a way, the perfect exemplars of this new class of people are persons like Ralph Nader and the graduates of Ivy League law schools. Having been born to middle-class, even affluent backgrounds on the whole, they are no longer interested in money, but are only interested in power, power to improve the world, power to make this a better place. How are they going to exercise this power? Through government, not by persuading you or me.

[...]

The notion of a "just society" existing on earth is a fantasy, a utopian fantasy. That is not what life on earth is like. The reason is that the world is full of other people who are different from you and me, alas, and we have to live with them. If they were all like us, we would live fine; but they are not all like us, and the point of a liberal society and of a market economy is to accept this difference and say, "Okay, you be you and I'll be I. We'll disagree, but we'll do business together. We'll mutually profit from doing business together, and we'll live not necessarily in friendship but at least in civility with one another."

I am not saying that capitalism is a just society. I am saying that there is a capitalist conception of justice which is a workable conception of justice. Anyone who promises you a just society on this earth is a fraud and a charlatan. I believe that this is not the nature of human destiny. It would mean that we all would be happy. Life is not like that. Life is doomed not to be like that. But if you do not accept this view, and if you really think that life can indeed be radically different from what it is, if you really believe that justice can prevail on earth, then you are likely to start taking phrases like "social justice" very seriously and to think that the function of politics is to rid the world of its evils: to abolish war, to abolish poverty, to abolish discrimination, to abolish envy, to abolish, abolish, abolish. We are not going to abolish any of those things. If we push them out one window, they will come in through another window in some unforeseen form. The reforms of today give rise to the evils of tomorrow. That is the history of the human race.

If one can be somewhat stoical about this circumstance, the basic precondition of social life, capitalism becomes much more tolerable. However, if one is not stoical about it, if one demands more of life than life can give, then capitalism is certainly the wrong system because capitalism does not promise that much and does not give you that much. All it gives is a greater abundance of material goods and a great deal of freedom to cope with the problems of the human condition on your own.

Robert Nozick, "The Entitlement Theory"*

The subject of justice in holdings consists of three major topics. The first is the *original acquisition of holdings*, the appropriation of unheld things. This includes the issue of how unheld things may come to be held, the process, or processes, by which unheld things may come to be held, the things that may come to be held by these processes, the extent of what comes to be held by a particular process, and so on. We shall refer to the complicated truth about this topic, which we shall not formulate here, as the principle of justice in acquisition. The second topic concerns the *transfer of holdings* from one person to another. By what processes may a person transfer holdings to another? How may a person acquire a holding from another who holds it? Under this topic come general descriptions of voluntary exchange, and gift and (on the other hand) fraud, as well as reference to particular conventional details fixed upon in a given society. The complicated truth about this subject (with placeholders for conventional details) we shall call the principle of justice in transfer. (And we shall suppose it also includes principles governing how a person may divest himself of a holding, passing it into an unheld state.)

If the world were wholly just, the following inductive definition would exhaustively cover the subject of justice in holdings.

1 A person who acquires a holding in accordance with the principle of justice in acquisition is entitled to that holding.
2 A person who acquires a holding in accordance with the principle of justice in transfer, from someone else entitled to the holding, is entitled to the holding.
3 No one is entitled to a holding except by (repeated) applications of 1 and 2.

The complete principle of distributive justice would say simply that a distribution is just if everyone is entitled to the holdings they possess under the distribution.

A distribution is just if it arises from another just distribution by legitimate means. The legitimate means of moving from one distribution to another are specified by the principle of justice in transfer. The legitimate first "moves" are specified by the principle of justice in acquisition. Whatever arises from a just situation by just steps is itself just. The means of change specified by the principle of justice in transfer preserve justice. As correct rules of inference are truth-preserving, and any conclusion deduced via repeated application of such rules from only true premises is itself true, so the means of transition from one situation to another specified by the principle of justice in transfer are justice-preserving, and any situation actually arising from repeated transitions in accordance with the principle from a just situation is

* Robert Nozick, extracted from *Anarchy, State, and Utopia* (Basic Books, Inc., 1974), pp. 149–63.

itself just. The parallel between justice-preserving transformations and truth-preserving transformations illuminates where it fails as well as where it holds. That a conclusion could have been deduced by truth-preserving means from premises that are true suffices to show its truth. That from a just situation a situation *could* have arisen via justice-preserving means does *not* suffice to show its justice. The fact that a thief's victims voluntarily *could* have presented him with gifts does not entitle the thief to his ill-gotten gains. Justice in holdings is historical; it depends upon what actually has happened. We shall return to this point later.

Not all actual situations are generated in accordance with the two principles of justice in holdings: the principle of justice in acquisition and the principle of justice in transfer. Some people steal from others, or defraud them, or enslave them, seizing their product and preventing them from living as they choose, or forcibly exclude others from competing in exchanges. None of these are permissible modes of transition from one situation to another. And some persons acquire holdings by means not sanctioned by the principle of justice in acquisition. The existence of past injustice (previous violations of the first two principles of justice in holdings) raises the third major topic under justice in holdings: the rectification of injustice in holdings. If past injustice has shaped present holdings in various ways, some identifiable and some not, what now, if anything, ought to be done to rectify these injustices? What obligations do the performers of injustice have toward those whose position is worse than it would have been had the injustice not been done? Or, than it would have been had compensation been paid promptly? How, if at all, do things change if the beneficiaries and those made worse off are not the direct parties in the act of injustice, but, for example, their descendants? Is an injustice done to someone whose holding was itself based upon an unrectified injustice? How far back must one go in wiping clean the historical slate of injustices? What may victims of injustices permissibly do in order to rectify the injustices being done to them, including the many injustices done by persons acting through their government? I do not know of a thorough or theoretically sophisticated treatment of such issues.[30] Idealizing greatly, let us suppose theoretical investigation will produce a principle of rectification. This principle uses historical information about previous situations and injustices done in them (as defined by the first two principles of justice and rights against interference), and information about the actual course of events that flowed from these injustices, until the present, and it yields a description (or descriptions) of holdings in the society. The principle of rectification presumably will make use of its best estimate of subjunctive information about what would have occurred (or a probability distribution over what might have occurred, using the expected value) if the injustice had not taken place. If the actual description of holdings turns out not to be one of the descriptions yielded by the principle, then one of the descriptions yielded must be realized.

The general outlines of the theory of justice in holdings are that the holdings of a person are just if he is entitled to them by the principles of justice in acquisition and transfer, or by the principle of rectification of injustice (as specified by the first two principles). If each person's holdings are just, then the total set (distribution) of holdings is just. To turn these general outlines into a specific theory we would have to specify the details of each of the three principles of justice in holdings; the principle of acquisition of holdings, the principle of transfer of holdings, and the principle of rectification of violations of the first two principles. I shall not attempt that task here. (Locke's principle of justice in acquisition is discussed below.)

Historical principles and end-result principles

The general outlines of the entitlement theory illuminate the nature and defects of other conceptions of distributive justice. The entitlement theory of justice in distribution is *historical*; whether a distribution is just depends upon how it came about. In contrast, *current time-slice principles* of justice hold that the justice of a distribution is determined by how things are distributed (who has what) as judged by some *structural* principle(s) of just distribution. A utilitarian who judges between any two distributions by seeing which has the greater sum of utility and, if the sums tie, applies some fixed equality criterion to choose the more equal distribution, would hold a current time-slice principle of justice. As would someone who had a fixed schedule of trade-offs between the sum of happiness and equality. According to a current time-slice principle, all that needs to be looked at, in judging the justice of a distribution, is who ends up with what; in comparing any two distributions one need look only at the matrix presenting the distributions. No further information need to be fed into a principle of justice. It

30 See, however, the useful book by Boris Bittker, *The Case for Black Reparations* (New York: Random House, 1973).

is a consequence of such principles of justice that any two structurally identical distributions are equally just. (Two distributions are structurally identical if they present the same profile, but perhaps have different persons occupying the particular slots. My having ten and your having five, and my having five and your having ten are structurally identical distributions.) Welfare economics is the theory of current time-slice principles of justice. The subject is conceived as operating on matrices representing only current information about distribution. This, as well as some of the usual conditions (for example, the choice of distribution is invariant under relabeling of columns), guarantees that welfare economics will be a current time-slice theory, with all of its inadequacies.

Most persons do not accept current time-slice principles as constituting the whole story about distributive shares. They think it relevant in assessing the justice of a situation to consider not only the distribution it embodies, but also how that distribution came about. If some persons are in prison for murder or war crimes, we do not say that to assess the justice of the distribution in the society we must look only at what this person has, and that person has, and that person has … at the current time. We think it relevant to ask whether someone did something so that he *deserved* to be punished, deserved to have a lower share. Most will agree to the relevance of further information with regard to punishments and penalties. […]

We construe the position we discuss too narrowly by speaking of *current* time-slice principles. Nothing is changed if structural principles operate upon a time sequence of current time-slice profiles and, for example, give someone more now to counterbalance the less he has had earlier. A utilitarian or an egalitarian or any mixture of the two over time will inherit the difficulties of his more myopic comrades. He is not helped by the fact that *some* of the information others consider relevant in assessing a distribution is reflected, unrecoverably, in past matrices. Henceforth, we shall refer to such unhistorical principles of distributive justice, including the current time-slice principles, as *end-result principles* or *end-state principles.*

In contrast to end-result principles of justice, *historical principles* of justice hold that past circumstances or actions of people can create differential entitlements or differential deserts to things. An injustice can be worked by moving from one distribution to another structurally identical one, for the second, in profile the same, may violate people's entitlements or deserts; it may not fit the actual history.

Patterning

The entitlement principles of justice in holdings that we have sketched are historical principles of justice. To better understand their precise character, we shall distinguish them from another subclass of the historical principles. Consider, as an example, the principle of distribution according to moral merit. This principle requires that total distributive shares vary directly with moral merit; no person should have a greater share than anyone whose moral merit is greater. (If moral merit could be not merely ordered but measured on an interval or ratio scale, stronger principles could be formulated.) Or consider the principle that results by substituting "usefulness to society" for "moral merit" in the previous principle. Or instead of "distribute according to moral merit," or "distribute to usefulness to society" we might consider "distribute according to the weighted sum of moral merit, usefulness to society, and need," with the weights of the different dimensions equal. Let us call a principle of distribution *patterned* if it specifies that a distribution is to vary along with some natural dimension, weighted sum of natural dimensions, or lexicographic ordering of natural dimensions. And let us say a distribution is patterned if it accords with some patterned principle. […]

Almost every suggested principle of distributive justice is patterned: to each according to his moral merit, or needs, or marginal product, or how hard he tries, or the weighted sum of the foregoing, and so on. The principle of entitlement we have sketched is *not* patterned. There is no one natural dimension or weighted sum or combination of a small number of natural dimensions that yields the distributions generated in accordance with the principle of entitlement. The set of holdings that results when some persons receive their marginal products, others win at gambling, others receive a share of their mate's income, others receive gifts from foundations, others receive interest on loans, others receive gifts from admirers, others receive returns on investment, others make for themselves much of what they have, others find things, and so on, will not be patterned. […] The process whereby the set of holdings is generated will be intelligible, though the set of holdings itself that results from this process will be unpatterned.

The writings of F. A. Hayek focus less than is usually done upon what patterning distributive justice requires. Hayek argues that we cannot know enough about each person's situation to distribute to each according to his moral merit (but would justice demand we do so if we did have this knowledge?); and he goes on to say "our objection is against all attempts to impress society a deliberately chosen pattern of distribution, whether it be an order of equality or of inequality."[31] However, Hayek concludes that in a free society there will be distribution in accordance with value rather than moral merit; that is, in accordance with the perceived value of a person's actions and services to others. Despite his rejection of a patterned conception of distributive justice, Hayek himself suggests a pattern he thinks justifiable: distribution in accordance with the perceived benefits given to others, leaving room for the complaint that a free society does not realize exactly this pattern. Stating this patterned strand of a free capitalist society more precisely, we get "To each according to how much he benefits others who have the resources for benefiting those who benefit them." [...]

To think that the task of a theory of distributive justice is to fill in the blank in "to each according to his ______" is to be predisposed to search for a pattern; and the separate treatment of "from each according to his ______" treats production and distribution as two separate and independent issues. On an entitlement view these are *not* two separate questions. Whoever makes something, having bought or contracted for all other held resources used in the process (transferring some of his holdings for these cooperating factors), is entitled to it. The situation is *not* one of something's getting made, and there being an open question of who is to get it. Things come into the world already attached to people having entitlements over them. From the point of view of the historical entitlement conception of justice in holdings, those who start afresh to complete "to each according to his ______" treat objects as if they appeared from nowhere, out of nothing. A complete theory of justice might cover this limit case as well; perhaps here is a use for the usual conceptions of distributive justice.

So entrenched are maxims of the usual form that perhaps we should present the entitlement conception as a competitor. Ignoring acquisition and rectification, we might say:

> From each according to what he chooses to do, to each according to what he makes for himself (perhaps with the contracted aid of others) and what others choose to do for him and choose to give him of what they've been given previously (under this maxim) and haven't yet expended or transferred.

This, the discerning reader will have noticed, has its defects as a slogan. So as a summary and great simplification (and not as a maxim with any independent meaning) we have:

> *From each as they choose, to each as they are chosen.*

How liberty upsets patterns

It is not clear how those holding alternative conceptions of distribute justice can reject the entitlement conception of justice in holdings. For suppose a distribution favored by one of these nonentitlement conceptions is realized. Let us suppose it is your favorite one and let us call this distribution D_1; perhaps everyone has an equal share, perhaps shares vary in accordance with some dimension you treasure. Now suppose that Wilt Chamberlain is greatly in demand by basketball teams, being a great gate attraction. (Also suppose contracts run only for a year, with players being free agents.) He signs the following sort of contract with a team: in each home game, twenty-five cents from the price of each ticket of admission goes to him. (We ignore the question of whether he is "gouging" the owners, letting them look out for themselves.) The season starts, and people cheerfully attend his team's games; they buy their tickets, each time dropping a separate twenty-five cents of their admission price into a special box with Chamberlain's name on it. They are excited about seeing him play; it is worth the total admission price to them. Let us suppose that in one season one million persons attend his home games, and Wilt Chamberlain winds up with $250,000, a much larger sum than the average income and larger even than anyone else has. Is he entitled to this income? Is this new distribution, D_2, unjust? If so, why? There is *no* question about whether each of the people was entitled to the control over the resources they held in D_1; because that was the distribution (your favorite) that (for the purposes of argument) we assumed was acceptable. Each of these persons *chose* to give twenty-five cents of their money to Chamberlain. They could have spent it on going to the movies, or on candy bars, or on copies of *Dissent* magazine, or of *Monthly Review*. But they all, at least one million of them, converged on giving it to Wilt Chamberlain in exchange for watching him play basketball. If D_1 was a just distribution, and people voluntarily moved from it to D_2, transferring parts of their shares they were given under D_1 (what was it for if not to do something with?), isn't D_2 also just? If the people were entitled (under D_1), didn't this

[31] F. A. Hayek, *The Constitution of Liberty* (Chicago: University of Chicago Press, 1960), p. 87.

include their being entitled to give it to, or exchange it with, Wilt Chamberlain? Can anyone else complain on grounds of justice? Each other person already has his legitimate share under D_1. Under D_1, there is nothing that anyone has that anyone else has a claim of justice against. After someone transfers something to Wilt Chamberlain, third parties *still* have their legitimate shares; *their* shares are not changed. By what process could such a transfer among two persons give rise to a legitimate claim of distributive justice on a portion of what was transferred, by a third party who had no claim of justice on any holdings of the others *before* the transfer? To cut off objections irrelevant here, we might imagine the exchanges occurring in a socialist society, after hours. After playing whatever basketball he does in his daily work, or doing whatever other daily work he does, Wilt Chamberlain decides to put in *overtime* to earn additional money. (First his work quota is set; he works time over that.) Or imagine it is a skilled juggler people like to see, who puts on shows after hours.

Why might someone work overtime in a society in which it is assumed their needs are satisfied? Perhaps because they care about things other than needs. I like to write in books that I read, and to have easy access to books for browsing at odd hours. It would be very pleasant and convenient to have the resources of Widener Library in my back yard. No society, I assume, will provide such resources close to each person who would like them as part of his regular allotment (under D_1). Thus, persons either must do without some extra things that they want, or be allowed to do something extra to get some of these things. On what basis could the inequalities that would eventuate be forbidden? Notice also that small factories would spring up in a socialist society, unless forbidden. I melt down some of my personal possessions (under D_1) and build a machine out of the material. I offer you, and others, a philosophy lecture once a week in exchange for your cranking the handle on my machine, whose products I exchange for yet other things, and so on. (The raw materials used by the machine are given to me by others who possess them under D_1, in exchange for hearing lectures.) Each person might participate to gain things over and above their allotment under D_1. Some persons even might want to leave their job in socialist industry and work full time in this private sector. [...] Here I wish merely to note how private property even in means of production would occur in a socialist society that did not forbid people to use as they wished some of the resources they are given under the socialist distribution D_1. The socialist society would have to forbid capitalist acts between consenting adults.

The general point illustrated by the Wilt Chamberlain example and the example of the entrepreneur in a socialist society is that no end-state principle of distributional patterned principle of justice can be continuously realized without continuous interference with people's lives....

Chapter 15
On Change

Introduction

The presidential campaign of Barack Obama emphasized the need for political change, and even his conservative opponent, John McCain, acknowledged that some changes are necessary. But what do such calls for change signify? Is "change" merely campaign rhetoric, and if not, what does it entail?

To political theorists, political change is not simply an alteration in political leadership or in specific policies; rather it is a summary concept that refers to numerous differences between what we have in political life and what we think would be good and just. It addresses the gap between our normative political principles and the problematic conditions in which we find ourselves. Any of our principles regarding community, citizenship, structure, rulers, authority, and justice might be insufficiently realized, and so we want those changes that will achieve our principles. Perhaps one principle is at the center of our political thinking and we are preoccupied with problems that we think arise from the failure of a political community to realize specific goals associated with that principle, and so our call for change can be quite limited. But perhaps we are more comprehensive political thinkers and hold dear many political principles, none of which we find realized, and so we call for more extensive and perhaps deeper changes.

But beyond the extensiveness of changes that are sought, political theorists must address questions of the means of pursuing change. We often think of revolutionary change as extensive and violent, but political communities can undergo extensive changes with little disruption and violence. Conversely, violence is often employed on behalf of very limited policy objectives and with little effect. Our concluding readings thus deal first with different perspectives on the desirability of extensive change and then with different views on the legitimacy of disruption and violence in achieving change.

Not everyone welcomes extensive change. According to Michael Oakeshott (1901–90), a noted philosopher at Cambridge, change is vexing to those with a conservative temperament. While recognizing that there is a certain intelligibility in a "glory style of politics" which seeks to mobilize social resources in pursuit of unrealized ideals, Oakeshott claims such a radical style of politics has resulted in great human suffering. In any event, the conservative is one who enjoys the blessings that one finds in present circumstances.

But even conservatives like Oakeshott recognize that "new activities are constantly appearing," making some innovations in governance appropriate. Assuming some reforms are always needed, how should we approach these possibilities? Richard Rorty, whose pragmatism we encountered in Chapter 8, suggests that there are two basic modalities for bringing about change. Some embrace "movement politics" which thinks, "things will (or should be) changed utterly, that a terrible new beauty will be born." This is the view of the young, the hope arising from purity of heart. But perhaps as we age, we become more comfortable with "campaign politics," in which the changes sought are more specific, more finite, and perhaps more capable of realization. According to Rorty, the question that a person asks himself at the end of a career or perhaps at the end of life is not whether he was committed to some grand political scheme, but whether the actions he took produced some good for the political communities in which he lived and worked.

Everyday life inevitably thrusts us into situations where we can act to achieve some small beneficial changes in political life. Are more extraordinary efforts on behalf of momentous changes ever justified? The iconic figure of the American civil rights movement, Martin Luther King Jr., certainly thought so. In "Letter from a Birmingham Jail," he asserts that when there is oppression and injustice, as there certainly was in segregated Birmingham, Alabama, in 1963, it needs to be confronted through direct action. He goes on to outline the various steps that need to be taken to justify such direct actions as conducting sit-ins, strikes, and marches that raise community tensions. Facts must be collected to determine whether injustice exists. Negotiations with authorities must be conducted. Participants in direct action must be trained in "self-purification" so that their actions conform to the principles of nonviolence that are at the core of a strategy of civil disobedience. Only then can a person participate directly in direct action aimed at changing the unjust conditions in which they find themselves.

But are acts of violence on behalf of fundamental changes ever justified? Certainly the most prominent practitioners of violence today are advocates of *jihad*. Abd Al-Salam Faraj (1954–82) was an Egyptian Muslim who was executed for his part in the 1981 assassination of Egyptian President Anwar Sadat. Faraj is known to have had connections with such leaders of al-Qaeda as Ayman al-Zawabin, so the ideas expressed in Faraj's "The Neglected Duty" remain the basic ideas that are used to justify the contemporary wave of terrorism. Essentially his claim is that devout Muslims have a sacred duty to establish an Islamic State, and if this requires acts of violence or war, then engaging in violence is not only a possibility, but also a duty. Other nonviolent strategies for achieving God's Will cannot attain that end. Neglecting one's duty to engage in *jihad* has resulted in the conditions of "lowness, humiliation, division, and fragmentation in which Muslims live today."

Having lived through World War II, Albert Camus (1913–60), the Algerian–French philosopher who won the Nobel Prize for literature in 1957, presented in *The Rebel* (published in 1951) one of the most famed analyses of violence and political change ever penned. He claims that rebels must "struggle against servitude, falsehood, and terror." But we live in a world where all values are relative, even freedom. Absolute freedom asserts the right to kill and destroy, but that is illogical; the logic of life is creation, not destruction. Nevertheless, absolute nonviolence can condemn those who will not fight for their lives and freedoms to a condition of slavery under those who would employ coercion and violence against others. Violence can only be used to combat more extreme violence. And so Camus believes that if we are to be rebels against the forces that divide humans and that undermine our living in genuine community with each other, we must affirm a philosophy of limits. We must realize that there is no heaven to be attained on earth, no paradise to be sought that can justify our use of violence. Still, we must realize that there are evils to be confronted, and sometimes this means that we must put up a fight.

Michael Oakeshott, "On Being Conservative"*

[...] To be conservative is to be disposed to think and behave in certain manners; it is to prefer certain kinds of conduct and certain conditions of human circumstances to others; it is to be disposed to make certain kinds of choices. And my design here is to construe this disposition as it appears in contemporary character, rather than to transpose it into the idiom of general principles.

The general characteristics of this disposition are not difficult to discern, although they have often been mistaken. They centre upon a propensity to use and to enjoy what is available rather than to wish for or to look for something else; to delight in what is present rather than what was or what may be. Reflection may bring to light an appropriate gratefulness for what is available, and consequently the acknowledgment of a gift or an inheritance from the past; but there is no mere idolizing of what is past and gone. What is esteemed is the present; and it is esteemed not on account of its connections with a remote antiquity, nor because it is recognized to be more admirable than any possible alternative, but on account of its familiarity: not, *Verweile doch, du bist so schön*, but, *Stay with me because I am attached to you.*

* Michael Oakeshott, extracted from *Rationalism in Politics* (Methuen & Co. Ltd, 1962), pp. 168–99.

If the present is arid, offering little or nothing to be used or enjoyed, then this inclination will be weak or absent; if the present is remarkably unsettled, it will display itself in a search for a firmer foothold and consequently in a recourse to and an exploration of the past; but it asserts itself characteristically when there is much to be enjoyed, and it will be strongest when this is combined with evident risk of loss. In short, it is a disposition appropriate to a man who is acutely aware of having something to lose which he has learned to care for; a man in some degree rich in opportunities for enjoyment, but not so rich that he can afford to be indifferent to loss. It will appear more naturally in the old than in the young, not because the old are more sensitive to loss but because they are apt to be more fully aware of the resources of their world and therefore less likely to find them inadequate. In some people this disposition is weak merely because they are ignorant of what their world has to offer them: the present appears to them only as a residue of inopportunities.

To be conservative, then, is to prefer the familiar to the unknown, to prefer the tried to the untried, fact to mystery, the actual to the possible, the limited to the unbounded, the near to the distant, the sufficient to the superabundant, the convenient to the perfect, present laughter to utopian bliss. Familiar relationships and loyalties will be preferred to the allure of more profitable attachments; to acquire and to enlarge will be less important than to keep, to cultivate and to enjoy; the grief of loss will be more acute than the excitement of novelty or promise. It is to be equal to one's own fortune, to live at the level of one's own means, to be content with the want of greater perfection which belongs alike to oneself and one's circumstances. With some people this is itself a choice; in others it is a disposition which appears, frequently or less frequently, in their preferences and aversions, and is not itself chosen or specifically cultivated.

Now, all this is represented in a certain attitude towards change and innovation; change denoting alterations we have to suffer and innovation those we design and execute.

Changes are circumstances to which we have to accommodate ourselves, and the disposition to be conservative is both the emblem of our difficulty in doing so and our resort in the attempts we make to do so. Changes are without effect only upon those who notice nothing, who are ignorant of what they possess and apathetic to their circumstances; and they can be welcomed indiscriminately only by those who esteem nothing, whose attachments are fleeting and who are strangers to love and affection. The conservative disposition provokes neither of these conditions: the inclination to enjoy what is present and available is the opposite of ignorance and apathy and it breeds attachment and affection. Consequently, it is averse from change, which appears always, in the first place, as deprivation. A storm which sweeps away a copse and transforms a favourite view, the death of friends, the sleep of friendship, the desuetude of customs of behaviour, the retirement of a favourite clown, involuntary exile, reversals of fortune, the loss of abilities enjoyed and their replacement by others – these are changes, none perhaps without its compensations, which the man of conservative temperament unavoidably regrets. But he has difficulty in reconciling himself to them, not because what he has lost in them was intrinsically better than any alternative might have been or was incapable of improvement, nor because what takes its place is inherently incapable of being enjoyed, but because what he has lost was something he actually enjoyed and had learned how to enjoy and what takes its place is something to which he has acquired no attachment. Consequently, he will find small and slow changes more tolerable than large and sudden; and he will value highly every appearance of continuity. Some changes, indeed, will present no difficulty; but, again, this is not because they are manifest improvements but merely because they are easily assimilated: the changes of the seasons are mediated by their recurrence and the growing up of children by its continuousness. And, in general, he will accommodate himself more readily to changes which do not offend expectation than to the destruction of what seems to have no ground of dissolution within itself.

Moreover, to be conservative is not merely to be averse from change (which may be an idiosyncrasy); it is also a manner of accommodating ourselves to changes, an activity imposed upon all men. For, change is a threat to identity, and every change is an emblem of extinction. But a man's identity (or that of a community) is nothing more than an unbroken rehearsal of contingencies, each at the mercy of circumstance and each significant in proportion to its familiarity. It is not a fortress into which we may retire, and the only means we have of defending it (that is, ourselves) against the hostile forces of change is in the open field of our experience; by throwing our weight upon the foot which for the time being is most firmly placed, by cleaving to whatever familiarities are not immediately threatened and thus assimilating what is new without becoming unrecognizable to ourselves. The Masai, when they were moved from their old country to the present Masai reserve in Kenya, took with them the names of their hills and plains and rivers and gave them to the hills and plains and rivers of the new country. And it is by some such subterfuge of conservatism that every man or people compelled to suffer a notable change avoids the shame of extinction.

Changes, then, have to be suffered; and a man of conservative temperament (that is, one strongly disposed to preserve his identity) cannot be indifferent to them. In the main, he judges them by the disturbance they entail and, like everyone else, deploys his resources to meet them. The idea of innovation, on the other hand, is improvement. Nevertheless, a man of this temperament will not himself be an ardent innovator. In the first place, he is not inclined to think that nothing is happening unless great changes are afoot and therefore he is not worried by the absence of innovation: the use and enjoyment of things as they are occupies most of his attention. Further, he is aware that not all innovation is, in fact, improvement; and he will think that to innovate without improving is either designed or inadvertent folly. Moreover, even when an innovation commends itself as a convincing improvement, he will look twice at its claims before accepting them. From his point of view, because every improvement involves change, the disruption entailed has always to be set against the benefit anticipated. But when he has satisfied himself about this, there will be other considerations to be taken into the account. Innovating is always an equivocal enterprise, in which gain and loss (even excluding the loss of familiarity) are so closely interwoven that it is exceedingly difficult to forecast the final up-shot: there is no such thing as an unqualified improvement. For, innovating is an activity which generates not only the 'improvement' sought, but a new and complex situation of which this is only one of the components. The total change is always more extensive than the change designed; and the whole of what is entailed can neither be foreseen nor circumscribed. Thus, whenever there is innovation there is the certainty that the change will be greater than was intended, that there will be loss as well as gain and that the loss and the gain will not be equally distributed among the people affected; there is the chance that the benefits derived will be greater than those which were designed; and there is the risk that they will be off-set by changes for the worse.

From all this the man of conservative temperament draws some appropriate conclusions. First, innovation entails certain loss and possible gain, therefore, the onus of proof, to show that the proposed change may be expected to be on the whole beneficial, rests with the would-be innovator. Secondly, he believes that the more closely an innovation resembles growth (that is, the more clearly it is intimated in and not merely imposed upon the situation) the less likely it is to result in a preponderance of loss. Thirdly, he thinks that an innovation which is a response to some specific defect, one designed to redress some specific disequilibrium, is more desirable than one which springs from a notion of a generally improved condition of human circumstances, and is far more desirable than one generated by a vision of perfection. Consequently, he prefers small and limited innovations to large and indefinite. Fourthly, he favours a slow rather than a rapid pace, and pauses to observe current consequences and make appropriate adjustments. And lastly, he believes the occasion to be important; and, other things being equal, he considers the most favourable occasion for innovation to be when the projected change is most likely to be limited to what is intended and least likely to be corrupted by undesired and unmanageable consequences.

The disposition to be conservative is, then, warm and positive in respect of enjoyment, and correspondingly cool and critical in respect of change and innovation: these two inclinations support and elucidate one another. The man of conservative temperament believes that a known good is not lightly to be surrendered for an unknown better. He is not in love with what is dangerous and difficult; he is unadventurous; he has no impulse to sail uncharted seas; for him there is no magic in being lost, bewildered or shipwrecked. If he is forced to navigate the unknown, he sees virtue in heaving the lead every inch of the way. What others plausibly identify as timidity, he recognizes in himself as rational prudence; what others interpret as inactivity, he recognizes as a disposition to enjoy rather than to exploit. He is cautious, and he is disposed to indicate his assent or dissent, not in absolute, but in graduated terms. He eyes the situation in terms of its propensity to disrupt the familiarity of the features of his world.

[...]

How, then, are we to construe the disposition to be conservative in respect of politics? And in making this inquiry what I am interested in is not merely the intelligibility of this disposition in any set of circumstances, but its intelligibility in our own contemporary circumstances.

Writers who have considered this question commonly direct our attention to beliefs about the world in general, about human beings in general, about associations in general and even about the universe; and they tell us that a conservative disposition in politics can be correctly construed only when we understand it as a reflection of certain beliefs of these kinds. It is said, for example, that conservatism in politics is the appropriate counterpart of a generally conservative disposition in respect of human conduct: to be reformist in business, in morals or in religion and to be conservative in politics is represented as being inconsistent. It is said that the conservative in politics is so by virtue of holding certain religious beliefs; a belief, for example, in a natural law to be gathered from human experience, and in a providential order reflecting a divine purpose in nature and in human history to which it is the duty of mankind to conform its conduct and departure from which spells injustice and calamity. Further, it is said that a disposition to be conservative in politics reflects what is called an 'organic' theory of human society; that it is tied up with a belief in the absolute value of human personality, and with a belief in a primordial propensity of human beings to sin. And the 'conservatism' of an Englishman has even been connected with Royalism and Anglicanism.

Now, setting aside the minor complaints one might be moved to make about this account of the situation, it seems to me to suffer from one large defect. It is true that many of these beliefs have been held by people disposed to be conservative in political activity, and it may be true that these people have also believed their disposition to be in some way confirmed by them, or even to be founded upon them; but, as I understand it, a disposition to be conservative in politics does not entail either that we should hold these beliefs to be true or even that we should suppose them to be true. Indeed, I do not think it is necessarily connected with any particular beliefs about the universe, about the world in general or about human conduct in general. What it is tied to is certain beliefs about the activity of governing and the instruments of government, and it is in terms of beliefs on these topics, and not on others, that it can be made to appear intelligible. And, to state my view briefly before elaborating it, what makes a conservative disposition in politics intelligible is nothing to do with a natural law or a providential order, nothing to do with morals or religion; it is the observation of our current manner of living combined with the belief (which from our point of view need be regarded as no more than an hypothesis) that governing is a specific and limited activity, namely the provision and custody of general rules of conduct, which are understood, not as plans for imposing substantive activities, but as instruments enabling people to pursue the activities of their own choice with the minimum frustration, and therefore something which it is appropriate to be conservative about. [...]

Surveying the scene, some people are provoked by the absence of order and coherence which appears to them to be its dominant feature; its wastefulness, its frustration, its dissipation of human energy, its lack not merely of a premeditated destination but even of any discernible direction of movement. It provides an excitement similar to that of a stock-car race; but it has none of the satisfaction of a well-conducted business enterprise. Such people are apt to exaggerate the current disorder; the absence of plan is so conspicuous that the small adjustments, and even the more massive arrangements, which restrain the chaos seem to them nugatory; they have no feeling for the warmth of untidiness but only for its inconvenience. But what is significant is not the limitations of their powers of observation, but the turn of their thoughts. They feel that there ought to be something that ought to be done to convert this so-called chaos into order, for this is no way for rational human beings to be spending their lives. Like Apollo when he saw Daphne with her hair hung carelessly about her neck, they sigh and say to themselves: 'What if it were properly arranged.' Moreover, they tell us that they have seen in a dream the glorious, collisionless manner of living proper to all mankind, and this dream they understand as their warrant for seeking to remove the diversities and occasions of conflict which distinguish our current manner of living. Of course, their dreams are not all exactly alike; but they have this in common: each is a vision of a condition of human circumstance from which the occasion of conflict has been removed, a vision of human activity co-ordinated and set going in a single direction and of every resource being used to the full. And such people appropriately understand the office of government to be the imposition upon its subjects of the condition of human circumstances of their dream. To govern is to turn a private dream into a public and compulsory manner of living. Thus, politics becomes an encounter of dreams and the activity in which government is held to this understanding of its office and provided with the appropriate instruments.

I do not propose to criticize this jump to glory style of politics in which governing is understood as a perpetual take-over bid for the purchase of the resources of human energy in order to concentrate them in a single direction; it is not at all unintelligible, and there is much in our circumstances to provoke it. My purpose is merely to point out that there is another quite different understanding of government, and that it is no less intelligible and in some respects perhaps more appropriate to our circumstances.

The spring of this other disposition in respect of governing and the instruments of government – a conservative disposition – is to be found in the acceptance of the current condition of human circumstances as I have described it: the propensity to make our own choices and to find happiness in doing so, the variety of enterprises each pursued with passion, the diversity of beliefs each held with the conviction of its exclusive truth; the inventiveness, the changefulness and the absence of any large design; the excess, the over-activity and the informal compromise. And the office of government is not to impose other beliefs and activities upon its subjects, not to tutor or to educate them, not to make them better or happier in another way, not to direct them, to galvanize them into action, to lead them or to coordinate their activities so that no occasion of conflict shall occur; the office of government is merely to rule.

[...]

To govern, then, as the conservative understands it, is to provide a *vinculum juris* for those manners of conduct which, in the circumstances, are least likely to result in a frustrating collision of interests; to provide redress and means of compensation for those who suffer from others behaving in a contrary manner; sometimes to provide punishment for those who pursue their own interests regardless of the rules; and, of course, to provide a sufficient force to maintain the authority of an arbiter of this kind. Thus, governing is recognized as a specific and limited activity; not the management of an enterprise, but the rule of those engaged in a great diversity of self-chosen enterprises. It is not concerned with concrete persons, but with activities; and with activities only in respect of their propensity to collide with one another. It is not concerned with moral right and wrong, it is not designed to make men good or even better; it is not indispensable on account of 'the natural depravity of mankind' but merely because of their current disposition to be extravagant; its business is to keep its subjects at peace with one another in the activities in which they have chosen to seek their happiness. And if there is any general idea entailed in this view, it is, perhaps, that a government which does not sustain the loyalty of its subjects is worthless; and that while one which (in the old puritan phrase) 'commands for truth' is incapable of doing so (because some of its subjects will believe its 'truth' to be error), one which is indifferent to 'truth' and 'error' alike, and merely pursues peace, presents no obstacle to the necessary loyalty.

Now, it is intelligible enough that any man who thinks in this manner about government should be averse from innovation: government is providing rules of conduct, and familiarity is a supremely important virtue in a rule. Nevertheless, he has room for other thoughts. The current condition of human circumstances is one in which new activities (often springing from new inventions) are constantly appearing and rapidly extend themselves, and in which beliefs are perpetually being modified or discarded; and for the rules to be inappropriate to the current activities and beliefs is as unprofitable as for them to be unfamiliar. For example, a variety of inventions and considerable changes in the conduct of business, seem now to have made the current law of copyright inadequate. And it may be thought that neither the newspaper nor the motor-car nor the aeroplane have yet received proper recognition in the law of England; they have all created nuisances that call out to be abated. Or again, at the end of the last century our governments engaged in an extensive codification of large parts of our law and in this manner both brought it into closer relationship with current beliefs and manners of activity and insulated it from the small adjustments to circumstances which are characteristic of the operation of our common law. But many of these Statutes are now hopelessly out of date. And there are older Acts of Parliament (such as the Merchant Shipping Act), governing large and important departments of activity, which are even more inappropriate to current circumstances. Innovation, then, is called for if the rules are to remain appropriate to the activities they govern. But, as the conservative understands it, modification of the rules should always reflect, and never impose, a change in the activities and beliefs of those who are subject to them, and should never on any occasion be so great as to destroy the *ensemble*. Consequently, the conservative will have nothing to do with innovations designed to meet merely hypothetical situations; he will prefer to enforce a rule he has got rather than invent a new one; he will think it appropriate to delay a modification of the rules until it is clear that the change of circumstance it is designed to reflect has come to stay for a while; he will be suspicious of proposals for change in excess of what the situation calls for, of rulers who demand extra-ordinary powers in order to make great changes and whose utterances are tied to generalities like 'the public good' or 'social justice', and of Saviours of Society who buckle on armour and seek dragons to slay; he will think it proper to consider the occasion of the innovation with care; in short, he will be disposed to regard politics as an activity in which a valuable set of tools is renovated from time to time and kept in trim rather than as an opportunity for perpetual re-equipment.

Richard Rorty, "Movements and Campaigns"*

In 1954, the year in which he founded *Dissent*, Irving Howe published an essay called "This Age of Conformity" in *Partisan Review*.[1] There he contrasted the dynamism of *Partisan Review*'s glory days with the complacent passivity of the intellectuals at the beginning of the Eisenhower years.

[...]

But by the time he wrote *A Margin of Hope*, he was much more skeptical about the very idea of a "movement" than he had been thirty years before.

In that book, written in the early 1980s, he pokes gentle fun at Philip Rahv's insistence that *Partisan Review* should "always seem to be moving somewhere," and at the "imagery of politics" which his younger self shared with Rahv: "an imagery of definition, conflict, alliance, exclusion."[2]

[...]

What Howe says here was anticipated by his own practice in editing *Dissent*. The difference between that magazine and *Partisan Review* during its first decade is that *Dissent*, and the group of writers around it, felt able to dispense with membership in a movement. They were content simply to throw themselves into a lot of campaigns. By "campaign," I mean something finite, something that can be recognized to have succeeded or to have, so far, failed. Movements, by contrast, neither succeed nor fail. They are too big and too amorphous to do anything that simple. They share in what Kierkegaard called "the passion of the infinite." They are exemplified by Christianity and by Marxism, the sort of movements which enable novelists like Dostoevsky to do what Howe admiringly called "*feeling* thought."[3]

Membership in a movement requires the ability to see particular campaigns for particular goals as parts of something much bigger, and as having little meaning in themselves. Campaigns for such goals as the unionization of migrant farm workers, or the overthrow (by votes or by force) of a corrupt government, or socialized medicine, or legal recognition of gay marriage can be conducted without much attention to literature, art, philosophy, or history. But movements levy contributions from each of these areas of culture. They are needed to provide a larger context within which politics is no longer just politics, but rather the matrix out of which will emerge something like Paul's "new being in Christ" or Mao's "new socialist man." Movement politics, the sort which held "bourgeois reformism" in contempt, was the kind of politics which Howe came to know all too well in the Thirties, and was doubtful about when it was reinvented in the Sixties. This kind of politics assumes that things will be changed utterly, that a terrible new beauty will be born.

Howe knew so well what it was like to belong to a movement when he was young that he was able to do without movements when he was older. So he, and the magazine he founded, were able to stick to campaigning. But of course this does not mean that he turned away from literature, art, philosophy, and history. He stayed in contact with all of these, but he no longer felt the same need to link critical consciousness with political conscience, to synthesize perfection of the work with perfection of the life. The difference between reading *Partisan Review* under Rahv and reading *Dissent* under Howe was that one read the former in order to take one's own spiritual temperature, and the latter in order to get the details on how the strong were currently oppressing the weak, how the rich were currently cheating the poor. *Partisan Review* was something to be lived up to, but *Dissent* was, and is, a source of information and advice.

[...]

Most of us, when young, hope for purity of heart. The easiest way to assure oneself of this purity is to will one thing – but this requires seeing everything as part of a pattern whose center is that single thing. Movements offer such a pattern, and thus offer such assurance of purity. Howe's ability, in his later decades, to retain both critical consciousness and political conscience, while not attempting to fuse the two into something larger than either, showed his admirers how to forgo such purity and such a pattern.

When literature replaces the Bible, polytheism and its problems return: choices between Tolstoy and Dostoevsky, or between Proust and Genet, replace choices between Jaweh and Baal or between Apollo and Dionysus. The prominence of the literary critic in the culture of the past two centuries is a natural consequence of the Romantic apotheosis of the creative artist: gods require contemplators of their splendor and glosses on their pronouncements. But whereas worship of One God, especially a God modeled on a Platonic Idea, requires purity of heart, polytheism requires the ability

* Richard Rorty, extracted from *Achieving Our Country* (Harvard University Press, 1998), pp. 111–24.

1 Irving Howe, "This Age of Conformity," in Howe, *Selected Writings*, 1950–1990 (San Diego: Harcourt Brace, 1990), p. 46.

2 Irving Howe, *A Margin of Hope: An Intellectual Autobiography* (San Diego: Harcourt Brace Jovanovich, 1982), p. 160.

3 Irving Howe, *Politics and the Novel* (New York: New American Library, 1987; orig. pub. 1957), Epilogue, p. 254.

to internalize and tolerate oppositions – oppositions not just between novelists and novels, but within both.

Howe said that one of the "secrets" of the novel in general may be "the vast respect which the great novelist is ready to offer to the whole idea of *opposition* – the opposition he needs to allow for in his book against his own predispositions and yearnings and fantasies."[4] I suspect that Harold Bloom is right that this secret of the novel is the secret of literature, considered as the area of culture which finds itself in perpetual opposition to science and philosophy.[5] Literature, Bloom says, adheres to Protagoras' motto "Two logoi opposing one another," and thus is as inevitably polytheist and agonistic as Plato's invention, philosophy, is inevitably monistic and convergent. Movements are suited to onto-theological Platonists, campaigns to many-minded men of letters.

The specific sort of opposition which most interested Howe is the one described in the epigraph from Max Scheler which he chose for *Politics and the Novel*: "True tragedy arises 'when the idea of "justice" appears to be leading to the destruction of higher values.'" An aspirant to political sainthood can avoid that kind of tragedy by purifying his heart, having only one yearning and only one fantasy. Such an aspirant will repeat over and over, "Not my will, but the Movement's, be done." Part of what helped Howe turn from movements to campaigns was the lesson he learned from political novels: a lesson about the dangers of such attempts at self-purification and self-surrender. A multiplicity of campaigns has the same advantage as a plurality of gods or of novels: each campaign is finite, and there is always another campaign to enlist in when the first fails or goes rancid. The realized impurity of a movement can destroy the person who has identified himself with that movement, but the impurity of a campaign can be taken in one's stride: such impurity is just what one expects of something finite and mortal.

[...]

Such reflections suggest a more general question: What might the cultural history and sociopolitical history of the West look like if we tried to narrate both without mention of major turnings? What would they look like if they were written as the histories of a very large number of small campaigns, rather than as the history of a few great movements? What would our past look like if we decided that (in the words that Bruno Latour takes as the title of his brilliant book) "we have never been modern" – that history is an endless network of changing relationships, without any great climactic ruptures or peripeties, and that terms like "traditional society," "modern society," and "postmodern society" are more trouble than they are worth?

Let me offer some tentative answers to these questions. I suggest that the analogue of a sociopolitical campaign, such as that on behalf of the eight-hour workday or equal pay for equal work, is the career of an individual poet, novelist, dancer, critic, or painter. Such a career, like such a campaign, is finite and mortal, and can be seen to have succeeded or failed – or, more frequently, to have succeeded to a certain degree while still falling short of its initial aims. Careers, like campaigns, may borrow impetus and enthusiasm from, or may define themselves by opposition to, contemporary careers and campaigns. This is why there are artistic, as well as sociopolitical, alliances and struggles.

The reason I cite poets, critics, and painters, rather than dentists, carpenters, and laborers, as having careers is that the former, more typically than the latter, are trying to make the future different from the past – trying to create a new role rather than to play an old role well. The difference is obviously not hard and fast, since there are such things as hack poetry and creative dentistry. But the creative artist, in a wide sense that includes critics, scientists, and scholars, provides the paradigm case of a career whose conclusion leaves the world a bit different from what it used to be. If there is a connection between artistic freedom and creativity and the spirit of democracy, it is that the former provide examples of the kind of courageous self-transformation of which we hope democratic societies will become increasingly capable – transformation which is conscious and willed, rather than semiconsciously endured.

If, following Latour's and Descombes' suggestions, we were to start writing narratives of overlapping campaigns and careers which were not broken up into chapters with titles like "The Enlightenment," "Romanticism," "Literary Modernism," or "Late Capitalism," we would lose dramatic intensity. But we might help immunize ourselves against the passion of the infinite. If we dropped reference to movements, we could settle for telling a story about how the human beings in the neighborhood of the North Atlantic made their futures different from their pasts at a constantly accelerating pace. We could still, like Hegel and Acton, tell this story as a story of increasing freedom. But we could drop, along with any sense of inevitable progress, any sense of immanent teleology. We could drop any attempt to capitalize History, to view it as something as big and strong as Nature or God.

4 Howe, *Politics and the Novel*, p. 23.

5 See Harold Bloom, *Agon* (Oxford: Oxford University Press, 1982), p. 35.

Such narratives of overlapping campaigns and careers would contain no hint that a career could be judged by its success in aligning itself with the movement of history. Both political and cultural history would be seen as a tissue of chances, mischances, and lost chances – a tissue from which, occasionally and briefly, beauty flashes forth, but to which sublimity is entirely irrelevant. It would not occur to somebody brought up on this kind of narrative to ask whether Joyce, Proust, Schönberg, Bartók, Picasso, and Matisse signified one of the major turnings in the cultural history of the West, or to ask whether that turning was perhaps not better signified by Rilke, Valéry, Strauss, Eliot, Klimt, and Heidegger. It would never occur to such a person to ask whether *Dissent* was central or marginal to the cultural or political life of its day. She would ask only whether *Dissent* did some good, whether it contributed to the success of some of the campaigns in which it took part. The answer to that question is clear.

Martin Luther King Jr., "Letter from a Birmingham Jail"*

My Dear Fellow Clergymen:

While confined here in the Birmingham city jail, I came across your recent statement calling my present activities "unwise and untimely." Seldom do I pause to answer criticism of my work and ideas. If I sought to answer all the criticisms that cross my desk, my secretaries would have little time for anything other than such correspondence in the course of the day, and I would have no time for constructive work. But since I feel that you are men of genuine good will and that your criticisms are sincerely set forth, I want to try to answer your statements in what I hope will be patient and reasonable terms.

I think I should indicate why I am here in Birmingham, since you have been influenced by the view which argues against "outsiders coming in." I have the honor of serving as president of the Southern Christian Leadership Conference, an organization operating in every southern state, with headquarters in Atlanta, Georgia. We have some 85 affiliated organizations across the South, and one of them is the Alabama Christian Movement for Human Rights. Frequently we share staff, educational and financial resources with our affiliates. Several months ago the affiliate here in Birmingham asked us to be on call to engage in a nonviolent direct-action program if such were deemed necessary. We readily consented, and when the hour came we lived up to our promise. So I, along with several members of my staff, am here because I was invited here. I am here because I have organizational ties here.

But more basically, I am in Birmingham because injustice is here. Just as the prophets of the eighth century BC left their villages and carried their "thus saith the Lord" far beyond the boundaries of their home towns, and just as the Apostle Paul left his village of Tarsus and carried the gospel of Jesus Christ to the far corners of the Greco-Roman world, so am I compelled to carry the gospel of freedom beyond my own home town. Like Paul, I must constantly respond to the Macedonian call for aid.

Moreover, I am cognizant of the interrelatedness of all communities and states. I cannot sit idly by in Atlanta and not be concerned about what happens in Birmingham. Injustice anywhere is a threat to justice everywhere. We are caught in an inescapable network of mutuality, tied in a single garment of destiny. Whatever affects one directly, affects all indirectly. Never again can we afford to live with the narrow, provincial "outside agitator" idea. Anyone who lives inside the United States can never be considered an outsider anywhere within its bounds.

You deplore the demonstrations taking place in Birmingham. But your statement, I am sorry to say, fails to express a similar concern for the conditions that brought about the demonstrations. I am sure that none of you would want to rest content with the superficial kind of social analysis that deals merely with effects and does not grapple with underlying causes. It is unfortunate that demonstrations are taking place in Birmingham, but it is even more unfortunate that the city's white power structure left the Negro community with no alternative.

In any nonviolent campaign there are four basic steps: collection of the facts to determine whether injustices exist; negotiation; self-purification; and direct action. We have gone through all these steps in Birmingham. There can be no gainsaying the fact that racial injustice engulfs this community. Birmingham is probably the most thoroughly segregated city in the United States. Its ugly record of brutality is widely known. Negroes have experienced grossly unjust treatment in the courts. There have been more unsolved bombings of Negro homes and churches in Birmingham than in any other city in the nation. These are the hard, brutal facts of the case. On the basis of these conditions, Negro leaders sought to

* Martin Luther King Jr. "Letter from a Birmingham Jail," extracted from http://patriotpost.us/histdocs/Birmjail/html, accessed April 29, 2008. The letter is dated April 16, 1963.

negotiate with the city fathers. But the latter consistently refused to engage in good-faith negotiation.

[...]

As in so many past experiences, our hopes had been blasted, and the shadow of deep disappointment settled upon us. We had no alternative except to prepare for direct action, whereby we would present our very bodies as a means of laying our case before the conscience of the local and the national community. Mindful of the difficulties involved, we decided to undertake a process of self-purification. We began a series of workshops on nonviolence, and we repeatedly asked ourselves : "Are you able to accept blows without retaliating?" "Are you able to endure the ordeal of jail?"

[...]

You may well ask: "Why direct action? Why sit-ins, marches and so forth? Isn't negotiation a better path?" You are quite right in calling for negotiation. Indeed, this is the very purpose of direct action. Nonviolent direct action seeks to create such a crisis and foster such a tension that a community which has constantly refused to negotiate is forced to confront the issue. It seeks so to dramatize the issue that it can no longer be ignored. My citing the creation of tension as part of the work of the nonviolent-resister may sound rather shocking. But I must confess that I am not afraid of the word "tension." I have earnestly opposed violent tension, but there is a type of constructive, nonviolent tension which is necessary for growth. Just as Socrates felt that it was necessary to create a tension in the mind so that individuals could rise from the bondage of myths and half-truths to the unfettered realm of creative analysis and objective appraisal, so must we see the need for nonviolent gadflies to create the kind of tension in society that will help men rise from the dark depths of prejudice and racism to the majestic heights of understanding and brotherhood.

The purpose of our direct-action program is to create a situation so crisis-packed that it will inevitably open the door to negotiation. I therefore concur with you in your call for negotiation. Too long has our beloved Southland been bogged down in a tragic effort to live in monologue rather than dialogue.

[...]

We know through painful experience that freedom is never voluntarily given by the oppressor; it must be demanded by the oppressed. Frankly, I have yet to engage in a direct-action campaign that was "well timed" in the view of those who have not suffered unduly from the disease of segregation. For years now I have heard the word "Wait!" It rings in the ear of every Negro with piercing familiarity. This "Wait" has almost always meant "Never." We must come to see, with one of our distinguished jurists, that "justice too long delayed is justice denied."

We have waited for more than 340 years for our constitutional and God-given rights. The nations of Asia and Africa are moving with jetlike speed toward gaining political independence, but we still creep at horse-and-buggy pace toward gaining a cup of coffee at a lunch counter. Perhaps it is easy for those who have never felt the stinging dark of segregation to say, "Wait." But when you have seen vicious mobs lynch your mothers and fathers at will and drown your sisters and brothers at whim; when you have seen hate-filled policemen curse, kick and even kill your black brothers and sisters; when you see the vast majority of your 20 million Negro brothers smothering in an airtight cage of poverty in the midst of an affluent society; [...] when you are harried by day and haunted by night by the fact that you are a Negro, living constantly at tiptoe stance, never quite knowing what to expect next, and are plagued with inner fears and outer resentments; when you are forever fighting a degenerating sense of "nobodiness" then you will understand why we find it difficult to wait. There comes a time when the cup of endurance runs over, and men are no longer willing to be plunged into the abyss of despair. I hope, sirs, you can understand our legitimate and unavoidable impatience.

You express a great deal of anxiety over our willingness to break laws. This is certainly a legitimate concern. Since we so diligently urge people to obey the Supreme Court's decision of 1954 outlawing segregation in the public schools, at first glance it may seem rather paradoxical for us consciously to break laws. One may well ask: "How can you advocate breaking some laws and obeying others?" The answer lies in the fact that there are two types of laws: just and unjust. I would be the first to advocate obeying just laws. One has not only a legal but a moral responsibility to obey just laws. Conversely, one has a moral responsibility to disobey unjust laws. I would agree with St. Augustine that "an unjust law is no law at all"

Now, what is the difference between the two? How does one determine whether a law is just or unjust? A just law is a man-made code that squares with the moral law or the law of God. An unjust law is a code that is out of harmony with the moral law. To put it in the terms of St. Thomas Aquinas: An unjust law is a human law that is not rooted in eternal law and natural law. Any law that uplifts human personality is just. Any law that degrades human personality is unjust. All segregation statutes are unjust because segregation distort the soul and damages the personality. It gives the segregator a false sense of superiority and the segregated a false sense of inferiority. Segregation, to use the terminology of the Jewish philosopher Martin Buber, substitutes an "I–it" relationship for an "I–thou" relationship and ends up relegating persons to the status of things. Hence segregation is not only politically, economically and sociologically unsound, it is morally wrong and awful.

[...]

Sometimes a law is just on its face and unjust in its application. For instance, I have been arrested on a charge of parading without a permit. Now, there is nothing wrong in having an ordinance which requires a permit for a parade. But such an ordinance becomes unjust when it is used to maintain segregation and to deny citizens the First Amendment privilege of peaceful assembly and protest.

I hope you are able to face the distinction I am trying to point out. In no sense do I advocate evading or defying the law, as would the rabid segregationist. That would lead to anarchy. One who breaks an unjust law must do so openly, lovingly, and with a willingness to accept the penalty. I submit that an individual who breaks a law that conscience tells him is unjust and who willingly accepts the penalty of imprisonment in order to arouse the conscience of the community over its injustice, is in reality expressing the highest respect for law.

Of course, there is nothing new about this kind of civil disobedience. It was evidenced sublimely in the refusal of Shadrach, Meshach and Abednego to obey the laws of Nebuchadnezzar, on the ground that a higher moral law was at stake. It was practiced superbly by the early Christians, who were willing to face hungry lions and the excruciating pain of chopping blocks rather than submit to certain unjust laws of the Roman Empire. To a degree, academic freedom is a reality today because Socrates practiced civil disobedience. In our own nation, the Boston Tea Party represented a massive act of civil disobedience.

We should never forget that everything Adolf Hitler did in Germany was "legal" and everything the Hungarian freedom fighters did in Hungary was "illegal." It was "illegal" to aid and comfort a Jew in Hitler's Germany. Even so, I am sure that, had I lived in Germany at the time, I would have aided and comforted my Jewish brothers. If today I lived in a Communist country where certain principles dear to the Christian faith are suppressed, I would openly advocate disobeying that country's antireligious laws.

I must make two honest confessions to you, my Christian and Jewish brothers. First, I must confess that over the past few years I have been gravely disappointed with the white moderate. I have almost reached the regrettable conclusion that the Negro's great stumbling block in his stride toward freedom is not the White Citizen's Counciler or the Ku Klux Klanner, but the white moderate, who is more devoted to "order" than to justice; who prefers a negative peace which is the absence of tension to a positive peace which is the presence of justice; who constantly says: "I agree with you in the goal you seek, but I cannot agree with your methods of direct action"; who paternalistically believes he can set the timetable for another man's freedom; who lives by a mythical concept of time and who constantly advises the Negro to wait for a "more convenient season." Shallow understanding from people of good will is more frustrating than absolute misunderstanding from people of ill will. Lukewarm acceptance is much more bewildering than outright rejection.

I had hoped that the white moderate would understand that law and order exist for the purpose of establishing justice and that when they fail in this purpose they become the dangerously structured dams that block the flow of social progress. I had hoped that the white moderate would understand that the present tension in the South is a necessary phase of the transition from an obnoxious negative peace, in which the Negro passively accepted his unjust plight, to a substantive and positive peace, in which all men will respect the dignity and worth of human personality. Actually, we who engage in nonviolent direct action are not the creators of tension. We merely bring to the surface the hidden tension that is already alive. We bring it out in the open, where it can be seen and dealt with. Like a boil that can never be cured so long as it is covered up but must be opened with all its ugliness to the natural medicines of air and light, injustice must be exposed, with all the tension its exposure creates, to the light of human conscience and the air of national opinion before it can be cured.

[...]

You speak of our activity in Birmingham as extreme. At first I was rather disappointed that fellow clergymen would see my nonviolent efforts as those of an extremist. I began thinking about the fact that stand in the middle of two opposing forces in the Negro community. One is a force of complacency, made up in part of Negroes who, as a result of long years of oppression, are so drained of self-respect and a sense of "somebodiness" that they have adjusted to segregation; and in part of a few middle-class Negroes who, because of a degree of academic and economic security and because in some ways they profit by segregation, have become insensitive to the problems of the masses. The other force is one of bitterness and hatred, and it comes perilously close to advocating violence. It is expressed in the various black nationalist groups that are springing up across the nation, the largest and best-known being Elijah Muhammad's Muslim movement. Nourished by the Negro's frustration over the continued existence of racial discrimination, this movement is made up of people who have lost faith in America, who have absolutely repudiated Christianity, and who have concluded that the white man is an incorrigible "devil."

I have tried to stand between these two forces, saying that we need emulate neither the "do-nothingism" of the complacent nor the hatred and despair of the black nationalist. For there is the more excellent way of love and nonviolent protest.

[...]

But though I was initially disappointed at being categorized as an extremist, as I continued to think about the matter I gradually gained a measure of satisfaction from the label. Was not Jesus an extremist for love: "Love your enemies, bless them that curse you, do good to them that hate you, and pray for them which despitefully use you, and persecute you." Was not Amos an extremist for justice: "Let justice roll down like waters and righteousness like an ever-flowing stream." Was not Paul an extremist for the Christian gospel: "I bear in my body the marks of the Lord Jesus." Was not Martin Luther an extremist: "Here I stand; I cannot do otherwise, so help me God." And John Bunyan: "I will stay in jail to the end of my days before I make a butchery of my conscience." And Abraham Lincoln: "This nation cannot survive half slave and half free." And Thomas Jefferson: "We hold these truths to be self-evident, that all men are created equal ..." So the question is not whether we will be extremists, but what kind of extremists we will be. Will we be extremists for hate or for love? Will we be extremist for the preservation of injustice or for the extension of justice? [...]

Abd Al-Salam Faraj, "The Neglected Duty"*

[...]

(3) *Jihad* (struggle) for God's cause, in spite of its extreme importance and its great significance for the future of this religion, has been neglected by the '*ulama*' (leading Muslim scholars) of this age. They have feigned ignorance of it, but they know that it is the only way to the return and the establishment of the glory of Islam anew. Every Muslim preferred his own favorite ideas and philosophies above the Best Road, which God – Praised and Exalted He is – drew Himself (a road that leads back) to (a state of) Honor for His Servants.

(4) There is no doubt that the idols of this world can only be made to disappear through the power of the sword. It is therefore that (the Apostle Muhammad) – God's peace be upon him – said: "I have been sent with the Sword at this Hour, so that God alone is worshiped, without associate to Him, He put my daily bread under the shadow of my lance, He brings lowness and smallness to those who disagree with what I command.

[...]

(15) God gave a promise to a group of believers in His – Glorious and Majestic He is – word: "God has promised to those of you who have believed and wrought the works of righteousness, that He will surely make them successors (to power) in the land as He made those before them successors, and he will surely establish for them their religion which He has approved for them, and after their fear will give them in exchange security; 'They shall serve Me not associating anything with Me.'" (This Qur'an quotation) is taken from verse 55 of Surah 24. God does not break His promises. We ask Him – Majestic and Supreme He is – that He make us one of them (who are mentioned in the beginning of this Qur'an quotation).

(16) This is a duty which is rejected by some Muslims and neglected by others although the proof for the obligatory character of the establishment of a state is clear, and made obvious by the (text of the) Book of God – Blessed and Supreme He is, – for God – Glory to Him – says: "and that you must rule between them according to what God sent down," and He says: "Whosoever does not rule by what God sent down, those, they are the unbelievers." He says – Glorious and Majestic He is – in (the first verse of) Surah 24 (of which we quoted verse 55 in the previous paragraph), about the obligatory character of the prescripts of Islam: "a Surah which we sent down and which we made obligatory." From this (verse) (it follows) that the establishment of the Rule of God over this earth (mentioned in verse 55 of this Surah) must be considered to be obligatory for the Muslims. God's prescripts are an obligation for the Muslims. Hence, the establishment of an Islamic

* Abd Al-Salam Faraj, extracted from *The Neglected Duty: The Creed of Sadat's Assassins and the Emergence of Islamic Militancy in the Middle East,* by Johannes J. G. Jensen (Macmillan Reference, 1986).

State is an obligation for the Muslims, for something without which something which is obligatory cannot be carried out becomes (itself) obligatory. If, moreover, (such a) state cannot be established without war, then this war is an obligation as well.

(17) Muslims are agreed on the obligatory character of the establishment of an Islamic Caliphate. To announce a Caliphate must be based on the existence of a (territorial) nucleus (from which it can grow). This (nucleus) is the Islamic State. "Whosoever dies without having taken upon himself (the obligation of) a pledge of allegiance does not die as a Muslim." So, it is obligatory for every Muslim to seriously strive for the return of the Caliphate in order not to fall into the category of people (mentioned in the) Tradition (quoted in this paragraph). By "pledge of allegiance" (the text of the Tradition) means "allegiance to the Caliphate."

(18) Here a question appears: do we live in an Islamic State? One of the characteristics of such a state is that it is ruled by the laws of Islam. The Imam Abu Hanifah gave us his opinion that the House of Islam changes into the House of Unbelief if three conditions are fulfilled simultaneously: 1. if it is ruled by other laws than those of Islam, 2. the disappearance of safety for the Muslim inhabitants, 3. its being adjacent or close … and this (means) that the House (of Islam) is close to the house of Unbelief to such an extent that this is a source of danger to the Muslims and a cause for the disappearance of their safety.

[…]

(21) The laws by which the Muslims are ruled today are the laws of Unbelief, they are actually codes of law that were made by infidels who then subjected the Muslims to these (codes) although God – Praised and Exalted He is – says in Surah 5 (of the Qur'an): "Whosoever does not rule … by what God sent down, those are the Unbelievers … ." (This quotation is taken from Qur'an 5.44.) After the disappearance of the Caliphate definitively in the year 1924, and (after) the removal of the laws of Islam in their entirety, and (after) their substitution by laws that were imposed by infidels, the situation (of the Muslims) became identical to the situation of the Mongols.

[…]

(25) The rulers of this age are in apostasy from Islam. They were raised at the tables of imperialism, be it Crusaderism, or Communism, or Zionism. They carry nothing from Islam but their names, even though they pray and fast and claim … to be Muslim. It is a well-established rule of Islamic Law that the punishment of an apostate will be heavier than the punishment of someone who is by origin an infidel (and has never been a Muslim), and this in many respects. For instance, an apostate has to be killed even if he is unable to (carry arms and) go to war. Someone, however, who is by origin an infidel and who is unable to (carry arms and) go to war (against the Muslims) should not be killed, according to leading Muslim scholars like Abu Hanifah and Malik and Ahmad (ibn Hanbal).

[…]

(52) There are those who say: "We must establish an Islamic political party (and add this party) to the list of extant political parties." It is true that this is better than benevolent societies, because a party at least talks about politics. However, the purpose of the foundation (of such a party) is the destruction of the infidel State (and to replace it by an Islamic theocracy). To work through a political party will, however, have the opposite effect, since it means building the pagan State and collaborating with it … . (Moreover, such an Islamic political party) will participate in the membership of legislative councils that enact laws without consideration for God's Laws.

(53) There are those who say that the Muslims should do their best in order to obtain (socially) important positions. Only when all important centers are filled with Muslim doctors and Muslim engineers, will the existing pagan order perish automatically and the Muslim Ruler … establish himself … . Someone who hears this argument for the first time will think it is a fantasy or a joke, but there are, as a matter of fact, people in the Muslim world who embrace such philosophies and arguments, although there is nothing in the Book (of God) or the Example (of the Prophet) which supports or proves the(se arguments). Moreover, reality prevents (such aspirations) from ever coming true … . No matter how many Muslim doctors and Muslim engineers there are, they too will help to build the (pagan) State. Moreover, things will never go so far as to permit a Muslim personality to reach a ministerial post when he is not a 100 percent supporter of the existing order.

(54) Some of them say the right road to the establishment of an (Islamic) State is (nonviolent) propaganda … only, and the creation of a broad base. This, however, does not bring about the foundation of an (Islamic) State. Nevertheless, some people make this point the basis for their withdrawal from (true) *jihad*. The truth is that an (Islamic) State can only be founded by a believing minority … . Those who follow the straight path that is in accordance with the Command of God and the Example of the Apostle of God – May God's Peace be upon Him – are always a minority. Scriptural proof of

this is found in the Word of God – Exalted and Majestic He is – : "Few among my servants are thankful" (Qur'an 34.12) and in His Word – He be Praised – : "If thou obey the majority of those who are in the land they will lead thee astray from the Way of God" (Qur'an 6.116). This is the Custom of God … with regard to His World … . From where will we get this hoped-for majority? (Did not God) also say: "Most of the people, even though thou shouldst be zealous, are not believers"? (Qur'an 12.103).

(55) Islam does not triumph by (attracting the support of) the majority. Did not God – Praised and exalted He is – say: "How many a small band has, by the permission of God, conquered a numerous band?" (Qur'an 2.249)? And also: "(God has already helped you on many fields) and on the Day of Hunayn when ye prided yourselves on your numbers but they did not benefit you at all, and the land, wide as it was, became too narrow for you" (Qur'an 9.25) … .

[…]

(63) There are some who say that at present the true road is the quest for knowledge. "How can we fight when we have no knowledge (of Islam and its prescripts)? The quest for knowledge is an obligation …, too." But we shall not heed the words of someone who permits the neglect of a religious command or one of the duties of Islam for the sake of (the quest for religious) knowledge, certainly not if this duty is the duty of *jihad*. How could we possibly neglect a personal individual duty (like *jihad*) for the sake of a collective duty (like the quest for knowledge)?

How can it have come about that we got to know the smallest (details of the Islamic doctrine of duties like) recommendable and desirable acts, and call upon people to perform these acts, but at the same time neglect a duty which the Apostle – May God's Peace be upon Him – glorified?

How can someone who has specialized in (Islamic) religious studies and who really knows all about small and great sins not have noticed the great importance of *jihad*, and the punishment for postponing or neglecting it?

Someone who says that (the quest for) knowledge (also) is (a form of) *jihad* has to understand that the duty (which is indicated by the Arabic word *jihad*) entails the obligation of fighting, for God – Praised and Exalted He is – says: "Prescribed for you is fighting" (Qur'an 2.216) … .

[…]

(65) God – Exalted He is – made it clear that this Community differs from the other (religious) Communities as far as Fighting is concerned. In the case of earlier communities God – Praised and Exalted He is – made His punishment come down upon the infidels and the enemies of His religion by means of natural phenomena like eclipses (of the moon), floods, shouts and storms … . With regard to the Community of Muhammad – God's Peace be upon Him – this differs, for God – Praised and Exalted He is – addressed them saying: "Fight them and God will punish them at your hands, will humiliate them and aid you against them, and will bring healing to the breasts of people who are believers" (Qur'an 9.14).

This means that a Muslim has first of all the duty to execute the command to fight with his hands. (Once he has done so) God – Praised and Exalted He is – will then intervene (and change) the laws of nature. In this way victory will be achieved through the hands of the believers by means of God's – Praised and Exalted He is – (intervention) … .

[…]

(68) It is said that the battlefield of *jihad* today is the liberation of Jerusalem since it is (part of) the Holy Land. It is true that the liberation of the Holy Land is a religious command, obligatory for all Muslims, but the Apostle of God – May God's Peace be upon Him – described the believer as "sagacious and prudent"…, and this means that a Muslim knows what is useful and what is harmful, and gives priority to radical definitive solutions. This is a point that makes the explanation of the following necessary:

(69) First: To fight an enemy who is near is more important than to fight an enemy who is far.

Second: Muslim blood will be shed in order to realize this victory. Now it must be asked whether this victory will benefit the interests of an Islamic State? Or will this victory benefit the interests of Infidel Rule? It will mean the strengthening of a State which rebels against the Laws of God … . These rulers will take advantage of the nationalist ideas of these Muslims in order to realize their un-Islamic aims, even though at the surface (these aims) look Islamic. Fighting has to be done (only) under the Banner of Islam and under Islamic Leadership. About this there is no difference of opinion.

(70) Third: The basis of the existence of Imperialism in the Lands of Islam are (precisely) these Rulers. To begin by putting an end to imperialism is not a laudatory and not a useful act. It is only a waste of time. We must concentrate on our own Islamic situation: we have to establish the Rule of God's Religion in our own country first, and to make the Word of God supreme … . There is no doubt that the first battlefield for *jihad* is the extermination of these infidel leaders and to replace them by a complete Islamic Order. From here we should start.

[...]

The question now is: when is *jihad* an individual duty? *Jihad* becomes an individual duty in three situations:

(85) First, when two armies meet and their ranks are facing each other, it is forbidden to those who are present to leave, and it becomes an individual duty to remain standing, because God – Exalted He is – says: "O ye who have believed, when ye meet a hostile party, stand firm, and call God frequently to mind" (Qur'an 8.45) and also: "O ye who have believed, when ye meet those who have disbelieved moving into battle, turn them not your backs" (Qur'an 8.15).

Second, when the infidels descend upon a country, it becomes an individual duty for its people to fight them and drive them away.

Third, when the Imam calls upon a people to fight, they must depart into battle, for God – Exalted He is – says (Qur'an 9.38–39): "O ye who have believed, what is the matter with you? When one says to you: 'March out in the way of God,' ye are weighed down to the ground; are you so satisfied with this nearer life as to neglect the Hereafter? The enjoyment of this nearer life is in comparison with the Hereafter only a little thing. If ye do not march out He will inflict upon you a painful punishment, and will substitute (for you) another people; ye will not injure Him at all; God over everything has power." The Apostle – God's Peace be upon Him – says: "When you are called upon to fight, then hasten."

[...]

(100) Neglecting *jihad* is the cause of the lowness, humiliation, division and fragmentation in which the Muslims live today ... .

Albert Camus, "Rebellion Beyond Nihilism"*

Plato is right and not Moses and Nietzsche. Dialogue on the level of mankind is less costly than the gospel preached by totalitarian regimes in the form of a monologue dictated from the top of a lonely mountain. On the stage as in reality, the monologue precedes death. Every rebel, solely by the movement that sets him in opposition to the oppressor, therefore pleads for life, undertakes to struggle against servitude, falsehood, and terror, and affirms, in a flash, that these three afflictions are the cause of silence between men, that they obscure them from one another and prevent them from rediscovering themselves in the only value that can save them from nihilism – the long complicity of men at grips with their destiny.

In a flash – but that is time enough to say, provisionally, that the most extreme form of freedom, the freedom to kill, is not compatible with the sense of rebellion. Rebellion is in no way the demand for total freedom. On the contrary, rebellion puts total freedom up for trial. It specifically attacks the unlimited power that authorizes a superior to violate the forbidden frontier. Far from demanding general independence, the rebel wants it to be recognized that freedom has its limits everywhere that a human being is to be found – the limit being precisely that human being's power to rebel. The most profound reason for rebellious intransigence is to be found here. The more aware rebellion is of demanding a just limit, the more inflexible it becomes. The rebel undoubtedly demands a certain degree of freedom for himself; but in no case, if he is consistent, does he demand the right to destroy the existence and the freedom of others. He humiliates no one. The freedom he claims, he claims for all; the freedom he refuses, he forbids everyone to enjoy. He is not only the slave against the master, but also man against the world of master and slave. Therefore, thanks to rebellion, there is something more in history than the relation between mastery and servitude. Unlimited power is not the only law. It is in the name of another value that the rebel affirms the impossibility of total freedom while he claims for himself the relative freedom necessary to recognize this impossibility. Every human freedom, at its very roots, is therefore relative. Absolute freedom, which is the freedom to kill, is the only one which does not claim, at the same time as itself, the things that limit and obliterate it. Thus it cuts itself off from its roots and – abstract and malevolent shade – wanders haphazardly until such time as it imagines that it has found substance in some ideology.

It is then possible to say that rebellion, when it develops into destruction, is illogical. Claiming the unity of the human condition, it is a force of life, not of death. Its most profound logic is not the logic of destruction: it is the logic of creation.

[...]

In reality, the purely historical absolute is not even conceivable. Jaspers's thought, for example, in its essentials underlines the impossibility of man's grasping totality, since he lives in the midst of this totality. History, as an entirety, could exist only in the eyes of an observer outside it and outside the world. History only exists, in the final analysis, for God. Thus it is impossible to act

* Albert Camus, extracted from *The Rebel* (Vintage Books, 1956), pp. 283–5, 289–92, 302–6.

according to plans embracing the totality of universal history. Any historical enterprise can therefore only be a more or less reasonable or justifiable adventure. It is primarily a risk. In so far as it is a risk it cannot be used to justify any excess or any ruthless and absolutist position.

If, on the other hand, rebellion could found a philosophy it would be a philosophy of limits, of calculated ignorance, and of risk. He who does not know everything cannot kill everything. The rebel, far from making an absolute of history, rejects and disputes it, in the name of a concept that he has of his own nature. He refuses his condition, and his condition to a large extent is historical. Injustice, the transcience of time, death – all are manifest in history. In spurning them, history itself is spurned. Most certainly the rebel does not deny the history that surrounds him; it is in terms of this that he attempts to affirm himself. But confronted with it, he feels like the artist confronted with reality; he spurns it without escaping from it. He has never succeeded in creating an absolute history. [...]

Rebellion itself only aspires to the relative and can only promise an assured dignity coupled with relative justice. It supposes a limit at which the community of man is established. Its universe is the universe of relative values. Instead of saying, with Hegel and Marx, that all is necessary, it only repeats that all is possible and that, at a certain point on the farthest frontier, it is worth making the supreme sacrifice for the sake of the possible. Between God and history, the yogi and the commissar, it opens a difficult path where contradictions may exist and thrive. [...]

To kill freedom in order to establish the reign of justice comes to the same as resuscitating the idea of grace without divine intercession and of restoring by a mystifying reaction the mystic body in its basest elements. Even when justice is not realized, freedom preserves the power to protest and guarantees human communication. Justice in a silent world, justice enslaved and mute, destroys mutual complicity and finally can no longer be justice. The revolution of the twentieth century has arbitrarily separated, for overambitious ends of conquest, two inseparable ideas. Absolute freedom mocks at justice. Absolute justice denies freedom. To be fruitful, the two ideas must find their limits in each other. No man considers that his condition is free if it is not at the same time just, nor just unless it is free. Freedom, precisely, cannot even be imagined without the power of saying clearly what is just and what is unjust, of claiming all existence in the name of a small part of existence which refuses to die. Finally there is a justice, though a very different kind of justice, in restoring freedom, which is the only imperishable value of history. Men are never really willing to die except for the sake of freedom: therefore they do not believe in dying completely.

The same reasoning can be applied to violence. Absolute non-violence is the negative basis of slavery and its acts of violence; systematic violence positively destroys the living community and the existence we receive from it. To be fruitful, these two ideas must establish final limits. In history, considered as an absolute, violence finds itself legitimized; as a relative risk, it is the cause of a rupture in communication. It must therefore preserve, for the rebel, its provisional character of effraction and must always be bound, if it cannot be avoided, to a personal responsibility and to an immediate risk. Systematic violence is part of the order of things; in a certain sense, this is consolatory. *Führerprinzip* or historical Reason, whatever order may establish it, it reigns over the universe of things, not the universe of men. Just as the rebel considers murder as the limit that he must, if he is so inclined, consecrate by his own death, so violence can only be an extreme limit which combats another form of violence, as, for example, in the case of an insurrection. If an excess of injustice renders the latter inevitable, the rebel rejects violence in advance, in the service of a doctrine or of a reason of State.

[...]

There does exist for man, therefore, a way of acting and of thinking which is possible on the level of moderation to which he belongs. Every undertaking that is more ambitious than this proves to be contradictory. The absolute is not attained nor, above all, created through history. Politics is not religion, or if it is, then it is nothing but the Inquisition. How would society define an absolute? Perhaps everyone is looking for this absolute on behalf of all. But society and politics only have the responsibility of arranging everyone's affairs so that each will have the leisure and the freedom to pursue this common search. History can then no longer be presented as an object of worship. It is only an opportunity that must be rendered fruitful by a vigilant rebellion.

"Obsession with the harvest and indifference to history," writes René Char admirably, "are the two extremities of my bow." If the duration of history is not synonymous with the duration of the harvest, then history, in effect, is no more than a fleeting and cruel shadow in which man has no more part. He who dedicates himself to this history dedicates himself to nothing and, in his turn, is nothing. But he who dedicates himself to the duration of his life, to the house he builds, to the dignity of mankind, dedicates himself to the earth and reaps from it the harvest that sows its seed and sustains the world again and again. Finally, it is those who know how to rebel, at the appropriate moment, against history who really advance its interests. To rebel against it supposes an interminable tension and the agonized serenity of which René Char also speaks. But the true life is present in the heart of this dichotomy. Life is this dichotomy itself, the mind soaring over volcanoes of light, the madness of justice, the extenuating intransigence of moderation. The words that reverberate for us at the confines of this long adventure of rebellion are not formulas for optimism, for which we have no possible use in the extremities of our unhappiness, but words of courage and intelligence which, on the shores of the eternal seas, even have the qualities of virtue.

No possible form of wisdom today can claim to give more. Rebellion indefatigably confronts evil, from which it can only derive a new impetus. Man can master in himself everything that should be mastered. He should rectify in creation everything that can be rectified. And after he has done so, children will still die unjustly even in a perfect society. Even by his greatest effort man can only propose to diminish arithmetically the sufferings of the world. But the injustice and the suffering of the world will remain and, no matter how limited they are, they will not cease to be an outrage. Dimitri Karamazov's cry of "Why?" will continue to resound; art and rebellion will die only with the last man.

There is an evil, undoubtedly, which men accumulate in their frantic desire for unity. But yet another evil lies at the roots of this inordinate movement. Confronted with this evil, confronted with death, man from the very depths of his soul cries out for justice. Historical Christianity has only replied to this protest against evil by the annunciation of the kingdom and then of eternal life, which demands faith. But suffering exhausts hope and faith and then is left alone and unexplained. The toiling masses, worn out with suffering and death, are masses without God. Our place is henceforth at their side, far from teachers, old or new. Historical Christianity postpones to a point beyond the span of history the cure of evil and murder, which are nevertheless experienced within the span of history. Contemporary materialism also believes that it can answer all questions. But, as a slave to history, it increases the domain of historic murder and at the same time leaves it without any justification, except in the future – which again demands faith. In both cases one must wait, and meanwhile the innocent continue to die. For 20 centuries the sum total of evil has not diminished in the world. No paradise, whether divine or revolutionary, has been realized. An injustice remains inextricably bound to all suffering, even the most deserved in the eyes of men. The long silence of Prometheus before the powers that overwhelmed him still cries out in protest. But Prometheus, meanwhile, has seen men rail and turn against him. Crushed between human evil and destiny, between terror and the arbitrary, all that remains to him is his power to rebel in order to save from murder him who can still be saved, without surrendering to the arrogance of blasphemy.

Then we understand that rebellion cannot exist without a strange form of love. Those who find no rest in God or in history are condemned to live for those who, like themselves, cannot live: in fact, for the humiliated. The most pure form of the movement of rebellion is thus crowned with the heart-rending cry of Karamazov: if all are not saved, what good is the salvation of one only? Thus Catholic prisoners, in the prison cells of Spain, refuse communion today because the priests of the regime have made it obligatory in certain prisons. These lonely witnesses to the crucifixion of innocence also refuse salvation if it must be paid for by injustice and oppression. This insane generosity is the generosity of rebellion, which unhesitatingly gives the strength of its love and without a moment's delay refuses injustice. Its merit lies in making no calculations, distributing everything it possesses to life and to living men. It is thus that it is prodigal in its gifts to men to come. Real generosity toward the future lies in giving all to the present.

Rebellion proves in this way that it is the very movement of life and that it cannot be denied without renouncing life. Its purest outburst, on each occasion, gives birth to existence. Thus it is love and fecundity or it is nothing at all. Revolution without honor, calculated revolution which, in preferring an abstract concept of man to a man of flesh and blood, denies existence as many times as is necessary, puts resentment in the place of love. Immediately rebellion, forgetful of its generous origins, allows itself to be contaminated by resentment; it denies life, dashes toward destruction, and raises up the grimacing cohorts of petty rebels, embryo slaves all of them, who end by offering themselves for sale, today, in all the marketplaces of Europe, to no matter what form of servitude. It is no longer either revolution or rebellion but rancor, malice, and tyranny. Then, when revolution in the name of power and of history becomes a murderous and immoderate mechanism, a new rebellion is consecrated in the name of moderation and of life. We are at that extremity now. At the end of this tunnel of darkness, however, there is inevitably a light, which we already divine and for which we only have to fight to ensure its coming. All of us, among the ruins, are preparing a renaissance beyond the limits of nihilism. But few of us know it.

Already, in fact, rebellion, without claiming to solve everything, can at least confront its problems. From this moment high noon is borne away on the fast-moving stream of history. Around the devouring flames, shadows writhe in mortal combat for an instant of time and then as suddenly disappear, and the blind, fingering their eyelids, cry out that this is history. The men of Europe, abandoned to the shadows, have turned their backs upon the fixed and radiant point of the present. They forget the present for the future, the fate of humanity for the delusion of power, the misery of the slums for the mirage of the eternal city, ordinary justice for an empty promised land. They despair of personal freedom and dream of a strange freedom of the species; reject solitary death and give the name of immortality to a vast collective agony. They no longer believe in the things that exist in the world and in living man; the secret of Europe is that it no longer loves life. Its blind men entertain the puerile belief that to love one single day of life amounts to justifying whole centuries of oppression. That is why they wanted to efface joy from the world and to postpone it until a much later date. Impatience with limits, the rejection of their double life, despair at being a man, have finally driven them to inhuman excesses. Denying the real grandeur of life, they have had to stake all on their own excellence. For want of something better to do, they deified themselves and their misfortunes began; these gods have had their eyes put out. Kaliayev, and his brothers throughout the entire world, refuse, on the contrary, to be deified in that they refuse the unlimited power to inflict death. They choose, and give us as an example the only original rule of life today: to learn to live and to die, and, in order to be a man, to refuse to be a god.

At this meridian of thought, the rebel thus rejects divinity in order to share in the struggles and destiny of all men. We shall choose Ithaca, the faithful land, frugal and audacious thought, lucid action, and the generosity of the man who understands. In the light, the earth remains our first and our last love. Our brothers are breathing under the same sky as we; justice is a living thing. Now is born that strange joy which helps one live and die, and which we shall never again postpone to a later time. On the sorrowing earth it is the unresting thorn, the bitter brew, the harsh wind off the sea, the old and the new dawn. With this joy, through long struggle, we shall remake the soul of our time, and a Europe which will exclude nothing. Not even that phantom Nietzsche, who for 12 years after his downfall was continually invoked by the West as the blasted image of its loftiest knowledge and its nihilism; nor the prophet of justice without mercy who lies, by mistake, in the unbelievers' plot at Highgate Cemetery; nor the deified mummy of the man of action in his glass coffin; nor any part of what the intelligence and energy of Europe have ceaselessly furnished to the pride of a contemptible period. All may indeed live again, side by side with the martyrs of 1905, but on condition that it is understood that they correct one another, and that a limit, under the sun, shall curb them all. Each tells the other that he is not God; this is the end of romanticism. At this moment, when each of us must fit an arrow to his bow and enter the lists anew, to reconquer, within history and in spite of it, that which he owns already, the thin yield of his fields, the brief love of this earth, at this moment when at last a man is born, it is time to forsake our age and its adolescent furies. The bow bends; the wood complains. At the moment of supreme tension, there will leap into flight an unswerving arrow, a shaft that is inflexible and free.

Lightning Source UK Ltd.
Milton Keynes UK
UKHW030200051218
333471UK00002B/9/P

9 781405 189965